ZAGATSURVEY®

2007

MOVIE GUIDE

Editor: Curt Gathje

Coordinator: Larry Cohn

Published and distributed by
ZAGAT SURVEY, LLC
4 Columbus Circle
New York, New York 10019
Tel: 212 977 6000
E-mail: movies@zagat.com
Web site: www.zagat.com

Acknowledgments

We appreciate the help of the DC Independent Film Festival, as well as the Arizona Film Society, MSC Film Society, Olympia Film Society, Peachtree Film Society, University Film Society and Yale Film Society.

Thanks also to the following who worked on this guide: our assistant editor, Josh Rogers, as well as Carol Bialkowski, Jason Briker, Kimberly Butler, Ed Dwyer, Gwen Hyman, Marilyn Laurie, David Margolick, Joshua Mooney, Pia Nordlinger, Maura O'Connell, Bernard Onken, Jane Rosenthal, Arthur Schlesinger Jr. and Bill Wolf. In addition, this guide would not have been possible without the hard work of our staff, especially Reni Chin, Liz Daleske, Jeff Freier, Shelley Gallagher, Natalie Lebert, Mike Liao, Dave Makulec, Emily Parsons, Becky Reimer, Troy Segal, Robert Seixas, Daniel Simmons, Sharon Yates and Kyle Zolner.

Contents

About This Survey

Over the past 27 years, Zagat Survey has become the leading publisher of consumer-based leisure guides. Starting in 1989, we gradually expanded our scope beyond restaurants and hotels to cover entertaining, golf, music, movies, nightlife, shopping, theater and tourist attractions. Now we are proud to bring you this fifth edition of the ultimate moviegoers guide, a compilation of 1,600 outstanding films, as rated by our surveyors.

With nearly 15,000 participants in this *Survey*, seeing an average of 2.2 movies per week (or 1.7 million films annually), and with each surveyor separately rating the films they've seen for Overall Quality, Acting, Story and Production Values, we hope to have achieved a uniquely reliable guide.

Of our surveyors, 54% are women, 46% men; the breakdown by age is 15% in their 20s; 33%, 30s; 21%, 40s; 18%, 50s; and 13%, 60s or above. Though living in all parts of the country and coming from highly diverse backgrounds, these people share one common trait – they are all movie lovers. In producing the reviews contained in this guide, our editors have done their best to synopsize these surveyors' opinions, with exact comments shown in quotation marks. We thank each of these participants. Being based entirely on their ratings and comments, this guide is really "theirs."

To help you find the best movie for any occasion, we have prepared a number of Top Ratings lists (pages 8–32), as well as 69 handy indexes. Though the vast majority of films in this book are currently available on DVD, we have flagged those that are not yet available with the following icon – Ø.

To vote in any of our upcoming *Surveys*, just register at zagat.com. Each voter will receive a free copy of the resulting guide when it is published. Subscribers to zagat.com have access to restaurant, nightlife, attractions and hotel ratings and reviews for 80 cities worldwide and receive ZagatWire, our monthly e-mail newsletter, as well as getting 25% off on purchases at our online Shop.

Since there is always room for improvement, we invite your comments, suggestions and even criticisms of this guide so that we can revise future editions. Please contact us at movies@zagat.com or by mail at Zagat Movies, 4 Columbus Circle, New York, NY 10019. We look forward to hearing from you.

New York, NY
September 6, 2006

Nina and Tim Zagat

What's New

For this fifth edition of our Movie Guide, we've surveyed the new releases of the last 12 months and included the Top 40 herein (see page 8). We think our surveyors' choices say much about the national moviegoing mood.

While it didn't seem to be a stellar year, it was a banner one for **documentaries,** with both *March of the Penguins* and *Murderball* placing in the Top 10 (and *Penguins* taking the Top Film of the year honors, the first time a documentary has done so in any of our *Surveys*). **Politics** also placed well, with *The Constant Gardener, Good Night, and Good Luck, Munich, Syriana* and *Thank You for Smoking* represented. **Animation** (*Chicken Little, The Corpse Bride, Ice Age: The Meltdown, Over the Hedge, Wallace & Gromit in the Curse of the Were-Rabbit*) was strong, ditto **sci-fi** (*Serenity, V for Vendetta, X Men: The Last Stand*). **Bios** played big, with a writer (Capote), a boxer (Cinderella Man) and a singer (Walk the Line) getting the widescreen treatment.

The Year's Hottest Players: Seven actors garnered double berths in the Top 40: **Maria Bello** (*A History of Violence, Thank You for Smoking*), **George Clooney** (*Good Night, and Good Luck, Syriana*), **Jeff Daniels** (*Good Night, and Good Luck, The Squid and the Whale*), **Katie Holmes** (*Batman Begins, Thank You for Smoking*), **William Hurt** (*A History of Violence, Syriana*), **Catherine Keener** (*Capote, The 40 Year Old Virgin*) and **Reese Witherspoon** (*Just Like Heaven, Walk the Line*). In the director's chair, **Ron Howard** scored twice with *Cinderella Man* and *The Da Vinci Code*.

New to This Edition: In addition to the past year's Top 40, we've added 205 additional reviews (see page 329), for a grand total of 1,600 titles, making this edition our largest ever. We've also created a few new indexes: Coming of Age, High School, Office Politics and Road Movies.

DVD Candidates: We again asked voters to name their favorite films not available on DVD that should be. This year's touts included *The African Queen, Becket, Bedazzled, The Conformist, El Cid, Enchanted April, The Gang's All Here, The Heiress, Isadora, Kiss of the Spider Woman, Let It Be, The Magnificent Ambersons, Mame, 1900, O Lucky Man!, Performance, Personal Best, Sergeant York, Shoot the Moon, Song of the South, Yentl* and "more foreign language movies." Here's hoping that Hollywood is listening.

New York, NY   Curt Gathje
September 6, 2006

Ratings & Symbols

Film Name, U.S. Release Date, Director & Cast, Running Time, MPAA Rating

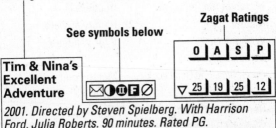

Zagat Ratings

See symbols below

O	A	S	P

| ▽ | 25 | 19 | 25 | 12 |

Tim & Nina's Excellent Adventure ✉ ◐ Ⅱ Ｆ ∅

2001. Directed by Steven Spielberg. With Harrison Ford, Julia Roberts. 90 minutes. Rated PG.

This "stirring" story of a couple's "epic struggle to build a movie studio" "against all odds" divides critics: "inspiring" ("outdoes *Citizen Kane*") vs. "strictly snoozeville" ("Bill and Ted's adventure was much better"); while most applaud Harrison Ford's "sensitive" portrayal of Tim ("amazing makeup job"), some feel Julia Roberts' take on Nina is just a "reprise of her role in *Pretty Woman*"; P.S. the black-and-white 3-D shots can be "nauseating", especially the dinner scenes in bed.

Review, with surveyors' comments in quotes

Top Movies: Films with highest overall ratings, popularity and scores are listed in BLOCK CAPITAL LETTERS.

✉ Oscar winner for Picture, Acting, Direction, Screenplay
◐ Filmed in Black & White
Ⅱ Inspired a Sequel
Ｆ Foreign Language film
∅ Not yet on DVD

Ratings are on a scale of **0** to **30**.

O	Overall	A	Acting	S	Story	P	Production Values
25		19		25		12	

0–9 poor to fair   **20–25** very good to excellent
10–15 fair to good   **26–30** extraordinary to perfection
16–19 good to very good   ▽ low response/less reliable

Top Ratings

Excluding films with low voting, unless indicated.

New Releases

26 March of the Penguins
Capote
25 Walk the Line
Cinderella Man
Good Night, and Good Luck
Murderball
24 Harry Potter/Goblet of Fire
Wallace & Gromit/Were-Rabbit
TransAmerica
Brokeback Mountain
23 Pride & Prejudice
Chronicles of Narnia
Munich
Batman Begins
Constant Gardener
Mrs. Henderson Presents
Serenity
Over the Hedge
Inside Man
Thank You for Smoking

Hustle & Flow
22 History of Violence
V for Vendetta
North Country
Match Point
21 Syriana
Wedding Crashers
Memoirs of a Geisha
Ice Age: The Meltdown
Squid and the Whale
Junebug
20 Corpse Bride
X-Men: The Last Stand
King Kong
19 40 Year Old Virgin
Rent
Da Vinci Code
Sisterhood/Traveling Pants
Just Like Heaven
Chicken Little

Favorite Films of All Time

Each surveyor has named his or her five favorite films. The following is a list of the 100 most popular.

1. Godfather, The
2. Casablanca
3. Star Wars
4. Gone with the Wind
5. Shawshank Redemption
6. Braveheart
7. Lord of Rings/Fellowship
8. Citizen Kane
9. Godfather Part II
10. Raiders of the Lost Ark
11. American Beauty
12. When Harry Met Sally
13. Beautiful Mind
14. It's a Wonderful Life
15. African Queen
16. Schindler's List
17. Matrix, The
18. Princess Bride
19. Wizard of Oz
20. Annie Hall
21. Usual Suspects*
22. Pretty Woman
23. Sound of Music
24. Moulin Rouge!
25. Pulp Fiction
26. 2001: A Space Odyssey
27. Gladiator
28. Affair to Remember
29. Breakfast at Tiffany's
30. Goodfellas*
31. Almost Famous
32. Saving Private Ryan
33. Singin' in the Rain*
34. Apocalypse Now
35. Lawrence of Arabia
36. Bridget Jones's Diary
37. Star Wars V/Empire*
38. Shrek
39. Silence of the Lambs*
40. Animal House
41. Forrest Gump
42. All About Eve
43. Top Gun
44. Blade Runner
45. Memento*
46. E.T.
47. Chocolat
48. Graduate, The
49. Dr. Strangelove
50. To Kill a Mockingbird*
51. Dirty Dancing
52. Airplane!
53. Blazing Saddles*
54. Shakespeare in Love*
55. Die Hard
56. Doctor Zhivago*
57. Harry Potter/Sorcerer's Stone
58. American Pie
59. American President
60. Willy Wonka
61. 12 Angry Men
62. As Good As It Gets
63. English Patient*
64. Ferris Bueller's Day Off
65. Rear Window
66. Amadeus
67. Caddyshack
68. Chinatown*
69. Fargo
70. Good Will Hunting*
71. Maltese Falcon
72. Sixth Sense
73. Dead Poets Society
74. Grease*
75. Great Escape
76. Producers, The
77. Roman Holiday
78. Bridge on the River Kwai
79. L.A. Confidential
80. Moonstruck*
81. My Fair Lady*
82. Fight Club
83. Fugitive, The
84. Hunt for Red October*
85. One Flew Over Cuckoo's…*
86. Being John Malkovich
87. Out of Africa*
88. Birdcage, The
89. Cast Away*
90. Sleepless in Seattle*
91. Some Like It Hot*
92. Titanic*
93. Young Frankenstein
94. Gosford Park
95. West Side Story
96. Billy Elliot
97. Clockwork Orange
98. Thelma & Louise*
99. Breakfast Club
100. North by Northwest

---

* Indicates a tie with film above

Overall Quality

(See page 32 for Top Foreign Language Films.)

Classic (Pre-1960)

29 Casablanca	Snow White
28 Wizard of Oz	Philadelphia Story
Lady Eve	Woman of the Year
Singin' in the Rain	Treasure of Sierra Madre
Rear Window	Notorious
It Happened One Night	Searchers, The*
Citizen Kane	Brief Encounter
All About Eve	Duck Soup
African Queen	It's a Wonderful Life
Third Man	Christmas Carol
Best Years of Our Lives	Great Expectations
Grapes of Wrath	Witness for the Prosecution
On the Waterfront	Big Sleep
Paths of Glory	Night of the Hunter
Fantasia	Streetcar Named Desire
Bridge on the River Kwai	Stalag 17
Some Like It Hot	How Green Was My Valley
Sunset Boulevard	Quiet Man
All Quiet/Western Front	Top Hat
Gone with the Wind	Vertigo
North by Northwest	Rebecca
High Noon	Roman Holiday
12 Angry Men	Gun Crazy
Double Indemnity	Place in the Sun*
Maltese Falcon	Wuthering Heights*
27 Sweet Smell of Success	Now, Voyager

Modern (1960 to Date)

29 Godfather	Manchurian Candidate (1962)
Godfather Part II	Chinatown
Schindler's List	Apocalypse Now
Lawrence of Arabia	Lord of Rings/Fellowship
To Kill a Mockingbird	Patton
28 Star Wars	Annie Hall
Shawshank Redemption	Sting, The
Pianist, The	Chicago
Finding Nemo	Lord of Rings/Two Towers
Dr. Strangelove	Gandhi
Lord of Rings/Return	Great Escape
Spellbound	Million Dollar Baby
Man for All Seasons	Wild Bunch
Lion in Winter	Princess Bride
Hotel Rwanda	Graduate, The
Sound of Music	Goodfellas
Psycho	Toy Story
Raiders of the Lost Ark	Days of Wine and Roses
27 One Flew Over Cuckoo's…	Doctor Zhivago
My Fair Lady	Breaker Morant
Usual Suspects	Fitzcarraldo
West Side Story	Mary Poppins
Taxi Driver	**26** March of the Penguins
Young Frankenstein	E.T.
Silence of the Lambs	Shrek

By Genre

Action/Adventure

Classic
- 27 Treasure of Sierra Madre
- 25 Adventures of Robin Hood
  - Mutiny on the Bounty
  - King Kong
  - Captains Courageous
- 23 Captain Blood
  - War of the Worlds
- 22 Mark of Zorro
  - Around the World in 80 Days
- 21 Tarzan and His Mate

Modern
- 29 Lawrence of Arabia
- 28 Star Wars
  - Lord of Rings/Return
  - Raiders of the Lost Ark
- 27 Lord of Rings/Fellowship
  - Lord of Rings/Two Towers
  - Great Escape
  - Fitzcarraldo
- 26 Star Wars V/Empire
  - Papillon

Americana

Classic
- 28 Best Years of Our Lives
  - Grapes of Wrath
- 27 It's a Wonderful Life
- 26 Shadow of a Doubt
  - Meet Me in St. Louis
  - Mr. Smith Goes to Washington
- 25 Yankee Doodle Dandy
  - Mr. Deeds Goes to Town
  - All the King's Men
- 24 Oklahoma!

Modern
- 29 To Kill a Mockingbird
- 26 Christmas Story
- 25 Music Man
  - Badlands
  - Seabiscuit
- 24 Stand by Me
  - American Graffiti
  - Far From Heaven
  - Forrest Gump
  - Straight Story

Animated

Classic
- 28 Fantasia
- 27 Snow White
- 26 Pinocchio
  - Cinderella
  - Bambi
  - Lady and the Tramp
- 25 Peter Pan
  - Sleeping Beauty
- 24 Dumbo
  - Alice in Wonderland

Modern
- 28 Finding Nemo
- 27 Toy Story
- 26 Shrek
  - Beauty and the Beast
  - Shrek 2
  - Incredibles, The
  - Monsters, Inc.
- 25 Lion King
- 24 Iron Giant
  - Little Mermaid

Biography

Classic
- 25 Yankee Doodle Dandy
- 24 Scarlet Empress▽
  - Sergeant York▽
- 23 Diary of Anne Frank
  - Anastasia
- 22 Song of Bernadette
  - Pride of the Yankees

Modern
- 29 Lawrence of Arabia
- 28 Man for All Seasons
- 27 Patton
  - Gandhi
- 26 Raging Bull
  - Amadeus
  - Becket
  - Ray
  - Last Emperor
  - Capote

Top Overall

Children/Family

Classic
28 Wizard of Oz
27 It's a Wonderful Life
Christmas Carol
David Copperfield▽
24 Jungle Book▽
National Velvet
Old Yeller
23 Father of the Bride
22 20,000 Leagues Under Sea
19 Journey to Center of Earth

Modern
28 Sound of Music
27 Princess Bride
Mary Poppins
26 E.T.
Christmas Story
Willy Wonka
25 Babe
Whale Rider
24 Harry Potter/Goblet of Fire
Oliver!

Comedy

Classic
28 Some Like It Hot
27 Woman of the Year
Mister Roberts
26 Adam's Rib
Great Dictator
Harvey
25 Auntie Mame
Lavender Hill Mob
Mr. Deeds Goes to Town
Desk Set

Modern
27 Young Frankenstein
Annie Hall
Graduate, The
26 This Is Spinal Tap
When Harry Met Sally
Manhattan
Local Hero
25 Waiting for Guffman
Blazing Saddles
Tootsie

Crime

Classic
28 Rear Window
On the Waterfront
26 Arsenic and Old Lace
Anatomy of a Murder
25 Lavender Hill Mob
Dial M for Murder
To Catch a Thief
24 Little Caesar
Angels with Dirty Faces
I Want to Live!

Modern
29 Godfather, The
Godfather Part II
27 Usual Suspects
Sting, The
Chicago
Goodfellas
26 Pulp Fiction
Capote
Mystic River
25 Fargo

Cult

Classic
29 Casablanca
28 Wizard of Oz
All About Eve
Fantasia
27 It's a Wonderful Life
Gun Crazy
26 Red Shoes
25 Forbidden Planet
23 Freaks
20 7th Voyage of Sinbad

Modern
28 Star Wars
Shawshank Redemption
Dr. Strangelove
Sound of Music
27 Manchurian Candidate (1962)
Princess Bride
26 Monty Python/Holy Grail
Breakfast at Tiffany's
Blade Runner
Willy Wonka

Drama

Classic
- 28 Citizen Kane
  Best Years of Our Lives
  Grapes of Wrath
  On the Waterfront
  Paths of Glory
  High Noon
  12 Angry Men
- 27 Great Expectations
  Witness for the Prosecution
  Streetcar Named Desire

Modern
- 29 Godfather, The
  Godfather Part II
  Schindler's List
  To Kill a Mockingbird
- 28 Shawshank Redemption
  Pianist, The
  Lion in Winter
  Hotel Rwanda
- 27 Taxi Driver
  Million Dollar Baby

Dramedy

Classic
- 28 All About Eve
  African Queen
- 27 It's a Wonderful Life
  Stalag 17
  Sullivan's Travels▽
  Women, The*▽
- 26 Mr. Smith Goes to Washington
- 25 Sabrina
- 24 Limelight
- 21 Bus Stop

Modern
- 27 One Flew Over Cuckoo's…
  Sting, The
- 26 Breakfast at Tiffany's
  Crimes and Misdemeanors
  Sense and Sensibility
  Charade
  Bend It Like Beckham
  Cool Hand Luke
- 25 Apartment, The
  Fargo

Epic

Classic
- 28 Bridge on the River Kwai
  Gone with the Wind
- 26 Ben-Hur
- 25 Mutiny on the Bounty
  Gunga Din
- 24 Ten Commandments
  Giant
- 23 Duel in the Sun
- 22 Around the World in 80 Days
- 20 King Solomon's Mines

Modern
- 29 Lawrence of Arabia
- 27 Gandhi
  Doctor Zhivago
- 26 Last Emperor
  Braveheart
  Spartacus
- 25 Empire of the Sun
- 24 Longest Day
  Zulu
  Once Upon a Time/America

Fantasy

Classic
- 28 Wizard of Oz
- 27 Christmas Carol
- 26 Harvey
- 25 Miracle on 34th Street
  King Kong
  Lost Horizon
- 24 Ghost and Mrs. Muir
  Brigadoon
- 20 Topper
  7th Voyage of Sinbad

Modern
- 28 Lord of Rings/Return
  Raiders of the Lost Ark
- 27 Lord of Rings/Fellowship
  Lord of Rings/Two Towers
  Princess Bride
  Mary Poppins
- 26 Willy Wonka
- 24 Indiana Jones/Last Crusade
  Harry Potter/Goblet of Fire
  Pirates of the Caribbean

Top Overall

Film Noir

Classic
- 28 Third Man
- Sunset Boulevard
- Double Indemnity
- Maltese Flacon
- 27 Sweet Smell of Success
- Big Sleep
- Night of the Hunter
- Gun Crazy
- Laura
- 26 Out of the Past

Modern
- 27 Chinatown
- 26 Blade Runner
- L.A. Confidential
- Memento
- 25 Cape Fear
- 24 Body Heat
- Blood Simple
- 23 Seven
- 22 Last Seduction
- Dead Again

Horror

Classic
- 25 Frankenstein
- Bride of Frankenstein
- 24 Dracula
- Invasion of Body Snatchers
- 23 Freaks
- Thing, The
- 22 Invisible Man
- 21 House of Wax
- 20 Wolf Man
- Fly, The

Modern
- 25 Exorcist, The
- Shining, The
- 24 Rosemary's Baby
- 23 Thing, The
- 22 Poltergeist
- Halloween
- Carrie
- Evil Dead
- Night of the Living Dead
- 21 Omen, The

Musical

Classic
- 28 Wizard of Oz
- Singin' in the Rain
- 27 Top Hat
- King and I
- 26 American in Paris
- Band Wagon
- Meet Me in St. Louis
- 25 Yankee Doodle Dandy
- White Christmas
- 24 Gigi

Modern
- 28 Sound of Music
- 27 My Fair Lady
- West Side Story
- Chicago
- Mary Poppins
- 26 Fiddler on the Roof
- Cabaret
- Funny Girl
- 25 Music Man
- That's Entertainment!

Romance

Classic
- 29 Casablanca
- 28 Lady Eve
- It Happened One Night
- African Queen
- Gone with the Wind
- 27 Philadelphia Story
- Notorious
- Brief Encounter
- How Green Was My Valley
- Quiet Man

Modern
- 27 Annie Hall
- Graduate, The
- Doctor Zhivago
- 26 Room with a View
- Charade
- Manhattan
- Romeo and Juliet
- 25 Harold and Maude
- Apartment, The
- Walk the Line

Sci-Fi

Classic
- 26 On the Beach
- 25 Forbidden Planet
- Day the Earth Stood Still
- 24 Invasion of Body Snatchers
- 23 War of the Worlds
- Thing, The
- 22 20,000 Leagues Under Sea
- 20 Fly, The
- 19 Journey to Center of Earth
- 16 Godzilla

Modern
- 28 Star Wars
- 26 E.T.
- Stars Wars V/Empire
- Blade Runner
- 2001: A Space Odyssey
- 25 Matrix, The
- Alien
- 24 Star Wars VI/Return of Jedi
- Close Encounters
- Terminator, The

Thriller

Classic
- 28 Rear Window
- Third Man
- North by Northwest
- 27 Notorious
- Night of the Hunter
- Vertigo
- 39 Steps
- 26 Shadow of a Doubt
- Gaslight
- Strangers on a Train

Modern
- 28 Psycho
- 27 Taxi Driver
- Silence of the Lambs
- Manchurian Candidate (1962)
- 26 Jaws
- Pulp Fiction
- Memento
- Seven Days in May
- Sixth Sense
- 25 Counterfeit Traitor

War

Classic
- 29 Casablanca
- 28 Paths of Glory
- Bridge on River Kwai
- All Quiet/Western Front
- 27 Stalag 17
- Caine Mutiny
- Mister Roberts
- 26 Twelve O'Clock High
- 25 Mrs. Miniver
- Beau Geste

Modern
- 29 Schindler's List
- 28 Pianist, The
- Hotel Rwanda
- 27 Apocalypse Now
- Patton
- Great Escape
- 26 MASH
- Saving Private Ryan
- Henry V
- Deer Hunter

Western

Classic
- 28 High Noon
- 27 Searchers, The
- Stagecoach
- 26 Red River
- Shane
- 25 Destry Rides Again
- 24 Oklahoma!
- She Wore a Yellow Ribbon
- 23 Fort Apache
- Duel in the Sun

Modern
- 27 Wild Bunch
- 26 Butch Cassidy
- Hud
- Unforgiven
- Magnificent Seven
- 25 Outlaw Josey Wales
- Once Upon a Time/West
- Man Who Shot Liberty Valance
- 24 Good, the Bad and the Ugly
- Little Big Man

Top Overall

By Decade

1910s/1920s

- *29* Napoléon▽
- *28* Greed▽
  General, The
  Gold Rush▽
- *27* Intolerance▽
  Potemkin
  Metropolis
- *26* Cabinet of Dr. Caligari
- *25* Birth of a Nation
- *24* Cocoanuts, The

1930s

- *28* Wizard of Oz
  It Happened One Night
  All Quiet/Western Front
  Modern Times
  Gone with the Wind
- *27* Snow White
  Duck Soup
  Top Hat
  Wuthering Heights
  39 Steps

1940s

- *29* Casablanca
- *28* Lady Eve
  Citizen Kane
  Third Man
  Best Years of Our Lives
  Grapes of Wrath
  Fantasia
  Double Indemnity
  Maltese Falcon
- *27* Philadelphia Story

1950s

- *28* Singin' in the Rain
  Rear Window
  All About Eve
  African Queen
  On the Waterfront
  Paths of Glory
  Bridge on the River Kwai
  Some Like It Hot
  Sunset Boulevard
  North by Northwest

1960s

- *29* Lawrence of Arabia
  To Kill a Mockingbird
- *28* Dr. Strangelove
  Man for All Seasons
  Lion in Winter
  Sound of Music
  Psycho
- *27* My Fair Lady
  West Side Story
  Manchurian Candidate

1970s

- *29* Godfather, The
  Godfather Part II
- *28* Star Wars
- *27* One Flew Over Cuckoo's...
  Taxi Driver
  Young Frankenstein
  Chinatown
  Apocalypse Now
  Patton
  Annie Hall

1980s

- *28* Raiders of the Lost Ark
- *27* Gandhi
  Princess Bride
  Breaker Morant
  Fitzcarraldo
- *26* E.T.
  Raging Bull
  Amadeus
  Star Wars V/Empire
  Right Stuff

1990s

- *29* Schindler's List
- *28* Shawshank Redemption
- *27* Usual Suspects
  Silence of the Lambs
  Goodfellas
  Toy Story
- *26* Saving Private Ryan
  Beauty and the Beast
  Hoop Dreams
  Pulp Fiction

2000s

- *28* Pianist, The
  Finding Nemo
  Lord of Rings/Return
  Spellbound
  Hotel Rwanda
- *27* Lord of Rings/Fellowship
  Chicago
  Lord of Rings/Two Towers
  Million Dollar Baby
- *26* March of the Penguins
  Shrek
  Shrek 2
  Beautiful Mind
  Incredibles, The
  Crash
  Ray
  Rabbit-Proof Fence
  Fog of War
  In America
  Monsters, Inc.
  Memento

By Director

Robert Aldrich
25 Flight of the Phoenix
24 Kiss Me Deadly
22 Whatever Happened to . . .

Woody Allen
27 Annie Hall
26 Crimes and Misdemeanors
   Manhattan

Pedro Almodóvar
26 Talk to Her
25 All About My Mother
24 Women on the Verge . . .

Robert Altman
26 MASH
23 McCabe & Mrs. Miller
   Player, The

Wes Anderson
23 Rushmore
20 Royal Tenenbaums
16 Life Aquatic/Steve Zissou

Hal Ashby
26 Being There
25 Harold and Maude
23 Coming Home

Bruce Beresford
27 Breaker Morant
24 Driving Miss Daisy
16 Double Jeopardy

Ingmar Bergman
27 Seventh Seal
26 Wild Strawberries
   Fanny and Alexander

Bernardo Bertolucci
26 Conformist, The
   Last Emperor
17 Last Tango in Paris

Peter Bogdanovich
23 Last Picture Show
22 Paper Moon
21 What's Up, Doc?

Kenneth Branagh
26 Henry V
24 Hamlet (1996)
22 Dead Again

James L. Brooks
25 Terms of Endearment
23 Broadcast News
22 As Good As It Gets

Mel Brooks
27 Young Frankenstein
26 Producers, The
25 Blazing Saddles

Richard Brooks
25 Elmer Gantry
   In Cold Blood
   Cat on a Hot Tin Roof

Tim Burton
22 Big Fish
21 Edward Scissorhands
20 Corpse Bride

James Cameron
24 Terminator, The
23 Aliens
   Terminator 2: Judgement Day

Frank Capra
28 It Happened One Night
27 It's a Wonderful Life
26 Arsenic and Old Lace

Charlie Chaplin
28 City Lights
   Modern Times
26 Great Dictator

Joel Coen
25 Fargo
24 Blood Simple
23 Raising Arizona

Chris Columbus
24 Harry Potter/Sorcerer's
   Harry Potter/Chamber
20 Mrs. Doubtfire

Francis Ford Coppola
29 Godfather, The
   Godfather Part II
27 Apocalypse Now

George Cukor
27 My Fair Lady
   Philadelphia Story
26 Adam's Rib

Michael Curtiz
29 Casablanca
26 Mildred Pierce
25 Yankee Doodle Dandy

Jonathan Demme
27 Silence of the Lambs
25 Stop Making Sense
24 Philadelphia

Brian De Palma
28 Scarface
   Carrie
   Untouchables, The

Stanley Donen
28 Singin' in the Rain
26 Charade
24 Funny Face

Top Overall

Clint Eastwood
27 Million Dollar Baby
26 Unforgiven
　　 Mystic River

Blake Edwards
27 Days of Wine and Roses
26 Breakfast at Tiffany's
25 Experiment in Terror

Federico Fellini
27 La Strada
　　 Nights of Cabiria
26 8½

Victor Fleming
28 Wizard of Oz
　　 Gone with the Wind
25 Captains Courageous

John Ford
28 Grapes of Wrath
27 Searchers, The
　　 How Green Was My Valley

Milos Forman
27 One Flew Over Cuckoo's...
26 Amadeus
20 Hair

Bob Fosse
26 Cabaret
24 Lenny
　　 All That Jazz

John Frankenheimer
27 Manchurian Candidate (1962)
26 Seven Days in May
22 Birdman of Alcatraz

Stephen Frears
24 Dangerous Liaisons
23 Dirty Pretty Things
　　 Mrs. Henderson Presents

Terry Gilliam
26 Monty Python/Holy Grail
24 Brazil
22 Twelve Monkeys

Christopher Guest
25 Waiting for Guffman
24 Best in Show
23 Mighty Wind

Lasse Hallström
25 My Life As a Dog
22 Chocolat
　　 What's Eating Gilbert Grape

Curtis Hanson
26 L.A. Confidential
21 Wonder Boys
19 8 Mile

Howard Hawks
27 Big Sleep
　　 Bringing Up Baby
26 Red River

Werner Herzog
27 Fitzcarraldo
25 Aguirre: The Wrath of God
22 Nosferatu the Vampyre

George Roy Hill
27 Sting, The
26 Butch Cassidy
22 Slap Shot

Alfred Hitchcock
28 Rear Window
　　 North by Northwest
　　 Psycho

Ron Howard
26 Beautiful Mind
25 Cinderella Man
24 Apollo 13

John Hughes
23 Ferris Bueller's Day Off
22 Breakfast Club
　　 Sixteen Candles

John Huston
28 African Queen
　　 Maltese Falcon
27 Treasure of Sierra Madre

James Ivory
26 Room with a View
24 Remains of the Day
22 Howards End

Peter Jackson
28 Lord of Rings/Return
27 Lord of Rings/Fellowship
　　 Lord of Rings/Two Towers

Lawrence Kasdan
24 Body Heat
　　 Silverado
23 Big Chill

Philip Kaufman
26 Right Stuff
21 Unbearable Lightness of Being
19 Invasion/Body Snatchers (1978)

Elia Kazan
28 On the Waterfront
27 Streetcar Named Desire
25 Splendor in the Grass

Stanley Kramer
26 Inherit the Wind
　　 On the Beach
　　 Judgment at Nuremberg

Stanley Kubrick
28 Dr. Strangelove
    Paths of Glory
26 2001: A Space Odyssey

Akira Kurosawa
29 Seven Samurai
    Rashomon
27 Ran

David Lean
29 Lawrence of Arabia
28 Bridge on the River Kwai
27 Brief Encounter

Ang Lee
26 Sense and Sensibility
25 Eat Drink Man Woman
24 Crouching Tiger

Spike Lee
23 Malcolm X
    Do the Right Thing
    Inside Man

Mike Leigh
24 Vera Drake
    Secrets and Lies
23 Topsy-Turvy

Sergio Leone
25 Once Upon a Time/West
24 Good, the Bad and the Ugly
    Once Upon a Time/America

Richard Lester
24 Hard Day's Night
22 Three Musketeers
    Funny Thing Happened . . .

Barry Levinson
25 Rain Man
    Diner
23 Natural, The

George Lucas
28 Star Wars
24 American Graffiti
23 Star Wars III/Revenge of Sith

Baz Luhrmann
23 Moulin Rouge!
    Strictly Ballroom
19 Romeo + Juliet

Sidney Lumet
28 12 Angry Men
26 Pawnbroker, The
24 Fail-Safe

David Lynch
24 Elephant Man
    Straight Story
22 Blue Velvet

Terrence Malick
25 Badlands
23 Days of Heaven
19 Thin Red Line

Louis Malle
27 Au Revoir Les Enfants
24 Atlantic City
21 My Dinner with Andre

Joseph L. Mankiewicz
28 All About Eve
25 Sleuth
24 Ghost and Mrs. Muir

Michael Mann
25 Insider, The
22 Last of the Mohicans
    Heat

Anthony Minghella
22 Cold Mountain
    English Patient
18 Talented Mr. Ripley

Vincente Minnelli
26 American in Paris
    Band Wagon
    Meet Me in St. Louis

Michael Moore
24 Roger & Me
22 Bowling for Columbine
21 Fahrenheit 9/11

Mike Nichols
27 Graduate, The
25 Who's Afraid of V. Woolf?
22 Silkwood

Alan J. Pakula
26 Sophie's Choice
25 All the President's Men
20 Klute

Alan Parker
24 Midnight Express
23 Mississippi Burning
21 Life of David Gale

Alexander Payne
23 Sideways
22 Election
21 About Schmidt

Arthur Penn
25 Miracle Worker
    Bonnie and Clyde
24 Little Big Man

Roman Polanski
28 Pianist, The
27 Chinatown
24 Rosemary's Baby

Top Overall

Sydney Pollack
25 Tootsie
   Out of Africa
24 Way We Were

Otto Preminger
27 Laura
26 Anatomy of a Murder
23 Carmen Jones

Robert Redford
25 Ordinary People
22 River Runs Through It
21 Quiz Show

Rob Reiner
27 Princess Bride
26 This Is Spinal Tap
   When Harry Met Sally

John Sayles
25 Lone Star
23 Brother from Another Planet
18 Sunshine State

Franklin J. Schaffner
27 Patton
26 Papillon
23 Planet of the Apes

Martin Scorsese
27 Taxi Driver
   Goodfellas
26 Raging Bull

Ridley Scott
26 Blade Runner
25 Alien
23 Gladiator

Bryan Singer
27 Usual Suspects
24 X2
19 X-Men

Steven Soderbergh
23 Traffic
21 Out of Sight
   Erin Brockovich

Steven Spielberg
29 Schindler's List
28 Raiders of the Lost Ark
26 E.T.

George Stevens
27 Woman of the Year
   Place in the Sun
26 Shane

Oliver Stone
25 Platoon
22 Wall Street
20 Born on the Fourth of July

John Sturges
27 Great Escape
26 Magnificent Seven
24 Bad Day at Black Rock

Preston Sturges
28 Lady Eve
27 Sullivan's Travels▽
25 Palm Beach Story

Quentin Tarantino
26 Pulp Fiction
25 Kill Bill Vol. 2
24 Reservoir Dogs

François Truffaut
27 400 Blows
   Day for Night
25 Shoot the Piano Player

Gus Van Sant
24 Good Will Hunting
19 My Own Private Idaho
   Elephant

Peter Weir
25 Gallipoli
24 Year of Living Dangerously
   Dead Poets Society

Orson Welles
28 Citizen Kane
26 Touch of Evil
25 Lady from Shanghai

Wim Wenders
25 Buena Vista Social Club
24 Wings of Desire
22 Paris, Texas

Billy Wilder
28 Some Like It Hot
   Sunset Boulevard
   Double Indemnity

Robert Wise
28 Sound of Music
27 West Side Story
25 Day the Earth Stood Still

William Wyler
28 Best Years of Our Lives
27 Roman Holiday
   Wuthering Heights

Robert Zemeckis
24 Forrest Gump
   Who Framed Roger Rabbit
23 Back to the Future

Fred Zinnemann
28 Man for All Seasons
   High Noon
26 From Here to Eternity

Acting

29 Godfather Part II	Now, Voyager
Godfather, The	Raging Bull
All About Eve	Adam's Rib
One Flew Over Cuckoo's...	Philadelphia Story
Monster	Sweet Smell of Success
Capote	Inherit the Wind
Ray	White Heat
Lion in Winter	Mystic River
Taxi Driver	Sophie's Choice
On the Waterfront	Prime of Miss Jean Brodie
Becket	My Left Foot
To Kill a Mockingbird	Night of the Hunter
Schindler's List	Midnight Cowboy
Pianist, The	TransAmerica
Brief Encounter	Born Yesterday
African Queen	Kind Hearts and Coronets
28 Hotel Rwanda	Grapes of Wrath
Casablanca	Chinatown
Beautiful Mind	Vera Drake
Million Dollar Baby	Woman of the Year
Streetcar Named Desire	Apartment, The
Silence of the Lambs	Hud
Days of Wine and Roses	Caine Mutiny
12 Angry Men	Walk the Line
Gandhi	Sunset Boulevard
Man for All Seasons	Sleuth
Lady Eve	Witness/Prosecution
Patton	Bridge on the River Kwai
Shawshank Redemption	American History X
Lawrence of Arabia	Raisin in the Sun

By Lead Actor

Ben Affleck
25 Good Will Hunting
19 Chasing Amy
Changing Lanes

Woody Allen
26 Annie Hall
Crimes and Misdemeanors
24 Manhattan

Julie Andrews
25 Sound of Music
24 Mary Poppins
Victor/Victoria

Ann-Margret
26 Carnal Knowledge
24 Grumpy Old Men
18 Bye Bye Birdie

Fred Astaire
26 On the Beach
24 Funny Face
23 Top Hat

Lauren Bacall
27 To Have and Have Not
Big Sleep
26 Key Largo

Alec Baldwin
27 Glengarry Glen Ross
Cooler, The
24 Hunt for Red October

Anne Bancroft
28 Miracle Worker
27 Graduate, The
Elephant Man

Antonio Banderas
24 Women on the Verge
21 Tie Me Up! Tie Me Down!
19 Interview with the Vampire

Drew Barrymore
23 Confessions of a Dangerous Mind
22 E.T.
19 Fever Pitch

Top Acting

Alan Bates
27 Zorba the Greek
26 King of Hearts
   Women in Love

Kathy Bates
26 About Schmidt
25 Fried Green Tomatoes
24 Misery

Warren Beatty
25 Bonnie and Clyde
   Splendor in the Grass
23 McCabe and Mrs. Miller

Annette Bening
27 Being Julia
   American Beauty
26 Grifters, The

Ingrid Bergman
28 Casablanca
27 Notorious
   Gaslight

Gael García Bernal
26 Bad Education
25 Motorcycle Diaries
24 Y Tu Mamá También

Juliette Binoche
24 English Patient
   Unbearable Lightness of Being
   Chocolat

Humphrey Bogart
29 African Queen
28 Casablanca
   Caine Mutiny

Helena Bonham Carter
26 Howards End
   Room with a View
25 Fight Club

Kenneth Branagh
28 Henry V
26 Hamlet (1996)
25 Rabbit-Proof Fence

Marlon Brando
29 Godfather, The
   On the Waterfront
28 Streetcar Named Desire

Jeff Bridges
25 Seabiscuit
24 Fisher King
23 Last Picture Show

Matthew Broderick
26 Glory
24 Election
22 Ferris Bueller's Day Off

Yul Brynner
27 Anastasia
26 King and I
22 Magnificent Seven

Richard Burton
29 Becket
27 Who's Afraid of V. Woolf?
26 Spy Who Came in from Cold

Nicolas Cage
26 Adaptation
25 Moonstruck
24 Leaving Las Vegas

James Cagney
28 White Heat
27 Mister Roberts
25 Yankee Doodle Dandy

Michael Caine
28 Sleuth
26 Man Who Would Be King
   Quiet American

Leslie Caron
23 Gigi
   Lili▽
   American in Paris

Jim Carrey
24 Eternal Sunshine
22 Truman Show
   Man on the Moon

Charlie Chaplin
28 City Lights
27 Great Dictator
26 Modern Times

Don Cheadle
28 Hotel Rwanda
27 Crash
17 Family Man

Cher
26 Silkwood
25 Moonstruck
24 Mask

Julie Christie
26 Doctor Zhivago
   Billy Liar
   Don't Look Now

Montgomery Clift
27 From Here to Eternity
   Place in the Sun
26 Suddenly, Last Summer

George Clooney
27 Good Night, and Good Luck
24 Syriana
23 O Brother, Where Art Thou?

Glenn Close
26 Dangerous Liaisons
24 Big Chill
23 Fatal Attraction

Jennifer Connelly
28 Beautiful Mind
27 House of Sand and Fog
Requiem for a Dream

Sean Connery
26 Man Who Would Be King
25 Wind and the Lion
24 Hunt for Red October

Gary Cooper
26 High Noon
For Whom the Bell Tolls
Mr. Deeds Goes to Town

Kevin Costner
26 Upside of Anger
24 Silverado
22 Bull Durham

Joseph Cotten
28 Third Man
27 Gaslight
26 Shadow of a Doubt

Joan Crawford
26 Women, The▽
25 Grand Hotel▽
Mildred Pierce

Russell Crowe
28 Beautiful Mind
Insider, The
27 Cinderella Man

Tom Cruise
27 Rain Man
26 Few Good Men
24 Collateral

Billy Crystal
25 When Harry Met Sally
21 Analyze This
20 City Slickers

Tony Curtis
28 Sweet Smell of Success
27 Some Like It Hot
19 Operation Petticoat

John Cusack
26 Grifters, The
24 Being John Malkovich
23 Bullets Over Broadway

Willem Dafoe
25 Platoon
Shadow of the Vampire
24 Mississippi Burning

Matt Damon
25 Good Will Hunting
24 Syriana
21 Talented Mr. Ripley

Bette Davis
29 All About Eve
28 Now, Voyager
27 Dark Victory

Geena Davis
25 Thelma & Louise
24 Accidental Tourist
20 League of Their Own

Daniel Day-Lewis
28 My Left Foot
25 In the Name of the Father
24 Age of Innocence

James Dean
27 East of Eden
24 Rebel Without a Cause
23 Giant

Benicio Del Toro
28 Usual Suspects
27 21 Grams
24 Traffic

Judi Dench
28 Mrs. Brown
27 Mrs. Henderson Presents
25 Shakespeare In Love

Catherine Deneuve
25 Last Metro
Belle de Jour
Indochine

Robert De Niro
29 Taxi Driver
28 Raging Bull
Deer Hunter

Johnny Depp
27 Finding Neverland
25 Pirates of the Caribbean
What's Eating Gilbert Grape

Cameron Diaz
24 Being John Malkovich
19 There's Something About Mary
18 Mask, The

Leonardo DiCaprio
25 What's Eating Gilbert Grape
Aviator, The
24 Catch Me If You Can

Kirk Douglas
27 Paths of Glory
26 Out of the Past
25 Bad and the Beautiful

Top Acting

Michael Douglas
25 China Syndrome
24 Traffic
    Wonder Boys

Richard Dreyfuss
24 Apprenticeship of D. Kravitz
23 Goodbye Girl
    American Graffiti

Faye Dunaway
28 Chinatown
25 Network
    Bonnie and Clyde

Clint Eastwood
28 Million Dollar Baby
26 Unforgiven
23 Outlaw Josey Wales

Dakota Fanning
25 I Am Sam
    Man on Fire
16 Uptown Girls

Mia Farrow
26 Crimes and Misdemeanors
25 Hannah and Her Sisters
    Rosemary's Baby

Sally Field
27 Norma Rae
25 Steel Magnolias
    Absence of Malice

Ralph Fiennes
29 Schindler's List
26 Constant Gardener
24 End of the Affair

Albert Finney
27 Two for the Road
24 Tom Jones
    Big Fish

Laurence Fishburne
26 What's Love Got to Do with It
22 Boyz N the Hood
19 Matrix, The

Henry Fonda
28 12 Angry Men
    Lady Eve
    Grapes of Wrath

Jane Fonda
27 On Golden Pond
26 Coming Home
25 China Syndrome

Harrison Ford
24 Fugitive, The
    Raiders of the Lost Ark
    Witness

Jodie Foster
28 Silence of the Lambs
    Accused, The
26 Alice Doesn't Live Here

Brendan Fraser
27 Gods and Monsters
26 Quiet American
16 Mummy, The

Morgan Freeman
28 Million Dollar Baby
    Shawshank Redemption
27 Driving Miss Daisy

Clark Gable
28 It Happened One Night
27 Gone with the Wind
25 Mutiny on Bounty (1935)

Judy Garland
26 Wizard of Oz
    Star is Born
24 Meet Me in St. Louis

Richard Gere
26 Chicago
25 Primal Fear
24 Unfaithful

Mel Gibson
25 Year of Living Dangerously
    Gallipoli
24 Braveheart

Whoopi Goldberg
27 Color Purple
21 Ghost
18 Sister Act

Cuba Gooding Jr.
25 Radio
22 Boyz N the Hood
    Jerry Maguire

Cary Grant
28 Philadelphia Story
    His Girl Friday
27 Bringing Up Baby

Hugh Grant
23 Bridget Jones's Diary
    Love Actually
    About a Boy

Alec Guinness
28 Kind Hearts and Coronets
    Bridge on the River Kwai
26 Lavender Hill Mob

Jake Gyllenhaal
26 Brokeback Mountain
23 Donnie Darko
22 Good Girl

Gene Hackman
26 Conversation, The
Unforgiven
French Connection

Tom Hanks
27 Philadelphia
26 Road to Perdition
Forrest Gump

Ed Harris
28 Beautiful Mind
27 Glengarry Glen Ross
26 Pollock

Rex Harrison
27 My Fair Lady
25 Ghost and Mrs. Muir
18 Cleopatra

Ethan Hawke
27 Training Day
25 Dead Poets Society
23 Before Sunset

Audrey Hepburn
27 My Fair Lady
Two for the Road
26 Roman Holiday

Katharine Hepburn
29 Lion in Winter
African Queen
28 Adam's Rib

Charlton Heston
24 Touch of Evil
23 Ben-Hur
21 Ten Commandments

Dustin Hoffman
28 Midnight Cowboy
27 Graduate, The
Rain Man

Philip Seymour Hoffman
29 Capote
25 Happiness
25th Hour

William Holden
28 Born Yesterday
Sunset Boulevard
Bridge on the River Kwai

Judy Holliday
28 Adam's Rib
Born Yesterday
24 Bells Are Ringing

Anthony Hopkins
28 Silence of the Lambs
27 Elephant Man
Remains of the Day

Dennis Hopper
23 Easy Rider
Blue Velvet
22 Hoosiers

Holly Hunter
26 Thirteen
25 Broadcast News
24 Piano, The

William Hurt
25 Children of a Lesser God
Body Heat
Kiss of the Spider Woman

Angelica Huston
26 Crimes and Misdemeanors
Grifters, The
24 Prizzi's Honor

Jeremy Irons
27 Being Julia
25 French Lieutenant's Woman
24 Mission, The

Scarlett Johansson
26 Ghost World
24 Lost in Translation
23 Girl with a Pearl Earring

Shirley Jones
27 Elmer Gantry
24 Music Man
22 Oklahoma!

Tommy Lee Jones
27 Coal Miner's Daughter
24 Fugitive, The
22 Missing, The

Diane Keaton
26 Annie Hall
Something's Gotta Give
24 Manhattan

Gene Kelly
28 Inherit the Wind
26 Singin' in the Rain
23 American in Paris

Grace Kelly
27 Rear Window
26 High Noon
25 To Catch a Thief

Deborah Kerr
27 From Here to Eternity
26 King and I
25 Affair to Remember

Nicole Kidman
28 Hours, The
25 Others, The
Dogville

Top Acting

Ben Kingsley
29 Schindler's List
28 Gandhi
27 House of Sand and Fog

Kevin Kline
28 Sophie's Choice
24 Fish Called Wanda
Big Chill

Burt Lancaster
28 Sweet Smell of Success
27 Elmer Gantry
Atlantic City

Jessica Lange
27 Tootsie
24 Cape Fear
23 All that Jazz

Jude Law
26 Road to Perdition
24 Cold Mountain
23 Closer

Janet Leigh
26 Psycho
24 Touch of Evil
18 Bye Bye Birdie

Jack Lemmon
28 Days of Wine and Roses
Apartment, The
27 Odd Couple

Laura Linney
26 You Can Count on Me
Kinsey
25 Squid and the Whale

Myrna Loy
27 Best Years of Our Lives
25 Thin Man
24 Mr. Blandings . . .

Shirley MacLaine
28 Apartment, The
27 Being There
26 Terms of Endearment

Fred MacMurray
28 Apartment, The
27 Double Indemnity
17 Absent-Minded Professor

Tobey Maguire
25 Seabiscuit
24 Wonder Boys
Cider House Rules

John Malkovich
26 Dangerous Liaisons
Killing Fields
25 Shadow of the Vampire

Fredric March
28 Inherit the Wind
27 Best Years of Our Lives
24 Seven Days in May

Marx Brothers
25 Duck Soup
Night at the Opera
24 Animal Crackers

James Mason
26 North by Northwest
Star Is Born
24 Lolita

Matthew McConaughey
25 Lonestar
24 Amistad
21 Contact

Frances McDormand
27 Fargo
26 North Country
25 Man Who Wasn't There

Ewan McGregor
24 Big Fish
23 Moulin Rouge!
22 Trainspotting

Ian McKellen
27 Gods and Monsters
26 Lord of Rings/Return
25 Lord of Rings/Fellowship

Steve McQueen
27 Papillon
26 Sand Pebbles
Great Escape

Ray Milland
25 Lost Weekend▽
24 Dial M for Murder
23 Beau Geste

Liza Minnelli
25 Cabaret
21 Arthur
19 New York, New York▽

Marilyn Monroe
27 Some Like It Hot
24 Misfits, The
23 Seven Year Itch

Yves Montand
27 Jean de Florette
26 Wages of Fear
25 Z

Julianne Moore
28 Hours, The
27 Far From Heaven
24 End of the Affair

Viggo Mortensen
26 Lord of Rings/Return
25 Lord of Rings/Fellowship
   Lord of Rings/Two Towers

Bill Murray
25 Rushmore
24 Lost in Translation
20 Caddyshack

Liam Neeson
29 Schindler's List
26 Kinsey
24 Mission, The

Paul Newman
28 Hud
27 Cat on a Hot Tin Roof
   Cool Hand Luke

Jack Nicholson
29 One Flew Over Cuckoo's...
28 Chinatown
27 Five Easy Pieces

Nick Nolte
25 Affliction
24 Cape Fear (1991)
21 Prince of Tides

Edward Norton
28 American History X
25 Fight Club
   Primal Fear

Kim Novak
26 Vertigo
24 Picnic
22 Bell, Book and Candle

Laurence Olivier
28 Sleuth
27 Wuthering Heights
   Rebecca

Ryan O'Neal
23 Paper Moon
20 What's Up, Doc?
18 Barry Lyndon

Haley Joel Osment
25 Sixth Sense
   Secondhand Lions
20 A.I.: Artificial Intelligence

Peter O'Toole
29 Lion in Winter
   Becket
28 Lawrence of Arabia

Clive Owen
27 Gosford Park
25 Inside Man
23 Closer

Al Pacino
29 Godfather Part II
   Godfather, The
28 Insider, The

Gwyneth Paltrow
25 Shakespeare In Love
24 Royal Tenenbaums
23 Emma

Guy Pearce
27 L.A. Confidential
25 Memento
24 Adventures of Priscilla...

Gregory Peck
29 To Kill a Mockingbird
26 Cape Fear (1962)
   Roman Holiday

Sean Penn
28 Mystic River
27 21 Grams
26 Dead Man Walking

Joe Pesci
28 Raging Bull
27 Goodfellas
24 Casino

Michelle Pfeiffer
26 Dangerous Liaisons
25 I Am Sam
24 Age of Innocence

Brad Pitt
25 Fight Club
23 Seven
   Twelve Monkeys

Christopher Plummer
28 Insider, The
26 Man Who Would Be King
25 Sound of Music

Sidney Poitier
28 Raisin in the Sun
27 In the Heat of the Night
   Guess Who's Coming...

William Powell
27 Mister Roberts
25 Thin Man
   My Man Godfrey

Dennis Quaid
27 Far From Heaven
23 Postcards from the Edge
22 Rookie, The

Robert Redford
26 Sting, The
   Butch Cassidy
   All the President's Men

Top Acting

Vanessa Redgrave
26 Julia▽
23 Blowup
21 Camelot

Lee Remick
28 Days of Wine and Roses
27 Anatomy of a Murder
24 Experiment in Terror

Burt Reynolds
26 Deliverance
21 Boogie Nights
15 Longest Yard (1974)

Tim Robbins
28 Shawshank Redemption
    Mystic River
23 Player, The

Julia Roberts
23 Closer
    Erin Brockovich
22 Pretty Woman

Edward G. Robinson
27 Double Indemnity
26 Key Largo
    Little Caesar

Geoffrey Rush
27 Elizabeth
25 Pirates of the Caribbean
    Shine

Kurt Russell
26 Silkwood
23 Miracle
22 Tombstone

Rosalind Russell
28 His Girl Friday
25 Auntie Mame
24 Picnic

Meg Ryan
25 When Harry Met Sally
22 Sleepless in Seattle
20 You've Got Mail

Eva Marie Saint
29 On the Waterfront
26 North by Northwest
23 Exodus

Adam Sandler
20 Punch-Drunk Love
    Spanglish
18 50 First Dates

Susan Sarandon
27 Atlantic City
26 Dead Man Walking
25 Thelma & Louise

Peter Sellers
28 Dr. Strangelove
27 Being There
24 Lolita

Omar Sharif
28 Lawrence of Arabia
26 Doctor Zhivago
25 Funny Girl

Martin Sheen
27 Apocalypse Now
    Badlands
23 Wall Street

Jean Simmons
27 Elmer Gantry
24 Spartacus
21 Guys and Dolls

Frank Sinatra
27 From Here to Eternity
26 Manchurian Candidate (1962)
23 On the Town

Will Smith
24 Six Degrees of Separation
21 Hitch
20 Men In Black

Sissy Spacek
27 Badlands
    Coal Miner's Daughter
26 In the Bedroom

Kevin Spacey
28 Usual Suspects
27 L.A. Confidential
    American Beauty

James Spader
24 Secretary
20 Sex, Lies and Videotape
17 Stargate

Rod Steiger
29 On the Waterfront
28 Pawnbroker, The
27 In the Heat of the Night

James Stewart
28 Philadelphia Story
27 Rear Window
    Anatomy of a Murder

Ben Stiller
21 Meet the Fockers
    Meet the Parents
19 There's Something About Mary

Meryl Streep
28 Sophie's Choice
    Hours, The
26 Adaptation

Barbra Streisand
25 Funny Girl
   Way We Were
21 Prince of Tides

Donald Sutherland
27 Ordinary People
26 Don't Look Now
25 MASH

Hilary Swank
28 Million Dollar Baby
27 Boys Don't Cry
22 Insomnia

Elizabeth Taylor
27 Who's Afraid of V. Woolf?
   Cat on a Hot Tin Roof
   Place in the Sun

Charlize Theron
29 Monster
26 North Country
24 Cider House Rules

Emma Thompson
27 Sense and Sensibility
   Remains of the Day
26 Howards End

Billy Bob Thornton
27 Sling Blade
26 Monster's Ball
25 Man Who Wasn't There

Uma Thurman
26 Pulp Fiction
24 Kill Bill Vol. 2
22 Kill Bill Vol. 1

Spencer Tracy
28 Adam's Rib
   Inherit the Wind
   Woman of the Year

John Travolta
26 Pulp Fiction
21 Ladder 49
19 Saturday Night Fever

Kathleen Turner
25 Body Heat
24 Prizzi's Honor
   Accidental Tourist

Jon Voight
28 Midnight Cowboy
26 Coming Home
   Deliverance

Max Von Sydow
27 Seventh Seal
24 Exorcist, The
20 Minority Report

Christopher Walken
28 Deer Hunter
25 Man on Fire
24 Catch Me If You Can

Denzel Washington
27 Philadelphia
   Training Day
26 Hurricane

John Wayne
25 Red River
   Searchers, The
   Quiet Man

Sigourney Weaver
25 Year of Living Dangerously
23 Holes
22 Alien

Orson Welles
28 Third Man
27 Citizen Kane
   Jane Eyre

Gene Wilder
26 Producers, The
   Young Frankenstein
22 Blazing Saddles

Robin Williams
26 Awakenings
25 Dead Poets Society
   Good Will Hunting

Bruce Willis
26 Pulp Fiction
25 Sixth Sense
23 Twelve Monkeys

Kate Winslet
27 Finding Neverland
   Sense and Sensibility
25 Heavenly Creatures

Reese Witherspoon
28 Walk the Line
24 Election
23 Importance of Being Earnest

Natalie Wood
25 Splendor in the Grass
24 West Side Story
   Rebel Without a Cause

Renée Zellweger
27 Cinderella Man
26 Chicago
24 Cold Mountain

Catherine Zeta-Jones
26 Chicago
24 Traffic
22 Terminal, The

Top Story

Classic (Pre-1960)

28 Casablanca
All Quiet/Western Front
Paths of Glory
Witness for the Prosecution
Grapes of Wrath
Wizard of Oz
Great Expectations
Best Years of Our Lives
Double Indemnity
Rear Window
Christmas Carol

27 All About Eve
Wuthering Heights
On the Beach
Citizen Kane
12 Angry Men
Bridge on the River Kwai
39 Steps
Place in the Sun
Strangers on a Train
Dial M for Murder
Gone with the Wind
It's a Wonderful life
Rebecca
Searchers, The

Gun Crazy
Sunset Boulevard
Third Man
Brief Encounter
Maltese Falcon
Anatomy of a Murder
North by Northwest
Stalag 17
Laura
Lady Eve
Vertigo

26 Sweet Smell of Success
Some Like It Hot
Diary of Anne Frank
Twelve O'Clock High
Gaslight
D.O.A.
Notorious
Oliver Twist
High Noon
Pinocchio
Woman of the Year
How Green Was My Valley
Caine Mutiny
Jane Eyre

Modern (1960 to Date)

29 Godfather, The
To Kill a Mockingbird

28 Schindler's List
Godfather Part II
Shawshank Redemption
Usual Suspects
Star Wars
Manchurian Candidate (1962)
Hotel Rwanda
Seven Days in May

27 Man for All Seasons
Henry V
Great Escape
Dr. Strangelove
Raiders of the Lost Ark
Breaker Morant
Romeo and Juliet
Lord of Rings/Return
Psycho
Christmas Story
Pianist, The
House of Games
Sting, The
One Flew Over Cuckoo's...
Killing Fields

Lord of Rings/Fellowship
Princess Bride
Lawrence of Arabia
Inherit the Wind
Spellbound*
Sixth Sense
Lion in Winter
West Side Story*
Gandhi
My Fair Lady
Memento
Sound of Music
Wait Until Dark
Fiddler on the Roof
Silence of the Lambs

26 Doctor Zhivago
Lord of Rings/Two Towers
Chinatown
Hoop Dreams
All the President's Men
Producers, The
Sleuth
Star Wars V/Empire
E.T.
Willy Wonka

Top Production Values
Classic (Pre-1960)

29 Fantasia
Wizard of Oz
Gone with the Wind
28 Singin' in the Rain
Citizen Kane
Ben-Hur
Bridge on the River Kwai
Third Man
27 North by Northwest
Searchers, The
King and I
American in Paris
Casablanca
Quiet Man
Sunset Boulevard
Snow White
Red River
Ten Commandments
Rear Window
26 Band Wagon
Paths of Glory
Top Hat
Great Expectations
Some Like It Hot
Notorious

Lady from Shanghai
Vertigo
African Queen
Bambi
Night of the Hunter
Touch of Evil
Sweet Smell of Success
Gigi
All About Eve
Moulin Rouge
Red Shoes
Cinderella
Star Is Born
Woman of the Year
Pinocchio
42nd Street
Laura
Meet Me in St. Louis
How Green Was My Valley
On the Waterfront
Lady Eve
Song of the South
25 Double Indemnity
Lady and the Tramp
Around the World in 80 Days

Modern (1960 to Date)

29 Lord of Rings/Return
Finding Nemo
Lord of Rings/Two Towers
Lawrence of Arabia
Lord of Rings/Fellowship
Godfather, The
Star Wars
Chicago
Godfather Part II
Schindler's List
28 Winged Migration
Star Wars V/Empire
Matrix, The
Last Emperor
March of the Penguins
Saving Private Ryan
Toy Story
Raiders of the Lost Ark
Pianist, The
Shrek 2
Doctor Zhivago
Sound of Music
Shrek
Monsters, Inc.
Incredibles, The

Apocalypse Now
Star Wars VI/Return of Jedi
Star Wars III/Revenge of Sith
Nightmare Before Christmas
27 2001: A Space Odyssey
Beauty and the Beast
West Side Story
Jurassic Park
My Fair Lady
Patton
Braveheart
Brazil
Gandhi
Last Samurai
Blade Runner
Harry Potter/Sorcerer's
Wild Bunch
Harry Potter/Goblet of Fire
E.T.
Who Framed Roger Rabbit
Fantasia 2000
Psycho
Lion King
Frida
Harry Potter/Prisoner

Top Foreign Language Films

29	Seven Samurai		Babette's Feast
	Rashomon		8½
	Sorrow and the Pity		Wild Strawberries
28	Shoah		Amarcord
	Children of Paradise		Black Orpheus
	Beauty and Beast (1947)		Fanny and Alexander*
	Grand Illusion		Z
	Das Boot		Cries and Whispers
27	Ran		Talk to Her
	Bicycle Thief		Smiles of a Summer Night
	Seventh Seal		Alexander Nevsky
	Life Is Beautiful		Amélie
	La Strada		M
	Au Revoir Les Enfants		Diabolique
	Jean de Florette	**25**	Blue Angel
	Nights of Cabiria		Antonia's Line
	Triumph of the Will*		Garden of Finzi-Continis
	400 Blows		Leopard, The
	Wages of Fear		Hiroshima, Mon Amour
	Spirited Away		Aguirre: The Wrath of God
	Day for Night		Maria Full of Grace
26	Cinema Paradiso		Farewell My Concubine
	Conformist, The		La Dolce Vita
	King of Hearts		Marriage of Maria Braun
	City of God		All About My Mother

By Country

France

29	Sorrow and the Pity
28	Shoah
	Children of Paradise
	Beauty and Beast (1947)
	Grand Illusion
27	Au Revoir Les Enfants
	Jean de Florette
	400 Blows
	Wages of Fear
	Day for Night
26	King of Hearts
	Black Orpheus
	Z
	Amélie
	Diabolique
25	Hiroshima, Mon Amour

Germany

28	Das Boot
27	Triumph of the Will
26	M
25	Blue Angel
	Aguirre: The Wrath of God
	Marriage of Maria Braun

Italy

27	Bicycle Thief
	Life Is Beautiful
	La Strada
	Nights of Cabiria
26	Cinema Paradiso
	Conformist, The
	8½
	Amarcord
25	Garden of Finzi-Continis
	Leopard, The

Japan

29	Seven Samurai
	Rashomon
27	Ran
	Spirited Away
23	Akira

Sweden

27	Seventh Seal
26	Wild Strawberries
	Fanny and Alexander
	Cries and Whispers
	Smiles of a Summer Night
25	My Life As a Dog

Movie Directory

About a Boy   21 | 23 | 22 | 21
2002. Directed by Chris Weitz, Paul Weitz. With Hugh Grant, Toni Collette, Nicholas Hoult, Rachel Weisz. 101 minutes. Rated PG-13.
This "wonderfully funny romantic comedy" features Grant's "best work" as a "rich, self-absorbed" "skirt-chaser pretending to be a single dad" who strikes up a "sweet friendship" with a "lonely young boy" and "redeems himself in the end"; those who "expect the usual superficial" "chick-flick fluff" are "pleasantly surprised" by this "clever" adaptation of the Nick Hornby novel.

About Schmidt   21 | 26 | 20 | 21
2002. Directed by Alexander Payne. With Jack Nicholson, Kathy Bates, Hope Davis, Dermot Mulroney. 125 minutes. Rated R.
It's a "change of pace for Nicholson" ("no eyebrow raising"), who plays a "lethargic" "Middle America everyman" trying "to give his life purpose before it's too late" in this "heartbreaking" yet "hilarious" dramedy "guaranteed to scare anyone approaching retirement"; though it "drags at times", the "brilliant acting overcomes any plot shortcomings" – and the "Kathy Bates hot-tub scene" "will leave your head spinning."

Absence of Malice   21 | 25 | 21 | 20
1981. Directed by Sydney Pollack. With Paul Newman, Sally Field, Bob Balaban. 116 minutes. Rated PG.
"Newman and Field ignite the screen" in this "textured" "hard-hitting" courtroom drama demonstrating how "guilt by association" causes a "newspaper to ruin a man's career"; most say that the "irresponsible press" is a topic made for the movies, but some feel this "slight" effort "should have been better" – starting with the "not-believable ending."

Absent-Minded Professor, The ❶⓫   19 | 17 | 19 | 17
1961. Directed by Robert Stevenson. With Fred MacMurray, Nancy Olson, Keenan Wynn. 97 minutes. Rated PG.
Despite its "charming", "classic Disney" formula, this "bouncy tale" involving an invention dubbed "flubber" divides voters: flubbergasted fans claim it "stands up well over time", but deflators find it "kinda corny", adding it "may not appeal" to small fry, since its black-and-white cinematography "looks old"; although popular enough to inspire a couple of remakes, the "original is the best."

Abyss, The   20 | 19 | 19 | 25
1989. Directed by James Cameron. With Ed Harris, Mary Elizabeth Mastrantonio. 146 minutes. Rated PG-13.
"Eye-popping" special effects – notably the "breakout use of morphing" – are the raison d'être of this "underwater opus", a "fun" cocktail comprised of a "little sci-fi, a little action and a little romance"; it's also a little "long" and "sputters" at the finale, so diehards recommend the (even longer) "director's cut", which "fleshes out the far-too-abrupt ending in the original version."

Accidental Tourist, The   20 | 24 | 21 | 19
1988. Directed by Lawrence Kasdan. With William Hurt, Kathleen Turner, Geena Davis. 121 minutes. Rated PG.
This "zany" romantic drama about love, loss and "alphabetizing the groceries in your cupboard" is "as good as" Anne Tyler's best-seller and might "break and mend your heart in one sitting"; its "perfect cast" includes a "terrific" Hurt and an "offbeat", "pitch-

perfect" Davis (who "copped an Oscar"), though some argue the picture is "too quirky" and "inert" for mainstream audiences.

Accused, The ✉   23 | 28 | 23 | 21
1988. Directed by Jonathan Kaplan. With Kelly McGillis, Jodie Foster, Bernie Coulson. 108 minutes. Rated R.
Not for the "faint of heart", this "white-knuckle" thriller about a gang rape and its courtroom consequences is "based on true events" and dominated by a "phenomenal" Foster, who won a "thoroughly deserved" Oscar for her "captivating performance"; the "excruciating", "very graphic" reenactment of the crime is "definitely for mature audiences" – but far from gratuitous given the picture's "socially responsible" message.

Ace Ventura: Pet Detective ⓤ   15 | 16 | 12 | 14
1994. Directed by Tom Shadyac. With Jim Carrey, Courteney Cox, Sean Young. 86 minutes. Rated PG-13.
The "vulgar", "puerile humor" of this "silly, turn-your-brain-off" comedy about a pet detective tracking down a kidnapped dolphin was "Carrey's breakthrough", though some would "rather eat dirt" than sit through it; still, the "rubber-faced" star is so "over the top" that few notice this venture is "inanely short on plot."

Adam's Rib ◐   26 | 28 | 25 | 23
1949. Directed by George Cukor. With Spencer Tracy, Katharine Hepburn, Judy Holliday. 101 minutes. Not Rated.
"Chemistry abounds" in this "sparkling" matchup of Tracy and Hepburn, "probably the best pairing" of these "two pros", who are so "delightful" that many "wish they'd made even more movies together"; plotwise, this "battle-of-the-sexes" comedy concerns "married attorneys on opposing sides of a case", but fans say it's worth watching for the "effortless comedic timing" alone.

ADAPTATION   22 | 26 | 21 | 22
2002. Directed by Spike Jonze. With Nicolas Cage, Meryl Streep, Chris Cooper. 114 minutes. Rated R.
"You'll either love or hate" this "story within a story within a story", a "dark", "twisted" "head trip" about a screenwriter trying to adapt an unadaptable book; some find it "confusing", and even fans feel the "ending seemed to belong to a different film" ("perhaps that's the point"), but still "it's one of the most original movies ever made", bolstered by "superb acting."

Addams Family, The ⓤ   17 | 19 | 16 | 20
1991. Directed by Barry Sonnenfeld. With Anjelica Huston, Raul Julia, Christopher Lloyd. 102 minutes. Rated PG-13.
That "creepy, kooky" family spawned from the "*New Yorker* cartoons" and popularized by the '60s TV series makes its "ookie" screen debut with all its "madcap", ghoulish antics intact; "like MTV's *The Osbournes*", the story revolves around "misunderstood but lovable" types doing "quirky, offbeat" things.

Adventures of Priscilla, Queen of the Desert, The   23 | 24 | 22 | 22
1994. Directed by Stephan Elliott. With Terence Stamp, Guy Pearce, Hugo Weaving. 104 minutes. Rated R.
"Outlandish drag queens" and the "Australian outback" collide in this "razor-sharp" road comedy, a "flaming romp" about "boas, false eyelashes" and a bus "ride through the desert"; highlights

include Stamp's "campy" performance as a "post-op transsexual looking for love" and a "fabulous" soundtrack that will thrill "ABBA fans"; P.S. yup, "that's really Guy Pearce!"

Adventures of Robin Hood, The ⬚ 25 | 22 | 24 | 24
1938. Directed by Michael Curtiz, William Keighley. With Errol Flynn, Olivia de Havilland. 102 minutes. Not Rated.
This "swashbuckliest swashbuckler of them all" is the "definitive telling" of the tale, filmed in "gorgeous Technicolor" and "acted with verve" by a "charismatic" Flynn and a "perfect" de Havilland; ok, it might be "a bit dated", but its "lightning-quick dialogue", "exciting" swordplay and those famous "green tights" are "still engaging" enough to inspire a "whole genre of films" – plus a "whole lot of parodies."

AFFAIR TO REMEMBER, AN 26 | 25 | 25 | 23
1957. Directed by Leo McCarey. With Cary Grant, Deborah Kerr, Richard Denning. 119 minutes. Not Rated.
The "ultimate chick flick", this "three-hankie tearjerker" begins with a "glamorous" "shipboard romance" that turns "tragic" after an "unexpected twist" at the "Empire State Building"; though the "inspiration for many other weepies" (notably *Sleepless in Seattle*), this one's the "standard", thanks to the "captivating banter", ultra-"suave Grant" and some "classic NY" scenery; just don't bother to see it with your boyfriend – men "don't get it."

Affliction 20 | 25 | 19 | 19
1998. Directed by Paul Schrader. With Nick Nolte, Sissy Spacek, James Coburn. 113 minutes. Rated R.
Granted, it's "grim, grim, grim", but this "disquieting" adaptation of Russell Banks' novel of "family dysfunction" in New Hampshire is still "eminently watchable" due to its "strong performances": Nolte's "wrenching" work and Coburn's "scary", Oscar-winning turn in particular; though admittedly a "great exposé on abuse", some of the afflicted find it so "mind-numbingly downbeat" that they want to "slash their wrists" afterward.

AFRICAN QUEEN, THE ⬚∅ 28 | 29 | 26 | 26
1951. Directed by John Huston. With Humphrey Bogart, Katharine Hepburn, Robert Morley. 105 minutes. Not Rated.
"Curmudgeonly riverboat captain" Bogie and "feisty missionary" Hepburn "sizzle" as they take a "trip up a hellish river" and "discover love, courage" and the "best use of leeches since the Middle Ages" in this "beautifully crafted" drama; its "legendary reputation" owes a lot to Huston's "no-nonsense direction", James Agee's "witty" screenplay, the fine "location shots" of "deepest Africa" and, of course, that "undeniable chemistry" between the two shining stars; in sum, "they don't make 'em like this anymore."

After Hours 21 | 20 | 22 | 19
1985. Directed by Martin Scorsese. With Griffin Dunne, Rosanna Arquette, Teri Garr. 96 minutes. Rated R.
From the ever-"creative" Scorsese comes this "offbeat" cult curio, a "pitch-black comedy" set in '80s SoHo recounting the after-hours adventures of a "straight-laced guy" out on the town and out of cash in a "pre-ATM" world; the "numerous subplots" (involving an "ice cream truck", a "headbanger nightclub" and a potty-mouthed sculptress) strike some as "confusing" verging on "weird", but most tout its "razor-sharp performances" and "deft" wit.

Age of Innocence, The

1993. Directed by Martin Scorsese. With Daniel Day-Lewis, Michelle Pfeiffer, Winona Ryder. 139 minutes. Rated PG.

"Scorsese does Edith Wharton justice" in this "exquisite period drama" concerning "forbidden love" among "upper-class NYers" in the "Gilded Age"; Day-Lewis does a "subtle" job as the "tortured" lover, while the "gorgeous production" supplies a "sumptuous feast for the eyes" that "captures the smallest details in a languorous way" – maybe that's why the pace is a little on the "slow" side.

Agnes of God

1985. Directed by Norman Jewison. With Jane Fonda, Anne Bancroft, Meg Tilly. 98 minutes. Rated PG-13.

Make sure to "be in a serious mood" for this "disturbing" yet "powerful" drama about a "hysterical nun who may or may not be pregnant"; while there's some mighty "serious acting by some great women", voters split on the story ("compelling" vs. "convoluted") and the overall quality ("thought-provoking" vs. "underbaked"); either way, it's "worth sitting through just for the ending."

Aguirre: The Wrath of God 🇫

1977. Directed by Werner Herzog. With Klaus Kinski, Helena Rojo. 100 minutes. Not Rated.

"Shot on a small budget under unbelievable conditions", this "staggering" saga of 16th-century Spaniards seeking El Dorado in the Andes stars Kinski as a "hopelessly mad" "megalomaniac conquistador" opposite "more monkeys than you can shake a stick at"; the film's "hauntingly beautiful" but "static" pacewise, and it's "hard to tell who's more obsessed – the characters in the movie or the director and actors who made it."

A.I.: Artificial Intelligence

2001. Directed by Steven Spielberg. With Haley Joel Osment, Jude Law, Frances O'Connor. 146 minutes. Rated PG-13.

"Pinocchio" meets "Blade Runner" in this "mesmerizing" tale of a "robot boy who wants to be loved" in a devastated, tech-sprawled future; while the "brilliant" Osment brings real life to this artificial world, the scenario is a "strange mélange", one part Stanley Kubrick's "brooding" vision (he first optioned the story), one part Spielberg's "sugar"-coated "sentimentalism"; biggest "downer": that "Amazingly Inept ending."

Air Force One

1997. Directed by Wolfgang Petersen. With Harrison Ford, Gary Oldman, Glenn Close. 124 minutes. Rated R.

The "furrowed-browed" Ford plays a "butt-kicking" American president whose plane is hijacked by a "Russian madman" in this "escapist" thriller, a gripping mix of "edge-of-your-recliner suspense" and multi-"million-dollar stunts"; cynics nix its "action-by-the-numbers" plot but admit that this piece of "harmless, jingoistic fun" "works best with a big bowl of popcorn" nearby.

AIRPLANE! ⓤ

1980. Directed by Jim Abrahams, David Zucker, Jerry Zucker. With Robert Hays, Julie Hagerty, Lloyd Bridges, Leslie Nielsen, Peter Graves, Robert Stack. 88 minutes. Rated PG.

"Funny as heck", this "laugh-a-second spoof" mocks "'70s-era disaster films" with a "scatter-gag" barrage of "relentless slapstick", "constant plays on words" and the "best appearance by Ethel Merman in decades"; granted, it's "infantile" and some of the humor may be "politically incorrect" today, but there are so many "one-liners you'll remember years later" – 'don't call me Shirley!' – that it's no surprise this flick "launched a thousand imitators."

Airport ⓤ
17 | 15 | 18 | 18

1970. Directed by George Seaton. With Burt Lancaster, Helen Hayes, Dean Martin, George Kennedy. 137 minutes. Rated G.
The "first" and arguably the "best" of the "disaster flick" genre, this "gripping", "old-fashioned" drama unfolds on one particular night when nothing's going right at a major airport; given the "big, lumbering production" with a bevy of nearly "out-of-work actors" spouting "soap opera–city" dialogue, it's become a "guilty pleasure", though in its heyday it inspired "myriad sequels and spoofs."

Akira ⓕ
23 | – | 21 | 26

1988. Directed by Katsuhiro Otomo. Animated. 124 minutes. Rated R.
"Defining the anime genre", this "groundbreaking" "classic" "based on the Japanese comic book" is "blazingly kinetic", though "more violent than it needs to be" and thus "not for younger viewers"; the "confusing" sci-fi plot (something to do with "how power corrupts") might "make you wonder if something was lost in translation", but it's so "visually stunning" you won't care.

Aladdin
24 | – | 22 | 25

1992. Directed by Ron Clements, John Musker. Animated. 90 minutes. Rated G.
Disney's "fast-moving" animated Aladdin story is "stolen" by Robin Williams' "infectiously manic", "whirlwind" vocal performance as a "genius" genie; overall, its "likable characters" and "humorous storyline" appeal to both "adults and kids", while the "enchanting" Oscar-winning soundtrack will leave you "singing for days."

Alamo, The
18 | 18 | 20 | 21

1960. Directed by John Wayne. With John Wayne, Richard Widmark, Laurence Harvey. 167 minutes. Not Rated.
A "big-as-Texas" slice of "Americana", this "entertaining" rendition of the Battle of the Alamo still "appeals as a period film", although it strikes some as "overblown", "hokum history" with a "surprisingly boring" Wayne as Davy Crockett; even so, that "slam-bang, operatic finale" "mostly justifies" the "dreary opening hour."

Alexander Nevsky ⓞⓕ
26 | 22 | 25 | 26

1938. Directed by Sergei Eisenstein. With Nikolai Cherkassov. 107 minutes. Not Rated.
"Propaganda" was never better than this "exceptional" war epic, made to rally Soviet support for Stalin; shot in "haunting" black-and-white and set to a "superb Prokofiev score", it recounts the trials and tribulations of a 13th-century Russian prince, and even if the "clanky" script "ultimately collapses under the weight of all the ideological baggage", it's still a "triumph of expressionism."

Alfie ⓤ
22 | 26 | 22 | 20

1966. Directed by Lewis Gilbert. With Michael Caine, Shelley Winters, Vivien Merchant. 114 minutes. Not Rated.
This "little charmer" of a drama stars the "phenomenal" Caine in the career-making role of a "philandering playboy who gets his comeuppance" after dalliances with a flock of '60s birds; although

it seems "a bit dated" and might be "politically incorrect" today, its "brutally honest" script still "asks the important questions" – and there's an "excellent" Sonny Rollins score as a bonus.

Alice Doesn't Live Here Anymore ✉ | 24 | 26 | 23 | 21 |

1974. Directed by Martin Scorsese. With Ellen Burstyn, Kris Kristofferson, Jodie Foster. 112 minutes. Rated PG.

In this "early Scorsese" drama, Burstyn won an Oscar for her role as a "blue-collar" gal "trying to find herself" after a marriage breakup, and the "poignant" outcome marked a "watershed" for feminists in a "time when men and women were changing roles."

Alice in Wonderland | 24 | – | 25 | 25 |

1951. Directed by Clyde Geronimi, Wilfred Jackson, Hamilton Luske. Animated. 75 minutes. Rated G.

Disney's wonderfully "wacky" animation transforms Lewis Carroll's children's book into an "intelligent cartoon" rife with "hidden messages" and a slightly "schizophrenic" edge to boot; indeed, "family entertainment" mavens say this "imaginative" production is such a "terrific adaptation" that it "almost makes you forget the classic Tenniel illustrations."

Alien Ⅱ | 25 | 22 | 25 | 26 |

1979. Directed by Ridley Scott. With Sigourney Weaver, Tom Skerritt, Veronica Cartwright. 117 minutes. Rated R.

"Often imitated but never equaled", this "fierce" sci-fi "horror classic" could pass as a "Hitchcock-in-space" thriller thanks to its "jaw-dropping visuals" and "heart-pounding" plot about an outer space "survey team" that inadvertently brings a "new guest" home to dinner; "Weaver rocks" in "macho-man" mode and is only upstaged by the "slimy", "really gross" title character, the "best movie monster this side of Frankenstein."

Aliens Ⅱ | 23 | 21 | 22 | 26 |

1986. Directed by James Cameron. With Sigourney Weaver, Michael Biehn, Bill Paxton. 137 minutes. Rated R.

This "second installment" in the *Alien* franchise is just as "scream-out-loud scary" as its predecessor, with a *Rambo*-esque" emphasis; expect the "same high-quality production values" and "edge-of-your-seat tension", and if there's debate as to whether it "trumps" or "just lives up to" the original, one thing's certain: Weaver is still one "bad-ass" chick.

ALL ABOUT EVE ✉◑ | 28 | 29 | 27 | 26 |

1950. Directed by Joseph L. Mankiewicz. With Bette Davis, Anne Baxter, Gary Merrill. 138 minutes. Not Rated.

"Fasten your seatbelts" – the "ladies lunch on each other" in this "scalding", "wickedly funny" look at the "vicious world of show-biz"; a "boffo" Davis is "electrifying" as the "fading star" (opposite a "strong" Baxter as the rising one), but both are indebted to Mankiewicz's "perfect script", a "catty" catalog of "sharp-tongued dialogue" that "puts today's scenarios to shame"; in sum, this is one of the "best backstage bitchfests of all time."

All About My Mother ✉🅵 | 25 | 26 | 25 | 23 |

1999. Directed by Pedro Almodóvar. With Cecilia Roth, Penélope Cruz, Marisa Paredes. 101 minutes. Rated R.

Though "all the major characters are women", this "captivating story" via Spanish director Almodóvar is definitely "not a chick flick": rather, this "unusual", Oscar-winning drama about a mother searching for her dead son's transsexual dad provides a very "modern definition of what makes a family"; fans single out Roth's "stunning" work and Cruz's "breakout performance" – that is, when they're not "crying their hearts out" or "laughing their heads off."

All Dogs Go to Heaven ⑪   17 | – | 17 | 18

1989. Directed by Don Bluth, Gary Goldman, Dan Kuenster. Animated. 89 minutes. Rated G.

"Great for toddlers and young children", this "cute" animated flick about a "ghostly canine" sent from heaven to do good on earth might be a "non-Disney film" but still boasts "Disney quality"; surveyors split on the end result: a "listless, uninspired cartoon" vs. a "wonderfully sweet tearjerker."

ALL QUIET ON THE   28 | 26 | 28 | 25
WESTERN FRONT ✉◑

1930. Directed by Lewis Milestone. With Lew Ayres, Louis Wolheim, Raymond Griffith. 131 minutes. Not Rated.

"One of the first anti-war films" (and the "last word" on the subject for many), this "devastating" WWI saga is a "harrowing" glimpse at the "unglorious nature" of battle; over 75 years later, it "still packs a wallop", and though a bit "slow" by modern standards, this "faithful adaptation of the novel" will "stay with you."

All That Jazz   24 | 23 | 22 | 26

1979. Directed by Bob Fosse. With Roy Scheider, Jessica Lange, Ann Reinking, John Lithgow. 123 minutes. Rated R.

A "brilliantly original" "autobiopic" from Bob Fosse about Bob Fosse, this "prescient" drama might be "self-indulgent" and plainly "inspired by 8½", but it's also a "warts-and-all" "character sketch", with no surprise, "imaginative choreography"; look for a "great star turn" by Scheider and lots of "sardonic" dialogue.

All the King's Men ✉◑   25 | 26 | 25 | 22

1949. Directed by Robert Rossen. With Broderick Crawford, John Ireland, Mercedes McCambridge. 109 minutes. Not Rated.

The "American dream goes sour" in this "classic political drama" adapted from the Pulitzer Prize–winning novel about the rise and fall of a Huey Long–esque politician "corrupted by power"; this Best Picture winner is memorable for its "strong story" – and "even stronger acting by Crawford" (who also won a statuette).

All the President's Men   25 | 26 | 26 | 23

1976. Directed by Alan J. Pakula. With Robert Redford, Dustin Hoffman, Jason Robards. 138 minutes. Rated PG.

"History comes alive" in this "truth-is-stranger-than-fiction" account of the "Watergate" scandal, a "riveting", torn-"from-the-headlines thriller" that "captures you every time" "even though you know the outcome"; as reporters Woodward and Bernstein, Redford and Hoffman are truly "memorable" (ditto those "ties and sideburns"), and in the end this "gripping" effort brings "clarity to the events of that confusing time."

Almost Famous ✉   23 | 24 | 24 | 22

2000. Directed by Cameron Crowe. With Billy Crudup, Frances McDormand, Kate Hudson. 122 minutes. Rated R.

"Almost perfect" filmmaking, director Crowe's "feel-good" "semi-autobiographical story" about his work as a "teenage

Rolling Stone reporter" "on the road with a rock band" is half "coming-of-age" romance, half unadulterated "love song" to the '70s; while Crudup's "underrated" portrayal of a rocker and McDormand's "outstanding" mom earn kudos, "Hudson steals the show" as the "vulnerable groupie."

Along Came a Spider
16 | 20 | 18 | 18

2001. Directed by Lee Tamahori. With Morgan Freeman, Monica Potter, Michael Wincott. 104 minutes. Rated R.
Playing a forensic psychologist trying to rescue a senator's daughter from a psychopathic kidnapper, "Freeman carries" this "better-than-average" thriller adapted from the James Patterson book; but even though this "prequel of sorts to *Kiss the Girls*" is "competent" enough, foes fret it's "pretty predictable" and "close to thrill-free", except for that "nice twist at the end."

Altered States
19 | 20 | 20 | 20

1980. Directed by Ken Russell. With William Hurt, Blair Brown, Bob Balaban. 102 minutes. Rated R.
"Sometimes you don't know which end is up" in this "mind-bending" sci-fi "journey" starring Hurt as a scientist experimenting with sensory deprivation via an isolation chamber and select hallucinogens; although the "trippy" visuals and "convoluted" plot were considered "shocking" at the time, it may now look "like a relic from another era."

AMADEUS ✉
26 | 27 | 25 | 27

1984. Directed by Milos Forman. With F. Murray Abraham, Tom Hulce, Elizabeth Berridge. 158 minutes. Rated PG.
"Genius thwarted by mediocrity" is the theme of this "lively" Mozart biopic that's admittedly "not historically accurate", given its depiction of the "tortured" composer as something of a cross between a "twerp" and a "rock god"; awash in "lush period details", "timeless music" and "surprisingly nuanced performances" by Abraham and Hulce, it even manages to "make classical music seem racy" – and was quite the Oscar magnet, taking home eight of them.

Amarcord ✉🅕
26 | 25 | 25 | 26

1975. Directed by Federico Fellini. With Magali Noël, Bruno Zanin, Pupella Maggio. 127 minutes. Rated R.
"Fellini's warmhearted look back to his childhood", this Foreign Language Oscar winner is a "wonderful depiction" of "small-town life" in 1930s "fascist Italy", an "evocative" film that's simultaneously "lyric, tragic, vulgar and comic"; fans say this "beautiful reminiscence" reveals the famed director "at his most accessible" – and most "surreal."

Amélie 🅕
26 | 26 | 24 | 25

2001. Directed by Jean-Pierre Jeunet. With Audrey Tautou, Mathieu Kassovitz. 122 minutes. Rated R.
"Sweet as *sucre*", this "candy-coated" "picture postcard" of a romance concerns a "modern-day Pollyanna from Montmartre" "who wants to fix everyone's life" to make up for "what's missing in hers"; in the title role, a "new star has arrived" in "gamine" Tautou, a "21st-century Audrey Hepburn" whose "doe-eyed", "cute-as-a-button" looks alone will "put a huge grin on your face"; indeed, this "brimming-with-goodwill" picture is so "magical", you'll "hardly notice the subtitles."

AMERICAN BEAUTY ✉   24 | 27 | 23 | 24
1999. Directed by Sam Mendes. With Kevin Spacey, Annette Bening, Wes Bentley, Thora Birch. 121 minutes. Rated R.
The "desperation of modern suburban life" is the theme of this "engrossing" Best Picture winner that polarizes viewers: fans hail this tale of a man's "midlife awakening" and "resurrection" as a "truthful commentary on American society", but thornier types fuss it's a "pretentious", "angry" tract "disguised as existentialist philosophy"; nonetheless, there are plenty of bouquets for Spacey's "dead-on" performance and Alan Ball's "seriously meaty", "rapierlike screenplay."

American Graffiti ⓫   24 | 23 | 23 | 23
1973. Directed by George Lucas. With Richard Dreyfuss, Ron Howard, Cindy Williams. 110 minutes. Rated PG.
"Spot future stars" (including an early Harrison Ford) in this "end-of-an-era" dramedy that "launched a dozen careers" and proves that "Lucas once directed actors, not just pixels"; "covering one night" in 1962 – "but what a night" – it "captures a time and place" in teenage, West Coast America by mixing "cool cars", "period jukebox hits" and "Wolfman Jack" into a "classic growing-up story" that really "makes nostalgia compelling."

American History X   25 | 28 | 24 | 23
1998. Directed by Tony Kaye. With Edward Norton, Edward Furlong, Beverly D'Angelo. 119 minutes. Rated R.
"Neo-Nazi violence" and "racism" lie at the heart of this "scalding" drama about "white supremacists" that's "like a punch in the gut" thanks to the "gifted" Norton's "all-too-convincing" portrait of a "scary" "skinhead"; though surely "horrifying", this "powerful" film will also "make you think."

American in Paris, An ✉   26 | 23 | 22 | 27
1951. Directed by Vincente Minnelli. With Gene Kelly, Leslie Caron, Oscar Levant. 113 minutes. Not Rated.
A "debonair" Kelly and "beautiful Caron" "dance up a storm" in this "unforgettable" Gershwin musical that might tempt you to "visit Paris"; sure, the "silly story" is a bit "hackneyed", but "who cares?" when the production's so "visually compelling" (especially that climactic ballet "integrating Impressionist art" in its settings); no surprise, it took home six Oscars, including Best Picture.

American Pie ⓫   19 | 16 | 18 | 18
1999. Directed by Paul Weitz. With Jason Biggs, Shannon Elizabeth, Tara Reid. 95 minutes. Rated R.
"You'll never look at an apple pie the same way" after a gander at this "drop-dead funny" slice of "raunch" about some teenage dudes, "hormones a-raging", who "vow to lose their virginity on prom night"; while bluenoses berate its "toilet humor" as "moronic", "baked-goods" buyers say its "laugh-a-minute" plot is an "intelligent gross-out", the "Gen-X" version of "*Porky's*."

American President, The   21 | 22 | 21 | 21
1995. Directed by Rob Reiner. With Michael Douglas, Annette Bening, Martin Sheen. 114 minutes. Rated PG-13.
"Only in Hollywood" could the "President openly date a lobbyist", but no one "believes it for a second – or cares" – since this "feel-good" romance is so darned "entertaining"; voters like Douglas'

"humanized" Chief Exec and Bening's "luminous" gal pal but reject the "rose-colored" script and its "telegraphed happy ending", sighing "pass the popcorn."

American Splendor | 23 | 25 | 22 | 22 |

2003. Directed by Shari Springer Berman, Robert Pulcini. With Paul Giamatti, Hope Davis, Harvey Pekar. 101 minutes. Rated R.
An "average slob" gets the big-screen treatment in this "subversive" biopic of underground comics scribe Harvey Pekar, a "schlubby" "anti-hero" complete with a "file-clerk" day job; deftly employing "three parallel realities" – "actors, cartoons" and Harvey himself – to tell its story, this "offbeat" picture is nothing if not "original", though some feel it "falls short of its potential" and wonder "what does it amount to in the end?"

American Tail, An Ⅱ | 21 | – | 21 | 22 |

1986. Directed by Don Bluth. Animated. 77 minutes. Rated G.
"One of the first good non-Disney" pieces of animation, this "wonderful" "story of the immigrant experience" follows the adventures of a Russian mouse separated from his kin after arriving in America; a "real family favorite", its "clever" concept with a "touch of pathos" makes many "hearts melt."

American Werewolf in London, An Ⅱ | 20 | 17 | 21 | 21 |

1981. Directed by John Landis. With David Naughton, Jenny Agutter, Griffin Dunne. 97 minutes. Rated R.
"Filmed with style and wit", this "tragicomic gorefest" "shows some bite" as it follows the misadventures of two American "zombies" abroad; best remembered for its "transformation scene" combining "superior makeup" and "amazing special effects" – and second-best known for Agutter's "hot shower scene" – this one's so "suspenseful and creepy" that it "helped revitalize the horror genre" in the early '80s.

Amistad | 21 | 24 | 22 | 24 |

1997. Directed by Steven Spielberg. With Morgan Freeman, Djimon Hounsou, Matthew McConaughey. 152 minutes. Rated R.
Examining the "dark underside of American history", this "little-known" true story of 19th-century "Africans forced into slavery" "starts on a slave ship and culminates in court"; while some say this "gripping", "difficult" story is an "underappreciated" Spielberg opus, others find it so "heavy-handed" and "manipulative" that they're left "out to sea."

Analyze That | 14 | 17 | 12 | 15 |

2002. Directed by Harold Ramis. With Robert De Niro, Billy Crystal, Lisa Kudrow, Joe Viterelli, Cathy Moriarty. 96 minutes. Rated R.
That the "novelty" of mobsters in therapy is "worn out beyond belief" doesn't stop Billy and Bobby from reuniting for this "lame" sequel to *Analyze This*, a "profanity"-fest with "few laughs" fashioned from a "one-joke concept"; in the final analysis, most shrink from recommending this "disappointment", saying they'd rather "sleep with the fishes."

Analyze This Ⅱ | 18 | 21 | 18 | 18 |

1999. Directed by Harold Ramis. With Robert De Niro, Billy Crystal, Lisa Kudrow, Chazz Palminteri. 103 minutes. Rated R.
"*Sopranos*" nuts see some familiar plot threads in this "funny Mafia movie" featuring the "hilarious pairing" of "De Niro as a

mobster with anxiety attacks" and Crystal as his reluctant shrink; though some analysts shrug it off as a "flat" "trifle", supporters call it an "amusing send-up" that may be "ridiculous, but it works."

Anastasia ✉

23	27	24	23

1956. Directed by Anatole Litvak. With Ingrid Bergman, Yul Brynner, Helen Hayes. 105 minutes. Not Rated.

The Oscar-winning, ever "appealing" Bergman and a "great" Brynner make quite a "combo" in this dramatic biography of Anastasia, the legendary daughter of the last Russian czar and pretender to the throne – or is she?; told with "sympathy and empathy", it's a "cuddle-up-with-your-honey" picture with acting "so good you find yourself rooting for those inept royals"; "is it true?" – c'mon, "does it matter?"

Anastasia

20	–	19	22

1997. Directed by Don Bluth, Gary Goldman. Animated. 94 minutes. Rated G.

"Disney isn't the only one" making "amazing animation" these days: this cartoon version of a lost (and found) Russian princess is an "astonishingly good feature", although it "doesn't seem to be kid material"; still, it's a "visually appealing" extravaganza oozing "style", even if the "bat steals the show."

Anatomy of a Murder ◑

26	27	27	24

1959. Directed by Otto Preminger. With James Stewart, Lee Remick, Ben Gazzara. 160 minutes. Not Rated.

Stewart "pulls out all the stops" as a "down-to-earth" lawyer in this courtroom drama that's "spellbinding" look at a "sensational" "backwoods" revenge killing; "considered risqué" in the '50s given Remick's "sultry" turn and its use of the then-verboten word "'panties'", it remains as "riveting" as ever; P.S. "Duke Ellington and his band" lay down the cool progressive jazz soundtrack.

Andromeda Strain, The

20	18	25	20

1971. Directed by Robert Wise. With Arthur Hill, David Wayne, James Olson, Kate Reid. 131 minutes. Rated G.

"Science provides the thrills" in this piece of "thinking man's sci-fi" based on the early "Michael Crichton thriller" concerning a "dangerous" virus from outer space; though it may be "low-tech" (with "out-of-date special effects" and "sprayed-on perspiration"), it supplies enough "palpable tension" to keep things "interesting."

Angels with Dirty Faces ◑

24	24	22	20

1938. Directed by Michael Curtiz. With James Cagney, Pat O'Brien, Humphrey Bogart. 97 minutes. Not Rated.

Two toughs from the slums take different career paths – one becoming a "lowlife", the other a priest – in this "cautionary melodrama" from the days when "good was good and bad was bad"; "cliché-ridden" though it may be, it was designed to "scare the bejesus out of would-be delinquents" – or at least have them "doing Cagney impersonations for weeks" afterward.

Anger Management

13	18	13	16

2003. Directed by Peter Segal. With Adam Sandler, Jack Nicholson, Marisa Tomei. 106 minutes. Rated PG-13.

The "unlikely" pairing of "silly" Sandler with "versatile" Nicholson as patient and therapist is a "cute idea gone awry" in this "disappointing" comedy flush with "juvenile bathroom humor"; when

44

cooler heads prevail, primary blame goes to the "ridiculous premise", which neither "great cameos" (Heather Graham, Woody Harrelson) nor a "surprise ending" can temper.

Animal Crackers ◑

| 26 | 24 | 18 | 20 |

1930. Directed by Victor Heerman. With the Marx Brothers, Lillian Roth, Margaret Dumont. 97 minutes. Rated G.

"Hooray for Captain Spaulding!"; this "timeless" Marx Brothers "romp" is best remembered for Groucho's "priceless entrance" and "fabulously stupid" quips ("I shot an elephant in my pajamas, but how he got in my pajamas, I'll never know"); needless to say, the "storyline isn't the point" here.

ANIMAL HOUSE

| 24 | 20 | 21 | 20 |

1978. Directed by John Landis. With John Belushi, Tim Matheson, Tom Hulce, John Vernon. 109 minutes. Rated R.

"Raunchy and vulgar", this much-admired "granddaddy of the frat boy gross-out comedies" features the much-"missed" Belushi "at his side-splitting best" as Bluto Blutarsky, a "seven-year college" vet; "no, it ain't Shakespeare", but rather a "textbook" study of "toga parties", "road trips", "food fights" and "anarchic libidos on parade" that's so much of a "guy's movie" that some fellas say they "thought it was a documentary."

Anna and the King

| 19 | 21 | 21 | 24 |

1999. Directed by Andy Tennant. With Jodie Foster, Chow Yun-Fat, Tom Felton. 148 minutes. Rated PG-13.

Take a "trip to Thailand" via this "touching" romance that's a "nonmusical rendition" of *The King and I*, based on the true story of Brit school teacher Anna Leonowens; though "slow" pacing and the "absence of chemistry" between Foster and Yun-Fat leave things "rather flat", at least this "lush" production ("magnificent scenery", "elaborate costumes") is "gorgeous to look at."

Annie

| 19 | 19 | 20 | 20 |

1982. Directed by John Huston. With Albert Finney, Carol Burnett, Aileen Quinn, Tim Curry. 126 minutes. Rated PG.

Little Orphan Annie's "rags-to-riches" saga morphs into a "colorful" "children's musical" with a "splendid cast" in this "stylized" "adaptation of the comic strip" that first bowed on Broadway; parents say it's "perfect for kids", and even those who find it "bloated" and "boring" find themselves leaving the theater humming 'Tomorrow.'

ANNIE HALL ✉

| 27 | 26 | 25 | 24 |

1977. Directed by Woody Allen. With Woody Allen, Diane Keaton, Tony Roberts. 93 minutes. Rated PG.

"Every neurotic's favorite comedy", this Oscar-winning Allen film about an "insecure" "Jewish nebbish" smitten with a nutty, "la-di-da"–spouting "shiksa" is "among his deftest creations"; its "pitch-perfect NY" setting, "pure-genius script" and "very funny" set pieces (the "lobster-cooking episode", the "split-screen family dinner scene") make for "essential Woody."

Anniversary Party, The

| 18 | 23 | 17 | 17 |

2001. Directed by Alan Cumming, Jennifer Jason Leigh. With Alan Cumming, Jennifer Jason Leigh, Phoebe Cates, Kevin Kline, Jennifer Beals, Gwyneth Paltrow. 115 minutes. Rated R.

"Hollywood shallowness" gets the "cinema verité" treatment in this "dark", "low-budget" tale of a "dysfunctional" writer and actress celebrating their wedding anniversary with various friends and hangers-on; party-poopers don't dig the "unsympathetic" characters and all that "talk, talk, talk", but others relish the "smart" skewering of "Southern California culture."

Antonia's Line ✉ 🇫

25 | 26 | 25 | 24

1995. Directed by Marleen Gorris. With Willeke van Ammelrooy, Els Dottermans. 102 minutes. Rated R.
"About women and for women", this "liberating" drama recounts 50 years in one lady's life, told in "flashback" from her "death bed"; "shockingly feminist" to chauvinists, its "charming performances" and "empowering message" are so "unforgettable" that it more than "deserves the Best Foreign Film Oscar" it received.

Antwone Fisher

23 | 26 | 24 | 22

2002. Directed by Denzel Washington. With Derek Luke, Denzel Washington, Joy Bryant. 120 minutes. Rated PG-13.
"Buy a box of tissues before you rent" this "inspiring true-life story about a boy from the 'hood who makes something of himself despite many obstacles"; this "emotional roller coaster" is "wonderfully acted" and represents a "terrific directorial debut by Denzel", who "manages to bring realism to what could have been a manipulative storyline."

Antz

20 | – | 19 | 23

1998. Directed by Eric Darnell, Tim Johnson. Animated. 87 minutes. Rated PG.
Opinion splitz on this fully computer-animated feature about an insect's "rebellion" against conformity; fans buzz that this "highly creative" film "for all ages" tells a "well-executed" story, yet drones swat it for "ugly animation" and a "subversive socialist subtext" that's "not recommended" for "younger children"; P.S. Woody Allen's voice-over as a "neurotic ant is a must-hear."

Apartment, The ✉ ◐

25 | 28 | 25 | 23

1960. Directed by Billy Wilder. With Jack Lemmon, Shirley MacLaine, Fred MacMurray. 125 minutes. Not Rated.
"Sex in the big, bad city" has never been as "realistic" or "touching" as in this "sad-edged romance", recounting the exploits of a "hapless" "junior exec in love with his boss' mistress"; it pits a "baby-faced" Lemmon opposite a "tender" MacLaine and "understated" MacMurray, and besides being "very amusing", it's also a "powerful social comment masquerading as comedy."

APOCALYPSE NOW

27 | 27 | 25 | 28

1979. Directed by Francis Ford Coppola. With Martin Sheen, Marlon Brando, Robert Duvall. 153 minutes. Rated R.
The "Vietnam nightmare" meets Joseph "Conrad's *Heart of Darkness*" in this "landmark" Coppola opus that's one part "gut churner", one part "acid trip" as it examines the "insanity of war"; true, it's "long", the "last half hour is disappointing" and many wonder "what the heck Brando's saying", but ultimately this "sprawling" "meditation on the human mind" just plain "grabs you."

Apollo 13

24 | 24 | 25 | 26

1995. Directed by Ron Howard. With Tom Hanks, Bill Paxton, Kevin Bacon, Gary Sinise. 140 minutes. Rated PG.
"Even though you [presumably] know the outcome", this "space race" drama based on the "remarkable true story" of the "peril-

ous voyage of Apollo 13" stays "suspenseful"; with a roster of "big-name actors" exuding the "right stuff", it delivers "get-up-and-cheer escapism" that might be "a tad corny" but will "make you proud to be an American" – "isn't history wonderful?"

Apprenticeship of Duddy Kravitz, The ∅

22 | 24 | 24 | 20

1974. Directed by Ted Kotcheff. With Richard Dreyfuss, Micheline Lanctôt, Jack Warden. 120 minutes. Rated PG.

A "nice Jewish boy in Montreal comes of age" and tries to ascend the "slippery slope of success" in this "little-known comic gem" "tinged with sadness"; a "moving" adaptation of Mordecai Richler's novel, it's a "genius" "showcase for Dreyfuss" as the titular "hustling" "mensch."

Armageddon

15 | 14 | 14 | 21

1998. Directed by Michael Bay. With Bruce Willis, Billy Bob Thornton, Ben Affleck, Liv Tyler. 144 minutes. Rated PG-13.

An "asteroid hurtles toward the earth" in this "high testosterone" "explosionfest" with a "far-fetched" "patriotic story" involving a "*Dirty Dozen*–style space mission" and "tongue-in-cheek heroics"; foes say this "blockbuster" is "all budget and no brain" with "state-of-the-art special effects as the real star of the film."

Around the World in 80 Days ✉

22 | 20 | 22 | 25

1956. Directed by Michael Anderson. With David Niven, Cantinflas, Shirley MacLaine. 175 minutes. Rated G.

"It's the scenery, stupid" that makes this globe-trotting "epic" "travelogue" based on "Jules Verne's classic book" "worth watching", though lots of "stars popping up in cameo roles" add to the "visual cornucopia"; however, some find it a "boring", "three-hour ride" and "can't believe" it snagged a Best Picture Oscar.

Arsenic and Old Lace ◐

26 | 26 | 25 | 22

1944. Directed by Frank Capra. With Cary Grant, Priscilla Lane, Raymond Massey. 118 minutes. Not Rated.

"Elderberry wine" makes for "murderous fun" in this "macabre" black comedy about two "vengeful old ladies" killing off bachelors while "chewing the scenery"; as their nephew, a "frantic" Grant "hams it up unashamedly" and delivers the "world's best double takes" in this "funny" adaptation of the Broadway hit.

Arthur ⑪

20 | 21 | 19 | 19

1981. Directed by Steve Gordon. With Dudley Moore, Liza Minnelli, John Gielgud. 117 minutes. Rated PG.

There's "not a dull moment" in this "silly" yet "tender" romantic comedy about a "falling-down-drunk" millionaire looking for love; although top billing goes to "sexy short guy" Dudley Moore opposite "Liza Minnelli as Liza Minnelli", this "priceless" picture arguably belongs to Gielgud, who delivers its most "classic line" – "I'll alert the media" – "as if he were playing Hamlet."

AS GOOD AS IT GETS ✉

22 | 25 | 21 | 21

1997. Directed by James L. Brooks. With Jack Nicholson, Helen Hunt, Greg Kinnear. 139 minutes. Rated PG-13.

Fans feel the "title says it all": this "smart comedy" about the "unlikely pairing" of a "cantankerous" "obsessive-compulsive jerk" and a "kooky" "single-mom waitress" crackles with "sharp", "NY neurotic" dialogue; but even though both Hunt and Nicholson grabbed Oscars for their "tour-de-force" turns, some shrug they "play themselves" in this "overhyped" and "overrated" flick.

Asphalt Jungle, The ◑ 24 | 24 | 24 | 23
1950. Directed by John Huston. With Sterling Hayden, Louis Calhern, Sam Jaffe. 112 minutes. Not Rated.
Sure, this "prime example of juicy film noir" is one of the "original caper" pictures, about a "carefully planned" "jewel heist gone terribly wrong", but it's also appealing for an "early" turn by Marilyn Monroe in a "blow-you-away" bit part; otherwise, this "dark tale" of "greed" and "emotion" supplies enough "twists and compelling characters" to make it "one of Huston's most underrated films."

Atlantic City 24 | 27 | 22 | 22
1980. Directed by Louis Malle. With Burt Lancaster, Susan Sarandon, Kate Reid. 104 minutes. Rated R.
This "valentine to a lost city" pairs a "stunning" Lancaster and Sarandon as unlikely lovers "trying to redeem their lives" in the "bleak atmosphere" of a "dying" town; "sad, bittersweet" and "overlooked", it boasts a "superb" John Guare script full of "characters worth caring about" but is most remembered for the scene of "our heroine bathing herself with sliced lemons."

Atlantis: The Lost Empire 16 | – | 14 | 21
2001. Directed by Gary Trousdale, Kirk Wise. Animated. 95 minutes. Rated PG.
Centering on the search for the "legendary" sunken civilization, this "sophisticated action" flick is a Disney production featuring elements of "Jules Verne" and "Japanese anime" but no "song-and-dance numbers" or cute talking animals; though its blend of traditional and CGI animation is "visually stunning", some say the story's "subpar" and a bit "too violent for minors."

Auntie Mame 25 | 25 | 24 | 25
1958. Directed by Morton DaCosta. With Rosalind Russell, Forrest Tucker, Coral Browne. 143 minutes. Not Rated.
"Defining diva-dom for generations", this "stylish" comedy about a wide-eyed kid's "wacky rich" auntie stars a "larger-than-life Russell" as a "great old broad"–cum–"force of nature"; it might be "overlong and underplotted", but "great one-liners" barbed with "sharp wit" ("life is a banquet and most poor suckers are starving to death") assure its rep as the "campiest of camp classics."

Au Revoir Les Enfants 🇫 27 | 26 | 27 | 24
1987. Directed by Louis Malle. With Gaspard Manesse, Francine Racette. 104 minutes. Rated PG.
"Powerful and haunting", this "must-see" drama explores "anti-Semitism" in WWII "occupied France" via its depiction of a "Jewish boy hidden" in a French school; though there's certainly "no happy ending" here, it "brings the events of the Holocaust to a personal level" so devastatingly that you'll "never forget" it.

Austin Powers: 19 | 18 | 17 | 19
International Man of Mystery ⑪
1997. Directed by Jay Roach. With Mike Myers, Elizabeth Hurley, Michael York. 90 minutes. Rated PG-13.
"No-brainer" alert: this "shagadelic" "spoof of James Bond movies" delivers "tons of laughs" with "dumb" jokes and overall "retro '60s silliness" – "oh, behave!" – courtesy of "comic genius"

Myers in a dual role as a spy with "mossy teeth" and a villain with a pet pussycat; there's debate over its "crude" "toilet humor" but wide agreement that you needn't "bother with the sequel."

Auto Focus
| 16 | 22 | 17 | 18 |

2002. Directed by Paul Schrader. With Greg Kinnear, Willem Dafoe, Rita Wilson, Maria Bello. 105 minutes. Rated R.
The "rise and fall" of "sick puppy" sitcom star Bob Crane is charted in this "raw" look at a "mid-level actor turned sex addict" and his enabler buddy; even though Kinnear and Dafoe are "suitably creepy" as "partners in grime", foes find it "hard to empathize with the characters and their obsessions" and feel the film is "devoid of any uplifting moments" – it's "like watching a train wreck."

Aviator, The
| 23 | 25 | 22 | 27 |

2004. Directed by Martin Scorsese. With Leonardo DiCaprio, Cate Blanchett, Kate Beckinsale, John C. Reilly, Alec Baldwin, Alan Alda. 170 minutes. Rated PG-13.
Martin Scorsese takes off with a "bottomless budget" in this "sweeping" biopic of "eccentric" gazillionaire Howard Hughes, where the lift-off is supplied by "sumptuous" production design (including one of the "most realistic plane crashes" ever filmed) and Cate Blanchett's "dead-on" take on Kate Hepburn; more debatable is Leo's title turn ("formidable" or "hollow"), though most agree on the "too-long" running time and "soulless", "conventional" windup.

Awakenings
| 22 | 26 | 23 | 20 |

1990. Directed by Penny Marshall. With Robert De Niro, Robin Williams, John Heard. 121 minutes. Rated PG-13.
A true story about the search for a "cure for comatose patients" gets "thought-provoking" treatment in this "touching" drama, featuring Williams "playing it straight" for a change opposite a "memorable" De Niro; while some berate its "sentimental", "hanky-wringing" edge, most find it both "amusing and moving", despite the "potentially mawkish" subject matter.

Awful Truth, The ✉◐
| ▽ 25 | 25 | 24 | 22 |

1937. Directed by Leo McCarey. With Irene Dunne, Cary Grant, Ralph Bellamy, Alexander D'Arcy. 91 minutes. Not Rated.
"Two spoiled rich people" on the verge of divorce try to "win each other back" in this "laugh-out-loud" romantic comedy top-billing the "classic combo" of Grant and Dunne; it's "one of the better screwball" pictures "from the golden age of Hollywood" loaded with "crackling dialogue" and sheer "fun."

Babe Ⓤ
| 25 | 22 | 25 | 26 |

1995. Directed by Chris Noonan. With James Cromwell, Magda Szubanski, Danny Mann. 89 minutes. Rated G.
"Believe the hype": fans are in "hog heaven" over this "porcine" comedy about a "talking pig" who "wants to be a sheepherder so he won't get eaten"; "cute without being cutesy", it features Oscar-winning "computer effects" that allow "animals to interact" with humans so realistically that it may "turn you into a vegetarian."

Babette's Feast ✉Ⓕ
| 26 | 26 | 26 | 25 |

1987. Directed by Gabriel Axel. With Stéphane Audran, Bibi Andersson, Jarl Kulle. 102 minutes. Rated G.
"Sumptuous enough to make vegetarians drool" (though "slow as molasses"), this "classic foodie" dramedy is an "unusual" tale

based on the Isak Dinesen story about the "power of redemption" cooked up in one "magnificent meal"; "still mouthwatering after all these years", this "intriguing" Danish treat is so "delectable" and "savory" that it could be the "Zagat signature movie."

Baby Boom   19 | 20 | 20 | 18
1987. Directed by Charles Shyer. With Diane Keaton, Sam Shepard, Harold Ramis. 103 minutes. Rated PG.
"Career vs. home and family" is the theme of this "very '80s" "light comedy" starring a "sharp, understated" Keaton as a "woman who wants it all" – and gets it when she inherits a baby and hooks up with Shepard; though tough guys dismiss it as a "feel-good chick flick", "warm-and-fuzzy" folk find it a "likable" tale of "triumphant romance."

Backdraft   18 | 18 | 18 | 23
1991. Directed by Ron Howard. With Kurt Russell, William Baldwin, Scott Glenn, Robert De Niro. 132 minutes. Rated R.
"Big fires and cute firemen" sum up the appeal of this disaster thriller aflame with a "stellar cast" and some mighty "eye-opening", "amazingly realistic" FX; ok, the "melodramatic storyline's a bit soft" and the actors struggle with the "moronic dialogue", but the action sequences will "keep you hanging on until the end."

Back to the Future ⑪   23 | 20 | 25 | 24
1985. Directed by Robert Zemeckis. With Michael J. Fox, Christopher Lloyd, Lea Thompson. 111 minutes. Rated PG.
A "time-traveling DeLorean" propels the "delectably dimpled Fox" into a "fun ride to the past" (and an opportunity to observe his parents as "goofy teenagers") in this "perfect blend of sci-fi, fantasy and pop culture"; "irrepressibly entertaining" and very popular, it spawned an "incredible ride" at the Universal theme park as well as two "terrible sequels."

Bad and the Beautiful, The ✉◗   24 | 25 | 24 | 24
1952. Directed by Vincente Minnelli. With Lana Turner, Kirk Douglas, Walter Pidgeon, Dick Powell, Gloria Grahame. 118 minutes. Not Rated.
Douglas is at his "jaw-clenching best" playing a "manipulative producer" in this knowing, "behind-the-scenes" look at Tinseltown that could be "Hollywood's best movie about itself"; told in a series of flashbacks by a director, an actress and a screenwriter, it's "lush, hammy" stuff that's "over the top in just the right way"; P.S. "never loan Lana Turner your car."

Bad Day at Black Rock   24 | 28 | 24 | 22
1955. Directed by John Sturges. With Spencer Tracy, Robert Ryan, Anne Francis. 81 minutes. Not Rated.
This "taut little thriller" is a "mean, lean" film about "bigotry" in a "small town with a secret", starring an "excellent" Tracy in "one of his more unusual roles"; although somewhat "forgotten" today, it's "just as relevant as it was in the post-McCarthy '50s", "giving you plenty to think about" as it "profiles American prejudices."

Bad Education 🄴   23 | 26 | 23 | 24
2004. Directed by Pedro Almodóvar. With Gael García Bernal, Fele Martínez, Daniel Giménez Cacho. 106 minutes. Rated R.
"Bad boy" director Almodóvar proves he's at the "head of the class" with this "visually hypnotic", "gender-bending" mystery

that pays homage to both "film noir" and "Hitchcock"; boasting a "bravura" performance by rising star Bernal (who's just as "sexy in drag"), this "out-there" flick is rife with "racy", "taboo"-smashing material (e.g. "drugs", "transvestites", "priest abuse") and "not for the easily offended."

Badlands

25	27	24	24

1973. Directed by Terrence Malick. With Martin Sheen, Sissy Spacek, Warren Oates. 95 minutes. Rated PG.
The "banality of evil" is dissected in this "dark, disturbing" depiction of a true-life teen crime spree; playing "shallow", "disaffected" lovers on the run, a "very young" Spacek and Sheen are "first rate", while Malick's "trademark sweeping cinematography" acts as "visually stunning" counterpoint to the "bitingly tragic" story; in short, it's "gutsy", "twisted" and "not nearly as well known as it should be."

Bad News Bears, The ⊞

18	16	19	15

1976. Directed by Michael Ritchie. With Walter Matthau, Tatum O'Neal, Vic Morrow. 102 minutes. Rated PG.
A "must-see for any Little Leaguer", this "cute" sports comedy pitches a story about a curmudgeonly drunk roped into coaching a "truly awful" kids' baseball team; though perhaps "better then than now" (with "foul but funny language" that might raise parental eyebrows), its sequels are definitely "bad news for moviegoers."

Bad Santa

18	20	17	17

2003. Directed by Terry Zwigoff. With Billy Bob Thornton, Tony Cox, John Ritter, Bernie Mac. 91 minutes. Rated R.
"Rude, crude and awfully funny", this "fearless" black comedy toplines Thornton as a "burnt-out", "mean-spirited" Santa who robs department stores with his partner, a "potty-mouthed" elf; no question, it's "sick, sick, sick" and "definitely not for kids", but cynics label it the "perfect antidote to phony Christmas cheer."

Bad Seed, The ❶

22	23	25	20

1956. Directed by Mervyn LeRoy. With Nancy Kelly, Patty McCormack, Eileen Heckart. 129 minutes. Not Rated.
"Not for the faint of heart", this "very creepy" thriller is the story of a "perky little deranged girl" who's the "world's most evil child" (think "Ted Bundy in a pinafore"); "unsettling and unforgettable" in its time, it's still "way, way over the top", and even if the Broadway play "had a better ending", this one will positively "send chills down your spine."

Bambi

26	–	25	26

1942. Directed by David Hand. Animated. 70 minutes. Rated G.
"Don't forget those tissues" before settling into this dear coming-of-age story that's best remembered for the "absolutely heart-wrenching" "death of Bambi's mother", a "cruel lesson in life" that will "make you think twice about showing it" to young children; otherwise, it's arguably the "most beautiful" example of vintage Disney animation, "warm and fuzzy" but "not mawkish."

Bananas

23	20	22	19

1971. Directed by Woody Allen. With Woody Allen, Louise Lasser, Carlos Montalban. 82 minutes. Rated PG-13.
"For Allen purists mostly", this "early" comic romance "relies heavily on sight gags and slapstick humor" in its "anarchic" story of

a nebbish turned "Latin American dictator" that's a "zany" satire to some, but "intermittently funny shtick" to others; P.S. hang on for a "young" Sylvester Stallone's cameo as a "thug on the subway."

Band Wagon, The
26 | 21 | 20 | 26

1953. Directed by Vincente Minnelli. With Fred Astaire, Cyd Charisse, Nanette Fabray. 111 minutes. Not Rated.
A "worthy companion to *Singin' in the Rain*", this "solid musical" comedy boasts the "most romantic moment in movie history" – the "hauntingly lovely 'Dancing in the Dark' number in Central Park" – performed by Astaire and Charisse in "top form"; thanks to its "fantastic music" and "delightful cast", nostalgists sigh "they don't make 'em like this anymore."

Bang the Drum Slowly
23 | 25 | 24 | 18

1973. Directed by John Hancock. With Michael Moriarty, Robert De Niro, Vincent Gardenia. 96 minutes. Rated PG.
Moriarty and De Niro deliver "two moving performances" in this memorably "sad" drama about a hayseed baseball catcher with a terminal illness and the star pitcher who befriends him; both a "real tearjerker" and a "powerful story of friendship", it's a "well done", "humbling" experience that still has "staying power."

Barbarella
13 | 9 | 11 | 15

1968. Directed by Roger Vadim. With Jane Fonda, John Phillip Law, Anita Pallenberg, Milo O'Shea. 98 minutes. Rated PG.
Über-"babe" Fonda "pushes the boundaries of sexuality" (at least the 1968 boundaries) with her "zero-g striptease" and other "amusing" outfit-free antics in this "campy" but "influential" sci-fi "cult classic"; if you can just "forget the story" and the "terrible", "bad-high-school-play" production values, you'll have "great fun" with all that young Jane "eye candy."

Barbershop ⅠⅠ
20 | 20 | 20 | 18

2002. Directed by Tim Story. With Ice Cube, Cedric the Entertainer, Eve. 102 minutes. Rated PG-13.
An "old-time barbershop where everyone hangs out" is the centerpiece of this "enjoyable, day-in-the-life" comedy that may be "set in a black neighborhood" but will "appeal to all hair colors"; Cedric the Entertainer's "timing steals the show", and even if the "Rosa Parks" and "Jesse Jackson" gibes seem "politically incorrect", the picture ultimately offers a "solid message about community."

Barfly
18 | 21 | 17 | 16

1987. Directed by Barbet Schroeder. With Mickey Rourke, Faye Dunaway, Frank Stallone. 100 minutes. Rated R.
"Down and out" in LA the Charles Bukowski way, this "painful look" at "burnt-out alcoholics" stars Rourke and Dunaway as "rummies on the skids" uttering "heavy dialogue" over "tacky/cool" background music; some swat it for being "relentlessly depressing", but for most it's a "gritty, poignant look at the fringes of society" with some mighty "great acting" as a bonus.

Barry Lyndon
20 | 18 | 21 | 27

1975. Directed by Stanley Kubrick. With Ryan O'Neal, Marisa Berenson, Leon Vitali. 184 minutes. Rated PG.
"Kubrick's classic adaptation" of the Thackeray novel depicts the "rise and fall of an Irish lad whose luck finally runs dry" with "amazing period detail" and "gorgeous photography"; but al-

though this "thing of beauty" is a "feast for the eyes", the "acting's from hunger" and the "dull, plodding" pace leaves some sighing "what you see isn't what you get."

Barton Fink   20 | 24 | 19 | 22
1991. Directed by Joel Coen. With John Turturro, John Goodman, Judy Davis, Michael Lerner. 116 minutes. Rated R.
"Delightfully weird", this Coen brothers drama about a gone-Hollywood playwright with a colossal case of writer's block "alternates between fascinating and frustrating" given a "surreal", "terribly odd" storyline that's "brain candy" for intellectuals; despite "fantastic acting" from an "exceptional" Turturro and "absolutely sinister" Goodman, this "out-there" picture is "not for everyone."

Basic Instinct   19 | 19 | 20 | 19
1992. Directed by Paul Verhoeven. With Michael Douglas, Sharon Stone, Jeanne Tripplehorn. 123 minutes. Rated R.
Aside from Stone's notorious "uncrossed legs" "money shot", this "leering erotic thriller" offers enough "noir-esque dialogue" and "gratuitous sex" to make for one "highly provocative" "hormone movie"; though detractors deem it "unintentionally funny trash", "mired in leftover '80s hedonism", fans find it "surprisingly entertaining" – just "don't watch it with your parents."

Basquiat   17 | 20 | 19 | 17
1996. Directed by Julian Schnabel. With Jeffrey Wright, Benicio Del Toro, David Bowie. 108 minutes. Rated R.
It "feels as though you've lived, not just watched", this "insightful biopic" about the rise and fall of a "promising prodigy imploding" in the NY art scene; directed by fellow artist Schnabel, "excellently scored" by ex–Velvet Undergrounder John Cale and featuring a "beautifully cast" Bowie as pop conduit Andy Warhol, it's a "dark", tragic ride that "ends abruptly – like Basquiat's life did."

Batman Ⓤ   20 | 19 | 19 | 24
1989. Directed by Tim Burton. With Michael Keaton, Jack Nicholson, Kim Basinger. 126 minutes. Rated PG-13.
The "first and best of the bat franchise", this "brilliantly shot" fantasy-adventure flick reflects the "dark side of the comic book" thanks to the "dynamic duo" of "visionary" director Burton and "top-notch" "caped crusader" Keaton; Nicholson's an "awesome" Joker and the *Blade Runner*–esque Gotham City is "realized to stunning effect", so even if the "sequels stink", this one "rocks."

Batman Begins   23 | 21 | 23 | 26
2005. Directed by Christopher Nolan. With Christian Bale, Michael Caine, Katie Holmes. 141 minutes. Rated PG-13.
After a "worrisome decline" into "cartoonish goofery", the Batman franchise is "back on track" with this "quality" revival, a "rollicking ride" that recounts the Caped Crusader's "early years"; as for acting, the "brooding" Bale "soars" in the lead role, shedding new "insight" into his character's "inner turmoil", though romantic interest Holmes is deemed the "weak link."

Batman Returns Ⓤ   16 | 17 | 15 | 21
1992. Directed by Tim Burton. With Michael Keaton, Danny DeVito, Michelle Pfeiffer. 126 minutes. Rated PG-13.
The "last of the dark deco Batman" pictures, this "freak show of a sequel" is "another atmospheric Burton production" that keeps

Keaton as the caped crusader and is "spiced up" by a "sizzling" Pfeiffer playing an "S&M version of Catwoman"; spoilsports say "they should've stopped" after the original, bemoaning what happens when "marketing takes over a movie."

Battle of Algiers, The ◐🅵   ▽ 28 | 23 | 27 | 27

1967. Directed by Gillo Pontecorvo. With Jean Martin, Yacef Saadi. 117 minutes. Not Rated.
"Terrorism and military response" are the up-to-the-minute subjects of this "decades-ahead-of-its-time" feature delineating the Algerian struggle for independence from French rule; the "riveting" footage is "so lifelike" that it "looks like a documentary", but even as a "docudrama" it remains "timely, essential" viewing.

Beau Geste ◐   25 | 23 | 25 | 22

1939. Directed by William A. Wellman. With Gary Cooper, Ray Milland, Robert Preston. 120 minutes. Not Rated.
"Heroic heroes and villainous villains" populate this "ultimate" war picture about "friendship and honor" that's "perhaps the best Foreign Legion movie" ever made; ok, there are "no special effects" and it might seem "corny" today, but it still supplies plenty of "first-class adventure" right up to that "majestic ending."

BEAUTIFUL MIND, A ✉   26 | 28 | 25 | 25

2001. Directed by Ron Howard. With Russell Crowe, Ed Harris, Jennifer Connelly. 134 minutes. Rated PG-13.
"What *Rain Man* did for autism", this "absorbing" Oscar winner about a "brilliant mathematician's" battle with mental illness "does for schizophrenia", revealing the "thin line between genius and insanity"; "phenomenally acted" by Crowe and Connelly, it "celebrates the triumph of the human spirit" – though foes say its "Hollywoodized" script "strays too far from historical accuracy."

Beauty and the Beast ◐🅵   28 | 25 | 27 | 28

1947. Directed by Jean Cocteau. With Jean Marais, Josette Day, Marcel André. 93 minutes. Not Rated.
Enter a "highly stylized universe" in this "hallucinatory" take on the classic "fairy tale" that's both "dreamlike" and "complex" owing to "Cocteau's wit and imagination"; "still unsurpassed by more lavish productions", this "amazing visual feast" demonstrates the artistry possible with "ancient technology" – and enough "sexuality beneath the surface" to keep things throbbing.

Beauty and the Beast   26 | – | 25 | 27

1991. Directed by Gary Trousdale, Kirk Wise. Animated. 84 minutes. Rated G.
A "sensational score" complements the cast of "lovable characters" in this "magical milepost" that "set the bar for a new wave of animated classics"; told with a "fresh approach", it has an "intelligent" "heroine with chutzpah" trilling "catchy", "singable songs" that will "keep tots of all ages entranced"; in short, this "modern masterpiece" – the first animated film ever nominated for Best Picture – is nothing less than "Disney at its high-flying best."

Becket ✉⊘   26 | 29 | 26 | 26

1964. Directed by Peter Glenville. With Richard Burton, Peter O'Toole, John Gielgud. 148 minutes. Not Rated.
"Big drama writ large", this biopic about England's King Henry II and his "deep bond with Thomas Becket" features the "brilliant

teaming" of "two high-powered actors" – the "winning" O'Toole and "wonderful" Burton – in "histrionic, bellowing performances"; sure, it's "a bit talky", but otherwise this "beautifully filmed period piece" is living proof of the way "history should be experienced."

Bedazzled ∅
20 | 19 | 21 | 16

1967. Directed by Stanley Donen. With Dudley Moore, Peter Cook, Raquel Welch. 104 minutes. Not Rated.
This "immensely clever" "takeoff on the Faust legend" relocated to "swinging '60s London" is a "wickedly funny" comedy full of "vintage Brit humor" and "witty" "double entendres" in its story of "poor dweeb Moore selling his soul" to the devil in exchange for "true love"; ok, it may be "slow in spots", but it's still "far superior to the 2000 remake."

Beethoven ❿
16 | 14 | 16 | 16

1992. Directed by Brian Levant. With Charles Grodin, Dean Jones, Bonnie Hunt, Stanley Tucci. 87 minutes. Rated PG.
"Dog lovers" dig this "cute" exercise in "good, clean family fun" about a "slobbery", "scene-stealing" St. Bernard who wreaks havoc in the house while deftly avoiding the clutches of an evil vet; though grumps growl about the "average acting", "predictable storyline" and "laboratory villains", "kids love it" – enough said.

Beetlejuice
20 | 19 | 21 | 22

1988. Directed by Tim Burton. With Michael Keaton, Geena Davis, Alec Baldwin, Winona Ryder. 92 minutes. Rated PG.
"Netherworld antics" animate this "demented haunted-house comedy", a "bizarre" yet "enchanting" flick from "twisted" director Burton that's "endlessly inventive and endearingly funny"; built around a "genius" performance by Keaton as the "wonderfully disgusting" title character, it's also notable for a "macabre" turn from Ryder as a very "unusual teenager."

Before Night Falls
22 | 26 | 22 | 20

2000. Directed by Julian Schnabel. With Javier Bardem, Johnny Depp, Olivier Martinez. 133 minutes. Rated R.
Based on the true life story of "gay Cuban poet" Reinaldo Arenas, this "historically significant" biodrama is a "serious" reminder not to "take freedom for granted" as it details the hero's struggles against an "oppressive regime" bent on "silencing" him; look for an "excellent" Bardem in a "beautiful", "fully realized" performance.

Before Sunset
21 | 23 | 20 | 21

2004. Directed by Richard Linklater. With Ethan Hawke, Julie Delpy. 80 minutes. Rated R.
After their "magical" one-night "chance encounter" in *Before Sunrise*, Hawke and Delpy – now "older and somewhat wiser" – meet again in "atmospheric" Paris for a one-day "second chance" in this "intelligent romance"; while their "nonstop", "meandering" conversation seems to "drag" for some, it's like a "fairy tale" for those mesmerized by the stars' "amazing chemistry."

Being John Malkovich
22 | 24 | 24 | 22

1999. Directed by Spike Jonze. With John Cusack, Cameron Diaz, John Malkovich, Catherine Keener. 112 minutes. Rated R.
"'Original' does not even begin to describe" this "surreal romp" that mixes "dark fantasy" with "smart comedy" in its "off-the-wall" story of a regular guy who finds a portal that takes him "in-

side the head" of actor John Malkovich; though it "rewards rather than insults the audience's intelligence", it's definitely "not for everybody", being either "engrossing", "audacious fun" or "confusing as hell."

Being Julia 23 | 27 | 21 | 24
2004. Directed by István Szabó. With Annette Bening, Jeremy Irons. 104 minutes. Rated R.
Bening "steals the show" with her "luminous" portrayal of a "fading English actress undertaking one last fling" with a young Yank in this "enjoyable" Brit "comedy of manners" based on the Somerset Maugham novella; overall, it's a "fluffy period piece" perhaps best suited for devotees of the "theatuh", but it's still "worth watching" all the way through for that "deliciously wicked climax."

Being There 26 | 27 | 25 | 23
1979. Directed by Hal Ashby. With Peter Sellers, Shirley MacLaine, Melvyn Douglas. 130 minutes. Rated PG.
"Politics and hypocrisy" get a skewering in this "classic allegory" about a "slow-thinking" gardener who proves that "80 percent of life is just showing up"; "Sellers glows" in this "faithful" adaptation of Jerzy Kosinski's story, which "requires patience with its slow pace" but does "allow you to form your own conclusions."

Bell, Book and Candle 22 | 22 | 22 | 21
1958. Directed by Richard Quine. With Kim Novak, James Stewart, Jack Lemmon. 106 minutes. Not Rated.
Stewart and Novak "have fun with witchcraft" in this romantic comedy based on the Broadway hit about a "man falling for a woman who's a witch"; fans claim that this "old chestnut" was responsible for many cats being "named Pyewacket" and note that the "enchanting" title refers to the Roman Catholic rite of exorcism.

Belle de Jour 🄵 24 | 25 | 23 | 23
1968. Directed by Luis Buñuel. With Catherine Deneuve, Jean Sorel. 101 minutes. Rated R.
Deneuve was "never sexier" than in this "marvelously perverse" French drama, a peek at the "dark side" of a "chichi housewife" pent up in "bourgeois" wedlock whose "S&M fantasies" compel her to take a "side job" at the local bordello; more "Dali painting" than *Playboy* centerfold, it's a "stylish", "complex" window into director Buñuel's "surreal world", and the leading lady's "intense", "alluring" performance spices up the "slow" spots.

Bells Are Ringing 24 | 24 | 22 | 22
1960. Directed by Vincente Minnelli. With Judy Holliday, Dean Martin, Fred Clark. 127 minutes. Not Rated.
A "funny" Broadway musical becomes a "fine vehicle" for the "wonderful" Holliday in this story of a singing switchboard girl hung up on a playwright (the slightly "out-of-his-league" Martin); yet despite a "classic" score and a "famous song" ('The Party's Over'), some say this "stage-bound" production's "outdated."

Bend It Like Beckham 26 | 24 | 25 | 23
2003. Directed by Gurinder Chadha. With Parminder K. Nagra, Keira Knightley, Jonathan Rhys-Meyers. 112 minutes. Rated PG-13.
"Bend it like anything you want" – this "thoroughly entertaining", "cross-cultural feel-good movie" about an "Indian girl in England who wants to play soccer" scores with its "empowering" story-

line and "fantastic ensemble acting"; a "true delight" "for young and old alike", it's the "best ethnic-themed movie since *My Big Fat Greek Wedding*" – "but no TV series, please."

Ben-Hur ✉   26 | 23 | 25 | 28
1959. Directed by William Wyler. With Charlton Heston, Jack Hawkins, Stephen Boyd. 212 minutes. Rated G.
Unleashed four decades "before *Gladiator*", this "bigger than big" sword-and-sandals "masterpiece" features Heston exuding "hammy", bare-chested "bravura" as a Judean prince betrayed into Roman slavery only to seek payback via "breathtaking" bouts of action (including that "stunner" of a "chariot race"); a colossal hit and major Oscar magnet, it epitomizes the "grand Hollywood historical epic", built on "biblical" bedrock.

Benji ⑪   19 | 16 | 18 | 17
1974. Directed by Joe Camp. With Patsy Garrett, Peter Breck. 86 minutes. Rated G.
The "must-see" flick for the "mid-'70s" single-digit demo, this fetching "doggy adventure" features a star turn from a "cute", shaggy-browed mutt who trots to the rescue after his young owners are kidnapped; nostalgists recall a "sappy" but "wonderful" "childhood favorite", albeit with "low-rent" production values.

Best in Show   24 | 25 | 23 | 22
2000. Directed by Christopher Guest. With Christopher Guest, Eugene Levy, Catherine O'Hara. 90 minutes. Rated PG-13.
"Three woofs" and "four paws up" for this "quirky riot" of a mockumentary about a "gaggle of fanatical dog show participants" and their "pedigreed pooches"; the wacky repartee makes for a "beautifully inappropriate", "laugh-a-minute satire" that "can be viewed 100 times without becoming dog-eared."

BEST YEARS OF OUR LIVES, THE ✉◑   28 | 27 | 28 | 25
1946. Directed by William Wyler. With Myrna Loy, Fredric March, Dana Andrews, Teresa Wright. 172 minutes. Not Rated.
"Have the Kleenex handy" – there's no denying the "pure heart" of this "compelling" drama exploring the "uneasy readjustment" of WWII "vets coming home" to Main Street USA; its all-around "riveting" acting and "no-miss script" perfectly capture the "next-door" post-war mood, taking Best Picture (plus six more Oscars) and resonating as a "quintessentially American period piece."

Beverly Hills Cop ⑪   20 | 19 | 19 | 19
1984. Directed by Martin Brest. With Eddie Murphy, Judge Reinhold, John Ashton. 105 minutes. Rated R.
This action/comedy "breakthrough" is a "star vehicle" for Murphy, cast as an "inner-city" flatfoot with a "trademark laugh" who upstages his "goofy" El Lay counterparts in pursuit of a friend's killer; though the typically "'80s" foolery and "cheesy storyline" have cooled over time, this "hoot" still works as "feel-good" fare to fill a "Saturday afternoon."

Beyond the Sea   19 | 22 | 19 | 20
2004. Directed by Kevin Spacey. With Kevin Spacey, Kate Bosworth, John Goodman. 118 minutes. Rated PG-13.
A bona fide "labor of love", this "enjoyable" bio of '50s bopper Bobby Darin was directed, co-written and enacted by the "many hat"–wearing Spacey, who's his "usual riveting self" – and even

does his own "first-rate singing"; still, sinkers say Kevin's "too old for the part" and compare this "self-indulgent" "vanity project" to "singing into a hairbrush in front of a mirror."

Bicycle Thief, The ✉ ◑ 🄵   27 | 26 | 27 | 24
1948. Directed by Vittorio De Sica. With Lamberto Maggiorani, Enzo Staiola. 93 minutes. Not Rated.
"Poetry put on film", this early slice of "Italian neorealism" is "so sad" but so "beautifully executed" that it's ultimately "not a downer"; using "nonprofessional actors" in a drama of a father and son searching impoverished post-war Rome for the stolen bike that's key to their livelihood, De Sica tugs hearts with a "timeless pathos" that's most "affecting" for its "charm and simplicity."

Big   23 | 24 | 24 | 22
1988. Directed by Penny Marshall. With Tom Hanks, Elizabeth Perkins, Robert Loggia. 104 minutes. Rated PG.
Getting literal with its "inner child", this "cute" "kid-in-a-man's-body" comedy stars a "winning", "never-so-lovable" Hanks, who "makes the movie" (and moves into the big time) as a 13-year-old who "becomes an adult overnight" and gains entrée to NYC's corporate playground; though some of the "fantasy" is "on the sappy side", a large contingent calls it "most rewatchable."

Big Business   19 | 20 | 18 | 18
1988. Directed by Jim Abrahams. With Bette Midler, Lily Tomlin, Fred Ward. 97 minutes. Rated PG.
Playing "two sets of twins" separated at birth, "Midler & Tomlin and Midler & Tomlin" star in this "hilariously cheesy" mistaken identity comedy set in NY's Plaza Hotel; a "guilty pleasure" for fans of '80s "polyester clothes and big hair", it "doesn't really hold up" for others who sniff it's "silly" and say that "Bette should stick to music."

Big Chill, The   23 | 24 | 22 | 21
1983. Directed by Lawrence Kasdan. With Glenn Close, William Hurt, Kevin Kline, Jeff Goldblum, Mary Kay Place, JoBeth Williams, Tom Berenger. 105 minutes. Rated R.
Trace the tracks of their tears as this '60s-era "nostalgia" trip tries to "define a generation" via a "superb ensemble", an "iconic soundtrack" and the "soul-searching" premise of "boomers re-gathering" at a friend's funeral (fun fact: Kevin Costner "plays the stiff"); anyone bummed by the "contrived" setup and "smug" "yuppie angst" can still groove to the "perfect" tune selection.

Big Fish   22 | 24 | 23 | 25
2003. Directed by Tim Burton. With Ewan McGregor, Albert Finney, Billy Crudup, Jessica Lange. 125 minutes. Rated PG-13.
The "guy equivalent of a chick flick", this "bittersweet" story of a "complicated father-and-son relationship" reels in sentimentalists with equal parts of "whimsy and schmaltz"; "less twisted" than director Burton's usual fare, it still has its "oddball" moments via a "*Forrest Gump*"–like script, and if cynics yawn it's "sappy" and "slow", many more laud its "vivid imagery and good message."

Big Heat, The ◑   ▽ 24 | 23 | 25 | 23
1953. Directed by Fritz Lang. With Glenn Ford, Gloria Grahame, Lee Marvin, Carolyn Jones. 90 minutes. Not Rated.
"Considered daring in its time", this "ultimate noir picture" features a rogues' gallery of hard-boiled "tough guys" and

gals in a story about an honest cop "obsessed with getting revenge" following his wife's murder; though tepid types say the heat's "cooled off over the years", there's "one horrifying scene" involving a pot of "scalding hot coffee" that's still one heck of a "shocker."

Big Lebowski, The
20 | 22 | 19 | 20

1998. Directed by Joel Coen. With Jeff Bridges, John Goodman, Julianne Moore, Steve Buscemi. 117 minutes. Rated R.
The brothers Coen "strike again" with this "shaggy-dog" comedy, an "homage to slobs" that gets rolling when Bridges' "aging" "slacker/stoner character" and his "bizarre bowling buddies" become embroiled in a surreal kidnapping; though an "acquired taste" and certainly "strange for its own sake" ("dude, where's my plot?"), it has "cult" followers citing "quotable" lines and swearing "you'll laugh."

Big Night
24 | 26 | 23 | 23

1996. Directed by Campbell Scott, Stanley Tucci. With Stanley Tucci, Tony Shalhoub, Minnie Driver. 107 minutes. Rated R.
"Yum": this "quirky", "thoroughly enjoyable" dramatic "feast" tracks two "Italian immigrant brothers" in their "endearing" effort to keep their restaurant and culinary "vision" alive on the '50s-era Jersey coast; hailed as an "overlooked gem", its slow-simmering pace allows admirers to "savor" "brilliant performances" that are rivaled only by "stunning food shots" – "don't catch it on an empty stomach."

BIG SLEEP, THE ◑
27 | 27 | 24 | 24

1946. Directed by Howard Hawks. With Humphrey Bogart, Lauren Bacall, Martha Vickers. 114 minutes. Not Rated.
"Whodunit? who cares?" as long as the legendary Bogie and Bacall keep up the "snappy" patter and "heavy-lidded" "chemistry" in this "dizzying" film noir "classic" featuring Bogart as "fast-talking" gumshoe Philip Marlowe prowling Raymond Chandler territory (1940s Los Angeles at its most "atmospheric"); if the notoriously "incomprehensible plot" is seriously in need of a clue, at least the "crackling" pace and "salty" repartee always "entertain and enthrall."

Bill & Ted's Excellent Adventure ⑪
15 | 10 | 15 | 13

1989. Directed by Stephen Herek. With Keanu Reeves, Alex Winter, George Carlin. 90 minutes. Rated PG.
"Two goof-offs" about to flunk out of high school time-travel to the past in a desperate attempt to graduate in this "totally tubular" slacker comedy, a budding "cult classic" that just may be "better than you remember it"; sure, this "sophomoric", "truly mindless" flick could have "typecast Keanu" forever, and even if it's "not very good, it's still lots of fun, dude."

Billy Elliot
25 | 26 | 25 | 23

2000. Directed by Stephen Daldry. With Julie Walters, Jamie Bell. 110 minutes. Rated PG-13.
It takes *Swan Lake* to break the "working-class shackles" of a Northern England mining town in this "coming-of-age" drama about a "boy who loves ballet" and his hardscrabble dad; behind the "thick British accents", fans discover a "captivating" if "unlikely tale" propelled by "talent, desire" and lots of "fancy footwork", with an "uplifting" finale that's apt to inspire "a good cry."

Billy Liar ◑   22 | 26 | 23 | 20
1963. Directed by John Schlesinger. With Tom Courtenay, Julie Christie, Wilfred Pickles. 98 minutes. Not Rated.
A prime example of British "kitchen-sink realism", this "poignant comic gem" relates the story of a daydreamer–cum–pathological liar itching to escape his humdrum, blue-collar existence; in the "challenging" title role, Courtenay's a "charmer", but the picture is stolen by the "scrumptious young" Christie in her first major film role.

Birdcage, The   22 | 25 | 22 | 22
1996. Directed by Mike Nichols. With Robin Williams, Nathan Lane, Gene Hackman, Dianne Wiest. 117 minutes. Rated R.
Reset in South Beach, director Nichols' "slick" take on the "classic" French farce La Cage aux Folles soars "over the top" on the wings of the "perfect comedic combination" of Williams and Lane, cast as a pair of "flamboyant" gay cabaret owners obliged to "play it straight" for their son's "uptight" in-laws-to-be; busy with burlesque and "insight", it's widely welcomed as a "laugh-out-loud" "blast", though holdouts chirp "stick with the original."

Birdman of Alcatraz ◑   22 | 25 | 22 | 20
1962. Directed by John Frankenheimer. With Burt Lancaster, Karl Malden, Thelma Ritter. 147 minutes. Not Rated.
Lancaster is "at the top of his game" in this saga of "a man, a prison and some birds", the "fascinating" bio of Rock lifer Robert Stroud who struggles under the screws' authority but "finds love and friendship" when he becomes a famed ornithologist; it's generally judged a "keeper" as a "gritty" but "entertaining" penal drama that's also a "touching" "examination of survival."

Birds, The   24 | 20 | 24 | 25
1963. Directed by Alfred Hitchcock. With Tippi Hedren, Rod Taylor, Jessica Tandy. 119 minutes. Rated PG-13.
"Nature strikes back, Hitchcock style", in this "improbably terrifying" "nail-biter" about "birds gone mad" that "still packs enough of a punch" to leave the timid "traumatized"; though critics aren't chirping about the "hokey", "no-rhyme-or-reason" plot that takes "too long to get going", ultimately you'll "never think of pigeons in the same way" after a gander at this one.

Birth of a Nation, The ◑   25 | 20 | 19 | 27
1915. Directed by D.W. Griffith. With Lillian Gish, Mae Marsh, Henry B. Walthall. 190 minutes. Not Rated.
A "masterful" technical feat that could be the "most influential movie ever made", Griffith's "landmark" silent epic "wrote the book" on "camera movement" and "cinema as storytelling" while offering a "morally irresponsible" version of Reconstruction replete with "blatantly racist" "stereotyping" and the "Ku Klux Klan presented as heroes"; so even though this work marks the "birth of the feature" film, be prepared for a storyline that's a "mess" – "even by 1915" standards.

Bishop's Wife, The ◑   24 | 24 | 24 | 23
1947. Directed by Henry Koster. With Cary Grant, Loretta Young, David Niven. 105 minutes. Not Rated.
Although "less well known" than some of its "holiday movie" peers, this "Christmasy" romance stars Grant as a "guardian an-

jel" blessed with "elegance and style" ("duh!") who's sent to "restore faith" to a clergyman and his spouse but "falls in love" along the way; overall, it's an "amusing, touching" display of "old-fashioned" "star power" that sentimental souls will "never forget."

Blackboard Jungle ◐

23 | 24 | 22 | 19

1955. Directed by Richard Brooks. With Glenn Ford, Anne Francis, Vic Morrow, Sidney Poitier. 101 minutes. Not Rated.

See "the '50s in a new way" via this "gritty" drama, a standout of the "juvenile delinquent genre" set in an "inner-city school" where "danger is only a heartbeat away" as idealistic teacher Ford is forced to "tame" a horde of punks; notable for Hollywood's "first use of a rock 'n' roll" soundtrack, it may "feel a bit dated", though cynics shrug "schools haven't changed" that much.

Black Hawk Down

23 | 21 | 23 | 26

2001. Directed by Ridley Scott. With Josh Hartnett, Ewan McGregor, Tom Sizemore. 144 minutes. Rated R.

It's "hard to watch, but it's even harder to turn away" from this "astoundingly gripping" (and "surprisingly accurate") account of a 1993 Mogadishu "military misadventure", which pitted a handful of U.S. Army Rangers against a huge enemy force; "Scott puts you on the ground with the soldiers", "brilliantly showing the total chaos of the Somalian battle" in all its "gory", "graphic" and "grueling" detail; indeed, even peaceniks agree this "salute to our servicemen" "doesn't simplify or sensationalize" combat.

Black Orpheus ✉ 🄵

26 | 23 | 25 | 25

1959. Directed by Marcel Camus. With Marpessa Dawn, Breno Mello. 100 minutes. Rated PG.

"Brazilian backdrops" and "bossa nova" rhythms cast their "spell" over Greek legend in this "enchanting", "lyrical" foreign flick, an "exotic retelling" of the Orpheus and Eurydice myth transposed to "modern-day Rio" during Carnival; "sexy", "lush" and full of "beautiful shots" of "cinema verité" revelry, it takes its Dionysian devotees to Hades and back in "unmatched" style – and oh, that "moving-in-your-seat" soundtrack!

Black Stallion, The ⓤ

24 | 20 | 23 | 25

1979. Directed by Carroll Ballard. With Mickey Rooney, Kelly Reno, Teri Garr. 118 minutes. Rated G.

Equestrians of "all ages" ponder the "bond between boy and horse" in this "captivating" family film about an Arabian steed who's shipwrecked with a youngster on a desert island only to be entered in a turf race after they're rescued and resettled to a Western ranch; though saddled with a "somber" side, it "wins the roses" with a "skillful blend" of "breathtaking" scenery and "luminous cinematography."

BLADE RUNNER

26 | 22 | 25 | 27

1982. Directed by Ridley Scott. With Harrison Ford, Rutger Hauer, Sean Young, Daryl Hannah. 117 minutes. Rated R.

This "awesome" "blueprint" for "modern sci-fi" is a "visually stunning" picture best watched with "your brain switched on"; an ultra-"stylish" "noir take" on LA as a 21st-century "dystopia" where "commercialism and biotech run amok", it's also a "hard-boiled" "morality play" with one of "Ford's best acting jobs" as a PI "hunting cyborg replicants while falling in love with one"; connoisseurs run right for the "superior director's cut."

BLAZING SADDLES
25 | 22 | 23 | 23

1974. Directed by Mel Brooks. With Cleavon Little, Gene Wilder, Harvey Korman, Madeline Kahn. 93 minutes. Rated R.

"You'll never look at a horse the same way" after a peek at this "hilarious", "decidedly un-PC" comedy via Mel Brooks, an "off-the-wall" Wild West "spoof" that "insults everyone" with a mix of "slapstick", "eminently quotable one-liners" and infamously "tasteless" routines (like the sound effects–ridden "campfire scene"); most call it "enjoyable" if "overdone."

Blood Simple
24 | 25 | 25 | 22

1984. Directed by Joel Coen. With Frances McDormand, John Getz, Dan Hedaya. 97 minutes. Rated R.

"Complex" is more like it as the Coen brothers' first feature "pumps new blood" into the "low-budget crime thriller" in this "brilliant" "film noir homage" filled with "wicked" "thrills delivered with a drawl"; it's a "twisty", "nerve-jangling" tale of betrayal and revenge in a dusty Texas town, told with a "quirky" slant that "foreshadows" the filmmakers' "masterpiece, *Fargo*."

Blowup
26 | 23 | 25 | 25

1966. Directed by Michelangelo Antonioni. With David Hemmings, Vanessa Redgrave, Sarah Miles. 111 minutes. Not Rated.

"Forget *Austin Powers*", baby, "this is the *real* Swinging London": a "riveting existential thriller" that tracks a happening fashion photographer obsessed with both Redgrave and a "mysterious death in a park"; hipsters hail it as an "enigmatic" (or "infuriating") milestone of the "alienation genre" possessed by the "spirit of the '60s" – and that tasty "period flavor" is still "too cool for words."

Blue Angel, The **O F**
25 | 27 | 24 | 22

1931. Directed by Josef von Sternberg. With Marlene Dietrich, Emil Jannings. 99 minutes. Not Rated.

Behold the "magnificent Dietrich" "at her best" in this "Weimar-era" German drama, the story of "naughty Lola", a garter-flashing chanteuse who "seduces an old fool" of a schoolmaster and expedites his "descent into the gutter"; though it's a "dated" dose of "ennui and moral rot" in a "world now lost", fräulein Marlene's "tour-de-force", career-launching turn is "music to the eyes."

Blues Brothers, The **11**
22 | 19 | 19 | 21

1980. Directed by John Landis. With John Belushi, Dan Aykroyd, John Candy. 133 minutes. Rated R.

"Ignore the plot" and "get out the popcorn" for this "good-time" comedy, powered by Belushi and Aykroyd on a "full tank of gas" as siblings who accept a "mission from God" to provoke "hilarity" and find out "how many cars they can wreck"; if it's (ahem) "not a critics' choice", those with a hankering for "hot" "soul 'n' blues" numbers liberally chased with "dumb fun" insist "you gotta love it."

Blue Velvet
22 | 23 | 20 | 23

1986. Directed by David Lynch. With Kyle MacLachlan, Isabella Rossellini, Dennis Hopper. 120 minutes. Rated R.

"One sick puppy of a movie", this pretty "kinky" yet totally "enthralling" look at the "seedy underbelly" "beneath the surface of suburbia" is "love-it-or-hate-it" filmmaking from the "warped" mind of "surrealist auteur Lynch"; despite applause for Hopper's "creepy" portrayal of the "gas-inhaling pervert" ("worth seeing for the Pabst Blue Ribbon scene alone"), sensitive souls find the flick "ugly, pointless" and "not as good as its reputation."

Bob and Carol and Ted and Alice   17 | 19 | 17 | 17
1969. Directed by Paul Mazursky. With Natalie Wood, Robert Culp, Elliott Gould, Dyan Cannon. 104 minutes. Rated R.
"Remember the '60s?" – this "social satire" of wannabe swingers experimenting with free love "captures the era to a T", though what was once "hip 'n' happening" seems more "quaint" today; still, many find themselves "laughing at the outfits, the decor", the "dated" dialogue and that "priceless" ending.

Body Heat   24 | 25 | 25 | 23
1981. Directed by Lawrence Kasdan. With William Hurt, Kathleen Turner, Richard Crenna, Mickey Rourke. 113 minutes. Rated R.
"Whew!" this "palpably steamy" "noir thriller" stars "what-a-babe" Turner as a trophy wife who "burns up the screen" as she seduces "small-town lawyer" Hurt into a "spiraling" web of "de-ceit" that "keeps you guessing" to the last frame; in short, it's a sexed-up "version of the old help-me-kill-my-husband story", a kind of *Double Indemnity* for a new generation."

Bonnie and Clyde   25 | 25 | 24 | 25
1967. Directed by Arthur Penn. With Warren Beatty, Faye Dunaway, Gene Hackman, Estelle Parsons. 111 minutes. Not Rated.
More a piece of "film history than real history", this "stunning" 1930s "crime-spree" biopic "broke a lot of old rules" in its "revi-sionist" take on the title characters, real-life "losers" recon-ceived by Beatty and Dunaway as the "screen's best-ever antiheroes"; the "letter-perfect" cast, "impeccable" direction and "gorgeously gory" photography all add up to way-"ahead-of-its-time" moviemaking, even if the "indelible images" of the "bloody ballet at the end" unsettle the squeamish.

Boogie Nights   19 | 21 | 19 | 19
1997. Directed by Paul Thomas Anderson. With Mark Wahlberg, Burt Reynolds, Julianne Moore. 152 minutes. Rated R.
Set in the '70s "disco era", this "dead-on look" at the "ins and outs (so to speak) of the porn industry" features "inspired performances" – "Burt returns!", "Marky Mark grows up!" – even if the "XXX film stars" portrayed "don't have much going on upstairs"; though the "sex-drugs-and-roller-skates" plot is "shamelessly entertaining" for the "first 2/3" of the picture, the "violent", "depressing" final act can be "emotionally draining."

Born Free ⑪   24 | 19 | 24 | 23
1966. Directed by James Hill. With Virginia McKenna, Bill Travers, Geoffrey Keen. 95 minutes. Rated PG.
The "theme song alone" is enough to set off "shameless weeping" as this "well-told" family flick unfolds, focusing on a husband and wife in "wild Africa" and their effort to "protect the lioness Elsa"; a "major tearjerker" in its day, it remains "vivid" for boomers who tell of "loving it as a child" even though it's "so sad."

Born on the Fourth of July ✉   20 | 21 | 20 | 20
1989. Directed by Oliver Stone. With Tom Cruise, Kyra Sedgwick, Willem Dafoe. 145 minutes. Rated R.
"Cruise excels" in one of Stone's "most accomplished works", a "potent", "well-done" bio of Vietnam vet Ron Kovic that's an "in-

tense", "heart-wrenching" study of "flag-waving patriotism"; though it draws fire for being "contrived" and "overwrought", it does offer convincing "proof that Tom can act."

Born Yesterday ✉◑   26 | 28 | 25 | 23
1950. Directed by George Cukor. With Judy Holliday, Broderick Crawford, William Holden. 103 minutes. Not Rated.
"Still magical today", this "zany" screwball comedy has to do with a "not-so-dumb blonde" who undergoes a *My Fair Lady*–like transformation and "breaks out of her bimbo chains"; thanks to a unique voice and "great timing", the "perfectly cast" Holliday took home an Oscar for her "pure gold" performance, a "pièce de résistance" that the 1993 remake "can't match."

Bourne Identity, The ⑪   20 | 19 | 20 | 21
2002. Directed by Doug Liman. With Matt Damon, Franka Potente, Chris Cooper. 119 minutes. Rated PG-13.
An "amnesiac" CIA assassin struggles to recover his identity in this "adrenaline-rush" thriller based on the Robert Ludlum best-seller that features "riveting action" scenes (including "one of the better car chases in recent memory"), but only "decent chemistry" between the leads; though Matt's performance provokes debate – "cool and capable" versus "lightweight" – in the end the scenic European "locations redeem the picture."

Bourne Supremacy, The   21 | 21 | 21 | 23
2004. Directed by Paul Greengrass. With Matt Damon, Joan Allen, Julia Stiles. 108 minutes. Rated PG-13.
Damon is "re-Bourne" as a "secret agent turned wanted man" out for "payback" in this "sharp-shooting sequel", a "spy caper with a brain" that's "as good as the original", packing fresh "cat-and-mouse action", "high-tech twists" and "gorgeous" Euro backdrops; its "herky-jerky" camera coverage can be "dizzying", though, so "take Dramamine" during those "fantastic" car chases.

Bowling for Columbine   22 | – | 21 | 19
2002. Directed by Michael Moore. Documentary. 120 minutes. Rated R.
Moore's "provocative" yet "surprisingly funny" docudrama is a "punch in the jaw to anyone who is completely pro-gun"; "even if the events were staged, the message massaged and the view decidedly one-sided", it's still an "important movie" that "everyone should see", so "watch it before passing judgment" – "you'll have something to talk about for hours."

Boys Don't Cry ✉   23 | 27 | 23 | 21
1999. Directed by Kimberly Peirce. With Hilary Swank, Chloë Sevigny, Peter Sarsgaard. 118 minutes. Rated R.
Turning a "dark situation" into a "tough" study of "intolerance", this "disturbing" drama is a "faithful telling of the story of Teena Brandon", a small-town girl who "dresses and acts the part" of a boy, leading to "powerful" complications; though the Oscar-winning Swank is "beyond convincing", the "brutal" ending is "not easy to watch", but "will stay with you" – "unfortunately, it's true."

Boys on the Side   15 | 18 | 15 | 16
1995. Directed by Herbert Ross. With Whoopi Goldberg, Mary-Louise Parker, Drew Barrymore. 117 minutes. Rated R.
"Girl power" is alive and well in this "epitome of a chick flick" charting the offbeat adventures of three gals headed cross coun-

try; the "touching" story, one part road movie and one part feminist tract, proves that "friendship is a great thing", while also demonstrating that "Drew can act if she picks the right material."

Boyz N the Hood
23 | 22 | 24 | 21

1991. Directed by John Singleton. With Ice Cube, Cuba Gooding Jr., Laurence Fishburne. 107 minutes. Rated R.
The "gangsta flick" that "sets the bar" for the competition "keeps it real" as it takes a "hard-core" look at ghetto "gang wars in South Central" LA; an "important" breakthrough with some "surprising acting turns", it's a "fantastic first film" from Singleton, whose later work doesn't "get anywhere near this one."

BRAVEHEART ✉
26 | 24 | 25 | 27

1995. Directed by Mel Gibson. With Mel Gibson, Sophie Marceau, Catherine McCormack. 177 minutes. Rated R.
"It's got everything" say fans of this "awe-inspiring" medieval "history lesson" about an "underdog" Scottish hero ("Mel in a kilt" and "war paint") "knocking heads" in an anti-Brit "rebellion"; the "gory", "hackin'-and-hewin'" battles, "heartfelt" acting and "huge scope" help justify Gibson's Best Director win, even if some warn of three "long", "melodramatic" hours.

Brazil
24 | 23 | 23 | 27

1985. Directed by Terry Gilliam. With Jonathan Pryce, Robert De Niro, Bob Hoskins. 131 minutes. Rated R.
Even as "fantasy", Monty Python alum Gilliam's "twisted", "utterly original" vision of a "part-Orwell, part-Python" future is "a little out there"; it demands "perseverance" – what with its "baffling" "whirlwind" of "bizarre" effects and chin-scratching "black comedy" plot about one man's struggle with a "Kafkaesque" "bureaucracy" – but rewards those who hang in there with a "totally crazy ride."

BREAKER MORANT
27 | 27 | 27 | 24

1980. Directed by Bruce Beresford. With Jack Thompson, Edward Woodward, Bryan Brown. 107 minutes. Rated PG.
"Guy's-flick" fans salute this "solid Aussie" drama of "kangaroo" justice, a "small masterpiece" in its "gripping" depiction of "betrayal" at a military trial during the Boer War; told with "moving realism", it tackles the "question of morals in warfare" using a "top-notch" cast to "demonstrate bravery" and "bravura", turning the fate of "appointed scapegoats" into an "inspiration."

BREAKFAST AT TIFFANY'S
26 | 26 | 24 | 24

1961. Directed by Blake Edwards. With Audrey Hepburn, George Peppard, Patricia Neal. 115 minutes. Rated PG.
In the "role she was born to play", a "mesmerizing" Hepburn brings Truman Capote's "messed-up" "free spirit" Holly Golightly to life in "peerless style"; fans find everything about it "irresistible" – "Henry Mancini's divine score", the "timeless clothes", the "love-letter-to-NY" cinematography – and call this "dream-making, heartbreaking" tribute to the "power of romance" their "all-time fave."

Breakfast Club, The
22 | 21 | 22 | 19

1985. Directed by John Hughes. With Emilio Estevez, Anthony Michael Hall, Judd Nelson, Molly Ringwald. 92 minutes. Rated R.
Any card-carrying "child of the '80s" is apt to "know all the lines" of this "engaging" high school yukfest, a "Gen-X" "time capsule"

about a group of "Brat Pack all-stars" "stuck in detention" and left to compare and contrast "confused personalities"; a "hoot" with a "sensitive" side, it's rerun "ad infinitum", since it "speaks to teenagers in a way that *American Pie* will never be able to."

Breaking Away ✉

24 | 21 | 24 | 20

1979. Directed by Peter Yates. With Dennis Christopher, Dennis Quaid, Daniel Stern. 100 minutes. Rated PG.
A "rousing ride", this "*Rocky*-esque" "Hoosier tale" is a "coming-of-age" drama on two wheels, with Christopher leading a cast of "cutie-pie" "underdogs" as a cyclist who pedals straight into a "town-and-gown" "class conflict"; it's cheered on as a "big-hearted" "buddy film" that delivers a "socko" bike race finale.

Breaking the Waves

23 | 27 | 20 | 20

1996. Directed by Lars von Trier. With Emily Watson, Stellan Skarsgård. 153 minutes. Rated R.
"Be prepared" for "emotionally devastating" doings in this "raw" drama of "delusion" and "doomed romance" about a "dimwitted girl" who "sacrifices everything for her paralyzed husband"; most pronounce it "strange" yet "so well done it's painful" (the "musical interludes give one time to weep"), though foes call it a "silly" parable that's a most "depressing" picture of "female martyrdom."

Breathless ◑ 🅵

25 | 24 | 21 | 23

1961. Directed by Jean-Luc Godard. With Jean-Paul Belmondo, Jean Seberg. 87 minutes. Not Rated.
"So hip" and as "refreshing" now as at its debut, this French "New Wave masterpiece" breathes "pure pleasure" into a "silly gangster story" with "luscious" leads Belmondo and Seberg as lovers on the lam (even the late-'50s Paris setting is a "terrific character"); while scholars speak of genre-"defining" technical feats – the "jump cut is born!" – most simply find it "charming" and way "ahead of its time."

Bride of Frankenstein, The ◑

25 | 21 | 23 | 23

1935. Directed by James Whale. With Boris Karloff, Colin Clive, Elsa Lanchester. 75 minutes. Not Rated.
Bolt-necked Frankie gets "his one shot at love" in this "excellent sequel" to the hoary "'30s horror classic", wherein Karloff reprises his signature role with "panache" and Lanchester's shocked fiancée simply has "great hair"; fright fiends cherish the "creepy" results as "campy", "funny" and not a little "whacked."

Bride Wore Black, The 🅵

▽ 25 | 26 | 25 | 22

1968. Directed by François Truffaut. With Jeanne Moreau, Michel Bouquet, Jean-Claude Brialy. 107 minutes. Not Rated.
The "original *Kill Bill*", this psychological thriller stars a "sterling" Moreau as a widow hell bent on avenging her husband's murder; it's an out-and-out "homage to Hitchcock" and plain that director Truffaut "knows the territory well", even engaging Hitch favorite Bernard Herrmann as its composer.

BRIDGE ON THE RIVER KWAI, THE ✉

28 | 28 | 27 | 28

1957. Directed by David Lean. With William Holden, Alec Guinness, Jack Hawkins. 161 minutes. Rated PG.
Those "stiff upper lips" do some "memorable" whistling in director Lean's "grand", "engrossing" Japanese POW camp epic, an "old-fashioned" yarn about the "timeless themes" of "honor",

"conviction" and the "madness" of war; a lock for the top Oscars of 1957, it "succeeds" mightily with "great performances" – led "heart and soul" by a "hubris"-afflicted Guinness – enhanced by "splashy" scenery and an "explosive ending."

Bridges of Madison County, The
19 | 23 | 20 | 20

1995. Directed by Clint Eastwood. With Clint Eastwood, Meryl Streep, Annie Corley. 135 minutes. Rated PG-13.
Director/leading man Eastwood unveils his "gentle side" in this "bittersweet" romance recounting the "middle-aged" passion between a "roving" photographer and a "lonely housewife"; some cite the "banal", "snail's-pace" plot as a big "yawn", but to fans it's "lovably sappy" – and "way better" than the "treacly" book.

Bridget Jones's Diary
21 | 23 | 22 | 21

2001. Directed by Sharon Maguire. With Renée Zellweger, Hugh Grant, Colin Firth. 97 minutes. Rated R.
This "everygirl" "chick flick" is a "charming" romance that logs the progress of the "fab" Zellweger, doing a "knockout job" in the title role as a "twentysomething singleton" "desperately seeking a spouse" but beleaguered by "faux pas", "weight gain" and a "perfect cad" of a boss; followers find it "hilarious yet so true" but won't commit as to whether it "nails the book" or not.

BRIEF ENCOUNTER ◗
27 | 29 | 27 | 25

1946. Directed by David Lean. With Celia Johnson, Trevor Howard, Stanley Holloway. 86 minutes. Not Rated.
For a "truly romantic" fix, this "quiet" "masterpiece of yearning" from David Lean (via Noël Coward) is "right up there" in the running as the "definitive tearjerker"; the "never better" Johnson and Howard play "ordinary people" whose meeting on a commuter line develops into a "short but intense" "connection", with swells of Rachmaninoff to seal the deal; in brief, an "unforgettable" trip.

Brigadoon
24 | 21 | 22 | 24

1954. Directed by Vincente Minnelli. With Gene Kelly, Van Johnson, Cyd Charisse. 108 minutes. Not Rated.
A Lerner and Loewe "stage show turned into a movie", this "lesser-known" MGM musical is set in a mythical Scottish town that can be visited by outsiders only once every 100 years; though some criticize the "corny" concept, "phony accents" and "cardboard back-lot" sets, most "suspend disbelief" once the music starts and the "magical" Kelly and Charisse begin "dancing in the heather."

Bringing Down the House
19 | 21 | 17 | 19

2003. Directed by Adam Shankman. With Steve Martin, Queen Latifah, Eugene Levy, Joan Plowright. 105 minutes. Rated PG-13.
Steve and Queenie are a "modern day George and Gracie" in this "laugh-out-loud" comedy about a "staid" lawyer and an "outrageous" bank robber who meet in an online chat room; the script may be "vulgar" with too many "outdated racial stereotypes", but at least it's "equal opportunity offensive" – and it's always "nice to see plus-size girls get their props."

Bringing Up Baby ◗
27 | 27 | 24 | 24

1938. Directed by Howard Hawks. With Katharine Hepburn, Cary Grant. 102 minutes. Not Rated.
"One continuous roar", director Hawks' "screwiest of screwball comedies" is propelled at a "frenetic pace" by the Hepburn-

Grant "chemistry" and a "tons-of-fun" scenario touching on "dinosaur bones, crazy rich folk" and a lost leopard; it's an old-school "madcap" "champ", and fans of "farce" still bring it up as the "funniest movie ever."

Broadcast News
23 | 25 | 22 | 20

1987. Directed by James L. Brooks. With William Hurt, Albert Brooks, Holly Hunter. 127 minutes. Rated R.

"Appearance over substance" is the subject of this "smart" "send-up of the media" about a "love triangle" in a "career-driven", *Network*-esque TV newsroom that hums with "behind-the-scenes" one-upmanship; nominated for a slew of Oscars (but winner of none), this "ahead-of-its-time" comedy remains "totally engaging", due to the efforts of its "sharp-as-a-tack" cast.

Broadway Danny Rose ◑
22 | 22 | 22 | 20

1984. Directed by Woody Allen. With Woody Allen, Mia Farrow, Nick Apollo Forte. 84 minutes. Rated PG.

Woody and Mia (in rosier days) light up this comedy about a "Mafia tootsie who melts" for the "ultimate mensch", a small-time talent agent clinging to the "underbelly" of "borscht-belt" showbiz; although infused with a "NY sensibility", some say the "shaggy-dog" plot "doesn't quite deliver."

Brokeback Mountain ✉
24 | 26 | 23 | 26

2005. Directed by Ang Lee. With Heath Ledger, Jake Gyllenhaal, Michelle Williams, Anne Hathaway. 134 minutes. Rated R.

Widely pegged as the "gay cowboy movie", this "star-crossed" "Romeo-and-Romeo" romance is as "controversial" as they come, yet its "gimmick-free" rendition of "forbidden love" "avoids sensationalism" thanks to an "understated" performance by Ledger (and an "underrated" one by Gyllenhaal), backed up by "stunning scenery", a "ravishing score" and "Angst" Lee's "heartfelt", Oscar-winning direction; ultimately, this "timeless" film has had a "real cultural influence", even if it's best remembered for the "most spoofed line of the year": "I don't know how to quit you."

Brother Bear
21 | – | 21 | 23

2003. Directed by Aaron Blaise, Bob Walker. Animated. 85 minutes. Rated G.

"Sweet" yet "not overly sentimental", this "politically correct" Disney feature tells the tale of a boy turned into a bear, learning to "respect all living things" along the way; despite "old-fashioned" animation and a "slow-moving" pace, it redeems itself with a "message of love"; P.S. a pair of moose voiced by SCTV's McKenzie brothers provide a breath of "over-the-top" relief for grown-ups.

Brother from Another Planet, The
23 | 22 | 23 | 19

1984. Directed by John Sayles. With Joe Morton, Steve James, Bill Cobbs. 108 minutes. Rated R.

"Truly original for its time", this "low-budget" "cult favorite" via John Sayles examines "race relations and urban life" in its "off-beat" story of a black extraterrestrial who lands in Harlem; despite the sci-fi underpinnings, it's more of a "funny social commentary" about "what it means to be human", with a mute title character (the very "likable" Morton) and one of the "greatest on-screen card tricks ever."

Bruce Almighty   18 | 20 | 18 | 19
2003. Directed by Tom Shadyac. With Jim Carrey, Jennifer Aniston, Morgan Freeman. 101 minutes. Rated PG-13.
"Heaven help us": Carrey of the renown "rubber face" portrays an "ordinary man" turned Supreme Being and actually "delivers laughs" plus a "positive message" in this "enjoyable", "light-hearted" chuckler co-starring the "lovable" Aniston and "elegant" Freeman; a warning to those who pray for "something edgy": this one might feel like "religion class."

Buck Privates ❶ ⓫   22 | 19 | 16 | 18
1941. Directed by Arthur Lubin. With Abbott & Costello, the Andrews Sisters. 84 minutes. Not Rated.
A coupla clowns go to boot camp and "frivolity" ensues in this "classic Abbott and Costello" comedy, which "evokes an era" thanks to the "duo's rapid-fire patter" and USO-worthy tunes by the "Andrews Sisters at their peak"; despite "patchwork" plotting, it "ranks up there" in Bud and Lou's oeuvre and works as a swell "Sunday morning" indulgence.

Buena Vista Social Club   25 | – | 24 | 24
1999. Directed by Wim Wenders. Documentary. 101 minutes. Rated G.
"Revelatory – and danceable" – this documentary is a "love letter to a vanishing breed" of musicians, "aging" vets of the "Afro-Cuban jazz" scene who volunteer "personal histories" of "trials and tribulations" in the "shadow of Castro", interspersed with "irresistible" live jams; it "builds slowly" in a haze of "washed-out tropical colors" to a narrative of "great charm" and "insight", backed by a soundtrack that's as "captivating" as they come.

Bug's Life, A   24 | – | 22 | 26
1998. Directed by John Lasseter, Andrew Stanton. Animated. 96 minutes. Rated G.
"Even parents" bug out on the "mind-blowing creativity" of the Disney/Pixar team's "step-ahead animation" in this "cute" parable of "insect politics" rendered in "sharp, colorful" computer graphics that "look incredible", even if the "social satire" is "geared for kids"; most maintain it's "superior to *Antz*" and advise sticking around for the fake outtakes as the credits roll (the "best part").

Bugsy   18 | 19 | 18 | 19
1991. Directed by Barry Levinson. With Warren Beatty, Annette Bening, Harvey Keitel, Ben Kingsley. 135 minutes. Rated R.
"Long but fascinating", this bio of mobster Bugsy Siegel (the "gangster who created Las Vegas out of desert dust") is a "graphic" film about high-rolling "lowlifes"; though a few yawn it's a "Beatty vanity project", at least the "bewitching cinematography" makes the already "beautiful cast even more ravishing"; fave line: "why don't you run outside and jerk yourself a soda?"

Bull Durham   22 | 22 | 22 | 20
1988. Directed by Ron Shelton. With Kevin Costner, Susan Sarandon, Tim Robbins. 108 minutes. Rated R.
"Life and love in minor-league baseball" equal "diverting" comedy in this "funny and realistic" sports pic, juiced by "sexy", "laid-back acting" from Sarandon and Costner, a "great pair" out to take the "American spirit" into extra innings; fans cheer it on as a "smart home run" that's "one of the best" of the hardball yarns.

Bullets Over Broadway

1994. Directed by Woody Allen. With John Cusack, Dianne Wiest, Jennifer Tilly, Chazz Palminteri. 98 minutes. Rated R.

A "quirky, colorful" shot of "period" atmosphere, this "backstage comedy" concerns a Jazz Age dramatist and a "gangster who rewrites his Broadway play"; it's "likable" enough for its "witty dialogue" and "over-the-top" cast, though as usual for a "post-*Hannah*" Allen opus, some wish it were "just a little funnier."

Bullitt

1968. Directed by Peter Yates. With Steve McQueen, Robert Vaughn, Jacqueline Bisset. 113 minutes. Rated PG.

Arguably "the mother of all cop films", this "solid" action thriller stars an "icy-cool" McQueen, "acting by not acting" as a no-bull SFPD detective who takes on a corrupt system; set in Frisco "before too many high-rises" arrived, it's famed for a "definitive car chase" ("whee!") that's "still the best" after "countless" knock-offs, though some find the ride "pretty straightforward" plotwise.

Bus Stop

1956. Directed by Joshua Logan. With Marilyn Monroe, Don Murray, Eileen Heckart. 96 minutes. Not Rated.

Proving herself "at home on the range", Monroe brings "depth" to romantic comedy as a "vulnerable" "Western chantoosie" with "impossible dreams" adrift in an otherwise "slightly sappy" tale of a cowpoke's "crazy love" (via a William Inge play); though Marilyn proves she's more than "just a pretty face", skeptics of her "serious actress" mode say they "want to get off."

Butch Cassidy & the Sundance Kid ✉ Ⓘ

1969. Directed by George Roy Hill. With Paul Newman, Robert Redford, Katharine Ross. 110 minutes. Rated PG.

"Compulsive charmers" Newman and Redford play a pair of wise-cracking, "magnetic" "antiheroes" trying to stay ahead of the law in this "outstanding" Western "buddy movie", loaded with "adventure and humor"; it fuses a "snappy" script, Burt Bacharach soundtrack and "too many classic scenes to count" into a "sentimental favorite" that's "never boring" from start to "unforgettable" finish.

Bye Bye Birdie

1963. Directed by George Sidney. With Janet Leigh, Dick Van Dyke, Ann-Margret. 112 minutes. Rated G.

The high "fun quotient" bolsters this "upbeat" musical from the "long-ago", faraway world of 1963, a look at the hoopla surrounding an Elvis-like singer's farewell gig before he goes off to the army; though Ann-Margret is "one heck of a talented sex kitten" doing some athletic song-and-dance numbers that – whew! – "stay with you", detractors wave it off as "cheesy" fare that's "woefully dated now."

Cabaret ✉

1972. Directed by Bob Fosse. With Liza Minnelli, Michael York, Joel Grey. 124 minutes. Rated PG.

Comprised of equal parts "love, angst", "singing, dancing and Nazis", this "seminal modern musical" set in pre-WWII Berlin is a "touchstone" of the genre that "hasn't lost its luster"; old chums cheer Fosse's "superb direction" and the "starmaking performances" from Minnelli and Grey (who all took home Oscars), and even though the mood of the piece can careen from "dark" to "raunchy", it's always "fun to watch."

Cabinet of Dr. Caligari, The ◑   26 | 21 | 24 | 26
1921. Directed by Robert Wiene. With Conrad Veidt, Werner Kraus. 67 minutes. Not Rated.
"They don't get any freakier" than this "fascinating antique", a "menacingly atmospheric" silent horror flick that uses "German expressionism" and "twisted sets" to kindle a "nightmare" tale of murder told by a "tortured mind"; "stark, powerful" and "spooky" right down to the pioneering "surprise ending", it's "still being imitated" and still makes many modern chillers "look lame."

Cactus Flower   ▽ 17 | 20 | 18 | 17
1969. Directed by Gene Saks. With Walter Matthau, Ingrid Bergman, Goldie Hawn. 103 minutes. Rated PG.
This "cute" if "dated" comedy about the affairs of a philandering dentist might be "romantic fluff", but it's redeemed by a "strong cast", particularly the "radiant" Bergman and the "delightful", Oscar-winning Hawn "in her screen debut"; sticklers say "even Matthau can't save" the "weak story", though "he does try."

CADDYSHACK ⑪   24 | 20 | 19 | 19
1980. Directed by Harold Ramis. With Chevy Chase, Rodney Dangerfield, Bill Murray. 99 minutes. Rated R.
"Dumb as it is", this "goofy" comedy of "golfers gone amok" is a "classic" of "un-ironic" (some say "sophomoric") humor featuring a "priceless" ensemble cast and a fake gopher; "ok, it's a guy thing", but it "stands the test of time" as "oft-quoted" "mindless fun."

Caine Mutiny, The   27 | 28 | 26 | 23
1954. Directed by Edward Dmytryk. With Humphrey Bogart, Jose Ferrer, Van Johnson. 124 minutes. Not Rated.
This "briny" blend of "powerful wartime story" and "engrossing" courtroom drama gets its ballast from Bogart's "brilliant", "pull-out-all-the-stops" turn as Queeg, the "demented sea captain" compulsively "click, click, clicking" a set of "steel balls"; the "classic script" follows a "totally believable" high-seas rebellion to a court-martial and is "must-see" material for maritime mavens.

Calendar Girls   23 | 25 | 23 | 22
2003. Directed by Nigel Cole. With Helen Mirren, Julie Walters, John Alderton. 108 minutes. Rated PG-13.
"Older can be beautiful" is the "serious message behind the tea and scones" of this comic tale of "plucky", middle-aged English gals who pose for a nude calendar to raise funds for a cancer center; the "talent-laden cast" does a "charming" job with this "female version of *The Full Monty*", and let's face it, "who doesn't love Helen Mirren naked?"; wags note certain parts "sag" a bit.

Camelot   21 | 21 | 23 | 23
1967. Directed by Joshua Logan. With Richard Harris, Vanessa Redgrave, Franco Nero. 179 minutes. Rated G.
Lerner and Loewe's Broadway musical of the "well-worn" King Arthur legend receives "faithful" treatment in this tale of pomp and "passion in medieval England"; admirers of the "gorgeous" sets and "beautiful music" sing its praises as a "magical" "diver-

sion", though dissenters take a tilt at the "ponderous" "excess" and note "no one in the cast can carry a tune."

Candidate, The ✉   20 | 22 | 22 | 20
1972. Directed by Michael Ritchie. With Robert Redford, Peter Boyle, Melvyn Douglas. 109 minutes. Rated PG.
A "prescient" civics lesson, this political drama tracks a "social activist seduced into selling his soul" when he runs for the Senate from California; a "most convincing" Redford leads the pack of "top-notch performances" as the novice campaigner who's "in far over his head", presenting an "accurate" if "cynical view" of the process that registers as "timely" over 30 years later.

Cape Fear ◑   25 | 26 | 26 | 23
1962. Directed by J. Lee Thompson. With Gregory Peck, Robert Mitchum, Polly Bergen. 105 minutes. Not Rated.
It's high tide for "rage and revenge" in this "doozy" of a noir thriller, a real "nail-biter" starring Peck as an upright dad who "gets down in the gutter" to protect his family from a "deeply frightening" ex-con at large in the marsh and "as evil as they come"; most rate it "scarier than the remake", "without the histrionics."

Cape Fear   20 | 24 | 21 | 20
1991. Directed by Martin Scorsese. With Robert De Niro, Nick Nolte, Jessica Lange, Juliette Lewis. 128 minutes. Rated R.
Count on "fear for sure" as Scorsese's "well-done" redo of the killer '62 thriller heads for "over-the-top territory", working up "sustained suspense" as a "terrifying" De Niro "has a ball" portraying a vengeance-bent "wacko"; it's an "edge-of-your-seat" ride, with the "cameos" from the "previous cast" that are a "nice touch."

CAPOTE ✉   26 | 29 | 24 | 25
2005. Directed by Bennett Miller. With Philip Seymour Hoffman, Catherine Keener, Chris Cooper. 114 minutes. Rated R.
Not content to do a mere "uncanny impression", "genius" Hoffman delves "inside the mind" of "flamboyant" writer Truman Capote to render the "iconoclast" "in all his complexity" – while nabbing a "well-deserved" Oscar along the way – in this "fascinating" biopic, a behind the scenes look at the writing of Tru's "watershed" book *In Cold Blood*; abetted by Keener's "sturdy" supporting turn, this "world-class study" also works well as a "meditation on journalistic ethics."

Captain Blood ◑   23 | 21 | 20 | 21
1935. Directed by Michael Curtiz. With Errol Flynn, Olivia de Havilland, Basil Rathbone. 119 minutes. Not Rated.
Avast, there's "salty" "popcorn fun" aplenty in this "smashing" swashbuckler, featuring "Flynn's first starring role" as an enslaved wretch who becomes a "devil-may-care" pirate of the Caribbean; armchair buccaneers jump on board for the "roguish" baddies, "high-seas action" and "men in tights", not minding that the old vessel is "on the creaky side."

Captains Courageous ✉◑   25 | 26 | 24 | 21
1937. Directed by Victor Fleming. With Spencer Tracy, Freddie Bartholomew, Lionel Barrymore. 115 minutes. Not Rated.
Fashioned from a Kipling tale that's "every boy's dream of excitement", this "tearjerker"-cum–adventure story stars Bartholomew as a bratty rich kid who's rescued at sea and matures under the

helm of a salty sailor, the Oscar-winning Tracy; the lad's "highly touching" transformation is conveyed through "phenomenal" acting that's "too often forgotten."

Carmen Jones | 23 | 23 | 23 | 23 |

1954. Directed by Otto Preminger. With Dorothy Dandridge, Harry Belafonte, Pearl Bailey. 105 minutes. Not Rated.

A "modern", "Americanized" version of Bizet's "classic" *Carmen*, this "beautiful reimagining" was a "breakthrough for its time" given its all-black cast, led by the "sassy" Dorothy and "hot" Harry; while the concept's "superb" and the music "beautiful", it's docked a few points since the stars' songs were dubbed by "real opera singers."

Carnal Knowledge | 22 | 26 | 21 | 21 |

1971. Directed by Mike Nichols. With Jack Nicholson, Candice Bergen, Art Garfunkel, Ann-Margret. 98 minutes. Rated R.

"Literate people talk dirty" in this "bitter but engrossing" look at "two self-absorbed buddies who measure life in terms of their sexual conquests", and though these "pretty sad characters" can be "hard to watch", the "perfect cast" expertly evokes its theme of "innocence lost"; still, the jaded jeer what was "bold for its time" is now rather "tame."

Carousel | 24 | 22 | 22 | 25 |

1956. Directed by Henry King. With Gordon MacRae, Shirley Jones, Cameron Mitchell. 128 minutes. Not Rated.

"Girl meets wrong boy" at the traveling show in this silver screen go-round of Rodgers and Hammerstein's "sentimental" musical, which draws on a "lovely" score and "fine cast" of "first-rate" singers to spin a tale that's "romantic, sad" and "not always pretty"; while it's regarded as a "neglected great" to devotees, it's also seen as a squandering of "talent" on a "corny", "tarnished-with-age" storyline.

Carrie ⓘ | 22 | 22 | 23 | 21 |

1976. Directed by Brian De Palma. With Sissy Spacek, Piper Laurie, Amy Irving, John Travolta. 98 minutes. Rated R.

"Stephen King done right", this "bloody good" horror pic headlines Spacek as a "bug-eyed" "telekinetic outcast" (with a "nut bar" of a mom) who repays the "casual cruelty of high-schoolers" with a prom-night "flip-out" that's gorier than a bucket of "pig's blood"; with "character-oriented" carnage that's a cut above "shock schlock", it's "white knuckles all the way" to that "grabber" of an ending.

CASABLANCA ✉◑ | 29 | 28 | 28 | 27 |

1942. Directed by Michael Curtiz. With Humphrey Bogart, Ingrid Bergman, Paul Henreid, Claude Rains. 102 minutes. Rated PG.

We'll always have the "magic" of this "most compelling" of romances, a showcase for "legendary" turns from an "enigmatic" Bogart, "radiant" Bergman and "top-shelf" supporting cast set against the "unforgettable" backdrop of WWII occupied North Africa; the "fast-paced" plot of passion and "intrigue" is an "unsurpassed" model of good, "old-fashioned storytelling" and a bona fide "runner-up to Shakespeare" in the "classic lines" department – ultimately, there's no choice but to "play it again and again."

Casper

| 21 | 24 | 21 | 22 |

Casino

1995. Directed by Martin Scorsese. With Robert De Niro, Sharon Stone, Joe Pesci. 178 minutes. Rated R.

A crash course in "pre-corporate casino management", this "flashy" crime saga of "mob life" in "seedy Vegas" relates a "dark" tale that deals out "violence, drugs and self-loathing" in spades; proponents lay their money down for De Niro as a dapper hood, Pesci's "insane mob guy" bit and a "sizzling" Stone proving she "can actually act"; still, those who yawn it's "way too long" say bets are off, since they could be "watching *Goodfellas* instead."

Casper

| 15 | 14 | 15 | 19 |

1995. Directed by Brad Silberling. With Christina Ricci, Bill Pullman, Cathy Moriarty. 100 minutes. Rated PG.

The "special effects are worth the ticket price" of this "typical family movie" "appropriate for all ages" that's also notable for its "really cute" title character, a ghost who's referred to as 'living impaired'; though some say the "sappy" storyline's "charmless", at least it's "not annoyingly adorable."

Cast Away

| 20 | 25 | 18 | 23 |

2000. Directed by Robert Zemeckis. With Tom Hanks, Helen Hunt. 143 minutes. Rated PG-13.

"Hanks does Crusoe" in this "well-made" adventure based on Tom's "almost-one-man show" as a "pudgy FedEx" pilot marooned after a crash landing and forced to "slim down", don a "loincloth" and start "talking to a volleyball"; though "feeling his loneliness" may be "inspiring", foes say the action's beached by "slow-moving" stretches and a "trite" windup that's too "predictable."

Cat Ballou ✉

| 21 | 22 | 19 | 20 |

1965. Directed by Elliot Silverstein. With Lee Marvin, Jane Fonda, Michael Callan. 97 minutes. Not Rated.

"Not your typical Western", this comic oater "with a heart" stars Fonda as a righteous lady outlaw but is stolen by Oscar-winner Marvin, who horses around in two roles, including that of a whiskey-addled gunslinger; a "hoot in its day", it's nearing its ninth life but is still "fun to watch."

Catch Me If You Can

| 23 | 24 | 25 | 24 |

2002. Directed by Steven Spielberg. With Leonardo DiCaprio, Tom Hanks, Christopher Walken. 141 minutes. Rated PG-13.

Spielberg's "witty, fast-paced" "cat-and-mouse game" ("based on a true story" about a charming con man) is "mischievous, delicious fun from the delightful opening credits until the final frame", with "lots of '60s color" and "awesome acting" by the "engaging DiCaprio" and "rock-solid" Hanks; it's an "exciting, wild ride" that shows us "sometimes crime *does* pay."

Cat on a Hot Tin Roof

| 25 | 27 | 24 | 23 |

1958. Directed by Richard Brooks. With Elizabeth Taylor, Paul Newman, Burl Ives. 108 minutes. Not Rated.

"Man, these people have problems": "steamy" Liz "in that white slip" and a "dynamite" Newman "couldn't possibly look better" as they "burn up the screen" in this "sex-soaked" Tennessee Williams drama of "love, rejection" and "Southern family politics"; the "towering" Ives presides as the ragin' Big Daddy, adding an "incredibly interesting" *Lear*-like thread to all that "eye candy."

Cat People
16 | 17 | 18 | 18

1982. Directed by Paul Schrader. With Nastassja Kinski, Malcolm McDowell, John Heard, Annette O'Toole. 118 minutes. Rated R.

"Pretty on the eye if fuzzy on the brain", this "atmospheric" remake of the 1942 "Simone Simon cult classic" is a "stylish but forgettable" fantasy having to do with panthers and "sexual politics"; fans purr about its "creepy", "feline performances" and "nifty special effects", but seen-it-alls say the "David Bowie theme song" is the "best thing about this movie."

Celluloid Closet, The
25 | – | 25 | 24

1995. Directed by Robert Epstein, Jeff Friedman. Documentary. 102 minutes. Rated R.

Learn to "appreciate" certain classics in a "whole new" way via this documentary "revelation" that traces "gay themes and undercurrents" in Hollywood history using film clips and "insightful" interviews; it takes an "unsparing look at prejudice" that's also a "very entertaining" glimpse into a "crowded closet" – even if some wish there were more than "mild surprises behind the door."

Changing Lanes
16 | 19 | 17 | 17

2002. Directed by Roger Michell. With Ben Affleck, Samuel L. Jackson. 99 minutes. Rated R.

A freeway fender-bender turns into "road rage" of epic proportions in this "fast-moving" "urban melodrama" pitting an "affluent", "smarmy" lawyer against a "poor, down-and-out" dad, both suffering from "too much testosterone" and bent on one-upmanship; admirers like its "small scope" and Jackson's "fine" performance but not the "just-along-for-the-ride" Affleck or that "wussy", "cop-out" ending.

Charade
26 | 25 | 26 | 25

1963. Directed by Stanley Donen. With Cary Grant, Audrey Hepburn, Walter Matthau. 113 minutes. Not Rated.

Expect "plenty of plot twists" in this "quintessential romantic comedy/thriller" (the "best Hitchcock flick that Hitchcock didn't make") about the scramble for a missing fortune; its very "easy-on-the-eyes" stars, "luscious Paris" scenery, magical "Mancini melodies" and "Audrey's fab wardrobe" make for "perfect" moviemaking – "murder was never so much fun."

Chariots of Fire ✉
26 | 25 | 25 | 25

1981. Directed by Hugh Hudson. With Ben Cross, Ian Charleson, Ian Holm. 123 minutes. Rated PG.

Remembered for "running off with" a Best Picture Oscar, this "inspiring" drama paces itself in "superb" style as it follows the "trials and triumph" of a British track team bound for the 1924 Olympics; thanks to "uplifting" legwork and a very "hummable" soundtrack, it breaks the tape as a "never boring" movie.

Charlie's Angels ⑪
13 | 11 | 10 | 17

2000. Directed by McG. With Cameron Diaz, Drew Barrymore, Lucy Liu, Bill Murray. 98 minutes. Rated PG-13.

"Girl power" gets a glam "MTV" makeover replete with "bootylicious" babes and "high-flying action" in this "fluffy", "nonsensical" send-up of the '70s TV series about foxy femme crime-fighters; no doubt, "it doesn't have the best acting ever" ("did Murray lose a bet?") and the "storyline's completely far-fetched", but charitable souls say it's "good when you want something mind-numbing."

Charly ✉   21 | 25 | 22 | 17
1968. Directed by Ralph Nelson. With Cliff Robertson, Claire Bloom, Leon Janney. 103 minutes. Rated PG.
A bright idea grafting drama onto a "believable" sci-fi scenario, this "original" flick gives Best Actor honoree Robertson a chance to "shine" in his "best performance" as a "man who goes from retardation to genius and back again" after a round of brain surgery; tutor Bloom adds romantic interest to make the doings "supremely touching" – "if a bit sappy" for cynics.

Chasing Amy   20 | 19 | 20 | 17
1997. Directed by Kevin Smith. With Ben Affleck, Joey Lauren Adams, Jason Lee. 111 minutes. Rated R.
Director Smith's trademarks – "Jersey-speak", "coarse humor", "semi-realistic situations" – are all apparent in this "offbeat" romantic comedy, featuring Affleck in the role of a comic-book scribe bewitched by a lesbian with a "nails-on-chalkboard" voice; it "rocks" fans with an "entertainingly different" mix of "smart" talk and "slacker cool", but foes claim it's a "sentimental" ode to "geek life" that's "not really funny."

Cheaper By the Dozen ⑪   22 | 22 | 23 | 19
1950. Directed by Walter Lang. With Clifton Webb, Jeanne Crain, Myrna Loy. 85 minutes. Not Rated.
Set at the turn of the last century, this "warm family comedy" relates the "wonderful", fact-based story of a pair of efficiency experts bringing up 12 "cute" children, with a "droll" Webb stealing the show as the "pompous" head of the brood; sure, it strays into "precious" territory but oldsters attest it "wears well over time."

Cheaper By the Dozen ⑪   17 | 18 | 16 | 18
2003. Directed by Shawn Levy. With Steve Martin, Bonnie Hunt, Piper Perabo, Hilary Duff. 98 minutes. Rated PG.
For a "good, old-fashioned movie experience", try this "wholesome" comedy about a "big crazy family" uprooted by dad and mom's new jobs; granted, it's "very different" from the original 1950 flick and "not really a remake except for the number of children", but the "kids are cute" and there are "some funny moments."

CHICAGO ✉   27 | 26 | 25 | 29
2002. Directed by Rob Marshall. With Renée Zellweger, Catherine Zeta-Jones, Richard Gere, Queen Latifah. 113 minutes. Rated PG-13.
"Bob Fosse would have been proud" of this "absolutely brilliant" adaptation of his boffo Broadway "tale of murder, greed and corruption" in 1920s Chicago; "astounded" surveyors swear this "razzle-dazzle" "visual masterpiece" "deserved every Oscar it won" thanks to its "phenomenal acting", "sexy cinematography", "spine-tingling music" ("who knew the big three could sing?") and "major dance moves that'll leave you gasping for air"; even critics who complain of "miscasting" and "MTV camerawork" hope it sparks a "return to old-fashioned movie musicals."

Chicken Little   19 | – | 17 | 22
2005. Directed by Mark Dindal. Animated. 81 minutes. Rated G.
Disney lays a "*War of the Worlds*" spin on a "classic" children's fable and hatches some "good clean fun" in this "cute" cartoon

featuring "excellent" animation and some "amusing" moments; the scattered nuggets of adult "belly laughs" earn parental praise, though a few critics chirp it "should have spent a little more time in the incubator."

Chicken Run   23 | – | 23 | 27
2000. Directed by Peter Lord, Nick Park. Animated. 84 minutes. Rated G.
Pure "poultry in motion", this "ingenious", "touching" barnyard saga uses "fantastic" claymation to portray a "darn appealing" bunch of British fowl and their "valiant struggle" to get off the farm; "subtle references" make it a "hilarious take" on all the *Stalag 17*–style POW pics, so while kids can enjoy the "innocent" animated escapade, it "doesn't chicken out" on "tongue-in-cheek", grown-up undertones; in an eggshell, a "good run for the money."

Children of a Lesser God ✉   23 | 25 | 22 | 21
1986. Directed by Randa Haines. With Marlee Matlin, William Hurt, Piper Laurie. 119 minutes. Rated R.
This "touching" drama "does justice to the original play" on the strength of "sexy, compelling" turns from Hurt as a speech teacher at a school for the deaf and Best Actress winner Matlin, "signing throughout" as a hearing-impaired woman with a complex past; expect "moving scenes" as their intimacy develops, and though an "enjoyable" intro to the "deaf community", it might be a "little overdramatized."

CHILDREN OF PARADISE ⓞⒻ   28 | 27 | 27 | 26
1946. Directed by Marcel Carné. With Arletty, Jean-Louis Barrault, Pierre Renoir. 190 minutes. Not Rated.
Filmed in France "under the noses of the Nazis", this "legendary" romance "lovingly re-creates 1840s Paris" in a "multilayered" story of a "lovesick" mime's passion for a vampish stage siren; built on "profound" themes and "stylized" performances (that come off as "melodramatic" but are rich with "beauty and feeling"), it "continues to fascinate" as a "masterpiece of world cinema" and the big screen's "greatest tribute to live theater."

China Syndrome, The   22 | 25 | 24 | 20
1979. Directed by James Bridges. With Jack Lemmon, Jane Fonda, Michael Douglas. 122 minutes. Rated PG.
The going gets "scary" as a nuclear power facility heads for meltdown in this "intelligent thriller" with a "solid" cast, including a "terrific" Lemmon as the plant supervisor and "Fonda at her peak" as a frustrated TV reporter; the "could-happen" story is "well-crafted", but conservatives contend that the "melodramatic" matchup of "bad-guy corporate players" against "good-guy idealists" makes it into the "definitive liberal" "message film."

CHINATOWN ✉Ⓤ   27 | 28 | 26 | 26
1974. Directed by Roman Polanski. With Jack Nicholson, Faye Dunaway, John Huston. 131 minutes. Rated R.
This "taut drama" about "stolen water" and "bottled-up emotion" in 1930s LA is a "nearly perfect" exercise in "Technicolor film noir" that's simultaneously "funny, bleak and knowing"; credit the "dynamite" cast, "ravishingly beautiful" cinematography and "superb script" (that ends with a "shocking", "untypical-Hollywood ending") for its success; most memorable scene: Dunaway's "slap"-happy "she's-my-sister-she's-my-daughter" tour de force.

Chocolat
22 | 24 | 22 | 23

2000. Directed by Lasse Hallström. With Juliette Binoche, Alfred Molina, Johnny Depp. 121 minutes. Rated PG-13.

A "yummy escape" "bordering on a fairy tale", this "funny" romance finds "lovely" "rebel spirit" Binoche pitted against "petty-minded villagers" when she opens a chocolate shop in a French hamlet and takes up with Depp; the blend of a "beautiful setting" mixed with some "uplifting whimsy" makes for one "tasty bonbon."

CHRISTMAS CAROL, A ◐
27 | 26 | 28 | 23

1951. Directed by Brian Desmond Hurst. With Alastair Sim, Kathleen Harrison, Mervyn Johns. 86 minutes. Not Rated.

"Sim is the best Scrooge ever" in this Dickens of a "holiday delight", a "magical adaptation" of the "timeless" fable concerning a rich old paragon of "grouchiness" transformed by a Yuletide visit from a posse of ghosts; cherished as "superb" family fare, it has fans replaying it "religiously" because there's "no way" to do "Christmas without it."

Christmas Story, A
26 | 23 | 27 | 22

1983. Directed by Bob Clark. With Peter Billingsley, Melinda Dillon, Darren McGavin. 94 minutes. Rated PG.

A "sweet but not sugary" look at the "debacle that's Christmas in America", this "irresistible" family fave takes a "fond glimpse back" with a "funny-till-it-hurts" "exposition of a '40s childhood" centered on a kid bent on a "BB gun" under the tree; "most rewatchable" and "quotable" thanks to its "excellent cast and script", it's "good clean fun" and deemed a seasonal "must."

Chronicles of Narnia: The Lion, the Witch & the Wardrobe
23 | 21 | 24 | 26

2005. Directed by Andrew Adamson. With Georgie Henley, Skandar Keynes, Tilda Swinton. 140 minutes. Rated PG.

C.S. Lewis' "classic" children's fantasy is "faithfully" rendered on celluloid via this "masterful production", a veritable "feast for the eyes" whose mane highlights include "lovely" performances, "beautiful" costumes and "spectacular" effects ("you can almost touch Aslan"); its "religious overtones" court controversy, however, with defenders declaring the "Christian themes are dealt with appropriately" and skeptics suggesting "it feels like a sermon."

Cider House Rules, The ✉
22 | 24 | 23 | 22

1999. Directed by Lasse Hallström. With Tobey Maguire, Charlize Theron, Michael Caine. 126 minutes. Rated PG-13.

Presenting "life choices" in a '30s-era Maine orphanage, this "thought-provoking tearjerker" is a story of "compassion" with some "tough subject matter sneaked in" that gives Maguire his "breakout role" and proves "Caine really can act"; despite a few objections to the "cloying" tone and "watered-down" treatment of John Irving's novel, "satisfied" customers rule it an "absorbing" "feel-good" flick that "doesn't pander to the Hallmark crowd."

Cinderella
26 | – | 25 | 26

1950. Directed by Clyde Geronimi, Wilfred Jackson, Hamilton Luske. Animated. 74 minutes. Rated G.

"You know the drill": "breathtaking" animation from "Disney's golden age" merges with the stuff "countless girlish dreams" are made of in this "beautiful fantasy" about an "overworked, abused orphan" who bags her Prince Charming, with a little help from her fairy godmother and some "industrious", very finely feathered friends; if "short on characterization", it remains an "old-fashioned favorite" that's a shoe-in to be a "classic for generations to come."

Cinderella Liberty ∅

19 | 23 | 20 | 17

1973. Directed by Mark Rydell. With James Caan, Marsha Mason, Kirk Calloway. 117 minutes. Rated R.
"Great chemistry" between the leads buoys this "honest" but "overlooked" romance about a lonesome shore-patrol swabbie who falls for a "tender-hearted prostitute" and becomes a real father figure to her "mixed-race son"; an "excellent" Caan plays well against Mason's "sympathetic" portrayal of the "hooker who doesn't know any other way to live"; all in all, a shipshape effort.

CINDERELLA MAN

25 | 27 | 25 | 25

2005. Directed by Ron Howard. With Russell Crowe, Renée Zellweger, Paul Giamatti. 144 minutes. Rated PG-13.
The "dreary" "look of the Great Depression" permeates this "superbly crafted" sports biopic 'bout James Braddock, the "down-on-his-luck pug" who "battled back" from poverty and injury for a "shot at the heavyweight title"; given its "superb" combo of the "incredibly believable" Crowe and "wonderful" Giamatti, fans feel this "worthy" contender "should have been a bigger hit."

Cinema Paradiso ✉ F

26 | 26 | 26 | 25

1988. Directed by Giuseppe Tornatore. With Philippe Noiret, Jacques Perrin. 123 minutes. Rated R.
This Italian "heart-warmer" is an "endearing" look at "love and loss" that's based on the "utterly charming" story of a "projectionist in the local movie house" who "mentors a fatherless child"; it rolls a "colorful" cast, "*bellissimo*" camerawork and a "lovely" score into an "engrossing", frankly "sentimental" film.

CITIZEN KANE ✉◐

28 | 27 | 27 | 28

1941. Directed by Orson Welles. With Orson Welles, Joseph Cotten, Agnes Moorehead, Everett Sloane. 119 minutes. Rated PG.
"Loosely based on the life of William Randolph Hearst", this "magnum opus" about a "ruthless megalomaniac" who "mourns the loss of his innocent childhood" is an "undisputed masterpiece" that's "often imitated, never duplicated" and "as fresh as ever"; starring and directed by wunderkind Welles, it "revolutionized the cinema" and forever changed the meaning of the word "rosebud" – "by comparison, all other films are home movies."

City Lights ◐

28 | 28 | 26 | 25

1931. Directed by Charles Chaplin. With Charles Chaplin, Virginia Cherrill. 87 minutes. Not Rated.
"Humor, pathos and poignancy" make this silent "Chaplin masterpiece" glow with "old-fashioned sentimentality" as the Little Tramp's love for a "blind flower girl" leads to a series of "classic" scenes; from the "balletic boxing match" to the "heartbreaking" closing, this early flicker shows the master "on top of his game."

City of God F

26 | 25 | 26 | 25

2003. Directed by Kátia Lund, Fernando Meirelles. With Matheus Nachtergaele, Seu Jorge. 130 minutes. Rated R.
"Even those who are allergic to subtitles" will be more than "captivated" by this "shattering portrait" of "street kids in Brazil" who

"grow up to become a gang of murderous drug dealers"; it's a "harrowing, gut-wrenching" "tour de force" that's "dynamically acted" by "nonactors" and made "edgy and fresh" by "hypnotic visuals"; the "extreme violence and brutality" may "leave you feeling ill", but "you can't look away."

City Slickers ⑪   20 | 20 | 20 | 19

1991. Directed by Ron Underwood. With Billy Crystal, Daniel Stern, Jack Palance. 112 minutes. Rated PG-13.
"Yee-haw!"; a "super" Crystal rides high in this "tons-of-fun" "buddy comedy" about three NYers who go west for a dude-ranch vacation and wind up having a "midlife crisis during a cattle drive"; the "right-on" cast (particularly the "just-too-funny Palance") has a way with "wisdom and great one-liners", rounding up applause for "good fun" that doesn't shy from its "moving" side.

Claire's Knee 🄵   23 | 24 | 22 | 23

1971. Directed by Eric Rohmer. With Jean-Claude Brialy, Aurora Cornu, Laurence de Monaghan. 105 minutes. Rated PG.
The "antithesis of an action movie", this "insightful" look at "erotic desire done without conventional sex scenes" tells the story of a "midlife crisis"–bound Frenchman "obsessed with, well, the title says it all"; knockers rap all the "cerebral ooh-la-la" as too "talky", though admirers insist this "sweet paean to romantic longing" is "probably the high point of Rohmer's career."

Clear and Present Danger   20 | 21 | 22 | 20

1994. Directed by Phillip Noyce. With Harrison Ford, Willem Dafoe, Anne Archer. 141 minutes. Rated PG-13.
Clearly "great popcorn fodder", this "provocative action" flick is "one of the better Clancy adaptations", with Ford in "fine form" reprising his role as "what-a-man" CIA agent Jack Ryan going *mano a mano* with a Colombian dope cartel; though some call it "escapist stuff", it's so "exciting" and "patriotic", you can't help but root for this "smart movie hero" who "really kicks butt."

Cleopatra   19 | 18 | 19 | 25

1963. Directed by Joseph L. Mankiewicz. With Elizabeth Taylor, Richard Burton, Rex Harrison. 192 minutes. Not Rated.
"Grand, gaudy and tons of fun", this epic bio of the queen of the Nile (renowned for "breaking all production-cost records") is either a "guilty pleasure" or an "incredible waste of time"; devotees dig its "huge scale", over-the-top "entertainment" value and Liz's "exquisite" eye makeup, but cynics nix the flick's "bloated" look and "draggy" pace, advising that you "hit the clicker" immediately after Cleo's "showstopping entrance into Rome."

Clerks ◖   23 | 17 | 22 | 16

1994. Directed by Kevin Smith. With Brian O'Halloran, Jeff Anderson, Marilyn Ghigliotti. 92 minutes. Rated R.
"Crude" acting and "bottom-of-the-barrel production" values are redeemed by "wicked black humor" and "inspired", "raunchy" dialogue in this "microbudget indie" effort, a "fast-paced" comedy that pumps life into the "dead-end job" scene with a "realistic" look at "minimart" wage slavery; the "first foray" in Smith's "New Jersey series", it's a "slacker" "cult classic" that's "painfully funny" but unsafe for the "squeamish."

Client, The
17 | 19 | 19 | 18

1994. Directed by Joel Schumacher. With Susan Sarandon, Tommy Lee Jones, Brad Renfro. 120 minutes. Rated PG-13.

Ok, it's "not great literature or art", but this adaptation of the John Grisham best-seller makes for a "good evening of entertainment" with its "linear story" of a youngster fleeing mobsters *and* the FBI; though too "predictable" for some, the "enjoyable Sarandon" and "impressive Renfro" keep things "interesting" enough.

Clockwork Orange, A
25 | 24 | 24 | 25

1971. Directed by Stanley Kubrick. With Malcolm McDowell, Patrick Magee. 137 minutes. Rated R.

"Not for the weak of heart", this "ingenious Kubrick" cult parable is a "bold", "nightmarish" "mix of sex, ultraviolence" and "mind control" set in a "freaky", "futuristic" Britain; following the travails of "unhinged" "bad boy" McDowell (the "sinister yet strangely likable" head of a "vicious gang of droogies") through his "chilling" crimes to his "brainwashing" rehab, it threads "brilliant visuals" and "twisted" "social satire" into "riveting", "artful stuff" – helped by a bit of the old "Ludwig van."

Close Encounters of the Third Kind
24 | 22 | 25 | 27

1977. Directed by Steven Spielberg. With Richard Dreyfuss, François Truffaut, Teri Garr. 135 minutes. Rated PG.

"It's ok to believe in UFOs" thanks to this "landmark" sci-fi "spectacle", a "mesmerizing", "believable contact film" wherein Spielberg's "sense of wonder" first embraces the "aliens-come-to-earth" formula; the "hopeful" plotline involves a race to "figure it all out" when strange signals arrive from the sky, and the result is a "mind-blowing" "visual treat" with plenty of "heart" (and "mountains of mashed potatoes") that delivers a "jaw-dropping" climax with a "sentimental streak" a light-year wide.

Closer
19 | 23 | 18 | 19

2004. Directed by Mike Nichols. With Jude Law, Julia Roberts, Natalie Portman, Clive Owen. 104 minutes. Rated R.

"Possibly the worst first-date movie ever", this "chilly", "caustic" look at four "seriously flawed" folks involved in a "love trapezoid" is a "feel-bad flick", though defenders "love that Clive" and the "brutally honest" script; but many find the "dirty talk", "unlikable characters" and "joyless" mood too "uncomfortable to watch."

Clueless
21 | 19 | 20 | 20

1995. Directed by Amy Heckerling. With Alicia Silverstone, Paul Rudd, Brittany Murphy. 97 minutes. Rated PG-13.

Totally "sneaky-smart", this "lively" "update of *Emma*" with a "*90210*" twist is a "winning" comedy about LA's "spoiled rich" kids and stars a "delightful", "not-quite-acting" Silverstone, who juggles romantic uncertainty, a variety of "Valley catch phrases" and a "'90s" wardrobe "to die for"; despite a few hints of "fluff" – "whatever" – it offers "pure enjoyment" as a "pivotal teen movie" and some of the "sharpest" "bubblegum" out there.

Coach Carter
21 | 22 | 21 | 20

2005. Directed by Thomas Carter. With Samuel L. Jackson. 136 minutes. Rated PG-13.

"Reliably cool" Jackson hits nothin' but net with this "inspiring" tale ("based on a true story") of a "get-tough" high school hoops coach who leads his "underdog" squad to the Big Game; sure, the "feel-good" outcome may be "a bit predictable", but at the final buzzer fans cheer the "valuable" stay-in-school message, not to mention those "slam 'n' jam" B-ball scenes.

Coal Miner's Daughter ✉   24 | 27 | 23 | 22
1980. Directed by Michael Apted. With Sissy Spacek, Tommy Lee Jones, Levon Helm. 125 minutes. Rated PG.
Kentucky moonshine and "bravura performances" brighten this "charming biopic" of country crooner Loretta Lynn, led by the Oscar-winning Spacek as the daughter of Appalachia who "makes it huge" in Nashville; a down-home, "down-to-earth fairy tale", its "realistic portrayal" of a star's "rise to fame" and bout with burnout plays like an "interesting" C&W take on *Behind the Music*.

Cocoanuts, The ◑   24 | 22 | 19 | 19
1929. Directed by Robert Florey, Joseph Santley. With the Marx Brothers, Kay Francis. 96 minutes. Not Rated.
Never mind the "technical primitiveness", this first Marx Brothers comedy is as "zany" as their later work; though this "crude" rendering of the sibs' Broadway show is burdened with "trite musical numbers" and a "weak" story involving Florida real estate, die-hard Marxists say ya "gotta love" it as an "intriguing mess" that's at worst a guarantee of "better things to come."

Cocoon ⓫   20 | 21 | 21 | 20
1985. Directed by Ron Howard. With Don Ameche, Wilford Brimley, Hume Cronyn. 117 minutes. Rated PG-13.
"Old duffers" meet "pod people" in this "warm" sci-fi tale, which spins a "clever story" of an intergalactic meet-up between extraterrestrials and Florida rest-home residents, whose backyard pool becomes a fountain of youth; the "delightful" setup and "complete characters" give some of Hollywood's elder statesmen room to "romp", while director Howard makes it all "credible" – if a bit too "warm and cuddly" for some.

Coffee and Cigarettes ◑   18 | 20 | 16 | 19
2003. Directed by Jim Jarmusch. With Roberto Benigni, Cate Blanchett, Iggy Pop, Tom Waits, Bill Murray. 95 minutes. Rated R.
Filmed episodically over 17 years, this collection of 11 black-and-white vignettes depicting conversations over caffeine and ciggies is a "hit-or-miss" proposition: sometimes "brilliant", sometimes "monotonous"; fans single out Blanchett's "amazing" double role and that "hoot" of a scene pairing Bill Murray with Wu-Tang Clan, but ultimately this one's "more for Jarmusch fans than for the general public."

Cold Mountain   22 | 24 | 22 | 26
2003. Directed by Anthony Minghella. With Jude Law, Nicole Kidman, Renée Zellweger. 152 minutes. Rated R.
The "cinematic equivalent of a coffee table book", this "beautifully shot" Civil War saga of separated lovers "adapted from Homer's *Odyssey*" stars a "smokin'" Law opposite a "too-beautiful" Kidman, ever the "fashion plate" when she's "supposed to be starving"; never mind the too-"long" running time, "watching-the-grass-grow" pacing and controversy over Renée's Oscar win ("much deserved" vs. "Granny Clampett"), at the very least, this one is certainly "worth falling asleep on the sofa for."

Collateral
21 | 24 | 21 | 22

2004. Directed by Michael Mann. With Tom Cruise, Jamie Foxx, Jada Pinkett Smith. 120 minutes. Rated R.
Cruise sports a silver hairdo and plays "against type" as a "psychopathic" contract killer pitted against Foxx's "unassuming everyman" for one "nightmare evening" in this "taut", "edge-of-your-seat" thriller from "master-of-moods" auteur Mann; devotees say the "incongruous plot", "tacked-on romance" and "generic conclusion" are "forgivable" due to the "morally challenging" situations – and "LA never looked so beautiful and dangerous."

Collector, The
▽ 23 | 26 | 23 | 22

1965. Directed by William Wyler. With Terence Stamp, Samantha Eggar. 119 minutes. Not Rated.
A "deeply disturbed recluse" kidnaps a "lovely young woman" in this "chilling story of obsession" adapted from John Fowles' "devastating" first novel; "terrific acting by Stamp and Eggar" keeps folks "fascinated", and if this "creepy stalker film" can be "hard to watch" at times, it's still "wonderfully done."

Color of Money, The ✉
16 | 21 | 16 | 17

1986. Directed by Martin Scorsese. With Paul Newman, Tom Cruise, Mary Elizabeth Mastrantonio. 119 minutes. Rated R.
Something different from Martin Scorsese, this "generation-later" "follow-up to *The Hustler*" details how a washed-up billiards baron molds an up-and-comer into his protégé; though somewhat "predictable", "excellent acting" from the "powerhouse Cruise" and the "finely tuned", Oscar-winning Newman "saves it."

Color Purple, The
26 | 27 | 26 | 25

1985. Directed by Steven Spielberg. With Whoopi Goldberg, Danny Glover, Oprah Winfrey. 154 minutes. Rated PG-13.
A "heartfelt" reading of Alice Walker's "breakthrough" bestseller, this "moving" drama of "empowerment" "really hits home" with its depiction of a "post-slavery black family" in the Deep South and a wronged woman's "redemption and liberation"; the "breathtaking" lenswork, "Goldberg's best-ever showing" and a "brilliant" supporting cast ("Oprah can act!") make for a "teary" "triumph" that some cite as "Oscar's biggest snub."

Coming Home ✉
23 | 26 | 23 | 21

1978. Directed by Hal Ashby. With Jane Fonda, Jon Voight, Bruce Dern, Penelope Milford. 126 minutes. Rated R.
"Jon and Jane are magic together" in this "ultimate anti-war message" drama–cum–love triangle involving a paraplegic Vietnam vet, an "inconveniently married" hospital volunteer and a gung-ho marine; expect "moving performances" (Voight and Fonda took home Oscars) and "loads of emotion" that manage to convey a "coming of age for both the characters – and the times."

Coming to America
18 | 18 | 17 | 17

1988. Directed by John Landis. With Eddie Murphy, Arsenio Hall, James Earl Jones. 116 minutes. Rated R.
"Sidesplitting", "multiple-character tour de force" showcasing the talents of "total riot" Murphy and "hilarious" Hall in a "goofy", "fish-out-of-water" comedy about an African prince who logically "heads to Queens" to find a royal mate; hard-core groupies can "repeat the whole movie by heart."

Con Air
14 | 15 | 14 | 18

1997. Directed by Simon West. With Nicolas Cage, John Cusack, John Malkovich, Steve Buscemi. 115 minutes. Rated R.
"Hardened criminals" en route to a "high-security prison" skyjack their plane in this "popcorn action flick" that's a "no-brainer" if you're ready for an "enjoyably obnoxious" experience; foes protest this "testosteronefest" has "little plot" and "just-collecting-a-paycheck" acting, but worst of all is Cage's "horrific mullet."

Conan the Barbarian ⏻
16 | 9 | 15 | 18

1982. Directed by John Milius. With Arnold Schwarzenegger, James Earl Jones. 129 minutes. Rated R.
The flick that "brought Arnold to everyone's attention", this "archetypal sword-and-sorcery fantasy" about a "barbarian butt-kicker" is "all a teenage boy could want" in a movie, conjuring up a pulpy, "no-holds-barred world of lust and vengeance"; even though Schwarzenegger's "acting isn't that great" – it was "before he learned to talk" – his "muscles are expressive" enough.

Confessions of a Dangerous Mind
19 | 23 | 19 | 20

2003. Directed by George Clooney. With Sam Rockwell, Drew Barrymore, George Clooney. 113 minutes. Rated R.
"Odd but oddly compelling", this bio of "game show guru" Chuck Barris is a "real eyebrow-raiser", intercutting his antics as host of *The Gong Show* with his "secret life" as a "CIA hit man"; while the dual careers are too "preposterous" and "bizarro" for many to swallow ("puh-leeze"), some confess the picture "grows on you the more you watch it" – what it lacks in logic, "it makes up for in nerve."

Conformist, The 🅵⊘
26 | 26 | 27 | 26

1971. Directed by Bernardo Bertolucci. With Jean-Louis Trintignant, Stefania Sandrelli, Dominique Sanda. 115 minutes. Rated R.
Director "Bertolucci is at his absolute best" in this "supercool, superstylized" Italian psychological drama set in the '30s about an "emotionally troubled civil servant" turned "fascist agent"; nonconformists warn "beware the dubbed version" but concur that Vittorio Storaro's "haunting" cinematography transcends dialogue; hottest moment: that "erotic tango" between Sanda and Sandrelli.

Constant Gardener, The
23 | 26 | 23 | 24

2005. Directed by Fernando Meirelles. With Ralph Fiennes, Rachel Weisz. 129 minutes. Rated R.
The "politically pertinent" topic of pharmaceutical companies' alleged "exploitation of third-world citizens" forms the "fascinating" backdrop of this "tautly woven" thriller–cum–"haunting" love story featuring the "ever dependable" Fiennes as an "uptight English diplomat" who unravels a "mystery" involving his activist wife (the "fabulous" Weisz); based on John Le Carré's "complex" novel, it's undoubtedly "more exciting than its title might suggest", and provides plenty of "food for thought."

Contact
20 | 21 | 20 | 22

1997. Directed by Robert Zemeckis. With Jodie Foster, Matthew McConaughey, Tom Skerritt. 153 minutes. Rated PG.
This "thinking person's" sci-fi flick asks the "Big Question" – "are we alone" in the universe?; true believers cite the "excellent special effects", "fascinating" story and a fine Foster "near the top

of her form", but the alienated dismiss it as "long-winded" and "preachy", opting to "read Carl Sagan's excellent book" instead.

Contempt F

25 | 24 | 22 | 24

1964. Directed by Jean-Luc Godard. With Brigitte Bardot, Michel Piccoli, Jack Palance, Fritz Lang. 104 minutes. Not Rated.
The "struggle between commerce and artistic integrity" gets the Godard treatment in this "scathing" "movie about movies" that details a screenwriter's struggle to adapt James Joyce's *Ulysses* and keep his marriage together; with a "coquettish" Bardot and a "full-throttle" Palance on board, and "stunning" Mediterranean vistas in CinemaScope, it's a fine example of "classic French New Wave" that's "showy, smart" and "enjoyably pretentious."

Contender, The

19 | 23 | 20 | 19

2000. Directed by Rod Lurie. With Joan Allen, Gary Oldman, Jeff Bridges, Christian Slater. 126 minutes. Rated R.
In this Clinton White House–ish "Washington soap opera" (with enough "twists and turns" to keep you "guessing till the end"), a "scrappy" female pol "stays true to her principles" at great cost to her reputation and career; though Allen is "superb" and Bridges would make a "fine" real-life prez, some pundits protest the drama's "tackling of big issues" as "overblown melodrama."

Conversation, The

25 | 26 | 25 | 23

1974. Directed by Francis Ford Coppola. With Gene Hackman, John Cazale, Frederic Forrest. 113 minutes. Rated PG.
A "brilliant" thriller about a "paranoid" surveillance specialist who comes undone, this "little-known" Coppola feature features a "virtuoso performance by Hackman", whose gradual "deterioration is amazing" (there's also an appearance by a very young Harrison Ford); though a bit "slow-moving", the script is so "superbly constructed" that "if this flick doesn't put you on edge, nothing will."

Cooler, The

22 | 27 | 22 | 21

2003. Directed by Wayne Kramer. With William H. Macy, Maria Bello, Alec Baldwin. 101 minutes. Rated R.
"Losing is winning" for the perpetually "unlucky" title character in this "quirky" dramedy about a Vegas shill hired by a casino to "jinx high-rollers' winning streaks"; an "unglamorous" spin on the usual gambling yarn, it boasts "riveting acting" and a "believable love story", though some say the "gratuitous violence" and Macy's "racy" nude scenes are more of a "crapshoot."

Cool Hand Luke

26 | 27 | 24 | 22

1967. Directed by Stuart Rosenberg. With Paul Newman, George Kennedy, Strother Martin. 126 minutes. Not Rated.
"One of the best movie lines ever" ('what we have here is a failure to communicate') and that "famous hard-boiled egg eating scene" make this "damn great" Deep South prison drama memorable – not to mention the efforts of "consummate pro" Newman playing one cool con on a "chain gang", abetted by a "strong" Kennedy, who grabbed an Oscar for his supporting work.

Cool Runnings

18 | 16 | 21 | 17

1993. Directed by Jon Turteltaub. With John Candy, Doug E. Doug, Leon, Malik Yoba. 98 minutes. Rated PG.
Granted, it might be "silly", but this "cute", "underrated" comedy "based on the true" tale of the '88 Olympics' "Jamaican bobsled

team" is "fun for the whole family" (despite "a bit too much profanity"); cheerleaders say its "come-from-behind" story will "touch anyone's heart", particularly those who "miss John Candy."

Corpse Bride, The
| 20 | – | 19 | 25 |

2005. Directed by Tim Burton, Mike Johnson. Animated. 76 minutes. Rated PG.

From the "macabre" mind of Tim Burton and in the spirit of "*The Nightmare Before Christmas*" comes this "ghoulishly entertaining" fairy tale pulsing with "eye-popping" stop-motion animation and "raucous" musical numbers; make no bones about it, Johnny Depp's voicing of a "groom who's stolen away to the world of the dead" is an added "pleasure", though some mourn the "trite" story.

Counterfeit Traitor, The
| 25 | 25 | 26 | 23 |

1962. Directed by George Seaton. With William Holden, Lili Palmer, Hugh Griffith. 140 minutes. Not Rated.

"Based on a true story", this "classy" (albeit "forgotten") WWII spy thriller revolves around a Swedish "quisling" blacklisted by the Allies after trading with the Nazis; the "dashing" Holden is in his "gracefully aging prime" here, though some say the "deeply moving" Palmer steals the show as his "noble" confederate.

Count of Monte Cristo, The
| 19 | 20 | 22 | 22 |

2002. Directed by Kevin Reynolds. With James Caviezel, Guy Pearce, Richard Harris. 131 minutes. Rated PG-13.

"Revenge is sweet" in this "well-crafted" swashbuckler about a man wrongfully imprisoned plotting epic payback; fans like its "old-fashioned", "golden-age-of-Hollywood" approach ("great swordplay", "excellent production values", "enough romance to keep the girls interested"), but foes yawn that this "500th remake of the Dumas classic" is "nothing new" and "not particularly engaging."

Cousin, Cousine 🇫 ⊘
| 21 | 20 | 21 | 19 |

1975. Directed by Jean-Charles Tacchella. With Marie-Christine Barrault, Victor Lanoux. 95 minutes. Rated R.

This "sweet but naughty" French farce about romantically involved cousins-by-marriage offers a "refreshing" take on family dynamics; while some say it's "much better than the American" remake (*Cousins*), those suffering from memory lapses "can't recall anything" except – *zut alors!* – Barrault's "naked breasts."

Crash ✉
| 26 | 27 | 26 | 25 |

2005. Directed by Paul Haggis. With Sandra Bullock, Don Cheadle, Matt Dillon, Brendan Fraser, Terrence Howard, Ludacris, Thandie Newton, Ryan Phillippe. 113 minutes. Rated R.

"Everyone's a little bit racist" according to this "provocative" treatment of "prejudice in America", a Best Picture Oscar grabber about "intertwined lives" in LA that "damn near hits the mark" in its attempts to "break down stereotypes" and "make you rethink your values"; with a "dream-team cast" enlivening the "incredible writing", expect to collide with some "tough", "wonderfully unpredictable" scenes that deliver a "powerful message."

Cries and Whispers 🇫
| 26 | 28 | 24 | 26 |

1972. Directed by Ingmar Bergman. With Harriet Andersson, Liv Ullmann, Ingrid Thulin. 106 minutes. Rated R.

"Compelling is an understatement" when it comes to this "tortured masterpiece", a "raw", "close-in study of three sisters and their prickly relationship" that's "quintessential Bergman"; although it's "well acted" and "handsomely mounted", its depiction of "pain" is so "hard to watch" that some ask "are you sure 'angst' isn't a Swedish word?"

Crimes and Misdemeanors
26 | 26 | 25 | 24

1989. Directed by Woody Allen. With Woody Allen, Mia Farrow, Anjelica Huston, Martin Landau. 107 minutes. Rated PG-13.
"Crime does pay" in this "deeply serious" Allen dramedy with dual plotlines, one about a murderous philanderer, the other a "socially inept" filmmaker; "ruthlessly truthful", it manages to be alternately "scathing", "thought-provoking" and "hilarious", with "dead-on casting" and an "expert" scenario to boot.

Crimson Tide
21 | 24 | 22 | 22

1995. Directed by Tony Scott. With Denzel Washington, Gene Hackman, George Dzundza. 116 minutes. Rated R.
"Gripping", "tightly plotted" action flick relating the "macho machinations aboard a submarine" as two officers square off over a nuclear launch that could trigger an "unprovoked war"; given the "smart", "thought-provoking" acting of "big-screen titans" Washington and Hackman, you can expect a "first-rate" ride, even if some shrug it off as a *Hunt for Red October* wannabe."

Crocodile Dundee II
17 | 14 | 17 | 16

1986. Directed by Peter Faiman. With Paul Hogan, Linda Kozlowski. 98 minutes. Rated PG-13.
This "surprise hit from Down Under" is a classic "fish-out-of-water" comedy about a transplanted Aussie "clashing with the ways of the modern world"; though critics split on Hogan's appeal – "charming" vs. "better in Subaru commercials."

Crouching Tiger, Hidden Dragon ✉ F
24 | 23 | 21 | 28

2000. Directed by Ang Lee. With Chow Yun-Fat, Michelle Yeoh, Zhang Ziyi. 120 minutes. Rated PG-13.
Whether it's a "kung fu chick flick", a "thinking person's" martial arts film or "'chop-socky' translated into art", this "surreal" fantasy is full of "eye-popping fight sequences" that are half "ballet", half "Bruce Lee"; most memorable for its "strong female characters" and that "encounter in the bamboo forest", it's nothing less than a "breath of fresh air on the stale movie landscape."

Crying Game, The ✉
22 | 24 | 24 | 20

1992. Directed by Neil Jordan. With Stephen Rea, Miranda Richardson, Jaye Davidson. 112 minutes. Rated R.
"Violence and pathos" are served in the "right amounts" in this "disturbing" British drama about an "IRA recruit who's not really committed to his cause"; most famed for its whopper of a "surprise twist" (that leaves some "still flabbergasted"), this "intense vision of terrorism" offers enough nuanced "questions about race, sex and country" to justify a Best Screenplay Oscar.

Damned, The
23 | 24 | 21 | 23

1969. Directed by Luchino Visconti. With Dirk Bogarde, Helmut Berger, Ingrid Thulin, Helmut Griem, Charlotte Rampling. 157 minutes. Rated R.
Steel yourself for "decadence on parade" in this "sick, slick" look at a family of "jaded" German industrialists who ally themselves with the Nazis on the eve of WWII; both "absorbing and repellent in equal measure", it's "kinky" alright, though "outstanding pro-

duction values" and the "beautiful Rampling" make it slightly more palatable for general audiences.

Damn Yankees
| 24 | 23 | 23 | 24 |

1958. Directed by George Abbott, Stanley Donen. With Gwen Verdon, Tab Hunter, Ray Walston. 111 minutes. Not Rated.
This screen adaptation of the Faust-influenced Broadway musical recounts how a "man makes a pact with the devil" to guarantee that the "Washington Senators win the pennant"; reprising their stage roles, Walston is at his "evil best" as Lucifer, while the "too-rarely-seen" Verdon gets what she wants as his sidekick, Lola; it's a "perfect evocation of the national optimism of the '50s" with a "great score" and a bonus: "Bob Fosse's mambo."

Dancer in the Dark
| 22 | 23 | 20 | 22 |

2000. Directed by Lars von Trier. With Björk, Catherine Deneuve, David Morse. 140 minutes. Rated R.
A "musical like no other", this "dynamic" if "depressing" film "pushes the genre to the limit" in its account of an immigrant Czech "factory worker going blind who finds redemption only in music"; while foes find it "difficult to watch" – "even painful" – artistes laud its "wondrously strange" feel and praise pop star Björk's "amazing acting chops" and "compelling" vocal work.

Dances with Wolves ✉
| 23 | 20 | 22 | 25 |

1990. Directed by Kevin Costner. With Kevin Costner, Mary McDonnell, Graham Greene. 183 minutes. Rated PG-13.
For once, American Indians are portrayed in a "human light" in this "picturesque, sweeping epic" about a Civil War soldier who goes West, joins the Sioux and finds love along the way; although "beautifully shot" and quite the Oscar magnet (seven statuettes, including Best Picture), this "guy flick that women love" has critics citing a "monotonous", way-"too-long" running time.

Dangerous Liaisons ✉
| 24 | 26 | 24 | 26 |

1988. Directed by Stephen Frears. With Glenn Close, John Malkovich, Michelle Pfeiffer. 119 minutes. Rated R.
"Malkovich quietly chews up the scenery" opposite "perfectly evil" "ice queen" Close in this "flawless" drama set in "decadent", 17th-century France rife with "treachery, betrayal and sexual games" among the "upper classes" ("no wonder the peasants revolted"); still, its "sumptuous production" and Oscar-winning screenplay make the "manipulating" characters more palatable.

Daredevil
| 14 | 14 | 14 | 19 |

2003. Directed by Mark Steven Johnson. With Ben Affleck, Jennifer Garner, Colin Farrell. 103 minutes. Rated PG-13.
"Ben Affleck in tights" may be a "big draw in Greenwich Village", but he's pretty "disappointing" everywhere else as the title character of this action/adventurer based on Marvel Comics' blind superhero, a lawyer by day turned freelance vigilante at night; despite the "delicious" Garner, "over-the-top" Farrell and "high-energy", Hong Kong–style fight scenes, most advise "watch *Spiderman* instead."

Dark Crystal, The
| 24 | – | 24 | 26 |

1982. Directed by Jim Henson, Frank Oz. With puppet characters. 93 minutes. Rated PG.
"Sinister muppets" take the stage in this "classic" "all-puppet feature", a "magical fairy tale" with an "otherworldly good and

evil" storyline that represents the "culmination of Jim Henson's imagination"; while the "stunning visuals" please crowds, some warn that the "dark" plot "may be too scary" for smaller fry.

Dark Victory ◑
25 | 27 | 23 | 23

1939. Directed by Edmund Goulding. With Bette Davis, George Brent, Humphrey Bogart. 104 minutes. Not Rated.

"Sensational" Bette at her "Warner Brothers peak" "turns camp into classic" in this melodramatic "tearjerker" about an heiress who's got everything – including a brain tumor; sob sisters say it's "worth every hanky" for Davis' "valiant" turn (one of the "best performances of 1939") and keep their eye out for a "young Ronald Reagan" in a supporting role.

Darling ✉◑
22 | 25 | 20 | 21

1965. Directed by John Schlesinger. With Julie Christie, Dirk Bogarde, Laurence Harvey. 128 minutes. Not Rated.

Get a "glimpse of the Swinging '60s" via this "quintessential" story of a "self-absorbed" "model/party girl" who "makes it to the top" only to find "there's nothing there"; if the film feels "a bit dated", at least it's "cast to perfection" – the "smashing", Oscar-winning Christie is "at the height of her beauty and acting powers" here.

Das Boot 🇫
28 | 26 | 26 | 27

1982. Directed by Wolfgang Petersen. With Jürgen Prochnow, Herbert Grönemeyer. 149 minutes. Rated R.

When it comes to "underwater über alles" action, it's hard to top this "sweaty, claustrophobic" saga of "doomed German sailors" engaged in a "battle of egos" in a U-boat at the "bottom of the ocean"; though it's almost an "anti-recruiting film" given its "harrowing" realism, it exhibits enough "depth" to prove that "fear has no nationality" – you'll almost "root for" the Nazis.

Dave
21 | 22 | 22 | 20

1993. Directed by Ivan Reitman. With Kevin Kline, Sigourney Weaver, Frank Langella. 110 minutes. Rated PG-13.

"Kline's adorable, as usual" in this "funny" political satire about an average "doofus" who looks so much like the President that he's asked to pinch-hit and winds up putting "faith back in government"; a latter-day "*Mr. Smith Goes to Washington*", this comedy has a "serious message", though conspiracy theorists say the message is "proof that liberals really do run Hollywood."

David Copperfield ◑
▽ 27 | 26 | 27 | 25

1935. Directed by George Cukor. With Freddie Bartholomew, W.C. Fields, Lionel Barrymore. 130 minutes. Not Rated.

"One of the gems" of the Hollywood versions of "classic novels", this "wonderfully atmospheric", "very Dickensian" production may be a bit "creaky", though ultimately most of its "scenes are truly effective"; credit the "brilliant acting" from the MGM "repertory company", an "inspired" bunch headed up by Fields, whose "agile, hilarious" performance as Mr. Micawber is a "joy to watch."

Da Vinci Code, The
19 | 18 | 21 | 22

2006. Directed by Ron Howard. With Tom Hanks, Audrey Tautou, Ian McKellen. 149 minutes. Rated PG-13.

Despite "all the hype", surveyors split on this "glossy" adaptation of Dan Brown's mega-popular "page-turner" about a "human"

Jesus who "married Mary Magdalene": admirers call it a "well-crafted" thriller packed with "fun puzzles", "magnificent" European settings and "intriguing" "intellectual banter", but contras say the "hard-to-follow" story "leaves little room" for the actors to strut ("Hanks is sleepwalking"), feeling that what was "fast-paced" in the novel is "lumberingly slow" here; ultimately, the "book was better" – "aren't they always?"

Day After Tomorrow, The   16 | 14 | 14 | 24

2004. Directed by Roland Emmerich. With Dennis Quaid, Jake Gyllenhaal, Emmy Rossum, Ian Holm. 124 minutes. Rated PG-13.

"Weather is the enemy" in this "high-gloss" sci-fi "thrill ride" with a "virtuous environmental message" underlying its story of a "killer ice age" ironically brought on by "global warming"; alright, the "impressive special effects" are a "helluva lot of fun" (notably the "destruction of all your favorite landmarks"), but critics "cringe" at the "bad science", "hammy acting" and "check-your-brain-at-the-door" plot; for many, this one's "not a disaster movie", simply a "disaster."

Day at the Races, A ◑   24 | 21 | 20 | 19

1937. Directed by Sam Wood. With the Marx Brothers, Maureen O'Sullivan, Margaret Dumont. 111 minutes. Not Rated.

The "Marx Brothers at their zenith of zaniness" horse around in this "very funny" comedy about a veterinarian turned human doctor; though some say it's a "slightly second-tier" also-ran (only "sporadically funny" and even a tad "racist"), it was nevertheless one of the boys' "biggest box office hits."

Day for Night ✉ 🄵   27 | 25 | 25 | 25

1973. Directed by François Truffaut. With Jacqueline Bisset, Valentina Cortese, Jean-Pierre Léaud. 115 minutes. Rated PG.

"Truffaut's homage to American filmmaking", this "quintessential movie about making movies" "perfectly captures" all the "behind-the-scenes" "neuroses" and "joy" from an insider's point of view; though it shows the director "at his lightest", the "magical" result was both "charming" and "wacky" enough for it to take home a Best Foreign Language picture Oscar.

Days of Heaven   23 | 21 | 20 | 25

1978. Directed by Terrence Malick. With Richard Gere, Brooke Adams, Sam Shepard. 95 minutes. Rated PG.

"Underseen but not underappreciated", this "gorgeous" if "bleak" drama detailing a love triangle between two dirt-poor migrant workers and a loaded landowner "broke new ground" in its use of "beautiful cinematography" to take the place of conventional exposition; though it "speaks volumes without much dialogue", low-attention-span types yawn "not terribly compelling."

DAYS OF WINE AND ROSES ◑   27 | 28 | 25 | 24

1962. Directed by Blake Edwards. With Jack Lemmon, Lee Remick, Charles Bickford. 117 minutes. Not Rated.

For a "tough look" at a "serious issue", this "harrowing" drama about the "ravages of alcoholism" was a "huge breakthrough in its day" and remains "relevant" thanks to "tear-your-heart-out" performances from Lemmon and Remick as "desperate" young marrieds "lost in the bottom of the bottle"; "Henry Mancini's haunting title song" won the Oscar and "says it all."

Day the Earth Stood Still, The ◑ | 25 | 20 | 26 | 21 |
1951. Directed by Robert Wise. With Michael Rennie, Patricia Neal, Sam Jaffe. 92 minutes. Rated G.
"Fifties-era real-life fears about the fate of humanity" are the backbone of this "Cold War sci-fi" flick about a "benevolent alien" invasion of Washington DC; sure, the "less-is-more special effects" seem "dated" and "primitive by today's standards", but the "underlying message" – "world peace or else!" – makes this one "very enlightened for its time."

Dead Again | 22 | 24 | 24 | 22 |
1991. Directed by Kenneth Branagh. With Kenneth Branagh, Andy Garcia, Emma Thompson. 107 minutes. Rated R.
There are "good twists and mind tricks" aplenty in this "stylish, pseudo-noir thriller" about a detective drawn into a decades-old murder mystery; deadheads dig its "riveting performances", "Dali-esque imagery" and that "wonderful twist at the end", swearing you'll never look at a "pair of scissors" the same way after seeing this "over-the-top" "nail-biter."

Dead Man Walking ✉ | 23 | 26 | 23 | 21 |
1995. Directed by Tim Robbins. With Susan Sarandon, Sean Penn, Robert Prosky. 122 minutes. Rated R.
"Based on a true story", this "enlightening" study of capital punishment is also a "profound lesson in human compassion" thanks to "poignant" turns from a "riveting" Penn as a "condemned killer" and the Oscar-winning Sarandon as a nun bent on leading him to "redemption"; although "unsettling and disturbing" overall, the picture "provides both sides of the death-penalty argument" in an "objective", "unflinching" manner.

DEAD POETS SOCIETY ✉ | 24 | 25 | 24 | 23 |
1989. Directed by Peter Weir. With Robin Williams, Robert Sean Leonard, Ethan Hawke. 128 minutes. Rated PG.
"Living with rules" vs. "living with passion" gets the big-screen treatment in this "uplifting" drama about an "inspirational teacher" who admonishes his students with a ringing "'carpe diem!'"; thanks to the Oscar-winning screenplay and Williams' ultra-"convincing" turn as the "influential mentor", many say this "wake-up call" of a movie should be "mandatory classroom viewing."

Dead Ringers | 18 | 23 | 19 | 19 |
1988. Directed by David Cronenberg. With Jeremy Irons, Geneviève Bujold. 115 minutes. Rated R.
Ok, it's "beyond weird", but this "cold, clinical" tale of "twin gynecologists" "descending into madness" strikes followers of things "depraved" as a "deliciously creepy" picture, given its fascination with "prescription drugs", "kinky sex" and some mighty "bizarre" surgical instruments; despite Irons' "astounding dual performance", very vocal opponents call it "really offensive" with "no redeeming value", maybe the "ickiest movie ever"; proceed at your own risk.

Death in Venice | 24 | 26 | 24 | 24 |
1971. Directed by Luchino Visconti. With Dirk Bogarde, Marisa Berenson, Bjorn Andresen, Silvana Mangano. 130 minutes. Rated PG.
"Delicious but depressing", this "exquisitely sad meditation on love and loss" adapted from the Thomas Mann novella stars a

"memorable" Bogarde as a man who becomes obsessed by a boy while on holiday in circa-1910 Venice; though the scenery's certainly "beautiful to look at" (and the "take-your-breath-away" Mahler soundtrack equally "haunting"), the film's "slow" pace and long, "languid" shots make some shrug "gorgeous but tedious."

Death on the Nile
19 | 20 | 23 | 21

1978. Directed by John Guillermin. With Peter Ustinov, Bette Davis, Angela Lansbury. 140 minutes. Rated PG.
"Everyone looks properly shifty-eyed and guilty" in this "decent" enough adaptation of the Agatha Christie whodunit that takes place on a Nile River cruise; though foes grouse it's a "lightweight" "follow-up to *Murder on the Orient Express*", cast with "out-of-work actors", fans find it "suspenseful" enough and single out the "outrageous" Lansbury and Oscar-winning costumes for praise.

Death Wish ⓫
16 | 14 | 17 | 15

1974. Directed by Michael Winner. With Charles Bronson, Hope Lange, Vincent Gardenia. 93 minutes. Rated R.
"Brash, politically incorrect and extremely macho", this '70s "revenge fantasy" was quite "scary" (and controversial) in its time, given its story of a "do-gooder" architect turned vicious "vigilante" after the murder of his wife; in the role that made him a star, Bronson is "more bad-ass than Clint Eastwood ever was", although four sequels later some say "he should have stopped after the first one."

Deconstructing Harry
16 | 19 | 17 | 17

1997. Directed by Woody Allen. With Woody Allen, Richard Benjamin, Kirstie Alley, Judy Davis. 96 minutes. Rated R.
"Uncompromising self-examination" is the heart of this "dark" Woody Allen film about a "neurotic" novelist; though the finicky fuss about his "treatment of women" and all the "dirty-mouthed" talk, fans call it his "strongest work in the last decade"; favorite character: Robin Williams' (literally) "unfocused" actor.

Deep, The
17 | 16 | 17 | 19

1977. Directed by Peter Yates. With Robert Shaw, Jacqueline Bisset, Nick Nolte. 123 minutes. Rated PG.
From the "same era" that gave us *Jaws* comes this "underwater" adventure about "dangerous sunken treasure", a damp "guilty pleasure" best remembered for that "infamous" image of "Jackie Bisset in a sopping-wet T-shirt"; though "not a match" for Peter Benchley's best-selling novel, it's still "solid", "cheesy fun."

Deep Impact
15 | 14 | 15 | 19

1998. Directed by Mimi Leder. With Robert Duvall, Téa Leoni, Elijah Wood, Vanessa Redgrave. 120 minutes. Rated PG-13.
Impending "mass destruction" (via a comet plummeting toward the earth) is the subject of this "world-coming-to-an-end" "disaster flick", a "strangely moving" endeavor portraying "people preparing for a known death"; though there are comparisons to *Armageddon*'s "similar storyline", "this one has heart, a brain and a bonus – no bad Bruce Willis performance."

Deer Hunter, The ✉
26 | 28 | 24 | 24

1978. Directed by Michael Cimino. With Robert De Niro, Christopher Walken, Meryl Streep, John Cazale, John Savage. 183 minutes. Rated R.
"Ordinary guys from an ordinary American town" undergo the "ravages" of Vietnam in this "unforgettable war film", a "deeply

moving", "epic-in-every-way" work that netted five Oscars (including Best Picture); brace yourself for "tough-as-nails" performances from De Niro and Walken, some "profound" if "heavy-handed symbolism" plotwise and a wrenching "Russian roulette scene" that will "leave you drained"; P.S. it also features "someone new named Streep."

Deliverance
| 25 | 26 | 25 | 23 |

1972. Directed by John Boorman. With Jon Voight, Burt Reynolds, Ned Beatty, Ronny Cox. 109 minutes. Rated R.
This "allegorical nightmare" about four "city slickers" on a "weekend canoe trip" "did for camping in the woods what *Jaws* did for swimming in the ocean", mainly because of that infamous "squeal-like-a-pig" "rape scene" (to the tune of "those damn 'Dueling Banjos'"); more important, it also "proves that thought and testosterone can coexist" and "debunks the long-held myth that Reynolds can't act."

De-Lovely
| 20 | 22 | 19 | 22 |

2004. Directed by Irwin Winkler. With Kevin Kline, Ashley Judd. 125 minutes. Rated PG-13.
"You can hum along (if you're old enough)" to the "wonderful score" of this Cole Porter biopic, an "informative" effort that doesn't shy away from the composer's "messy" love life; while some are "desappointed" by the "movie-of-the-week" screenplay and "gimmicky" musical numbers "decimated by modern singers", at least Kline's "usual fine performance" "gets the beguine begun."

Desk Set
| 25 | 27 | 23 | 23 |

1957. Directed by Walter Lang. With Katharine Hepburn, Spencer Tracy, Gig Young, Joan Blondell. 103 minutes. Not Rated.
Set in the "dawn of the computer age", this "brisk" romantic comedy brings the "battle of the sexes into the workplace" by pitting "efficiency expert" Tracy against "research librarian" Hepburn; while the "two pros" display "perfect chemistry" and "flawless timing", a few folks say it's "not their finest hour" – though "Kate's wardrobe" alone makes it "worth the rental" for fashionistas.

Desperately Seeking Susan
| 15 | 13 | 14 | 13 |

1985. Directed by Susan Seidelman. With Rosanna Arquette, Madonna, Aidan Quinn. 104 minutes. Rated PG-13.
This "quintessential '80s" flick set in NYC's SoHo has to do with a case of mistaken identity but is best known as Madonna's "breakout vehicle" (despite Arquette's "underappreciated" starring role); though the verdict on the Material Girl's thespian abilities is rather lukewarm – she "basically plays herself" – the picture's still "fun."

Destry Rides Again ◑
| 25 | 25 | 23 | 23 |

1939. Directed by George Marshall. With Marlene Dietrich, James Stewart, Mischa Auer. 94 minutes. Not Rated.
A "surprisingly modern approach to the code of the Old West", this "funny" oater tells the tale of a "reluctant", "soft-spoken" lawman aiming to tame a corrupt town; there's "strong chemistry" between Stewart's "aw-shucks" deputy and Dietrich's "heart-of-gold" floozy, not to mention a "classic saloon fight" and an "irresistible" song – 'The Boys in the Backroom' – later "parodied in *Blazing Saddles*."

Diabolique ❶ 🄵
26 | 25 | 28 | 23

1955. Directed by Henri-Georges Clouzot. With Simone Signoret, Véra Clouzot. 116 minutes. Not Rated.

"Leave it to the French" to serve up this "nasty little thriller" about a murderous love triangle set in a boarding school that "scares the socks" off surveyors; granted, it "looks pretty primitive today", but ultimately "Signoret still smolders", the "clever plot twists" keep coming and "whoa, what an ending!"

Dial M for Murder
25 | 24 | 27 | 24

1954. Directed by Alfred Hitchcock. With Ray Milland, Grace Kelly, Robert Cummings. 105 minutes. Rated PG.

A "jilted husband seeks revenge on his philandering wife" in this "taut" Hitchcock thriller, a "stagey story" transformed into a "suspenseful" movie (fun fact: it was "originally shot in 3-D"); actingwise, "Kelly shines", Milland is "subtly sinister" and Cummings "drags down every scene he appears in."

Diamonds Are Forever
20 | 18 | 18 | 21

1971. Directed by Guy Hamilton. With Sean Connery, Jill St. John, Charles Gray. 125 minutes. Rated PG.

"007 goes Vegas, baby" in this sixth installment of the series, chock-full of the usual "gadgets" and gals, including the "hot", high-"cheekboned" St. John; in his next-to-last appearance as the stirred-but-never-shaken spy, Connery's at his "dashing, womanizing best" while Gray, as a "hilarious Howard Hughes type", makes a "great villain"; still, Fleming fanatics fret it's "one of the sillier" in the canon.

Diary of Anne Frank, The ❶
23 | 23 | 26 | 21

1959. Directed by George Stevens. With Millie Perkins, Shelley Winters, Richard Beymer. 180 minutes. Not Rated.

"Every young person should see" this true story of a Jewish family hiding from the Nazis in an Amsterdam attic that "brings to life a dark time in history"; "man's inhumanity to man" is depicted "from a child's point of view" and "though we know the outcome", the "suspense" is truly "heartbreaking."

Dick Tracy
13 | 13 | 13 | 20

1990. Directed by Warren Beatty. With Warren Beatty, Madonna, Al Pacino, Glenne Headly. 105 minutes. Rated PG.

It's "visually stunning", it's "star-studded", it's got "great Sondheim songs" – but this "classy", "colorful" adaptation of the long-running comic strip is still "nothing special" due to a "vapid" script and an overall sense of "wretched excess"; the good news: this could be "Madonna's best film appearance."

Die Another Day ⓫
19 | 17 | 16 | 23

2002. Directed by Lee Tamahori. With Pierce Brosnan, Halle Berry, Toby Stephens. 133 minutes. Rated PG-13.

Equipped with "everything you expect from a James Bond film", this 20th installment in the series sports "cool gadgets", "fast cars", "easy-on-the-eyes" stars and "Schwarzenegger-like one-liners" in a story that has something to do with the "current political crisis with North Korea"; despite quibbles about an "absurd plot" and "too many CGI effects", diehards declare there's nothing wrong with the "yummy" Halle and her "homage-to-Ursula-Andress" bikini.

Die Hard ❶

23 | 19 | 22 | 24

1988. Directed by John McTiernan. With Bruce Willis, Bonnie Bedelia, Alan Rickman. 131 minutes. Rated R.

This "flawless" "granddaddy of the '80s action" flick spawned "countless imitations but no equals" thanks to its "thrill-a-minute" mix of suspense, explosions and "comic one-liners"; die-hard diehards tout Willis' "ass-kicking" turn as a "loser whom fate requires to be a hero" as well as "chic bad guy" Rickman, who supplies the "cool quips and fashion tips."

Diner

25 | 25 | 23 | 22

1982. Directed by Barry Levinson. With Steve Guttenberg, Mickey Rourke, Kevin Bacon, Ellen Barkin. 110 minutes. Rated R.

Levinson's first Baltimore drama "centers on the lives of a group of '50s high school grads" "who spent their youth in diners"; a "finely observed" flick that's both "smart and funny", it features a "wonderful ensemble cast" that delivers the snappy patter so "brilliantly" it served as a "springboard" for the careers of "many future stars."

Dinner at Eight ◐

▽ 27 | 27 | 26 | 25

1933. Directed by George Cukor. With Marie Dressler, John Barrymore, Jean Harlow. 113 minutes. Not Rated.

It seems as if "every star at MGM appears" in this frothy dramedy about a social-climbing hostess' "high society" dinner party where nothing goes as planned; look for plenty of "art deco sparkle" productionwise, a "joy" of a script and "suave, understated" performances from Dressler and John Barrymore; biggest surprise: Harlow's "snappy" turn as a gum-popping, gold-digging hussy.

Dinosaur

19 | – | 17 | 24

2000. Directed by Eric Leighton, Ralph Zondag. Animated. 82 minutes. Rated PG.

"Kids interested in dinosaurs" dig this Disney flick for its "extraordinary animation", "wonderful music" and "fabulous" meteor shower scene; but despite some "exciting moments", soreheads lament that it's "lacking in the plot department" and not much more than a "dull remake of *The Land Before Time.*"

Dirty Dancing

21 | 17 | 20 | 20

1987. Directed by Emile Ardolino. With Patrick Swayze, Jennifer Grey, Jerry Orbach. 96 minutes. Rated PG-13.

Whether it's a "girls'-night-in" "entertainment" or a "Sunday afternoon vacation", this "cult classic" is the cinematic equivalent of "comfort food" and even works as an "excellent date movie" after all these years; its "heart-melting story" centers on the romance between "hot, sexy teen dream" Swayze and "cute gamine" Grey, who "shake their booties" just "like the Solid Gold dancers" used to do to pop hits in a "'60s Catskills resort."

Dirty Dozen, The

21 | 19 | 22 | 20

1967. Directed by Robert Aldrich. With Lee Marvin, Ernest Borgnine, Charles Bronson. 145 minutes. Not Rated.

This "delightful" war adventure exudes a "healthy dose of cynicism" in telling the tale of a "merry band of cutthroats" "brought together to do good in WWII"; the "early-in-their-careers" actors are "awesome", "super-macho" types (particularly "ultimate tough guy" Marvin playing as their leader), while the "rough-and-tumble", action-packed plot still seems "fun after all these years."

Dirty Harry ⓫
21 | 18 | 20 | 19

1971. Directed by Don Siegel. With Clint Eastwood, Harry Guardino, Reni Santoni. 102 minutes. Rated R.
Clint's at his "steely-eyed, gravelly voiced best" in this "modern cop" flick that "struck a chord in the '70s" and "created a fast-and-furious" subgenre "solid" enough to "spawn a host of imitators"; throw in some "great views of San Francisco" and a moodily "muted jazz score" and you just might "feel lucky, punk."

Dirty Pretty Things
23 | 24 | 24 | 21

2003. Directed by Stephen Frears. With Chiwetel Ejiofor, Audrey Tautou, Sergi López. 97 minutes. Rated R.
London's illegal "immigrant underworld" goes under the microscope in this "atmospheric", "suspenseful" crime thriller detailing "shady goings-on" (think prostitution, drug dealing and "macabre" trafficking in human organs) at a "swanky UK hotel"; the "low-budget look" works well with the "gritty performances", "thought-provoking" scenario and "unexpected ending."

Discreet Charm of the Bourgeoisie, The ✉🅵
24 | 23 | 23 | 22

1972. Directed by Luis Buñuel. With Fernando Rey, Delphine Seyrig, Stéphane Audran. 102 minutes. Rated PG.
"Controversial" in its day, this "satirical portrait of the French bourgeoisie" tells the "elliptical" tale of "six people in search of a hot meal" who are "confounded at every turn" by bizarre goings-on; Buñuel serves up enough "dream-within-a-dream sequences" to turn this dark comedy into a "thoughtful, surreal delight" that further enhances his reputation as the "Dali of cinema."

Diva 🅵
24 | 20 | 24 | 24

1982. Directed by Jean-Jacques Beineix. With Wilhelmenia Fernandez, Frederic Andrei. 123 minutes. Rated R.
Perhaps the "greatest opera/action flick ever", this "oh-so-stylish" French thriller creates a "complicated world" about a "scooter-riding kid" obsessed by a "reclusive soprano"; "glorious to look at", with "wonderful images of Paris", it's most memorable for that "fast-paced motorcycle chase" in the Métro.

Divine Secrets of the Ya-Ya Sisterhood
16 | 20 | 17 | 17

2002. Directed by Callie Khouri. With Sandra Bullock, Ellen Burstyn, James Garner, Ashley Judd. 116 minutes. Rated PG-13.
A "disappointing adaptation of an amazing book", this Southern-fried "quintessential chick flick" tells the tale of a complicated "mother-and-daughter relationship" with "not a whit of the sass or charm of the novel"; though many find the performances "terrific" ("older actresses rock"), the "schmaltzy", "*Fried Green Magnolias*" script strikes some sisters as "more yo-yo than ya-ya."

Divorce Italian Style ✉🄐🅵
24 | 25 | 23 | 22

1962. Directed by Pietro Germi. With Marcello Mastroianni, Daniela Rocca, Stefania Sandrelli. 104 minutes. Not Rated.
"Mastroianni's a hoot" playing an "unfortunately married" man "lusting for greener pastures" in this "*molto bene*" comedy set way back when divorce was illegal in Italy; its "silly but sweet" screenplay is both a "condemnation of the law" as well as a "nice satire", and if it "loses a little in translation", it compensates with black-and-white cinematography that's "lusher than most color films."

D.O.A. ◑

22 | 22 | 26 | 21

1950. Directed by Rudolph Maté. With Edmond O'Brien, Pamela Britton, Luther Adler. 83 minutes. Not Rated.

A great opening line ("I want to report a murder...mine") sets in motion the "intriguing plot" of this "time-runs-backward" drama in which an "innocent man must find his own killer before he dies"; set against a backdrop of "great location shots of LA and San Fran", it's "gritty, bleak" noir that's "compelling as hell", even if a few deadbeats declare it "promises more than it delivers."

DOCTOR ZHIVAGO ✉

27 | 26 | 26 | 28

1965. Directed by David Lean. With Omar Sharif, Julie Christie, Geraldine Chaplin, Rod Steiger. 197 minutes. Rated PG-13.

Lean's "timeless" – others say "long" – Oscar-winning evocation of Boris Pasternak's "sweeping" novel of "love and war" is the "epic to end all epics", merging "brilliant historical storytelling" with "romantic extravaganza"; set during the Russian Revolution, it "humanized the USSR during the Cold War" due to the "tear-erking" relationship between Christie and Sharif – though its "balalaika"-heavy theme song and the scenes in that "winter wonderland" of an "ice palace" resonate most.

Dog Day Afternoon ✉

24 | 27 | 22 | 20

1975. Directed by Sidney Lumet. With Al Pacino, John Cazale, Chris Sarandon, Charles Durning. 124 minutes. Rated R.

This "funny/sad" true tale of a botched "bank heist" committed by "hapless" amateurs is transformed into a "deep, character-driven" example of director Lumet "at his best"; expect "great performances from the entire cast" (from the nervous bank tellers "right down to the pizza delivery guy"), with particular kudos to an "ass-kicking" Pacino and a "brilliant" Sarandon as his gay lover.

Dogville

21 | 25 | 20 | 21

2004. Directed by Lars von Trier. With Nicole Kidman, Harriet Andersson, Lauren Bacall, Paul Bettany. 178 minutes. Rated R.

Decidedly "not for everyone", this avant-garde "morality play" about a woman on the run taken in by a small town is "risky", "controversial" stuff, starting with its "minimalist", stagelike setting and "terribly long" running time; some growl it's too "self-important" (and maybe even "anti-American"), but those willing to "take a deep breath and plunge in" find it "daring" and "thought-provoking" – "art films don't get much artier than this."

Donnie Brasco

20 | 24 | 22 | 20

1997. Directed by Mike Newell. With Al Pacino, Johnny Depp, Anne Heche. 127 minutes. Rated R.

In this true story, an undercover FBI agent "befriends the man he's supposed to entrap" and takes you "inside the inner workings of the mob" to reveal a "more realistic side to the underworld"; a "sympathetic", "nuanced" Pacino does the "gangster-as-loser" thing right, while Depp's titular turn is similarly "excellent"; like the 'family' it portrays, this one "never lets go of you."

Donnie Darko

22 | 23 | 23 | 21

2001. Directed by Richard Kelly. With Jake Gyllenhaal, Drew Barrymore, Mary McDonnell. 113 minutes. Rated R.

"Harvey" meets "Psycho" in this indie "cult favorite" that combines "trippy sci-fi" FX with "John Hughes high-school angst" in

its story of a "delusional" teen who sees visions of "demoni
bunny rabbits"; sure, you might "need a few viewings to under
stand it" (after which it may still "make no sense"), but its "hug
fan base" goes bonkers over the "original" script, "top-notc
soundtrack" and the "solid" Jake, in the breakout role that mad
him a star.

Don't Look Back ◑   ▽ 25 | – | 20 | 23
*1967. Directed by D.A. Pennebaker. Documentary. With Bob Dylan
Joan Baez, Donovan. 96 minutes. Not Rated.*
This "revealing" "slice of musical history" "captures the youn
Bob Dylan in all his churlishness" as an "artist in transition" an
is an "indelible" "reminder of what all the fuss was about"; per
haps the "most referenced rockumentary ever, "it's improve
with time" and includes one of the "first music videos" ever: th
famed cue-cards clip for 'Subterranean Homesick Blues.'

Don't Look Now   24 | 26 | 24 | 24
*1974. Directed by Nicolas Roeg. With Julie Christie, Donald
Sutherland. 110 minutes. Rated R.*
"Venice at its most eerie" is the backdrop for this "disturbing
psychological thriller with an "atmosphere of dread" so perva
sive that you'll be "on the edge of your gondola" throughout
based on a Daphne du Maurier story about "grieving parents
mourning the death of their child, it weaves a "blind clairvoyant
and a "murderous dwarf" into its "thoroughly adult" web – and top
things off with "one of the best sex scenes in the history of cinema.

Door in the Floor, The   19 | 23 | 19 | 19
*2004. Directed by Tod Williams. With Jeff Bridges, Kim Basinger,
Jon Foster. 111 minutes. Rated R.*
"Nice looking and well acted", this "textured" adaptation of "th
first third of John Irving's novel *A Widow for One Year*" relates the
"sad, bleak" tale of a successful, "self-centered author whose
marriage has fallen apart"; Bridges is "brilliant" ("when is he go
ing to win an Oscar?"), Basinger the "same vulnerable mess, as
usual", and although the picture certainly "has its moments"
some slam it as "ultimately unengaging."

Do the Right Thing   23 | 23 | 22 | 21
*1989. Directed by Spike Lee. With Spike Lee, Danny Aiello, Ossie
Davis, Ruby Dee. 120 minutes. Rated R.*
"Italian-American pizza parlor owners" and the "African-American
community who patronize the shop" clash "on the hottest day o
the year" in this "anatomy of a race riot" from Spike Lee, wh
"deftly balances tragedy with comedy" to telegraph a "message as
clear as black and white" that still "resonates years later."

DOUBLE INDEMNITY ◑   28 | 27 | 28 | 25
*1944. Directed by Billy Wilder. With Fred MacMurray, Barbara
Stanwyck, Edward G. Robinson. 107 minutes. Not Rated.*
"From the chiaroscuro settings to the world-weary voice-over",
Wilder's "refreshingly sour" slice of "hard-boiled" noir "sets the
standard for the genre"; the story of "another dumb cluck done in
by a woman", it features a "fast-talking" MacMurray, a "knockout" Stanwyck ("love the anklet") and a "fantastic" Robinson,
with enough plot "twists" and sly "killer banter" to make it the
cinematic equivalent of "bonded bourbon"; best scene: shopping
at the "supermarket."

Double Jeopardy
16 | 18 | 19 | 18

1999. Directed by Bruce Beresford. With Tommy Lee Jones, Ashley Judd, Annabeth Gish. 105 minutes. Rated R.
"Diverting" enough, this "clever" thriller finds Judd playing a "kick-ass bitch" wrongfully imprisoned for murder and hell-bent on "revenge"; legal eagles rule it's "completely implausible" (even its title "premise is false") and add that "Jones' cop thing is getting old", but it's "enjoyable nonetheless" if you like "a lot of twists."

Down and Out in Beverly Hills
17 | 19 | 17 | 17

1986. Directed by Paul Mazursky. With Nick Nolte, Richard Dreyfuss, Bette Midler. 103 minutes. Rated R.
The "Jean Renoir classic" *Bondu Saved from Drowning* is "given an American spin" in this "spoof of the upper class", Beverly Hills–style, wherein a "bum interacts in the lives of a wealthy family" with "hilarious" results; Bette's "divine" as a "neurotic wife who undergoes an amazing transformation", and even if the humor verges on the "crude", it's still "winning" enough.

Down by Law ◐
24 | 23 | 23 | 22

1986. Directed by Jim Jarmusch. With Tom Waits, John Lurie, Roberto Benigni. 107 minutes. Rated R.
A "trio of unlikely fugitives" – a DJ, a pimp and an Italian tourist – takes it on the lam from a Louisiana slammer in this "odd", "brooding" comedy from indie king Jarmusch that's best remembered for "introducing Benigni" to American audiences; but even though this B&W "original" has attained "compulsory" "cult classic" status over time, a few say its "slow pace is not for everyone."

Down with Love
18 | 19 | 17 | 23

2003. Directed by Peyton Reed. With Renée Zellweger, Ewan McGregor, David Hyde Pierce. 101 minutes. Rated PG-13.
"Not everyone's cup of tea", this "stylized homage" spoofs "Camelot-era" sex comedies with its "frothy" tale of a "lady-killer" journalist out to seduce a "wily" writer, and fans "dig the clothes", the wink-wink "double entendres" and the "split-screen telephone conversations"; but foes fume "fluffy", citing a "thin" plot and "little chemistry" between the leads ("Doris and Rock did it better"), although Pierce "out–Tony Randalls Tony Randall."

Dracula ◐Ⅱ
24 | 21 | 23 | 20

1931. Directed by Tod Browning. With Bela Lugosi, Helen Chandler, Dwight Frye. 75 minutes. Not Rated.
Granted, the "special effects are nonexistent", but this "definitive Dracula" is still "scarier than anything made today", leaving "plenty of room for imagination" thanks to Lugosi's "riveting" take on the "immortal vampire"; though it uses music sparingly to evoke an "eerie atmosphere", a new, souped-up DVD with a "Philip Glass score" is highly touted; best line: "I never drink . . . wine."

Dracula
20 | 19 | 22 | 25

1992. Directed by Francis Ford Coppola. With Gary Oldman, Winona Ryder, Anthony Hopkins, Keanu Reeves. 130 minutes. Rated R.
"You can sink your teeth" into Coppola's "highly underrated" "retelling of Bram Stoker's tale" of a "lovelorn", bloodthirsty Romanian count; "stylish" costumes, a "stunning" Oldman and the spectacle of "Tom Waits eating bugs" make for "visionary" moviemaking, even if some nix the "laughable miscasting" of Reeves.

Dr. Dolittle ⓞ
16 | 17 | 17 | 18

1998. Directed by Betty Thomas. With Eddie Murphy, Ossie Davis, Peter Boyle. 85 minutes. Rated PG-13.

Both "kids and kids at heart" "crack up" over this "priceless" Murphy vehicle in which he "shines" playing a doc who can "talk to animals"; based vaguely on Hugh Lofting's "perennially popular" children's stories, this update employs state-of-the-art animatronics and computer graphics to make the animalspeak both realistic and "entertaining."

Dressed to Kill
20 | 22 | 19 | 20

1980. Directed by Brian De Palma. With Michael Caine, Angie Dickinson, Nancy Allen. 105 minutes. Rated R.

"Swirling camerawork, split screens, tracking shots that go on for miles" – yup, it's another "stylishly bloody" De Palma thriller, replete with "violent slashings, sensuous showers and sexual confusion" as it tells the adventures of a "happy hooker, an unhappy housewife and a shrink"; though an "inspiring" Angie provides the "sexy" "goose bumps", foes say it's "too derivative of Hitchcock."

Driving Miss Daisy ✉
24 | 27 | 23 | 22

1989. Directed by Bruce Beresford. With Morgan Freeman, Jessica Tandy, Dan Aykroyd. 99 minutes. Rated PG.

"Race relations" in the South and the "loss of dignity" that can come with aging are "wonderfully depicted" in this "heartwarming" story of an "unconventional friendship" between a matriarch and her chauffeur; the "sterling" Tandy and Freeman exhibit "incredible onscreen chemistry" (she drove home with an Oscar) in this "uplifting yet down-to-earth" drama.

Dr. No
23 | 20 | 22 | 23

1963. Directed by Terence Young. With Sean Connery, Ursula Andress, Jack Lord. 110 minutes. Rated PG.

The "first Bond outing" is a "lean and mean" thriller "unhindered by political correctness", with "fewer gadgets" and gals than usual (though the image of Andress in that "white bikini" is "seared forever onto many a man's brain"); while the "dashing" Connery "makes it all look effortless", "purists" note this "unadulterated" "template" is the "closest they ever came to Ian Fleming's vision."

DR. STRANGELOVE ◑
28 | 28 | 27 | 26

1964. Directed by Stanley Kubrick. With Peter Sellers, George C. Scott, Sterling Hayden. 93 minutes. Rated PG.

"Nuclear annihilation was never funnier" than in Kubrick's "stinging Cold War satire", a "chillingly comic" examination of "distressingly familiar government officials" and their "precious bodily fluids"; as members of "our military at work", Scott is "magnificent" and Sellers "phenomenal" (in "three, count 'em, roles"), while "Slim Pickens riding the bomb" remains one of the cinema's most indelible images; doomsday devotees dub it "apocalypse now and forever."

Drugstore Cowboy
19 | 21 | 19 | 18

1989. Directed by Gus Van Sant. With Matt Dillon, Kelly Lynch, James Le Gros. 100 minutes. Rated R.

Van Sant's grittily "accurate depiction" of narcotics addicts robbing drugstores for drugs is loaded with "precise, unexpected performances" and a surprise bonus: William Burroughs as a junkie ex-priest; though habit-ues hail it as a "highly original dark comedy", nonsupporters say it "doesn't hold up well."

DUCK SOUP ◑

`27` `25` `23` `22`

1933. Directed by Leo McCarey. With the Marx Brothers, Margaret Dumont. 70 minutes. Not Rated.

"Hail, hail Freedonia" cry fans of the "anarchic" Marx foursome, whose trademark "lunacy" is at its "peak" in this "political satire" about a "mythical dictatorship"; "absurdly funny" – it includes the "legendary mirror scene with Groucho and Harpo" – it's the brothers' "finest hour" and voted top of the Marxes in this *Survey*.

Duel in the Sun

`23` `22` `22` `24`

1946. Directed by King Vidor. With Jennifer Jones, Gregory Peck, Joseph Cotten, Lillian Gish. 146 minutes. Not Rated.

Producer David O. Selznick "goes for baroque" in this "overripe", "overacted", "overly long" horse opera about a "hot" half-breed and the two brothers who desire her; its "shockingly sexual" undercurrent led to its "nickname, *Lust in the Dust*", though what's "campy" and "over the top" for some is "epic" and "operatic" to others; no question, "they don't make 'em like this anymore."

Dumb and Dumber ⓤ

`15` `16` `12` `14`

1994. Directed by Peter Farrelly, Bobby Farrelly. With Jim Carrey, Jeff Daniels, Lauren Holly. 106 minutes. Rated PG-13.

No duh, the "title says it all" in this maiden effort from the Farrelly brothers, a "gross-out" "guilty pleasure" about a "moronic duo" "traveling cross country" with a briefcase stuffed with cash; fans say the "vulgar" antics (think "potty jokes", "disgusting noises") "grow on you", though foes sneer the "puerile", "not-for-adults" storyline makes for the "ultimate" in "lowbrow humor."

Dumbo

`24` `–` `23` `24`

1941. Directed by Ben Sharpsteen. Animated. 64 minutes. Rated G.

"Elephants fly" in this "short but sweet" animated Disney classic message movie "about the importance of being yourself"; though the politically correct disparage its "racist undertones" and find it "too sad" for smaller fry, fans laud its "fabulous", Oscar-winning score and "unforgettable sequences" – particularly the "tripped-out" "hallucination" of those pink pachyderms on parade.

Dune

`14` `13` `18` `18`

1984. Directed by David Lynch. With Kyle MacLachlan, Francesca Annis, Jürgen Prochnow, Sting. 137 minutes. Rated PG-13.

"Beautiful to look at but incoherent" plotwise, this "problematic" adaptation of Frank Herbert's "iconic" sci-fi novel is either a "heroic mess" or an "unjustly maligned" work that "gets better after repeated viewings"; many argue that the "complicated storyline" (something to do with warring factions in the far-off year of 10191) is practically "unfilmable", but whether the end result is worth seeing for director Lynch's trademark "high weirdness" or just a "waste of celluloid" is up to you.

Easter Parade

`22` `21` `17` `24`

1948. Directed by Charles Walters. With Judy Garland, Fred Astaire, Ann Miller. 107 minutes. Not Rated.

"It isn't really Easter" till you've watched this "grand Irving Berlin musical" boasting 17 songs and "lots of frills upon it" – including Fred and Judy at their "singing and dancing best" in their "only screen appearance together"; the slender story has Astaire trying to make a star out of chorus girl Garland, but this "wonderful" MGM "showcase" transcends its plot with sheer star power.

East of Eden 24 | 27 | 24 | 23
1955. Directed by Elia Kazan. With James Dean, Julie Harris, Raymond Massey, Jo Van Fleet. 115 minutes. Not Rated.
An "unforgettable" Dean eats "every actor on the set for breakfast" in his "searing" big-screen debut as the "proverbial bad seed" in this adaptation of John Steinbeck's tale of "sibling rivalry"; sure, there are also "beautiful" CinemaScope panoramas and an Oscar-winning turn from Van Fleet, but Jimmy makes it "memorable" – "to think he only made three films is amazing."

Easy Rider 23 | 23 | 20 | 20
1969. Directed by Dennis Hopper. With Peter Fonda, Dennis Hopper, Jack Nicholson. 94 minutes. Rated R.
"Sex, drugs and rock 'n' roll" explode on the silver screen in this "seminal" "road movie" that "defined a generation" by capturing the essence of the "tumultuous" '60s; famed for "Nicholson's starmaking performance" and Hopper's "manic", "revolutionary" direction, this "trippy" "time capsule" might have also "invented the music video" thanks to that "amazing soundtrack"; still, Gen-Y types protest it "doesn't hold up" today, unless you "get high" first.

Eat Drink Man Woman 🅵 25 | 24 | 24 | 24
1994. Directed by Ang Lee. With Sihung Lung, Wu Chien-Lien, Yang Kuei-Mei, Wang Yu-Wen. 123 minutes. Not Rated.
Gourmands eat up this "tasty" Taiwanese look at a "different culture" that tells the story of a traditional "Asian father who shows his love by cooking for his daughters"; director Lee's "visual feast" contrasts "ticklish relationships" with "stupendous food scenes" so adroitly that many "get hungry just thinking about it."

Eating Raoul 18 | 18 | 21 | 15
1982. Directed by Paul Bartel. With Paul Bartel, Mary Woronov, Robert Beltran. 90 minutes. Rated R.
"Not everyone can stomach" this "blacker-than-black" "bizarro" "cult" comedy, but there's agreement that its "absurd" plot (about a Moral Majority–esque couple luring swingers to their deaths) is the "trailer-park" version of *"Sweeney Todd"*; "kind of sick", this "deadpan" "low-budget" "B movie" is also kind of "fun" – and "probably for grown-ups only."

Educating Rita 18 | 21 | 19 | 18
1983. Directed by Lewis Gilbert. With Michael Caine, Julie Walters. 110 minutes. Rated PG-13.
Caine and Walters exhibit "great chemistry" in this "interesting" tale of an "alcoholic professor" who tutors a "working-class" gal; though the "pseudo-*Pygmalion*" plot "isn't quite convincing" for some, others relate perfectly to the "believable" title character, a "woman who won't allow herself to be held back by social class."

Edward Scissorhands 21 | 22 | 22 | 24
1990. Directed by Tim Burton. With Johnny Depp, Winona Ryder, Dianne Wiest. 100 minutes. Rated PG-13.
Burton's "oddball" opus spins a "delightfully bent" "love story" around an ultimate "outsider" – a "misfit boy with garden tools for hands" – living in "conformist suburbia"; "Depp shows he has

the big-screen stuff" (and "makes a hell of a topiary"), while the "primary-colored" art direction creates an "alternative universe disturbingly close to home"; best line: Wiest's perky "Avon calling!"

Ed Wood ◑   20 | 23 | 19 | 21

1994. Directed by Tim Burton. With Johnny Depp, Martin Landau, Sarah Jessica Parker. 127 minutes. Rated R.
"Schlockmeister" director Ed Wood gets the full Tim Burton treatment in this "loving tribute" that's also an "entertaining glimpse into grade Z filmmaking"; look for an "enthusiastic", "totally sympathetic" Depp in the title role opposite an Oscar-winning Landau as a "drugged-out" Bela Lugosi – "never before have the talentless been so brilliantly rendered by the talented."

8½ ✉◑🄵   26 | 26 | 24 | 26

1963. Directed by Federico Fellini. With Marcello Mastroianni, Claudia Cardinale, Anouk Aimée. 145 minutes. Not Rated.
"Navel-gazing has never been more profound" than in this "semi-autobiographical" "Italian masterpiece" from the "extraordinary" Fellini about a blocked "director trying to make a film" by using his "life as material for his work"; told in "stream of consciousness", it also features "luscious" art direction and a "career-defining turn by Mastroianni" – no wonder many call this "heartfelt" flick the "definitive movie about movies."

8 Mile   19 | 18 | 17 | 19

2002. Directed by Curtis Hanson. With Eminem, Kim Basinger, Brittany Murphy, Mekhi Phifer. 110 minutes. Rated R.
Take "*Rocky*", add "*Purple Rain*", "go to Detroit" and top it off with "sweet freestyle scenes", and you've got this "quality" "retread" of the "poor-boy-claws-his-way-out-of-the-hood" story; while Eminem's "semi-autobiographical" performance is ("surprise!") "raw and touching", this "gritty" flick (and its "7 mile"–long string of "F-words") gets truly "compelling" in the last "rap-off."

El Cid ∅   19 | 16 | 20 | 23

1961. Directed by Anthony Mann. With Charlton Heston, Sophia Loren, Raf Vallone. 182 minutes. Not Rated.
This early '60s epic is a "guy's delight" that finds Heston once again inhabiting the skin of a "larger-than-life" figure, this time the legendary 11th-century Spaniard who defended his country against the Moors; "lots of action" elates thrill-seekers, though foes lambaste it as "bombastic and overblown."

Election   22 | 24 | 22 | 20

1999. Directed by Alexander Payne. With Reese Witherspoon, Matthew Broderick. 103 minutes. Rated R.
"Student council elections" as an "allegory for real political life" underscore this "whip-smart" "black comedy" about a "goody two-shoes" "high-school overachiever" and a teacher bent on putting a stop to her rise; voters find "no fraud" in this "spot-on" "social satire", adding that "unless you were home-schooled, you'll relate."

Elephant   19 | 18 | 19 | 21

2003. Directed by Gus Van Sant. With Alex Frost, Eric Deulen. 81 minutes. Rated R.
"Wildly original", this "disturbing" examination of a "Columbine-esque" high-school massacre splits surveyors: fans praise the "dreamlike" plot, "cinema verité"–style photography and "mov-

ing" work by a cast of "nonprofessionals", but cynics say it's "in-sightless" and "boring"; both sides agree it's "tough to watch" and "definitely open to interpretation."

Elephant Man, The ◗

1980. Directed by David Lynch. With Anthony Hopkins, John Hurt, Anne Bancroft. 125 minutes. Rated PG.
The "dignity in deformity" is defined in this "unflinching" true story about a "Victorian-era" freak who "tests the compassion of a horrified society"; "brilliant acting and makeup" make it a "glo-riously Gothic" "voyage into the human heart" – a "perfect match of director and material", it will "touch you deep inside."

Elf

2003. Directed by Jon Favreau. With Will Ferrell, James Caan, Bob Newhart, Zooey Deschanel. 95 minutes. Rated PG.
Imbued with the "real spirit of Christmas", this "surprisingly sweet-natured" holiday comedy stars "funny man Ferrell" as a "human being raised by elves" at the North Pole who travels to NYC to find his birth parents; granted, there's "nothing to tax your mind" in this "old-fashioned romp", but Will's a "hoot", "Deschanel looks gor-geous" and the "deadpan" Newhart is "consistently hilarious."

Elizabeth

1998. Directed by Shekhar Kapur. With Cate Blanchett, Geoffrey Rush, Joseph Fiennes. 124 minutes. Rated R.
"Captivating" Cate displays "unbelievable range" in this bio of England's "Virgin Queen" that follows her progress from "lusty young woman" to "ice-cold, calculating icon"; though it "feels like a fantasy version of Elizabeth I's life" to skeptics, scholars swear it's "historically on the mark", with "beautiful sets", "ex-cellent costume design" and a "gripping" storyline.

Elmer Gantry ✉

1960. Directed by Richard Brooks. With Burt Lancaster, Jean Simmons, Shirley Jones. 146 minutes. Not Rated.
Disciples of this "rip-roaring" adaptation of the Sinclair Lewis novel testify that Lancaster's Oscar-winning, "fire-and-brimstone" performance as a "street preacher"–cum–"con man" in a "hypocritical" traveling ministry is the "best of his ca-reer" (while some "get religion" watching Jones' take on a jilted prostitute); its "excellent script" detailing a "flesh vs. the spirit" conflict also took home a statuette.

Elvira Madigan 🄵

1967. Directed by Bo Widerberg. With Pia Degermark, Thommy Berggren. 91 minutes. Rated PG.
Both "visually stunning" and "wonderfully dated", this Swedish sobfest recounts the "heartbreaking" affair between "two AWOL lovers" – a tightrope walker and a married army officer – who are "beautiful" and, of course, "doomed"; although memorable for its "lovely scenery" and the Mozart piano concerto it popularized, it's forgettable to those who see it as "tiresome" "romantic fluff."

Emma

1996. Directed by Douglas McGrath. With Gwyneth Paltrow, Jeremy Northam, Greta Scacchi. 121 minutes. Rated PG.
Jane Austen's "charming" story of "matchmaking at its best and worst" gets an "engaging" spin in this "delightful period piece"

starring a "perfect" Paltrow opposite a "charming" Northam; its "cheery" tone and dry humor make it a natural to "watch back-to-back with *Clueless,* since they're both based on the same novel."

Emperor's New Groove, The | 20 | – | 18 | 20 |

2000. Directed by Mark Dindal. Animated. 78 minutes. Rated G.
A "selfish, smart-mouthed emperor becomes a llama" with extremely humbling results in this "quirky", "overlooked cartoon" that effortlessly merges both "standard and CGI animation" with "superb voice acting"; sure, aesthetes complain of a "low-budget", "slapped-together" look, but most find it "highly entertaining" with "lots of great gags" and a script that's "actually funny."

Empire of the Sun | 25 | 23 | 24 | 26 |

1987. Directed by Steven Spielberg. With Christian Bale, John Malkovich. 154 minutes. Rated PG.
Perhaps Spielberg's most "underappreciated" picture, this "touching story of a British child's internment in a World War II Japanese prison camp" is an "ambitious" epic replete with "dazzling" acting, "David Lean–worthy" imagery and an "especially moving John Williams score"; maybe the "storyline drags" a bit midway, but overall its "sheer power" supplies the "magic moments."

Enchanted April ∅ | 24 | 26 | 22 | 25 |

1992. Directed by Mike Newell. With Joan Plowright, Miranda Richardson, Josie Lawrence. 95 minutes. Rated PG.
For a "wonderfully rich pick-me-up", take a look at this "genteel" "getaway" of a movie about four "risk-taking" women who decide to "leave their dreary English lives behind" and are "transformed" during an April vacation in "lush, sunny" Tuscany; the perfect "antidote to winter", it's "more complex than it first appears", and Plowright's "terrific performance" will brighten any "rainy day."

End of the Affair, The | 20 | 24 | 20 | 22 |

1999. Directed by Neil Jordan. With Ralph Fiennes, Julianne Moore, Stephen Rea. 102 minutes. Rated R.
"Faith, love and loss" underlie this "terrific" adaptation of Graham Greene's "tragic romance" set in "rainy" WWII London about a "conflicted, adulterous Englishwoman" and her "jealous, angry lover"; this "difficult story" succeeds thanks to a "flashback"-heavy, "multilayered" scenario and "wonderful screen chemistry" between a "powerful" Fiennes and a "smoldering" Moore modeling "glamorous slips and retro suits."

Enemy of the State | 19 | 19 | 20 | 21 |

1998. Directed by Tony Scott. With Will Smith, Gene Hackman, Jon Voight. 131 minutes. Rated R.
"Privacy and civil liberties" issues take center stage in this ultra-"engaging", ultra-"paranoid" thriller about "Big Brother"–ish "government agents" pursuing a DC lawyer who's unwittingly holding an incriminating videotape; extremely "fast moving", it mixes "high-tech" effects with a "low-concept" idea to come up with something that's "very exciting" indeed.

English Patient, The ✉ | 22 | 24 | 21 | 25 |

1996. Directed by Anthony Minghella. With Ralph Fiennes, Juliette Binoche, Kristin Scott Thomas. 160 minutes. Rated R.
"Love it or hate it", there's no question that this "lush" WWII romance (winner of nine Oscars) boasts an "old-Hollywood scope",

swoonworthy cinematography, "brilliant writing" and "magnetic" performances from Fiennes and Scott Thomas as star-crossed lovers "in the desert sands of North Africa"; but those who "agree with Elaine on *Seinfeld*" claim this patient requires "patience", thanks to a pace so "laborious" that it's "recommended for treating insomnia."

Enron:
The Smartest Guys in the Room
25 | – | 26 | 22 |

2005. Directed by Alex Gibney. Documentary. 109 minutes. Not Rated.
Learn how "arrogant corruption" and "greed run amok" led to the collapse of energy trader Enron's "house of cards" in this "compelling" documentary that "reveals the downside of American corporate culture"; "full of information", it reduces a "complicated", "numbers-centered" scheme into an "easy-to-follow" account that manages to both "disgust and fascinate", without resorting to "Michael Moore hysteria."

Enter the Dragon
23 | 16 | 17 | 20 |

1973. Directed by Robert Clouse. With Bruce Lee, John Saxon, Jim Kelly. 98 minutes. Rated R.
"Martial arts" mavens maintain that this "all-time best kung fu" flicker is "butt-kicker" Lee's "magnum opus", the "standard by which all karate films are judged"; sure, the "production's cheesy" and its "James Bond" "rip-off" plot is "unoriginal", but the "balletic, ballistic" fight scenes are so "spectacular" that this one "spawned many forgettable imitators" – not to mention many "video games."

Eraserhead ◑
21 | 17 | 17 | 19 |

1977. Directed by David Lynch. With Jack Nance, Charlotte Stewart. 90 minutes. Not Rated.
Director Lynch's "trippy", "dread-inducing" debut is an "eerie glimpse of a marriage gone horribly awry" that "replicates the logic of a nightmare" (i.e. "you don't know what's going on half the time"); gird yourself for some "disturbing pictures, disturbing music" and "no discernable plot", but at least this "cult classic" is "willing to take risks."

Erin Brockovich ✉
21 | 23 | 23 | 21 |

2000. Directed by Steven Soderbergh. With Julia Roberts, Albert Finney, Aaron Eckhart. 130 minutes. Rated R.
"Roberts proves her worth" with a "boffo", Oscar-winning turn in this "uplifting", "push-up bra"–laden true story about "standing up to a big corporation and winning"; ok, its "socially conscious", "don't-mess-with-the-little-people" screenplay might owe a lot to "*Norma Rae*", but ultimately this "polished production" works as both a "star vehicle and a compelling story."

Escape from New York ⓣ
15 | 13 | 17 | 18 |

1981. Directed by John Carpenter. With Kurt Russell, Lee Van Cleef, Ernest Borgnine. 99 minutes. Rated R.
A "hoot and a half", this "tongue-in-cheek" action-adventurer is set in "post-apocalyptic" Manhattan that has morphed into a maximum security prison where the President is being held hostage; to the rescue comes Russell as Snake Plissken, a "cartoon character" but still a "very appealing hero", who manages to keep the "novel premise amusing" enough to make for some "silly", "cheesy fun."

Eternal Sunshine of the Spotless Mind 23 | 24 | 24 | 23
2004. Directed by Michel Gondry. With Jim Carrey, Kate Winslet, Tom Wilkinson, Mark Ruffalo, Kirsten Dunst. 108 minutes. Rated R.
A "one-of-a-kind experience", this "quirky, deeply romantic" fantasy follows a "balanced" Carrey and "winning" Winslet as broken-up lovers who biologically erase their memories of each other, then struggle to erase the erasure; though "not likely to be everyone's cup of tea", the "zany", "head-trip" script is "cerebral", "comical" and "complex" (given a "juggled time sequence" à la "*Memento*"), yet skillfully steered by director Gondry's "deft hand."

E.T. THE EXTRA-TERRESTRIAL 26 | 22 | 26 | 27
1982. Directed by Steven Spielberg. With Dee Wallace, Henry Thomas, Drew Barrymore. 115 minutes. Rated PG.
Arguably the "*Wizard of Oz* for a brand-new generation", this "irresistible" sci-fi "fairy tale" is the "endearing story of a boy", the "cutest alien of all time" and their attempts to "phone home"; there's agreement that Spielberg's "incredibly imaginative" "genius strikes again", managing to express "every human emotion in less than two hours", so gather the "entire family" along with a "big bowl of Reese's Pieces" and get ready for some "true magic."

Evil Dead, The ⑪ 22 | 14 | 18 | 17
1982. Directed by Sam Raimi. With Bruce Campbell, Ellen Sandweiss, Betsy Baker. 85 minutes. Rated NC-17.
"Not for the weak-stomached", this "scary, scary, scary" "gorefest" with "abundant blood" and lots of "energy" is "dumb", "campy horror at its best"; alright, the acting's "questionable", the dialogue "lame", the story "hackneyed" and the effects very "low-budget", but it "blows Hollywood blockbusters away" because it's "so much fun."

Evita 19 | 17 | 21 | 24
1996. Directed by Alan Parker. With Madonna, Antonio Banderas, Jonathan Pryce. 134 minutes. Rated PG.
"Sleazy politics come alive" in this "visually rich" celluloid version of the Andrew Lloyd Webber stage musical based on the life of Argentina's Eva Peron, an all-singing, dialogue-free production that seems to some like an "extended MTV video"; though surveyors split on Madonna's title turn ("surprisingly good" vs. "doesn't have the chops"), the "smoldering", "powerful" Banderas is a hit and overall this "entertaining" epic is at the very least "watchable."

Exodus 23 | 23 | 26 | 25
1960. Directed by Otto Preminger. With Paul Newman, Eva Marie Saint, Sal Mineo. 210 minutes. Not Rated.
An "all-star cast" drives this story of the "founding of modern Israel", a "stunning", "satisfying" Preminger epic "faithfully" adapted from Leon Uris' best-seller; fans single out the star turn from a "too-gorgeous-for-words" Newman "in his prime", and if the plot has some "bathos" mixed into its "high drama", it's ultimately a "moving" moving picture.

Exorcist, The ✉⑪ 25 | 24 | 26 | 25
1973. Directed by William Friedkin. With Ellen Burstyn, Max von Sydow, Linda Blair. 122 minutes. Rated R.
"Horror and religion" collide in this "head-spinning", "nightmare-inducing" "shocker" about a child possessed by the devil that

"grossed out America" with its "revolting" language and that infamous "pea-soup vomit scene"; though some say it's "slid into camp" over the years, most maintain it's still "one of the scariest movies ever" – but stick to the "original" cut that's much more "terrifying" than the recent 'restored' reissue.

Experiment in Terror ◑
25 | 24 | 25 | 23

1962. Directed by Blake Edwards. With Glenn Ford, Lee Remick, Stefanie Powers, Ross Martin. 123 minutes. Not Rated.

A rare thriller from Blake Edwards, this "little-known gem" is "one of the better woman-in-danger pictures" thanks to "chilling" performances by Remick as a "sexy" bank teller and Martin as an "asthmatic" extortionist; a jazzy Henry Mancini soundtrack and "mesmerizing" San Francisco settings (particularly that knockout windup at Candlestick Park) supply the atmosphere.

Eyes Wide Shut
13 | 15 | 12 | 19

1999. Directed by Stanley Kubrick. With Tom Cruise, Nicole Kidman, Sydney Pollack. 159 minutes. Rated R.

"Stanley Kubrick's final hurrah", this "would-be erotic thriller" about "marital infidelity" disappoints most voters, especially given the big "buildup before its release"; critics condemn Cruise's "cardboard-cutout" acting, the "plodding" plot, the "Chinese water torture" soundtrack and the director's "overall failure of vision" – but not the "polished, sexy" Kidman, who's the "only thing worth watching" in this "maddening" picture.

Fabulous Baker Boys, The
20 | 22 | 18 | 19

1989. Directed by Steven Kloves. With Jeff Bridges, Michelle Pfeiffer, Beau Bridges. 114 minutes. Rated R.

"Sibling rivalry" gets "compelling" treatment in this "great date movie" about two "journeyman musicians" competing for the attentions of their "slinky, sexy" girl singer; the Bridges brothers exude the "art of cool" and Pfeiffer "slithers around so deliciously" that no one minds that this "slice-of-life" story "doesn't go anywhere", given the "enjoyable" ride; most memorable scene, no question: Michelle "draped over a piano" crooning 'Makin' Whoopee' – "who knew she could sing?"

Face/Off
18 | 19 | 18 | 21

1997. Directed by John Woo. With John Travolta, Nicolas Cage, Joan Allen, Gina Gershon. 138 minutes. Rated R.

"Hong Kong auteur" John Woo "goes Hollywood" in this "hyperkinetic" action flick that "fires on all pistons", despite an "unashamedly preposterous scenario" in which "over-the-top" archenemies Travolta and Cage "switch places" (and faces); be prepared for "twists and turns galore", "lots of violence" and enough "mindless fun" to put this one at the very top of your "guilty pleasures list."

Faces ◑
22 | 27 | 18 | 19

1968. Directed by John Cassavetes. With John Marley, Gena Rowlands, Lynn Carlin, Seymour Cassel. 130 minutes. Rated PG-13.

The "beginning of independent filmmaking as we know it", this "ultra-low-budget" drama really "put Cassavetes on the map as a director" with its "revealing" insights on infidelity and the meaninglessness of life; it "remains as avant-garde" as ever thanks to the "fierce performances" alone, and is just the thing "when you want to take a breather from feel-good fare."

Fahrenheit 451

21	19	25	19

1966. Directed by François Truffaut. With Oskar Werner, Julie Christie, Cyril Cusack. 110 minutes. Not Rated.
"Truffaut's first English-language picture" is an "excellent adaptation" of Ray Bradbury's "Big Brother"–ish sci-fi novel, a "social commentary" about "censorship by book burning" in the not-too-distant future (the title is the temperature at which paper ignites); though zealots praise the "thoughtful" presentation of an "important topic", nonbelievers flame it as "plodding" and suggest you "read the book" instead.

Fahrenheit 9/11

21	–	22	19

2004. Directed by Michael Moore. Documentary. 122 minutes. Rated R.
Conveyed "with all the subtlety of a carpet bombing", Moore's "unapologetically biased" polemic against George W. Bush's "policies and leadership" elicits passionate praise and bitter condemnation alike, with defenders calling it a "daring exposé" of the "real truth" and foes crying it's a "complete fraud on every level"; though unlikely to "change your opinion", it's still a "must-see for anyone remotely interested in what's going on in the Washington world of today."

Fail-Safe ◑

24	25	26	21

1964. Directed by Sidney Lumet. With Henry Fonda, Walter Matthau, Larry Hagman. 112 minutes. Not Rated.
The "Cold War gets hot" in this "chilling", "hypnotic" nuclear-war melodrama about an American President forced to make some "horrifying choices" as an atom bomb hurtles its way toward Moscow; devotees note that the storyline is strikingly similar to that of *Dr. Strangelove* (though decidedly laugh-free) but insist its "what if?" plot is especially "gripping – and hopefully not prophetic."

Fame

21	18	21	20

1980. Directed by Alan Parker. With Irene Cara, Lee Curreri, Eddie Barth, Laura Dean. 134 minutes. Rated R.
"Little girls who sing in front of the mirror" relate to this "feel-good" musical set in "NY's High School of Performing Arts", where "talented", "leg warmer–wearing teenagers" spend their days "dancing in the streets" and "struggling for fame"; ok, it's a bit "overdone" and "very dated now", but "crank up the volume" and you'll "enjoy the energy" all the same.

Family Man, The

16	17	18	17

2000. Directed by Brett Ratner. With Nicolas Cage, Téa Leoni, Don Cheadle. 125 minutes. Rated PG-13.
A "harried, unmarried exec wakes up with a new life and family" in this "what-if?" picture, an "update of *It's a Wonderful Life*" that may be "a bit far-fetched" but still "questions all the choices we make"; Leoni is "adorable", Cage "more affecting than expected" and despite the "slow" pace, most leave "believing wholeheartedly in true love."

Fanny and Alexander ✉ 🎬

26	25	25	26

1982. Directed by Ingmar Bergman. With Pernilla Allwin, Bertil Guve, Gunn Wallgren. 188 minutes. Rated R.
"Proof that Bergman wasn't miserable all the time", this "semi-autobiographical look back at his childhood" in Sweden "told from two siblings' point of view" features the "master" "at his most ac-

cessible"; sure, the "pacing's slow" and the film "long" (in fact, it's a pared-down version of a six-hour TV miniseries), yet the overall "visual magnificence" makes for something "rich and interesting."

FANTASIA ① `28 | – | – | 29`

1940. Directed by Ben Sharpsteen et al. Animated. 120 minutes. Rated G.

Disney's "magnificent merger" of "mind-blowing" animation with a symphonic orchestra conducted by "maestro Leopold Stokowski" is a piece of "unbeatably creative" "eye candy" that's "never been equaled"; though a "flop when it first came out", it was later revived as a "'60s head movie" (thanks to trippy sequences like those "dancing hippos in tutus" and "Mickey Mouse as the sorcerer's apprentice"); modernists maintain this "original music video" remains a "perfect way to introduce a child to classical" sounds.

Fantasia 2000 `24 | – | – | 27`

1999. Directed by James Algar et al. Animated. 75 minutes. Rated G.

The "perfect companion" to the 1940 "classic", this "worthy" sequel marrying animation to music of great composers is "terrific Disney" that might be "more for adults than kids" for a change; it "keeps the spirit of the original beautifully" (right down to the "cloying celebrity" intros to each vignette), and although the "flamingo-with-the-yo-yo" scene enthralls many, the "best segment" is "'Rhapsody in Blue' via Al Hirschfeld."

Fantastic Voyage `19 | 12 | 23 | 21`

1966. Directed by Richard Fleischer. With Stephen Boyd, Raquel Welch, Edmond O'Brien. 100 minutes. Rated PG.

"Outrageous in its day", this sci-fi fantasy for "thinking" folks "still wows" the wide-eyed with its story about scientists shrunken and then "injected into a human body" to repair a blood clot; despite "wooden acting" and a "dumb ending", the "special effects are impressive for its time" – and Raquel sure looks swell in and out of that skintight diving outfit.

Farewell My Concubine 🅕 `25 | 26 | 24 | 26`

1993. Directed by Chen Kaige. With Leslie Cheung, Gong Li, Zhang Feng-Yi. 171 minutes. Rated R.

"Worthy of David Lean on every level", this "sumptuous", "epic achievement" traces a complex friendship between two Peking Opera singers over a "fascinating sweep of history" from the '30s to the '70s; "stunning both visually and emotionally", it boasts "superb acting" and "outstanding scenery", but make sure to sit up straight: its "overlong" running time can be "draining."

Far From Heaven `24 | 27 | 23 | 26`

2002. Directed by Todd Haynes. With Julianne Moore, Dennis Quaid, Dennis Haysbert. 107 minutes. Rated PG-13.

Haynes' "gorgeous homage to director Douglas Sirk's '50s melodramas" takes a "grippingly bittersweet" look at the "reality of the suburban picket-fence dream" and "genteel Northern racism"; though the pace is "slow" and the story "a little weak", it remains a "must-see" thanks to "flawless performances" from Moore and Quaid as well as "colorful", "stunning cinematography" that "captures the time period with brilliance" – the "costumes alone are close to heaven."

FARGO ✉ | 25 | 27 | 25 | 25 |
1996. Directed by Joel Coen. With Frances McDormand,
William H. Macy, Steve Buscemi. 98 minutes. Rated R.
This "comic noir" treatment of "crime in the heartland" shows
"how funny Minnesota can be" in the hands of the Coen brothers,
who "spin a folksy", violent yarn that makes the "outrageous
seem everyday" and the "mundane interesting"; but the pièce de
résistance is McDormand's "deadpan", Oscar-winning turn as a
"pregnant" "crime-stopper" whose "goofy dialogue" alone is –
"you betcha" – worth the price of admission.

Fast Times at Ridgemont High | 22 | 19 | 21 | 18 |
1982. Directed by Amy Heckerling. With Sean Penn, Judge Reinhold,
Jennifer Jason Leigh. 92 minutes. Rated R.
One of the "crown jewels of the teen-comedy" genre, this "totally
killer" "coming-of-age" "favorite" is an indelible "snapshot of the
'80s" that made a star of Penn in the immortal role of "surfer
stoner dude" Jeff Spicoli; adapted from Cameron Crowe's book, it
showcases a "sprawling cast in interweaving stories" (like a kind
of "teenage *Nashville*") and, among other things, "inspired a generation of in-school pizza orderers"; best "gratuitous scene":
"Phoebe Cates on the diving board."

Fatal Attraction | 22 | 23 | 23 | 21 |
1987. Directed by Adrian Lyne. With Michael Douglas, Glenn Close,
Anne Archer. 119 minutes. Rated R.
"Anyone contemplating an extramarital affair" should take a hard
look at this "genuinely creepy" "cautionary tale", dominated by a
"demented" Close as a "licentious hubby's worst nightmare";
though the plot "goes overboard" occasionally and Douglas "plays
the same character as in 47 other movies", the picture had tremendous "cultural impact" in its day and is "still hair-raising" –
particularly the "yikes"-inducing "boiled-bunny" scene.

Father of the Bride ❶❷ | 23 | 25 | 21 | 20 |
1950. Directed by Vincente Minnelli. With Spencer Tracy, Joan
Bennett, Elizabeth Taylor. 92 minutes. Not Rated.
Hollywood legends Tracy (in the "harried" title role) and Taylor (as
the bride) walk down the aisle together in this "heartwarming"
chestnut about the "havoc surrounding the planning of a wedding"; while most vow it's something that "all fathers and daughters
should watch" together, a few pronounce it "dated and slow."

Father of the Bride ❷ | 20 | 20 | 19 | 20 |
1991. Directed by Charles Shyer. With Steve Martin, Diane Keaton,
Martin Short. 105 minutes. Rated PG.
"Faster-moving than the original", this "thoroughly engaging"
comedy captures the "chaos of wedding planning" thanks to a
"hilarious" Martin (as the "clueless dad") and an equally "hysterical" Short; sure, it can be "tame" and rather "silly", but ultimately it
goes down "like soothing chocolate pudding"; better yet, it "won't
inflict pain on guys", even though it's a bona fide "chick flick."

Fear and Loathing in Las Vegas | 15 | 20 | 15 | 18 |
1998. Directed by Terry Gilliam. With Johnny Depp, Benicio Del Toro,
Craig Bierko. 119 minutes. Rated R.
"You'll either love or loathe" this "whirlwind cult film", a "faithful
adaptation" of Hunter S. Thompson's "unadaptable" book detail-

ing his "psychedelic" escapades in Las Vegas; despite kudos for Depp and Del Toro's "bizarre but authentic" performances, loathers find the film "essentially unpleasant" with "no plot", just a bunch of "idiots doing drugs."

Ferris Bueller's Day Off
23 | 22 | 23 | 21

1986. Directed by John Hughes. With Matthew Broderick, Alan Ruck, Mia Sara. 98 minutes. Rated PG-13.

"Every teenager's fantasy" of "ditching high school" for the day is realized in this "brilliant comedy" about a "sly slacker" on the loose in Chicago who "gets away with everything" and "does it with style"; the "smug-mugged" Broderick exudes "bravado" in the role that "launched his career", while "underappreciated" director Hughes offhandedly produces a picture so "influential" that it "belongs in a time capsule of the '80s."

Fever Pitch
20 | 19 | 21 | 19

2005. Directed by Bobby Farrelly, Peter Farrelly. With Drew Barrymore, Jimmy Fallon. 103 minutes. Rated PG-13.

"Sports and love" are the themes of this "surprisingly tame outing" from the Farrelly brothers, a "feel-good" romantic comedy about an alpha gal who falls for an "obsessed" Red Sox fan; even though the "chemistry's believable" between the "watchable" Fallon and the "adorable as always" Barrymore, the overall call is "harmless" – "not a home run", but maybe a "solid triple."

Few Good Men, A
23 | 26 | 23 | 22

1992. Directed by Rob Reiner. With Tom Cruise, Jack Nicholson, Demi Moore, Kevin Bacon. 138 minutes. Rated R.

"Star-driven", "crackerjack courtroom drama" about a military murder investigation that's both "intelligent and entertaining"; no question, there are more than a few good performances, especially the "adorable-as-ever" Cruise in a "gritty", change-of-pace role playing against Nicholson's "riveting" if "pompous" marine colonel, who delivers the picture's most "infamous line: 'you can't handle the truth.'"

Fiddler on the Roof
26 | 25 | 27 | 26

1971. Directed by Norman Jewison. With Topol, Leonard Frey, Norma Crane. 181 minutes. Rated G.

One of the "last of the epic musicals", this "uplifting" adaptation of the "Broadway classic" finds "wide-screen resonance" in its "memorable" score and "elaborate production" values; despite the unmusical subject matter (19th-century "Jews fleeing the pogroms"), it's still a "joyous" film that's as "moving as a moving picture can be."

Field of Dreams
22 | 21 | 23 | 22

1989. Directed by Phil Alden Robinson. With Kevin Costner, Amy Madigan, Ray Liotta, James Earl Jones. 107 minutes. Rated PG.

"Even non–sports fans can love" this "feel-good" fantasy/drama about "baseball, ghosts" and "one man's search to find himself" in an Iowa cornfield; its "realistic sporting sequences, great storyline" and a "touching" turn from Costner ("before he lost it") make for a flick that "gets better every time you see it"; even those who find it too "sentimental" agree it's a "must-see for any father and son."

Fifth Element, The

19 | 15 | 19 | 23

1997. Directed by Luc Besson. With Bruce Willis, Gary Oldman, Milla Jovovich. 126 minutes. Rated PG-13.

"Hyperkinetic", "loud" and "fast-paced", this "slick" sci-fi "actionfest" is about as substantial as a "big ball of cotton candy, but a hoot nonetheless"; sure, "Willis saves the planet – again" – but in this "loopy" "send-up of the genre", the "tongue-in-cheek" plot plays a distinct second fiddle to the "visually spectacular" effects; still, shirkers shrug it off as a "messy example of why more isn't always better."

50 First Dates

18 | 18 | 19 | 19

2004. Directed by Peter Segal. With Adam Sandler, Drew Barrymore, Rob Schneider. 99 minutes. Rated PG-13.

"Comedy power couple" Sandler and Barrymore have the "chemistry" down pat in this "surprisingly touching" romance about a womanizer enthralled by a woman with short-term memory loss (i.e. she can't remember what she did on her last date); fans sigh it's "sweet" and "light-hearted", foes say "juvenile" and "farfetched", but at least they "didn't cop out with a cheap Hollywood ending."

Fight Club

23 | 25 | 24 | 24

1999. Directed by David Fincher. With Brad Pitt, Edward Norton, Helena Bonham Carter. 139 minutes. Rated R.

"Love-it-or-hate-it" moviemaking is alive and well in this "testosterone-ridden" "cult classic" that uses "top-notch effects", "twisted humor" and a "killer" soundtrack in its depiction of "ultraviolent, disenfranchised males"; an "amazing Norton" and "underrated Pitt" provide the fireworks in this "gore"-drenched drama, with a "surprise finish" that's either "mind-blowing" or "nonsensical", depending on who's talking.

FINDING NEMO

28 | – | 25 | 29

2003. Directed by Andrew Stanton, Lee Unkrich. Animated. 100 minutes. Rated G.

"No matter what your age", you'll be "riveted to your seat" by this "Pixar masterpiece" about a "neurotic father fish searching for his son" in a "beautifully rendered undersea world"; voters insist it's "one of the best animated films of all time", blending "superb visual effects" with a "touching" yet "hilarious script" (laced with "adult references that the tots will certainly miss") and "fully developed, brilliantly voiced characters."

Finding Neverland

25 | 27 | 24 | 26

2004. Directed by Marc Forster. With Johnny Depp, Kate Winslet, Julie Christie. 106 minutes. Rated PG.

"Even if you're a rock-hearted cynic", get out your handkerchiefs for this "pixie dust–coated", "semi-biographical" reflection on *Peter Pan* playwright J.M. Barrie's "fantastic imagination" and the people who inspired it; "do-no-wrong" Depp and Winslet "fly high" with "stellar performances", though most agree it's the "adorable child" actors who "steal the show."

Finian's Rainbow

▽ 20 | 19 | 19 | 20

1968. Directed by Francis Ford Coppola. With Fred Astaire, Petula Clark, Tommy Steele, Keenan Wynn. 141 minutes. Rated G.

This "last musical" starring "lighter-than-air Fred Astaire" was "directed by Francis Ford Coppola, of all people", who supplies an "inventive" take on the genre in this story of Irish folks (and a leprechaun) transplanted to a small Southern town; although "dated" to a few, it's "underrated" to others.

Firm, The
17 17 20 18

1993. Directed by Sydney Pollack. With Tom Cruise, Jeanne Tripplehorn, Gene Hackman. 154 minutes. Rated R.
"Nail-biters" say this "slick" adaptation of John Grisham's "solid" best-seller about an "honest lawyer and his evil employers" succeeds mainly because of its "quirky supporting performances"; but foes argue this "not-too-thrilling thriller" "rarely lives up to the book", particularly since they went and "changed the ending."

First Blood: Rambo ❶
18 13 19 18

1982. Directed by Ted Kotcheff. With Sylvester Stallone, Richard Crenna, Brian Dennehy. 97 minutes. Rated R.
A "great kick-butt movie" "bolstered by a muscular score", this "simplistic but satisfying revenge tale" about a Vietnam vet harassed by small-town cops "delivers some punch"; the "studly", "steroidal" Stallone makes a bloody decent "action god", if not a silver-tongued thespian ("he should never talk"), though compadres caution it's his "last good movie before getting lost in sequel land."

First Wives Club, The
17 19 18 17

1996. Directed by Hugh Wilson. With Bette Midler, Goldie Hawn, Diane Keaton, Maggie Smith. 102 minutes. Rated PG.
The "heavyweight talent" of its "all-star cast" made this "lightweight battle-of-the-sexes farce", a revenge comedy pitting "strong women" against "rotten men", into a big hit at the box office; still, foes say it's as "fluffy as Goldie's lips", citing a "ridiculous plot" that's an "embarrassment for all involved"; P.S. it's "not a good date movie" either.

Fish Called Wanda, A
23 24 22 21

1988. Directed by Charles Crichton. With John Cleese, Jamie Lee Curtis, Kevin Kline. 108 minutes. Rated R.
It's easy getting hooked on this "nonstop", "kitchen-sink comedy" about a heist perpetrated by a "bumbling gang" portrayed by a "few chaps of Python fame" as well as the "show-stealing", Oscar-winning Kline; be prepared for "lots of giggles", but "forget political correctness", as "stutterers" and some unfortunate "goldfish" are gleefully abused.

Fisher King, The
21 24 21 21

1991. Directed by Terry Gilliam. With Jeff Bridges, Robin Williams, Mercedes Ruehl, Amanda Plummer. 137 minutes. Rated R.
Grail-seekers gravitate to this "strange" mix of "comedy, fantasy and drama", a "powerful" story of a high-flying radio shock jock who falls to earth only to be rescued by a homeless man; some find the plot "confusing" and "a little too out there", but loyal subjects say the "incredible visual effects in the Grand Central Station" scene alone "make it worth watching."

Fistful of Dollars, A ❶
19 17 18 17

1967. Directed by Sergio Leone. With Clint Eastwood, Marianne Koch, Mario Brega. 99 minutes. Rated R.
The "pasta flows" in this "early spaghetti Western" as Clint "defines coolness" with his "prototypical" "Man With No Name" caught between two rival families; though a "couple notches down

from *The Good, the Bad and the Ugly*" ("maybe something was lost in the translation"), this "classic" is "still fun" on a rainy day.

FITZCARRALDO
27 | 26 | 26 | 27

1982. Directed by Werner Herzog. With Klaus Kinski, Claudia Cardinale. 158 minutes. Rated PG.
"Absolute perseverance" verging on "outlandish obsession" is the theme of this "very bizarre" story of a "quixotic" fellow determined to "build an opera house in the middle of the South American jungle"; "awe-inspired" types say "you've never seen anything like it", starting with that "scene of a ship being carried over a mountain", done with "no special effects"; P.S. try it as a "double feature with *Burden of Dreams*", the "spectacular making-of documentary."

Five Easy Pieces
24 | 27 | 22 | 21

1970. Directed by Bob Rafelson. With Jack Nicholson, Karen Black, Lois Smith. 96 minutes. Rated R.
"Nicholson's at the height of his powers" in this "deliberately paced character study" about "disaffection", "wasted ambition and dreams" that's a "must-see" for die-hard Jack fans; it "captures the restlessness of its era" with an expert "mix of comedy and serious drama" – and offers explicit instructions on "how not to be a waitress" in that "unforgettable chicken-salad sandwich" scene.

5,000 Fingers of Dr. T., The
▽ 21 | 15 | 21 | 24

1953. Directed by Roy Rowland. With Tommy Rettig, Hans Conried, Peter Lind Hayes. 88 minutes. Not Rated.
"Imaginative, absurd, trippy and a million other crazy things", this "ahead-of-its-time" musical "written by Dr. Seuss" depicts a "bizarre world" where a boy battles a piano teacher bent on world domination; though this "quirky little masterpiece" boasts a "growing cult following", it might be a little too "dark" for smaller fry.

Flashdance
16 | 14 | 15 | 18

1983. Directed by Adrian Lyne. With Jennifer Beals, Michael Nouri. 96 minutes. Rated R.
"Break dancing, leg warmers and sweatshirts worn off the shoulder" got their start in this "breakthrough" musical about a "Cinderella"-esque steel worker yearning to be a ballerina; granted, the "politically incorrect" story is "somewhat lacking", yet this "guilty pleasure" features a "soundtrack that nails the early '80s" and was "one of the highest grossing films" of its time – "what a feeling", indeed.

Fletch ⑪
19 | 18 | 18 | 16

1985. Directed by Michael Ritchie. With Chevy Chase, Joe Don Baker, Tim Matheson. 98 minutes. Rated PG.
This "goofball" "cult" comedy represents "Chase's peak" in his "ultimate" role as an "undercover reporter who changes his ID more often than his underwear"; fools for "tomfoolery" swear it's "possibly the most quotable movie" ever, thanks to a flurry of "great one-liners" that only get "funnier every time you see it."

Flight of the Phoenix, The
25 | 26 | 24 | 21

1965. Directed by Robert Aldrich. With James Stewart, Richard Attenborough, Peter Finch. 147 minutes. Not Rated.
"Jimmy Stewart can fly anything" and does in this post–*Spirit of St. Louis* adventure flicker about a desert plane crash that leaves

its survivors facing a "seemingly hopeless future"; "realistically shot" and "brilliantly acted", it's a "feel-good", "can-do" kind o picture "without violence" that "really stays with you."

Fly, The ❶   20 | 18 | 22 | 18
1958. Directed by Kurt Neumann. With Vincent Price, David Hedison, Patricia Owens. 94 minutes. Not Rated.
The "golden age of B movies" lives on in this wonderfully "camp classic" about a scientist "who pushes the envelope too far and becomes a fly"; fans buzz it remains "truly horrifying", especially that "unforgettable" shot of our hero "stuck in the spider's web" ("*help me!*") that "makes up for any quaintness in the execution."

Fly, The ❶   16 | 17 | 17 | 20
1986. Directed by David Cronenberg. With Jeff Goldblum, Geena Davis. 96 minutes. Rated R.
A "reinterpretation, not a rehash" of the "campy original", this "graphic, gruesome" remake explores Cronenberg's "obsession about the relationship between biology and technology"; sure, "special effects rule the day" here, yet there's also an "effective" love story amid the otherwise "dark" doings.

Fly Away Home   22 | 20 | 24 | 24
1996. Directed by Carroll Ballard. With Anna Paquin, Jeff Daniels, Dana Delany. 107 minutes. Rated PG.
Get out your "biggest bowl of popcorn" for this "deeply felt family film" about a young girl, her estranged dad and the flock of baby geese she takes under her wing; fans "honk" about its "captivating story" and "beautiful" Canadian scenery, saying it's "not just for kids", but rather a "quite uplifting", "lovely movie for all."

Fog of War, The   26 | – | 25 | 23
2003. Directed by Errol Morris. Documentary. 95 minutes. Rated PG-13.
"Controversial" former U.S. Secretary of Defense Robert S. McNamara recounts his involvement in WWII and the Cuban missile crisis, as well as his role as one of the "architects of the Vietnam War", in this "eye-opening", Oscar-winning documentary that's "amazingly relevant considering the current political climate"; director Morris' "fascinating yet maddening" work underscores McNamara's "brilliance and fallibility" while "neither condemning nor excusing him entirely."

Footloose   17 | 15 | 16 | 17
1984. Directed by Herbert Ross. With Kevin Bacon, Lori Singer, John Lithgow, Dianne Wiest. 107 minutes. Rated PG.
A "town that's banned dancing" is the setting for this "classic '80s rebellion flick", a "guilty pleasure" that "started it all for Kevin Bacon" and is best remembered for its hit-heavy soundtrack and "jumping" theme song; though "silly fluff" to detractors, it's "all-around fun" for "toe-tappers" who "take it for what it is."

For a Few Dollars More ❶   23 | 21 | 21 | 20
1967. Directed by Sergio Leone. With Clint Eastwood, Lee Van Cleef, Gian Maria Volontè. 130 minutes. Rated R.
"No one's tougher than Clint" (who "doesn't smile once" but sure "looks good in a poncho") in this "tasty spaghetti western", the second installment in the Man With No Name trilogy; even though the dialogue's "dubbed", the characters "cardboard" and the

bounty-hunter plot "weird", this "guilty pleasure" is still "fun to watch" – and "oh, that music!"

Forbidden Planet
25 | 18 | 25 | 24

1956. Directed by Fred M. Wilcox. With Walter Pidgeon, Anne Francis, Leslie Nielsen. 98 minutes. Rated G.
Its long-before-digital FX "may seem quaint" today, but this "top-notch psychological thriller" represents the "true start of the sci-fi genre" to many; despite a compelling storyline "based on Shakespeare's *Tempest*" and some halfway decent acting from the humans, "Robby the Robot is the real star" here.

FORREST GUMP ✉
24 | 26 | 24 | 25

1994. Directed by Robert Zemeckis. With Tom Hanks, Robin Wright, Gary Sinise. 142 minutes. Rated PG-13.
"Even macho guys" get misty over this "sentimental" story of "hope and perseverance" that explores recent American history through the "unlikely eyes" of a "simple-minded", Zelig-like hero (the "triumphant", Oscar-winning Hanks); though picky viewers find "not much assortment in this box of chocolates", they're overruled by "enchanted" believers who say its "basic good-heartedness" makes it "remarkably touching."

Fort Apache ◑
23 | 22 | 23 | 22

1948. Directed by John Ford. With John Wayne, Henry Fonda, Shirley Temple, Ward Bond. 125 minutes. Not Rated.
This "great" Golden-Age-of-Hollywood Western is the first of the Ford trilogy that both mythologized and humanized the cavalry; Fonda's effectively "cast against type" as a by-the-numbers commander who takes over a frontier fort and can't connect with his men or the local Indians, while Wayne is "perfect" as the more understanding captain with whom he clashes; tame for the TV generation, its fight scenes are "remarkable for its era."

Fortune Cookie, The ◑
▽ 21 | 25 | 20 | 19

1966. Directed by Billy Wilder. With Walter Matthau, Jack Lemmon. 125 minutes. Not Rated.
The first (and many say the "best") pairing of the Lemmon-Matthau combo", this biting black comedy via Billy Wilder takes aim at our litigious society in its story of a sports cameraman faking an injury in exchange for insurance money; a "top-notch script" intertwining "big laughs" and "nonstop snickers" keeps things moving, even if the ending "veers uncomfortably between drama and humor."

48 HRS. ⓘ
19 | 18 | 18 | 17

1982. Directed by Walter Hill. With Nick Nolte, Eddie Murphy, Annette O'Toole. 92 minutes. Rated R.
The "blueprint" for "buddy action flicks", this "entertaining" crime thriller about a "surly white cop teaming up with a loud-mouthed black convict" features "stroke-of-genius" casting pairing Nolte and Murphy; ok, it's "brainless fun" and a "little too violent", but worth catching for Eddie's "starmaking" screen debut alone – especially his "great rendition of 'Roxanne.'"

42nd Street ◑
24 | 18 | 20 | 26

1933. Directed by Lloyd Bacon. With Ruby Keeler, Ginger Rogers, Bebe Daniels. 89 minutes. Not Rated.
Alright, it's a "bit corny by modern standards", but this "brassy" "mother of all backstage musicals" showcases choreographer

"Busby Berkeley at his glossy best" applying his "inventive" genius to all those "dancing feet"; "every actress' dream" come true, it's a real "classic", so just ignore the "hackneyed" plot and Keeler's "clunky" footwork.

40 Year Old Virgin, The
19 | 20 | 19 | 18

2005. Directed by Judd Apatow. With Steve Carell, Catherine Keener, Paul Rudd. 116 minutes. Rated R.

Alright, the title portends a hopeless "one-trick pony", but funnyman Carell actually "pulls it off", delivering "loads of laughs" and even some "surprising charm" as a "sweet", middle-aged "nerd" chasing his first score in this "wickedly funny" sex farce; no surprise, prudes protest the "unapologetically vulgar" content and complain the story takes "too long" to climax; P.S. "body wax", anyone?

For Whom the Bell Tolls
25 | 26 | 26 | 22

1943. Directed by Sam Wood. With Gary Cooper, Ingrid Bergman, Katina Paxinou. 170 minutes. Not Rated.

Fans swear this adaptation of Hemingway's Pulitzer Prize–winner about an American fighting fascism in '30s Spain "gets every single nuance right", starting with its "poignant", "old-fashioned love story" right down to the very convincing battle sequences; though a minority dubs it "schmaltz in macho drag", it strikes a chord as a "true classic by any measure" for most bell-ringers.

For Your Eyes Only
18 | 16 | 18 | 21

1981. Directed by John Glen. With Roger Moore, Carole Bouquet, Topol, Julian Glover. 127 minutes. Rated PG.

A "solid" entry in the Bond blitz, this spy flicker focuses less on "supergadgets" and more on Moore, leading many to label it his "best" outing as the ever-suave 007; the "realistic villains", "exotic locations" and "jaw-dropping" ski chases entice "even die-hard nonfans" – although the "fight scenes are never believable."

Foul Play
21 | 19 | 20 | 19

1978. Directed by Colin Higgins. With Goldie Hawn, Chevy Chase, Dudley Moore. 116 minutes. Rated PG.

Goldie "at her cute, giggly best" and a "terrific" Chevy make a "charming couple" in this "lightweight murder mystery" that's a loose "takeoff on Hitchcock's *The Man Who Knew Too Much*"; its "international-assassination plot" seesaws between "hilarity and suspense", while Moore deftly walks away with the picture as a lecherous swinger with a memorably equipped bachelor pad.

Fountainhead, The ❶∅
▽ 22 | 21 | 23 | 20

1949. Directed by King Vidor. With Gary Cooper, Patricia Neal, Raymond Massey. 114 minutes. Not Rated.

Ayn Rand's mammoth novel "brought to life", this Hollywood version fortunately "doesn't take six months to watch" as it profiles the life of an independent, "Frank Lloyd Wright"–esque architect intent on being a "genuine individual"; foes find it too talky and "hokey" (except for the "delicious Neal") and advise you "read the book before seeing the movie."

400 Blows, The ❶Ⅲ🅕
27 | 26 | 25 | 24

1959. Directed by François Truffaut. With Jean-Pierre Léaud, Robert Beauvais. 94 minutes. Not Rated.

"Anyone who survived adolescence" can relate to this French "coming-of-age" film, a "semi-autobiographical" effort that marked

Truffaut's directorial debut; as his "great alter ego", Léaud "depicts the pain and joy of growing up" in a winsomely "giddy" turn, though the picture earned its "place in film history" by "breaking a lot of rules" while demonstrating a "true love of movies."

Four Weddings and a Funeral

21 | 21 | 21 | 20

1994. Directed by Mike Newell. With Hugh Grant, Andie MacDowell, Kristin Scott Thomas. 117 minutes. Rated R.

This "entertaining" marriage of "sweet and savvy" wrings "unexpected" laughs out of "modern love" and "every bad wedding" you've ever endured; notable for "putting Hugh Grant on the map", it also boasts a "sparkling script" and a "quirky" ensemble cast, though the less said about the "wooden" MacDowell the better.

Fox and the Hound, The

18 | – | 19 | 18

1981. Directed by Ted Berman, Richard Rich, Art Stevens. Animated. 83 minutes. Rated G.

As the title canines become unlikely pals, kids can learn about the "meaning of friendship" from this "cute" Disney film, but it's not all tail-wagging "family" fun: the "bittersweet" tone "tugs at those heartstrings with no mercy", and bashers bark at the "copy-machine" quality of the early '80s animation.

Frances

▽ 22 | 28 | 23 | 20

1982. Directed by Graeme Clifford. With Jessica Lange, Kim Stanley, Sam Shepard. 140 minutes. Rated R.

"Disturbing" but still "quite fine", this "harrowing" biography of "Hollywood nonconformist" Frances Farmer pulls no punches in its exploration of the actress' "demons" and "society's response to her mental illness"; in the title role, Lange is "magical" (and "matched by Stanley as her mother"), but this one's "not for the timid" given its ultimately "desperate, depressing" tone.

Frankenstein ◑ ⅠⅠ

25 | 21 | 25 | 23

1931. Directed by James Whale. With Boris Karloff, Colin Clive, Mae Clarke. 71 minutes. Not Rated.

The "granddaddy of all horror films" adds a touch of "pathos" and "camp" to its story of a mad scientist who "goes against nature" and builds a creature "prone to violence"; beyond monster-mashing, it also explores the "theme of loneliness" via Karloff's "heartbreaking" ghoul, and though "a bit overacted", it's still "goose-bumps time when Colin Clive shouts *'it's alive!'*"

Freaks ◑

23 | 18 | 22 | 19

1932. Directed by Tod Browning. With Wallace Ford, Leila Hyams, Olga Baclanova. 64 minutes. Not Rated.

"Dated" perhaps, but "as creepy as ever", this "subversive" look at "circus sideshow" performers still shocks 75 years later since it casts "actual human oddities" – real midgets, pinheads and Siamese twins – in leading roles; "banned for years" after its initial release and "hardly politically correct", it's either "exploitative", "sympathetic" or a "nightmare-inducing" "train wreck" that "you can't take your eyes off of."

Freaky Friday

18 | 17 | 21 | 16

1976. Directed by Gary Nelson. With Barbara Harris, Jodie Foster, John Astin. 95 minutes. Rated G.

A "kooky" idea – a teenage girl and her mom trade bodies for a day – powers this "fun" '70s "family film" that's a step up from the "usual body-swapping" comedies; thanks to a "smart script" and "brilliant" performances from Harris and Foster, some mothers and daughters watch it together for a "great bonding experience."

Freaky Friday | 21 | 22 | 20 | 20 |

2003. Directed by Mark Waters. With Jamie Lee Curtis, Lindsay Lohan, Mark Harmon. 97 minutes. Rated PG.

"Nicely adapted to the 21st century", this "surprisingly entertaining" remake of the '70s comedy about mother-and-daughter body-swapping is "in many ways better than the original" thanks to "smart, funny" performances by the "spirited" Lindsay and "still-a-babe" Jamie Lee; it's just the ticket when "you don't feel like thinking too hard", with plenty of "family appeal" that extends beyond the "Disney Channel crowd."

Free Willy ⑪ | 17 | 14 | 18 | 18 |

1993. Directed by Simon Wincer. With Jason James Richter, Lori Petty. 112 minutes. Rated PG.

"Everyone cries at the end" of this "family favorite", the "touching" story of an unhappy street kid who befriends an unhappy "killer whale" to "inspiring" results; it's "captivating" enough to work as a good "babysitter" for the kiddies, though seen-it-all types find it too "simplistic and message-laden."

French Connection, The ✉⑪ | 25 | 26 | 25 | 24 |

1971. Directed by William Friedkin. With Gene Hackman, Roy Scheider, Fernando Rey. 104 minutes. Rated R.

Famed for the "most harrowing car chase ever", this "seminal hard-boiled cop drama" is a "fast-paced" "exposé of the drug underworld" that's also "superbly cast and acted", starting with Hackman's "explosive", Oscar-winning turn as the tough-talking 'Popeye' Doyle; sure, it might seem "dated" to modernists, but that's "only because it's aped so frequently."

French Lieutenant's Woman, The | 22 | 25 | 21 | 23 |

1981. Directed by Karel Reisz. With Meryl Streep, Jeremy Irons, Hilton McRae. 127 minutes. Rated R.

"Streep is fantastic" in this "original" romance detailing parallel relationships: one involving an upper-class gentleman and a lower-class lass in Victorian England, the other between the contemporary actors playing them; granted, Harold Pinter's scenario might be "a bit confusing at the get-go", but ultimately this "excellent" adaptation of John Fowles' novel is both "really cool and worthwhile."

Frequency | 19 | 20 | 22 | 19 |

2000. Directed by Gregory Hoblit. With Dennis Quaid, James Caviezel. 118 minutes. Rated PG-13.

Sure, it might be "unbelievable", but this "time-travel" tale generates lots of "surprise" with its "truly original story" about a young man who talks to his late father via ham radio; despite "metropolis-size plot holes", it's still "touching", with a baseball subplot that's "especially fun" for fans of NY's 1969 "Miracle Mets."

Frida | 25 | 27 | 25 | 27 |

2002. Directed by Julie Taymor. With Salma Hayek, Alfred Molina. 123 minutes. Rated R.

"Fiery" Hayek "put her heart and soul" into this "underrated little" bio of "eccentric" Mexican artist Frida Kahlo, "and it shows"; she delivers her "finest performance", capturing the "pain, grief and ersonal tragedy that the painter expressed in her art" against a "visually stunning tapestry" of "color and texture" in which her "actual paintings come to life"; "wonderful" acting by Molina and an "amazing soundtrack" are more reasons "not to miss it."

Friday Night Lights
21 | 21 | 21 | 20

2004. Directed by Peter Berg. With Billy Bob Thornton, Derek Luke, Jay Hernandez. 118 minutes. Rated PG-13.
"Football fanatics" feel the "mojo" of this "gritty", "documentary-style" look at a Texas town's "bigger than life" devotion to high school gridiron; as an "embattled" coach preaching "love for the game", Thornton shows his "versatility", but some Monday morning quarterbacks are "unimpressed with the character development" and the "headache-inducing" camerawork.

Friday the 13th ⑪
16 | 9 | 15 | 13

1980. Directed by Sean S. Cunningham. With Betsy Palmer, Adrienne King, Harry Crosby. 95 minutes. Rated R.
The "granddaddy of modern-day horror films", this "cult slasher flick" "spawned an entire franchise" of "wretched sequels" that don't hold a candle to its "unrelenting creepiness"; set in a summer camp populated by "stupid, horny teenagers" who "scream a lot", it might "succeed more on a comedic level" today, but that "twist at the end" still "scares the hell" out of everybody.

Fried Green Tomatoes
23 | 25 | 23 | 22

1991. Directed by Jon Avnet. With Kathy Bates, Jessica Tandy, Mary Stuart Masterson. 130 minutes. Rated PG-13.
"Southern-fried memories" are the basis of this "heartwarming" dramedy detailing how a "pathetic excuse for a woman" transforms herself into a "take-charge wonder"; its "sweet story" might feature a dash of "male bashing", but it's "genuinely touching and involving" – no wonder many fried-food fans find this "feel-good" "tear-jerking" "chick flick" so gosh darn "yummy."

Friendly Persuasion
▽ 24 | 25 | 24 | 23

1956. Directed by William Wyler. With Gary Cooper, Dorothy McGuire, Anthony Perkins. 140 minutes. Not Rated.
"One for thy heart", this story of "Quakers during the Civil War" "trying to be pacifists" is an "all-around solid" picture thanks to a "strong storyline"; its "endearing characters" include the ultra-"believable" Cooper (the "Harrison Ford of his time") as well as a "moving" McGuire and Oscar-nominated Perkins.

From Here to Eternity ✉◑
26 | 27 | 24 | 24

1953. Directed by Fred Zinnemann. With Burt Lancaster, Montgomery Clift, Deborah Kerr, Frank Sinatra, Donna Reed. 118 minutes. Not Rated.
Based on James Jones' "powerful" novel, this "gold standard" of war dramas depicts military life in Honolulu's Pearl Harbor just before the Japanese attack; the "all-star cast" (including an Oscar-winning "Ol' Blue Eyes") and a "technically brilliant" production make this a "compelling classic" – though it's best remembered for Burt and Deborah's iconic "kissing-on-the-beach" scene.

From Russia With Love
23 | 21 | 23 | 23

1964. Directed by Terence Young. With Sean Connery, Robert Shaw, Lotte Lenya. 115 minutes. Rated PG.
Ride the "Orient Express from Istanbul to Venice" – with plenty of stops for "exotic locales", "scantily clad" gals and "great fight

scenes" – in this early James Bonder; the "formula never work§ better" thanks to an "incomparable" Connery pitted against "non¶ cartoon" villains, especially Lenya at her most "sadomasochistic."

Front Page, The ◐   ▽ 22 | 19 | 21 | 15
1931. Directed by Lewis Milestone. With Adolphe Menjou, Pat O'Brien, Edward Everett Horton. 101 minutes. Not Rated.
Based on the timeless stage comedy from Ben Hecht and Charles MacArthur, this zany satire of tabloid journalism is propelled by a fast-moving plot delivered with rapid-fire, overlapping dialogue; since it's an early talkie, it hasn't aged well, but the story was well-regarded enough to inspire three remakes, including *His Girl Friday,* arguably the best of the bunch.

Fugitive, The   23 | 24 | 24 | 23
1993. Directed by Andrew Davis. With Harrison Ford, Tommy Lee Jones, Sela Ward, Julianne Moore. 127 minutes. Rated PG-13.
From the "ultimate adrenaline rush" of the opening "train wreck" to the "smashing grand finale", you'll be "on the edge of your seat" throughout this "thinking person's action flick", based on the "long ago" TV series about a doctor unjustly accused of murder; the "cat-and-mouse" plot lends a "Hitchcockian" feel to the proceedings while Ford and Jones deliver "pitch-perfect performances."

Full Metal Jacket   24 | 25 | 22 | 25
1987. Directed by Stanley Kubrick. With Matthew Modine, Adam Baldwin, Vincent D'Onofrio. 116 minutes. Rated R.
"Kubrick does Vietnam" in this "intense" war picture that's really "two amazing films in one": first up is the "disturbingly funny" depiction of "boot-camp" basic training, followed by an abrupt about-face to the "total hell" of the front-line war; "first-rate production and acting" keep things "compelling" throughout, even if peaceniks feel the "uneven" second half is a tad too "violent."

Full Monty, The   22 | 22 | 24 | 19
1997. Directed by Peter Cattaneo. With Robert Carlyle, Mark Addy, Tom Wilkinson. 91 minutes. Rated R.
Out-of-work, out-of-shape blokes put together a "Chippendale's-type" strip act as a "creative response to unemployment" in this "riotous" English comedy that mixes "bumps and grinds" with "serious social themes"; its "enthusiastic" if "unknown" ensemble cast shake their booties to a "terrific" pop soundtrack, though most prefer it "with subtitles" to decipher those "British accents."

Funny Face   24 | 24 | 21 | 25
1957. Directed by Stanley Donen. With Audrey Hepburn, Fred Astaire, Kay Thompson. 103 minutes. Not Rated.
"Cinderella" goes to Paris in this "fashion industry musical" wherein a "gracefully aging", "debonair" Astaire turns a "bookish" Hepburn into an "ethereal", "luminous" supermodel; despite "no story to speak of", it's "thoroughly enchanting" thanks to "magic" dancing and Gershwin's "s'wonderfully" "dreamy" score; best number: Thompson's "steal-the-movie" rendition of 'Think Pink.'

Funny Girl ✉❶   26 | 25 | 24 | 26
1968. Directed by William Wyler. With Barbra Streisand, Omar Sharif, Walter Pidgeon. 151 minutes. Rated G.
"Hello, gorgeous!"; Babs' "big movie debut" in one of the "last great traditional Hollywood musicals" made her the "greatest

star" thanks to some "chutzpah", some "charm" and a voice "like buttah"; indeed, her Oscar-winning turn as comedienne Fanny Brice is so "socko" that it's easy to ignore the "schmaltzy" plot about the "man who got away."

Funny Lady
15 | 17 | 14 | 18

1975. Directed by Herbert Ross. With Barbra Streisand, James Caan, Omar Sharif. 136 minutes. Rated PG.

This "not-as-good follow-up to *Funny Girl*" (they should have "quit while they were ahead") strikes some as a Streisand "vanity production" trying to "milk the success" of the original, with "everything in excess – except the story and acting"; on the positive side, there are a couple of "sparkling Kander and Ebb" tunes.

Funny Thing Happened on the Way to the Forum, A
22 | 22 | 21 | 20

1966. Directed by Richard Lester. With Zero Mostel, Phil Silvers, Buster Keaton. 99 minutes. Not Rated.

For "comedy tonight", try this "total farce" of a musical that depicts Ancient Rome as a freewheeling toga party; sure, "Zero's the greatest" at provoking "laugh after laugh", but fans of the "quite different" stage version find it "stupid" "schlock" with "a lot lost in the translation to the screen."

Fury ◑
▽ 25 | 25 | 25 | 23

1936. Directed by Fritz Lang. With Spencer Tracy, Sylvia Sidney, Bruce Cabot. 90 minutes. Not Rated.

"Paranoia master" Lang's first American film, this "chilling depiction of mob violence and collective hysteria" remains "as fresh today as it was in 1936" thanks to the director's "skillful manipulation of sympathies"; a "nice and bitter" Tracy is its lynchpin, playing a "morally ambiguous" everyman caught up in a "social tragedy."

Gallipoli
25 | 25 | 25 | 24

1981. Directed by Peter Weir. With Mel Gibson, Mark Lee, Bill Kerr, David Argue. 110 minutes. Rated PG.

A "fresh-faced" Gibson "comes of age" as an actor in this "oh-so-sad war movie" about a "disastrous WWI" battle in Turkey that points out the "pointlessness" of combat; "one of the best of the Australian New Wave" films, it winds up with a "10-hanky tragic ending" that "tugs at the heartstrings without being corny."

GANDHI ✉
27 | 28 | 27 | 27

1982. Directed by Richard Attenborough. With Ben Kingsley, Candice Bergen, Edward Fox. 188 minutes. Rated PG.

"Big Hollywood at its best", this "meticulously detailed" bio of the Indian leader is "*The Ten Commandments* of the '80s", "long but riveting" and "emotionally wrenching"; Kingsley's "searing", Oscar-winning portrayal of the figure "who brought the British Empire to its knees" is the movie's "glorious centerpiece", and if a few find it "ponderous" and "overblown", there's no debate that it "captures the spiritual essence of the man perfectly."

Gangs of New York
21 | 23 | 20 | 25

2002. Directed by Martin Scorsese. With Leonardo DiCaprio, Daniel Day-Lewis, Cameron Diaz. 166 minutes. Rated R.

The "corrupt world" of "Civil War–era New York" is the backdrop for this "bloody good" "love and revenge" picture via Martin Scorsese that's "overwhelming visually" but "wholly uneven" plotwise; cynics skewer the "unnecessary violence", "moldy love story" and "way too long" running time, while fans counter Day-Lewis' "vivid" performance is the picture's "saving grace"; in sum, "flawed, but worth it."

Garden of the Finzi-Continis, The ✉🅵 | 25 | 24 | 27 | 25 |
1971. Directed by Vittorio De Sica. With Dominique Sanda, Lino Capolicchio, Helmut Berger. 94 minutes. Rated R.
"Complacency leads to disaster" in this "haunting" WWII drama about "upper-class Italian Jews" who "close their eyes to the looming evil" of fascism by believing that "money and position will insulate them"; "gripping and emotional", it's notable for making the "beautiful" young Sanda a star.

Garden State | 22 | 23 | 21 | 20 |
2004. Directed by Zach Braff. With Zach Braff, Natalie Portman, Peter Sarsgaard. 102 minutes. Rated R.
Think of it as "*The Graduate* for a new century": this "quirky" dramedy directed, written and starring Zach Braff is pitched to "disillusioned twentysomethings" with its depiction of the ultimate "quarter-life crisis sufferer"; despite mixed notices for the "enchanting" (or "annoying") Portman and catcalls for that "fake Hollywood ending", it's worth renting for the "kick-ass soundtrack" alone.

Gaslight ✉◐ | 26 | 27 | 26 | 24 |
1944. Directed by George Cukor. With Ingrid Bergman, Charles Boyer, Joseph Cotten. 114 minutes. Not Rated.
Anything but light, this "high-tension" thriller stars a "glowing", Oscar-winning Bergman as a newlywed who thinks she's "going insane – or is she?"; "mesmerized" fans say the "original" storyline "maintains the suspense to the end", helped by an atmospheric "Victorian setting" and a particularly "villainous villain" in Boyer; P.S. look for a "very young Angela Lansbury" in her screen debut.

Gay Divorcee, The ◑ ▽ | 22 | 19 | 17 | 23 |
1934. Directed by Mark Sandrich. With Fred Astaire, Ginger Rogers, Edward Everett Horton. 107 minutes. Not Rated.
"No one could dance like Fred and Ginger", and this footloose '30s musical "whirls" with production numbers "par excellence" as Rogers plays a spouse untying the knot in high style as Astaire duly falls into step; the "silly story" is trumped by the "dreamy" tunes and, of course, that terpsichorean team-up "can't be beat."

General, The ◑ | 28 | 27 | 26 | 27 |
1927. Directed by Clyde Bruckman, Buster Keaton. With Buster Keaton, Marion Mack. 75 minutes. Not Rated.
One of the "most remarkable" silent films, this pioneering effort "establishes gags still used today" in its story of a Civil War–era Southern engineer in relentless, hapless pursuit of a stolen locomotive; the "Great Stoneface's" most "ambitious" work, it also incorporates some "amazing physical comedy" (Keaton "does all his own stunts") that must be "seen to be believed."

Gentleman's Agreement ✉◐ ▽ | 25 | 26 | 27 | 23 |
1947. Directed by Elia Kazan. With Gregory Peck, Dorothy McGuire, Celeste Holm. 118 minutes. Not Rated.
A once-"controversial exposé" of "American anti-Semitism", this "earnest" "message drama" offers Peck in a "wonderfully emo-

tional" turn as an investigative reporter who passes himself off as Jewish and becomes a first-hand witness to "subtle prejudice"; if the final result seems a bit "dated" and "simplistic" today, it's still "interesting" as an early attempt at social criticism.

Gentlemen Prefer Blondes

23 | 21 | 20 | 24

1953. Directed by Howard Hawks. With Jane Russell, Marilyn Monroe, Charles Coburn. 91 minutes. Rated PG.

You'll probably prefer Monroe's "ingenious, ingenuous" "dumb blonde" to the "nonexistent storyline" in this "guilty-pleasure" musical comedy, a "deliciously over-the-top" story of "gold diggers" on the make made all the more vivid in "spectacular Technicolor"; it's "one for the time capsule", if only for Marilyn's "dazzling", iconic rendition of 'Diamonds Are a Girl's Best Friend.'

George of the Jungle

17 | 16 | 16 | 17

1997. Directed by Sam Weisman. With Brendan Fraser, Leslie Mann, Thomas Haden Church. 91 minutes. Rated PG.

Young chimps and big apes who "remember the cartoon" have "goofy fun" with this comedy featuring "Fraser in a loincloth" as a "moronic", secondhand Tarzan; cynics say Disney grabs for the vine and "falls short", but it is "surprisingly entertaining", even if the theme ditty will stay "in your head for days."

Getaway, The

22 | 22 | 21 | 21

1972. Directed by Sam Peckinpah. With Steve McQueen, Ali MacGraw, Ben Johnson. 122 minutes. Rated PG.

"Steve and Ali sizzle" with their "onscreen (and offscreen) love affair" in this "essential" "crime spree road trip" flick about an ex-con and his missus "on the run from basically everyone they know"; McQueen is his "usual stoic yet likable self", MacGraw's deliciously "icy" and director Peckinpah provides enough "slo-mo" action to make for "exciting B-movie" thrills.

Ghost ✉

21 | 21 | 22 | 21

1990. Directed by Jerry Zucker. With Patrick Swayze, Demi Moore, Whoopi Goldberg. 128 minutes. Rated PG-13.

There's "action for the boys and romance for the girls" in this comic "tearjerker" that's got "hot date movie" written all over it; sure, its story of a dead man watching over his surviving lover is "improbable" (and "sappy and manipulative", according to cynics), yet Moore and Swayze make it seem so "sexy", while the "priceless", Oscar-winning Goldberg "delivers the laughs."

Ghost and Mrs. Muir, The ◑

24 | 25 | 25 | 22

1947. Directed by Joseph L. Mankiewicz. With Rex Harrison, Gene Tierney, George Sanders. 104 minutes. Not Rated.

This "timeless" fantasy details the unlikely "love story" between a widow and a "crusty old" sea captain who's "full of life" – even though he's a ghost; the "otherworldly" romance that ensues avoids being "sentimental goop" thanks to "superb performances" from Tierney, Harrison and little "eight-year-old Natalie Wood."

Ghostbusters ⓫

21 | 18 | 21 | 23

1984. Directed by Ivan Reitman. With Bill Murray, Dan Aykroyd, Sigourney Weaver, Harold Ramis. 107 minutes. Rated PG.

"Kooky, spooky" and flat-out "funny", this "classic '80s" "sci-fi comedy" about 'paranormal investigators' banishing ghosts from

NYC is "one of the best stupid movies ever", so "not much thinking is required"; "wonderful special effects" and a brilliantly "sarcastic Murray" are its highlights, though its most lasting achievement is that it "made the word 'slime' into a verb."

Ghost World   23 | 26 | 22 | 21
2001. Directed by Terry Zwigoff. With Thora Birch, Steve Buscemi, Scarlett Johansson. 111 minutes. Rated R.
A "witty" look at two "nonconformist" girls in a "homogenized" suburb, this "random" comedy is a "nice departure from the typical teen angst film"; the "quirky" characters sport "great thrift-store clothes", while the "phenomenal Buscemi" is "pitch-perfect."

Giant ⊠   24 | 23 | 24 | 24
1956. Directed by George Stevens. With Elizabeth Taylor, Rock Hudson, James Dean, Dennis Hopper. 201 minutes. Rated G.
As "sprawling" as the Lone Star state itself, this "all-out wonderful" Texas "epic" about money, love and oil "burns with star power", featuring some mighty "big names" – Liz, Rock and Jimmy (in his last role) – "in their prime"; cynics say this "way too long" example of "Hollywood bloat" is just "cornball hooey", but fans insist this "colossal '50s production" "holds your interest."

Gigi ⊠   24 | 23 | 23 | 26
1958. Directed by Vincente Minnelli. With Leslie Caron, Maurice Chevalier, Louis Jourdan. 119 minutes. Rated G.
"Thank heaven" for this "fine rendering" of Lerner and Loewe, an "unorthodox love story" about a "turn-of-the-century" Parisian courtesan and the client who wants to marry her; winner of nine Oscars, this "stunner" boasts a "radiant" Caron, suave Jourdan and "*amusant*" Chevalier, so even if the end result might look like a "lavish" wad of "cotton candy", "just give in" and enjoy it.

Gilda ◐   24 | 23 | 21 | 23
1946. Directed by Charles Vidor. With Rita Hayworth, Glenn Ford, George Macready. 110 minutes. Not Rated.
Noir was never more "delectable" than in this "solid" love triangle starring a "delicious" "Hayworth in her signature role" as the "glamorous", hair-tossing Gilda; though her "modified striptease" in the 'Put the Blame on Mame' number is the "only reason to see it" for some, others find enough "mystery and suspense" to make it "memorable."

Gimme Shelter   25 | – | 21 | 22
1970. Directed by Albert Maysles, David Maysles, Charlotte Zwerin. Documentary. With The Rolling Stones. 91 minutes. Rated R.
Originally commissioned by the Rolling Stones as a "simple concert" flick, this "rockumentary" took on a "darker side" after filmmakers inadvertently recorded a "real murder" at the group's infamous Altamont gig; the result is a "grim, gritty look" at the "turbulent '60s" "spiraling out of control", with a "complicated storyline" and "classic" soundtrack that put modern "music videos to shame"; hottest moment: the "amazing" Tina Turner at the mike.

Girl, Interrupted   18 | 22 | 18 | 18
1999. Directed by James Mangold. With Winona Ryder, Angelina Jolie, Brittany Murphy. 127 minutes. Rated R.
"Haunting if overwrought" drama providing a "hair-raising glimpse" inside a mental institution headlining a "convincing"

Ryder as a "troubled" patient, though Jolie "steals the show" portraying the "sexiest crazy person" ever captured on film; fans insist it's a "compelling" "emotional trip", but others say it's so insanely "soapy" that it "should have been a 'Cosmo' article."

Girl with a Pearl Earring

21 | 23 | 19 | 25

2003. Directed by Peter Webber. With Colin Firth, Scarlett Johansson, Tom Wilkinson. 95 minutes. Rated PG-13.
A "true art movie", this "beautifully photographed" period piece set in 17th-century "bourgeois Holland" is based on a Vermeer painting (and a novel of the same name) and explores the artist's "possible relationship" with a "lovely muse" played by Johansson, "who wows with her nearly wordless performance" as his "shy" servant; though the "slow" pacing is "like watching paint dry", enough "sexual tension abounds" to keep the interest level up.

GLADIATOR ✉

23 | 23 | 22 | 27

2000. Directed by Ridley Scott. With Russell Crowe, Joaquin Phoenix, Oliver Reed, Richard Harris. 155 minutes. Rated R.
"Everything a big Hollywood blockbuster should be", this "old-fashioned" "sword-and-sandal" extravaganza features lots of "action, adventure and backstabbing" in its story of a Roman general turned wretched slave; the "intense", Oscar-winning Crowe oozes "testosterone" and the "lavish re-creation of Ancient Rome" brings the "Coliseum to life", but thumbs-downers dismiss it as "bombastic beefcake."

Glengarry Glen Ross

23 | 27 | 22 | 20

1992. Directed by James Foley. With Al Pacino, Jack Lemmon, Ed Harris, Alec Baldwin. 100 minutes. Rated R.
"High-pressure" real-estate salesmen "with an axe about to fall on their jobs" get the David Mamet treatment in this "dark" drama about the "predatory world of business"; its "talky", expletive-laden scenario can be "disturbing", but ultimately it "shows what can be done with a small cast, limited sets and Godzilla talent."

Gloria

22 | 26 | 22 | 20

1980. Directed by John Cassavetes. With Gena Rowlands, John Adames, Buck Henry. 123 minutes. Rated PG.
A "retired gun moll" and a six-year-old orphan go "on the run from the mob" in this "gritty" Cassavetes drama that manages to be both hard-boiled and "surprisingly moving" (with a "mystery ending" to boot); similarly, "tough cookie" Gena ranges from "fierce" to "maternal" in the "kick-butt" title turn.

Glory

25 | 26 | 26 | 26

1989. Directed by Edward Zwick. With Matthew Broderick, Denzel Washington, Morgan Freeman. 122 minutes. Rated R.
Based on the "true tale" about the "first black Civil War regiment and the white Union officer who led them", this "period piece" is a fine "evocation of a story few people know"; expect "great battle scenes", even if it "doesn't end the way you want it to."

GODFATHER, THE ✉⓫

29 | 29 | 29 | 29

1972. Directed by Francis Ford Coppola. With Marlon Brando, Al Pacino, Diane Keaton, Robert Duvall, James Caan, John Cazale. 175 minutes. Rated R.
Perhaps the "best three hours you can spend sitting still", this "ultimate gangster film" and "cultural phenomenon" is ranked

both Top Overall and Most Popular film in this *Survey*; an "absolutely flawless" "American epic", it recounts the "operatic" lives of the Corleone family via an "intricate" plot, "bravura photography" and "iconic performances" from Brando and Pacino; in fact, the end result is so "killer" that "nothing else comes close – except maybe the sequel"; favorite line: "leave the gun, take the cannoli."

GODFATHER PART II, THE ✉ 🅤   29 | 29 | 28 | 29

1974. Directed by Francis Ford Coppola. With Al Pacino, Robert Duvall, Diane Keaton, Robert De Niro, John Cazale. 200 minutes. Rated R.
A "real rarity – a sequel as good as the original" – this "true masterpiece" "stands on its own laurels" as it "delves deeper into the Corleone family" saga; a "moody meditation on the emptiness of power", its "complex" plot "masterfully intercuts" two stories separated by a half-century into a "taut", "heartbreaking tale of innocence lost", and though "never overshadowing its big brother", it just might be "even more subtle and sublime"; most chilling moment: the "kiss between Michael and Fredo."

Godfather Part III, The   16 | 18 | 16 | 21

1990. Directed by Francis Ford Coppola. With Al Pacino, Diane Keaton, Talia Shire, Andy Garcia. 161 minutes. Rated R.
"Conspiracy, mayhem, opera, revenge": the "prime American" crime "saga" concludes with this "flawed" but "watchable" sequel as Pacino's don Michael aims to take the Corleones legit, despite beefs from both the old guard and his own clan; though it's a "must-see" for diehards, some say the "forced" plotting and "miscasting" ("two words: Sofia Coppola") are a "disgrace to the Family"; in short, it doesn't fill the "enormous shoes" of I and II.

Gods and Monsters ✉   23 | 27 | 23 | 22

1998. Directed by Bill Condon. With Ian McKellen, Brendan Fraser, Lynn Redgrave. 105 minutes. Rated R.
McKellen's "brilliant" performance is the backbone of this "innovative biopic" detailing an "encounter between a hedge clipper and a has-been" moviemaker that's based on the life of 1930s "gay director" James Whale; partisans point to the Oscar-winning script as proof of why "indie films are such a delight."

Gods Must Be Crazy, The 🅤   22 | 17 | 23 | 18

1981. Directed by Jamie Uys. With Marius Weyers, Sandra Prinsloo, N!xau. 109 minutes. Rated PG.
"Consumerism meets primitive African bushmen" when a Coke bottle "falls out of the sky" in this "cult" "culture-clash" comedy that "proves you don't need a big Hollywood budget" to be "original and witty"; despite bare-bones production and middling acting, this "diamond in the rough" still exhibits "universal appeal" thanks to "creative" ideas and "more sight gags than the Marx Brothers."

Godzilla ◑ 🅤   16 | 10 | 16 | 14

1956. Directed by Terry Morse, Ishiro Honda. With Raymond Burr, Takashi Shimura. 80 minutes. Not Rated.
The menace of the atom age hovers over this sci-fi "classic" about a colossal, radiation-spawned lizard who rises up to become the "prototypical city-destroying" beast, doing the "monster mash" through a model-train-gauge Tokyo; "laugh if you want" at the "camp-to-the-max" "Japanese footage" (with "Burr spliced in"), but the "bleak, creepy" A-bomb "echoes" throughout still have a "hold over our imaginations."

Going My Way ✉ ◑ ⓤ
▽ 21 | 19 | 21 | 18

1944. Directed by Leo McCarey. With Bing Crosby, Barry Fitzgerald, Risë Stevens. 126 minutes. Not Rated.

"Sing along with Bing" in this "hokey but pleasant" musical drama showcasing Crosby "at his best" as a "popular priest" with heavenly pipes who converts a parish house choir to his feel-good philosophy; though multiple Oscars came its way, it looks "very dated" now since they "stopped making" this brand of "engaging schmaltz" "long ago."

GoldenEye
19 | 19 | 19 | 23

1995. Directed by Martin Campbell. With Pierce Brosnan, Sean Bean, Famke Janssen. 130 minutes. Rated PG-13.

"Born to play the part" of the "never-fazed secret agent", Pierce Brosnan brings the 007 "franchise" "back from the dead" with an ultra-"suave" turn opposite Janssen's "great villainess" in this "modern Bond" flick; though the "convoluted storyline" (something having to do with globe-busting weaponry in post-Soviet Russia) is a "little clunky", overall it "gets the job done" with "outstanding action", "amazing special effects" and a "refreshing lack of hokeyness."

GOLDFINGER
26 | 23 | 25 | 25

1964. Directed by Guy Hamilton. With Sean Connery, Honor Blackman, Gert Frobe. 112 minutes. Rated PG.

Rated the Top 007 picture in this *Survey,* this "classic" has it all: "formidable villains", the "coolest gadgets", an "out-of-this-world", "robbing-Fort-Knox" plot, a "fabulous theme song" "belted out by Shirley Bassey" and perhaps the "best-named" babe of them all, the one-and-only "Pussy Galore"; most memorable exchange: "do you expect me to talk? – no, Mr. Bond, I expect you to *die!*"

Gold Rush, The ◑
▽ 28 | 28 | 26 | 27

1925. Directed by Charles Chaplin. With Charles Chaplin, Mack Swain. 82 minutes. Not Rated.

Chaplin's "amazing talent" (as a writer, director and actor) is evident in this "brilliant" silent flicker, featuring the Little Tramp as a prospector "fighting the elements in the Klondike" and "overcoming all hurdles to get the girl" – and the gold; rife with "classic sequences" (the "bread-roll dance", the boiled "shoe for dinner", the cabin teetering on the edge of a cliff), it doesn't need dialogue "to evoke both laughter and pathos" – indeed, over 80 years later, many report a "lasting emotional impact."

GONE WITH THE WIND ✉
28 | 27 | 27 | 29

1939. Directed by Victor Fleming. With Clark Gable, Vivien Leigh, Leslie Howard, Olivia de Havilland, Hattie McDaniel, Butterfly McQueen. 238 minutes. Rated G.

A bona fide piece of "American pop culture", this Civil War melodrama based on Margaret Mitchell's "beloved" book is a "timeless", "sweeping", saga of love and loss in dwindling Dixieland; frankly, legions of admirers "do give a damn", rating it an "epic with a capital E" for its incredibly "beautiful production", "amazing" costumes and "perfect cast", especially Gable's "dashing" Rhett and Leigh's "performance of a lifetime" as the "feisty", "fiddle-dee-deeing" Scarlett; sure, it's a "long sit", yet in the end this "gorgeous triumph" "still thrills."

Goodbye, Columbus
19 | 19 | 20 | 19

1969. Directed by Larry Peerce. With Richard Benjamin, Ali MacGraw, Jack Klugman. 102 minutes. Rated PG.
Based on Philip Roth's once-provocative novella, this frank romantic comedy "might seem dated" now, but nostalgists remember its "good performances", especially MacGraw's tour-de-force turn as a "crush"-worthy "Jewish princess"; foes say that it "should have been better", considering the source material.

Goodbye Girl, The ✉
21 | 23 | 20 | 20

1977. Directed by Herbert Ross. With Richard Dreyfuss, Marsha Mason, Paul Benedict. 110 minutes. Rated PG.
"Exactly what a romantic comedy should be", this "feel-good movie" is about a "likable", lovelorn single mom forced to share an apartment with an unlikable, "lovable actor"; one of "Neil Simon's best" screenplays, this surprise hit garnered a clutch of Oscar nominations and won one for Dreyfuss' "charismatic" turn.

Goodbye, Mr. Chips ✉◑
▽ 25 | 25 | 25 | 22

1939. Directed by Sam Wood. With Robert Donat, Greer Garson, Paul Henreid. 114 minutes. Not Rated.
More proof for the theory that "1939 was the best film year ever", this "touching" tale depicting 40 years in the life of everyone's "favorite" British schoolmaster is an unabashedly "sentimental story that will leave nary an eye dry"; credit "wonderful turns" from both Garson (in her screen debut) and Donat (who copped an Oscar) for making this "classic" "withstand the test of time."

GOODFELLAS
27 | 27 | 26 | 25

1990. Directed by Martin Scorsese. With Robert De Niro, Ray Liotta, Joe Pesci. 146 minutes. Rated R.
"Not for the faint of heart", "mob-master" Scorsese's "harrowing modern gangster" classic careens from "hysterically funny to terrifyingly violent" owing to an "electrifying" screenplay based on the true story of "'made' guys and greed" that reveals "mobsters as human beings" – albeit "vicious and heartless" ones; "beautiful lensing" and "stellar performances" make this one boil with "brutal power."

Good Girl, The
18 | 22 | 17 | 17

2002. Directed by Miguel Arteta. With Jennifer Aniston, Jake Gyllenhaal, Zooey Deschanel, John C. Reilly. 93 minutes. Rated R.
"Escaping the dreariness of real life" is the theme of this "downbeat" dramedy about a "disillusioned" shopgirl living in "Nowheresville" and "dreaming of better things"; it's "better than it had any right to be" thanks to Jake's "childish charm" and Jen's "nuanced", "low-key" work – there is "life after *Friends*" – even if foes find it "slow going" and saddled with an "oversupply of angst."

Good Morning, Vietnam
22 | 24 | 22 | 22

1987. Directed by Barry Levinson. With Robin Williams, Forest Whitaker, Bruno Kirby. 119 minutes. Rated R.
Get a "different perspective on the Vietnam war" from this "bittersweet" tale of an army radio DJ in Saigon that "strikes just the right balance between comedy and drama", capturing the "reality" while still provoking beaucoup "laughs"; Williams "at his manic best" not only supplies the expected "hilarious ad-libbing" but shows off some "impressive acting skills" too.

GOOD NIGHT, AND GOOD LUCK ◑   25 | 27 | 24 | 26

2005. Directed by George Clooney. With David Strathairn, George Clooney, Robert Downey Jr. 93 minutes. Rated PG.
"History doesn't get much better" than George Clooney's re-creation of the "tense", "smoke-filled" ambiance of CBS's 1950s-era newsroom, scene of an "intriguing showdown" between Senator Joseph McCarthy and broadcaster Edward R. Murrow ("they don't make journalists like that anymore"); crackling with "sharp dialogue" and blessed with a "sterling cast" headlined by the "phenomenal" Strathairn, it raises enough "thoughtful criticism" to incite "discussion about government censorship."

Good, the Bad and the Ugly, The   24 | 21 | 23 | 23

1967. Directed by Sergio Leone. With Clint Eastwood, Lee Van Cleef, Eli Wallach. 161 minutes. Rated R.
A "delicious spaghetti Western" drenched in "tasty dramatic marinara sauce", this Clint-essential "Man-With-No-Name" oater about a trio of Civil War–era gunmen battling over Confederate treasure is a "true classic"; sure, Eastwood's "penetrating glare" is "hypnotic", but some say Wallach "steals the show" by injecting some "subtle comedy" into the mix, while composer Ennio Morricone's "memorable score" will "stick in your head for days."

GOOD WILL HUNTING ✉   24 | 25 | 24 | 22

1997. Directed by Gus Van Sant. With Robin Williams, Matt Damon, Ben Affleck. 126 minutes. Rated R.
Written by the "then-unknown" team of Damon and Affleck, this "intelligent" drama is built on an "uplifting", "powerful" screenplay about a "troubled petty criminal" who's coincidentally a "brilliant math genius"; its "searing yet subtle" performances include an Oscar-winning turn from Williams at his "most moving", and though the ill-willed badmouth it as "predictable", overall most folks "like them apples."

Goonies, The   23 | 19 | 23 | 21

1985. Directed by Richard Donner. With Sean Astin, Josh Brolin, Corey Feldman. 114 minutes. Rated PG.
One of the "best kids' adventures ever", this "smart, finely crafted" "family movie" about a gang of "pre-teen treasure hunters" who wield "go-go gadgets" and thwart bad guys is a fun "roller-coaster ride" "for all ages" (and a bona fide "nostalgia" trip for "Gen-Xers"); ok, it may have "some flaws", but at least it "doesn't take itself too seriously."

Gorillas in the Mist   19 | 21 | 20 | 21

1988. Directed by Michael Apted. With Sigourney Weaver, Bryan Brown, Julie Harris. 129 minutes. Rated PG-13.
"African jungles" supply the "beautiful setting" in this bio of primatologist Dian Fossey, the story of a complex woman who abandons humanity in favor of a group of endangered mountain gorillas; Weaver delivers a "great performance", and the special effects blend real and artificial apes seamlessly.

Gosford Park ✉   23 | 27 | 21 | 25

2001. Directed by Robert Altman. With Clive Owen, Alan Bates, Maggie Smith, Helen Mirren, Kristin Scott Thomas. 137 minutes. Rated R.
"Agatha Christie meets *Upstairs, Downstairs*" in this "jolly good show" of a "whodunit" that's an "insightful", "behind-the-scenes

skewering of the British class system" set in a "'30s country estate";
"one of Altman's best", it boasts "rich atmosphere", "scintillating
dialogue" and a "bloody great" ensemble cast all "acting up a
storm", and if contrarians complain about its "convoluted", "hard-
to-follow" plot, fans claim it "gets better every time you see it."

Gothika
17 | 19 | 17 | 19

*2003. Directed by Mathieu Kassovitz. With Halle Berry, Robert
Downey Jr., Penélope Cruz. 98 minutes. Rated R.*
Surveyors split on this "supernatural thriller" in which a shrink in a
psycho ward wakes up one day to find herself an inmate accused of
murder: fans praise the "heebie-jeebie"-inducing cinematography
and "keeps-you-guessing" plot, but foes find "very few scares"
in this "standard" effort – even the "hot Halle can't heat it up."

GRADUATE, THE ✉
27 | 27 | 26 | 24

*1967. Directed by Mike Nichols. With Dustin Hoffman, Anne Bancroft,
Katharine Ross. 105 minutes. Rated PG.*
The "benchmark coming-of-age comedy", this "knowing" look at
a "confused young man" and his "older seductress" is the "definitive '60s alienation" flick and "somehow never ages"; credit
its "witty script", Mike Nichols' "ahead-of-its-time direction", a
"groovy" Simon-and-Garfunkel soundtrack and "superb" turns
from the "fab" Hoffman and the "unforgettable" Bancroft as –
"koo-koo-ka-choo" – Mrs. Robinson; best word: "plastics."

Grand Canyon
18 | 21 | 18 | 18

*1991. Directed by Lawrence Kasdan. With Danny Glover, Kevin
Kline, Steve Martin, Mary McDonnell. 134 minutes. Rated R.*
In this ambitious "meaning-of-life" drama, director Kasdan brings
together a group of "average people leading average lives" to tell
some "extraordinary stories" about "destiny and hope"; though
some find the "fragmented" result too "out there", most allow that
this "surprisingly moving" moving picture "just misses being great."

Grand Hotel ✉◑
▽ 24 | 25 | 22 | 25

*1932. Directed by Edmund Goulding. With Greta Garbo, John Barrymore,
Joan Crawford, Lionel Barrymore. 112 minutes. Not Rated.*
"Intertwined lives" are the basis of this star-studded "early MGM
talkie", one of the first multicharacter dramas set in a hotel; in addi-
tion to its "sumptuous" production and "literate" screenplay, it's en-
dured thanks to a "brilliant" cast, particularly an "amazing"
Crawford, the "show-stealing" Barrymores and the "breathtaking"
Garbo", who utters her most famous line here: "I vant to be alone."

Grand Illusion ◑F
28 | 28 | 27 | 26

*1938. Directed by Jean Renoir. With Jean Gabin, Erich von Stroheim,
Pierre Fresnay. 114 minutes. Not Rated.*
"It's no illusion": this "compelling" WWI "masterpiece" has "inspired generations" with its "crushing portrayal of the futility of
war" and is "still as powerful as ever"; Renoir "shows how it should
be done" in this "ahead-of-its-time" picture that's on "everyone's
greatest list" simply because it "touches on every human emotion."

GRAPES OF WRATH, THE ✉◑
28 | 28 | 28 | 25

*1940. Directed by John Ford. With Henry Fonda, Jane Darwell,
John Carradine. 128 minutes. Not Rated.*
"Every frame is a work of art" in this "faithful rendition" of
Steinbeck's "eloquent" novel about dispossessed Depression-

era farmers living through "desperate" times; quite possibly "Ford's best", it's a "classic for a reason" and "ranks high on the list of great American films" as an "important statement about life", the "depth of man's sorrow and the zenith of man's spirit."

GREASE ⓫ | 23 | 19 | 21 | 23 |
1978. Directed by Randal Kleiser. With John Travolta, Olivia Newton-John, Stockard Channing. 110 minutes. Rated PG.
"Fun" is the word for this "campy" comedy "classic", a "high-energy" "adaptation of the Broadway musical" that's a "'70s take on a "hokey '50s" story enacted by some of the "oldest high-school students ever"; still, the "hunky Travolta" and "stunning Newton-John" "light up the screen", and the "slick production" numbers are so "irresistible" that "cult followers" watch this "guilty pleasure" "over and over."

Great Dictator, The ◑ | 26 | 27 | 25 | 23 |
1940. Directed by Charles Chaplin. With Charles Chaplin, Jack Oakie, Paulette Goddard. 124 minutes. Not Rated.
The normally "silent Chaplin" "fearlessly" takes "aim at Hitler" in this rare talkie, a "scathing satire of fascist tyranny" in which he "plays two roles": a Jewish barber and "rabid" dictator Adenoid Hynkel, a "brilliant parody" of Der Führer; although "overly sentimental" and "preachy" to some, most find this "masterpiece of physical comedy" "thought-provoking and perpetually relevant."

GREAT ESCAPE, THE | 27 | 26 | 27 | 26 |
1963. Directed by John Sturges. With Steve McQueen, James Garner, Richard Attenborough. 169 minutes. Not Rated.
"Guy movies don't get any better" than this "absorbing" "prison break" flick "based on a true escape" from a WWII "German war camp"; featuring McQueen backed up by an "all-star" ensemble, it also boasts "excellent writing", a "hummable score" and "flawless action" scenes, including the "best motorcycle scene ever filmed"; though on the "long" side, it's "worth every minute."

GREAT EXPECTATIONS ◑ | 27 | 27 | 28 | 26 |
1947. Directed by David Lean. With John Mills, Valerie Hobson, Alec Guinness, Jean Simmons. 118 minutes. Not Rated.
A "pip of a movie", David Lean's "superb realization" of Dickens' novel about an orphan and his mysterious benefactor is a "masterpiece in every sense of the word"; it's "hauntingly shot" in "living black and white", and memorable moments include the "stunning graveyard sequence", Miss Havisham's "cobwebby wedding table" and "wonderful early performances by Simmons and Guinness"; in sum, "when they talk about a classic, this is what they mean."

Great Gatsby, The | 22 | 22 | 24 | 23 |
1974. Directed by Jack Clayton. With Robert Redford, Mia Farrow, Bruce Dern, Karen Black, Sam Waterston. 144 minutes. Rated PG.
"Wealth doesn't buy happiness" in this "opulent" adaptation of Scott Fitzgerald's classic 1920s novel that's sure "gorgeous to look at" but otherwise splits surveyors: fans feel its "gangster-in-love" story is "wonderfully mounted" and the "hot blond" Redford and "luminous" Farrow are "superbly cast", but opponents say "overblown", "shallow" and distinctly "bottom drawer, old sport."

Great Race, The
20 | 18 | 20 | 20

1965. Directed by Blake Edwards. With Jack Lemmon, Tony Curtis, Natalie Wood, Peter Falk. 150 minutes. Not Rated.
Director Edwards revs up the engines in this "kitschy" "family" comedy about a turn-of-the-century auto race from NY to Paris, with plenty of "must-see" settings along the way; a tip-top cast supplies "over-the-top" performances, but the pièce de résistance is the "best pie fight in movie history"; in a word, it's a "hoot."

Great Santini, The
22 | 27 | 21 | 21

1979. Directed by Lewis John Carlino. With Robert Duvall, Blythe Danner, Michael O'Keefe. 115 minutes. Rated PG.
"Adapted from the painful Pat Conroy novel", this intense "dissection" of a "dysfunctional family" offers a "look inside the mind" of a "domineering" marine – "outstandingly" played by the "frighteningly good Duvall" – who treats his wife and kids like soldiers under his command; you'll "love him or hate him (or maybe both)", but in any event his "imperfect life" will "stay with you."

Greed ◑∅
▽ 28 | 27 | 27 | 29

1925. Directed by Erich von Stroheim. With Gibson Gowland, ZaSu Pitts, Jean Hersholt. 140 minutes. Not Rated.
Originally "exceedingly long" (clocking in at 10 hours), this silent "tour de force" from Erich von Stroheim is famous for the studio's "hatchet job" to trim it to a commercially viable length; still, even in a "truncated" form, this "dark masterpiece" about a down-and-out dentist and his lottery-winning wife remains an exercise in "gritty realism", right down to that "stunning finale" in Death Valley.

Green Mile, The
23 | 25 | 23 | 24

1999. Directed by Frank Darabont. With Tom Hanks, David Morse, Michael Clarke Duncan. 188 minutes. Rated R.
Stephen King's "harrowing" serial novel is now "wonderfully translated to the screen" in this "disturbing drama" that "tugs at your emotions" with its "touching depiction" of "humanity at its best and worst"; despite "fine acting", this "very long" Mile makes some "wish it was an hour shorter."

Gremlins ⓫
19 | 14 | 20 | 20

1984. Directed by Joe Dante. With Zach Galligan, Phoebe Cates, Hoyt Axton. 106 minutes. Rated PG.
This "black comedy" features a "cuddly", "too-cute-for-words" pet who breeds "scary" offspring when exposed to bright light, water or being "fed after midnight"; although "lots of fun", some parents warn "proceed with caution": it has a "dark side", i.e. those "mean-spirited", "nightmare"-inducing gremlins who are too violent for smaller fry.

Greystoke: The Legend of Tarzan
15 | 14 | 17 | 19

1984. Directed by Hugh Hudson. With Christopher Lambert, Andie MacDowell, Ian Holm. 130 minutes. Rated PG.
Don't expect much monkey business in this "lush" drama, a "compelling retelling" of Edgar Rice Burroughs' ape-man tale that adds class-system critique and "animal welfare overtones" to the mix; there's plenty of "gorgeous" scenery as Lambert's jungle-bred hunk is introduced into English aristocracy, but even though it's "pretty to look at", many see an "overlong mess."

Grifters, The

22 26 23 21

1990. Directed by Stephen Frears. With Anjelica Huston, John Cusack, Annette Bening. 119 minutes. Rated R.

Despite "soulless characters" and a "cynical" theme, this very "adult" piece of "hard-core film noir" is a "first-class" study of "lowlife culture" (the "twisted" plot concerns a "mommy and her long-lost son who are reunited" only to "go down in flames"); while the "film gels" around the "powerhouse work of all three leads", some say the "real star" is "Donald Westlake's superb" script.

Groundhog Day

22 20 24 20

1993. Directed by Harold Ramis. With Bill Murray, Andie MacDowell, Chris Elliott. 101 minutes. Rated PG.

An "intelligent existential romp", this "literate comedy" has an "original concept": a "jerk" is forced to "live the same day over and over until he gets it right" and "becomes a lovable man"; ok, it's a "one-joke premise" that gets "tedious", but for most it "works like a charm" thanks to the "hilarious" Murray, who exchanges his "usual smart-ass" persona for something "surprisingly deep."

Grumpy Old Men ⊕

21 24 20 20

1993. Directed by Donald Petrie. With Jack Lemmon, Walter Matthau, Ann-Margret. 103 minutes. Rated PG-13.

Though "made for the *Murder, She Wrote*" set, this "lighthearted comedy" works for both "young and old", reuniting the "classic Matthau-and-Lemmon" team playing retired Minnesotans "vying for the affections" of a "comely" new neighbor (the "not-hard-to-watch Ann-Margret"); sure, "we've seen it all before", but these "well-loved icons" still provoke a "ton of laughs."

Guess Who's Coming to Dinner ✉

25 27 25 22

1967. Directed by Stanley Kramer. With Spencer Tracy, Sidney Poitier, Katharine Hepburn. 108 minutes. Not Rated.

"Daring for its day", this '60s "commentary on race relations" is the "final film of Hollywood's finest couple", "class acts Hepburn and Tracy", at their most "powerful"; sure, its "controversial subject" of "interracial marriage" might seem "dated" now, but its "poignant and charming" treatment assures that the "issues remain" relevant.

GUN CRAZY ◑

27 24 27 22

(aka Deadly Is the Female)
1949. Directed by Joseph H. Lewis. With Peggy Cummins, John Dall. 86 minutes. Not Rated.

"Eat your heart out, *Bonnie and Clyde*" – this "tight little thriller" about "gun-toting lovers on the run" is film noir at its most "brilliant" and "economical", despite its "B-list stars" and "zero-budget" budget; there's plenty of "subtly kinky" innuendo too, but it's best remembered for an "influential" robbery sequence, shot in one take from the backseat of a car.

Gunfight at the O.K. Corral

20 21 20 21

1957. Directed by John Sturges. With Burt Lancaster, Kirk Douglas, Rhonda Fleming. 122 minutes. Not Rated.

Always "entertaining", this Western recounts the famed 19th-century shoot-out between rival gangs in Tombstone, AZ; despite two Hollywood icons "playing off each other wonderfully" – the rugged Lancaster and the cleft-chinned Douglas – foes fume this "too-long" production doesn't "move the way it should."

Gunga Din ◑   25 | 24 | 25 | 24
1939. Directed by George Stevens. With Cary Grant, Victor McLaglen, Douglas Fairbanks Jr. 117 minutes. Not Rated.
This "rousing adventure flick" from "Hollywood's golden age" recounts the "golden age of the British Empire" via the "story of three soldiers in imperial India" and the titular native lad who befriends them; some snappy "byplay between Grant, McLaglen and Fairbanks" makes it a "buddy film" prototype, though a few are troubled by the "superior", "racist attitude" of the colonialists.

Guns of Navarone, The ⓫   23 | 22 | 24 | 23
1961. Directed by J. Lee Thompson. With Gregory Peck, David Niven, Anthony Quinn. 158 minutes. Rated PG.
"Even people who hate war movies love" this "star-studded" production about WWII Allied commandos plotting to destroy Nazi artillery; "pounding" suspense and a "splendid cast" put this action-adventurer "head-and-shoulders above" the rest – and that "climactic sequence" will have you "holding your breath."

Guys and Dolls   24 | 21 | 24 | 24
1955. Directed by Joseph L. Mankiewicz. With Marlon Brando, Jean Simmons, Frank Sinatra. 150 minutes. Not Rated.
"Brando sings!" in this "colorful" musical rendition of the "Damon Runyon stories" about "gamblers, evangelists" and racehorses, all dolled up into one "heavyweight" extravaganza set around Times Square, rife with "catchy tunes" and "show-stopping" numbers; foes think Marlon's "miscast", pointing to his "bored", "sexually smug" rendition of 'Luck Be a Lady.'

Gypsy   20 | 21 | 22 | 22
1962. Directed by Mervyn LeRoy. With Rosalind Russell, Natalie Wood, Karl Malden. 143 minutes. Not Rated.
"Stripper Gypsy Rose Lee's life" is the basis of this "terrific" musical bio about the "original backstage mother" and her "passionate" efforts to mold her kids into stars; ok, it's "kind of windy" and Wood (in the title role) "doesn't really strip", while the "brilliant miscasting" of a "shrill" Russell leads many to say the part "should have gone to Ethel Merman", who delivered the "real goods" on Broadway.

Hair   20 | 18 | 21 | 21
1979. Directed by Milos Forman. With John Savage, Treat Williams, Beverly D'Angelo. 121 minutes. Rated PG.
The groovy "Broadway musical" that "defined the psychedelic '60s" gets a "terrific" big-screen transfer in this story of a draftee bound for Vietnam dallying with Central Park hippies; even though "Treat's a treat" in a role that "epitomizes the loving craziness" of the time, some say the "flower-child imagery" is "sadly faded."

Hairspray   19 | 17 | 18 | 18
1988. Directed by John Waters. With Divine, Ricki Lake, Sonny Bono, Ruth Brown, Debbie Harry. 91 minutes. Rated PG.
"Grab a can of Aquanet" and get ready to "shake a tailfeather": this "hilariously campy" story of a "fat girl who lives to dance" is underground director Waters' "mainstream" ode to his "beloved Baltimore" in the '60s and his "most family-friendly" flick (it even "unflinchingly looks at racism"); though "Divine's divine" and the "absolutely perfect" Lake wears her "big hair" well, "deviant" devotees hedge it's "kind of tame, but still fun."

Halloween ❶
22 | 16 | 20 | 19

1978. Directed by John Carpenter. With Donald Pleasence, Jamie Lee Curtis. 91 minutes. Rated R.

"Changing the face of horror movies forever", this "almost blood-less chiller shows that gore doesn't equal terror" as it depicts a "masked psycho stalker" who preys on "rowdy teens"; despite "zero-budget" production values and so-so acting (but mighty "great screaming by Jamie Lee"), this "influential" "slasher" flick spawned a slew of sequels and "still holds up."

Hamlet ✉◐
▽ 26 | 28 | 28 | 23

1948. Directed by Laurence Olivier. With Laurence Olivier, Eileen Herlie, Basil Sydney, Jean Simmons. 153 minutes. Not Rated.

"Probably the best Shakespeare film ever made with the greatest Shakespearean actor", this Oscar-winning epic is a "brilliantly vi-sual" take on the Bard's "greatest drama"; director/producer/star Olivier does Hamlet as a blond "as only he can do it", and if the action scenes are less vivid than in other versions, overall it's still considered "unfailingly great."

Hamlet
24 | 26 | 26 | 25

1996. Directed by Kenneth Branagh. With Kenneth Branagh, Julie Christie, Derek Jacobi. 242 minutes. Rated PG-13.

This oft-done (maybe "overdone") Shakespearean tragedy gets "expansive" treatment from "modern master" Branagh, who uses the Bard's full text, resulting in a "four-hour adaptation"; though "engrossing, suspenseful" and "beautifully reimagined" to fans, those who say "enough already" call it "*too much* of a good thing."

Hand That Rocks the Cradle, The
16 | 16 | 17 | 16

1992. Directed by Curtis Hanson. With Annabella Sciorra, Rebecca De Mornay. 110 minutes. Rated R.

It's De Mornay who "rocks" as the "world's most warped nanny" nursing a "psychopathic" grudge in this "well-done" thriller, a "real nail-biter" despite "huge plot holes" and "overwrought" sit-uations; the ultimate in "working-mom paranoia", it delivers a "chilling" moral: "always check references!"

Hannah and Her Sisters ✉
24 | 25 | 23 | 23

1986. Directed by Woody Allen. With Mia Farrow, Barbara Hershey, Dianne Wiest. 103 minutes. Rated PG-13.

A "nice balance of jokes and philosophy", this "pertinent" romantic comedy about three sisters and their "struggle with the meaning of life" "brims with so much heart" that many call it "Allen's most life-affirming" picture; featuring "all-around wonderful" acting, it's a "valentine" to "NYers in all their neurotic glory" that manages to "convey a message without tempering the laugh-out-loud humor."

Hannibal ❶
15 | 21 | 14 | 19

2001. Directed by Ridley Scott. With Anthony Hopkins, Julianne Moore, Ray Liotta, Gary Oldman. 131 minutes. Rated R.

Sure, it's "not the same without Jodie", but this "grisly" *Silence of the Lambs* sequel lets the "fascinating" Hopkins chew the scenery as a refined psycho dreaded for his "wry comments" – "bon appétit!" – and "unspeakable" cravings; buckets of "ba-roque gore" help distract from the "inferior story", yet many say it "crosses the line" into a "pointless ickfest" with a "tasteless (no pun intended)" climax better suited to "*Fear Factor.*"

Happiness

1998. Directed by Todd Solondz. With Jane Adams, Jon Lovitz, Philip Seymour Hoffman. 134 minutes. Not Rated.
Forget the "truly ironic title": this extremely "dark" "feel-bad" comedy is "*American Beauty* with a lot more acid" and so "unrelentingly bleak" that it's "not for the faint of heart"; given some "taboo subject matter", the unhappy call it a "sicko train wreck" that's "probably the worst first-date movie ever", but fans tout its "brave" if "perverted" take on the "middle classes."

Hard Day's Night, A ◑

1964. Directed by Richard Lester. With The Beatles, Wilfrid Brambell. 87 minutes. Rated G.
"Before there was MTV", there was this "best rock movie ever", an "ahead-of-its-time groundbreaker" shot with documentary-style "quick edits" that convey the "lunacy" and the "pure joy of Beatlemania" in the "days of innocence"; it's "still a film of wonder", and then there's that "incredible soundtrack" of "Fab Four" classics.

Harold and Maude

1972. Directed by Hal Ashby. With Ruth Gordon, Bud Cort, Vivian Pickles. 91 minutes. Rated PG.
Ok, it "starts with a hanging", but this "counterculture cult classic gets funnier", managing to be both "morbid" and "absurdly wonderful" in its "May-December story" of a "death-obsessed" kid who finds love with a "free-spirited old lady"; while "not for everyone", this "original" features a "phenomenal" Gordon and a "gem" of a "Cat Stevens soundtrack."

Harry Potter and the Chamber of Secrets ⓤ

2002. Directed by Chris Columbus. With Daniel Radcliffe, Rupert Grint, Emma Watson, Kenneth Branagh. 161 minutes. Rated PG.
This "rare spectacular sequel" is "much darker and scarier than the first", but "fantastic fantasy fare for the family" nevertheless and an "excellent adaptation of the book" "within the limits of time"; the special effects are "amazing", of course, and "the young stars have grown into their roles and do an even better job" this time around, but fans who "can't wait for the next one" admit that "Dumbledore is going to be tough to replace."

Harry Potter and the Goblet of Fire ⓤ

2005. Directed by Mike Newell. With Daniel Radcliffe, Rupert Grint, Emma Watson, Gary Oldman. 157 minutes. Rated PG-13.
"Dragons", a giant "maze" and "puberty" spell trouble for Harry and the Hogwart gang in this "fine addition" to a series that's "progressed beyond the kids movie" milieu and ventured into "darker" territory thanks to the maturing Potter's "increasing angst"; a "faithful compression" of Rowling's tome, it summons more "impressive" effects wizardry and "strong acting", keeping the franchise "on fire" as the wand passes to future episodes.

Harry Potter and the Prisoner of Azkaban ⓤ

2004. Directed by Alfonso Cuarón. With Daniel Radcliffe, Rupert Grint, Emma Watson. 141 minutes. Rated PG.
Rowling's third installment in the "beloved" series of children's books about a triumvirate of young wizards is "as wonderful and

fanciful as the others", with particularly "fabulous production values"; featuring just the "right touch of menace and darkness" to win over "older moviegoers", it has appeal for all ages, but since the "kids are growing up", some wonder "will Harry have a beard in the next one?"

HARRY POTTER AND THE SORCERER'S STONE ⓫

24 | 23 | 25 | 27

2001. Directed by Chris Columbus. With Daniel Radcliffe, Rupert Grint, Emma Watson. 152 minutes. Rated PG.

It's "Hogwarts brought to magic life": this "reverent" screen adaptation of the ultra-"popular children's book" about a school for young witches and wizards is simply "spellbinding" – nothing less than a "21st-century *Wizard of Oz*"; fans zero in on the "eye-popping special effects", "outstanding" ensemble cast and "perfect" scenario that "gets every character right", "just like you imagined them"; still, the "length and scariness factors" might mean it's "wasted on little kids."

Harvey ◑

26 | 27 | 25 | 22

1950. Directed by Henry Koster. With James Stewart, Josephine Hull, Peggy Dow. 104 minutes. Not Rated.

"So sweet and genuine that it's never become dated", this ever "classic comedy" concerning an "adorable sot" and his "imaginary six-foot rabbit" is such an "enchanting, grown-up fairy tale" that the "word 'heartwarming' was coined for it"; "delightful performances" elevate this "feel-good" flick into the "can't-miss" category.

Hatari!

21 | 17 | 18 | 23

1962. Directed by Howard Hawks. With John Wayne, Hardy Kruger, Elsa Martinelli. 157 minutes. Not Rated.

"Great African location shots" and a "fab" Henry Mancini score make this "somewhat forgotten" action/adventurer "better than its reputation" (even if its rather "dull" plot about "wild animal" trappers lacks "political correctness"); though it's a "lesser" vehicle for the "bigger-than-life" Wayne, at least the "beautiful photography" supplies some real "entertainment value."

Heartbreak Kid, The

20 | 20 | 21 | 19

1972. Directed by Elaine May. With Charles Grodin, Cybill Shepherd, Jeannie Berlin, Eddie Albert. 106 minutes. Rated PG.

"Not your traditional romantic comedy", this "biting satire" tells the story of a "NY Jewish guy" who falls for a Midwestern "shiksa goddess" – while on his honeymoon; it's "hysterical" albeit "cringe-making" stuff, with Grodin appropriately "smarmy" in his "bulldoggish pursuit" of the "unobtainable" Shepherd, but the "fabulous" Berlin (director May's daughter) steals the picture, leaving many with a "complex about egg salad sandwiches."

Heartburn

19 | 24 | 19 | 19

1986. Directed by Mike Nichols. With Meryl Streep, Jack Nicholson, Jeff Daniels, Maureen Stapleton. 108 minutes. Rated R.

The "ups and downs of married life" are dissected in this "comedic" yet "acidic" story of "revenge" that's a "thinly veiled account" of writer Nora Ephron's relationship with "Watergate reporter" Carl Bernstein; still, some say the "slight" story is "unworthy" of its "divine" stars, and outside of a memorable "Key lime pie", much of the movie is "tripe."

Heat
22 | 25 | 19 | 22
1995. Directed by Michael Mann. With Al Pacino, Robert De Niro, Val Kilmer, Jon Voight. 171 minutes. Rated R.
"Both the cop and robber are heroes" in this "operatic" crime epic, a "star-studded killfest" that's cinematically historic, since "legends" Pacino and De Niro are "finally on-screen together" (their "face-to-face" "coffeehouse scene" is a "knockout"); yet "despite a captivating cast and storyline", "they could have done a better job in the editing room" – "there's a perfect two-hour movie" lurking in this sprawling, 171-minute marathon.

Heathers
21 | 19 | 22 | 18
1989. Directed by Micheal Lehmann. With Winona Ryder, Christian Slater, Shannen Doherty. 102 minutes. Rated R.
The "pinnacle of '80s dark humor" – maybe even "before its time" – this "out-there" "black comedy" is "twisted" and "proud of it" as it provides an important lesson in "teen peer pressure": "popularity can kill"; though "not for everyone" (especially the "lighthearted or light-stomached"), it did "launch Slater's and Ryder's careers", and the "deliciously biting dialogue is full of comebacks you wish you'd thought of."

Heaven Can Wait
24 | 24 | 24 | 22
1943. Directed by Ernst Lubitsch. With Gene Tierney, Don Ameche, Charles Coburn. 112 minutes. Not Rated.
The famed "Lubitsch touch" is rendered in Technicolor in this "witty, unsentimental" comedy about a deceased playboy at the gate of Hell hoping to be admitted by listing his many transgressions; it's a "clever" yet "charming" trifle about how "life doesn't meet up to one's expectations", with a "devilishly nice ending."

Heaven Can Wait
21 | 19 | 22 | 19
1978. Directed by Warren Beatty, Buck Henry. With Warren Beatty, Julie Christie, Dyan Cannon. 101 minutes. Rated PG.
An "enjoyable remake of *Here Comes Mr. Jordan*", this comedy-fantasy mix of true love and the afterlife is kind of "far-fetched, but it works"; sure, "Buck Henry's script is as good as the original" and a "likable" Beatty at least "tries to be sincere", but the "hysterical" Charles Grodin "steals the show."

Heavenly Creatures
24 | 25 | 26 | 24
1994. Directed by Peter Jackson. With Kate Winslet, Melanie Lynskey, Clive Merrison. 99 minutes. Rated R.
One part "fantasy", one part "true crime", this "absolutely riveting" drama about two teens plotting "matricide" is a "surreal", "haunting descent into the imagination" as it details an "attachment that turns deadly"; Winslet's "career-launching" performance is so "astounding" that some say "*this* is the movie" that the *Titanic* star "should have gotten an Oscar nomination for."

Heavy Metal ⑫
20 | – | – | 21
1981. Directed by Gerald Potterton. Animated. 86 minutes. Rated R.
"Based on the sci-fi comic book of the same name", this "cult" cartoon "classic" is a novel "departure for animation", given its "adult-oriented" content and "heavy metal" score; some shrug it "wavers between entertaining and dull", since this "strung-together anthology" of hard-rock-flavored "vignettes" is more than "a little choppy" (it "makes no sense without alcohol").

Hello, Dolly!

| 20 | 19 | 20 | 23 |

1969. Directed by Gene Kelly. With Barbra Streisand, Walter Matthau, Michael Crawford. 146 minutes. Rated G.

This "big, over-the-top" musical concerning a turn-of-the-century matchmaker is a "colorful" romp with all the "beautiful music from the Broadway show"; but goodbye Charlies call it an "overblown spectacle", citing "one of the most unappealing romantic couplings imaginable": a "miscast" Streisand ("who knew Dolly Levi was 25 years old?") playing opposite an "embarrassing" Matthau.

Help!

| 19 | 16 | 15 | 20 |

1965. Directed by Richard Lester. With The Beatles, Leo McKern, Eleanor Bron. 90 minutes. Rated G.

"Sing along with the hits from 1965" that enliven this "zany musical comedy", a "perfectly enjoyable" if "silly John-Paul-George-and-Ringo romp" that's really not much more than a "platform to take advantage of the Beatles' popularity"; still, the "story's ok" ("at least there's a plot this time"), the international "locations are great" and, "of course, the soundtrack is terrific."

Henry & June

| ▽ 18 | 21 | 19 | 19 |

1990. Directed by Philip Kaufman. With Fred Ward, Uma Thurman, Maria de Medeiros. 136 minutes. Rated NC-17.

"Not for the prudish", this "lushly produced" drama explores the libidinous "literary underbelly" of Paris in the '30s, where burgeoning bohemian scribe Henry Miller, his alluring wife June and their groupie Anaïs Nin indulge in a steamy triangle fueled by "curiosity and lust"; an ultra-"erotic lesbian love scene" helped tag this "perverse gem" with the "first NC-17 rating" ever.

Henry V

| 26 | 28 | 27 | 26 |

1989. Directed by Kenneth Branagh. With Kenneth Branagh, Derek Jacobi. 137 minutes. Rated PG-13.

"Brush up on your Shakespeare" via this "revisionist" adaptation of the Bard's "difficult" history play about an English monarch at war with France; "both spectacular and approachable", it makes the 17th-century dialogue "completely understandable to modern ears", and first-time director Branagh's "lavish, lusty" brio is so "brilliant" that many acolytes ask "Sir Laurence who?"

Hercules

| 17 | – | 17 | 21 |

1997. Directed by Ron Clements, John Musker. Animated. 92 minutes. Rated G.

To "Disney-fy" Greek mythology risks the wrath of Zeus, but this "witty", "well-told" animated saga is "elevated" Olympusward by a "strong voice cast", "great songs" and enough "jokes for adults" to make for "stylish family fun" with "an edge"; like its brawny hero fending off superhuman foes, it "stands up well" and marks a "departure from the usual formula."

Hero 🇫

| 25 | 22 | 23 | 27 |

2004. Directed by Zhang Yimou. With Jet Li, Zhang Ziyi. 99 minutes. Rated PG-13.

"Not your typical martial-arts movie", this Chinese "homage to *Rashomon*" told from multiple perspectives in "non-linear" format explodes with "luscious visuals", "chop-'em-up kung fu" fight scenes and even some "noble" performances ("Jet Li can act!"); still, while fans see a "thought-provoking" epic about "politics, loyalty and truth", a few Sinophobes can't help but read a "propaganda" message in the "nationalist storyline."

Hidalgo
20 | 21 | 21 | 23

2004. Directed by Joe Johnston. With Viggo Mortensen, Omar Sharif. 136 minutes. Rated PG-13.

"*The Little Engine That Could* meets *Lawrence of Arabia*" with "not quite epic" results in this "old-fashioned" story about an "underdog" cowboy undertaking a 3,000-mile horse race across the North African desert; while the scenery's "sumptuous" and Viggo's a "god" as the "handsome daredevil hero", neigh-sayers say the plot's "weak" and the running time "a little long."

High Anxiety
21 | 19 | 19 | 19

1977. Directed by Mel Brooks. With Mel Brooks, Madeline Kahn, Cloris Leachman. 94 minutes. Rated PG.

"Hitch would have laughed" at this "totally goofy" comic homage from the "totally insane" Mel Brooks that's a "send-up" of the Hitchcockian oeuvre, particularly *Psycho* and *Vertigo*; only problem is, "you must know the material he's spoofing in order to get the jokes" or else this "silly" picture "doesn't really hang together."

HIGH NOON ✉ ◐
28 | 26 | 26 | 25

1952. Directed by Fred Zinnemann. With Gary Cooper, Grace Kelly, Lloyd Bridges. 85 minutes. Not Rated.

Voted the "best Western" in this *Survey*, this "tense drama" filmed in "real time" "breaks the mold" by combining all the "grit of the West" with a "strong comment on the McCarthyist '50s" and a touch of "Greek drama" to boot; as a "single-minded sheriff" with "principles", Cooper took home an Oscar, though many admit they're drawn to this "classic" "allegory" for its "theme song" alone; in short, it's "absolutely tops" – nothing else "comes close."

High Plains Drifter
18 | 19 | 20 | 19

1972. Directed by Clint Eastwood. With Clint Eastwood, Verna Bloom, Marianna Hill. 105 minutes. Rated R.

"Perennial badass" Eastwood plays a "violent" "avenging angel" in this "powerful" if by-the-numbers Western in which "everyone gets what they deserve"; connoisseurs say it's Clint's "defining moment", though the less enamored rate it an "acquired taste", "not up to the standard of some of his others."

High Sierra ◐
▽ 23 | 25 | 23 | 19

1941. Directed by Raoul Walsh. With Humphrey Bogart, Ida Lupino, Alan Curtis. 100 minutes. Not Rated.

Hard-boiled with a heart, this "gritty gangster pic" features a sneering Bogie in a "part made for him" as a "bad crook gone worse" who puts on a "tough" front to cover up the sentimental sap underneath; noir connoisseurs call it "dated but great", heaping high praise on Lupino's incredibly "hot" performance.

High Society
23 | 22 | 22 | 23

1956. Directed by Charles Walters. With Bing Crosby, Grace Kelly, Frank Sinatra, Celeste Holm. 107 minutes. Not Rated.

"What a swell party" is this Cole Porter "musical rendition of *The Philadelphia Story*", a "sophisticated comedy of manners" set in a "Newport mansion" inhabited by some "fantastic talent": a "gorgeous Grace", "swingin' Bing" and "delightful Sinatra"; sure, the original might be "far superior" plotwise, but fans dub this "softer" take the "Tiffany" of the singing-and-dancing genre.

Hilary and Jackie
21 | 26 | 22 | 21
1998. Directed by Anand Tucker. With Emily Watson, Rachel Griffiths, David Morrissey. 121 minutes. Rated R.
"Poignant and touching", this "overlooked" biodrama tells the true story of the prickly "relationship between two sisters", one a cellist who's "battling MS" as well as other "personal" demons; "outstanding lead performances from Watson and Griffiths" lend appeal to more than just "classical music fans", though some say it can be "difficult to watch", given the "tragic" storyline.

Hiroshima, Mon Amour ◑🅵
25 | 24 | 24 | 23
1960. Directed by Alain Resnais. With Emmanuelle Riva, Eiji Okada. 90 minutes. Not Rated.
Simultaneously "harrowing and beautiful", this "inventive", "intellectual" drama "explores the tragedies of war and the meaning of memory" by intercutting an "interracial love story" with "documentary footage" of the ruins of Hiroshima; though too "enigmatic" and "arty" for some ("I really want to like it, but . . ."), others tout the "cinematic importance" of this French New Wave "masterpiece."

His Girl Friday ◑
26 | 28 | 24 | 22
1940. Directed by Howard Hawks. With Cary Grant, Rosalind Russell, Ralph Bellamy. 92 minutes. Not Rated.
"Pay attention" now: the "superfast-moving plot" "comes at you at 100 mph" in this "biting" screwball comedy that's a "wonderful adaptation" of *The Front Page*; Grant and Russell "snap and crackle" as a "newspaper editor and star reporter chasing the story of a lifetime – and each other" – and if the "breakneck speed" of this zippy "roller-coaster ride" can be "exhausting", the payoff is "absolute hilarity."

History of Violence, A
22 | 25 | 22 | 22
2005. Directed by David Cronenberg. With Viggo Mortensen, Maria Bello, Ed Harris, William Hurt. 96 minutes. Rated R.
Examining the "brutal violence underlying a serene landscape", this "taut", "pitch-perfect" thriller from David Cronenberg asks the question "do you really know anyone?" in its story of a "quiet family man" who may be a "cold-blooded killer"; Viggo's "awesome" as the "ambiguous average Joe", "Hurt's a hoot" in a "scene-stealing" turn and that "blatant" "stairway sex scene" is just plain "hot."

Hitch
21 | 21 | 20 | 20
2005. Directed by Andy Tennant. With Will Smith, Eva Mendes, Kevin James. 118 minutes. Rated PG-13.
A "charismatic" "date doctor" tutoring a "down-on-his-luck guy" on the "NYC singles scene" loses his cool in the face of true love in this "light" romantic comedy; while a tad "trite and silly" for those who disparage the "no-brainer" "Hollywood heart-tugger" ending, it's "no disappointment" for chuckleheads thanks to that "unforgettable dance scene."

Hoffa
▽ 16 | 22 | 17 | 17
1992. Directed by Danny DeVito. With Jack Nicholson, Danny DeVito, Armand Assante. 140 minutes. Rated R.
DeVito's laborious, "uneven" drama delivers a "real dose of reality" as it traces the rise and demise of notorious union boss Jimmy

Hoffa, who uses rough justice and mob connections to win the Teamsters their due; though it's "very well-acted and photographed", critics call it an overlong, "flawed" piece of work.

Holes
23 | 23 | 24 | 22

2003. Directed by Andrew Davis. With Sigourney Weaver, Jon Voight, Tim Blake Nelson. 117 minutes. Rated PG.
The "wonderful children's book" about a boy punished for a crime he didn't commit has been "faithfully adapted" into this "excellent movie for the whole family"; a "creative, interesting story", "outstanding" performances by "old pros" and "young actors" alike and an "awesome soundtrack" that will keep "the kids singing all week" add up to a "highly entertaining" two hours.

Holiday Inn ◑
23 | 20 | 20 | 23

1942. Directed by Mark Sandrich. With Bing Crosby, Fred Astaire, Marjorie Reynolds. 100 minutes. Not Rated.
"Crooner Bing" and "hoofer Astaire" are "rivals" in this "lively" "musical romance" that's chock-full of "Irving Berlin favorites" but most remembered for introducing 'White Christmas'; sure, the plot's pretty "lightweight", but at least the songs of this "holiday bonbon" will "stick in your brain well into the new year."

Hollywood Ending
15 | 18 | 16 | 17

2002. Directed by Woody Allen. With Woody Allen, Téa Leoni, George Hamilton, Debra Messing. 112 minutes. Rated PG-13.
Ok, it has "a few memorable bon mots", but otherwise this "Woody-Allen-on-cruise-control" comedy about a has-been director who goes "hysterically blind" is "pretty bland" stuff; most say his shtick is "wearing a bit thin" (casting himself opposite "women a third of his age" is distinctly "unfunny") and feel he's "not having fun" anymore: "what happened?"

Home Alone ⓫
19 | 17 | 20 | 19

1990. Directed by Chris Columbus. With Macaulay Culkin, Joe Pesci, Daniel Stern. 103 minutes. Rated PG.
"Every parent's nightmare" – and "every child's fantasy" – this "ultimate sleepover movie" made Culkin a star as a "self-sufficient kid who defends himself against robbers" after his vacation-bound family accidentally "leaves him at home"; though its "loony premise" is "full of sight gags", some warn it can be too "violent" for smaller fry: "this is Bugs Bunny vs. Yosemite Sam for real."

Honey, I Shrunk the Kids ⓫
16 | 14 | 18 | 19

1989. Directed by Joe Johnston. With Rick Moranis, Matt Frewer, Marcia Strassman. 101 minutes. Rated PG.
A "cute", "creative idea" that "grows on you", this "wacky family" comedy concerns a "friendly mad scientist" dad whose "experiments go awry" when his kids are zapped down to sub-pint size; with "inventive" special effects to "overcome lame acting", it's "always good for some laughs", though most shrink from the "next two installments."

Hook
17 | 18 | 17 | 21

1991. Directed by Steven Spielberg. With Robin Williams, Dustin Hoffman, Julia Roberts. 144 minutes. Rated PG.
Presenting "Peter Pan if he grew up", this "clever" '90s "twist" on the adventure finds Williams' cynical adult Peter activating his "inner child" for a rematch with Hoffman's "memorable" Hook; if

often a "pleasure to watch", it's also panned as a "bloated", "PC version" of the fairy tale and "one of Spielberg's rare mistakes."

Hoop Dreams
| 26 | – | 26 | 23 |

1994. Directed by Steve James. Documentary. 170 minutes. Rated PG-13.

"Two young athletes who dream of NBA fame" as a way "to escape the inner city" are the subjects of this "gritty" documentary, a "slam-dunk exposé" of "naive boys" that's "quite moving" if a "tad long"; "superb editing" makes it feel more like a "drama" than a real-life story, but don't look for a "Hollywood ending": this one's so "devastatingly real", it just might "break your heart."

Hoosiers
| 23 | 22 | 24 | 19 |

1986. Directed by David Anspaugh. With Gene Hackman, Barbara Hershey, Dennis Hopper. 114 minutes. Rated PG.

A modern-day "David and Goliath on the basketball court", this "inspirational" "classic of the small-town-team-rises-up genre" is a "corporate team builder" kind of flick; as the "motivational" but "down-and-out coach trying to make a comeback in the boonies", Hackman captures the spirit of "rural" hoops culture and supplies this "underdog story" with some "real heart."

Horse Feathers ◐
| 24 | 22 | 20 | 18 |

1932. Directed by Norman Z. McLeod. With the Marx Brothers, Thelma Todd. 68 minutes. Not Rated.

"One of the Marxes' zaniest comedies" showcases the boys in "peak form" in a college setting, in which Groucho is the incoming university president; expect the usual "breezy lunacy" "based on years of vaudeville antics" – especially the "hilarious" "French-farcical wooing of Todd" – and ignore that "abrupt ending."

Horse Whisperer, The
| 17 | 19 | 18 | 20 |

1998. Directed by Robert Redford. With Robert Redford, Kristin Scott Thomas, Sam Neill. 169 minutes. Rated PG-13.

"Redford and horses" are "so right" together in this "tearjerker" romance, with Bob taking a "real star turn" as a Montana cowpoke whose way with the "healing process" sweeps city gal Scott Thomas right out of her saddle; it's all "uplifting", "tender" and "lovingly" shot, and if some bridle at the "boring", "interminable" pace, stay awake and you'll "learn a lot about horses."

HOTEL RWANDA
| 28 | 28 | 28 | 26 |

2004. Directed by Terry George. With Don Cheadle, Sophie Okonedo, Joaquin Phoenix, Nick Nolte. 121 minutes. Rated PG-13.

A "heartwrenching" reminder of the "horrors" committed during the 1994 Rwandan genocide ("a modern-day Holocaust"), this "true story" of a hotel manager who "helped save 1,200 lives" eschews "preachy" moralizing and overt carnage in order to emphasize the "redemptive" notion that "courage can turn the tide"; the "magnificent" Cheadle and "brilliant" supporting cast "do a great service" to this "important piece of history", inspiring "much hope" that such an "appalling" tragedy "doesn't happen again."

Hound of the Baskervilles, The ◐
▽ | 21 | 21 | 24 | 19 |

1939. Directed by Sidney Lanfield. With Basil Rathbone, Nigel Bruce, Richard Greene. 80 minutes. Not Rated.

Critics call this the "most successful" take on Arthur Conan Doyle's "classic" thriller, featuring Rathbone's "quintessential" Sherlock

Holmes sleuthing around an English castle; it's "must" viewing for most, with "campy" ambiance and "over-the-top" emoting.

Hours, The ✉   25 | 28 | 24 | 25
2002. Directed by Stephen Daldry. With Nicole Kidman, Julianne Moore, Meryl Streep, Ed Harris. 114 minutes. Rated PG-13.
There's "no action, only acting" in this "intelligent, challenging" adaptation of the "brilliant" book about three women of different generations whose "not perfect" lives are linked by a Virginia Woolf novel – and the "acting by all three leading ladies" "deserved an Oscar" (Kidman "won by a nose"); "don't watch it if you're in a good mood", however, because it's "hopelessly depressing" and "so slow moving it should have been called *The Days*."

House of Flying Daggers ▣   24 | 22 | 21 | 27
2004. Directed by Zhang Yimou. With Takeshi Kaneshiro, Zhang Ziyi, Andy Lau. 119 minutes. Rated PG-13.
"Exhilarating fight sequences" and "feast-for-the-eyes" scenery team up with a "tearjerker" story of "star-crossed lovers" in this "outstanding" Chinese epic that kicks the martial arts genre to "new heights"; still, visual beauty aside, not everyone's flying high over the kung-fusing plot (with "more twists and turns than the Yangtze River"), ditto the seemingly "interminable" ending.

House of Games   24 | 23 | 27 | 21
1987. Directed by David Mamet. With Lindsay Crouse, Joe Mantegna, Lilia Skala. 102 minutes. Rated R.
"Cold characters and clipped conversations" make this "mind-bending thriller" pure Mamet "at his most manipulative"; its "twisty" con-game plot (something like "*The Sting*, all grown-up") "keeps you guessing", and though the dialogue reminds some critics of "cartoons talking", it's "chilling on many levels", with a "head-spinning" ending that stays with you "long after the movie's over."

House of Sand and Fog   23 | 27 | 22 | 23
2003. Directed by Vadim Perelman. With Jennifer Connelly, Ben Kingsley, Shoreh Aghdashloo. 126 minutes. Rated R.
A "brilliant rendering" of the "moral stand-off" between a "slacker who loses her home" and a "desperate" Iranian who purchases it for his exiled family, this "taut", "heart-wrenching" drama explores "everything that the American dream is – and isn't"; "balanced directing" and "amazingly nuanced performances" by Kingsley, Connelly and Aghdashloo turn this inherently "dour material" into a "gripping", "haunting" tragedy.

House of Wax   21 | 18 | 21 | 20
1953. Directed by Andre de Toth. With Vincent Price, Frank Lovejoy, Phyllis Kirk. 90 minutes. Rated PG.
"Look out for the giant vat of wax!": this "entertaining" horror picture was one of the first flicks made in 3-D, but modern-day fans say it's "still fun" "even without the glasses"; featuring a "priceless Price", a "chiller"-diller story and "atmospheric", "gaslight-era" settings, it's the "stuff of nightmares" and always "spooky."

Howards End ✉   22 | 26 | 21 | 25
1992. Directed by James Ivory. With Anthony Hopkins, Emma Thompson, Helena Bonham Carter. 140 minutes. Rated PG.
"Another Merchant-Ivory masterpiece", this "period piece" adaptation of the E.M. Forster novel concerns a "snobby upper-

class" British family scheming to cut an interloper out of their mother's will; though Anglophiles laud the lovely cinematography and appearances by "some of the best actors of our time" (including a "superb" Hopkins and Oscar-winning Thompson), phobes fret it's "way too slow."

HOW GREEN WAS MY VALLEY ✉◐   27 | 26 | 26 | 26

1941. Directed by John Ford. With Walter Pidgeon, Maureen O'Hara, Anna Lee, Donald Crisp. 118 minutes. Not Rated.
Director Ford's "gentler side" is showcased in this "sentimental", "soulful" story of a Welsh mining family over the course of 50 years; renowned as the movie that "beat out *Citizen Kane*" for the year's Best Picture Oscar, it may seem a tad "corny" to modernists, but traditional types laud its "compassion, humanity" and "old-fashioned values."

How the Grinch Stole Christmas   17 | 18 | 19 | 23

2000. Directed by Ron Howard. With Jim Carrey, Jeffrey Tambor, Christine Baranski. 105 minutes. Rated PG.
Dr. Seuss gets the "grand production" treatment in this mighty "enjoyable" comedy featuring "great visuals" and a "scary" Carrey as a "perfect Grinch" plotting Yuletide vengeance on the "über-commercialized" "world of the Whos"; while it's hailed as a "holiday keeper" that stands "heart to heart" with the "classic cartoon", some viewers see a "heavy-handed" effort that's a few sizes too "overinflated."

How the West Was Won ✉   ▽ 22 | 20 | 21 | 25

1963. Directed by John Ford, Henry Hathaway, George Marshall. With Gregory Peck, Henry Fonda, James Stewart, George Peppard, Carroll Baker, Eli Wallach. 162 minutes. Rated G.
A "true epic" that feels like "five films in one", this "sprawling Western" boasts an "all-star cast" hitting the trail to follow "compelling storylines" ranging from the Civil War to a prairie-schooner drive, all in blazing "Cinerama"; the "long overview" of the "taming" of the territories makes for a grand, "sweeping tale" that's "plenty entertaining", but see it in "wide-screen" or else "don't bother."

How to Lose a Guy in 10 Days   19 | 20 | 19 | 19

2003. Directed by Donald Petrie. With Kate Hudson, Matthew McConaughey. 116 minutes. Rated PG-13.
"Cute" Kate "carries on her mother's legacy" in this high-concept romantic comedy, a kind of "*Losing Mr. Goodbar*" story about a journalist trying to get dumped so she can write about it; maybe it's a "total chick flick" with a "typical Hollywood ending", but both leads are so "likable" and "easy on the eyes" that it also works as a "surprisingly good" date movie.

How to Marry a Millionaire   22 | 20 | 19 | 22

1953. Directed by Jean Negulesco. With Betty Grable, Marilyn Monroe, Lauren Bacall. 95 minutes. Not Rated.
"Fabulous gowns and mink coats are the stars" of this "rather entertaining" romantic comedy, a "guilty pleasure" about three gold diggers on the loose in Manhattan; "Lauren and Marilyn are charming in their own ways", while its "fascinating look" at women's roles in "'50s society" makes many feminists sigh "thank goodness for progress."

Hud ✉◑ 26 | 28 | 24 | 24
1963. Directed by Martin Ritt. With Paul Newman, Melvyn Douglas, Patricia Neal, Brandon De Wilde. 112 minutes. Not Rated.
"Stud muffin" Newman is at his "bad boy best" playing an "alienated", "black-hearted" cowboy in this "truly adult" "modern Western" about a "struggle between a father and son"; sure, "Neal got the Oscar" (as did "heartbreaker Douglas" and that "gorgeous black-and-white cinematography"), but in the end, Paul's "heartbreakingly cool" anti-hero gets the most reaction.

Hunchback of Notre Dame, The ◑ ▽ 26 | 27 | 26 | 25
1939. Directed by William Dieterle. With Charles Laughton, Cedric Hardwicke, Maureen O'Hara. 116 minutes. Not Rated.
One of the more "remarkable" adaptations of the much-filmed Victor Hugo novel of 15th-century Paris, this "timeless" picture about a hunchback's love for a gypsy girl garners praise for its "terrific story and wonderful production"; in the flashy title role, the "spectacular" Laughton gives Lon Chaney's 1923 silent performance a run for its money; best word: "sanctuary!"

Hunchback of Notre Dame, The 19 | – | 19 | 21
1996. Directed by Gary Trousdale, Kirk Wise. Animated. 91 minutes. Rated G.
"Disney does Victor Hugo" in this "underrated" bell-ringer that's "edgier than most animated fluff" and thus "more rewarding" for adults, given its "opera"-esque feel and "dark subtleties"; but cynics nix it as a bit "too sinister for children" and fear that the "forgettable songs" and "stupid talking gargoyles" must have the author "turning in his grave."

Hunger, The 20 | 21 | 20 | 20
1983. Directed by Tony Scott. With Catherine Deneuve, David Bowie, Susan Sarandon. 100 minutes. Rated R.
Deliciously "scary and erotic", this "stylish" "modern-day vampire film" "gets the blood moving" with a "to-die-for cast", including a "surprisingly effective Bowie" opposite Deneuve and Sarandon as two very "hot" vamps ("Buffy wouldn't stand a chance against them"); a pop Goth score by Bauhaus helps the atmospherics, but ultimately this one's best remembered for that notorious "lesbian" interlude.

Hunt for Red October, The 24 | 24 | 25 | 24
1990. Directed by John McTiernan. With Sean Connery, Alec Baldwin, Scott Glenn. 134 minutes. Rated PG.
The "first and best Jack Ryan thriller", this "entertaining" "Cold War guy flick" about a "renegade Russian submarine captain" combines "heart-pounding" suspense with "characters you can root for" (i.e. the "powerhouse" Connery and "holding-his-own" Baldwin); the "twisting plot" supplies enough "white-knuckle" moments to make it every bit "as good as the book."

Hurricane, The 21 | 26 | 21 | 21
1999. Directed by Norman Jewison. With Denzel Washington, Liev Schreiber. 145 minutes. Rated R.
Denzel's "excellent", "Oscar-worthy" performance is the glue in this true story about a hardscrabble middleweight boxer wrongly convicted of a triple murder; alternately "exciting and poignant", the script "really emphasizes human emotion", but it's Washington's

"tremendous" performance that makes this miscarriage-of-justice movie so moving.

Hustle & Flow
`23` `26` `21` `21`

2005. Directed by Craig Brewer. With Terrence Howard, Anthony Anderson, Taryn Manning, Ludacris. 116 minutes. Rated R.
This "gritty", "gutter-to-glory" story of a Southern "street hustler" chasing "rap star" dreams has a simple message: "it's tough out there for a pimp"; "emerging star" Howard turns in a "hard-to-the-bone" performance that morphs an "unlovable" character into "someone you root for", while his chief co-star – that "catchy soundtrack" – will "stick in your head for days."

Hustler, The ❶⓫
`25` `26` `24` `22`

1961. Directed by Robert Rossen. With Paul Newman, Jackie Gleason, Piper Laurie. 134 minutes. Not Rated.
"Dark, tense and beautifully delivered", this "ultimate movie about winning" is also a "love poem to the game of pool", featuring "Newman on a roll" opposite Gleason in a rare dramatic turn that nearly "steals the picture"; it's "convincing", "gripping" stuff, and though Paul reprised the character of Eddie Felson in *The Color of Money*, connoisseurs claim this first take is so "much better."

I Am Sam
`21` `25` `21` `21`

2001. Directed by Jessie Nelson. With Sean Penn, Michelle Pfeiffer, Dakota Fanning. 132 minutes. Rated PG-13.
Nary an emotion's left untouched in this "enjoyable, if predictable tearjerker" about a "mentally handicapped man's struggle to raise his child"; while it does "make one ponder the rights of the retarded", it's basically "a Barney movie for grown-ups" abetted by an "amazing soundtrack of Beatles remakes"; what saves it are the "luminous performances" from a "poignant" Penn and Fanning as "his darling daughter" ("I want one like her").

Ice Age ⓫
`23` `–` `21` `25`

2002. Directed by Chris Wedge, Carlos Saldanha. Animated. 81 minutes. Rated G.
The "oddest combination" of ice-age mammals sets out to save a little girl in this "cute", "cross-generational animated flick" featuring a "perfectly chosen" "all-star" vocal cast (e.g. Ray Romano as a "whiney" woolly mammoth); although it's "not up to the current high animated film standards", the "laugh-out-loud-funny" script and "well-done graphics" certainly "won't leave you cold."

Ice Age: The Meltdown
`21` `–` `19` `24`

2006. Directed by Carlos Saldanha. Animated. 91 minutes. Rated PG.
With a "cute" nod to "Noah's Ark", this "enjoyable", "family"-friendly animated sequel dishes out "lots of laughs" ("even for adults") as it sends a "mishmash" of "prehistoric animals" fleeing from the watery "doom" wrought by a "melting glacier"; if a few cynics smell a "warmed-over rehash" of the original, at least the "impressive visuals" help the adventure "stay fresh."

Identity
`18` `20` `19` `20`

2003. Directed by James Mangold. With John Cusack, Ray Liotta, Amanda Peet, John Hawkes. 90 minutes. Rated R.
"Ten strangers are stuck in a rained-out motel" – and "one of them is a killer" – in this "tricky", "twisty" thriller that owes a lot to "Agatha Christie's *10 Little Indians*"; though there's plenty of

"razzle-dazzle" and an "amazing ensemble cast", the "surprise ending" is debatable: either "well thought out" or a "disappointing" "audience-cheater" that's "too clever for its own good."

Igby Goes Down
20 | 23 | 19 | 19

2002. Directed by Burr Steers. With Kieran Culkin, Claire Danes, Jeff Goldblum, Amanda Peet, Ryan Phillippe. 97 minutes. Rated R.
"Hints of *Catcher in the Rye*" permeate this "quirky" coming-of-ager featuring the "terrific" Culkin ("Macaulay, eat your heart out") as a Caulfield-esque teen coping with his "rich, dysfunctional family" and other "messed-up" folk; its "touching moments" and "fabulously dark" flourishes unfold at a "slow" pace that "loses energy" at times, so stay alert to "pick up where it's going."

Il Postino 🅵
24 | 25 | 24 | 24

1995. Directed by Michael Radford. With Massimo Troisi, Philippe Noiret. 108 minutes. Rated PG.
A "charming" mix of "poetry and postal services", this "small treasure" "could only have been made in Italy", given its "lyrical", "humble" airs; the "sweet tale" of a "simple" postman "with the heart of a poet", it manages to be both a "great love story" and a "haunting" tale of "inspiration", with "bravura" acting and "beautiful scenery" that come together for "winning" moviemaking.

Imitation of Life
21 | 22 | 23 | 22

1959. Directed by Douglas Sirk. With Lana Turner, John Gavin, Sandra Dee. 125 minutes. Not Rated.
Bring "two boxes of Kleenex" before viewing this melodramatic Turner vehicle, a "classy" if "campy" "B movie" about a black woman who passes for white; a remake of the 1934 Claudette Colbert "tearjerker", this time around it's "all gussied up in pretty color" with the "racial theme toned down", leading realists to rate it a "ridiculous", "sudsy" soap opera.

Importance of Being Earnest
21 | 23 | 23 | 22

2002. Directed by Oliver Parker. With Rupert Everett, Colin Firth, Frances O'Connor, Reese Witherspoon, Judi Dench. 97 minutes. Rated PG.
This "undemanding" production of Oscar Wilde's "comedy of mistaken identities, romance and your typical weekend at an English manor" scores with "gorgeous sets" and "wonderful" acting from a "cast that looks like they're enjoying themselves"; but purists who prefer the "perfect 1952 version" insist the "magically funny play didn't need 'opening up'" by the screenwriter.

In America
26 | 27 | 25 | 24

2003. Directed by Jim Sheridan. With Paddy Considine, Samantha Morton, Djimon Hounsou. 107 minutes. Rated PG-13.
Sheridan's "beautiful" retelling of the "immigrants-come-to-NY" story is brought to life by an "exceptional ensemble" cast in this "small movie with a big heart"; while its "bittersweet" scenario of a poor Irish family trying to "rebuild after the tragic loss" of a child has many "crying like babies", it's executed so "brilliantly" that even the dry-eyed concur it's "without a single false moment."

In & Out
17 | 19 | 17 | 17

1997. Directed by Frank Oz. With Kevin Kline, Joan Cusack, Matt Dillon, Tom Selleck. 90 minutes. Rated PG-13.
"Is he gay or not?", that is the question: a Midwestern drama teacher protests too much after being outed at the Oscars in this

"lighthearted" comedy that's like an extended "*Saturday Night Live* skit"; though "well-acted" by an ace "ensemble cast", it's Kline's "inspired" lead – capped by a "scene-stealing boogie session" – that's the "very funny" payoff.

In Cold Blood ◑

| 25 | 26 | 26 | 22 |

1967. Directed by Richard Brooks. With Robert Blake, Scott Wilson, John Forsythe. 134 minutes. Rated R.
Brooks' "brilliant" adaptation of Truman Capote's "true-crime" "spellbinder" is "one of the most chilling films" about random murders ever made ("remember when not showing blood was more scary than showing it?"); shot "in almost documentary style" and all the more frightening thanks to Quincy Jones' evocative, spine-tingling score, it "still works today" as "powerful" albeit "disturbing" moviemaking.

Incredibles, The

| 26 | – | 25 | 28 |

2004. Directed by Brad Bird. Animated. 115 minutes. Rated PG.
"Not everyone can be Batman", and this animated Pixar satire "with brains" depicts the everyday "humdrum" lives of "has-been superheroes" suddenly drawn into an "edge-of-your-seat" rescue; it's "not just for kids" what with its "existential take on superherodom", though its "stunning animation" and "witty" set pieces (like the "Jack Jack attack" and that "show-stealing costumer") appeal to "all ages"; in fact, its "old-fashioned" message – the "family comes first" – makes many "love cartoons again."

Independence Day

| 19 | 16 | 18 | 24 |

1996. Directed by Roland Emmerich. With Will Smith, Bill Pullman, Jeff Goldblum. 145 minutes. Rated PG-13.
"*E.T.* with an attitude", this "ultimate flying-saucer movie" might be a "remake of *War of the Worlds*" and "splashy trash" with a "plot as thin as a dime" that's "all noise and no substance", but at least it "doesn't take itself too seriously"; so grab some "popcorn" and hold on for a "helluva lot of fun."

Indiana Jones and the Last Crusade

| 24 | 23 | 23 | 26 |

1989. Directed by Steven Spielberg. With Harrison Ford, Sean Connery, Denholm Elliott. 127 minutes. Rated PG-13.
"Almost as good as the first" installment, this third foray in the "Indy adventure" series is a "search-for-the-Holy-Grail" tale that alternates "lighthearted humor" with plenty of "gee-whiz", "close-call action sequences"; Ford is the "perfect hero" as always, but Connery (as his dad) "takes the cake" in this fond salute to "old-fashioned Saturday afternoon movie serials" "brought up to date."

Indiana Jones and the Temple of Doom ⏏

| 22 | 21 | 21 | 25 |

1984. Directed by Steven Spielberg. With Harrison Ford, Kate Capshaw, Quan Ke Huy. 118 minutes. Rated PG.
"Ford rules the day and saves the world" – again – in this "take-me-away" action/adventure story, the "follow-up to *Raiders*" that "goes more for shock value than the original" (though as exhilaratingly "over the top" as ever); still, doomsayers say its "hooey"-heavy plot and "dark feel" can be "far too grisly for younger viewers", dismissing it as a "blip in the trilogy"; most indelible image: those "chilled monkey brains."

Indochine ✉🅵　　　23 | 25 | 23 | 25
1992. Directed by Régis Wargnier. With Catherine Deneuve, Vincent Perez. 152 minutes. Rated PG-13.
A "haunting", "epic" tale of French Indochina, this Foreign Language Oscar winner details an "enthralling romance" played out against the background of a country in turmoil; as a "beautiful" plantation owner, Deneuve "looks smashing in great clothes", though some say the end result is a "little too picture perfect."

Inherit the Wind ◐　　　26 | 28 | 27 | 22
1960. Directed by Stanley Kramer. With Spencer Tracy, Fredric March, Gene Kelly. 128 minutes. Rated PG.
"You'll go ape" for this "superb" "fictionalized account of the Scopes monkey trial", based on the true story of a teacher trying to bring Darwin into his Tennessee classroom; a "magnificent Tracy and March" are "at the top of their game" trying to "reconcile creationism with evolution" in this "relevant thought-provoker" that many call the "ultimate in intelligent courtroom drama."

In-Laws, The　　　24 | 24 | 24 | 20
1979. Directed by Arthur Hiller. With Peter Falk, Alan Arkin, Richard Libertini. 103 minutes. Rated PG-13.
If you have any "weird" relatives-by-marriage, you'll "laugh out loud" at this "sidesplitting" comedy pitting a "chameleonic Falk" against a "befuddled Arkin" ("one of the great pairings of the cinema") as about-to-be in-laws; "totally unpredictable", it's "worth watching" if only to "find out where *Meet the Parents* came from."

Innerspace　　　15 | 15 | 18 | 17
1987. Directed by Joe Dante. With Dennis Quaid, Martin Short, Meg Ryan, Kevin McCarthy. 120 minutes. Rated PG.
Far-out FX and "likable" characters keep this "charming" entry in the "comedy sci-fi category" inneresting as Quaid's top-gun pilot is shrunken and inadvertently sent into the bloodstream of nerdy clerk Short, who's "never been better"; the "cute-as-always" Ryan rounds out the cast for an excursion that's lightweight but "quite funny" as crackpot "fantasy" goes.

Inside Man　　　23 | 25 | 23 | 23
2006. Directed by Spike Lee. With Denzel Washington, Clive Owen, Jodie Foster. 129 minutes. Rated R.
A "clever bank robber" undertakes an "elaborate" heist and tries to elude the "embattled cop" sent after him in this "intense" thriller driven by a "tight", "fast-paced" script that "keeps you guessing until the end"; featuring a "top-flight" cast led by the "sensational" duo of Denzel and Clive, it marks a "graceful" foray into "mainstream commercial" fare for Spike Lee.

Insider, The　　　25 | 28 | 25 | 23
1999. Directed by Michael Mann. With Al Pacino, Russell Crowe, Christopher Plummer. 157 minutes. Rated R.
Crowe turns in a "quietly intense" performance (while Pacino is intense but definitely not quiet), in this dramatic thriller about a tobacco company "whistle-blower" trying to "do the right thing no matter what the consequences"; although a "disillusioning behind-the-scenes look" at "big business, the media and public opinion", it's "absolutely riveting" and an "inspirational" profile in "courage."

Insomnia
18 | 22 | 18 | 19

2002. Directed by Christopher Nolan. With Al Pacino, Robin Williams, Hilary Swank, Martin Donovan. 118 minutes. Rated R.

There's "a lot of high-powered talent" on board this "above-average" "mainstream thriller" about a "wayward cop investigating a murder in Alaska", where the "round-the-clock sunshine" and "tense" goings-on keep him wide awake; as the "droopy-eyed" protagonist, Pacino sure looks "tired" and Williams is a "surprisingly good bad guy", yet those who "expected more" yawn it's so "forgettable" that they "had no trouble sleeping right through it."

Interpreter, The
20 | 23 | 20 | 22

2005. Directed by Sydney Pollack. With Nicole Kidman, Sean Penn. 128 minutes. Rated PG-13.

A "United Nations interpreter overhears something she shouldn't and ends up under Secret Service protection" in this "promising" if "predictable" political thriller; while Kidman does the "classic movie heroine" thing well and Penn "seems to get better with age", the real star of the picture might be the "awe-inspiring" UN – this is the "first film shot inside the building."

Interview with the Vampire
19 | 19 | 20 | 22

1994. Directed by Neil Jordan. With Tom Cruise, Brad Pitt, Antonio Banderas, Christian Slater. 123 minutes. Rated R.

"Cover up your neck"; this "entertaining Gothic horror flick about a maladjusted trio of immortal vampires" is "almost as good" as Anne Rice's "overwrought" best-selling book; sure, it might be "too beautiful" for words and they "could have cut out some of the gore", but with "pretty boys" Brad, Tom and Antonio playing "yummy bloodsuckers", "what's not to like?"

In the Bedroom
22 | 26 | 20 | 21

2001. Directed by Todd Field. With Sissy Spacek, Tom Wilkinson, Marisa Tomei. 130 minutes. Rated R.

"Less is more" in this "intense" drama about murder, revenge and family "dysfunction" that's the kind of picture in which the "silences say more than any of the dialogue"; though "Spacek and Wilkinson are superb" and "first-time director" Field "does an amazing job", critics sigh it's a "made-for-Lifetime movie" that's "dark, depressing and 20 minutes too long."

In the Company of Men
▽ 21 | 23 | 22 | 17

1997. Directed by Neil LaBute. With Aaron Eckhart, Stacy Edwards, Matt Malloy. 95 minutes. Rated R.

A "manipulative", "seriously despicable" loser abuses his "power over men and women alike" and "plays them for fools" in this "nasty little" drama that unflinchingly depicts the "evil that lurks in the hearts of men"; even those who "left the movie with a scowl" and "felt like they needed a shower" afterward admit being "strangely affected" by this "underwatched work."

In the Heat of the Night ✉ ⓘ
24 | 27 | 24 | 22

1967. Directed by Norman Jewison. With Sidney Poitier, Rod Steiger, Warren Oates. 109 minutes. Rated PG.

The "faint smell of honeysuckle hangs over" this "excellent" crime drama, a "brave statement on race relations" about a "black Yankee cop" suspected of murder in a small Southern town; it "generated a fair amount of controversy in its day" and was quite the Oscar magnet, taking home five statuettes including Best Picture and Best Actor for the "perfect Steiger."

In the Line of Fire
20 | 20 | 21 | 19

1993. Directed by Wolfgang Petersen. With Clint Eastwood, John Malkovich, Rene Russo. 128 minutes. Rated R.
"Eastwood is perfect" as an "aging but resourceful" Secret Service agent – "vulnerable, tough and world-weary" – battling a "would-be Presidential assassin" in this "solid action" thriller; throw in a "truly creepy" Malkovich as the "coldly reptilian" villain and you have a "completely engrossing" flick that's more than "effective", right up to the "suspenseful climax."

In the Name of the Father
23 | 25 | 24 | 21

1993. Directed by Jim Sheridan. With Daniel Day-Lewis, Emma Thompson, Pete Postlethwaite. 133 minutes. Rated R.
This "shattering" look at "desperate times" in Northern Ireland is a "riveting" true story about a "father and son jailed for a crime they did not commit"; "Day-Lewis is mesmerizing" and "totally believable" in this "troubling" account of "love and respect" amid a "terrible civil war."

Intolerable Cruelty
15 | 18 | 15 | 17

2004. Directed by Joel Coen. With George Clooney, Catherine Zeta-Jones, Geoffrey Rush, Billy Bob Thornton. 100 minutes. Rated PG-13.
The Coen brothers go "mainstream" in this reworking of the "old war-between-the-sexes theme", a sporadically "snappy" screwball comedy involving a gold digger and a divorce attorney; critics complain "it's not Coen enough", citing a "rambling" story that "drags in parts", and even "gorgeous" George and "luscious" Catherine can't elevate its overall "tolerable" ratings.

Intolerance ◑
▽ 27 | 23 | 24 | 28

1918. Directed by D.W. Griffith. With Lillian Gish, Mae Marsh, Constance Talmadge. 178 minutes. Not Rated.
"D.W. Griffith's apology" for the racist subtext in his earlier film, *Birth of a Nation,* is this "monumental" silent "landmark", which intercuts four tales of intolerance set respectively in Babylon, Calvary, 15th-century France and contemporary California; the result is "grandiosity glorified" on a scale of "sheer staggering size" never seen before, and arguably the birth of "epic" filmmaking.

Invasion of the Body Snatchers ◑
24 | 19 | 25 | 19

1956. Directed by Don Siegel. With Kevin McCarthy, Dana Wynter, Larry Gates. 80 minutes. Not Rated.
"Don't fall asleep!"; this '50s slice of "paranoid science fiction" posits that there are "alien pod people among us" "plotting to take over our hearts and minds"; alright, it's a "classic Red Scare parable", but "still perfectly effective today" despite "wooden acting" and that studio-enforced optimistic ending.

Invasion of the Body Snatchers
19 | 18 | 21 | 18

1978. Directed by Philip Kaufman. With Donald Sutherland, Brooke Adams, Jeff Goldblum. 115 minutes. Rated PG.
You'll be "looking for pods in the basement" after seeing this "thought-provoking", "very different" remake of the "classic" sci-fi thriller about an insidious alien invasion; this time around, the McCarthyist subtext has been replaced by 'Me Decade' pop

psychobabble, and even if "less fun" than the original, it's still pretty darn "scary."

Invisible Man, The ◑⬚

22 | 20 | 21 | 20

1933. Directed by James Whale. With Claude Rains, Gloria Stuart, William Harrigan. 71 minutes. Not Rated.
"Fabulous effects" ("especially for its time") and some slyly "campy" moments make this "classic" creature feature worthy of "every movie lover's repertoire"; the tale of an inventor whose invisibility serum transforms him into a crazed killer, it stars an engrossing Rains in the "scary" title role, whose amazing acting has more to do with vocalizing than visibility.

Iris

▽ 23 | 27 | 20 | 20

2001. Directed by Richard Eyre. With Judi Dench, Kate Winslet, Jim Broadbent. 90 minutes. Rated R.
This "beautifully done" bio of English writer Iris Murdoch and her "spiral" into "frightening illness" shines with "amazing acting" and bookish wit; "flashbacks" follow her from a "sweet" Oxford courtship to later years when the "superb" Dench "realistically portrays" the onset of Alzheimer's in a "sad but finally uplifting" tribute to "true" fidelity.

Irma La Douce

21 | 23 | 20 | 21

1963. Directed by Billy Wilder. With Shirley MacLaine, Jack Lemmon, Lou Jacobi. 147 minutes. Not Rated.
A surprisingly "sweet" comedy from the acerbic Billy Wilder, this story of an honest Parisian cop who falls for a prostitute, becomes her unwilling pimp, then schemes to keep her off the streets is "funny and well done"; MacLaine plays the "hooker with a heart of gold" perfectly, while Lemmon mugs winningly in a dual role.

I, Robot

18 | 17 | 19 | 23

2004. Directed by Alex Proyas. With Will Smith, Bridget Moynahan. 115 minutes. Rated PG-13.
Master sci-fi author Isaac Asimov's futuristic "classic" of "robots turning against man" gets a "blockbuster" buff-up in this "fast, fun" action flick full of "dazzling effects", "over-the-top" stunts and "cool set design"; Smith does his "typical" routine as a "wise-cracking" cop, though that glimpse of his "bare" ro-butt in the shower is definitely "worth the money."

Iron Giant, The

24 | – | 25 | 25

1999. Directed by Brad Bird. Animated. 86 minutes. Rated PG.
"Markedly different from other animated films", this story of a "quirky boy and an enormous robot from outer space" is both a "sly satire of the '50s" and a "message" flick about "tolerance and non-violence"; "criminally underrated" (it "slipped through the cracks due to poor marketing"), it's "entertaining and deserves to be seen."

Italian Job, The

22 | 19 | 21 | 24

2003. Directed by F. Gary Gray. With Mark Wahlberg, Edward Norton, Charlize Theron. 111 minutes. Rated PG-13.
The "Mini Cooper is the real star" of this "edge-of-your-seat" remake that "fires on most, if not all, cylinders", as a "fast-moving", "action-packed" "heist film" "filled with plot twists, maniacal car chases", "high-tech gadgets" and "timely pop-culture refer-

ences"; while "not at all thought-provoking", it's "everything a summer movie should be."

IT HAPPENED ONE NIGHT ✉◑
28 | 28 | 26 | 25
1934. Directed by Frank Capra. With Clark Gable, Claudette Colbert. 105 minutes. Not Rated.
"Gable and Colbert are swell together" in this "great Depression spirit-lifter", the "mother of all screwball comedies" about a "wise-cracking tabloid reporter" and a "snooty heiress" "on the run"; the first picture to "sweep all the major Oscars", it was also considered rather "racy for its time": indeed, Gable's baring of his chest in the "walls of Jericho" scene sent the "undershirt industry" into a tizzy.

It's a Mad Mad Mad Mad World
24 | 21 | 22 | 23
1963. Directed by Stanley Kramer. With Spencer Tracy, Milton Berle, Sid Caesar, Buddy Hackett, Mickey Rooney, Ethel Merman, Edie Adams, Jonathan Winters. 192 minutes. Rated G.
The ultimate "car comedy", this "sprawling gut-buster" features a "huge cast" of "crème de la crème" comedians in an "every-man-for-himself" "race to find a hidden fortune"; sure, it's a "long long long long movie", but it's "still terrifically entertaining" with plenty of "silly slapstick" and "great cameos" to keep things lively.

IT'S A WONDERFUL LIFE ◑
27 | 27 | 27 | 25
1946. Directed by Frank Capra. With James Stewart, Donna Reed, Henry Travers. 130 minutes. Not Rated.
"Nobody tells a story like Capra", and this "inspirational" film "strikes a fundamental chord with lots of people" via its "small-town" tale about a "good guy" coping with "hard times" and proving "how one life can make a difference"; sure, it's a "little schmaltzy" and "surprisingly dark", but most say "it's a wonderful picture" and "Christmas wouldn't be Christmas without it" – even if you've seen it a "million times" on TV.

I Want to Live! ✉◑
24 | 27 | 25 | 23
1958. Directed by Robert Wise. With Susan Hayward, Simon Oakland, Theodore Bikel. 120 minutes. Not Rated.
For "Susan Hayward at her most Susan Hayward", check out her "scenery-chewing", Oscar-grabbing turn in this "gut-wrenching" true story about a "tough cookie" "party girl" headed for the gas chamber; though cynics hiss this overheated "potboiler" as "extremely dated", more feel it's "not easily forgotten", particularly its still "effective" "anti–death penalty" theme.

I Was a Male War Bride ◑
21 | 24 | 20 | 20
1949. Directed by Howard Hawks. With Cary Grant, Ann Sheridan. 103 minutes. Not Rated.
Maybe it's "pretty standard" stuff and "not in the pantheon of romantic comedies", but this "amusing little movie" is still "thoroughly watchable" thanks to the "debonair" Grant as a WWII French army captain who falls for an American lieutenant (the very "nice" Sheridan); it's best remembered for its sequences of "Cary in drag" – even in a skirt, he's as "irresistible" as ever.

Jackass: The Movie
13 | 9 | 7 | 11
2002. Directed by Jeff Tremaine. With Johnny Knoxville, Bam Margera, Steve-O, Chris Pontius. 87 minutes. Rated R.
Fans of "sheer stupidity" fall for this "dumb", "title-says-it-all" flick based on the MTV series, in which a few "sick", "not-too-

bright lads" perform "idiotic stunts" and "crude sight gags" for your amusement; while too "moronic" for highbrows and certainly not for those "squeamish about paper cuts and bodily fluids", it's "absolutely hilarious" to its "brainless" cult followers, who report that "alcohol helps" make it even funnier.

Jagged Edge

22 | 22 | 22 | 20 |

1985. Directed by Richard Marquand. With Glenn Close, Jeff Bridges, Peter Coyote. 108 minutes. Rated R.

This "entertaining murder" thriller tells the tale of a "grisly homicide, a sensational trial and a forbidden love affair"; "great performances" from "'80s diva" Close (as a lawyer with principles) and Bridges (as the client endowed with troubling "charm") keep it so "exciting" that you'll be "guessing to the very end."

Jailhouse Rock ◑

18 | 15 | 14 | 19 |

1957. Directed by Richard Thorpe. With Elvis Presley, Judy Tyler, Mickey Shaughnessy. 96 minutes. Not Rated.

The "only really good Elvis movie (and that's not saying much)", this "cheesy classic" about an ex-con turned crooner is "worth the price of admission alone" for its "big musical number" featuring chorus boys in prison stripes and the King in all his "hip-swiveling" glory; favorite lyric: "if you can't find a partner, use a wooden chair."

James and the Giant Peach

20 | – | 20 | 24 |

1996. Directed by Henry Selick. Animated. 79 minutes. Rated PG.

"Fantastic effects", a kinetic visual style and bushels of "charm" give this "quirky" cartoon a "different look from the typical animated movie"; the story of a boy and a house-size fruit, it blends "live-action" shots with animation, though the result is "too edgy" and "bizarre" for those who claim Roald Dahl's "book is much better."

Jane Eyre ◑∅

25 | 27 | 26 | 22 |

1944. Directed by Robert Stevenson. With Orson Welles, Joan Fontaine, Margaret O'Brien. 97 minutes. Not Rated.

A "moody rendition of the Brontë novel", this "damn good" Gothic romance concerns a "frail" governess, a rich landowner and a houseful of dark secrets; expect plenty of "gloom and doom from the get-go" followed by atmospheric "shadows" and "Orson scowling" throughout – but as for that "disappointingly contrived ending", blame the author, not Hollywood.

JAWS ⑪

26 | 22 | 25 | 26 |

1975. Directed by Steven Spielberg. With Roy Scheider, Robert Shaw, Richard Dreyfuss. 124 minutes. Rated PG-13.

"Sink your teeth" into this "classic summer" scarefest that "gets the adrenaline pumping", since it's got "everything": "horrifying shark attacks", "missing limbs", "crackling" John Williams music and even "fully developed characters"; it "launched the Spielberg juggernaut" by cleverly "making you fear what you don't see", and if the title character looks a bit dated today, the "seasick" wonder "will it ever be safe to go back in the water?"

Jean de Florette ⑪🄵

27 | 27 | 26 | 26 |

1987. Directed by Claude Berri. With Yves Montand, Gérard Depardieu. 120 minutes. Rated PG.

"As Balzacian as French cinema can get", this "epic" drama about farmers feuding over a natural spring in the "pastoral paradise of Provence" is "stunningly beautiful" and "totally compelling"; since it's only the "first half of a genuinely tragic tale", "make sure to see *Manon of the Spring*" (its sequel) afterward to get the full scope of this truly "unforgettable story."

Jeremiah Johnson
23 | 21 | 23 | 22

1972. Directed by Sydney Pollack. With Robert Redford, Will Geer, Stefan Gierasch. 108 minutes. Rated PG.
"One of the earliest Westerns to change the movie stereotypes of Indian ways", this saga relates the story of an American soldier turned "mountain man" and his pitched, emotional battle with Crow Nation warriors; a precursor of *Dances with Wolves,* it showcases Redford "at his best" and is a "classic" to true believers.

Jerk, The
22 | 21 | 19 | 18

1979. Directed by Carl Reiner. With Steve Martin, Bernadette Peters, Catlin Adams. 94 minutes. Rated R.
Opening with "one of the best lines ever" – "I was born a poor black child" – this "absolutely hysterical" "rags-to-riches-to-rags" comedy captures the "wacky early Steve Martin" in all his "zany" glory (with ample support from Peters as his "sweetly naive love interest"); some say it's "silly", but "that's exactly the point."

Jerry Maguire
21 | 22 | 21 | 20

1996. Directed by Cameron Crowe. With Tom Cruise, Cuba Gooding Jr., Renée Zellweger, Jonathan Lipnicki. 138 minutes. Rated R.
A "gutsy sports agent" "sees the light" and "rediscovers his soul" in this "crowd-pleasing" dramedy that blends "football and love" into an "honest", "better-than-average" brew; in the "tailor-made" title role, "Tom terrific" plays "Mr. Show Me the Money" with excellent backup from the Oscar-winning Gooding and "little kid" Lipnicki (who "steals the movie"); best line: "you had me at hello."

Jesus Christ Superstar
21 | 18 | 22 | 21

1973. Directed by Norman Jewison. With Ted Neeley, Carl Anderson, Yvonne Elliman. 108 minutes. Rated G.
"Old flower children" find religion in this "visually arresting" "rock opera", a "fantastic" depiction of "Christ's humanity" featuring "hottie" Neeley in the title role and possibly the "best Andrew Lloyd Webber score" ever; heretics say it's "overindulgent" and "not as good as the stage show", speculating that the "cast was stoned the entire time" and thus it all "made sense to them."

JFK
19 | 20 | 20 | 21

1991. Directed by Oliver Stone. With Kevin Costner, Kevin Bacon, Tommy Lee Jones, Gary Oldman. 189 minutes. Rated R.
This "riveting", "revisionist" "conspiracy theory" drama about "what really happened on November 22, 1963" is, at the very least, a look at "what might have happened"; zealots swear it "makes a pretty good case" and delivers some "pull-out-all-the-stops" punches, but debunkers dub it "powerful paranoia" with "too many ifs, buts and maybes to be credible"; in the end, "whether truth or fiction", it remains as "controversial" as ever.

Journey to the Center of the Earth
19 | 16 | 21 | 18

1959. Directed by Henry Levin. With James Mason, Pat Boone, Arlene Dahl. 132 minutes. Rated G.
"Bernard Herrmann's score lends enchantment" to this very "enjoyable" production based on "Jules Verne's fantastical tale" of

underground exploration that's a "fun" sci-fi "romp" worth seeking out in a "widescreen" format; sure, it's a tad "hokey", but kids like its "Disney-esque" flavor and "superior special effects."

Judgment at Nuremberg ✉ ◑   `26` `27` `25` `22`

1961. Directed by Stanley Kramer. With Spencer Tracy, Burt Lancaster, Richard Widmark. 178 minutes. Not Rated.

Based on the "historic" 1948 Nazi war criminal trials, this "excellent courtroom drama" "asks some tough questions" and boasts "uniformly fine" players "often cast against type", as well as a "brilliant", Oscar-winning script; though the issues it raises are "unsettling", it remains a "relevant flick that everyone should see."

Jules and Jim ◑ 🄵   `24` `26` `24` `23`

1962. Directed by François Truffaut. With Jeanne Moreau, Oskar Werner, Henri Serre. 100 minutes. Not Rated.

One of the "milestones of the French New Wave", this charming "Truffaut masterpiece" is the "ultimate" "love triangle", wherein Moreau's "enigmatic beauty" makes her the "elusive muse" of two best friends; the "chemistry" between the players is "haunting and lyrical", and though that "bad-dream" ending is mighty "sad", the "fascinating story" proves "how complicated life can be."

Julia ✉   ▽ `24` `26` `25` `23`

1977. Directed by Fred Zinnemann. With Jane Fonda, Vanessa Redgrave, Jason Robards. 118 minutes. Rated PG.

"Fonda and Redgrave are radiant" in this "fascinating" drama, a "superb pairing of two actresses" cast as playwright Lillian Hellman and her "beloved childhood friend" Julia, a lefty resisting the Nazis in '30s Europe; fans applaud the "nervous" suspense and "moving" moments in this "frightening portrayal" of fraught times.

Juliet of the Spirits 🄵   ▽ `24` `24` `21` `26`

1965. Directed by Federico Fellini. With Giulietta Masina, Mario Pisu, Sandra Milo. 142 minutes. Not Rated.

"Fellini's first color feature", this "dreamlike" tale is the story of an unhappy housewife who escapes her "dreary marriage" and slides into "fantasy" after a séance; it "still haunts" fans who dub it a "vivid" look at the power of "imagination", thanks to the performance of the director's "likable" real-life wife Masina, along with a "surrealistic platter" of "fascinating" character actors.

Jumanji   `18` `18` `19` `22`

1995. Directed by Joe Johnston. With Robin Williams, Bonnie Hunt, Kirsten Dunst. 104 minutes. Rated PG.

"You'll see rolling dice in a whole different light" after a look at this "smartly done" adventure fantasy about a "mysterious board game" that swallows a young boy and coughs him up a quarter-century later – "along with a number of rampaging animals"; despite a "very cool concept" with "lots of action" and "loud CGI effects", it's "too scary for younger children" and ultimately might be a "better theme-park ride than movie."

Junebug   `21` `25` `19` `19`

2005. Directed by Phil Morrison. With Embeth Davidtz, Alessandro Nivola, Amy Adams. 106 minutes. Rated R.

A "rural" North Carolina family welcomes home the "son who got away" and his new "Blue State" bride in this "sleeper" dramedy whose "excellent" ensemble cast – notably the "sensational"

Adams – manages to produce a "vivid", "lovingly" realized "slice of Southern life"; for most, the "non-formulaic" storyline is a "quirky delight", though a few fret it "rambles around with no discernible point."

Jungle Book, The   ▽ 24 | 22 | 25 | 25
1942. Directed by Zoltan Korda. With Sabu, Joseph Calleia, Rosemary DeCamp. 109 minutes. Not Rated.
Talk to the animals: this "great children's movie" is a picturesque take on the Kipling yarn of Mowgli, a lad reared by wolves who returns to village life only to face mercenary types hot on the scent of hidden riches; it's a wild eyeful of "classic" family fare that even outdoes "one of the best Disneys", the Mouse House's animated version made 25 years later.

Jungle Book, The   23 | – | 23 | 24
1967. Directed by Wolfgang Reitherman. Animated. 78 minutes. Rated G.
Kipling's "Tarzan-like character and all his friends" pop up in this "charming" Disney cartoon that "makes an impression" with a "crowd-pleasing" story full of "family fun"; it might not be the studio's "best animation", but its "enchanting" soundtrack has enough "delightful songs" to make for a thing of "pure joy."

Jurassic Park ⓮   22 | 16 | 22 | 27
1993. Directed by Steven Spielberg. With Sam Neill, Laura Dern, Jeff Goldblum. 127 minutes. Rated PG-13.
"Humans are upstaged by dinosaurs" in this sci-fi "thrill ride" from the "astounding" Spielberg set in an extinct-creatures-come-to-life theme park that's "every child's dream come true"; don't expect much from the "lame story" and "weak" actors (nothing more than "dinochow"), but hold on for "white-knuckle", "roller-coaster" pacing and "astounding special effects" so "truly frightening" that they "might scare younger viewers."

Just Like Heaven   19 | 20 | 19 | 19
2005. Directed by Mark Waters. With Reese Witherspoon, Mark Ruffalo. 95 minutes. Rated PG-13.
A slice of "date movie" heaven comes with this "fluffy" romantic comedy, provided "you're willing to ride along" with its "offbeat premise": a "cynical" San Fran man hooking up with the disembodied "spirit of a woman"; "couch-cuddling" couples ignore the "cutesy" script's "eye-rolling predictability."

Karate Kid, The ⓮   19 | 16 | 20 | 17
1984. Directed by John G. Avildsen. With Ralph Macchio, Pat Morita, Elisabeth Shue. 126 minutes. Rated PG.
"*Rocky* for teenagers", this "classic" "underdog-wins-the-day story" matches a "kid finding it hard to fit in" with a martial-arts "mentor" who teaches him control through "discipline and loyalty"; balancing "solid values" with "doses of action", this "not-typical teen movie" has the "coming-of-age" thing down pat while being "inspiring" and "entertaining throughout."

Key Largo ❶   26 | 26 | 23 | 23
1948. Directed by John Huston. With Humphrey Bogart, Edward G. Robinson, Lauren Bacall. 101 minutes. Not Rated.
"Tough guys and dolls bring back the golden Warner Brothers days" in this "hard-hitting" noir showcase about a group held

hostage by a "super-rat" of a gangster – until "anti-hero" Bogart shows up; near the "top of Huston's body of work", it features a "highly suspenseful" plot, "stellar performances" and some "vintage" Bogie and Bacall moments – "'nuff said."

Kid Stays in the Picture, The   21 – 22 20

2002. Directed by Nanette Burstein, Brett Morgen. Documentary. 93 minutes. Rated R.

The "rise and fall" of legendary producer/studio head Robert Evans (*Chinatown, The Godfather, Rosemary's Baby*) gets the big-screen treatment in this "stylish documentary", an "only-in-America story" that's "narrated by the subject himself"; although "self-congratulatory propaganda" to some, most find it a "fascinating", "inside" look at moviemaking – "if you can get past Evans' enormous ego", that is.

Kill Bill Vol. 1 🎦   23 22 21 25

2003. Directed by Quentin Tarantino. With Uma Thurman, Lucy Liu, Vivica A. Fox, Sonny Chiba. 111 minutes. Rated R.

"Violence and gore abound" in this "over-the-top", "occasionally ridiculous" first installment of Quentin Tarantino's two-part salute to "comic strips", "spaghetti westerns" and "grindhouse kung fu flicks"; starring a "butt-kicking" Uma as a "revenge"-seeking "killing machine", it's "not for everyone" what with all the "spurting blood", "flying limbs" and "gross sound effects", but thrill freaks purr its "adrenaline" rush is simply "cool as heck" – provided you "check your brains at the door" before viewing.

Kill Bill Vol. 2   25 24 24 26

2004. Directed by Quentin Tarantino. With Uma Thurman, David Carradine, Michael Madsen, Daryl Hannah. 136 minutes. Rated R.

A continuation that "improves upon the original", this "gentler cousin" of the "obscenely graphic" *Vol. 1* features "less red food coloring" and more "character development", while remaining a "wickedly referential" homage to martial arts movies; as the ever-vengeful assassin, Thurman still "burns bright" and despite "trademark" Tarantino dialogue that gets a bit "long-winded", fans say there's a "true heart beating at the center of all the fighting" that lends "emotional heft" to both parts.

Killers, The ◑   25 25 25 23

1946. Directed by Robert Siodmak. With Burt Lancaster, Ava Gardner, Edmond O'Brien. 105 minutes. Not Rated.

"Lancaster makes a powerful film debut" backed up by an "outstanding" Gardner in this "riveting" flick "expanded from the Hemingway short story" about a mysterious small-town murder and its aftermath; it gets to the "core of film noir" through a burbling mix of "moral ambiguity, sexual tension and crime."

Killing Fields, The   26 26 27 25

1984. Directed by Roland Joffé. With Sam Waterston, Haing S. Ngor, John Malkovich. 141 minutes. Rated R.

"Friendship is tested by war" in this "harrowing" true story "told through the eyes of a journalist" relating the "atrocities in Cambodia" and the "horrors of the Khmer Rouge" following the U.S. pullout from Vietnam; "worthy Oscar-winner Ngor" (a real-life survivor of this "holocaust") turns in an "honest" performance that "will move you to tears" and "make you think" a lot.

Kind Hearts and Coronets ◑
26 | 28 | 26 | 24

1949. Directed by Robert Hamer. With Alec Guinness, Dennis Price, Valerie Hobson. 106 minutes. Not Rated.

For "quintessential" "English humor" that "gets better with each viewing", check out this "matchless black comedy" about the disinherited scion of a noble family who tries to achieve dukedom through serial murder; in an inspired twist, his victims – all eight of them – are played by the one-and-only Alec Guinness, whose spot-on performance squarely places this one on the "forever best list."

King and I, The ✉
27 | 26 | 25 | 27

1956. Directed by Walter Lang. With Yul Brynner, Deborah Kerr, Rita Moreno. 133 minutes. Rated G.

The "'Shall We Dance' scene" alone is "worth the price of admission" to this regally "sumptuous" version of Rodgers and Hammerstein's "terrific, old-fashioned" Broadway musical; though it may be "historically inaccurate", "who cares?" given the "stunning production", "gorgeous score" and "totally engaging" team of the "lovely Kerr" "getting to know" Oscar-winner Brynner.

King Kong ◑⓪
25 | 15 | 24 | 24

1933. Directed by Merian C. Cooper, Ernest B. Schoedsack. With Fay Wray, Robert Armstrong, Bruce Cabot. 100 minutes. Rated PG.

This "granddaddy of all monster flicks" "still rules the roost" as an "essential piece of cinema history" and the inspiration for "countless" imitators; ok, the "stop-motion" special effects are "Stone Age stuff by today's standards", but this "warped beauty-and-the-beast saga" remains memorable for its "indelible" imagery, that iconic "climax atop the Empire State Building" and most of all for the "irreplaceable" Fay Wray, "filmdom's finest screamer."

King Kong
20 | 18 | 19 | 26

2005. Directed by Peter Jackson. With Naomi Watts, Jack Black, Adrien Brody. 187 minutes. Rated PG-13.

"Less would have been more" in this "bloated remake" of the '30s classic about a "big monkey coerced into show business" that many dub more "video game" than movie; though fans can't help but "love the big furball" and are awed by the "mega-bucks" production, "slow pacing" and endless "monkeying around before the inevitable climb up the Empire State Building" add up to one "way-too-long" flick; in sum, director Jackson should either "hire an editor" or "stick to Middle-Earth."

King of Comedy, The
23 | 26 | 23 | 21

1983. Directed by Martin Scorsese. With Robert De Niro, Jerry Lewis, Sandra Bernhard. 101 minutes. Rated PG.

"Sharp, insightful and totally original", this pitch-black comedy about a wannabe comedian and the talk-show host he stalks is a different kind of "De Niro psycho flick" that's "complex and unsettling, but kind of fun"; as the stalkee, Lewis is both "funny and sad" ("maybe the French do know something"), and the picture itself is the "most underrated of Scorsese's career."

King of Hearts ⬛
26 | 26 | 26 | 24

1967. Directed by Philippe de Broca. With Alan Bates, Geneviève Bujold, Pierre Brasseur, Adolfo Celi. 100 minutes. Not Rated.

One of the "best anti-war flicks", this "satiric" allegory tells of a WWI soldier's attempt to dismantle a bomb set in a village solely inhabited by "insane asylum inmates"; while some snort its "pacifist" message is too "heavy-handed", more say this "cult classic" is a "thought-provoking" indictment of the "madness of war."

King Solomon's Mines
20 | 18 | 20 | 22

1950. Directed by Compton Bennett, Andrew Marton. With Stewart Granger, Deborah Kerr. 103 minutes. Not Rated.
"Location filming on the beautiful African continent" is the raison d'être of this H. Rider Haggard "chestnut" that's "hardly the most realistic" action flick, but a "good enough rendition" for most; it delivers some "romance" (via its "matinee idol" marquee names) and some "camp" (that "noble savages" subtext), but whether it's truly "Indiana Jones *before* Indiana Jones" is your call.

Kinsey
22 | 26 | 22 | 22

2004. Directed by Bill Condon. With Liam Neeson, Laura Linney, Chris O'Donnell, Peter Sarsgaard, Timothy Hutton. 118 minutes. Rated R.
"Kinky", "controversial" sex therapist Alfred Kinsey is the subject of this "racy", "pulls-no-punches" biopic that details "how the sexual revolution started" as well as "how far we've progressed and how far we have to go"; Neeson is "arousing" and Linney ever the "acting goddess", but overall what's "provocative and poignant" to some is "sterile and congratulatory" to others; P.S. "don't watch it with your parents."

Kissing Jessica Stein
21 | 20 | 21 | 19

2001. Directed by Charles Herman-Wurmfeld. With Jennifer Westfeldt, Heather Juergensen, Tovah Feldshuh. 97 minutes. Rated R.
"Single women relate" to this "new-age chick flick", a "quirky romantic comedy" about a "likable" gal "discouraged by the dating scene" who embarks on a lesbian affair; it's done in such a "sensitive" way that it "transcends moral objections" (it "won't offend your mother"), and even if "not profound", it's "sweet and solid."

Kiss Me Deadly ◑
24 | 20 | 23 | 21

1955. Directed by Robert Aldrich. With Ralph Meeker, Albert Dekker, Paul Stewart, Marian Carr. 104 minutes. Not Rated.
"Cold War propaganda has never been more frightening" than in this "mesmerizing" example of "classic film noir" rife with girls, guns and "cynicism", topped off with some "nuclear paranoia"; based on Mickey Spillane's lurid best-seller, it "bears repeat viewing" thanks to Aldrich's "superb direction", a "memorable ending" and that famous "suitcase", later "paid homage to in *Pulp Fiction*."

Kiss Me Kate
24 | 21 | 24 | 25

1953. Directed by George Sidney. With Howard Keel, Kathryn Grayson, Ann Miller. 109 minutes. Not Rated.
"Cole Porter's Broadway smash" gets the "Hollywood treatment" in this "sparkling film version" that's a reworking of "*The Taming of the Shrew*"; even though the "principals lack star power", you can still "brush up on your Shakespeare" nicely with "great musical numbers" and "exciting dancing", which come together famously in Miller's "knock-'em-dead" turn in 'Too Darn Hot.'

Kiss of the Spider Woman ✉∅
22 | 25 | 22 | 21

1985. Directed by Hector Babenco. With William Hurt, Raul Julia, Sonia Braga. 120 minutes. Rated R.
An "odd couple" – a political activist and a gay pederast – inhabit the same prison cell in this "intense drama" based on the Manuel

Puig novel that deals with "love, corruption and redemption"; though "worth seeing" for its "moving" script and Hurt's Oscar-winning turn, it may be "too much" for mainstream audiences.

Klute ✉   20 | 23 | 21 | 19
1971. Directed by Alan J. Pakula. With Jane Fonda, Donald Sutherland, Roy Scheider. 114 minutes. Rated R.
Oscar-winner Fonda stars as an "unhappy hooker" in this "heart-pounding" thriller, where she's "stalked by a killer" but protected by an "excellent" Sutherland as the cop who humanizes her; it "avoids all the clichés" of the genre via a chillingly matter-of-fact script, and if a bit "forgotten", at least Jane's shag "hairdo" is memorable.

Knife in the Water ❶🄵   24 | 23 | 24 | 22
1963. Directed by Roman Polanski. With Leon Niemczyk, Jolanta Umecka, Zygmunt Malanowicz. 94 minutes. Not Rated.
Polanski's "breakthrough" movie achieves "suspense in a boat" via its story of a married couple who invite a hitchhiker along on their sailing expedition; despite a "small cast" and "obvious low budget", the "mesmerizing" result achieves "Hitchcock-level tension", no mean feat considering that it was the director's first feature.

Kramer vs. Kramer ✉   23 | 26 | 23 | 21
1979. Directed by Robert Benton. With Dustin Hoffman, Meryl Streep, Justin Henry. 105 minutes. Rated PG.
"All about the acting", this "riveting drama" won Oscars for Hoffman and Streep as a married couple undergoing the "trauma of divorce and child custody"; overturning the "gender-biased view of parenting", its depiction of a growing "father-son" bond is the core of the story, though its "heart-wrenching" theme "hits you hard" – "there are no winners" in this split-up.

Kung Fu Hustle 🄵   23 | 20 | 21 | 24
2005. Directed by Stephen Chow. With Stephen Chow, Yuen Wah, Qiu Yuen. 95 minutes. Rated R.
"Move over Jackie Chan!": this "wildly imaginative" piece of "chop-socky" merges "mind-boggling fight choreography" with "genre-blending" aplomb in its tale of "unlikely heroes" facing off against mobsters; its "spaghetti-western-meets-*Crouching-Tiger*" approach is equal parts "Bruce Lee, Wile E. Coyote and Quentin Tarantino", along with a dash of "Bob Fosse."

La Cage aux Folles ⓫🄵   24 | 26 | 25 | 22
1979. Directed by Edouard Molinaro. With Michel Serrault, Ugo Tognazzi, Remy Laurent. 100 minutes. Rated R.
"Funnier than the American remake", the "Broadway musical" and the "two sequels", this "absurd" French farce is "light-years ahead of its time" telling the story of two gay blades forced to "play it straight" in order to impress prospective in-laws; "over-acted to perfection" by an "unbeatable" cast, it defines flaming "frivolity", even if a few cluck it's become "a bit faded" with time.

L.A. CONFIDENTIAL ✉   26 | 27 | 25 | 26
1997. Directed by Curtis Hanson. With Kevin Spacey, Russell Crowe, Guy Pearce, Kim Basinger. 138 minutes. Rated R.
"Every nuance is perfect" in this "steamy" period crime drama, an "explosive exposé" about "crooks, hookers" and "police corruption" in '50s LA that's "sharp", "detailed" and "violent as hell"; though it "made a star of Crowe", the overall "dead-on casting"

advances the "case for an ensemble acting award", while the "smart", Oscar-winning script has "all the grit" of a "film noir" classic, boosted by "21st-century production values."

Ladder 49

| 19 | 21 | 19 | 22 |

2004. Directed by Jay Russell. With Joaquin Phoenix, John Travolta. 115 minutes. Rated PG-13.
"Hunky" Phoenix and Travolta battle blazes in this "stirring tribute to firefighters", which impresses with "frightening" infernos and "tugs at the heartstrings" with its looks at "camaraderie" and "sacrifice"; most feel its themes carry special "poignancy in post-9/11" times, though a few hose it for being a bit "predictable and corny."

La Dolce Vita ◐ **F**

| 25 | 25 | 23 | 25 |

1961. Directed by Federico Fellini. With Marcello Mastroianni, Anita Ekberg, Anouk Aimée. 167 minutes. Not Rated.
"Celebrity-obsessed culture" goes under the microscope in this "scandalous" study of "decadence", "damnation and redemption" as seen in '60s Rome through the eyes of a jaded gossip columnist (Mastroianni "at his best") fed up with the "sweet life"; arguably "Fellini's most famous" film, it's a "decidedly unglamorous look at glamour" that "introduced the word 'paparazzi'" into the world lexicon; most iconic scene: "Ekberg in the Trevi Fountain."

Lady and the Tramp

| 26 | – | 24 | 25 |

1955. Directed by Wilfred Jackson, Hamilton Luske, Clyde Geronimi. Animated. 75 minutes. Rated G.
Puppy love gets a "gorgeous vintage Disney" spin in this "cute" canine romance awash in "lush animation" and lensed in "beautiful" CinemaScope; doggy devotees adore its fetching characters, "endearing story" and "great songs" ("highlighted by Peggy Lee's" sultry rendition of 'He's a Tramp'), though the most unforgettable moment has to be its "famous spaghetti kiss."

LADY EVE, THE ◐

| 28 | 28 | 27 | 26 |

1941. Directed by Preston Sturges. With Barbara Stanwyck, Henry Fonda, Charles Coburn. 97 minutes. Not Rated.
"Steamy innuendo" and "wacky pratfalls" coexist in this "smart" Sturges "romp" about a "scheming con artist" out to snare an "unsuspecting" "wealthy geek", aided by an "outstanding supporting cast"; a "sassy", "shameless" Stanwyck does "that sultry thing" so well that Fonda's "bumbling rube" "doesn't stand a chance" in this "sly" screwball comedy that many call "perfect."

Lady from Shanghai, The ◐

| 25 | 23 | 22 | 26 |

1948. Directed by Orson Welles. With Orson Welles, Rita Hayworth, Everett Sloane. 87 minutes. Not Rated.
"Another Orson Welles achievement", this "bravura" "B movie" is "completely enjoyable" for many, thanks to some memorable "stand-out scenes": the "shootout in the hall of mirrors", "Rita Hayworth speaking Chinese"; still, skeptics shrug the plot is a "confusing mess" that "looks like it's been cut to death."

Ladykillers, The

| 21 | 23 | 21 | 20 |

1956. Directed by Alexander Mackendrick. With Alec Guinness, Cecil Parker, Peter Sellers, Katie Johnson. 97 minutes. Not Rated.
"Inspired lunacy" from Britain's Ealing Studios, this "really funny" black comedy tells the story of a band of "incompetent" con artists planning a heist but "done in by a sweet little old lady"; the

"marvelous" cast includes a "first-rate" Guinness and a "just-starting-out" Sellers, but many say the picture's "stolen" by Katie Johnson, who's a "brilliant foil" as the elderly dowager.

Ladykillers, The
| 15 | 19 | 16 | 18 |

2004. Directed by Ethan Coen, Joel Coen. With Tom Hanks, Irma P. Hall, Marlon Wayans. 104 minutes. Rated R.
"Trying to recapture the magic of *O Brother, Where Art Thou?*", the Coen brothers again head to the Deep South for this "flat" re-make of the British black comedy that has some "good single laughs" but ultimately seems "another lame attempt by Hollywood to co-opt a classic film"; playing a "witty" if "uncharacteristically evil" con man, the "over-the-top" Hanks doesn't fare well either: despite a "great set of false teeth", he's "no Alec Guinness."

Lady Sings the Blues
▽ | 20 | 21 | 21 | 19 |

1972. Directed by Sidney J. Furie. With Diana Ross, Billy Dee Williams, Richard Pryor. 144 minutes. Rated R.
"Sad yet real", this biography of songbird Billie Holiday moves to the tempo of the "commanding" Miss Ross' body-and-soul performance; following Lady Day from hard times to the big time to her "strung-out" decline, it "holds you from beginning to end", though for diva devotees it's Diana who's the "best part."

Lady Vanishes, The ◑
▽ | 25 | 24 | 26 | 24 |

1938. Directed by Alfred Hitchcock. With Margaret Lockwood, Michael Redgrave, Dame May Whitty. 97 minutes. Not Rated.
A first-class ticket to "intrigue", this "crackerjack Hitchcock classic" finds the master at his "most fleet" and "fascinating", cooking up a "sublime combination" of the comic and the thrilling; its story of a strange disappearance on a train full of "memorable characters" is such "sheer entertainment" that even those who "know the ending" "never tire" of jumping back aboard.

La Femme Nikita 🇫
| 23 | 22 | 24 | 23 |

1991. Directed by Luc Besson. With Anne Parillaud, Jean-Hugues Anglade, Jeanne Moreau. 115 minutes. Rated R.
The "intelligent foreign film" gets a "violent jolt of adrenaline" in this "fast-paced" but "thought-provoking" "tough chick" flick about a punk junkie turned professional assassin; as the "kick-ass" lead, the "mesmerizing" Parillaud performs "spectacular stunts" that "hold your attention" so completely that it's more than "worth the effort to read the subtitles."

Last Emperor, The ✉
| 26 | 24 | 25 | 28 |

1987. Directed by Bernardo Bertolucci. With John Lone, Joan Chen, Peter O'Toole. 160 minutes. Rated PG-13.
"Truly an epic, and a darned good one" at that, this "sweeping", "large-scale" bio tells the story of China's "final monarch" from his ascent to the throne at age three through war, occupation and "revolutionary changes" in his kingdom; credit "lavish" sets, "spectacular scenery" and "outstanding" acting by Lone and O'Toole for its winning an impressive "nine Academy Awards."

Last Metro, The 🇫
| 24 | 25 | 23 | 23 |

1981. Directed by François Truffaut. With Catherine Deneuve, Gérard Depardieu, Jean Poiret. 131 minutes. Rated PG.
"Love and loyalty" are the underlying themes of this "wistful" tale of a French theatrical troupe staging a play in Nazi-occupied Paris;

it's "vintage Truffaut" with "beautiful" work from the "haunting" Deneuve, and might work best as a "double bill with *Day For Night*", the same director's "tribute to movies and movie folk."

Last of the Mohicans, The
22 | 22 | 22 | 25

1992. Directed by Michael Mann. With Daniel Day-Lewis, Madeleine Stowe, Russell Means. 122 minutes. Rated R.
For a "realistic portrayal of the French and Indian War", this "historical adventure set in the battle-torn American colonies" doesn't stint on the "barbarism", though they're tempered by "beautiful scenery" and an "incredible score"; "truly evil villains and larger-than-life heroes" make this "wonderful realization of James Fenimore Cooper's book" "top-notch filmmaking."

L.A. Story
20 | 20 | 20 | 19

1991. Directed by Mick Jackson. With Steve Martin, Victoria Tennant, Sarah Jessica Parker. 95 minutes. Rated PG-13.
"Every LA stereotype is played for laughs" in this "on-point" romantic comedy that's a "biting" if "loving put-down" of the "outrageous city" where people "really do drive down the road to get the mail"; Martin's "effortlessly intelligent" script throws "wacky" curves – and foretells the Starbucks invasion with its priceless "half-caff-triple-shot-no-foam-cappuccino" scene.

Last Picture Show, The ❶❷
23 | 23 | 23 | 22

1971. Directed by Peter Bogdanovich. With Timothy Bottoms, Jeff Bridges, Cybill Shepherd, Ben Johnson. 118 minutes. Rated R.
This "gritty portrait of a small Texas town on the brink of extinction" is "stunningly realized" in Bogdanovich's "masterpiece" that captures the loss so well "you can practically hear the death rattle"; the "birthplace of many new stars", it features some mighty "raw performances" from its "marvelous ensemble", a "strong script" and ultra-"realistic production values"; in short, it's a "lovely" if "sad" tribute to "something intrinsically American."

La Strada ✉❶❑
27 | 28 | 26 | 25

1956. Directed by Federico Fellini. With Giulietta Masina, Anthony Quinn, Richard Basehart. 108 minutes. Not Rated.
Set in a "traveling circus", Fellini's "parable of goodness thwarted by cruelty" pairs a "strongman who's all muscle and no heart" with a "peasant girl who's nothing but heart"; the "waif-like" Masina is "luminous" opposite a "surprisingly good" Quinn, and combined with "beautiful imagery" and "sad" "music that will stay with you", it's plain to see why this "masterwork" won the very first Best Foreign Film Oscar.

Last Samurai, The
23 | 23 | 22 | 27

2003. Directed by Edward Zwick. With Tom Cruise, Ken Watanabe, Tony Goldwyn. 154 minutes. Rated R.
"*Shogun*" meets "*Dances with Wolves*" in this "rousing" epic, wherein a haunted, "drunken Civil War vet" goes to feudal Japan to fight the samurai and is instead taken hostage by their "honor and spirit"; while Cruise garners an equivocal appraisal ("bang-up job" vs. "doesn't cut it"), "Watanabe wildly outshines him" as the "noble, betrayed" samurai leader; despite "slow pacing" and way "too much blood", this "clash of cultures" still swells with "sweeping vistas", "beautiful cinematography" and "amazing fight scenes."

Last Seduction, The ⓤ
22 | 24 | 22 | 20

1994. Directed by John Dahl. With Linda Fiorentino, Peter Berg, Bill Pullman. 110 minutes. Rated R.

"Fiorentino sizzles" as a "bad"-to-the-bone "femme fatale" in this "deliciously wicked" neo-noir crime thriller about a "very sexy" gal who rips off her husband and takes cover with a love-struck doofus; sure, it's "low budget" and there may be more than a few "holes in the plot", but "man, what a ride!"

Last Tango in Paris
17 | 20 | 15 | 19

1973. Directed by Bernardo Bertolucci. With Marlon Brando, Maria Schneider. 129 minutes. Rated NC-17.

Definitely not about dance lessons, this "evocative blend" of the "romantic" and the "erotic" presents a "graphically sexual" Parisian pas de deux between a "compelling" Brando and a limber Schneider; scenes that "seemed steamy then" may come off as "pointless" now, but Marlon's "at his best" "mumbling in two languages" and dreaming up "risqué" ways to "use butter."

Last Temptation of Christ, The
22 | 23 | 25 | 22

1988. Directed by Martin Scorsese. With Willem Dafoe, Harvey Keitel, Barbara Hershey. 164 minutes. Rated R.

"Controversial" with a big C, this "intriguing" drama "reexamines Christian faith" by portraying "one of the most humanizing perspectives on Jesus" ever filmed; of course, those "rigid on the Scriptures" consider it blasphemous (and it's still not available in certain video chains to this day), but believers say this "absorbing", "important" Scorsese drama must "be seen to be criticized."

Last Waltz, The
26 | – | 20 | 26

1978. Directed by Martin Scorsese. Documentary. With The Band. 117 minutes. Rated PG.

In the running for "best concert movie of all time", this renowned documentary "captures the end of a rock 'n' roll era" in its recording of The Band's last gasp, abetted by a musical "dream team" that includes, among others, Bob Dylan, Eric Clapton, Joni Mitchell, Muddy Waters, Neil Young and Van Morrison; it's "clearly a labor of love from Scorsese" that "shouldn't be this good, but it is."

Laura ◐
27 | 25 | 27 | 26

1944. Directed by Otto Preminger. With Gene Tierney, Dana Andrews, Clifton Webb. 88 minutes. Not Rated.

A "suspenseful, elegant whodunit with a twist" – the "detective falls in love with the murder victim" – this "chic" take on film noir provides plenty of "romantic goose bumps" owing to the simmering "chemistry" between the "brooding" Andrews and "exquisite" Tierney; throw in some "haunting music" and a "nicely paced" if somewhat "silly plot", and the result is "Preminger's best flick."

Laurel Canyon
18 | 24 | 17 | 20

2003. Directed by Lisa Cholodenko. With Frances McDormand, Christian Bale, Kate Beckinsale. 103 minutes. Rated R.

A "dysfunctional family" is dissected in this "quirky" drama pitting an "aging hippie" record producer against her "conservative" son, who's moved back in with her; the "radiant" McDormand "carries the film" as the "hot, smart" mama, though she's up against a "predictable", "unfulfilling" story that "doesn't quite come together."

Lavender Hill Mob, The ✉◑   25 | 26 | 23 | 22
1951. Directed by Charles Crichton. With Alec Guinness, Stanley Holloway. 78 minutes. Not Rated.
"Wittily whimsical", this British comic "gem" helped introduce Alec Guinness – an "actor's actor with the most expressive raised eyebrow in film" – to America; the caper-gone-awry story involving a milquetoast bank clerk who dreams up the "perfect crime" is "delightfully funny" thanks to its "wonderful" script.

L'Avventura ◑🄵   ▽ 24 | 23 | 22 | 24
1961. Directed by Michelangelo Antonioni. With Gabriele Ferzetti, Monica Vitti, Lea Massari. 145 minutes. Not Rated.
A real art-house "landmark" and one of "Antonioni's most accessible" films, this "minimalist masterwork" follows a jaded playboy as he hunts for his missing mistress on a Mediterranean isle; its "stark visual and intellectual" values are hailed as "revolutionary", though literalists wading through the "ennui" come up "baffled and confused."

LAWRENCE OF ARABIA ✉   29 | 28 | 27 | 29
1962. Directed by David Lean. With Peter O'Toole, Omar Sharif, Alec Guinness. 222 minutes. Rated PG.
The "biggest epic of them all", this bio of WWI British soldier T.E. Lawrence "sets the standard for large-scale filmmaking" with its "stunning" desert cinematography, "suspense by the duneful" and "stupendous cast", led by the "perfect" O'Toole; thanks to Lean's "painterly techniques", the "background is as consistently amazing as the foreground" in this "gold standard" of an Oscar magnet that "demands to be seen on the big screen."

League of Their Own, A   20 | 20 | 22 | 20
1992. Directed by Penny Marshall. With Geena Davis, Tom Hanks, Madonna, Lori Petty, Rosie O'Donnell. 128 minutes. Rated PG.
"There's no crying in baseball", though this "nostalgic gem" about a WWII women's team has fans praising its "fantastic" ensemble cast ("even Madonna is good"); "bringing back the innocence" of simpler times, this "piece of history" might have a "sentimental epilogue", but its "feel-good" aura makes it "highly rewatchable."

Leaving Las Vegas ✉   20 | 24 | 18 | 18
1995. Directed by Mike Figgis. With Nicolas Cage, Elisabeth Shue, Julian Sands. 111 minutes. Rated R.
"Disturbing", "depressing" and "painful to watch", this "tragic love story" between a "suicidal alcoholic" and a "burned-out prostitute" is still "brilliant in all aspects", leaving viewers "emotionally drained"; while giddy fans agree the "damn good" Cage "deservedly won the Oscar" for his "best work thus far", soberer sorts call this "feel-bad" flick the "ultimate downer."

Legally Blonde ⑪   19 | 20 | 17 | 19
2001. Directed by Robert Luketic. With Reese Witherspoon, Luke Wilson. 96 minutes. Rated PG-13.
The near-unanimous verdict on this "*Clueless*-goes-to-law-school" comedy: "cute-as-a-button" Witherspoon is "irresistible" as a "Valley Girl" "bursting the stereotype" and proving that "anyone can achieve their dream"; though most jurors decree

that "even an intellectual can like" this "pink puffball of a movie", some say "there ought to be a law" against such "derivative piffle."

Legend 18 | 15 | 18 | 22

1986. Directed by Ridley Scott. With Tom Cruise, Mia Sara, Tim Curry, David Bennent. 94 minutes. Rated PG.

"Fantasy" fanatics adore this "mythical" tale of a quest to rescue an "innocent princess" and free the "last remaining unicorn" by a group of "bumbling elves" and a "forest boy"; while it's atmospheric enough to be a "guilty pleasure", "dippy" dialogue makes it a "winner in the unintentional humor" department for some.

Legends of the Fall 20 | 21 | 20 | 23

1994. Directed by Edward Zwick. With Brad Pitt, Anthony Hopkins, Aidan Quinn, Julia Ormond. 133 minutes. Rated R.

This "sweeping epic" set in "untamed 19th-century America" chronicles "one family's struggle in times of political turmoil" and the "moving" story of a woman "tragically passed between three brothers"; sure, a few label it "pretentious" and "no threat to the best Westerns", but there are no complaints about the "fantastic scenery" – and "nothing beats Pitt riding in on that horse!"

Lemony Snicket's A Series of Unfortunate Events 18 | 20 | 19 | 23

2004. Directed by Brad Siberling. With Jim Carrey. 107 minutes. Rated PG.

Brimming with "visually pleasing" sets and costumes à la "Tim Burton", this "dark yet heartwarming" orphan tale is distilled from the popular children's book series; while the kid actors fit their parts "to a tee", super-"ham" Carrey's "scenery-devouring" turn as villainous Count Olaf splits surveyors: supporters say it's "overacting at its best" but foes fume it "drags the movie down."

Lenny ◑ 24 | 27 | 23 | 21

1974. Directed by Bob Fosse. With Dustin Hoffman, Valerie Perrine. 111 minutes. Rated R.

"Blue comic" Lenny Bruce gets the Bob Fosse scrutiny in this "knockout", "ahead-of-its-time" biopic that's alternately "depressing and funny"; the amused applaud the "virtuoso" Hoffman, "excellent" Perrine ("who knew?") and "gritty" black-and-white cinematography that perfectly "captures the kind of seedy clubs" where the "self-destructive" comedian got his start.

Leopard, The 🇫 25 | 27 | 24 | 27

1963. Directed by Luchino Visconti. With Burt Lancaster, Claudia Cardinale, Alain Delon. 187 minutes. Rated PG.

"Historical sweep", "stunning visuals" and "personal reverie" combine in this "magnificent period piece" from Luchino Visconti, a "sumptuous" epic set in 19th-century Italy detailing the rise of Garibaldi and subsequent "decline of the aristocracy"; despite a "sluggish pace" and mixed marks for Lancaster's title turn as an Italian prince, "awesome" production values and the finale's "lauded" ballroom sequence make this one a "must-see" for cineasts.

Lethal Weapon ⑪ 21 | 19 | 20 | 21

1987. Directed by Richard Donner. With Mel Gibson, Danny Glover, Gary Busey. 112 minutes. Rated R.

"Top-notch" action peppered with "plenty of laughs" establishes this "classic buddy" flick as the "first and best of the franchise" (three sequels and counting); as "hard-bitten, job-weary" LA detectives, Gibson and Glover are "at the top of their form" with such "tremendous chemistry" that the picture became the "model for '80s cop movies", a "classic" of the genre.

Letter, The ◑
▽ 25 | 28 | 26 | 25

1940. Directed by William Wyler. With Bette Davis, Herbert Marshall, Gale Sondergaard. 95 minutes. Not Rated.
"Bette shines" as a cool customer in torrid British Malaya in this "superb" drama based on Somerset Maugham's story of a planter's wife who goes postal on her paramour; replete with "tinkling chimes and clouded full moons", the "exotic ambiance" lends "scary impact" to the proceedings, while Davis' "incredible" chops set the "standard for judging acting to this day."

Liar Liar
16 | 17 | 16 | 16

1997. Directed by Tom Shadyac. With Jim Carrey, Maura Tierney, Justin Cooper. 87 minutes. Rated PG-13.
Critics quibble over this "Carrey vehicle" about a lawyer compelled to tell the truth for 24 hours for the sake of his child; while some laud the star's "hilarious", "effective" performance shaded with some "poignant, non-hammy" moments, cynics nix the "not believable" (verging on "boring") story.

License to Kill ⑪
14 | 13 | 13 | 17

1989. Directed by John Glen. With Timothy Dalton, Carey Lowell, Robert Davi, Talisa Soto. 133 minutes. Rated PG-13.
Dalton's second turn as 007 is also "thankfully his last" as this "grim" Bonder bucks the franchise formula to show the normally suave spy "losing his cool" and going on a mission to "get even" with a drug lord; the violence is "too graphic" and the tone overly "mean spirited" gripe critics who lament "there's no fun in this one."

Life Aquatic with Steve Zissou, The
16 | 19 | 14 | 19

2004. Directed by Wes Anderson. With Bill Murray, Owen Wilson, Cate Blanchett, Anjelica Huston, Willem Dafoe. 119 minutes. Rated R.
"Quirk"-meister Anderson captains this "esoteric" undersea "parody of Jacques Cousteau" (and *Moby Dick*) that's awash in "droll" humor, "visual candy" and "great actors", chiefly the "brilliant" Murray; all told, what's "imaginative filmmaking" to some feels like "flat" "self-indulgence" to a majority who can't fathom "what all the fuss is about."

Lifeboat ◑
25 | 26 | 25 | 22

1944. Directed by Alfred Hitchcock. With Tallulah Bankhead, William Bendix, Walter Slezak. 96 minutes. Not Rated.
"Can a one-set movie hold your attention?": this "fascinating Hitchcock" war-era thriller does, providing "more drama per square inch", since the "entire picture takes place in a small lifeboat"; among the "bickering crew of castaways", Bankhead is "superb, dahling", but blink and you'll miss the director's "inspired" cameo.

Life Is Beautiful ✉️ 🅕
27 | 27 | 27 | 25

1998. Directed by Roberto Benigni. With Roberto Benigni, Nicoletta Braschi. 118 minutes. Rated PG-13.
Simultaneously "heart-wrenching" and "uplifting", this story about an Italian family's attempt to shelter their son from the Holocaust is a "bittersweet fable about the triumph of the human spirit"; Oscar-winner Benigni provides an "emotional roller-coaster

ride" with some "inspired comedic" touches, and though some "uncomfortable" viewers suggest a "trivialization" of a very serious subject, most agree "if you don't shed a tear, you're not human."

Life of Brian | 23 | 21 | 23 | 20 |
1979. Directed by Terry Jones. With Monty Python. 94 minutes. Rated R.
"Profane, sacrilegious and really funny", this "hysterical" "cult classic" about a Holy Land sad sack mistaken for the Messiah is "as bitingly original a spoof as has ever been made" and "probably one of God's favorites"; only "Monty Python at their finest" could "get away with" the final scene that "sends you off singing 'Always Look on the Bright Side of Life.'"

Life of David Gale | 21 | 24 | 22 | 20 |
2003. Directed by Alan Parker. With Kevin Spacey, Kate Winslet, Laura Linney. 130 minutes. Rated R.
Expect a "great shocker at the end" of this "compelling" capital punishment drama, "but getting there has some pretty dull moments"; "surprised" surveyors "love the twists and turns", while those who "figured things out ahead of time" find the story "predictable" and "contrived", but "interesting nonetheless."

Like Water for Chocolate 🇫 | 25 | 24 | 25 | 25 |
1993. Directed by Alfonso Arau. With Lumi Cavazos, Marco Leonardi. 123 minutes. Rated R.
"Ahh, food and sex" make a "lip-smacking" combination in this "mouthwatering" Mexican "foodie classic" that serves up an "eccentric" love story that's "as pleasing to the eye as it is to the palate"; "deliciously true to the novel", it offers "magical realism at its best" and, "like a warm dessert", leaves one feeling so "content and hopeful" that many show up for "another helping."

Lili ⊘ | ▽ 23 | 23 | 23 | 23 |
1953. Directed by Charles Walters. With Leslie Caron, Mel Ferrer, Jean-Pierre Aumont. 81 minutes. Rated G.
Walking a tightrope between "deep whimsy" and "endearing" drama, this ringside look at an "innocent" orphan follows "ultimate waif" Caron as she joins the circus; enlivened by "one song" and some occasional dancing, the story is almost "too cute", but an "outstanding" cast ensures it will "turn on the tears every time."

Lilies of the Field ✉◑ | 25 | 26 | 24 | 23 |
1963. Directed by Ralph Nelson. With Sidney Poitier, Lilia Skala, Stanley Adams. 94 minutes. Not Rated.
With his "flawless" performance in this "quiet, simple" tale about a handyman who helps refugee nuns build a chapel, Poitier became the first African-American to win a lead-role Oscar and also helped "open up racial dialogue" in the Civil Rights era; the film's many admirers hail a "sweet story" told with "heart and charm" that delivers a "lesson in dignity and trust."

Lilo & Stitch | 23 | – | 22 | 24 |
2002. Directed by Chris Sanders, Dean DeBlois. Animated. 85 minutes. Rated PG.
"Different from the usual Disney stuff", this "adorable" animated tale features a "spunky" orphaned Hawaiian girl who adopts a "lovable" blue 'dog' that turns out to be a space alien; it's a "heartwarming story" with "great life lessons" about "love", the

"meaning of family" and "finding your place in the world", as well as "laughs from beginning to end" and an Elvis-infused soundtrack; "beautiful watercolor backdrops" give the film its "distinctive look."

Limelight ◑
`24` `25` `22` `23`

1952. Directed by Charles Chaplin. With Charles Chaplin, Claire Bloom, Buster Keaton, Nigel Bruce. 137 minutes. Rated G.
"Chaplin's last great film", this "poignant" look at a British ballerina and a music hall clown draws mixed responses; foes call it "dated corn" and protest its "overstated" "self-indulgence", but fans counter it's "sensitive" stuff, and certainly worth watching to see "two giants of the silent film era [Charlie and Buster Keaton] on-screen together."

LION IN WINTER, THE ✉
`28` `29` `27` `26`

1968. Directed by Anthony Harvey. With Peter O'Toole, Katharine Hepburn. 134 minutes. Rated PG.
Hepburn and O'Toole give "performances so brilliant your eyes will hurt" as "two titans battling each other and history" in this "intelligent, delicious" drama that reigns as "one of the best historical films ever made"; indeed, this "masterful" look at Henry II and Eleanor of Aquitaine (the original "dysfunctional royal family") is so "superb" that it earned Kate her third Oscar, as well as statuettes for its "sparkling" screenplay and score.

Lion King, The
`25` `–` `25` `27`

1994. Directed by Roger Allers, Rob Minkoff. Animated. 89 minutes. Rated G.
Hakuna Matata!: this "crowning achievement" garners roars of approval as one of "Disney's best" thanks to its "breakthrough animation techniques", "toe-tapping" music and "exceptional voice characterizations by Matthew Broderick and Jeremy Irons"; though this "heartwarming" tale about an exiled lion cub (sort of the "same story as *Bambi*") is "touching" and often "comedic", the film has some bona fide "scary moments" and "may be too intense" for smaller fry.

Little Big Man
`24` `25` `24` `23`

1970. Directed by Arthur Penn. With Dustin Hoffman, Faye Dunaway, Chief Dan George. 147 minutes. Rated PG.
A "rousing" Wild West "saga", this "memorable period piece" concerns a "Forrest Gump–like" character with a knack for popping up at "famous historical moments"; plaudits go to its "engrossing blend of humor and drama" and "great" performances by George and Hoffman ("truly the man of 1,000 faces") – indeed, it's "one of the best looks at Native Americans" ever portrayed in moviedom.

Little Caesar ◑
`24` `26` `23` `22`

1931. Directed by Mervyn LeRoy. With Edward G. Robinson, Douglas Fairbanks Jr., Glenda Farrell. 79 minutes. Not Rated.
"Crime doesn't pay" in this "seminal" gangster flicker, a "fictionalized" version of the Al Capone story starring "true Hollywood tough guy" Robinson, who brings some "Greek tragedy" to the role of a "moiderous bum" on the way up ("Tony Soprano, eat your heart out"); it's a "gritty", "fast-paced" ride that's best remembered for its immortal last line: "mother of mercy, is this the end of Rico?"

Little Foxes, The ◑
▽ | 25 | 27 | 23 | 24

1941. Directed by William Wyler. With Bette Davis, Herbert Marshall, Teresa Wright, Dan Duryea. 116 minutes. Not Rated.

All the "power" of Lillian Hellman's "bitter little" stage drama is apparent in this "excellent" film adaptation via William Wyler, a showcase for "Bette at her bitchy best" as the mercenary missus in a shifty Southern family; the sly scheming and deadly betrayal make for such a bang-up "lesson in acting" that many wonder "why don't they make movies like this anymore."

Little Mermaid, The
24 | – | 23 | 25

1989. Directed by Ron Clements, John Musker. Animated. 82 minutes. Rated G.

This "first of the great second wave of Disney classics" manages to "hold its own against *Cinderella* and *Snow White*", what with its delightful cartoon "critters", "witty dialogue" and "upbeat", Oscar-winning music that "made animation sing again"; sure, feminists discern a "sexist message" ("why does the woman have to change for the man?"), but in the end "how could you not love this adorable redheaded mermaid?"

Little Princess, A
▽ | 26 | 24 | 25 | 26

1995. Directed by Alfonso Cuarón. With Liesel Matthews, Eleanor Bron. 97 minutes. Rated G.

"Shirley Temple's version has nothing on" this "sumptuous", "perfectly played" family fable of a "pampered" boarding-school lass with "mystical" leanings who goes from "riches to rags and back" after her dragoon dad is declared dead during WWI; though it attracts less than the "attention it deserves", loyalists label it a "top-flight tearjerker."

Little Shop of Horrors
19 | 19 | 20 | 21

1986. Directed by Frank Oz. With Rick Moranis, Ellen Greene, Steve Martin. 94 minutes. Rated PG-13.

If "campy" "sci-fi musicals" ring your bell, this "twisted" tale about a boy, a girl and a "smart-ass, man-eating plant" (based on an old Roger Corman B-movie) "ranks right up there with *The Rocky Horror Picture Show* as a cult classic"; credit the "great cast" and "humorously dark score" for the ensuing "goofy fun"; most "priceless" moment: Martin's "sadistic dentist" treating "masochist patient" Bill Murray.

Little Women
21 | 23 | 24 | 21

1994. Directed by Gillian Armstrong. With Winona Ryder, Susan Sarandon. 115 minutes. Rated PG.

Surveyors are split on this "feminist" adaptation of Louisa May Alcott's classic novel about a Civil War–era family: partisans of George Cukor's 1933 version dismiss this remake as "unnecessary", harrumphing that "Ryder can't compare to Katharine Hepburn", yet others swear it's "worth watching" for Sarandon's performance alone; there's no debate, however, that its "great message" – about a "family loving each other no matter what" – is "very well done."

Live and Let Die
19 | 17 | 20 | 21

1973. Directed by Guy Hamilton. With Roger Moore, Jane Seymour, Yaphet Kotto. 119 minutes. Rated PG.

Expect "beautiful women, fast cars", "snakes, voodoo and Yaphet Kotto" in this "exotic" James Bond caper set in the Caribbean and the "sultry South"; "nonstop" action sequences ("particularly the bayou boat chase"), "humor that's shaken (not stirred)" and Moore's first 007 impersonation make it worth watching – even if Sean Connery loyalists label it the "beginning of the decline."

Living Daylights, The ⑪

14 | 14 | 14 | 18

1987. Directed by John Glen. With Timothy Dalton, Maryam d'Abo, Jeroen Krabbé, Joe Don Baker. 130 minutes. Rated PG.
There's heated debate about Timothy Dalton's first stab at James Bond, with fans saying his "underrated", "hard-edged" performance is "very true to Ian Fleming", while foes fume his "brooding", "gritty" take does the character a "disservice" (007 "doesn't have to be politically correct"); as for the storyline, it's the usual over-the-top thrill ride involving a defecting Russian general, a shifty American arms dealer and a drop-dead gorgeous cellist/assassin.

Local Hero

26 | 24 | 26 | 23

1983. Directed by Bill Forsyth. With Burt Lancaster, Peter Riegert, Peter Capaldi. 111 minutes. Rated PG.
"The little people triumph over the money people" in this "understated but brilliant" comedy contrasting the differences between a "quaint Scottish town" and the "corporate world"; its "engaging characters", "quirky" storyline and Mark Knopfler's "great soundtrack" make for such "bighearted", "whimsical" fun that many argue it "deserves a larger following."

Lock, Stock and Two Smoking Barrels

23 | 22 | 25 | 23

1998. Directed by Guy Ritchie. With Jason Flemyng, Dexter Fletcher, Nick Moran. 105 minutes. Rated R.
"First-time director" Ritchie does a "brilliant job co-opting every gangster flick cliché" in this "violent but riveting" thriller that's a "Cockney" take on *Pulp Fiction*; agreed, it's "hard to understand the accents", but the "acting, setting and soundtrack are dead-on" and "super plot surprises" abound; all in all, this "fun romp with guns" is "lean", mean and "wonderfully produced."

Lolita ①

24 | 24 | 24 | 23

1962. Directed by Stanley Kubrick. With James Mason, Sue Lyon, Shelley Winters, Peter Sellers. 152 minutes. Not Rated.
Though this "fine adaptation of the Nabokov classic" might be somewhat "sanitized" ("it was made in 1962, after all"), it's still "slyly dirty" enough for its very adult subject, a middle-aged man's obsession with a barely teenaged girl; though ageists argue Lyon is "too old" for the title role, there still are plenty of "choice moments" supplied by an "extremely funny" Sellers and Winters, who "gives the performance of her life."

Lone Star

25 | 25 | 25 | 22

1996. Directed by John Sayles. With Kris Kristofferson, Matthew McConaughey, Chris Cooper. 135 minutes. Rated R.
Director Sayles' "overlooked masterpiece" is a "flawless murder mystery that digs deep into the American psyche" and "takes a hard look at race relations"; following the discovery of a buried skeleton in a small Texas town, the plot goes through "more twists and turns than the Rio Grande" but still "works on multiple levels" as it "seamlessly interweaves multiple characters" – and that "ending will make your jaw drop."

Longest Day, The ◑   24 | 20 | 25 | 26
1962. Directed by Ken Annakin, Andrew Marton et al. With John Wayne, Rod Steiger. 180 minutes. Rated G.
As far as "war-as-spectacle" epics go, this "sweeping" saga of the Normandy invasion sets the "standard by which all others are measured"; D-day devotees dig the "superb dedication to detail" and "all-star cast" that "really gets into their characters" thanks to a script that "includes the point of view of everyone involved"; still, foes snipe "too many cameos" turn it into a "cattle call."

Longest Yard, The   17 | 15 | 18 | 16
1974. Directed by Robert Aldrich. With Burt Reynolds, Eddie Albert, Michael Conrad. 121 minutes. Rated R.
A "guy's movie" Hall of Famer, this "prison football comedy" stars Reynolds as a pro quarterback sent to the big house only to "lead a Heisman-quality cast" of roughneck convicts in a game against the guards; scoring many "memorable lines", it has "Mean Machine" mavens ruling it "arguably the best" pigskin pic ever.

Longest Yard, The   17 | 16 | 17 | 18
2005. Directed by Peter Segal. With Adam Sandler, Chris Rock, Burt Reynolds, Nelly. 113 minutes. Rated PG-13.
A "decent remake of an already good film", this "mildly amusing" sports comedy about a prison football team "rehashes" the original, adding a "more modern soundtrack" and "cameos galore"; still, foes fret this "formulaic" flick "fumbles on every level", starting with Sandler, who's "unbelievable as a quarterback" – "once a waterboy, always a waterboy."

Longtime Companion   23 | 25 | 25 | 21
1990. Directed by Norman René. With Campbell Scott, Mary-Louise Parker, Bruce Davison. 100 minutes. Rated R.
"Love and heartbreak" are the themes of this "groundbreaking" film that follows seven gay men throughout a "specific time and place": '80s Manhattan during the "first wave of AIDS"; "just as devastating today as when first released", it "gives legitimacy" to a former "forbidden subject" but "doesn't pander or trivialize the issues" thanks to the "heartfelt performances", notably the "standout" Davison and "up-and-coming" Parker.

Looking for Mr. Goodbar ∅   18 | 21 | 19 | 18
1977. Directed by Richard Brooks. With Diane Keaton, Tuesday Weld, Richard Gere. 135 minutes. Rated R.
Powered by Keaton's "brilliant" turn as a "sexually repressed" teacher by day who "trolls the bars by night", this "sobering tale of '70s promiscuity" is a "dark primer for single women" that "sends chills down your spine" – with a "gruesome ending" delivered "like a sledgehammer upside the head."

Lord of the Flies ◑   ▽ 21 | 17 | 25 | 19
1963. Directed by Peter Brook. With James Aubrey, Tom Chapin, Hugh Edwards. 90 minutes. Not Rated.
The last word in youth gone wild, this "powerful" take on novelist William Golding's "modern classic" finds a pack of marooned British schoolboys slipping into "disturbing" behavior as barbarity overtakes breeding; the "realistic" style makes for an "unsettling" drama with bonus "social commentary buried within", though some savage the "incompetent acting" and sniff "read the book instead."

Lord of the Rings, The `15` – `22` `16`
1978. Directed by Ralph Bakshi. Animated. 132 minutes. Rated PG.
Graphics guru Bakshi's animated take on Tolkien is no "Fritz the Hobbit": it's "true to the books" in presenting the elfin Frodo's "epic" face-off with the forces of evil (even if it's "too bad" the "truncated storyline" "breaks off halfway" into the trilogy); but others say that this "muddled" "travesty" often "looks ridiculous."

LORD OF THE RINGS: THE FELLOWSHIP OF THE RING ⑪ `27` `25` `27` `29`
2001. Directed by Peter Jackson. With Elijah Wood, Ian McKellen, Viggo Mortensen, Sean Astin, Liv Tyler. 178 minutes. Rated PG-13.
This "enthralling", "true-to-the-book" retelling of Tolkien's classic epic "transcends the genre" and "sets the benchmark for fantasy films to come" with its "lovingly crafted" visualization of Middle Earth; despite a somewhat "slow beginning", "three hours of brilliant bliss" ensue that are "exhilaratingly" perfect, "right down to the hairy Hobbit feet."

LORD OF THE RINGS: THE RETURN OF THE KING ✉ `28` `26` `27` `29`
2003. Directed by Peter Jackson. With Elijah Wood, Ian McKellen, Viggo Mortensen, Sean Astin, Liv Tyler. 201 minutes. Rated PG-13.
Jackson "should be knighted" for this "history-making", Oscar-grabbing finale to the "superlative trilogy", a "paean to the goodness of good" in the Fellowship's "united allegiance against evil"; it "lives up to the hoopla" from its two "faithfully rendered" predecessors thanks to "mythic sweep and grandeur" and a "cast obviously devoted to the picture"; in sum, this "masterpiece" is a "cinematic monument" to Tolkien's original fantasy, capped by a "long ending" that nonetheless draws a "big round of applause."

LORD OF THE RINGS: THE TWO TOWERS ⑪ `27` `25` `26` `29`
2002. Directed by Peter Jackson. With Elijah Wood, Ian McKellen, Viggo Mortensen, Sean Astin, Liv Tyler. 179 minutes. Rated PG-13.
There's "much less exposition" and much "more testosterone" in the second "gripping" installment of the Tolkien trilogy, which "starts right where the last one ended"; grab a "comfortable chair" and brace yourself for three hours of "flawless special effects" ("Gollum rocks"), "wonderful" acting by "hot guys", "epic battles the likes of which have never before been captured on celluloid" and an "amazing storyline" that really "does justice" to the book.

Lost Horizon ◑ `25` `24` `26` `22`
1937. Directed by Frank Capra. With Ronald Colman, Jane Wyatt, Margo, Sam Jaffe. 138 minutes. Not Rated.
A "nostalgic reminder of Hollywood's Golden Age", this "moving" adaptation of James Hilton's best-seller still "casts a spell" thanks to the "irresistible" utopia known as "Shangri-la"; this "fairy tale" of a picture may seem "quaint" and "dated" now, but Colman's performance is "as contemporary as if it were made today."

Lost in America `20` `20` `21` `17`
1985. Directed by Albert Brooks. With Albert Brooks, Julie Hagerty, Garry Marshall. 91 minutes. Rated R.
Brooks' "seriously underrated" satire about a yuppie couple who chuck it all and hit the road is dryly "hilarious" filmmaking boast-

ing what may be the "funniest first 45 minutes in movie history"; though a few protest the "premise doesn't quite get there", the majority reports the "situations, characters and jokes are all in sync."

Lost in Translation ✉

21 | 24 | 19 | 21

2003. Directed by Sofia Coppola. With Bill Murray, Scarlett Johansson. 102 minutes. Rated R.

"Not much happens" in this "poignant" look at a young woman and a "has-been" movie star who meet out of "boredom and insomnia" in a Tokyo hotel; admirers say it's "eminently watchable" thanks to "talented" writer/director Coppola (it must "run in the family") as well as the "surprising chemistry" between the "world-weary" Murray and "enigmatic" Johansson; still, "baffled" viewers want to know "what the hoopla is all about" – and especially "what he whispers at the end"; best scene: the "Suntory commercial."

Lost Weekend, The ✉◑

▽ 23 | 25 | 23 | 21

1945. Directed by Billy Wilder. With Ray Milland, Jane Wyman, Phillip Terry. 101 minutes. Not Rated.

"Strong" stuff served neat, this "smart", sobering drama depicts the "terrifying inner world" of an alcoholic who "lives only" for the bottle, starring Milland in a "top-shelf", Oscar-winning turn as a barfly on a bender careening from double bourbons to detox to the d.t.'s; some maintain it "should be required viewing" at AA meetings – it's the "scariest movie of all time if you drink."

Love Actually

22 | 23 | 21 | 22

2003. Directed by Richard Curtis. With Hugh Grant, Liam Neeson, Colin Firth, Laura Linney, Emma Thompson, Alan Rickman, Keira Knightley, Bill Nighy. 135 minutes. Rated R.

"Intertwining" vignettes of lovesick Londoners meeting up "cute" and breaking up "sad" form the core of this "walk-away-smiling" romantic comedy; while Brit chick flick fans are "delighted" by the "great ensemble" with a special nod to the habitually "charming" Grant, those finding it "not that good actually" zap its "saccharine", "scattershot" script as barely "tolerable fluff."

Love Bug, The ⓫

18 | 15 | 16 | 17

1969. Directed by Robert Stevenson. With Dean Jones, Michele Lee, Buddy Hackett. 107 minutes. Rated G.

"They don't get much sillier" than this "imaginative" Disney "oldie" about Herbie, a "sweet"-talking VW bug that supplies boomers with plenty of "fond memories"; it still "stands the test of time" well enough for it to be a perennial "rainy-afternoon" rental.

Love in the Afternoon ◑

▽ 24 | 24 | 22 | 22

1957. Directed by Billy Wilder. With Gary Cooper, Audrey Hepburn, Maurice Chevalier. 130 minutes. Not Rated.

An "old-fashioned" romance set in "misty" Paree, this "witty" Wilder "treat" stars Coop as an "American playboy" who goes "mad with desire" for the much-younger Hepburn; if the "age difference" between the "odd couple" might seem "unspannable", the "bright cast" shows lots of "chemistry" – "isn't love grand?"

Love Is a Many-Splendored Thing

22 | 23 | 22 | 21

1955. Directed by Henry King. With Jennifer Jones, William Holden. 102 minutes. Not Rated.

"What drama! what heartbreak!" sigh admirers of this "classic" romantic "tearjerker", an "ahead-of-its-time" tale about an affair between a "liberated" Eurasian woman and a conflicted American war correspondent; ok, it's a little "soppy" and "Jones isn't believable as a Eurasian", but the "breathtaking" Hong Kong scenery and "memorable" theme song "make the whole thing worth it."

Love Story ⑪ | 19 | 18 | 20 | 18 |
1970. Directed by Arthur Hiller. With Ali MacGraw, Ryan O'Neal, Ray Milland. 99 minutes. Rated PG.
"Get out the Kleenex" – this "three-hanky chick flick" about a "rich boy, a poor girl" and an incurable disease is applauded for its "adorable" leads, the "cute" O'Neal and "divine" MacGraw; critics of this "shameless" "schmaltz"-fest sneer that "love means having to say you're sorry every five minutes", but even they admit "35 years of soggy-eyed females can't be wrong."

Love! Valour! Compassion! | 21 | 24 | 23 | 22 |
1997. Directed by Joe Mantello. With Jason Alexander, Stephen Spinella, John Glover. 108 minutes. Rated R.
Adapted from Terrence McNally's "Broadway smash", this "well-acted" dramedy follows eight gay men over three weekends in the country; alternately "funny, touching and sad", it's a "social commentary about the early years of the AIDS epidemic", but the compassionate claim it's "only peripherally about homosexuality" and really more about "the power of the human heart."

M ⓞⒻ | 26 | 26 | 26 | 23 |
1931. Directed by Fritz Lang. With Peter Lorre, Ellen Widmann, Gustaf Gründgens. 99 minutes. Not Rated.
Still "frightening seven decades later", this crime thriller features Lorre as a "nervous, sweaty little child killer" in a "riveting" performance that evokes "horror and pity at the same time"; set in "'30s Berlin" "plunging headlong into fascism", it's known for its "expressionistic" camerawork and montage sequences that "set the benchmark for film editing."

Madagascar | 21 | – | 19 | 24 |
2005. Directed by Eric Darnell, Tom McGrath. Animated. 86 minutes. Rated PG.
"NYC zoo animals" fly the coop and end up "in the wilds of Africa" in this "wholesome" cartoon rendered in "eye-popping colors", and with enough "zaniness for kids" (and "'in' jokes" for adults) to keep all ages happy; sure, its "uneven" storyline gets "tangled" in its own nets, so it's a good thing those "penguins steal the show."

Mad Max ⑪ | 20 | 17 | 19 | 19 |
1980. Directed by George Miller. With Mel Gibson, Joanne Samuel, Hugh Keays-Byrne. 93 minutes. Rated R.
"Raw" and thrillingly "underproduced", this "seminal" tale of "post-apocalyptic", "Darwinian doom" is one of the "all-time great low-budget fantasies", done with "conviction and style"; it pits a "fabulous Mel in tight black leather" against some "truly bad bad guys" and is so "ultimately effective" that it spawned two sequels (though connoisseurs claim the first is "the best").

Madness of King George, The | 22 | 26 | 23 | 24 |
1994. Directed by Nicholas Hytner. With Nigel Hawthorne, Helen Mirren, Ian Holm. 107 minutes. Rated PG-13.
"Insightful", "worthwhile" bio of the "mad, irascible" British monarch who, among other things, lost the American colonies;

though "history buffs" declare the "accuracy is debatable", there's no debate about Hawthorne's "superb" performance (that "almost makes George III sympathetic"), nor that it's "visually stunning."

Magdalene Sisters, The
25 | 26 | 26 | 23

2003. Directed by Peter Mullan. With Anne-Marie Duff, Dorothy Duffy, Eileen Walsh, Nora-Jane Noone. 119 minutes. Rated R.
"Quite an eye-opener", this Irish "exposé" tells the true story of young women "deemed immoral" and committed to asylums to "pay for their sins" "in the name of religion"; its "documentary-like style" and a strong cast of "little-known actors" make for "raw" filmmaking that "stays in your mind."

Magnificent Ambersons, The ❶∅
▽ 24 | 23 | 22 | 23

1942. Directed by Orson Welles. With Joseph Cotten, Dolores Costello, Anne Baxter, Agnes Moorehead. 88 minutes. Not Rated.
"In the shadow of *Citizen Kane*" stands Welles' "visually brilliant" but oft-"overlooked" follow-up, this "turn-of-the-century" drama detailing the "downfall of an Indiana family" whose spoiled scion can't "keep up with the times"; some magnificence is lost due to the "damage done by the studio's re-editing", but admirers say this "90% masterpiece" is still "brilliant filmmaking."

Magnificent Seven, The ❶
26 | 22 | 25 | 23

1960. Directed by John Sturges. With Yul Brynner, Steve McQueen, Eli Wallach, Charles Bronson. 128 minutes. Not Rated.
"Gunfighter cool" is alive and well in this "magnificent remake" of *The Seven Samurai* that "stands on its own" despite being "translated into a Western" and cast with "big stars of the '60s"; those who "never tire of watching it" "enjoy the adventure", "love the score" and attempt to "memorize the dialogue" that's become "fodder for countless movie trivia questions."

Magnolia
20 | 23 | 18 | 21

1999. Directed by Paul Thomas Anderson. With Tom Cruise, Julianne Moore, Philip Seymour Hoffman, Jason Robards Jr., John C. Reilly. 188 minutes. Rated R.
"Love-it-or-hate-it" filmmaking from auteur Anderson that's either a "compelling" study of "intersecting lives" in the San Fernando Valley or a "never-ending" "letdown" about a "bunch of dysfunctional people"; still, the direction is "energetic" and "Cruise actually acts", though some ask "what's up with the frogs?"

Maid in Manhattan
14 | 14 | 13 | 16

2002. Directed by Wayne Wang. With Jennifer Lopez, Ralph Fiennes, Natasha Richardson. 105 minutes. Rated PG-13.
"Warm and fuzzy" says it all about this "modern day Cinderella" story, a romantic comedy about a hotel chambermaid with a "great booty" who lands a "JFK Jr.–esque bachelor" (wags tag it "*Pretty Cleaning Woman*"); while it's certainly "harmless" enough "airline entertainment", cynics say "sappy", citing "no chemistry" between the leads, the "all-glammed-up-but-nowhere-to-go" J. Lo and "uncomfortable-looking" Fiennes.

Malcolm X
23 | 26 | 23 | 23

1992. Directed by Spike Lee. With Denzel Washington, Angela Bassett, Al Freeman Jr. 194 minutes. Rated PG-13.
In this "galvanizing", "probing" bio, the "transformation" of Malcolm X from "young hustler" to "outspoken" Civil Rights

180

leader is portrayed by an "emotional" Washington in such a "bravura", "sympathetic" way that many say he was "robbed of an Oscar"; still, this "profound" film is a "time capsule of black American style" that resolutely "captivates and educates."

MALTESE FALCON, THE ◑ 28 | 27 | 27 | 25

1941. Directed by John Huston. With Humphrey Bogart, Mary Astor, Peter Lorre. 101 minutes. Not Rated.

The "stuff movies should be made of", this "vintage noir gem" boasts an "unforgettable Bogie" as the "hard-boiled detective" Sam Spade, plus a "blue-ribbon" supporting cast of "creeps and crooks", all searching for a mysterious "rara avis"; although its "taut script" that "runs like a Swiss watch" and "keeps you guessing to the end" is "often imitated", this "perfect rendering" of Dashiell Hammett's novel has been "never duplicated."

Man and a Woman, A ✉◑◻ 24 | 24 | 24 | 24

1966. Directed by Claude Lelouch. With Anouk Aimée, Jean-Louis Trintignant. 102 minutes. Not Rated.

For "romance par excellence", this "touching", "very French" '60s "classic" is served with "panache" and is "still worth seeing" today – indeed, the "music alone can make you fall in love"; detailing an affair between a widow and widower, it stars a "beautiful Aimée" opposite "Trintignant at his best."

MANCHURIAN CANDIDATE, THE ◑ 27 | 26 | 28 | 25

1962. Directed by John Frankenheimer. With Frank Sinatra, Laurence Harvey, Angela Lansbury. 126 minutes. Rated PG-13.

As "perfectly paranoid" "Cold War" filmmaking, this provocative "conspiracy thriller" about Korean War–era "brainwashing" still packs a "wallop" due to a "twist"-laden script and a "take-your-breath-away" ending; Sinatra and Harvey are "electrifying", but the real revelation is Lansbury as an "evil", solitaire-playing mommy.

Manchurian Candidate, The 18 | 21 | 19 | 19

2004. Directed by Jonathan Demme. With Denzel Washington, Meryl Streep, Liev Schreiber. 129 minutes. Rated R.

"Cleverly updated" by substituting "corporate conspiracies" for "Cold War paranoia", this remake of the "classic" '60s political thriller is "different enough to be interesting", yet ultimately many wonder "why mess with perfection?"; even if Denzel "does his best" and Meryl "gives Angela Lansbury a run for her money", this "unnecessary" effort "doesn't hold a candle to the original."

MAN FOR ALL SEASONS, A ✉ 28 | 28 | 27 | 27

1966. Directed by Fred Zinnemann. With Paul Scofield, Wendy Hiller, Robert Shaw. 120 minutes. Rated G.

"Intelligent and riveting in a quiet way", this "literate" historical drama about the "conflict between conscience and convenience" between Henry VIII and Sir Thomas More garnered six Oscars, including Best Actor for the "magnificent Scofield"; a "rare film about integrity", "loyalty and betrayal", it serves as a "reminder of the days when the movies enlightened."

Man from Elysian Fields, The 21 | 23 | 21 | 21

2002. Directed by George Hickenlooper. With Andy Garcia, Mick Jagger, Julianna Margulies. 106 minutes. Rated R.

A "struggling writer" turns gigolo to make ends meet in this "sexy, stylish" variation on the "Faust legend"; although Garcia is a bit "one-note" and the "story falls off at the end", the big "surprise" here is Jagger, who "makes the whole thing worthwhile" portraying a "dapper", high-end pimp.

Manhattan ◑   26 | 24 | 23 | 24

1979. Directed by Woody Allen. With Woody Allen, Diane Keaton, Michael Murphy, Mariel Hemingway. 96 minutes. Rated R.
"Even NYers get all mushy" about this "love letter to the Big Apple" filmed in "fantastic black and white" and set to a thrilling "Gershwin soundtrack"; a romance laced with "angst", it appeals to those who like their "philosophy mixed with a little comedy" and is "more fully realized than *Annie Hall*"; in a nutshell, "it can be fun to be depressive."

Man on Fire   21 | 25 | 21 | 22

2004. Directed by Tony Scott. With Denzel Washington, Dakota Fanning, Christopher Walken. 146 minutes. Rated R.
"Revenge" is the emotion driving this "intense" thriller starring a "prime Denzel" as "one bad mother" bodyguard who turns "vigilante" after his charge is kidnapped; critics find the beginning "compelling" enough, but say the second half disintegrates into a "mindless shoot-'em-up" further muddied by "hyperactive" camerawork; "no lasting impact" is the final verdict.

Man on the Moon   16 | 22 | 15 | 17

1999. Directed by Milos Forman. With Jim Carrey, Danny DeVito, Courtney Love. 118 minutes. Rated R.
Carrey is "better as Andy than Andy himself" in this "affecting" bio of spaced-out '70s comic Andy Kaufman, whose "funny but strange" routines conclude with an early curtain after he succumbs to cancer; though it's heckled as a "disappointing, disjointed" portrait that "doesn't shed much light" on its "complicated" subject, it's still "entertaining" for Dada comedy fans.

Man Who Came to Dinner, The ◑   ▽ 26 | 27 | 25 | 23

1942. Directed by William Keighley. With Bette Davis, Ann Sheridan, Monty Woolley. 112 minutes. Not Rated.
Fans of "smart, hilarious" comedy relish the "unforgettable feast" in this screen treatment of Kaufman and Hart's stage play à clef, with Woolley "stealing the movie" as a "pompous radio personality" who visits a Midwestern household and "won't go home" after becoming wheelchair-bound; mixing "acid wit" with "fast-paced" dialogue, it's a "not-to-be-missed" "scream" from the "old school."

Man Who Fell to Earth, The   18 | 18 | 20 | 17

1976. Directed by Nicolas Roeg. With David Bowie, Rip Torn, Candy Clark. 140 minutes. Rated R.
Followers of this "way-ahead-of-its-time" sci-fi fantasy about an extraterrestrial "searching for water" to save his planet say it's "still relevant", citing its "inventive" storyline and "perfect casting" ("Bowie has no trouble playing a trippy alien"); however, some dismiss it as an "incoherent", "unwatchable mess" that's too "creepy and weird."

Man Who Knew Too Much, The   24 | 24 | 25 | 24

1956. Directed by Alfred Hitchcock. With James Stewart, Doris Day, Brenda de Banzie. 120 minutes. Rated PG.
A "Hitchcock remake of an earlier Hitchcock" thriller, this "more commercial" version plays up the "amazing ordinariness" of its

"everyman" stars as they seek their kidnapped son; for most, it's "very exciting" – especially the "unbearably suspenseful" "scene in Royal Albert Hall" – though a few "could do without" Day's "cornball" rendition of 'Que Sera, Sera' (which still snagged a Best Song Oscar).

Man Who Shot Liberty Valance, The ◑ | 25 | 24 | 25 | 23 |
1962. Directed by John Ford. With John Wayne, James Stewart, Vera Miles, Lee Marvin, Edmond O'Brien. 123 minutes. Not Rated.
The formidable Ford's "darkest Western" is illuminated by a "star-studded" cast featuring "all-time bad guy" Lee Marvin in his "finest performance", with "dynamic" backup from Wayne and Stewart; though a bit "claustrophobic" (it was filmed "mostly on Hollywood soundstages"), this is still "mythic" moviemaking that "works like a huge, sprawling novel"; biggest surprise: "Wayne loses the girl."

Man Who Wasn't There, The ◑ | 21 | 25 | 19 | 25 |
2001. Directed by Joel Coen. With Billy Bob Thornton, Frances McDormand, James Gandolfini. 116 minutes. Rated R.
This "quirky, haunting" take on vintage film noir ("as only the Coen brothers can re-create it") charts the last days of a "hapless" small-town barber whose "decline is a metaphor" for nothing less than "modern alienation"; the "stylistically incredible" cinematography is "so colorful you forget it's filmed in black and white", while Thornton's titular turn nearly manages to "out-Bogart Bogart."

Man Who Would Be King, The | 25 | 26 | 26 | 25 |
1975. Directed by John Huston. With Sean Connery, Michael Caine, Christopher Plummer. 129 minutes. Rated PG.
Based on Kipling's "epic of friendship and heroism", this "classic adaptation" is a "ripsnorting", "good-time adventure" chronicling the perils of a pair of "opportunistic" "British rogues" on a "grand lark" in 19th-century colonial India; the combination of "sweeping vistas", "incandescent chemistry" between Connery and Caine and a "haunting ending" make for a "buddy flick that rises way above the genre."

Man with the Golden Gun, The | 18 | 17 | 17 | 20 |
1974. Directed by Guy Hamilton. With Roger Moore, Christopher Lee, Britt Ekland. 125 minutes. Rated PG.
"Moore almost redeems himself" in his second stab at 007 ("much better than his debut"), though Lee steals the show as a "droll" assassin boasting "three nipples" as well as a golden gun; still, despite the sizzle supplied by Ekland and some "great Asian scenery", foes dismiss it as a "disjointed, inferior" misfire in the Bond canon.

Marathon Man | 24 | 27 | 24 | 22 |
1976. Directed by John Schlesinger. With Dustin Hoffman, Laurence Olivier, Roy Scheider. 125 minutes. Rated R.
"Just when you thought it was safe to go back to the dentist" comes this "nasty" little thriller about a "totally mad", "tooth-drilling" "Nazi on the loose" hell-bent on retrieving ill-gotten loot; the "huffing, puffing" Hoffman is "superlative" as a man "drawn into something way beyond his control", while set pieces like the "whining drill" scene and the "diamond-swallowing" finale raise enough "goose bumps" to make most "swear off checkups for life."

MARCH OF THE PENGUINS
26 | – | 25 | 28

2005. Directed by Luc Jacquet. Documentary. 85 minutes. Rated G.
The "majestic" emperor penguins who "struggle to survive and procreate" in the "hostile", "frigid ice fields" of Antarctica will "melt your heart" in this "superlative" documentary, an "entertaining, educational" dramatization of the "tuxedo-clad" critters' life cycle; mixing "breathtaking" footage with Freeman's "perfectly voiced" narration, it may paint an overly "anthropomorphized" picture – "they're just birds" – but somehow it manages to make "human problems seem petty" by comparison.

Maria Full of Grace 🅕
25 | 26 | 25 | 22

2004. Directed by Joshua Marston. With Catalina Sandino Moreno, Yenny Paola Vega. 101 minutes. Rated R.
The "horrific plight" of women desperate to "wean themselves from poverty" by becoming "pawns in the drug trade" is the "untold story" brought to light by this "raw", "impactful" indie; newcomer Moreno shows she's "full of talent" in the role of a Colombian cocaine mule, and while her near-"suicidal" mission "puts you through a wringer", it's worth it for the film's "unbleached message of hope."

Mark of Zorro, The ◑
22 | 19 | 22 | 19

1940. Directed by Rouben Mamoulian. With Tyrone Power, Linda Darnell, Basil Rathbone. 94 minutes. Not Rated.
This "rousing adventure" tale of "double identity and romance" has "hardly dated" thanks to the "dashing", buckle-swashing Power's "sexy swordfighting"; "lady-in-distress" Darnell is "unbelievably lovely", "fop" Rathbone "as dastardly as ever" and a "marvelous" Alfred Newman score provides the cinematic coup de grace.

Marriage of Maria Braun, The 🅕
25 | 25 | 24 | 23

1979. Directed by Rainer Werner Fassbinder. With Hanna Schygulla, Klaus Löwitsch, Ivan Desny. 120 minutes. Rated R.
This "scathing portrait" of "survival in postwar Germany" traces its gritty heroine's determined climb up the economic ladder with some "bitingly funny" scenes that demonstrate "you can't bury the past", no matter how hard you try to disguise it; "extraordinary" work from director Fassbinder and the "brilliant" Schygulla make up for that "letdown of an ending."

Married to the Mob
17 | 17 | 16 | 16

1988. Directed by Jonathan Demme. With Michelle Pfeiffer, Matthew Modine, Dean Stockwell. 103 minutes. Rated R.
'Family' fare à la Jonathan Demme, this "quirky" comedy stars a "gorgeous" Pfeiffer playing a "small-time mobster's wife" parting with The Life after a dishonored don rubs out her hubby; "silly" but "easy to watch", it features a "fine" ensemble cast "having a great time" as well as a "don't-miss-it" cameo from "Alec Baldwin's chest hair."

Marty ✉◑
25 | 27 | 24 | 21

1955. Directed by Delbert Mann. With Ernest Borgnine, Betsy Blair, Esther Minciotti. 91 minutes. Not Rated.
Ok, the story of a "sloppy butcher" who finds love with a "mousy clerk" might "never play", but this "poignant" Paddy Chayefsky drama proved naysayers wrong, garnering four Oscars (including Best Actor for Borgnine, who's "perfect" as an ordinary Brooklyn

schmo); shot in black and white, its "realistic style" "never gets old" – but be prepared for a feeling of "hopelessness" throughout.

MARY POPPINS ✉
27 | 24 | 25 | 27

1964. Directed by Robert Stevenson. With Julie Andrews, Dick Van Dyke, David Tomlinson. 140 minutes. Rated G.
Mix a "perky" Andrews (as an "odd" nanny with "magical powers") with a "cheeky" Van Dyke, "fantastic animation" and "catchy tunes", add a "spoonful of sugar" and the result is a "super-duper" Disney "treat"; a "technical marvel of its time", this "jolly" production "makes you feel good at any age" and serves as a dandy "introduction to musicals for kids."

MASH ✉
26 | 25 | 26 | 24

1970. Directed by Robert Altman. With Donald Sutherland, Elliott Gould, Sally Kellerman. 116 minutes. Rated PG.
"War is hell (and funny)" in this "groundbreaking" "black" satire about a dysfunctional Korean War medical unit that still "holds up" as "one of the smartest comedies ever written" – "once you get past all the blood", that is; maybe the "last third" goes "downhill" during the "lame" football game, but there's no doubt this is "Altman's breakthrough."

Mask
21 | 24 | 23 | 19

1985. Directed by Peter Bogdanovich. With Cher, Sam Elliott, Eric Stoltz. 120 minutes. Rated PG-13.
Proof that "Cher can act", this "touching tearjerker" showcases the diva in "top form" as a single biker mom "in a tough situation with a challenged kid" who's horribly disfigured; as the "grotesque" teen who just "wants to be treated normally", an "amazing" Stoltz radiates enough "inner beauty" to remind the rest of us "how lucky we are."

Mask, The ⑪
17 | 18 | 15 | 20

1994. Directed by Chuck Russell. With Jim Carrey, Cameron Diaz, Peter Riegert. 101 minutes. Rated PG-13.
A bedraggled schmo finds a magical mask that transforms him into a swinging, macho hero in this "entertaining" comedy that might hinge on a "ridiculous concept" but nevertheless "works" (thanks to Carrey's "funny" performance); though "kinda stupid" to brainiacs, fans are wowed by the "dazzling effects", including the "luminous Diaz", who makes her "delightful" screen debut here.

Mask of Zorro, The
18 | 17 | 18 | 21

1998. Directed by Martin Campbell. With Antonio Banderas, Catherine Zeta-Jones. 136 minutes. Rated PG-13.
This "big-budget" spin on the "Zorro legend" provokes dueling opinions: zealots admire its "old-school movie style" ("great swordfights", "breathtaking" production values) and ask "is there a better-looking cast ever assembled?"; but critics parry it's "lightweight fluff" that might work well with "popcorn" but "doesn't hold a candle to the 1940 version."

Master and Commander: The Far Side of the World
23 | 24 | 22 | 27

2003. Directed by Peter Weir. With Russell Crowe, Paul Bettany. 138 minutes. Rated PG-13.
For "textbook adventure filmmaking" sailing over the "bounding main", set your sights on this "visually extraordinary" nautical

epic depicting "cat-and-mouse" high-sea games during the Napoleonic War; the all-male cast includes the "great-as-usual" Crowe backed up by a "strong" Bettany, but despite "incredible battle scenes", "magnificent storms" and "stellar" special effects, mutineers say the "thin" storyline and "endless frigate jargon" simply "don't hold water"; other seafarers, however, "look forward to another installment."

Match Point 22 | 23 | 22 | 22
2005. Directed by Woody Allen. With Jonathan Rhys Meyers, Scarlett Johansson, Matthew Goode. 124 minutes. Rated R.
Breaking from his usual "silly slapstick", Woody Allen channels both "Hitchcock" and "Theodore Dreiser" to serve up this "mesmerizing", "keeps-you-guessing" London thriller whose "chilling portrait of a social climber" examines "the role of luck in life"; further assuring the film's place in the sun are the performances of the "outstanding" Rhys Meyers and "sumptuous" Scarlett, who simmer with "intense chemistry."

Matchstick Men 20 | 24 | 21 | 19
2003. Directed by Ridley Scott. With Nicolas Cage, Sam Rockwell, Alison Lohman. 116 minutes. Rated PG-13.
A "neurotic" con artist "with more tics than a time bomb" shows his "soft" side when he plays dad to a "junior swindler" in this "smart", "dark"-edged comic caper featuring "excellent" performances from Cage and the "stardom"-bound Lohman; it "takes a while" to get going, but don't fret – the "surprise twist" at the end will "hook you."

MATRIX, THE ⓘ 25 | 19 | 25 | 28
1999. Directed by Andy Wachowski, Larry Wachowski. With Keanu Reeves, Laurence Fishburne, Carrie-Anne Moss. 136 minutes. Rated R.
"Move over, *Star Wars*"; not even Reeves' "leaden" acting can sink this "mind-bending, reality-rocking" "new modern myth" of a movie that "raised the bar on special effects" and "revolutionized hand-to-hand combat in filmmaking"; even if its "intricate" plot (something about a computer hacker turned "humanity's last hope") verges on "incoherence", this "sci-fi shoot-'em-up for people with brains" just "gets better every time you see it."

Matrix Reloaded, The ⓘ 21 | 17 | 18 | 26
2003. Directed by Andy Wachowski, Larry Wachowski. With Keanu Reeves, Carrie-Anne Moss, Laurence Fishburne, Hugo Weaving. 138 minutes. Rated R.
The "conceptual novelty's gone", the "story is not as compelling as the original" and it "could have benefited from some editing", yet the "sexier" second installment of the "groundbreaking" sci-fi trilogy is still "worth a watch" for its "eye candy galore" – "off-the-charts special effects", "take-your-breath-away fight scenes" and a "car-chase scene that just blows your mind"; now if only there were "a *Matrix for Dummies* to explain what happened."

Matrix Revolutions, The 15 | 14 | 13 | 23
2003. Directed by Andy Wachowski, Larry Wachowski. With Keanu Reeves, Laurence Fishburne, Carrie-Ann Moss. 129 minutes. Rated R.
This "less than stellar end" to the martial-arts/sci-fi trilogy features the same "over-the-top CGI effects" and "garbled-but-intriguing philosophy" as the preceding installments, but this time out there's "too much action and not enough thought"; in fact, it's

such a "letdown" to a series that "started with so much potential" that many think "they should have stopped after the first one."

Maverick
18 | 20 | 17 | 19

1994. Directed by Richard Donner. With Mel Gibson, Jodie Foster, James Garner. 127 minutes. Rated PG.
As TV shows morphed into movies go, this "laid-back Western" based on ABC's '50s series "works well" by loading the deck with "escapism", "modern twists" and Gibson as a "tall, dark stranger" who's "having more fun than the audience"; but it's the "effortless style" of Garner (the original Maverick) that wins big.

McCabe & Mrs. Miller
23 | 23 | 23 | 24

1971. Directed by Robert Altman. With Warren Beatty, Julie Christie, Shelley Duvall. 120 minutes. Rated R.
Decidedly "not for conventional Western" fans, this "brilliantly directed", "postmodern deconstruction" of the genre "eliminates the clichés" and "faithfully re-creates what the West was really like": namely, "harsh, cruel and lacking true heroes"; despite one major drawback – "you can't understand what anyone is saying" – it's more than evident that the leads are "impossibly in love."

Mean Girls
20 | 19 | 20 | 19

2004. Directed by Mark Waters. With Lindsay Lohan, Rachel McAdams, Tina Fey. 97 minutes. Rated PG-13.
The "*Heathers* of the new millennium", this "smart teen comedy" brings back "painful high school memories" of the "trauma of trying to fit in" at a time when "social status seems so important"; as the new kid on the block, "goddess" Lohan demonstrates she's definitely "going places" and Tina Fey's "witty" script "hits the nail on the head" – even if the "sappy" finale is a tad too "preachy" for many.

Mean Streets
▽ 24 | 27 | 22 | 22

1973. Directed by Martin Scorsese. With Harvey Keitel, Robert De Niro. 110 minutes. Rated R.
"Gritty and graphic before that became the norm", Scorsese's breakout drama of hoods in the 'hood "rings with truth" as a "definitive slice of NY", with Keitel out to "make it in the mob" in spite of "Catholic guilt" and ties to De Niro's loose-cannon "loser"; it's a "grim" but "passionate" study of streetwise style, including some "pioneering" use of "oldies but goodies" on the soundtrack.

Meatballs ⑪
18 | 15 | 17 | 14

1979. Directed by Ivan Reitman. With Bill Murray, Harvey Atkin, Kate Lynch. 99 minutes. Rated PG.
A pre-"*Caddyshack*" Murray plays a wisecracking "summer camp counselor everyone would love to have" in this "underrated", lowbrow "comedy staple", later "ruined" by three sequels; ok, it might be a "little dated" and "poor production quality" detracts, but overall it conveys the "experience every camper hopes for."

Mediterraneo ✉️🎬∅
21 | 21 | 20 | 23

1991. Directed by Gabriele Salvatores. With Diego Abatantuono, Claudio Bigagli. 96 minutes. Rated R.
Sure, this "sweet" comedy about a group of WWII Italian soldiers "stranded" on a Greek isle is a "trifle", but the "beautiful cinematography" and "sweep-you-away" soundtrack nicely complement its assortment of "cute characters"; some report the story

"drags in some parts" (resulting in "awkward" scenes), but it offers enough "great escapism" to make for a primo "date flick."

Meet Me in St. Louis
26 | 24 | 23 | 26

1944. Directed by Vincente Minnelli. With Judy Garland, Margaret O'Brien, Mary Astor. 113 minutes. Not Rated.
Clang, clang, clang, here comes Garland "at her radiant finest" as a girl who "adores the boy next door" in this musical "treasure" about a "turn-of-the-century" American family; fans laud its "sumptuous" Technicolor production and "unforgettable" tunes, while brainiacs hint it's "darker and deeper than its rep suggests."

Meet the Fockers
18 | 21 | 17 | 19

2004. Directed by Jay Roach. With Robert De Niro, Ben Stiller, Dustin Hoffman, Barbra Streisand. 115 minutes. Rated PG-13.
There's "major star wattage" on display in this *Meet the Parents* sequel, starting with the "oy vey" pairing of "big names" Dusty and Babs, who "steal the show" along with a can of "whipped cream"; otherwise, this "crude" comedy about in-laws interacting for the first time earns mixed marks: it's either a "one-trick movie" with "too many potty jokes" or else "hilarious", "verging on ridiculous – what's wrong with that?"

Meet the Parents Ⓤ
19 | 21 | 19 | 19

2000. Directed by Jay Roach. With Robert De Niro, Ben Stiller, Blythe Danner. 108 minutes. Rated PG-13.
"Every guy's worst nightmare" about being introduced to his "prospective in-laws" comes true in this very "watchable" comedy that succeeds mainly because of the "brilliant pairing of Stiller and De Niro"; though the unamused frown it "relies too much on slapstick" and repeats the "same joke for two hours straight", most say it "pinpoints" an "all-too-real" situation.

Melinda and Melinda
17 | 21 | 18 | 18

2005. Directed by Woody Allen. With Radha Mitchell, Will Ferrell, Chloë Sevigny. 100 minutes. Rated PG-13.
"Two versions of the same tale" – one comic, one tragic – form the framework for this "intriguing" Woody Allen flicker about a "nervous" adulteress adrift in "ultrasophisticated Manhattan"; fans feel the Woodman "flits between the two stories with ease", but those who retitle it "*Monotonous and Monotonous*" advise he "join the 21st century" ("who can afford those apartments?") or else "retire."

Melvin and Howard ✉
22 | 23 | 22 | 19

1980. Directed by Jonathan Demme. With Paul Le Mat, Mary Steenburgen, Jason Robards. 95 minutes. Rated R.
A "small movie that landed in a big way", this "wacky" riff on the "Howard Hughes myth" tells the tale of a milkman who befriends a bum, who's really a gazillionaire, who wills the milkman a fortune; it's "funny", "off-the-wall" stuff that's "uplifting without being preachy or schmaltzy" and might be best enjoyed "as a companion piece to *The Aviator*."

MEMENTO
26 | 25 | 27 | 25

2000. Directed by Christopher Nolan. With Guy Pearce, Carrie-Anne Moss. 113 minutes. Rated R.
"Bring your brain to the theater, you'll need it" for this "exquisitely existential" "mind-bender" about a man who loses his "short-term memory" following his wife's murder; it "turns traditional

narrative on its head" by telling the story "in reverse" – so it may "require several viewings to get it all straight"; though there's applause for the "stunning" Pearce, befuddled folks "still trying to figure it out" wail it's too "gnisufnoc."

Memoirs of a Geisha
21 | 23 | 21 | 26

2005. Directed by Rob Marshall. With Zhang Ziyi, Ken Watanabe, Gong Li, Michelle Yeoh. 145 minutes. Rated PG-13.

"Beautiful costumes" and "breathtaking" cinematography ("every shot feels like a painting") shine in this "poignant", "rags-to-silks" period drama that offers a rare glimpse inside the "closed society" of Japan's geishas; despite some grumbling that "Chinese actors playing Japanese" characters may be "politically incorrect", overall most find the experience "transporting", albeit at a "slow" clip.

Men in Black ⏢
21 | 20 | 21 | 24

1997. Directed by Barry Sonnenfeld. With Tommy Lee Jones, Will Smith, Linda Fiorentino. 98 minutes. Rated PG-13.

"Wisecracking" Smith and "deadpan" Jones show "great chemistry" as they battle "slime, aliens and explosions" in this "action-packed" sci-fi "blockbuster" that's "delicious fun"; a "kids' movie for adults", it's a "hugely enjoyable spoof" that some find "silly" and may be a "little gross."

Men in Black II
14 | 16 | 12 | 20

2002. Directed by Barry Sonnenfeld. With Tommy Lee Jones, Will Smith, Rip Torn, Lara Flynn Boyle. 88 minutes. Rated PG-13.

An "overload of special effects", a "cast on autopilot" and "no real storyline" are the classic symptoms of "sequel syndrome" afflicting this "mediocre" encore to the hit sci-fi comedy; fortunately, a "few amusing sight gags" (i.e. the "worth-a-laugh Michael Jackson cameo") and the "short" running time "make it bearable."

Metropolis ◑
27 | 22 | 24 | 28

1927. Directed by Fritz Lang. With Alfred Abel, Gustav Froelich, Brigitte Helm. 153 minutes. Not Rated.

A "visionary" film of "magnitude, imagination and depth", this "sci-fi social commentary" about "oppression and uprising" set in a "futuristic city" "still retains its visual impact" seven decades later; indeed, Lang's "man-versus-machine" story (embodied by a "fetishized woman robot") remains "revolutionary in every sense of the word" – this is a "movie everybody should watch at least once."

Metropolitan
▽ 20 | 19 | 20 | 17

1990. Directed by Whit Stillman. With Carolyn Farina, Edward Clements, Christopher Eigeman. 99 minutes. Rated PG-13.

The "young and the privileged" in "present-day NY" get the Jane Austen treatment in this "charming" "coming-of-age" comedy with an "exciting young cast" spouting "intensely dry", "droll" dialogue; those fascinated by "rich kids and their problems" say it's one part "Woody Allen", one part "George Plimpton."

Midnight Cowboy ✉
26 | 28 | 24 | 24

1969. Directed by John Schlesinger. With Dustin Hoffman, Jon Voight, Sylvia Miles. 113 minutes. Rated R.

"Still as gritty as ever", this "unvarnished look at NYC street life" is a "touching" if "depressing" depiction of a pair of "down-and-out" losers "spiraling downward" that turns the "buddy-flick concept" on its ear; the first "X-rated" film to take Best Picture honors (and since re-rated), it continues to wow with "inner beauty", "haunting music" and "brilliant" turns from Hoffman and Voight – and that "ending on the bus is unforgettable."

Midnight Express ✉   24 | 24 | 25 | 22
1978. Directed by Alan Parker. With Brad Davis, Randy Quaid, John Hurt. 120 minutes. Rated R.
This "frighteningly realistic" drama about a not-so-innocent American abroad imprisoned for smuggling hash "should be required viewing for teens and travelers", even though this "eye-opener" might "induce nightmares for years to come"; it probably "did more to stop kids from doing drugs" than all of "Nancy Reagan's efforts" combined.

Mighty Aphrodite   18 | 21 | 18 | 18
1995. Directed by Woody Allen. With Woody Allen, Mira Sorvino, Michael Rapaport. 98 minutes. Rated R.
Maybe "not as incisive" as Allen's "best", this "minor Woody" work still exudes "inventive charm" in its story of a man seeking the biological mother of his adopted child; throw in an "inspired Greek chorus" providing commentary and Sorvino's Oscar-winning turn as a "ditzy hooker", and the result is "painless fun."

Mighty Wind, A   23 | 26 | 21 | 23
2003. Directed by Christopher Guest. With Bob Balaban, Christopher Guest, John Michael Higgins, Eugene Levy. 91 minutes. Rated PG-13.
"You'll have almost as much fun as the cast" watching this "hysterical mockumentary" about the "'60s folk music scene" full of "priceless material", a "hilarious cast of characters" and "lots of hidden humor"; while "not as good as *Best in Show*", "anything by Guest is better than most everyone else's work."

Mildred Pierce ✉◑   26 | 25 | 25 | 24
1945. Directed by Michael Curtiz. With Joan Crawford, Jack Carson, Ann Blyth, Eve Arden. 111 minutes. Not Rated.
Oscar-winner Crawford is in "full weeper bloom" (with "shoulder pads for days" and "star lighting to make sure you get the point") in this noir "sudser" based on the James M. Cain novel about a "mother who sacrifices everything for her daughter"; "camp" followers crack up over Arden's "witty repartee" (which "would put any drag queen to shame") and "rent it as a double feature with *Mommie Dearest* for full impact."

Miller's Crossing   22 | 23 | 22 | 22
1990. Directed by Joel Coen. With Gabriel Byrne, Albert Finney, Marcia Gay Harden. 115 minutes. Rated R.
"Don't give the high hat" to this "subtle", "criminally underrated" early Coen brothers "gem" about a gangland war between Irish and Italian mobsters that proves "betrayal can come back to haunt you"; devotees declare it "deserves to be up there with *Goodfellas*", given the worthiness of the "broody" Byrne, "knockout Finney" and "deliciously tangled" plot "larded with obscure underworld slang."

MILLION DOLLAR BABY ✉   27 | 28 | 25 | 26
2004. Directed by Clint Eastwood. With Clint Eastwood, Hilary Swank, Morgan Freeman. 132 minutes. Rated PG-13.
What begins as a boxing "Cinderella story" about a "guilt-racked coach" mentoring a "determined female fighter" takes a "sharp

turn" and becomes a "profound" meditation on "significant moral dilemmas" in this "knockout" Oscar magnet from "powerhouse" actor/director Eastwood; a "flawless Swank" and "quietly brilliant" Freeman round out the cast in this "simple", "less-is-more" production, with a "surprise" ending that "leaves you breathless."

Minority Report
21 | 20 | 22 | 25

2002. Directed by Steven Spielberg. With Tom Cruise, Colin Farrell, Samantha Morton, Max von Sydow. 145 minutes. Rated PG-13.
"Cruise and Spielberg are a great combo" in this "intelligent, exciting" sci-fi thriller with "stunning visual effects" and "a mind-bending premise" – catching murderers before they commit the actual crime; though the "original, chilling storyline" "moves at lightning speed", it's "hard to follow at times", making it more difficult to detect the "holes in the plot"; bottom line: "better than the box office would indicate."

Miracle
24 | 23 | 26 | 24

2004. Directed by Gavin O'Connor. With Kurt Russell, Patricia Clarkson. 135 minutes. Rated PG.
Although most already "know the ending", this "feel-good" "insider's look" at the U.S. hockey team's quest for gold at the 1980 Olympics keeps athletic supporters "riveted" with its taut "they-shoot-they-score" script; indeed, Kurt's "commanding performance" and the "realistic moments on and off the ice" keep its "inspirational" themes resonating long afterwards – "way to go, team."

Miracle on 34th Street ✉ ◐
25 | 23 | 26 | 23

1947. Directed by George Seaton. With Maureen O'Hara, Natalie Wood, Edmund Gwenn. 96 minutes. Not Rated.
It "can't be Christmas" without a screening of this "schmaltzy", "charming fantasy" that embodies a "child's belief in Santa Claus" so well that it's become an enduring "seasonal favorite" for "every generation"; true believers say the Oscar-winning screenplay is the key behind this "perfect" "holiday classic" that puts the remakes to shame.

Miracle Worker, The ✉ ◐
25 | 28 | 24 | 22

1962. Directed by Arthur Penn. With Anne Bancroft, Patty Duke, Victor Jory, Inga Swenson. 106 minutes. Not Rated.
"Beautifully transferred from stage to screen" by director Penn, this "moving" account of deaf-and-blind Helen Keller and her teacher Annie Sullivan garnered Oscars for both leads (who reprised their Broadway roles); while Duke is undeniably "superb", it's Bancroft who "dominates" this "fiercely acted", "exceptional" film; most memorable moment: at the water pump.

Misery ✉
21 | 24 | 23 | 19

1990. Directed by Rob Reiner. With James Caan, Kathy Bates, Richard Farnsworth. 107 minutes. Rated R.
This "freaky" yarn about an injured writer "rescued" from a snowstorm by a "seriously deranged" fan is a "hobbling", "cracking-with-tension" experience that really "packs a wallop"; Oscar-winner Bates is beyond "mesmerizing" as the seriously "obsessed", "sledgehammer-swinging" captor opposite Caan's "excellent", hapless hostage, though diehards say the real credit goes to Reiner's "great hand when it comes to directing Stephen King stories."

Misfits, The ◐
21 | 24 | 21 | 22

1961. Directed by John Huston. With Clark Gable, Marilyn Monroe, Montgomery Clift, Thelma Ritter, Eli Wallach. 124 minutes. Not Rated.
The "swan song of Gable and Monroe" (and the "last movie" for both), this "bittersweet" romance between a Reno divorcée and an aging cowboy has a big theme at its heart, the demise of the Old West; while Arthur Miller's script is "thought-provoking" and there's plenty of "chemistry" between the leads, some say this "famously troubled production" ("were they all as dead tired as they appeared?") has "taken on an aura it doesn't deserve."

Miss Congeniality
15 | 16 | 15 | 16

2000. Directed by Donald Petrie. With Sandra Bullock, Michael Caine, Benjamin Bratt. 109 minutes. Rated PG-13.
Action comedy meets "chick flick" in this "lighthearted send-up" of beauty-contest culture starring Bullock at her most "adorable" as a "tomboy FBI agent" who goes undercover as cheesecake in a national pageant; ok, it's "slight" and "sophomoric", but in the eyes of most beholders it's "endearing fun" – despite the absence of "Bert Parks."

Missing ✉
24 | 26 | 25 | 22

1982. Directed by Costa-Gavras. With Jack Lemmon, Sissy Spacek, John Shea. 122 minutes. Rated PG.
Based on "actual events in South America", this fictionalized account of a U.S.-sanctioned military coup and its bloody aftermath is a "riveting" yet "moving" political thriller with a "devastating" message: "governments lie"; given "strong" performances by Lemmon and Spacek that "save it from being too preachy", many wonder why this Best Picture nominee is so "unheralded" and "overlooked" 25 years later.

Missing, The
18 | 22 | 18 | 19

2003. Directed by Ron Howard. With Tommy Lee Jones, Cate Blanchett. 137 minutes. Rated R.
Helmer Howard goes for grit in this "entertaining" if "somewhat disturbing" Western that adds a "supernatural" slant to a "familiar" abducted-child storyline ("isn't this *The Searchers* in disguise?"); in spite of "great acting on all parts" and some "gorgeous scenery", those with reservations claim the "slow pace" sends things "a little off the mark."

Mission, The
24 | 24 | 22 | 25

1986. Directed by Roland Joffé. With Robert De Niro, Jeremy Irons, Liam Neeson. 126 minutes. Rated PG.
"Beautifully shot", Oscar-winning cinematography nearly steals the show in this "intriguing drama" about an 18th-century struggle between missionaries and mercenaries over the riches of South America; even though evangelist Irons and reformed slave trader De Niro turn out their usual "amazing" work, unfazed foes feel Ennio Morricone's "soundtrack is far better" than the picture itself.

Mission: Impossible ⅠⅠ
16 | 15 | 15 | 21

1996. Directed by Brian De Palma. With Tom Cruise, Jon Voight, Ving Rhames. 110 minutes. Rated PG-13.
Many "convoluted" plot "twists" make this "tense", "James Bond–ish" action/adventurer a "watchable" if "highly confusing" picture; while diehards "drool" over the "never-looking-better"

Tom in an "all-black DKNY-ish outfit" performing "amazing stunts", purists pronounce it "not as good as the TV show" and bawl "bring back Peter Graves."

Mississippi Burning
23 | 24 | 23 | 22

1988. Directed by Alan Parker. With Gene Hackman, Willem Dafoe, Frances McDormand. 128 minutes. Rated R.

A "story that needed to be told", this "powerful" depiction of '60s "racial unrest" focuses on an investigation of the murder of three Civil Rights workers; yet despite an "all-too-real glimpse of life in the Deep South", critics say it overemphasizes "white hate" to the point that there are few "speaking parts for black actors."

Mister Roberts ⑪
27 | 27 | 24 | 23

1955. Directed by John Ford, Mervyn LeRoy. With Henry Fonda, James Cagney, Jack Lemmon, William Powell. 123 minutes. Not Rated.

A Broadway hit transposed to the big screen, this "heartfelt" story about the misadventures of a WWII supply ship crew delivers "wonderful acting all around", from the "unforgettable" Cagney to the "perfect" Fonda and "no-slouch" Lemmon; a "great wartime comedy with a serious side", it leaves even tough guys with a "lump in their throat."

Modern Times ◑
28 | 26 | 26 | 25

1936. Directed by Charles Chaplin. With Charles Chaplin, Paulette Goddard. 87 minutes. Not Rated.

"Timelessly funny and resonant", this "man-vs.-machine" story runs on a "blend of slapstick and pathos" guaranteed to make you "smile . . . though your heart is breaking"; there's "little dialogue" (save for Chaplin's "singing waiter" "gibberish number"), but his "heartwarming" performance and sharp "swipes at the age of technology" transcend words; in short, this one's a "must-see in *these* times."

Mommie Dearest
17 | 19 | 16 | 17

1981. Directed by Frank Perry. With Faye Dunaway, Diana Scarwid, Steve Forrest. 129 minutes. Rated PG.

Right up there in the "camp classic" pantheon is this look at "ice lady" Joan Crawford and her adopted daughter Christina that's notorious for Dunaway's "uncanny", "over-the-top" title performance, a truly "scary" imagining of the "horror of being a fading star"; though some call it "exploitive", "bitter stuff", others insist it's "absorbing" and sometimes "terribly funny."

Mona Lisa Smile
16 | 19 | 16 | 18

2003. Directed by Mike Newell. With Julia Roberts, Kirsten Dunst, Julia Stiles, Maggie Gyllenhaal. 117 minutes. Rated PG-13.

Set "in the days before women's lib", this "female version of *Dead Poets Society*" tells the story of a "strong-willed", 1950s college professor hoping to inspire her Stepford-esque students; though some call it "superficial", "watered-down feminism for the masses", side benefits include "authentic period touches" and a "who's who of young actresses stealing scenes from Queen Julia."

Monkey Business ◑
▽ 25 | 24 | 19 | 20

1931. Directed by Norman Z. McLeod. With the Marx Brothers, Thelma Todd. 77 minutes. Not Rated.

This "early" Marx Brothers' "Hollywood vehicle" is both "solidly entertaining" and "suitably anarchic" as the sibs stow away on a luxury liner and much "hilarious" "shipboard mayhem" ensues; though maybe "not quite their best" work, this "could be their looniest" of all – especially Harpo's "Punch and Judy" riff.

Mon Oncle ✉ 🎬
▽ 25 | 24 | 22 | 24

1958. Directed by Jacques Tati. With Jacques Tati, Jean-Pierre Zola. 110 minutes. Not Rated.

A trove of "very French" folly to "tickle your brain" and "set you giggling", this "delightful" comedy has Tati reprising his "sad-sack" Hulot act as he "bumbles through life" in a series of "superb gags and set pieces"; his "everyman-as-a-buffoon" shtick is a trusty "chuckle producer", while the underlying "commentary on modernity gone awry" is "really funny" too.

Monsieur Verdoux ◑
▽ 25 | 25 | 23 | 22

1947. Directed by Charles Chaplin. With Charles Chaplin, Martha Raye, Isobel Elsom. 124 minutes. Not Rated.

Cynics who say "Chaplin's little tramp is too sentimental" relish this "wicked" comedy of murders, a "dark, dark, dark" tale in which Charlie plays a "serial-killing", modern-day "bluebeard"; admirers say it's way "ahead of its time", some find it "too preachy at the end", but most agree this "overlooked" work is still "very moving."

Monsoon Wedding 🎬
24 | 23 | 23 | 23

2002. Directed by Mira Nair. With Naseeruddin Shah, Lillete Dubey, Shefali Shetty, Vasundhara Das, Parvin Dabas. 114 minutes. Rated R.

A "feast for the funny bone, eyes and mind", this "charming" dramedy about a "dysfunctional" Indian family and the wedding of their daughter "proves that all families are the same no matter the ethnicity"; it's "a bit slow", but the "colorful cinematography" and "fantastic music" will make you "want to see it again."

Monster ✉
24 | 29 | 24 | 22

2003. Directed by Patty Jenkins. With Charlize Theron, Christina Ricci. 109 minutes. Rated R.

"Frighteningly believable" and thus "tough to watch", this bio of serial murderess Aileen Wuornos "pushes all the emotional buttons" thanks to a "complete immersion" in the role by the Oscar-winning, "makeup"-slathered Theron (with ample backup from the "unsung" Ricci as her girlfriend); though "not as gruesome as it could have been", this "downer" does deliver enough imagery so "violent" that many vow to "never pick up a hitchhiker again."

Monster's Ball ✉
22 | 26 | 21 | 21

2001. Directed by Marc Forster. With Billy Bob Thornton, Halle Berry. 111 minutes. Rated R.

A "redneck" prison guard and the widow of an inmate he helped execute fall in love in this "disturbingly good" drama, a "gritty depiction" of "two lost souls"; the "slow-moving" story sometimes seems "strained, but is redeemed by the acting" of a deglamorized, Oscar-winning Berry and a "solid" Thornton, who display "great chemistry" during that "steamy sex scene."

Monsters, Inc.
26 | – | 25 | 28

2001. Directed by Peter Docter, David Silverman, Lee Unkrich. Animated. 92 minutes. Rated G.

"Pixar does it again" with this "innovative" "animation gem" that "shows kids that the monsters in their closets are really harmless"; this time around, the "*Toy Story*" tech team alloy an "original" plot, "amazing attention to detail" and "ugly" but "cute" characters to create an "endearing" entertainment that works "for adults" too; P.S. the "blow-you-away" "flying door" sequence has got "theme-park ride" written all over it.

Monty Python & the Holy Grail | 26 | 22 | 23 | 21 |
1975. Directed by Terry Gilliam, Terry Jones. With Monty Python. 91 minutes. Rated PG.
By dint of "sheer tasteless genius", this "absurdly wacky" "burlesque of the King Arthur legend" turns "historic reverence" on its ear and rules among "true" Pythonettes as the "movie of a thousand quotes" ("bring out your dead!"); granted, it may be comprised of a series of "strung-together skits" involving "killer bunnies" and "knights who say 'ni'", but the array of "knee-slapping" characters provides enough "lunacy to last the ages."

Moonraker ❶ | 16 | 14 | 15 | 20 |
1979. Directed by Lewis Gilbert. With Roger Moore, Lois Chiles, Richard Kiel. 126 minutes. Rated PG.
A "stiff" Moore pursues the usual mad villain in this 007 picture that has a hard time living up to its "dynamite credits sequence"; most agree the "silly" scenario is "quite a stretch", what with metal-mouth "Jaws finding love" and a "laughable space battle" that "tries to cash in on *Star Wars*" but "plays more like a Bond spoof."

MOONSTRUCK ✉ | 24 | 25 | 24 | 22 |
1987. Directed by Norman Jewison. With Cher, Nicolas Cage, Olympia Dukakis. 102 minutes. Rated PG.
Both "Italians and wannabe Italians" fall for this "totally charming" "romp" that shows how "love can be found in the least likely places" – even Brooklyn; a "phenomenal" Cher and Cage (the "heat between them could peel wallpaper") combine with a "dead-on", "star-studded" ensemble to keep this "romance classic" shining bright; fave scene: the "snap-out-of-it" slap.

Motorcycle Diaries, The 🇫 | 23 | 25 | 23 | 24 |
2004. Directed by Walter Salles. With Gael García Bernal, Rodrigo de la Serna. 128 minutes. Rated R.
Witness the "seeds of social conscience" sprouting in "young Che Guevara" in this "poetic" road picture set amid "breathtaking South American scenery"; "ogle"-icious Bernal's "marvelous" turn as the future "legendary figure" stokes the revolutionary fire despite hitting a raw nerve with a few *capitalistas* who claim this "saintly" depiction fosters too much "undeserved attention."

Moulin Rouge | 21 | 22 | 20 | 26 |
1952. Directed by John Huston. With José Ferrer, Zsa Zsa Gabor, Colette Marchand. 119 minutes. Not Rated.
"Drenched in color and the excitement of belle epoque Paris", this "original" look at the tortured life of artist Toulouse-Lautrec is the "lush" product of an era when "movies were movies"; Ferrer's "entertaining" performance is the glue here, even if his gloomy portrayal might be at odds with the "eye-candy" production values.

Moulin Rouge! | 23 | 23 | 20 | 27 |
2001. Directed by Baz Luhrmann. With Nicole Kidman, Ewan McGregor, Jim Broadbent. 127 minutes. Rated PG-13.
This "dizzying, decadent" "fever dream of a musical" set in "bohemian Paris" earned a clutch of Oscar nominations and may

have "single-handedly revived and re-created the genre" for the "new millennium"; the ever-"ravishing" Kidman "sheds her icy image" in a "kaleidoscopic" turn as a notorious "shady lady" smitten by a "naive poet", and it turns out "McGregor can sing", but naysayers call it a "confusing", "overedited" "mishmash" that's "all glitter, no substance."

Mouse That Roared, The ⓊⒾ
`23` `23` `24` `19`

1959. Directed by Jack Arnold. With Peter Sellers, Jean Seberg, David Kossoff. 83 minutes. Not Rated.

"British humor has never been better" than in this "priceless" Cold War–era import about an impoverished nation that declares war on America, planning to lose in exchange for foreign aid; an "ingenious" satire that "pokes lots of holes" in a lot of targets, it's "worth seeing" for "Peter Sellers' expert multiple performances alone."

Mr. Blandings Builds His Dream House ◑
`23` `24` `23` `21`

1948. Directed by H.C. Potter. With Cary Grant, Myrna Loy, Melvyn Douglas. 94 minutes. Not Rated.

"If you're thinking of building or remodeling your home", "there's no funnier movie" than this "timeless" "cautionary tale" that proves the "perils haven't changed in the last 50 years"; "fixer-uppers" laugh along with this amusing view of the "suburban dream gone askew", most notably "Myrna's painting-the-living-room" scene.

Mr. Deeds Goes to Town ✉◑
`25` `26` `24` `23`

1936. Directed by Frank Capra. With Gary Cooper, Jean Arthur, George Bancroft, Lionel Stander. 115 minutes. Not Rated.

With "all the heart and soul" (and "schmaltz") that you expect from director "Capra-corn", this "sweet" tale of a "pixilated" eccentric who inherits a fortune and then tries to give it away is one of the "great populist films" of the '30s; thanks to the "feel-good" mood, "heartwarming ending" and Cooper's "trademark underplaying", it's become a "standard" and is "much superior" to the Adam Sandler remake, *Mr. Deeds.*

Mr. Holland's Opus
`21` `22` `21` `19`

1995. Directed by Stephen Herek. With Richard Dreyfuss, Glenne Headly. 143 minutes. Rated PG.

"Sweet, funny and insightful", this "uplifting" opus chronicles the career of a "reluctant" high-school music teacher "who makes a difference in the lives of his students" while "struggling to come to terms with his own deaf son"; though the hard-hearted fuss it's too "preachy", the soft-hearted swear that this "inspirational" story is well worth seeing for Dreyfuss' "superb" performance alone.

Mr. Hulot's Holiday ◑🅵
▽ `26` `25` `22` `22`

1954. Directed by Jacques Tati. With Jacques Tati, Nathalie Pascaud. 86 minutes. Not Rated.

Right "up there with Keaton and Chaplin", Tati's "irresistible" "comic masterpiece" is bound to "take away the worst blues" with some of the "best sight gags" delivered in "almost pure mime"; when its "hilariously" maladroit title character goes to a vacation retreat, whatever "could possibly go wrong does" and the payoff's a "quirky", "low-key" "laugh riot."

Mr. Mom ✉

| 18 | 18 | 20 | 17 |

1983. Directed by Stan Dragoti. With Michael Keaton, Teri Garr, Martin Mull. 91 minutes. Rated PG.

Mom and pop "switch roles" in this "fish-out-of-water" comedy detailing the misadventures of a "stay-at-home dad" reduced to "ironing grilled-cheese sandwiches" and "playing poker" with housewives for "shopping coupons"; but even though Keaton is a "likable" enough "slob" in the title role, rewinders report this "guilty pleasure" "doesn't hold up" to repeated viewings.

Mrs. Brown

| 22 | 28 | 23 | 23 |

1997. Directed by John Madden. With Judi Dench, Billy Connolly, Geoffrey Palmer. 103 minutes. Rated PG.

"Not widely seen", this "intelligent" drama detailing the platonic relationship between Queen Victoria and her groomsman shows that "even the most hardened heart can be changed by love"; naturally, many say that the "amazing" Dench is "the reason to see it", given her "poignant" performance, though the "intriguing" plot and "subtle" work from Connolly are equally "wonderful."

Mrs. Doubtfire

| 20 | 23 | 20 | 20 |

1993. Directed by Chris Columbus. With Robin Williams, Sally Field, Pierce Brosnan. 125 minutes. Rated PG-13.

This "laugh-out-loud" story of a man attempting to "win back his ex and kids" by impersonating a "nanny" manages to be "over-the-top", "subversive" and "endearing" all at once; sure, doubters snipe the "far-fetched" screenplay "can't decide if it's a farce or a tearjerker", but it's agreed that "riot" Williams is "at his manic best" when in "drag."

Mrs. Henderson Presents

| 23 | 27 | 22 | 23 |

2005. Directed by Stephen Frears. With Judi Dench, Bob Hoskins, Kelly Reilly, Christopher Guest. 103 minutes. Rated R.

"Dench didn't earn her reputation for nothing", as demonstrated by her "marvelous" performance in this British comedy about an "eccentric" theater owner whose "nude cuties" revue helps stiffen public resolve during WWII; co-star Hoskins is equally "wonderful" in support, and the pairing of "top-notch humor" with "poignant" meditations on "love and loss" strikes a "crowd-pleasing" balance.

Mrs. Miniver ✉◑❶

| 25 | 27 | 24 | 24 |

1942. Directed by William Wyler. With Greer Garson, Walter Pidgeon, Teresa Wright. 134 minutes. Not Rated.

For "WWII without the combat scenes", check out the "civilian side" in this "stirring" saga of Britain during the Blitz, starring Garson as a "stiff-upper-lipped" homemaker who stoically endures everything from "harrowing air raids" to "Nazi paratroopers" in the kitchen; while cynics say it seems "more propaganda than entertainment", the film was an Oscar magnet, taking home six statuettes, including Best Picture and Best Actress.

Mr. Smith Goes to Washington ◑

| 26 | 27 | 25 | 22 |

1939. Directed by Frank Capra. With James Stewart, Jean Arthur, Claude Rains. 125 minutes. Not Rated.

"As American as two slices of apple pie", Frank Capra's "rousing" "political fairy tale" about "one man's belief in goodness" and his eventual "triumph" "appeals to the idealist in each of us"; "corny", perhaps, but "you can't help but be moved" by Stewart waging the "filibuster to beat all filibusters" – and proving "you *can* beat City Hall."

Mulan
23 | – | 23 | 24

1998. Directed by Tony Bancroft, Barry Cook. Animated. 88 minutes. Rated G.
An "underrated" rarity, this "gorgeously realized" animated "Chinese folk tale" features a Disney heroine "who can carry a movie on her own"; its mix of "family honor" and "women power" make it "good for a girl's self-esteem", while "just the right balance of seriousness and humor" "sends its message without preaching."

Mulholland Dr.
20 | 22 | 19 | 22

2001. Directed by David Lynch. With Naomi Watts, Laura Harring, Justin Theroux. 145 minutes. Rated R.
"Another confusing but consuming Lynch production", this "intriguing", "utterly disquieting" "portrait of Hollywood losers" "requires contemplation" since it's "hard to follow"; sure, fans say its "smoldering" leads are so "beautiful" that their presence alone makes the film "visually worth it", but cynics feel "totally ripped off" by this "weird" "nonsense."

Mummy, The ◑
▽ 22 | 20 | 21 | 19

1932. Directed by Karl Freund. With Boris Karloff, Zita Johann. 72 minutes. Not Rated.
Fresh out of his Frankenstein boots, "master" of fear Karloff wraps himself around the role of an ancient Egyptian priest who's revived when foolhardy explorers open his crypt in this "standout" horror flick; indeed, Boris is "so very creepy" that many say this "original" version of the oft-filmed tale is still the "best."

Mummy, The ⓤ
19 | 16 | 18 | 24

1999. Directed by Stephen Sommers. With Brendan Fraser, Rachel Weisz. 124 minutes. Rated PG-13.
Archeologists ravage Egyptian tombs to disastrous results in this "cornball" "modern B movie" featuring "fancy CGI effects" and a plot that lurches between "scary and funny"; but foes who dis its "ridiculous" premise suggest you "rent the original – *Raiders of the Lost Ark.*"

Munich
23 | 24 | 23 | 24

2005. Directed by Steven Spielberg. With Eric Bana, Daniel Craig, Geoffrey Rush. 164 minutes. Rated R.
The "spiritually corrosive effects of revenge" come under Steven Spielberg's "soul-searching" lens in this "provocative", "action-packed" thriller modeled on the "real events" that followed the 1972 "massacre of Israeli Olympic athletes" by Palestinian terrorists; treating the "very sensitive issue" of the Middle East conflict in a "balanced" manner, it suggests there are "no easy answers", frustrating foes who prefer a less "muddy" moral message.

Muppet Movie, The ⓤ
24 | 23 | 23 | 25

1979. Directed by James Frawley. With Charles Durning, Austin Pendleton. 97 minutes. Rated G.
"You're never too old" to enjoy this "goofy" but "utterly delightful" romp that might unleash your "inner kid" thanks to some "wonderful puppetry" abetted by an array of star-studded cameos from everyone from Milton Berle to Steve Martin; fans say it's the "best" of the Muppet oeuvre, crediting the "genius" of "na-

tional treasure" Jim Henson for the "successful transition" of *Sesame Street*'s denizens to the big screen.

Murderball
25 | – | 25 | 22

2005. Directed by Henry Alex Rubin, Dana Adam Shapiro. Documentary. 88 minutes. Rated PG-13.
"Leave your pity at the door" and hold tight for this "hard-hitting" documentary profiling the "fierce competitors" of "quadriplegic rugby", a "rough" wheelchair sport with a rep for "demolition derby" intensity; smashing the conventional "clichés about the disabled", it's a "non-sentimental" glimpse at a "seldom seen" group whose "guts, strength and love of life" are an "inspiration" to all.

Murder by Death
21 | 21 | 22 | 19

1976. Directed by Robert Moore. With Peter Falk, Peter Sellers, Maggie Smith, Alec Guinness. 94 minutes. Rated PG.
A "kooky lampoon that hits the spot", this Neil Simon–penned whodunit "spoof" places a "diverse" group of private eyes in a castle where murder ensues; given the efforts of a Charlie Chan–esque Sellers and a Bogart-channeling Falk, this "madcap" exercise is a "must-see satire for mystery lovers", even if some turn up evidence of too many "good actors playing useless parts."

Murder, My Sweet ◑
24 | 24 | 24 | 22

1944. Directed by Edward Dmytryk. With Dick Powell, Claire Trevor, Anne Shirley, Otto Kruger. 95 minutes. Not Rated.
For "Dick Powell without Ruby Keeler", check out his "breakout" role as the "tough" private dick Philip Marlowe in this adaptation of Raymond Chandler's *Farewell, My Lovely*; it's a "quintessential" piece of "early noir", replete with a "perfect femme fatale", "unsurpassed" dialogue and a world-weary, "wisecracking" outlook on life.

Murder on the Orient Express
23 | 23 | 26 | 24

1974. Directed by Sidney Lumet. With Albert Finney, Lauren Bacall, Ingrid Bergman. 128 minutes. Rated PG.
"Agatha Christie hasn't been done better" than in this "fascinatingly complex, lushly produced" Hercule Poirot mystery set on-board the Orient Express; boasting a "crisply directed" "all-star" ensemble cast that "looks like they're having the time of their lives", this "luxuriously funny" "perfect thriller" certainly "won't bore you" – and "you'll never guess whodunit."

Music Man, The
25 | 24 | 25 | 26

1962. Directed by Morton DaCosta. With Robert Preston, Shirley Jones, Buddy Hackett. 151 minutes. Rated G.
Making an "exquisite, seamless transition from Broadway to the silver screen", this slice of "pure Americana" about a "traveling con man" let loose in River City, Iowa, hits "classic" notes with its "catchy" Meredith Willson score; thanks to a "tour-de-force" turn by a "mesmerizing" Preston, this "family treat" "never grows old."

Mutiny on the Bounty ✉◑
25 | 25 | 25 | 23

1935. Directed by Frank Lloyd. With Charles Laughton, Clark Gable, Franchot Tone. 132 minutes. Not Rated.
Despite being "a bit creaky" after all these years, this original version of a legendary clash of egos on the high seas remains "the one and only" simply because "you don't get acting like this anymore": Laughton is darn "grand" as "definitive villain"

Captain Bligh, and "Gable is, well, Gable" as Mr. Christian, his second-in-command.

Mutiny on the Bounty ∅   22 | 24 | 24 | 22
1962. Directed by Lewis Milestone. With Marlon Brando, Trevor Howard, Richard Harris. 178 minutes. Not Rated.
Ultra-"fabulous scenery" that will surely make you "want to move to Tahiti" and a "cast of thousands" collide in this "big-budget" MGM remake about an uprising at sea; Brando turns in "one of his most controversial roles" as a "foppish" Fletcher Christian, even if foes harrumph "I'll take Gable."

My Beautiful Laundrette   ∇ 21 | 22 | 21 | 19
1985. Directed by Stephen Frears. With Daniel Day-Lewis, Gordon Warnecke. 98 minutes. Rated R.
This "highly original" drama of "modern London" puts race and assimilation through a "wonderfully up-front" spin cycle in its story of "smart", "entrepreneurial" immigrants vs. the nativist "lower classes"; amid the many "honest" moments that come out in the wash is the "daring" bond between Warnecke's go-getting Pakistani and Day-Lewis' tough hooligan, resulting in some "steamy gay kissing."

My Best Friend's Wedding   19 | 19 | 19 | 19
1997. Directed by P.J. Hogan. With Julia Roberts, Dermot Mulroney, Rupert Everett. 105 minutes. Rated PG-13.
There's "no thinking required" in this "enjoyable if predictable" "chick flick" about a single gal bent on preventing her best male friend from getting hitched; while a "surprisingly funny Roberts" and "yummy Everett" "chew up the scenery" entertainingly, those through with love find this "anti-romance" "contrived" and "obvious" – except for the "'Say a Little Prayer'" sing-along.

My Big Fat Greek Wedding   23 | 22 | 23 | 21
2002. Directed by Joel Zwick. With Nia Vardalos, John Corbett, Lainie Kazan. 96 minutes. Rated PG.
It "doesn't matter whether you are Greek, Jewish, Italian or Albanian" – "we all see our crazy relatives up on the screen" in this "absolutely hilarious" "feel-good" look at Hellenic matrimony featuring a "likable cast of characters that you grow to love despite all their quirks"; critics claim "too much big fat hype", but they're outvoted by fans who "will never look at Windex the same way again."

My Bodyguard   18 | 18 | 19 | 16
1980. Directed by Tony Bill. With Chris Makepeace, Adam Baldwin, Matt Dillon. 96 minutes. Rated PG.
The "ultimate teenage revenge fantasy", this "feel-good" flick about an "underdog" high-schooler who hires a tough classmate to protect him from a bully "rings true" with "anyone who was ever picked on"; sure, there's a "silly, irrelevant" subplot about "eccentric grown-ups", but overall this "endearing" "coming-of-age saga" is "well done."

My Brilliant Career   25 | 28 | 25 | 23
1979. Directed by Gillian Armstrong. With Judy Davis, Sam Neill, Wendy Hughes. 100 minutes. Rated G.
A "headstrong young woman" coming of age in 19th-century Australia must choose between a man or a career in this "won-

derful" drama that's a bona fide "feminist favorite" ("it changed my life"); in the "brilliant performance" that made her a star, "Davis rules", and abetted by "lovely photography and scenery", the film's an "absorbing" testimony to "girl power."

My Cousin Vinny
22 | 24 | 21 | 19

1992. Directed by Jonathan Lynn. With Joe Pesci, Ralph Macchio, Marisa Tomei. 120 minutes. Rated R.

"Fuhgeddaboudit": this "laugh-out-loud", "quotable" "courtroom classic" about a novice "Noo Yawk lawyer" representing his cousin in an Alabama murder trial is a "cleverly written" comic look at "Southern justice"; a "perfect" Pesci "carries the show", amply assisted by Tomei, who earned a "well-deserved Oscar" just by "making a Brooklyn accent the sexiest sound around"; P.S. it works best with "ordered-in pizza."

My Dinner with Andre
21 | 21 | 18 | 19

1981. Directed by Louis Malle. With Wallace Shawn, Andre Gregory. 110 minutes. Not Rated.

Who'd have thought a movie that "consists entirely of a dinner conversation" between two acquaintances could keep you entertained for two hours?; although with talk "spanning every philosophical topic" that "captures the magic in the ordinary", Shawn and Gregory do just that; "remarkable for how little it works with", this "simple, unpretentious" art-house hit is "oddly fascinating" to those who wish their own dining companions "could be as interesting."

MY FAIR LADY ⊠
27 | 27 | 27 | 27

1964. Directed by George Cukor. With Audrey Hepburn, Rex Harrison, Stanley Holloway. 170 minutes. Rated G.

"Hollywood couldn't have done a better job" than this "grand, classy" version of Broadway's Lerner and Loewe musical "based on *Pygmalion*"; a "breathtaking" (but "dubbed") Hepburn is "incomparable" as the Cockney "guttersnipe turned into a lady", while Oscar-winner Harrison "at his tweedy best" plays her "superior yet vulnerable" teacher; "infectious" tunes and costumes that "leave you weak-kneed" ("those hats!") make this "luscious production" all the more "loverly."

My Favorite Year
22 | 25 | 22 | 20

1982. Directed by Richard Benjamin. With Peter O'Toole, Mark Linn-Baker, Jessica Harper. 92 minutes. Rated PG.

This "winning comedy" about the "early days of TV" involves a boozy matinee idol's appearance on a program that's a "great riff on the old Sid Caesar show"; although "O'Toole playing a drunk might not be a stretch", he "nails every nuance", turning this "affectionate period piece" into "one of the funniest movies no one has ever seen."

My Girl ⑪
20 | 18 | 19 | 18

1991. Directed by Howard Zieff. With Dan Aykroyd, Jamie Lee Curtis, Anna Chlumsky. 102 minutes. Rated PG.

Get out your handkerchiefs: this "make-you-cry" dramedy pulls out all the stops in its depiction of a motherless girl dealing with emotional awakening (and her father's new girlfriend); Chlumsky's "sweet", "heart-wrenching" turn nails the "innocence and complexity of childhood" so well that many would like to "have her as a daughter."

My Left Foot ✉   25 | 28 | 25 | 23

1989. Directed by Jim Sheridan. With Daniel Day-Lewis, Brenda Fricker, Hugh O'Conor. 98 minutes. Rated R.

It "could have been sappy and overly sentimental", but this "stereotype-smashing" true account of an Irish man born with cerebral palsy is "handled with unvarnished dignity" thanks to the Oscar-winning Day-Lewis, who "maintains the contorted body and emotional scars" of his condition so adeptly that "you forget you're watching an actor"; "very moving", this film's a "beacon of light for all."

My Life As a Dog 🅵   25 | 24 | 25 | 22

1987. Directed by Lasse Hallström. With Anton Glanzelius, Melinda Kinnaman. 101 minutes. Rated PG-13.

"For once, an adult really gets into a child's head" in this "enchanting" Swedish "coming-of-age" drama that devotees deem director "Hallström's best"; the "puckish" lead is both "complex" and "cute", his fellow villagers "wacky" and the story "heart-tugging" without a "single false note" – no wonder many say it's "goose bump–worthy."

My Man Godfrey ◑   25 | 25 | 23 | 21

1936. Directed by Gregory La Cava. With William Powell, Carole Lombard, Eugene Pallette. 94 minutes. Not Rated.

As an "unconventional love-struck heiress", Lombard displays "impeccable timing" opposite the "masterful" Powell as the "hobo hired to be the family butler" in this "ultimate screwball comedy", the standard by which "all others are measured"; of course, the "fast-paced", fast-talking "plot is absurd" (that's "precisely the point"), but the "charming" principals "make it look convincing."

My Night at Maud's ◑🅵   ▽ 26 | 26 | 23 | 23

1970. Directed by Eric Rohmer. With Jean-Louis Trintignant, Françoise Fabian, Marie-Christine Barrault. 105 minutes. Rated PG.

A "movie about grown-ups for grown-ups", this "rewarding philosophical" drama examines the "concept of morality" in its story of a man attracted to two very different women; it's "mostly an extended conversation" with *beaucoup* "talk, talk and more talk", but intellectuals insist "all of it is worth listening to" (or reading about in the subtitles).

My Own Private Idaho   19 | 21 | 19 | 19

1991. Directed by Gus Van Sant. With River Phoenix, Keanu Reeves, William Richert. 102 minutes. Rated R.

"Beautiful boys" work the streets of Portland in this "original modern romance" about a "narcoleptic hustler" (Phoenix, in a "heartbreaking" turn) who falls for a "man he can never have"; once the plot drifts off into a "pretentious" takeoff of *Henry IV*, some say it becomes "overreaching" and downright "depressing", but still there are "enough good moments to make it worthwhile."

Mystic Pizza   17 | 18 | 17 | 15

1988. Directed by Donald Petrie. With Annabeth Gish, Julia Roberts, Lili Taylor. 104 minutes. Rated R.

"Female friendships" and young romance are examined in this "coming-of-age charmer" set in a New England pizza parlor, an "authentic slice of life" that's also a "great Sunday afternoon chick flick"; notable for being "Julia's first major movie", it's "very fluffy", though its "sweetness" is very "winning."

Mystic River ✉   26 | 28 | 25 | 25
2003. Directed by Clint Eastwood. With Sean Penn, Tim Robbins, Kevin Bacon, Laurence Fishburne, Marcia Gay Harden, Laura Linney. 137 minutes. Rated R.
"Lots of angst and anger" lie beneath this "bleak" tale of childhood buddies reunited as adults in the aftermath of a murder; it really "packs a wallop" thanks to a "pitch-perfect" ensemble (with special kudos to Penn and Robbins for their "kick-in-the-gut" turns), not to mention Clint's "compelling" direction and "haunting score"; the only dissonant note is that "slightly off-the-mark" ending.

Naked Gun, The ❶   20 | 17 | 17 | 18
1988. Directed by David Zucker. With Leslie Nielsen, Priscilla Presley, George Kennedy. 85 minutes. Rated PG-13.
This "laugh-a-minute" "cop spoof" from the minds behind *Airplane!* stars a "deadpan" Nielsen, who "raises the bar for satirical comedy" with his "terrific" performance; sure, the "brilliantly dumb characters" and "loopy overlapping dialogue" are equally "riotous", but ultimately "you have to be a guy to enjoy this much stupidity."

Napoléon ❶◐∅   ▽ 29 | 22 | 22 | 29
1927. Directed by Abel Gance. With Albert Dieudonné, Antonin Artaud. 235 minutes. Rated G.
"Eye-popping even today", this bio of Napoléon Bonaparte from "audacious" director Gance is a "sweeping epic" from the silent era that had been truncated over time but then restored to its former glory; its "unsurpassed" camerawork includes shots made "from horseback" and on a "pendulum", but its "final triptych", predating widescreen photography, makes for a "rousing" windup.

Napoleon Dynamite   19 | 20 | 17 | 17
2004. Directed by Jared Hess. With Jon Heder, Jon Gries. 82 minutes. Rated PG.
"Gosh", the road to "cult classic" status was short for this "flippin' sweet" underdog comedy whose "deadpan" depiction of a "tater tot"–chomping "born loser" pays "honest" homage to that "nerdy kid you went to school with"; voters "love it or hate it": lovers like its "quotable lines" ("vote for Pedro") and the "best dance scene ever", though foes fret it "goes nowhere and does nothing."

Nashville   23 | 23 | 22 | 24
1975. Directed by Robert Altman. With Ronee Blakley, Keith Carradine, Lily Tomlin. 159 minutes. Rated R.
It's the "wonderful ensemble" cast that makes this comic "portrait of '70s America" set in Nashville "richer and funnier with every viewing"; though some find it "frustrating" ("too many people talking at once"), "black humor" fans dub it "Altman's best", with enough "interesting characters" and "smart observations" to make it the "country cousin of *Gosford Park*."

National Lampoon's Vacation ❶   22 | 17 | 20 | 17
1983. Directed by Harold Ramis. With Chevy Chase, Beverly D'Angelo, Randy Quaid. 98 minutes. Rated R.
"Bad taste has never been funnier" than in this "vacation-from-hell" comedy recounting a "dysfunctional family's" cross-country

road trip; as the beleaguered dad, Chase is at the "pinnacle of his career", though many say he's upstaged by fleeting glimpses of white-"hot" "Christie Brinkley in a red sports car."

National Treasure | 19 | 17 | 20 | 21 |
2004. Directed by John Turteltaub. With Nicolas Cage, Jon Voight. 131 minutes. Rated PG.
"Indiana Jones meets *The Da Vinci Code*" in this "helluva roller-coaster ride" hinged around a treasure map discovered "on the back of the Declaration of Independence" ("seriously") and other "far-fetched" clues geared toward "American history buffs"; granted, Nic may be "no Harrison Ford" and the flick an "utterly disposable" "no-brainer", but it's more than "ok for a little escapism" and works best with a "large bag of popcorn."

National Velvet ⓤ | 24 | 24 | 24 | 22 |
1945. Directed by Clarence Brown. With Elizabeth Taylor, Mickey Rooney, Anne Revere. 123 minutes. Rated G.
The movie equivalent of "comfort food", this "classic" "coming-of-age story" about a "girl and her horse" stars a "dazzlingly young Taylor" and a "scene-stealing" Rooney in a "feel-good" parable of "surmounting obstacles to make dreams come true"; maybe it's "corny", but any young lady "who ever dreamed of having a pony" can't help but "gush" over that climatic steeplechase race.

Natural, The | 23 | 21 | 23 | 22 |
1984. Directed by Barry Levinson. With Robert Redford, Robert Duvall, Glenn Close. 134 minutes. Rated PG.
"Every Little Leaguer's favorite flick", this mix of "magic" and "major league baseball" stars a "rugged Redford" as a "middle-aged rookie" who hits a "chill"-inducing "home run into the lights"; though some sigh it's too "sentimental", fans cheer this "solid period drama" (and Randy Newman's "unforgettable score").

Network ✉ | 24 | 25 | 24 | 22 |
1976. Directed by Sidney Lumet. With Faye Dunaway, William Holden, Peter Finch, Beatrice Straight. 120 minutes. Rated R.
Even 30 years later, newscaster Howard Beale's "fateful cry, 'I'm mad as hell, and I'm not going to take it anymore'" is still "relevant" to proponents of this "prophetic" dramedy about television's "battle between news and entertainment"; "expertly written" by Paddy Chayefsky and "brilliantly acted" by Finch, Dunaway and Straight (who all won Oscars), this "biting" dark comedy has surveyors citing *"Jerry Springer"* and sighing "it's all true now."

Never on Sunday ◑ | 24 | 26 | 23 | 21 |
1960. Directed by Jules Dassin. With Melina Mercouri, Jules Dassin. 91 minutes. Not Rated.
A "sensuous" Mercouri became an international star after illuminating the screen in this "delightful" drama about an "earthy" Greek prostitute and an uptight American (played by director Dassin) who tries to pull a Pygmalion on her; although once "shocking", some say it's now "delightfully dated."

Never Say Never Again | 18 | 20 | 17 | 19 |
1983. Directed by Irvin Kershner. With Sean Connery, Klaus Maria Brandauer, Barbara Carrera. 134 minutes. Rated PG.
Live-and-let-diehards declare it's "fun to see Connery reprise the role that made him famous (and rich)" in this "rehash of

Thunderball" featuring an "older" though "still studly" 007 who's "stunningly" teamed with Carrera; but foes say this "disappointing" picture "shouldn't be considered a Bond film", since it lacks the "appropriate music" and panache of producer Albert Broccoli.

New York, New York
▽ | 18 | 19 | 18 | 20

1977. Directed by Martin Scorsese. With Liza Minnelli, Robert De Niro, Mary Kay Place. 164 minutes. Rated PG.
Minnelli's "perfectly cast" and in "flawless voice" in this "post-modern musical from Martin Scorsese" about married musicians yearning for "fame in the 1940s"; still, many moan "De Niro's character is so unlikable" that the "picture never works", resulting in a "forgettable muddle" – "except for a certain song."

Niagara
21 | 22 | 20 | 22

1953. Directed by Henry Hathaway. With Marilyn Monroe, Joseph Cotten, Jean Peters. 92 minutes. Not Rated.
The movie that "made Monroe a star", this "twisted" Technicolor thriller is set back in the day when Niagara Falls was a "hot destination" for honeymooners; its "double-cross", "soap opera"-esque plot involves a "treacherous wife", a frustrated husband and a pair of naive newlyweds, but its most "unforgettable" moment is Marilyn's "famous walk" through a parking lot, which totally "overshadows" everything else in the picture.

Nicholas Nickleby
22 | 23 | 24 | 22

2002. Directed by Douglas McGrath. With Christopher Plummer, Jim Broadbent, Charlie Hunnam, Anne Hathaway. 132 minutes. Rated PG.
"Escape to another era" and follow the "wholesome" adventures of a "down-on-his-luck" bloke who "rises to the top" in this "rich", "intelligently pared-down" rendering of Dickens' "very long novel"; "outstanding performances" by the "wonderfully odious" Plummer and fellow "fine talents" contribute to an overall "solid" production, leaving fans to ponder why "nobody saw it."

Night at the Opera, A ◗
26 | 25 | 22 | 22

1935. Directed by Sam Wood. With the Marx Brothers, Kitty Carlisle, Margaret Dumont. 96 minutes. Not Rated.
"Inspired insanity" meets "Marxist lunacy" in this "nutty" comedy (the "origin of the term 'laugh riot'") from the brothers Marx, wherein Groucho persuades a social-climbing Dumont to invest in an opera production; fans fast-forward through the "saccharine musical moments" in favor of the "verbal dazzle" of the "contract routine", the "baseball-in-the-orchestra-pit" bit and, of course, that "not-to-be-believed stateroom scene."

Nightmare Before Christmas, The
24 | – | 22 | 28

1993. Directed by Henry Selick. Animated. 76 minutes. Rated PG.
The "perfect antidote to the holidays" may well be this "magical", "macabre masterpiece" of stop-motion animation that ideally epitomizes the "bizarre genius" of producer Tim Burton; with a "cool story" – Halloween meets Christmas – and "Danny Elfman's great score", it's a "must-see for kids of all ages."

Nightmare on Elm Street, A ⑪
19 | 14 | 19 | 18

1984. Directed by Wes Craven. With John Saxon, Ronee Blakley, Johnny Depp. 91 minutes. Rated R.
Built around the "concept that your nightmares are real", this "original splatter" flick "did for sleeping what *Jaws* did for swim-

ming" thanks to Freddy Krueger, its "pizza-faced" villain who sports "knives for fingers"; over 20 years later, this "darn scary" picture is now recognized as a "modern horror classic."

NIGHT OF THE HUNTER, THE ◑   27 | 28 | 25 | 26
1955. Directed by Charles Laughton. With Robert Mitchum, Shelley Winters, Lillian Gish. 93 minutes. Not Rated.
Playing a "semi-psychotic preacher" "personifying pure evil", the "mesmerizing" Mitchum "terrorizes a bunch of kids" (and "invents tattooed knuckles") in this "strange" film noir frightfest; it's a "pity this was Laughton's only directorial" effort, given the "exquisite cinematography" and "unforgettable" performances that add up to "stunningly innovative cinema."

Night of the Living Dead ◑ⅠⅠ   22 | 13 | 19 | 16
1968. Directed by George A. Romero. With Duane Jones, Judith O'Dea, Russ Streiner. 96 minutes. Not Rated.
Director Romero "does zombies right" in this "zero-budget" indie "landmark" that proves that even "schlocky" special effects, a "shabby storyline" and "bad acting" can produce what living dead–heads call the "scariest movie ever made"; the "grainy black-and-white film used adds to the creepy aura", right down to the "freak-you-out", "pj-wetting" finale.

Nights of Cabiria ✉ ◐ 𝐅   27 | 28 | 25 | 24
1957. Directed by Federico Fellini. With Giulietta Masina, François Périer. 117 minutes. Not Rated.
"Post-WWII Italy" as seen "through the eyes of a streetwalker" is the premise of this "simple, heartfelt" drama that's one of Fellini's "most moving" (and least "bizarre") films; as the "lovable girl of the streets", the "radiant" Masina is nothing less than a "female Charlie Chaplin", rendering an "amazing" performance that "ranges from tragedy to transcendence to flat-out comedy."

9½ Weeks ⅠⅠ   15 | 15 | 15 | 16
1986. Directed by Adrian Lyne. With Mickey Rourke, Kim Basinger. 113 minutes. Rated R.
"Groundbreaking for its time", this "steamy" rendering of an "obsessive relationship" remains a definite "third-date movie", what with the "twisted" Rourke and "hot! hot! hot!" Basinger engaged in "kinky sex" via blindfolds, "ice cubes" and peanut shells; still, bluenoses find it "dreary, numbing" "softcore porn" that's nowhere near "as sexy as *An Officer and a Gentleman*."

1900 𝐅 ∅   ▽ 22 | 24 | 19 | 23
1976. Directed by Bernardo Bertolucci. With Robert De Niro, Gérard Depardieu, Burt Lancaster. 243 minutes. Rated R.
This "sweeping epic" from Bernardo Bertolucci is a "sumptuous", "fascinating study of Italian society and politics in the first half of the 20th century"; "finely acted" by De Niro (playing an aristocrat) and Depardieu (as a proletariat labor leader), it might be "a bit long and self-indulgent", but most find its "operatic form" and "meticulous" camerawork completely "involving."

9 to 5   18 | 18 | 19 | 17
1980. Directed by Colin Higgins. With Jane Fonda, Lily Tomlin, Dolly Parton, Dabney Coleman. 110 minutes. Rated PG.
"Every secretary's dream" of "getting even with the boss" comes true in this "silly comedy", a "feminist classic" with a "relevant

message" (though chauvinists snicker it's "proof that women's lib can be sexist too"); still, its "strong" protagonists exhibit "amazing chemistry" and Parton's theme song sure is "catchy."

Ninotchka ◑
▽ 25 | 26 | 24 | 22

1939. Directed by Ernst Lubitsch. With Greta Garbo, Melvyn Douglas, Ina Claire. 110 minutes. Not Rated.
This "great American comedy" depicts Soviet comrades seduced by capitalism, but is best known as the picture in which "Garbo laughs" for the first time on-screen; playing a "woman who follows her heart rather than the Communist manifesto", she's "smooth and sexy" spouting "incredibly funny dialogue" courtesy of a group of ace scenarists including Billy Wilder.

Norma Rae ✉
24 | 27 | 24 | 21

1979. Directed by Martin Ritt. With Sally Field, Beau Bridges, Ron Leibman, Pat Hingle. 110 minutes. Rated PG.
A "stirring tale about ordinary people", this "uplifting" drama is a "painfully accurate look" at a "courageous" mill worker's "fight for justice" when caught between "unions and management"; in the title role, the "superb" Field really "earned her Oscar", and the "image of her holding up that sign" has become iconically "indelible."

NORTH BY NORTHWEST
28 | 26 | 27 | 27

1959. Directed by Alfred Hitchcock. With Cary Grant, Eva Marie Saint, James Mason. 136 minutes. Not Rated.
"James Bond, eat your heart out" – "no one is cooler than Cary Grant" in this "incredibly stylish" Hitchcock thriller, a "twisting story of mistaken identity" set "all over the country" involving a "cool blonde", a "smooth villain" and a "malevolent crop duster"; despite some "holes in the script", there's distraction via that "exhilarating" climb down Mount Rushmore and the "double entendre" scenario (e.g. the "train entering a tunnel" at the climax).

North Country
22 | 26 | 22 | 21

2005. Directed by Niki Caro. With Charlize Theron, Frances McDormand, Woody Harrelson, Sissy Spacek. 126 minutes. Rated R.
"Boy, can Theron act" declare devotees of her "fine performance" as a miner fighting "sexual harassment in the Minnesota iron range" in this "powerful" drama inspired by "real events"; highlighting a "piece of history few know about", this "message film" risks "heavy-handedness" to stand as a "harsh reminder" of "how hard it is for women to earn a living."

North Dallas Forty
19 | 18 | 20 | 18

1979. Directed by Ted Kotcheff. With Nick Nolte, Mac Davis, Charles Durning, Dayle Haddon. 119 minutes. Rated R.
"Way before the steroids controversy" was this "ahead-of-its-time" depiction of the "dirty underside of pro football" starring Nolte as an "aging", "medicated" player ("boy, those needles look like they hurt"); the "tell-it-like-it-is" script "doesn't have a storybook ending", and many are convinced the team is a "thinly disguised version of the Dallas Cowboys" in their '70s heyday.

Nosferatu ◑
▽ 26 | 22 | 23 | 24

1922. Directed by F.W. Murnau. With Max Schreck, Gustav von Wangenheim, Greta Schroeder. 84 minutes. Not Rated.
"Still creepy after all these years", this "important German horror film" (an "unauthorized version of *Dracula*") is "one spooky" silent

flick that can "evoke terror" thanks to the "genuinely scary Schreck"; it's the "most poetic of vampire films" and the "standard that others are measured against – and usually found lacking."

Nosferatu the Vampyre 🅕 22 | 24 | 22 | 25
1979. Directed by Werner Herzog. With Klaus Kinski, Isabelle Adjani, Bruno Ganz. 107 minutes. Rated PG.
A "stylish retelling" of the "familiar" Dracula story, this "great remake" via Werner Herzog owes a lot to the "mesmerizing", "out-there" Kinski who "stakes his claim" on the title role; "visually stunning" and imbued with a "strong political subtext", it's "reasonably creepy", but paced at such a "hypnotic crawl" that purists insist the Murnau original is "still the gold standard."

Notebook, The 23 | 24 | 24 | 23
2004. Directed by Nick Cassavetes. With Ryan Gosling, Rachel McAdams, James Garner, Gena Rowlands. 123 minutes. Rated PG-13.
Sweet enough to "dissolve a tooth", this "hauntingly beautiful" sob-o-rama based on the Nicholas Sparks best-seller might be the "ultimate chick flick", a "testament to the awesome power of love" as it endures "through the ages"; naturally, the dry-eyed cry "corny", but even they credit the "genuinely sad Alzheimer's storyline" for addressing an issue that's "not often given attention."

Nothing Sacred ▽ 23 | 23 | 20 | 20
1937. Directed by William Wellman. With Carole Lombard, Fredric March. 75 minutes. Not Rated.
The "notion of celebrity is lampooned" in this nutty screwball comedy, the story of a woman diagnosed with a terminal disease who's feted by a newspaper in exchange for her exclusive story – only to find out that she's been misdiagnosed; it's way "ahead of its time" in its arch analysis of the fame game alone.

No Time for Sergeants ◑∅ 23 | 22 | 22 | 19
1958. Directed by Mervyn LeRoy. With Andy Griffith, Myron McCornick, Nick Adams. 119 minutes. Not Rated.
Managing to be "endearing without being annoying", Griffith "delivers the goods" in this "hilarious" comedy about a "dim hayseed who nearly destroys the U.S. Air Force", abetted by "perfect foil" Don Knotts; the infamous "toilet-seat scene" is a "display of American ingenuity" at its finest.

NOTORIOUS ◐ 27 | 27 | 26 | 26
1946. Directed by Alfred Hitchcock. With Cary Grant, Ingrid Bergman, Claude Rains. 101 minutes. Not Rated.
"Fetching" Ingrid Bergman "goes under the sheets for her country and gets Cary Grant as a reward" in this "brilliantly subversive" Hitchcock spy thriller featuring equal parts of "suspense", "suspicion", "hurt pride" and "Nazis too"; best remembered for the leads' "lingering, smoldering love scene", it also boasts "topnotch" supporting work from Rains, who has the best line: "mother, I'm married to an American agent."

Notting Hill 19 | 19 | 18 | 19
1999. Directed by Roger Michell. With Julia Roberts, Hugh Grant, Rhys Ifans. 124 minutes. Rated PG-13.
"Straight-up chick flick" about a "hair-flicking" movie star who finds love with an "endearing" bookseller; though rotters relate it's "formulaic" (with "Roberts playing herself" and Grant in his

"stammering ingénue" mode), at least the supporting cast is "brilliantly funny"; the London scenery provides the "charm."

No Way Out
20 | 19 | 23 | 19

1987. Directed by Roger Donaldson. With Kevin Costner, Gene Hackman, Sean Young. 114 minutes. Rated R.
Perhaps "Costner's finest hour", this "entirely enjoyable military thriller" offers "wonderful intrigue" in its way-out plot, something to do with the KGB, the Pentagon, the backseat of a limousine and a classy call girl (the "very hot" Young); while coolly "tense" throughout, the "unexpected", "twisty" ending is still a "shocker."

NOW, VOYAGER ◑
27 | 28 | 26 | 25

1942. Directed by Irving Rapper. With Bette Davis, Paul Henreid, Claude Rains. 117 minutes. Not Rated.
"Break out the hankies" – this "chick flick extraordinaire" features "the moon, the stars and Bette Davis", who effects an "appealing transformation" as an "old maid" defecting from a "demanding mother" to find kismet with a "perfect" Henreid; though the "two-cigarette scene" is decidedly un-PC today, it's become a "sacred" (and paradoxically "life-affirming") moment in this "classy" "mature love story."

Nurse Betty
15 | 18 | 15 | 15

2000. Directed by Neil LaBute. With Renée Zellweger, Morgan Freeman, Chris Rock. 108 minutes. Rated R.
"Entertaining" but "unconventional", this "quirky black comedy" top-lines Zellweger as a "clueless blonde" soap opera buff pursued by vicious hitmen; foes find the wild mix of comedy and gore too "incongruous" and "unnecessarily violent" ("what planet did the screenwriter come from?"), and even fans admit it's "not for everyone" – just those who appreciate "inventive" filmmaking.

Nutty Professor, The
21 | 19 | 18 | 18

1963. Directed by Jerry Lewis. With Jerry Lewis, Stella Stevens, Del Moore. 107 minutes. Not Rated.
Jerry's "finest hour", this "can't-be-improved-upon" "wacky" comedy concerns a nerdy college prof who is transformed from Dr. Jerk-yll into Mr. Hyde after guzzling an exotic tonic; fans find it "sweet", foes shrug "typical Lewis shtick" and deep thinkers deem it a "metaphor for the monsters inside the greatest comedians."

Nutty Professor, The ⓫
15 | 18 | 14 | 18

1996. Directed by Tom Shadyac. With Eddie Murphy, Jada Pinkett, James Coburn. 95 minutes. Rated PG-13.
This "competent remake" of the Jerry Lewis comedy features Murphy in "amazingly versatile" mode, playing a seriously overweight professor (in a "great fat suit") in addition to six other minor characters; it may be "more sentimental and less sharp" than the original – and "probably not appreciated by the French" – but those "dinner table scenes" are "wet-your-pants funny."

O Brother, Where Art Thou?
22 | 23 | 22 | 24

2000. Directed by Joel Coen. With George Clooney, John Turturro, Tim Blake Nelson, John Goodman. 106 minutes. Rated PG-13.
"Who else but the Coen brothers could mix Greek mythology, bluegrass and George Clooney?" ask fans of this picaresque, "perversely funny" satire "based on Homer's *Odyssey*" that details the adventures of three Depression-era "hayseeds" who

bust out of prison; though a bit too "highbrow" for some, the "beautiful period detail" and "best roots music soundtrack ever" keep this "sweet" if "strange" genre-bender accessible.

Ocean's Eleven
16 | 15 | 19 | 18

1960. Directed by Lewis Milestone. With Frank Sinatra, Dean Martin, Sammy Davis, Jr., Peter Lawford. 127 minutes. Not Rated.
A "guilty pleasure to be sure", this "original version" of the casino heist caper features the "Rat Pack at their best" in a fab "1960 Las Vegas" setting ("when all the buildings were one story"); sure, it may be a bit "slow" in the beginning, but the look is "so stylish", the cast "so cool" and the ending so "clever" that it's always "entertaining."

Ocean's Eleven
19 | 19 | 19 | 22

2001. Directed by Steven Soderbergh. With George Clooney, Brad Pitt, Andy Garcia. 116 minutes. Rated PG-13.
"Fluffy fun" that "goes down smooth like a good martini", this "breezy caper" flick is "more lively than the original" version with its "great shots of Vegas", "never-a-dull-moment" plot and "lots of eye candy for the ladies"; ok, it might be "really silly", but the "slick", "all-star cast" and "genius director du jour Soderbergh" serve up something "wonderfully entertaining."

Octopussy ❶
17 | 15 | 16 | 19

1983. Directed by John Glen. With Roger Moore, Maud Adams, Louis Jourdan. 130 minutes. Rated PG.
James Bond goes to India in this "over-the-top" feature whose "name lets you know how silly it is"; it might have a rather "basic", "assembly-line" formula, a "hokey" script and a star "getting too old for the part", but fans say it's worth seeing just for a glimpse of 007 masquerading "as a clown."

Odd Couple, The ❶
25 | 27 | 25 | 21

1968. Directed by Gene Saks. With Jack Lemmon, Walter Matthau, John Fiedler. 105 minutes. Rated G.
Lemmon and Matthau are "brilliant" in this "timeless" Neil Simon "classic" (which spawned a sequel and a TV series) that poses the question 'can two divorced men share an apartment without driving each other crazy?'; the ensuing dilemma makes for "unbeatable" comedy that'll make your "sides hurt from laughter."

Officer and a Gentleman, An
22 | 21 | 21 | 20

1982. Directed by Taylor Hackford. With Richard Gere, Debra Winger, David Keith. 122 minutes. Rated R.
"What gal doesn't dream" of Richard Gere "sweeping" her into his arms and lifting her up where she belongs?; this "quintessential" '80s "date movie" provides plenty of fodder for "guilty-pleasure" fantasizing with its love story between a "young enlisted man" and a "poor" working girl, even if foes pan it as "a bit lame" and advise "fast-forward to the last scene that makes the rest worthwhile."

Oh, God! ❶
17 | 17 | 18 | 16

1977. Directed by Carl Reiner. With George Burns, John Denver, Teri Garr, Paul Sorvino. 104 minutes. Rated PG.
For pure "entertainment value", it's tough to top this "irresistible" comedy about an average Joe chosen by God to spread His word; believers say Burns is "perfectly cast" in the title role ("he's old

enough to be God") and Denver as his disciple is "surprisingly effective", but even though this "humanist" picture is "worth a watch", it "didn't deserve to launch a series of follow-ups."

Oklahoma!
24 | 22 | 23 | 25

1955. Directed by Fred Zinnemann. With Gordon MacRae, Shirley Jones, Gloria Grahame. 145 minutes. Rated G.
"Every song" in this "sprawling" Rodgers and Hammerstein musical/Western "makes you want to sing along" with the "lovely" voices of Jones and MacRae, plus there are "rousing dance numbers"; though modernists malign it as a "little dated", for most it's a whole lot "more than O-K", it's a pure "C-L-A-S-S-I-C."

Old School
20 | 19 | 18 | 17

2003. Directed by Todd Phillips. With Luke Wilson, Will Ferrell, Vince Vaughn. 91 minutes. Rated R.
"Ninth-grade cafeteria humor" underlies this "sophomoric" albeit "pee-your-pants-funny" comedy of "old frat guys who relive their youth" by opening an "adult fraternity"; sure, it's plenty "stupid" ("don't bring your brain") with a "derivative" plot that "couldn't exist without *Animal House*", but its "good-natured doofiness" and Ferrell's "manic performance" are both pretty "classic."

Old Yeller ⏏
24 | 20 | 24 | 20

1957. Directed by Robert Stevenson. With Dorothy McGuire, Fess Parker, Tommy Kirk. 83 minutes. Rated G.
"You can't help but cry your eyes out" after watching this "outstanding" Disney "tearjerker" about a "boy and his big yellow dog"; if a few find the acting "formulaic" and the plot "sappy", most agree it's an "all-time" children's "standard" that even adults "never tire of watching" – despite that gosh-darned "sad ending."

Oliver! ✉
24 | 23 | 24 | 26

1968. Directed by Carol Reed. With Mark Lester, Ron Moody, Shani Wallis, Oliver Reed. 153 minutes. Rated G.
Dickens' "bleak yet hopeful" novel is "lovingly brought to the screen" in this Oscar-winning adaptation of the "classic" stage musical; given the "incredible" production numbers, "wonderful" score and "just-about-perfect" cast, many "English orphan" wannabes beg 'please, sir can we watch it again?'

Oliver Twist ◗
25 | 26 | 26 | 24

1951. Directed by David Lean. With Robert Newton, Alec Guinness, John Howard Davies. 116 minutes. Not Rated.
David Lean's "classic" take on Dickens' ageless novel "stands up over time" so well that many consider it the "best version of the book" put onto celluloid (indeed, it's "almost as good as *Great Expectations*"); admirers applaud Newton's "stunning", "tug-at-the-heartstrings" title turn and the "jolly good" Guinness, whose "controversial" performance as Fagin (deemed anti-Semitic by some) delayed the film's U.S. release.

Omen, The ⏏
21 | 21 | 22 | 20

1976. Directed by Richard Donner. With Gregory Peck, Lee Remick, David Warner. 111 minutes. Rated R.
This "genuinely spooky" thriller has a "brilliant premise" – a couple unwittingly adopts the devil's child – and features an appropriately "satanic" storyline, "eerie" music and a frightening turn by the "scariest kid ever to be in a horror movie" (Harvey Stephens);

thrill-seekers also quiver in delight at its "terrifying" special effects that make the "unbelievable believable."

Once Upon a Time in America
24 | 26 | 24 | 24

1984. Directed by Sergio Leone. With Robert De Niro, James Woods, Elizabeth McGovern. 227 minutes. Rated R.

Some of De Niro's "most subtle and effective" acting is on display in this "unfairly neglected" crime epic spanning four decades, which hard-core cineasts hail as "truly remarkable" when "seen in the long [227-minute] director's cut"; but despite a "top-drawer cast" and "magnificent" direction, others are less enthused about the "flawed" end result that's awash in "too much blood."

Once Upon a Time in Mexico
15 | 18 | 14 | 18

2003. Directed by Robert Rodriguez. With Antonio Banderas, Salma Hayek, Johnny Depp. 102 minutes. Rated R.

A diet "light on plot, heavy on action" helps pulp director Rodriguez cap his Mariachi trilogy with a "bang bang", but this "lackluster" series finale shoots its way through a "muddled" revenge storyline rendered by mere "moments of visual brilliance"; *muchas gracias* go to Depp for his "outrageous" performance, even if his "scene-stealing" antics can't save this "disappointment."

Once Upon a Time in the West
25 | 24 | 23 | 25

1969. Directed by Sergio Leone. With Henry Fonda, Claudia Cardinale, Charles Bronson. 165 minutes. Rated PG-13.

This "ultimate Western" is "epic in every way", starting with its "big-name" cast, "long, long" running time and operatic plot about the struggle for a piece of land; throw in Fonda as an "amazingly evil" villain, Ennio Morricone's "magical score" and "one of the coolest opening scenes ever", and it's easy to see why many consider this "high-water mark" to be Leone's "definitive" work.

ONE FLEW OVER THE CUCKOO'S NEST ⊠
27 | 29 | 27 | 25

1975. Directed by Milos Forman. With Jack Nicholson, Louise Fletcher, Will Sampson. 133 minutes. Rated R.

"Life in a mental ward" gets the "stand-up-for-your-rights" treatment in this "absorbing, disturbing" and "influential" drama starring "national treasure" Nicholson at his "ornery best", backed up by an "amazing" ensemble cast; no surprise, it took five major Oscars, made Nurse Ratched a household name and is "hard to top" – folks are just plain "nuts about it."

One Hour Photo
18 | 23 | 18 | 18

2002. Directed by Mark Romanek. With Robin Williams, Connie Nielsen, Michael Vartan. 96 minutes. Rated R.

Williams "sheds his funny-man image" and "gives good villain" in this "super-creepy" psychological thriller about "Sy the photo guy", a "mega-mart" lab technician obsessed by an all-American family; despite a "slow" pace and "out-of-focus" script that "needed more time in the darkroom", the movie's ultimately "disturbing" enough for some to consider "switching to Polaroids" or "digital cameras."

101 Dalmatians
24 | – | 22 | 24

1961. Directed by Wolfgang Reitherman, Clyde Geronimi, Hamilton Luske. Animated. 79 minutes. Rated G.

Puppy proponents put their paws together for Pongo, Perdita and their prolific progeny when watching this "fast, funny" piece of

Disney animation; its "hugely entertaining" tale of a klatch of "cute" canines outrunning über-villainess Cruella De Vil appeals to the "little kid in everyone" and makes this one an "enduring winner."

101 Dalmatians ⓫ | 18 | 19 | 19 | 22 |

1996. Directed by Stephen Herek. With Glenn Close, Jeff Daniels, Joely Richardson. 103 minutes. Rated G.
"*The* reason" to see Disney's "cute" live-action "update" of their earlier animated feature is the "over-the-top" Close as the "truly wicked" Cruella De Vil (though there's also "dry humor" courtesy of the largely British supporting cast); still, cynics nix this "wholly unnecessary remake" as "not as good as the original."

One, Two, Three ◑ | ▽ 24 | 26 | 25 | 24 |

1961. Directed by Billy Wilder. With James Cagney, Horst Buchholz, Pamela Tiffin. 108 minutes. Not Rated.
"Billy Wilder scores in this Cold War comedy", a "fast and furious farce" set in Berlin about a "harried Coca-Cola executive" whose "world is collapsing around him"; Cagney's "machine-gun delivery is a scream", though diehards say the picture's "underrated" and "overshadowed" by the director's better-known films.

On Golden Pond ✉ | 24 | 27 | 23 | 23 |

1981. Directed by Mark Rydell. With Katharine Hepburn, Henry Fonda, Jane Fonda. 109 minutes. Rated PG.
A "beautiful tale of growing old and looking back on life", this "brilliant" drama features the "stunning", Oscar-winning Hank and Kate "pulling out all the stops" as an elderly couple coming to terms with their child and each other over one golden summer; the "real-life tension" between the real-life father-and-daughter Fondas supplies some "electric" moments, while its timeless theme about the "strength of the human spirit" "will appeal to all."

On Her Majesty's Secret Service | 19 | 15 | 21 | 20 |

1969. Directed by Peter R. Hunt. With George Lazenby, Diana Rigg, Telly Savalas. 140 minutes. Rated PG.
"James Bond gets married" in this "respectable" flick featuring "astonishing ski chases", "Swiss Alp views" and a "believable love story" for a change; still, opinion splits on Lazenby's one-time-only turn as 007 ("wooden" vs. "formidable"), and as for the end result, it's either "underrated" or "the worst" in the series.

On the Beach ◑ | 26 | 26 | 27 | 23 |

1959. Directed by Stanley Kramer. With Gregory Peck, Ava Gardner, Fred Astaire, Anthony Perkins. 134 minutes. Not Rated.
"Now dated, but still riveting", this "chilling" Cold War–era message picture details the "aftermath of a nuclear war", where the earth's sole survivors struggle to stay alive in Australia; it's an "intense" look at "how people spend their last days" that "isn't about explosions, but emotions", and many report "never listening to 'Waltzing Matilda' the same way again" after seeing it.

On the Town | 23 | 23 | 21 | 25 |

1949. Directed by Stanley Donen, Gene Kelly. With Gene Kelly, Frank Sinatra, Jules Munshin. 98 minutes. Not Rated.
Despite "wonderful dancing by Kelly" and some "funny" bits from the ensemble cast, "NYC is the real star" of this "exuberant" musical "celebrating the American spirit in the '40s"; "filmed partially on location" and juiced up by a "great Leonard Bernstein score", it

follows three sailors at liberty on the town, and although rather "silly", it effortlessly radiates the "pure joy" of simpler times.

ON THE WATERFRONT ✉◑
28 | 29 | 26 | 26

1954. Directed by Elia Kazan. With Marlon Brando, Karl Malden, Eva Marie Saint, Rod Steiger. 108 minutes. Not Rated.
Most decidedly a "candidate for all-time greatest" film, this "gritty tale of corruption on the NJ docks" is a "movie to turn you onto movies", with Oscar wins by the "phenomenal Brando" (as a "washed-up", "Palookaville"-bound boxer) and a "knockout" Saint (in her screen debut); indeed, this "gutsy", "brutal masterwork" "rings so true" and is so "emotionally satisfying" that it's "nothing less than brilliant"; best line: "I coulda been a contender."

Open City ◑🄵
▽ 28 | 29 | 28 | 25

1946. Directed by Roberto Rossellini. With Aldo Fabrizi, Anna Magnani. 105 minutes. Not Rated.
One of the major works of Italian neorealism, this "devastating" look at occupied Rome in the 1940s shows the "devastation that war produces and how people pick up the pieces that are left"; the "unforgettable" Magnani's performance "burns in one's memory", while the picture itself is credited for reawakening American interest in modern international films.

Operation Petticoat
19 | 19 | 18 | 19

1959. Directed by Blake Edwards. With Cary Grant, Tony Curtis, Joan O'Brien, Dina Merrill. 124 minutes. Not Rated.
"Feel-good" WWII comedy having to do with a Navy captain's "emergency" efforts to keep a gaggle of army nurses and a "pink submarine" afloat; despite smooth "chemistry" between Grant and Curtis resulting in some pretty "funny" situations (i.e. lots of tight-quarters gags), the unamused torpedo it as "contrived."

Ordinary People ✉
25 | 27 | 25 | 23

1980. Directed by Robert Redford. With Donald Sutherland, Mary Tyler Moore, Timothy Hutton. 124 minutes. Rated R.
"Every parent's nightmare" – the death of a child – is dissected in this "devastating" drama that goes below the "veneer of an upper-middle-class family" to plumb the "dysfunction" below; Redford's "deserving" directorial debut copped a Best Picture Oscar, but it's Moore's "playing-against-type" role as a "classy" but "coldhearted" mom that "steals the movie."

Others, The
23 | 25 | 23 | 24

2001. Directed by Alejandro Amenábar. With Nicole Kidman, Fionnula Flanagan. 101 minutes. Rated PG-13.
A "dynamic" Kidman delivers an "old-school movie star turn" in this "grand ghost story" about a mother protecting her children who suffer from a rare "photosensitive" condition (an "excellent excuse to keep the house dark and murky"); "wonderfully atmospheric" and "deliciously scary", it's "highbrow horror" with a "jeepers-creepers" ending that's a "real shocker."

Outbreak
16 | 18 | 17 | 18

1995. Directed by Wolfgang Petersen. With Dustin Hoffman, Rene Russo, Morgan Freeman. 127 minutes. Rated R.
"Cheer the hero and hiss the villain" in this "entertaining bio-thriller" where "time's running out" in a California community threatened by "wayward monkeys" and "airborne viruses"; in his

first "action hero" role, Hoffman is "realistic" enough, but foes say the upshot is "silly" – "more bad science" – and suggest you "read *The Hot Zone* instead."

Outlaw Josey Wales, The
25 | 23 | 24 | 23

1976. Directed by Clint Eastwood. With Clint Eastwood, Sondra Locke, Chief Dan George. 135 minutes. Rated PG.
Playing a renegade Confederate soldier seeking revenge after his wife and children are murdered, Eastwood is his "usual unreadable self" (though you "feel for his plight") in this "quirky" Western that's a "rural version of *Death Wish*"; fans rate it "better-than-usual Clint", given its "classic lines" and "profound issues."

OUT OF AFRICA ✉
25 | 25 | 24 | 27

1985. Directed by Sydney Pollack. With Meryl Streep, Robert Redford, Klaus Maria Brandauer. 150 minutes. Rated PG.
Supporters are "spellbound" by this "splendiferous" "love story played out against the mysterious continent" starring a "radiant" Streep as Danish writer Karen Blixen (aka Isak Dinesen) and a "great-looking" Redford as her paramour; the "beauty" of Africa and "soaring score" "amplify the emotion", and even though it's a "real tearjerker", most eat up this "treat" "again and again."

Out of Sight
21 | 21 | 21 | 22

1998. Directed by Steven Soderbergh. With George Clooney, Jennifer Lopez, Ving Rhames. 123 minutes. Rated R.
"Clooney and Lopez generate electricity aplenty" in this "smart caper" flick that "oozes cool" in its depiction of a "cocksure" con artist, his "eye-candy police pursuer" and "one of the sexiest love scenes" ever; a "crackling" story (via Elmore Leonard's novel) and "brilliant" direction from Soderbergh make this one an "overlooked gem."

Out of the Past ◑
26 | 26 | 25 | 25

1947. Directed by Jacques Tourneur. With Robert Mitchum, Jane Greer, Kirk Douglas. 97 minutes. Not Rated.
The "*Citizen Kane* of film noir", this "fabled" picture "sets the standard" for the genre by pitting a "classic antihero" ("Mitchum at his laconic best") against the "ultimate femme fatale" (the "beautiful but deadly" Greer); the "insanely labyrinthine plot" with "twists in all directions" is equally "note perfect", and perfumed with a "whiff of French existentialism."

Out-of-Towners, The
20 | 22 | 22 | 18

1970. Directed by Arthur Hiller. With Jack Lemmon, Sandy Dennis, Sandy Baron. 98 minutes. Rated G.
"They don't make comedies" like this Neil Simon–scripted "classic" anymore, the saga of an Ohio couple visiting "Fun City" only to discover that it's their "worst nightmare" as they endure one "hilariously miserable" mishap after another; "Lemmon and Dennis are perfection as the tortured tourists", leading many to wonder "why they remade this movie" at all.

Outrageous Fortune
15 | 14 | 14 | 13

1987. Directed by Arthur Hiller. With Shelley Long, Bette Midler, Peter Coyote. 100 minutes. Rated R.
"Midler and Long make a funny team" in this buddy comedy about two struggling actresses tracking down a mutual boyfriend turned espionage agent; though too "strident" and "formulaic"

for some, it's "guilty pleasure" time for those in the mood for something "silly."

Outsiders, The
22 | 21 | 22 | 19

1983. Directed by Francis Ford Coppola. With C. Thomas Howell, Matt Dillon, Ralph Macchio. 91 minutes. Rated PG.
Coppola "paints a great picture" of "teen angst" in this "coming-of-age story" that limns the "problems" between adolescent gangs in a '50s Oklahoma hamlet; what seems like the "entire Brat Pack" delivers such "outstanding" work that the end result is "almost as good" as S.E. Hinton's enduring novel.

Over the Hedge
23 | – | 22 | 25

2006. Directed by Tim Johnson, Karey Kirkpatrick. Animated. 83 minutes. Rated PG.
Their habitat "dwindling as suburbia spreads", a gang of animals "tries to get food from humans" in this "clever" cartoon powered by "fantastic" animation and "excellent" celeb voicings ("Steve Carell's squirrel steals the show"); a "real crowd-pleaser", it boasts an "easy-to-follow" story for small fry plus "commentary about society" that goes over well with adults.

Ox-Bow Incident, The ◗
▽ 27 | 26 | 27 | 23

1943. Directed by William Wellman. With Henry Fonda, Dana Andrews. 75 minutes. Not Rated.
"Decent, law-abiding folk never looked more pathetic" than in this message Western, a "gripping story of mob violence gone mad" that's a chilling indictment of American justice; there are no heroes in this dark "morality tale", though the "excellent ensemble" makes this "adaptation of the classic novel" come alive.

Paint Your Wagon
18 | 18 | 19 | 21

1969. Directed by Joshua Logan. With Lee Marvin, Clint Eastwood, Jean Seberg. 166 minutes. Rated PG-13.
"See Clint sing" in this tuneful Lerner and Loewe Western that cynics say is one fine "reason why musicals have had a hard time succeeding since the '60s"; but champions claim this story of bigamous Wild West gold miners "pokes fun at many cultures" and believe that the "non-singer" cast "does a surprisingly good job."

Palm Beach Story, The ◗
25 | 25 | 25 | 24

1942. Directed by Preston Sturges. With Claudette Colbert, Joel McCrea, Mary Astor, Rudy Vallee. 88 minutes. Not Rated.
Screwball comedies "don't get much better" than this "zany romp" about a married couple who separate over money troubles; the "smart" dialogue, "fast" pacing and "ridiculous" plot showcase director Sturges "at his wittiest and loopiest", and then there's the "irresistible" Colbert and "perfect" Rudy Vallee – "they don't write 'em like this anymore."

Panic Room
18 | 21 | 18 | 20

2002. Directed by David Fincher. With Jodie Foster, Kristen Stewart, Forest Whitaker, Jared Leto. 112 minutes. Rated R.
The "Hitchcockian opening credits" echo the "innovative camerawork" in this "state-of-the-art thriller" from "style-freak" director Fincher about a "resourceful" mother and daughter fending off burglars in their townhouse's "bulletproof safe room"; though the plot elicits mixed notices – a "real nail-biter" vs. "dis-

appointingly predictable" – Jodie's her usual "terrific" self as the "smart-thinking, anti-Buffy heroine."

Paper Chase, The
▽ 21 | 23 | 21 | 18

1973. Directed by James Bridges. With Timothy Bottoms, Lindsay Wagner, John Houseman. 111 minutes. Rated PG.
The "terrors and rigors of the first year of Harvard Law School" are revealed in this "seminal" '70s movie that re-creates the student "rat race" in an "entertaining" way; despite "outstanding performances by all", the Oscar-winning Houseman (as a "crusty professor") is the "main reason to see it."

Paper Moon ◖
22 | 23 | 21 | 22

1973. Directed by Peter Bogdanovich. With Ryan O'Neal, Tatum O'Neal, Madeline Kahn. 102 minutes. Rated PG.
Have "fun watching Ryan and Tatum acting together" in this "delightful" "father/daughter bonding flick", the "charming" story of a Depression-era con man and his equally manipulative offspring who "drift" through the Midwest in glorious black and white; though some say this "sweet little comedy" was "stolen by Madeline Kahn", it was the younger O'Neal who copped the Oscar.

Papillon
26 | 27 | 26 | 24

1973. Directed by Franklin J. Schaffner. With Steve McQueen, Dustin Hoffman. 150 minutes. Rated R.
It's hard to escape from this "powerful" tale of prisoners scheming to break out of Devil's Island, the French Guiana penal colony that makes "HBO's *Oz* look like Club Med"; a "consistently cool McQueen" and "heavyweight Hoffman" play "mistreated-but-not-defeated" inmates "determined to be free" in this "tight", taut drama that's all the more "scary" since it's "based on a true story."

Parenthood
22 | 22 | 22 | 20

1989. Directed by Ron Howard. With Steve Martin, Mary Steenburgen, Dianne Wiest. 124 minutes. Rated PG-13.
"Modern family life" gets "compelling" treatment in this "harrowing if affectionate look at being a parent", a "feel-good" dramedy that confirms "you need a sense of humor" when you have kids; "smart, insightful" and briskly paced thanks to "multiple plotlines", it features "one of Martin's better performances."

Parent Trap, The
23 | 21 | 23 | 21

1961. Directed by David Swift. With Hayley Mills, Maureen O'Hara, Brian Keith. 129 minutes. Rated G.
"Hayley Mills and Hayley Mills" star as "twins separated at birth plotting to bring their estranged parents together" in this "non-animated Disney classic", an "entertaining romp" that serves up "warmhearted family fare"; one of the "most remembered" movies in boomerdom, it boasts such a "timeless story" that most "stick to the original", having "no need for the remake."

Paris, Texas
22 | 24 | 21 | 20

1984. Directed by Wim Wenders. With Harry Dean Stanton, Nastassja Kinski, Dean Stockwell. 147 minutes. Rated R.
"Haunting landscapes" and "outstanding performances" are the hallmarks of this "unconventional" (verging on "totally bizarre") road movie about a lost soul rediscovering his wife and child; while there's praise for screenwriter Sam Shepard's "spare dialogue" and composer Ry Cooder's "perfect soundtrack",

many say the "drawn-out", "slow-moving" pace makes for "awfully strange" filmmaking.

Passion of the Christ, The ▣ 　　 22 | 23 | 21 | 23
2004. Directed by Mel Gibson. With James Caviezel, Monica Bellucci, Maia Morgenstern. 127 minutes. Rated R.
Echoing the "overblown controversy" surrounding its release, Mel Gibson's "brutal portrayal" of the last 12 hours of Christ's life similarly "polarizes" surveyors: proponents praise its "lengthy torture scenes" as "necessary to make the point" of "what Jesus went through", but "traumatized" viewers see a "slasher film" full of "prejudice and propaganda" that "preaches to the converted"; both sides concur it's "not for kids" (nor for subtitle-phobes, given the all-Aramaic/Latin/Hebrew dialogue).

Patch Adams 　　 16 | 18 | 17 | 15
1998. Directed by Tom Shadyac. With Robin Williams, Daniel London, Monica Potter. 115 minutes. Rated PG-13.
Laughter's the best medicine in this tale of a doctor who tries to heal patients with humor, an "inspiring" story that's both "funny and sad" but ultimately "uplifting"; eye-rollers counter that Williams "needs to get back to his roots" and avoid such "sappy" material.

PATHS OF GLORY ◑ 　　 28 | 27 | 28 | 26
1957. Directed by Stanley Kubrick. With Kirk Douglas, Ralph Meeker, George Macready. 86 minutes. Not Rated.
"All the hopelessness, folly and stupidity" of WWI is "dramatically" shown in Kubrick's "devastating" "anti-war" picture that "ruthlessly" depicts "corrupt" officers deploying "scapegoated enlisted men" as "cannon fodder"; even though this "grim" yet "moving" film is in black and white, the "story is full color", and it "really makes its point" and "stands the test of time."

Patriot, The 　　 21 | 21 | 21 | 23
2000. Directed by Roland Emmerich. With Mel Gibson, Heath Ledger, Joely Richardson. 164 minutes. Rated R.
Present-day patriots salute this "epic in the Gibson tradition" as an "inspiring portrait" of a reluctant American "hero" enmeshed in "gruesome Revolutionary War battles"; though turncoats dismiss it as typical "Hollywood good guy/bad guy nonsense" ("*Lethal Musket*"), they're outvoted by partisans who "feel liberated" by this "heartfelt" history jazzed up with some "entertainment value."

Patriot Games 　　 21 | 21 | 22 | 21
1992. Directed by Phillip Noyce. With Harrison Ford, Anne Archer, Patrick Bergin. 117 minutes. Rated R.
"Harrison gets cool again" as a "humble hero whose life is turned upside down by a crazed IRA terrorist" in this "slick" action-adventurer known for its "mind-spinning chase across oceans and freeways"; though it's as "thrilling on the screen as on the written page", traitors contend it's "cookie-cutter espionage" and say that Alec Baldwin is the "more believable Jack Ryan."

PATTON ✉ 　　 27 | 28 | 26 | 27
1970. Directed by Franklin J. Schaffner. With George C. Scott, Karl Malden. 170 minutes. Rated PG.
Legions salute "one of the best biopics ever made", this "hauntingly mounted character study" of fabled WWII General Patton, who's "superbly fleshed out" as both "monstrous and human";

though there's "lots of drama" throughout, it "doesn't get much better than that opening speech" by "Old Blood and Guts", probably the most "memorable" scene; P.S. the "convincing" portrayal won Scott an Oscar, which he famously rejected.

Pawnbroker, The ◐

| 26 | 28 | 24 | 22 |

1965. Directed by Sidney Lumet. With Rod Steiger, Geraldine Fitzgerald. 116 minutes. Not Rated.

This "disturbing", "depressing message picture", expertly rendered in "chilling black and white", shows the "horrors of the Holocaust" by focusing on one survivor, the owner of a Harlem pawnshop; in "one of the all-time great screen performances", Steiger is nothing short of "mesmerizing" in the title role – too bad it's been so "sadly neglected" over the years.

Pearl Harbor

| 14 | 14 | 13 | 21 |

2001. Directed by Michael Bay. With Ben Affleck, Josh Hartnett, Kate Beckinsale, Cuba Gooding Jr.. 183 minutes. Rated PG-13.

"*Titanic* meets *Saving Private Ryan*" in this "predictable", "heavy-handed" epic that juxtaposes a "romantic subplot" against a historic backdrop, the "horrific attack" that led the U.S. into WWII; most agree the "dumb", "cardboard-charactered" love story is completely "unnecessary", blown away by "breathtaking action" and "superior special effects", so for best results, "skip the first hour-and-a-half" and fast-forward to the "battle scenes only."

Pee-wee's Big Adventure ⓤ

| 19 | 17 | 17 | 20 |

1985. Directed by Tim Burton. With Paul Reubens, Elizabeth Daily, Diane Salinger. 90 minutes. Rated PG.

"Wacky", "campy", maybe even "inspired", this comic "cult classic" is a "work of the sublime from the ridiculous" team of "twisted" director Burton and "genius" performer Reubens; though ostensibly aimed at small fry, "adults love it" too, yet the pleasure is bittersweet for those who "miss Pee-wee" and "wish for another" installment; P.S. "Large Marge is worth the price of admission."

Peggy Sue Got Married

| 19 | 20 | 21 | 18 |

1986. Directed by Francis Ford Coppola. With Kathleen Turner, Nicolas Cage. 104 minutes. Rated PG-13.

Unhappily married Peggy Sue "magically enters her teenage self's world" in this "back-in-time" comedy "with a heart and a brain"; though ageists say Turner is "too old" for the role, the "original premise" and "nostalgic" mood provide ample distraction.

Pelican Brief, The

| 16 | 18 | 18 | 16 |

1993. Directed by Alan J. Pakula. With Julia Roberts, Denzel Washington, Sam Shepard. 141 minutes. Rated PG-13.

In this "fast-paced" adaptation of John Grisham's best-seller, an inventive law student posits a dangerously compelling conspiracy theory after two Supreme Court justices are murdered; while "terminally predictable" for "suspense-thriller" seekers, it has a "great team" in Julia and Denzel – even if their characters' book romance didn't make it to the silver screen.

People vs. Larry Flynt, The

| 18 | 21 | 18 | 18 |

1996. Directed by Milos Forman. With Woody Harrelson, Courtney Love, Edward Norton. 129 minutes. Rated R.

Forman's "daring movie" creates an unlikely "hero" out of a "less than excellent subject", "pornographer" Larry Flynt, whose "rags-to-riches-to-ruin story" is rendered in such "heartbreaking" but "inspiring" terms that you wind up "loving the bad guy"; Harrelson is "first-rate" in the title role, Love "really can act" and you might just come away with a "whole new outlook" on smut.

Perfect Storm, The
16 | 16 | 18 | 22

2000. Directed by Wolfgang Petersen. With George Clooney, Mark Wahlberg, John C. Reilly. 129 minutes. Rated PG-13.
There's "never a dull moment" in this "compelling" tale of an "ill-fated fishing boat crew" swept up in 1991's 'storm of the century'; no question, the deep-sea FX are "stunning", but the "unconvincing script" strikes some as "surprisingly shallow", "pulling the heartstrings" in a "dumbed-down", "big-budget Hollywood" way.

Persona ◑🄵
▽ **28 | 29 | 25 | 25**

1967. Directed by Ingmar Bergman. With Bibi Andersson, Liv Ullmann. 81 minutes. Not Rated.
Bergman's "plunge into the mysteries of the self" beguiles surveyors who say this "intense, very moving" film is the director's "best synthesis of symbolism and reality"; the story of a nurse and her patient (an actress who has gone mute) is "not rational but psychologically satisfying" as the two characters' identities "blend" together to make a "stunning" whole.

Peter Pan 🄸🄸
25 | – | 25 | 25

1953. Directed by Clyde Geronimi, Wilfred Jackson, Hamilton Luske. Animated. 76 minutes. Rated G.
Lost boys and girls who "never want to grow up" fly to this "simple", pixie dust–peppered tale concerning the eternally youthful Peter's adventures in Neverland; a "true classic" of Disney animation from the days when "Walt was running the show", it remains enough of an "important childhood film" for latter-day critics to ask "why did they bother with a remake?"

Peter Pan
20 | 19 | 21 | 23

2003. Directed by P.J. Hogan. With Jeremy Sumpter, Jason Isaacs, Rachel Hurd-Wood, Lynn Redgrave. 113 minutes. Rated PG.
"Move over, Disney": J.M. Barrie's oft-filmed children's classic gets a "beautiful live-action" retelling in this "well-done" movie that "really captures what it feels like to grow up"; a "seductive undertone" and some "darker aspects" make it a "bit more adult than previous versions", and if this puts off traditionalists ("after Mary Martin, why bother?"), most find it "thoroughly enjoyable."

Pete's Dragon
20 | – | 20 | 21

1977. Directed by Don Chaffey. Animated. With Helen Reddy, Jim Dale, Mickey Rooney. 128 minutes. Rated G.
Surveyors slayed by this "Disney classic" combining both animation and live action cheer its "heartwarming" story of a runaway orphan and his sometimes-invisible dragon companion; though fire-breathers blast it as "overlong" and "unmemorable", most agree the "kids will dig it", which is all that matters.

Peyton Place 🄸🄸
20 | 20 | 21 | 21

1957. Directed by Mark Robson. With Lana Turner, Hope Lange, Diane Varsi, Arthur Kennedy. 162 minutes. Not Rated.
"Ninety-nine and 44/100 percent melodrama", this campy "mother of all soap operas" based on Grace Metalious' "trashy"

mega-seller is set in a "small New England town" rife with "secrets and scandals" – or at least "what passed for scandalous in the 1950s"; in fact, most say what was "shocking" and "racy" then seems rather "timid" and "schmaltzy" now.

Phantom of the Opera, The   21 | 20 | 23 | 26

2004. Directed by Joel Schumacher. With Gerard Butler, Emmy Rossum, Patrick Wilson, Miranda Richardson, Minnie Driver. 143 minutes. Rated PG-13.

Towing along its "lavish sets" and "to-die-for" tunes, Andrew Lloyd Webber's "Gothic romance" hit musical leaps onto the silver screen in this "faithful adaptation" courtesy of "over-the-top" director Schumacher; castwise, Phantom fandom is "swept away" by Rossum's "starmaking performance" as the "angelic" ingénue, though some purists wince at "hunk" Butler's "rock 'n' roll" rendition of the titular masked marauder.

Phenomenon   18 | 18 | 19 | 17

1996. Directed by John Turteltaub. With John Travolta, Kyra Sedgwick, Forest Whitaker. 124 minutes. Rated PG.

This "inspirational" "tearjerker" "pulls at the heartstrings" and "makes you want to live a better, fuller life" by showcasing a "convincing" Travolta as a small-town schmo who acquires supernatural powers and becomes a benevolent hero; though the dubious dub it "new-age hooey", for true believers the "message is touching" and the "beautiful images" leave a "good feeling."

Philadelphia ✉   24 | 27 | 25 | 23

1993. Directed by Jonathan Demme. With Tom Hanks, Denzel Washington. 125 minutes. Rated PG-13.

"Hollywood takes on AIDS" in this "extraordinarily powerful and poignant" drama that "puts a human face" on a "depressing" subject thanks to Hanks' "brave", Oscar-winning portrayal of a gay lawyer battling the "double-edged sword of discrimination and physical deterioration"; the final result resonates with "thought-provoking" issues, but don't forget to "bring the tissues – it's painful to watch."

PHILADELPHIA STORY, THE ✉◑   27 | 28 | 26 | 25

1940. Directed by George Cukor. With Cary Grant, Katharine Hepburn, James Stewart. 112 minutes. Not Rated.

For the "sheer joy" of "listening to fast, furious dialogue" that "doesn't insult your intelligence", this "laugh-out-loud" screwball "comedy of manners" provides a "wild ride"; "you'll need a scorecard to keep up" with the "banter and spark" between the "classy" Kate, "acerbic" Grant and "underplaying" Stewart, uttered in settings so "perfectly frothy" that many wish that "life was really like that."

Phone Booth   18 | 20 | 18 | 18

2003. Directed by Joel Schumacher. With Colin Farrell, Kiefer Sutherland, Forest Whitaker. 81 minutes. Rated R.

You "don't see many original ideas anymore", so there's applause for this "implausible but diverting" thriller, a "tightly woven", high-concept "doozy" about a man trapped in a phone booth by a "really creepy" sniper; Farrell's "raw", "one-man-show" performance keeps most from hanging up, despite a script that "starts promisingly but runs out of steam toward the end."

PIANIST, THE ✉   28 | 29 | 27 | 28
2002. Directed by Roman Polanski. With Adrien Brody, Thomas Kretschmann. 150 minutes. Rated R.
"Agonizing and beautiful all at once", this "haunting" true story about a concert pianist's struggle to survive in Nazi-occupied Warsaw receives raves as "Polanski's historic achievement", a "masterpiece of filmmaking" that "will stay in your mind"; Brody's "brilliant", "subdued performance" "conveys so much without hardly saying a word", while the "depiction of the horror" is "accurate and harrowing in its detail"; in sum, both the director and star "deserved to win those Oscars."

Piano, The ✉   21 | 24 | 19 | 22
1993. Directed by Jane Campion. With Holly Hunter, Harvey Keitel, Sam Neill. 121 minutes. Rated R.
"Each frame could be a painting" in this "exquisitely shot" drama set in 19th-century New Zealand concerning a "mute woman" and her "search for fulfillment"; though Hunter delivers an "expressive", Oscar-winning performance (despite very "limited dialogue") opposite Keitel at his "sensual", "full-frontal" best, critics contend the "contrived" plot strikes flat notes.

Pickup on South Street ◑   23 | 24 | 24 | 22
1953. Directed by Samuel Fuller. With Richard Widmark, Jean Peters, Thelma Ritter, Richard Kiley. 80 minutes. Not Rated.
For "film noir at its best", check out this "knockout" flick about a pickpocket and a prostitute inadvertently mixed up with a "Communist spy" ring; it's an "old-school", Red-menace ride with fine work from the "consummate" Widmark and the overripe Peters, and if that's not enough for you, "there's Thelma Ritter too."

Picnic   24 | 24 | 24 | 24
1955. Directed by Joshua Logan. With William Holden, Kim Novak, Rosalind Russell. 115 minutes. Not Rated.
Darn "sexy for its time", this "star-crossed", "moonglow"-drenched romance relates the havoc that a "handsome drifter" wreaks upon a group of "small-town" gals; fans say it "retains its charm", since it "epitomizes the lush storytelling of the '50s", but admit it may be a "little too theatrical to appeal to today's audiences"; hottest scene, no contest: Novak and Holden's "sizzling dance on the bridge."

Pieces of April   21 | 24 | 21 | 19
2003. Directed by Peter Hedges. With Katie Holmes, Patricia Clarkson, Derek Luke. 80 minutes. Rated PG-13.
A Thanksgiving dinner rife with "family dysfunction" is the setting of this "hysterical yet heartbreaking" dramedy that's "touching without being overly sentimental"; while Holmes gives a "winning performance" as the estranged title character and an "off-the-wall" cast keeps pace, the "stunning" Clarkson as her cynical, cancer-stricken mother steals this "little film with a big heart."

Pillow Talk ✉   20 | 20 | 17 | 19
1959. Directed by Michael Gordon. With Doris Day, Rock Hudson, Tony Randall, Thelma Ritter. 103 minutes. Not Rated.
The "first – and best – of the Rock-Doris bedroom farces", this "gloriously goofy" romantic comedy about an "unlikely" pair who share a telephone party line is "good clean fun" with "no laugh

track needed"; alright, the "setup is a bit dated" (verging on "insipid"), but more than a few fess up it's a "true guilty pleasure" that they "never tire of watching."

Pink Flamingos
▽ 17 | 11 | 12 | 11

1972. Directed by John Waters. With Divine, David Lochary, Mink Stole, Edith Massey. 95 minutes. Rated NC-17.

Watch it "at your own risk": this "cult favorite from John Waters" is the rare flick with "something to offend absolutely everyone", with a plot incorporating a "demented" drag queen, a "filthy" motor home, a "gross" half-dead chicken and topped off by an "extreme" ending too "disgusting" to relate; it's "lowbrow" and ultra "low-budget", but it just may be the "best worst movie ever made."

Pink Panther, The ⓤ
24 | 24 | 21 | 21

1964. Directed by Blake Edwards. With Peter Sellers, David Niven, Robert Wagner. 113 minutes. Not Rated.

"Hilarity abounds" – "starting with the opening credits" – in this "outlandish" caper, the first production by the "comedy dream team" of director Edwards and actor Sellers (in his "brilliant" debut as "bumbling Jacques Clouseau"); "funny to this day", it marked the start of a "sequel brigade" that marched along for years afterward.

Pinocchio
26 | – | 26 | 26

1940. Directed by Hamilton Luske, Ben Sharpsteen. Animated. 88 minutes. Rated G.

"Forget the wooden kid with the schnoz" (who's a bit "dull" anyway) – this "wonderful" animated fantasy is more memorable for its introduction of the "classic" character of Jiminy Cricket and its Oscar-winning song, 'When You Wish Upon a Star'; otherwise, this story of a puppet transformed into a boy still "combines some of the sweetest and scariest scenes" in all of Disneydom.

Pirates of the Caribbean:
The Curse of the Black Pearl
24 | 25 | 22 | 27

2003. Directed by Gore Verbinski. With Johnny Depp, Geoffrey Rush, Orlando Bloom, Keira Knightley. 143 minutes. Rated PG-13.

"Eat your heart out, Errol Flynn" – Johnny Depp's a real "hoot" in this Disney high seas adventure, turning in an "over-the-top" performance as a pirate captain who's half "swashbuckling", half "swish" (think "Keith Richards with a cutlass"); though it "could have been fluff" given its "audio-animatronic", "theme-park-ride" origins, this "rollicking" romp keeps the violence "stylized" and rolls out enough "impressive" FX to provide lots of "salty fun."

Pit and the Pendulum, The
▽ 22 | 20 | 22 | 19

1961. Directed by Roger Corman. With Vincent Price, John Kerr, Barbara Steele. 80 minutes. Not Rated.

"Vincent Price does Edgar Allen Poe" in this low-budget "B-movie" that might bear little resemblance to the source material (save the climax), but is atmospheric and "scary" throughout; part of a series based on Poe stories, this one's the "all-time favorite" of dyed-in-the-wool Roger Corman fans.

PLACE IN THE SUN, A ✉◐
27 | 27 | 27 | 24

1951. Directed by George Stevens. With Montgomery Clift, Elizabeth Taylor, Shelley Winters. 122 minutes. Not Rated.

This "classic American" love triangle from Oscar-winning director Stevens might be a "glamorized version of the Dreiser novel" but was still rather daring for its time given the unwed-mother subplot; while it's hard to miss the "radiant Clift and Taylor" (thanks to some swoonworthy giant close-ups), "poor Shelley Winters'" role as the third wheel may well be the best performance; most famous line: Liz's smoldering "'tell mama all.'"

Places in the Heart ✉   20 | 22 | 20 | 18
1984. Directed by Robert Benton. With Sally Field, Lindsay Crouse, Ed Harris, Danny Glover. 112 minutes. Rated PG.
Softhearted souls really, really like this "moving Depression-era tale" of a Texas "woman alone with kids, a farm, a mortgage" and, thankfully, plenty of "courage"; though both Field and screenwriter Benton snagged Oscars for this "heartwarming" study, the hard-hearted nix it as too "depressing."

Planet of the Apes Ⓤ   23 | 20 | 25 | 23
1968. Directed by Franklin J. Schaffner. With Charlton Heston, Roddy McDowall, Kim Hunter. 112 minutes. Rated G.
"Darwin would have loved" this "thought-provoking" stew of "science fiction and pop culture" about an American astronaut who crashes on a simian-ruled planet; Heston's "brawny", "over-the-top" performance brings equal parts "paranoid power" and "Republican campiness" to the leading role, while that "wallop" of an ending remains one of the "most talked-about ever."

Platoon ✉   25 | 25 | 24 | 26
1986. Directed by Oliver Stone. With Tom Berenger, Willem Dafoe, Charlie Sheen. 120 minutes. Rated R.
"Disturbing" yet "unforgettable", this "almost-too-real" war picture offers a "raw" view of the Vietnam conflict as seen "through the eyes of a recruit just arrived in the jungle"; granted, it "fails to offer the slightest glimmer of hope", but it "captures the desperation" of battle "better than any other movie", with a clutch of Oscars (including Best Picture and Best Director) to prove it.

Player, The   23 | 23 | 23 | 22
1992. Directed by Robert Altman. With Tim Robbins, Greta Scacchi, Fred Ward. 124 minutes. Rated R.
"People who love movies about movies" love this "scathing satire" of "cutthroat" Hollywood, "perfectly directed" by "genius" Altman; cineasts cite the "excellent opening shot" (eight minutes "without a cut") and the "wonderful all-star cameo" appearances peppered throughout, but zero in on Robbins' "marvelous" portrayal of a "ne'er-do-well producer" as the real standout.

Play It Again, Sam   22 | 21 | 23 | 20
1972. Directed by Herbert Ross. With Woody Allen, Diane Keaton, Tony Roberts. 85 minutes. Rated PG.
Woody's "wonderful" in this "fine early comedy" adapted from his Broadway hit about a lovelorn film critic so enamored with *Casablanca* that he conjures up an imaginary Bogie for advice; though this spoof "works on every level" for "hard-core" Allen fans, purists protest there's one major problem: "he didn't direct it."

Play Misty for Me   22 | 20 | 23 | 19
1971. Directed by Clint Eastwood. With Clint Eastwood, Jessica Walter, Donna Mills. 102 minutes. Rated R.
The "original, much creepier" version of "*Fatal Attraction*", this "scary" erotic thriller concerns a 'Misty'-spinning DJ "stalked by a

deranged radio listener" (who supplies the "jump-out-at-you" moments); fans "get a thrill" out of Eastwood playing the "hunted instead of the hunter" for a change.

Pleasantville
20 | 21 | 22 | 23

1998. Directed by Gary Ross. With Tobey Maguire, Jeff Daniels, Joan Allen, Reese Witherspoon. 124 minutes. Rated PG-13.
"Two modern teens" are magically transported into the "world of a '50s sitcom" in this "totally disarming" parable about "American family" life that's enlivened by some "high-tech tricks" (notably the "imaginative" use of "color vs. black and white"); though a bit "heavy-handed" for some, its "clever premise" and "memorable Randy Newman score" make for "unique" moviemaking.

Pocahontas
17 | – | 16 | 20

1995. Directed by Mike Gabriel, Eric Goldberg. Animated. 82 minutes. Rated G.
"Disney does it again" with this "subtly beautiful" animated feature about American Indians and English invaders in the Virginia colonies that might be "not historically accurate" but does offer a "great message" vis-à-vis tolerance and true love; if too "bland and preachy" for some, at least the "music's exceptional."

Polar Express, The
21 | – | 21 | 25

2004. Directed by Robert Zemeckis. Animated. With Tom Hanks. 99 minutes. Rated G.
Showcasing an "impressive" new filming technique that drops a "CGI"-enhanced Hanks into "five roles", this "good-spirited" animated adaptation of the "classic" children's book about a little boy who "doesn't believe in Santa" is "destined to become a holiday classic"; still, concerned parents caution that while the "choo-choo magic" is "pretty to look at", there are a "few scary spots" that might creep out the "preschooler set."

Pollock
22 | 26 | 21 | 22

2000. Directed by Ed Harris. With Ed Harris, Marcia Gay Harden, Amy Madigan, Jennifer Connelly. 122 minutes. Rated R.
"Harris is uncanny" capturing the "essence of dark genius" Jackson Pollock, the "misunderstood" 20th-century artist/"self-destructive" individual who's the subject of this "unflashy" biopic; as his mate and fellow painter, "Harden matches him every step of the way" in a "deservedly Oscar-winning" performance that further transforms this "amazing life" story into a "real work of art."

Poltergeist ⏀
22 | 20 | 23 | 24

1982. Directed by Tobe Hooper. With JoBeth Williams, Craig T. Nelson, Beatrice Straight. 114 minutes. Rated PG.
"Half social satire, half haunted-house tale", this "vivid" "roller-coaster ride" of a horror flick has a "pure Spielberg" premise: "affluent parents and cute children" living in a home "built over a graveyard" chock-full of "pesky ghosts"; the "strong story", "ahead-of-its-time special effects" and that "little voice" squeaking "they're he-ere" still startle boo-mers over "20 years later."

Poseidon Adventure, The ⏀
19 | 18 | 20 | 22

1972. Directed by Ronald Neame. With Gene Hackman, Ernest Borgnine, Red Buttons. 117 minutes. Rated PG.
A "boat flips over" and the "actors flip out" in this "topsy-turvy" "granddaddy of Hollywood all-star disaster flicks" that's "more

fun in a campy way than you'd expect"; sure, the "phenomenal underwater footage" and "unforgettable (if not completely subtle) performances" are "entertaining" enough, but foes sneer this "kitschy" "sinking ship" defines the "true meaning of 'all wet.'"

Postcards from the Edge
| 18 | 23 | 19 | 18 |

1990. Directed by Mike Nichols. With Meryl Streep, Shirley MacLaine, Dennis Quaid. 101 minutes. Rated R.
Edgy types tout this "Hollywood insider story" as a "terrifically funny" look at the relationship between a "recovering-druggie" movie star and her scenery-chewing movie-star mom; though both the "biting" MacLaine and "brilliant" Streep "shine", fans say that the "sharp" script is as acidly "amusing" as they come.

Postman Always Rings Twice, The ◑
| 25 | 25 | 25 | 24 |

1946. Directed by Tay Garnett. With John Garfield, Lana Turner, Cecil Kellaway. 113 minutes. Not Rated.
Garfield and Turner "set off the smoke alarms" in this "steamy" slice of film noir, a "deliciously sinful" saga about a "married femme fatale", a "streetwise vagabond" and their simmering affair that "boils over into murderous passion"; though this "twisting" tale of "love, betrayal" and "homicide" is pretty "wonderful", one question remains: "didn't people know about divorce in those days?"

Postman Always Rings Twice, The
| 20 | 23 | 22 | 19 |

1981. Directed by Bob Rafelson. With Jack Nicholson, Jessica Lange, John Colicos. 122 minutes. Rated R.
Maybe it's "not as good as the original", but this "decent" enough remake of the film noir classic features "real sex" scenes instead of "implied" ones, most notably that display of "countertop love" that inspired many to install "butcher blocks in their kitchens"; "Jack is as creepy as ever", though purists pout "there's too much emphasis on sex at the expense of characterization" here.

Potemkin ◑
| 27 | 22 | 25 | 27 |

1925. Directed by Sergei Eisenstein. With Aleksandr Antonov, Vladimir Barsky. 75 minutes. Not Rated.
Over 80 years later, cineasts are still electrified by director Eisenstein's "influential" "triumph" that "put 'montage' into the filmmaking lexicon" and "forever set the standards for camerawork"; detailing the failed 1905 uprising against the Czar, it's best known for its "often copied baby-carriage-on-the-Odessa-steps sequence" that "paved the way for edit-happy MTV directors"; indeed, it's so "exciting" that many insist it "should be mandatory moviegoing."

Presumed Innocent
| 20 | 21 | 22 | 18 |

1990. Directed by Alan J. Pakula. With Harrison Ford, Brian Dennehy, Raul Julia. 127 minutes. Rated R.
Based on Scott Turow's best-seller, this "darkly powerful courtroom thriller" concerns a Philadelphia prosecutor whose life takes a "roller-coaster" turn after he's accused of murder; jurists say its "cliff-hanger" storyline boasts a "perfect surprise ending" that "keeps you guessing up till the last frame."

Pretty Baby
| 17 | 18 | 17 | 18 |

1978. Directed by Louis Malle. With Brooke Shields, Keith Carradine, Susan Sarandon. 109 minutes. Rated R.
Despite the "iffy" subject matter – "child prostitution in WWI-era New Orleans" – this "controversial" drama is "presented so

matter-of-factly" that jaded folks "may find it a bit dull"; starring a "very young Brooke" (who's "just fine" in the title role), it's "beautifully filmed" in "soft focus" and "not exploitative", though a few "shocked" sorts say it "could never be made today."

Pretty in Pink
19 | 18 | 19 | 18

1986. Directed by Howard Deutch. With Molly Ringwald, Harry Dean Stanton, Jon Cryer. 96 minutes. Rated PG-13.

For a most "entertaining" "glimpse into the horrors of teenage dating", try this "Brat Pack" comedy "classic" starring Ringwald (at her late-'80s "poutiest") as an "angst"-ridden gal from the "wrong side of the tracks" who falls for a "rich preppie"; ok, it's "sappy" and "not too original", but given all the "cute touches" and that "killer soundtrack", many call it a "guilty pleasure to the nth degree."

PRETTY WOMAN
23 | 22 | 22 | 22

1990. Directed by Garry Marshall. With Richard Gere, Julia Roberts, Jason Alexander. 119 minutes. Rated R.

Despite a premise somewhere between "Cinderella" and "Eliza Doolittle", this story of a "hooker with a heart of gold" who bags "Prince Charming" is a "happily-ever-after" romance that "put Julia (and her smile) on the map"; credit the "dizzying charisma" and "palpable chemistry between its stars" for its "believability", and though the "glamorization-of-prostitution" angle turns off bluenoses, "hopeless romantics" insist it will "steal your heart."

Pride and Prejudice ◑
▽ 24 | 24 | 26 | 23

1940. Directed by Robert Z. Leonard. With Greer Garson, Laurence Olivier, Mary Boland. 118 minutes. Not Rated.

A "lovely, headstrong heroine and a handsome haughty hero" make "sparks fly" in this "lush", "true-to-the-book" adaptation of the Jane Austen classic; "fabulous period costumes and sets" in high MGM style contribute to the "splendid" feel, while "Garson and Olivier play off each other wonderfully" – now, "that's style."

Pride & Prejudice
23 | 24 | 25 | 25

2005. Directed by Joe Wright. With Keira Knightley, Matthew Macfadyen, Donald Sutherland. 127 minutes. Rated PG.

"New insights into an old classic" flow from this "delightful" translation of Jane Austen's novel featuring a "radiant" Knightley as the "headstrong" heroine who finds a "sparring partner and true love" in "brooding English Lord" Mr. Darcy; a "lavish production" featuring "breathtaking scenery", "intelligent" dialogue and an "alluring soundtrack", it maintains a modern "freshness."

Pride of the Yankees, The ◑
22 | 22 | 23 | 20

1942. Directed by Sam Wood. With Gary Cooper, Teresa Wright, Walter Brennan. 127 minutes. Not Rated.

A "must" for both "baseball and Yankee fans", this "best sports" biopic virtually guarantees a "lump in the throat" as it delineates the life story of the "great Lou Gehrig" and his courage in the face of death; in the title role, Cooper is so effectively "self-effacing" that repeat viewers "cry every time" they hear his "farewell speech."

Primal Fear
22 | 25 | 23 | 21

1996. Directed by Gregory Hoblit. With Richard Gere, Laura Linney, Edward Norton. 129 minutes. Rated R.

The verdict's in: an "amazing" Norton "hits a home run" in his "stunning debut" as a "timid, stuttering" altar boy accused of killing an archbishop in this "unsettling" murder mystery/courtroom drama; otherwise, the "acting is on-point all around" (even "Gere is less dull than usual"), though the performances are nearly "blown away" by that "knock-you-for-a-loop" "surprise ending."

Primary Colors   16 | 19 | 17 | 17
1998. Directed by Mike Nichols. With John Travolta, Emma Thompson, Kathy Bates. 143 minutes. Rated R.
An "uncomfortable peek" into the '92 Presidential campaign, this "tight" political comedy stars a "right-on" Travolta as a "thinly disguised" Bill Clinton in all his "lovably infuriating" grandeur; though hindered by "unnecessary melodrama", this "underrated" picture works as a "good insider's view" of the "way things probably were – and you wish they weren't."

Prime of Miss Jean Brodie, The ✉   25 | 28 | 24 | 23
1969. Directed by Ronald Neame. With Maggie Smith, Robert Stephens, Pamela Franklin, Jane Carr. 116 minutes. Rated PG.
Transposing "*Dead Poets Society*" to a '30s-era Scottish boarding school, this portrait of a "free-thinking teacher" is "worth revisiting" for Dame Maggie's "towering" turn (which "does for Jean Brodie what Roz Russell did for Auntie Mame"); it's a "coming-of-age classic" crafted with "impressionable girls" in mind, despite its "heartbreaker" message: "idealism can be bad for you."

Prince of Egypt, The   19 | – | 19 | 23
1998. Directed by Simon Wells, Brenda Chapman, Steve Hickner. Animated. 99 minutes. Rated PG.
Respondents part like the Red Sea over this "history/cartoon combo" from the "then-fledgling Dreamworks": fans insist it's a "fascinating modern Bible retelling" of the story of Moses' exodus with the Jews from Egypt, with "terrific animation" and "beautiful songs", but foes say it's an "overwrought" derivation of the "Disney formula" that "lacks" in all areas "except special effects."

Prince of Tides, The   19 | 21 | 21 | 20
1991. Directed by Barbra Streisand. With Barbra Streisand, Nick Nolte, Blythe Danner. 132 minutes. Rated R.
In this "interesting story" about a "Southern football coach, his dysfunctional family" and the "NYC psychiatrist who sorts it all out", the "convincing Nolte really gives his all"; yet despite the "lyricism" and "stunning scenery", some say the "self-important" Babs "never should have directed herself" in this "vanity" production.

PRINCESS BRIDE, THE   27 | 23 | 27 | 24
1987. Directed by Rob Reiner. With Cary Elwes, Mandy Patinkin, Robin Wright. 98 minutes. Rated PG.
Despite the "chick-flick title", this "lighthearted" but "fractured fairy tale" defies any easy "categorization" and is admired by "even the most macho" guys for its "swordfights" and "verbal jousting"; thanks to an "intelligent" William Goldman script, "masterful" direction by Reiner and an "incredibly talented" cast, "finding a better movie is inconceivable" – "plus, it's got André the Giant."

Princess Diaries, The Ⓤ   18 | 19 | 17 | 18
2001. Directed by Garry Marshall. With Julie Andrews, Anne Hathaway, Hector Elizondo. 114 minutes. Rated G.
It's "every girl's dream" – to discover she's "actually a princess" (albeit of "some little country you've never heard of") – and this

"wholesome" "mom-and-daughter" comedy follows newcomer Hathaway's transformation from "high-school dork" to crowned head amusingly enough; but even though this "feel-good" flick appeals to the "teenager inside us all", critics complain it's a "little flat for older audiences."

Prisoner of Second Avenue, The   22 | 25 | 21 | 20

1975. Directed by Melvin Frank. With Jack Lemmon, Anne Bancroft, Gene Saks. 98 minutes. Rated PG.

There's "a lot of hollering out the window" going on in this Neil Simon comedy about a frustrated worker who loses his job and has a "classic breakdown" in circa-1970 New York; it's a "quintessential" Lemmon role (with Bancroft equally "awesome" as his put-upon wife), and if some dismiss it as a "not funny enough" "sitcom", at least it's a "well-acted one"; P.S. watch for a "fun cameo" from the then-unknown Sylvester Stallone.

Private Benjamin   17 | 19 | 17 | 16

1980. Directed by Howard Zieff. With Goldie Hawn, Eileen Brennan, Armand Assante. 100 minutes. Rated R.

"Goldie's golden" in this "funny, inspirational" comedy about a newly widowed Jewish princess who comes into her own after unwittingly enlisting in the army; a "lighthearted twist on women's liberation", it "shines" with "punchy" dialogue and a "charming" cast, particularly an acerbic Brennan and a "what-a-hunk" Assante as the romantic interest.

Prizzi's Honor   21 | 24 | 21 | 19

1985. Directed by John Huston. With Jack Nicholson, Kathleen Turner, Anjelica Huston. 130 minutes. Rated R.

This "terrific black comedy about a dysfunctional mob family" anticipates *The Sopranos* with "cynical", "give-and-take" dialogue delivered by the "perfect cast" (a "bright" Jack and a "stellar", Oscar-copping Anjelica); one of John Huston's "last masterpieces", this "whacked-out gangster farce" wrings laughs via a "play-it-straight" script peppered with "in-jokes"; biggest conundrum: "do I ice her? do I marry her?"

PRODUCERS, THE ✉   26 | 26 | 26 | 23

1968. Directed by Mel Brooks. With Zero Mostel, Gene Wilder, Kenneth Mars. 88 minutes. Rated PG.

Flaunting "silly and shocking originality" long before the "Broadway hoopla", this "anarchic", "appallingly funny" comedy boasts Mostel and Wilder "at their best" as perps of a "Ponzi scheme" to produce an "unbelievably over-the-top" musical winningly titled *Springtime for Hitler* and cash in on its failure; it earns an ovation as "unrelenting", "inspired lunacy" from the "warped mind" of Mel Brooks that still "holds up" as a manic "masterpiece."

PSYCHO ◐⓫   28 | 26 | 27 | 27

1960. Directed by Alfred Hitchcock. With Anthony Perkins, Vera Miles, John Gavin, Janet Leigh. 109 minutes. Rated R.

"Generations of moviegoers started double-locking their bathroom doors" after one look at the "famous shower scene" in this "classic Hitchcock" "psycho-logical thriller" that was "quite a shocker in its day" and "still packs a wallop" – "without the gross violence of modern flicks"; standouts include Bernard Herrmann's "scariest film score ever" and Perkins' "twitchy", "tour-de-force" performance as the ultimate "mama's boy."

Public Enemy ◑　　　　▽ 25 | 24 | 21 | 20
1931. Directed by William Wellman. With James Cagney, Jean Harlow, Edward Woods, Mae Clarke. 84 minutes. Not Rated.
"Cagney's spectacular" in this "classic '30s gangster flick" that made him a star in the role of a petty crook who evolves into a "dangerous" crime czar; the picture still delivers quite a punch, brimming with "energy", especially the famous scene in which the girlfriend gets it in the kisser with a grapefruit.

PULP FICTION ✉　　　　26 | 26 | 25 | 25
1994. Directed by Quentin Tarantino. With John Travolta, Samuel L. Jackson, Uma Thurman, Bruce Willis, Amanda Plummer, Tim Roth, Ving Rhames, Harvey Keitel. 154 minutes. Rated R.
A "pioneer of plot shuffling" and "twisty chronology", this "propulsive", "in-your-face" thriller is a "true original" with an "unpredictable storyline" and "dialogue that's like a punch in the face"; recounting the affairs of some "charming hit men", it stars a "rogues' gallery of actors" in memorable bits ("Travolta's dancing", Uma's overdose, Plummer's "psychotic rant") played out with "dark humor", "intense violence" and "foul language"; not only did it "put Tarantino on the map", it's in a "genre all by itself."

Pumping Iron Ⓤ　　　　17 | – | 18 | 15
1977. Directed by George Butler, Robert Fiore. Documentary. With Arnold Schwarzenegger, Lou Ferrigno. 85 minutes. Rated PG.
An "enlightening" look into the "world of competitive bodybuilding", this "muscle-bound" documentary "put working out on the map" but is better known for "introducing Arnold to the world" in all his "cocky" glory, full of the "charisma" and "ambition" that led to his "running the state of California" – "talk about foreshadowing!"

Punch-Drunk Love　　　　17 | 20 | 16 | 17
2002. Directed by Paul Thomas Anderson. With Adam Sandler, Emily Watson, Philip Seymour Hoffman. 95 minutes. Rated R.
"Not for everyone", this "quirky" "love story for losers" stars a "zombified" Sandler as an "angry, passive-aggressive type" who falls for an "adorable" if somewhat "weird" gal; foes find "more potential than payoff" here and say it's "about as self-important as movies get", while even fans admit it will "leave you scratching your head a little . . . kind of the way life does"; best line: "I beat up the bathroom."

Purple Rose of Cairo, The　　　　21 | 21 | 24 | 21
1985. Directed by Woody Allen. With Mia Farrow, Jeff Daniels, Danny Aiello. 84 minutes. Rated PG.
The Woodman rises to the occasion with this "clever", "not-self-absorbed" comedy, a "bittersweet tale" featuring "Farrow's best" work as a Depression-era moviegoer whose "fantasy world" merges with "real life" when an RKO star walks off the screen into her life; the "imaginative" plot takes an "inside-out" look at "love of the movies", with a last reel calculated to "break your heart."

Quiet American, The　　　　24 | 26 | 24 | 24
2002. Directed by Phillip Noyce. With Michael Caine, Brendan Fraser. 101 minutes. Rated R.
Delivering a "powerful performance", Caine demonstrates why he's "legendary" in this "highly underrated" adaptation of the Graham Greene novel about "America's involvement in the early

stages of the Vietnam War"; a "terrific" Fraser, a "wonderful story" and a "lavish" re-creation of 1950s Saigon are more reasons why many say "it's a shame" this "sleeper wasn't promoted enough."

QUIET MAN, THE ✉
27 | 25 | 25 | 27

1952. Directed by John Ford. With John Wayne, Maureen O'Hara, Barry Fitzgerald. 129 minutes. Not Rated.
"Every Irish cliché" is "alive and well" in this "romanticized" drama, starring the Duke as an American boxer who hangs up his gloves and settles in his Hibernian "ancestral home" only to be smitten by the "beautiful", "feisty" O'Hara; presenting a "postcard" Ireland populated by "enchanting townspeople", it's "witty" and – despite a wee bit o' "blarney" – judged "worthy of a yearly viewing."

Quiz Show
21 | 23 | 21 | 20

1994. Directed by Robert Redford. With Ralph Fiennes, John Turturro, Rob Morrow. 133 minutes. Rated PG-13.
"America's loss of innocence" is the subtext for this "intelligent" drama chronicling the '50s TV quiz-show scandals, a "blistering" commentary on the "mania for celebrity and money"; Turturro is the cast's "bright spot" as a bought-off contestant in a rigged high-brow showdown, and nostalgists prize the "vivid picture of the era", long before *Millionaire* – the "kicker is it really happened."

Rabbit-Proof Fence
26 | 25 | 26 | 24

2002. Directed by Phillip Noyce. With Everlyn Sampi, Tianna Sansbury, Laura Monaghan, Kenneth Branagh. 94 minutes. Rated PG.
Young Aboriginal girls "escape forced slavery" and trek 1,500 miles across the Australian outback to return home in this "heart-wrenching true story" "acted wonderfully" by "three unknowns"; "don't expect special effects", and make sure to "watch the credits and you'll see the real children, now in their 80s."

Radio
22 | 25 | 23 | 22

2003. Directed by Michael Tollin. With Cuba Gooding Jr., Ed Harris. 109 minutes. Rated PG.
"Small-scale" and proud of it, this "inspiring" sports drama recounts the true story of a "friendly football coach" who molds a "less fortunate", mentally disabled man into a popular mascot-cum-cheerleader (played by the "outstanding" Gooding, who "loses himself in the character"); parents say its "old-fashioned, feel-good" scenario teaches "great life lessons for kids."

Radio Days
23 | 23 | 23 | 23

1987. Directed by Woody Allen. With Mia Farrow, Julie Kavner, Dianne Wiest. 85 minutes. Rated PG.
Tune in for "fond memories" to this "charming" "family comedy", an "affectionate period piece" set in late-'30s Rockaway Beach, where "childhood innocence, neurotic relatives" and golden-age radio fill the airwaves in a series of "warm vignettes"; touted for "top-to-bottom acting excellence", it's a "funny", "free-form" sampler of "Allen at his sunniest" and "most enjoyable."

Raging Bull ✉◑
26 | 28 | 24 | 26

1980. Directed by Martin Scorsese. With Robert De Niro, Cathy Moriarty, Joe Pesci. 129 minutes. Rated R.
Perhaps the "best boxing movie of all time", this "riveting" biopic charts the "rise and fall" of former middleweight champion Jake LaMotta, whose toughest opponents were his own "self-

destructive tendencies"; shot in "beautiful black and white", it features a "primo De Niro", and though it can be "as painful as an open wound" to watch, most feel this is "knockout" filmmaking.

RAIDERS OF THE LOST ARK ⓤ   28 | 24 | 27 | 28
1981. Directed by Steven Spielberg. With Harrison Ford, Karen Allen, Paul Freeman. 115 minutes. Rated PG.
It doesn't get "more exciting" than this "benchmark" of "nonstop pulp-fiction action", Spielberg's "roller-coaster" homage to "Saturday matinee" serials that introduces the "rakish" Indiana Jones, a tweedy archaeologist with a "strapping-hero" alter ego who scraps with the Nazis over an "all-powerful artifact"; chock-full of "retro" delights like "tongue-in-cheek" humor, "improbable cliff-hanger escapes" and a "love interest" amid the "snakes, whips and guns", it's a "rousing blockbuster" that proves the "'80s weren't all bad."

Rain Man ✉   25 | 27 | 24 | 23
1988. Directed by Barry Levinson. With Dustin Hoffman, Tom Cruise, Valeria Golino. 133 minutes. Rated R.
This Best Picture winner is an unconventional "brothers bonding" drama driven by an Oscar-winning performance from Hoffman, who's "nothing short of incredible" as a full-grown "autistic savant" blessed with an endless supply of "quirky mannerisms" and "memorable lines"; Cruise shows off his own "acting chops" as the "scheming" sibling angling for half his inheritance, bringing on showers of "insight" that clear up to let a "feel-good" resolution shine through.

Raising Arizona   23 | 23 | 23 | 21
1987. Directed by Joel Coen. With Nicolas Cage, Holly Hunter, John Goodman. 94 minutes. Rated PG-13.
For a "completely original" and truly "bizarre" screwball comedy, check out this "hilarious white-trash" "cult classic" about a "childless", "criminal-class" couple (a policewoman married to a "failed convenience-store thief") that kidnaps a kid; Cage and Hunter are drolly "deadpan" delivering "dialogue that can't be beat", while the plot is typical Coen brothers: "goofy", "quirky" and gosh "darn funny."

Raisin in the Sun, A ◖   26 | 28 | 26 | 23
1961. Directed by Daniel Petrie. With Sidney Poitier, Claudia McNeil, Ruby Dee, Diana Sands. 128 minutes. Not Rated.
"Equal to" Lorraine Hansberry's award-winning Broadway play, this "groundbreaking" adaptation tells the story of a poor black family coping with a modest financial windfall; there's "emotional conflict" aplenty in its "dueling themes" of "racism, motherhood and manhood" and the "strong" cast is up to the challenge (particularly the "poignant Poitier"); pessimists say it's "sadly as applicable today as it was in the '60s."

Ran ⒡   27 | 25 | 27 | 29
1985. Directed by Akira Kurosawa. With Tatsuya Nakadai, Mieko Harada, Daisuke Ryu. 160 minutes. Rated R.
"Big, bold and beautiful", Kurosawa's "swan song" shows his "deft touch" intact in this "expansive retelling of *King Lear*" transformed into a "riveting" samurai "epic" involving a Shogun warlord whose decision to sheath his sword leads to intra-clan "betrayals"; suitably "Shakespearean" in scale, with "stunning" depictions of

"feudal society" and "incredible battle scenes", it's "slow"-running pacewise but most hail it as "brilliant almost beyond belief."

Ransom
16 | 18 | 17 | 17

1996. Directed by Ron Howard. With Mel Gibson, Rene Russo, Gary Sinise, Lili Taylor. 120 minutes. Rated R.
"Gripping", "sustained suspense" is tempered with "much emotion" in this "dark" tale of a kidnapped child, starring "Mel in a suit" as a "conflicted" dad; though some bluff-callers deem it "overblown" and "formulaic", others swear by its "realistic" tension that's "scary to every parent out there."

RASHOMON O F
29 | 27 | 29 | 25

1951. Directed by Akira Kurosawa. With Toshiro Mifune, Machiko Kyo, Masayuki Mori. 88 minutes. Not Rated.
Surely "truth is in the eye of the beholder", but most agree that Akira Kurosawa's "superb head-twister" of a Japanese drama should be "required viewing"; aided by "exquisite" camerawork and "fine medieval embellishments", it's a "simple story" about an ambush in the forest told from "four different points of view", proving that "self-interest" amounts to "nine-tenths of everything"; in sum, this "seminal" tale has been tirelessly "copied but never equaled."

Ray ✉
26 | 29 | 25 | 26

2004. Directed by Taylor Hackford. With Jamie Foxx. 152 minutes. Rated PG-13.
"Foxx almost disappears into the person of Ray Charles" in this "phenomenal" bio-"tribute" to the "legendary musician", nabbing a "well-deserved" Oscar for his "foot-stomping", "heartrending" portrayal of the superstar that's so convincing you'll "forget who you're really watching"; fans agree the "uncompromising" look at the soul man's "boozing, drugs and womanizing" is right on key, with additional hoorays going out to that "marvelous soundtrack."

Reality Bites
19 | 18 | 18 | 17

1994. Directed by Ben Stiller. With Winona Ryder, Ethan Hawke, Janeane Garofalo. 99 minutes. Rated PG-13.
"Escape with the losers" in this romantic comedy of "post-college" Gen-X existence as Winona and company find themselves "going nowhere" but obliged to deal when faced with "job woes", tainted love and "utter annoyance with life"; vets of the day say as a "portrayal of MTV and other pop-culture" touchstones, "nothing represents the '90s more accurately."

Real Women Have Curves
21 | 22 | 21 | 19

2002. Directed by Patricia Cardoso. With America Ferrera, Lupe Ontiveros, Ingrid Oliu, George Lopez. 90 minutes. Rated PG-13.
Those with "less-than-supermodel bodies" – "which is about 99 percent of the population" – will especially enjoy this "inspirational" coming-of-age story about a "courageous" Latina teen "who isn't a size eight" "caught between family traditions and modern mores"; "there needs to be more movies" like this "celebration of women."

REAR WINDOW
28 | 27 | 28 | 27

1954. Directed by Alfred Hitchcock. With James Stewart, Grace Kelly, Thelma Ritter. 112 minutes. Rated PG.
"Voyeurism" meets "suspense" in this "snooper's dream" about a "wheelchair-bound" photographer "spying on his neighbors"

and trying to "trap a killer" while fending off his girlfriend, who's tempting him into "another trap – marriage"; while the "crisp script" and "great NY set" draw huzzahs, fans tout its "perfectly cast" leads, the "solid" Stewart and "deeelicious" Kelly; so many find it "unsurpassed" that it was voted the top Hitchcock flick in this *Survey*.

REBECCA ✉◗
27 | 27 | 27 | 25

1940. Directed by Alfred Hitchcock. With Laurence Olivier, Joan Fontaine, Judith Anderson. 130 minutes. Not Rated.
Based on Daphne du Maurier's "ultimate romance novel", "Hitchcock's first American film" is a "dark, moody" tale of a woman living in the shadow of her new husband's old wife; "haunting" and "eerily captivating", it showcases an "excellent" Olivier and a "gorgeous" Fontaine; but it's the "over-the-top" Anderson who's the real "hoot" here.

Rebel Without a Cause
24 | 24 | 21 | 22

1955. Directed by Nicholas Ray. With James Dean, Natalie Wood, Sal Mineo. 111 minutes. Not Rated.
A "lost generation lives on" in this "terse drama" of "disaffected youth" and "family conflict", which elevated Dean to "icon" status as a "rebellious" juvenile delinquent who leads a "great cast" as they cope with "hope, fear and love" in the "inchoate Los Angeles" of the '50s; while all that acting out seems a bit "dated", most maintain it "lives up to its rep" as the "ultimate" ode to "teen alienation."

Recruit, The
17 | 20 | 18 | 19

2003. Directed by Roger Donaldson. With Al Pacino, Colin Farrell, Bridget Moynahan. 115 minutes. Rated PG-13.
"Nothing is what it seems" in this "keeps-you-guessing" spy thriller wherein a "secretive CIA" man attempts to enlist a promising recruit; though Farrell "holds his own" as the protégé, some say Pacino's "patented screaming mentor role" is "starting to sound the same in every movie", and despite all the "twists and turns", the "ending's kind of weak."

Red Dragon
19 | 22 | 20 | 20

2002. Directed by Brett Ratner. With Anthony Hopkins, Edward Norton, Ralph Fiennes, Harvey Keitel. 124 minutes. Rated R.
"Better than *Hannibal*" but "not as good as *Silence of the Lambs*" is this "engaging" prequel" wind-up of the "Lecter trilogy", a "suspenseful" thriller pitting a "stoic" G-man against a "disturbed murderer", and featuring the obligatory "mental chess match" with Hopkins' "good doctor" (albeit in a "minor role"); P.S. compare it with 1986's *Manhunter*, based on the same novel and often considered the "superior" version.

Red River ◗
26 | 25 | 25 | 27

1948. Directed by Howard Hawks. With John Wayne, Montgomery Clift, Joanne Dru. 133 minutes. Not Rated.
"Perhaps the grandest" Western of all, this cowpuncher "classic" breaks into a gallop when "lots of hunky men" saddle up for a dangerous cattle drive along the Chisholm Trail; Wayne "excels in an unsympathetic role" as a "stolid" rancher who turns against Monty, who "holds his own" as a buckaroo of "brooding sensitivity"; the result is a horn-lock that fans brand a grade-A prime "rewatcher."

Reds ✉ 21 21 20 22
1981. Directed by Warren Beatty. With Warren Beatty, Diane Keaton, Jack Nicholson. 194 minutes. Rated PG.
Agitprop meets "epic romance" in this "impressive" bio of writers John Reed and Louise Bryant that chronicles their courtship and activities as bolshie sympathizers during the Russian Revolution; "Beatty's labor of love", it's an "excellent re-creation" of the time, framed by "remembrances" of "largely forgotten men and women", but "major themes" or no, critics say this "big production" is "too long to keep you interested."

Red Shoes, The 26 24 24 26
1948. Directed by Michael Powell, Emeric Pressburger. With Anton Walbrook, Moira Shearer. 133 minutes. Not Rated.
With a tip of the slipper to Hans Christian Andersen, this "ageless" drama of "romance and ballet" "takes a fairy tale and creates magic" around the story of a young dancer who joins a celebrated troupe only to enter into a pas de deux with a composer; "sumptuous" staging and "dreamy choreography" make it a terpsichorean "benchmark", and fans "love every bit of it."

Red Violin, The 🄵 24 23 24 24
1999. Directed by François Girard. With Samuel L. Jackson, Greta Scacchi. 131 minutes. Rated R.
A "symphony" recounting the "many tales of a violin's life", this "intricate" drama "follows the path" of a "fabulous instrument" from its creation in Renaissance Italy though various owners, countries and epochs, up to Jackson's encounter as a present-day appraiser; in spite of "art-house" airs, boosters bow to a "twisting" story that "keeps you guessing" – backed by a really "stunning" soundtrack featuring "real music by a real composer."

Remains of the Day, The 24 27 23 25
1993. Directed by James Ivory. With Anthony Hopkins, Emma Thompson, Christopher Reeve. 138 minutes. Rated PG.
"If you loved *Howards End*", you'll dig this "complex and entertaining" drama of "two fragile souls" on a British estate in the late '30s; "repressed" head butler Hopkins "puts duty above all else", even his yen for housekeeper Thompson, and both give "precise, controlled performances" filled with "gripping silences" to suit its "nuanced" story of "unfulfilled love", "class-system" bias and the "obtuseness of the upper crust" – just "don't expect action."

Remember the Titans 20 21 21 19
2000. Directed by Boaz Yakin. With Denzel Washington, Will Patton, Wood Harris. 113 minutes. Rated PG.
"Denzel is the man" to knock a ball team into shape while tackling "racial fault lines" in this "inspirational" family drama about a black high-school coach taking over a newly integrated football squad; if the "feel-good" theme of "tolerance and social understanding" plays out as "hokey" and "about as deep as astroturf", fans "cheer anyway" for a "sleeper" that never fumbles its underlying "hope."

Rent 19 20 20 20
2005. Directed by Chris Columbus. With Anthony Rapp, Adam Pascal, Rosario Dawson, Jesse L. Martin, Taye Diggs. 135 minutes. Rated PG-13.
Of course, there's "nothing like the live Broadway show", but this stage-to-screen transfer of Jonathan Larson's "groundbreaking"

musical actually "holds its own" thanks to the casting of "most of the original" players (albeit "aged" some years) for an "energetic" reprise of those "rousing" song-and-dance numbers; if a few critics charge the AIDS-themed storyline "loses its punch" in translation, most proponents feel it's still as "poignant as ever."

Repo Man
17 | 15 | 17 | 16

1984. Directed by Alex Cox. With Harry Dean Stanton, Emilio Estevez. 92 minutes. Rated R.
A "cult classic with a serious following", this "wacko" comedy "captures the nihilism of the '80s punk scene" in its story of lowlifes repossessing cars and chasing after UFOs; with lots of "throwaway gags", "quotable lines" and an "overlooked soundtrack", this "silly delight" is proudly "over the edge" and "hard to resist."

Repulsion ◑
▽ 25 | 27 | 24 | 23

1965. Directed by Roman Polanski. With Catherine Deneuve, Ian Hendry. 105 minutes. Not Rated.
Polanski's first English-language feature, this "disturbing" psychological thriller top bills an "unbeatable" Deneuve as an unstable young woman slowly descending into madness; although made on a shoestring budget, it's still really "frightening" in its "depiction of insanity from the inside out" and is already showing "definite cult potential."

Requiem for a Dream
25 | 27 | 24 | 25

2000. Directed by Darren Aronofsky. With Ellen Burstyn, Jared Leto, Jennifer Connelly. 102 minutes. Not Rated.
"Heavy" and "altogether devastating", this "bleak" "druggy" drama "spirals into the depths of hell" on the back of some "scary", strung-out imagery and Burstyn's "amazing" turn as a magenta-maned diet-pill popper with a none-too-swift junkie son; a "stomach-churning" depiction of "major drug use" that pushes Aronofsky to the "cutting edge" of "directing talents", it's "not subtle" but lingers like a "brilliant", "unnerving nightmare" – "be prepared" for some "grueling" going.

Requiem for a Heavyweight ◑
26 | 28 | 26 | 23

1962. Directed by Ralph Nelson. With Anthony Quinn, Jackie Gleason, Mickey Rooney, Julie Harris. 95 minutes. Not Rated.
Adapted from Rod Serling's Emmy-winning television play, this "knockout" drama is "one of the best fight films around", detailing a punch-drunk boxer's "gut-wrenching" decline; maybe it's turned "dated" and "preachy" over time, but for diversion there's always that "superb" ensemble cast, especially the "amazing" Quinn; N.B. look for cameos from real-life heavyweight champs Jack Dempsey and Muhammad Ali (billed here as Cassius Clay).

Rescuers, The ⑪
▽ 20 | – | 21 | 20

1977. Directed by Wolfgang Reitherman, John Lounsbery, Art Stevens. Animated. 76 minutes. Rated G.
A "must-see for every child", this animated Disney feature stars a pair of "adorable" mice bent on rescuing a kidnapped little girl; although maybe not at the top of the Mouse House pantheon, it's still "cute and fun" with memorable voicework from Bob Newhart, Eva Gabor and Geraldine Page.

Reservoir Dogs   24 | 25 | 24 | 22
1992. Directed by Quentin Tarantino. With Harvey Keitel, Tim Roth, Michael Madsen, Steve Buscemi. 99 minutes. Rated R.
The Tarantino "template" for a "new" style of crime thriller splices "hip, sharp" dialogue with "hard-core violence" as a "dream cast" sporting two-tone threads turns a jewel heist into a "riveting" "bloody spectacle"; the "clever" script relies on diced chronology, "sly riffs" on pop culture and "psychological twists" to lend heart to the "vicious" gang, though many howl the "nasty" bits ("ear removal", anyone?) are still "painful to watch."

Reversal of Fortune ✉   ▽ 19 | 24 | 19 | 18
1990. Directed by Barbet Schroeder. With Jeremy Irons, Glenn Close, Ron Silver. 120 minutes. Rated R.
"You can't make this stuff up" – Oscar-winner Irons is "totally mesmerizing" in his "smarmy" take on the real-life Claus von Bulow, the high-society ladies' man accused of sending his heiress wife into an irreversible coma; Close and Silver also deliver the goods in this "solid" picture whose only drawback is "not having the ending that you want."

Right Stuff, The   26 | 24 | 26 | 26
1983. Directed by Philip Kaufman. With Sam Shepard, Scott Glenn, Ed Harris. 193 minutes. Rated PG.
"Exuberant", "involving" and "proud to be American", this "triumphant" drama "never flags" in launching Tom Wolfe's "snarky yet sincere" "epic of the space age" onto the big screen; a "retelling of true events" surrounding the evolution of test pilots into astronauts in the Mercury program, it pushes the envelope with "adventure, humor" and a cast that's "A-ok in every way."

Ring, The ⓤ   19 | 18 | 20 | 21
2002. Directed by Gore Verbinski. With Naomi Watts, Martin Henderson, David Dorfman, Brian Cox. 115 minutes. Rated PG-13.
Viewers of a "mysterious videotape" receive a "spooky" call and "die seven days later" in this "genuinely scary" ghost story that delivers its "spine-tingling" chills without the "gross-out effects" common to the genre; cynical cinephiles say the "convoluted" story "falls apart" toward the end (*Ringu*, the "original Japanese version, is better"), but most are still "clutching their armrests" and vowing "never to answer the phone again."

Rio Bravo   ▽ 23 | 22 | 23 | 23
1959. Directed by Howard Hawks. With John Wayne, Dean Martin, Ricky Nelson. 141 minutes. Not Rated.
"As Westerns go", this "entertaining" oater from the Hawks/Wayne team is an "expert reshuffling" of the plot of "*High Noon*", the story of a lone sheriff trying to hold a prisoner against a threatening mob; though the picture was remade as *El Dorado* (and later as *Rio Lobo*), fans say the original is the "best version."

Risky Business   20 | 18 | 19 | 18
1983. Directed by Paul Brickman. With Tom Cruise, Rebecca De Mornay, Bronson Pinchot. 98 minutes. Rated R.
"Every boy's dream" comes true in this "smart, sexy" "coming-of-age" comedy, with Cruise as the high-schooler who turns chez suburbia into party central when his parents leave town – only to fall into "the arms of a beautiful hooker" and venture into the brothel

business; it's a "funny" jibe at "upper-middle-class teenage life" with some "raging hormones" thrown in, and that celebrated scene of "Tom dancing in his Jockeys" is nothing short of "starmaking."

River Runs Through It, A · 22 | 23 | 21 | 25

1992. Directed by Robert Redford. With Brad Pitt, Craig Sheffer, Tom Skerritt. 123 minutes. Rated PG.
Sounding "deep" waters with a "pastoral" tale of "life as we no longer know it", Redford's "elegiac" drama of "family bonds" takes a "moving", "candid" look at the sibling rivalry between two small-town minister's sons; the "smooth" pace is set by the stars' "subtle emotion" and "striking" cinematography that captures the "Montana wilderness" in all of its full "majesty", though some clock-watchers find the running time a bit "too slow."

Road to Perdition · 23 | 26 | 22 | 25

2002. Directed by Sam Mendes. With Tom Hanks, Paul Newman, Daniel Craig, Jude Law. 117 minutes. Rated R.
"Hanks proves his versatility" in this "evocative period piece", playing a "cold-blooded hit man" for the Irish mafia during the Depression; the "intense journey" is "impeccably done", with Newman in "stellar form", Oscar-winning cinematography that will "take your breath away" (notably that "tommy gun scene in the rain") and "top-notch screenwriting" that "stays true to the novel."

Road Warrior, The ⑪ · 22 | 18 | 21 | 20

1982. Directed by George Miller. With Mel Gibson, Bruce Spence, Mike Preston. 94 minutes. Rated R.
"Road rage" kicks into overdrive in this "raw Aussie action flick", with "lean, mean" Gibson "at his baddest" as Mad Max, a "lone, reluctant cowboy" cruising a "post-apocalyptic" wasteland and upholding his "own brand of justice"; set in a "nihilistic" near-future when barbaric gangs comb the desert pestering decent folk for petrol, its combo of an "intriguing" setup and "incredible car stunts" makes it a "visceral" "cult favorite"; gas up.

Robe, The ⑪ · ▽ 19 | 19 | 20 | 21

1953. Directed by Henry Koster. With Richard Burton, Jean Simmons, Victor Mature. 135 minutes. Not Rated.
"Burton reigns" as a Roman centurion who oversees the crucifixion, then wins Christ's robe in a dice game in this '50s "religious movie" that inspired a slew of biblical flicks; most memorable for being the first feature shot in CinemaScope, it's "big" in every way, though some ask "can it really be an epic without Charlton Heston?"

Robin and Marian · ▽ 21 | 24 | 23 | 22

1976. Directed by Richard Lester. With Sean Connery, Audrey Hepburn, Robert Shaw. 106 minutes. Rated PG.
In "Robin Hood's later years" he resumes his affair with Maid Marian in this "wistful wisp" of a tale worth seeing for the "casting" alone; the "sadness of time passing is palpable" (right down to that "darkly romantic ending"), and if it's mainly a "woman's film", there's still "enough swordplay" to keep the guys happy.

Robin Hood: Prince of Thieves · 16 | 14 | 17 | 18

1991. Directed by Kevin Reynolds. With Kevin Costner, Morgan Freeman, Alan Rickman. 138 minutes. Rated PG-13.
This retelling of the spurned-lord-turned-benevolent-thief legend is "surprisingly original", with a "super villain" and enough

"tongue-in-cheek" antics to "keep it moving"; but Costner's "now-you-hear-it, now-you-don't English accent" and other "inaccuracies" make holdouts hold out for "Errol Flynn."

RoboCop ❶   16 | 13 | 17 | 19
1987. Directed by Paul Verhoeven. With Peter Weller, Nancy Allen, Ronny Cox. 103 minutes. Rated R.
"Ruthlessly smart and satirical", this "novel" sci-fi adventure flick tells the story of a cop killed in the line of duty then brought back to life as a bio-mechanical robot; alternately "violent and hilarious", this "live-action comic book" is a "thought-provoking look" at a "techno vigilante" and a lot "better than it should have been."

Robots   20 | – | 19 | 24
2005. Directed by Chris Wedge, Carlos Saldanha. Animated. 91 minutes. Not Rated.
"Dazzling", "Rube Goldberg-esque" animation "keeps the whole family entertained" in this "simple", "heartfelt" 'toon about a young 'droid who "leaves home to chase a dream" in the big city; ok, the "ho-hum" "fish-out-of-water" plotline is "as mechanical as the characters", 'bot at least it's got an "uplifting", "you-can-do-anything-you-put-your-mind-to" message for the kids.

Rock, The   20 | 21 | 20 | 22
1996. Directed by Michael Bay. With Sean Connery, Nicolas Cage, Ed Harris. 136 minutes. Rated R.
Find out who's got the biggest "fireballs" in this very "noisy testosterone fix", bringing "slick", "edge-of-your-seat action" to Alcatraz as "crusty" ex-spy Connery and "bumbling" weapons-expert Cage penetrate the prison walls to stop a mad general from blitzing the Bay Area with nerve gas; fans find the pair "amazing together", and despite the highly "not-likely" scenario, the "awesome locale" and "great FX" ensure a "kick-ass" good time.

Rocky ✉ ❶   25 | 20 | 25 | 21
1976. Directed by John G. Avildsen. With Sylvester Stallone, Talia Shire, Burt Young. 119 minutes. Rated PG.
This "red-blooded" ring drama (and Oscar champ) "goes the distance" with an "underdog-makes-good" theme as "two-bit" boxer Sly "wins over everyone's heart" when he "gets his shot" at the title, works up "lots of sweat" and "finds true love" along the way; though part "hokey" "Hollywood fantasy", it's also a "stirring confidence-booster" that packs an everlasting "wallop."

Rocky Horror Picture Show, The   21 | 18 | 19 | 22
1975. Directed by Jim Sharman. With Tim Curry, Susan Sarandon, Barry Bostwick. 100 minutes. Rated R.
"Beyond weird" to the uninitiated, this "camp classic" rock 'n' roll musical is famed for the "floor show" put on at "midnight screenings" by costumed carousers who pronounce it the "best trash ever"; a "pure B-movie" spoof involving a pair of innocents who stumble into the lair of a "sweet transvestite", it's "silly" but "entertaining on its own bizarre level", so "get out your toast, rice and lighter" and "sing along" with this "legendary mess."

Roger & Me   24 | – | 24 | 20
1989. Directed by Michael Moore. Documentary. 91 minutes. Rated R.
"Laugh and cringe" at this salvo of "guerrilla filmmaking", an "eye-opening" documentary chronicling both the "disintegration"

of a Michigan town after its GM plant pulls up stakes and "squeaky wheel" Moore's "quest to confront" the corporation's CEO; the "too-real" footage is "drop-dead funny" yet "sobering" ("rabbit lovers beware"), and if a few find the "irreverent" tone "annoying", progressives everywhere hail it as a "vital exposé" of the "new global economy" and a "stirring" fanfare for the "common man."

Roger Dodger
18 | 22 | 18 | 16

2002. Directed by Dylan Kidd. With Campbell Scott, Jesse Eisenberg, Isabella Rossellini. 104 minutes. Rated R.
Playing the "biggest cad since Alfie", the "underappreciated" Scott is "socko" in this "sharp little indie" that ventures into "Neil LaBute" territory in its story of a "smarmy", "lecherous adman" instructing his "wide-eyed teenage nephew" in the "art of seduction"; despite "lots of talk", it's "never dull", though some find this "bitter, mean-spirited rant" "hard to watch."

Romancing the Stone 🎬
20 | 19 | 21 | 20

1984. Directed by Robert Zemeckis. With Michael Douglas, Kathleen Turner, Danny DeVito. 105 minutes. Rated PG-13.
This "poor man's *Raiders of the Lost Ark*" turns a "lighthearted" adventure into a "fast-paced crowd-pleaser", with Turner cast as a "nerdy" romance novelist who hooks up with "tongue-in-cheek hero" Douglas down South America way; the two are "quite the duo", and some "humorous action sequences" with archrival DeVito "trying to keep up" make for "durable escapism."

ROMAN HOLIDAY ✉️◐
27 | 26 | 25 | 25

1953. Directed by William Wyler. With Gregory Peck, Audrey Hepburn. 118 minutes. Not Rated.
A "date movie without equal", this "frothy", "witty romance" presents a "radiant" Hepburn as the "rebellious" "gamine princess" with a "pixie cut" who plays hooky in the Eternal City, escorted by "charming", "not-so-hard-boiled reporter" Peck; helped along by "wondrous Roman scenery", their "coy" exchanges lead things on their natural "exhilarating" course, making for a "captivating fantasy" that draws to a "bittersweet", "refreshingly realistic" ending ("awww!").

Romeo and Juliet
26 | 24 | 27 | 26

1968. Directed by Franco Zeffirelli. With Olivia Hussey, Leonard Whiting. 138 minutes. Rated PG.
"Achingly beautiful" and played with "youthful vigor", this "faithful Zeffirelli" reading renders the "grand" romance of star-crossed love so "accessible" that "even boys cry" during the tragic last act; the "classic" production stays "true to the Bard" with "so-cute" teenage actors and "gorgeous" sets, pleasing "purists" as the "definitive film version" and surviving as the odds-on favorite to be the Shakespeare everyone's "made to watch in school."

Romeo + Juliet
19 | 17 | 22 | 23

1996. Directed by Baz Luhrmann. With Leonardo DiCaprio, Claire Danes, John Leguizamo. 120 minutes. Rated PG-13.
Flash master Luhrmann presents the ageless romance "in a different light" in this "daring updating", a "kinetic visual feast" that aims to please the "MTV generation" with "pop music" and "creative" modern-day staging; Leo and Claire lend the lovers "teen-idol" allure, and if some sniff at "style over substance" and say

the "acting seriously lacks", those who are "ok with extravagance" find it "effective" and "really cool."

Rookie, The
22 | 22 | 23 | 20

2002. Directed by John Lee Hancock. With Dennis Quaid, Rachel Griffiths, Brian Cox. 127 minutes. Rated G.
Quaid "hits a grand slam" as an over-the-hill major-league baseball rookie in this "feel-good movie for the whole family to enjoy" and "learn from"; it's a true story (with a "little Disney sprinkled on it") "that shows the importance of following your dreams" "even when it seems too late"; critics have just one quibble: it "drags on longer than a low-scoring doubleheader."

Room at the Top ⊠◑▥
24 | 27 | 24 | 23

1959. Directed by Jack Clayton. With Simone Signoret, Laurence Harvey, Heather Sears. 115 minutes. Not Rated.
Britain's "class struggle" is the subject of this "powerful" "drama of ambition" starring an "excellent" Harvey as an angry young man bent on improving his lot in life by wooing a naive heiress; along the way, he has some "provocative" moments with the "smoky" Signoret, who steals the picture (and copped a Best Actress Oscar) as his "sultry, world-weary" playmate.

Room with a View, A ⊠
26 | 26 | 24 | 27

1986. Directed by James Ivory. With Maggie Smith, Helena Bonham Carter, Denholm Elliott. 117 minutes. Not Rated.
"Florence looks like heaven" in this "crisp" costume drama about a "proper Victorian girl's" sightseeing tour that's considerably perked up by "friendships that form in a pensione", leading to her "romantic awakening"; the "brilliant acting" brings "wit and energy" to a "sunny" "study of class and character" that finds all kinds of room for "superb fin de siècle" touches and "seductive" shots of the Italian landscape.

Rope
22 | 21 | 23 | 22

1948. Directed by Alfred Hitchcock. With Farley Granger, James Stewart, John Dall. 80 minutes. Rated PG.
"One word – Hitchcock" – draws film buffs to this "chilling" reworking of the Leopold and Loeb murder case that's told with a "compelling gimmick": it was "shot entirely on one set" and "runs in real time"; though a few snore "slow and stagy", at least the master's "eye to detail" makes it an "interesting curiosity."

Rose, The
19 | 23 | 18 | 18

1979. Directed by Mark Rydell. With Bette Midler, Alan Bates, Frederic Forrest. 125 minutes. Rated R.
The "mesmerizing" Miss M makes the "most stunning movie debut since Streisand" in this rock-chanteuse drama, a "homage" to the wild-at-heart chronicling the life and times of a "self-destructive Janis Joplin type" as she barrels down the road to ruin; groupies who insist Midler's "strong performance" should have "won the Oscar" find consolation in that "great title song."

Rosemary's Baby ▥
24 | 25 | 25 | 22

1968. Directed by Roman Polanski. With Mia Farrow, John Cassavetes, Ruth Gordon. 136 minutes. Rated R.
A "glamorous horror" flick about a "naive" housewife duped into bearing "Satan's child", this "gut-wrenching classic" still "scares the hell out" of nearly everybody; "pro-choice" types tout Farrow's

"amazing" turn (and "faaabulous haircut") as well as Polanski's "very faithful adaptation" of Ira Levin's novel, but everyone says that the "devilishly good", Oscar-winning Gordon "steals the show."

Roxanne 21 | 21 | 21 | 19
1987. Directed by Fred Schepisi. With Steve Martin, Daryl Hannah, Rick Rossovich. 107 minutes. Rated PG.
Schnoz aficionados consider this "amusing" romance the "quint-essential Martin vehicle": a "modernization" of *Cyrano de Bergerac* concerning a fire chief cursed with a prodigious proboscis but blessed with a "grab bag of comic devices" with which he helps a surrogate court the highly "watchable" Hannah; though some find it too "cute", it's a "good-natured" yarn with a "ton of heart."

Royal Tenenbaums, The 20 | 24 | 18 | 21
2001. Directed by Wes Anderson. With Gene Hackman, Anjelica Huston, Ben Stiller, Gwyneth Paltrow. 109 minutes. Rated R.
This "very black" yet colorful "character-driven" comedy delineates the "humorous side of dysfunctionality" within a "wacky family of overachievers"; while the "Oscar-worthy" script and "stellar ensemble cast" draw applause, some shrug it's a "movie about nothing" that's "too clever" and "cynical" – the "reviewers liked it more than I did."

Rules of the Game, The ◖🅵 ▽ 27 | 24 | 25 | 26
1939. Directed by Jean Renoir. With Marcel Dalio, Nora Gregor, Mila Parély. 110 minutes. Not Rated.
"Always on the short list of the greatest films ever made" is this "scathing indictment of the French upper class" from "master" filmmaker Renoir, which "takes place at a weekend retreat in the country" and contrasts the romantic entanglements of both rich and poor alike; although "perfectly written, filmed and acted", it was not a hit in its initial release, and only garnered its rep after resurfacing at a film festival 20 years later.

Ruling Class, The 23 | 26 | 22 | 21
1972. Directed by Peter Medak. With Peter O'Toole, Alastair Sim, Arthur Lowe, Harry Andrews. 154 minutes. Rated PG.
Alternately "funny and disturbing", this black "social satire" takes on "the British upper class" in its story of a "delusional" fellow who becomes an earl after his father's death; the "bizarre" plot "moves like lightning", and as the "bonkers" nobleman, O'Toole's "totally over the top."

Runaway Jury 20 | 22 | 21 | 20
2003. Directed by Gary Fleder. With John Cusack, Gene Hackman, Dustin Hoffman. 127 minutes. Rated PG-13.
"Liberal Hollywood goes after the gun industry" in this courtroom drama pitting a "jury-stacking lawyer" against a "righteous underdog"; ok, it "doesn't follow the storyline" of its John Grisham origins, but devotees dig watching "old pros Hackman and Hoffman square off" just the same – even if they appear together on-screen in "just one scene."

Runaway Train 21 | 22 | 20 | 21
1985. Directed by Andrei Konchalovsky. With Jon Voight, Eric Roberts, Rebecca de Mornay. 111 minutes. Rated R.
"Surprisingly" stimulating despite "cheapish production values", this "stark", "existential actioner" keeps onlookers "enthralled"

with a "twist on the prison-break" scenario as a freight train carrying a pair of fugitive cons careens through the Alaskan wild ("bring a parka") while the law looks on; though "over the top" enough to nearly hop the rails, this "bleak masterwork" also offers "powerful" acting and "dark" themes.

Run Lola Run 🅵
23 | 21 | 24 | 24

1999. Directed by Tom Tykwer. With Franka Potente, Moritz Bleibtreu, Herbert Knaup. 81 minutes. Rated R.
There's "never a dull moment" in this "amped-up" German import involving the "sweat-dripping" effort of a fleet-footed fräulein to hustle a big pile of cash to save her boyfriend from a nasty mobster; "strongly driven" by an "adrenaline"-pumping "techno soundtrack" and "video-game" vibe, the "breathless" "nonlinear" narrative forges "different perspectives" and "time repeats" into a "pulse-pounding" "original" that's as "ultra-watchable" as it is "quirky."

Rush Hour Ⓤ
19 | 17 | 16 | 20

1998. Directed by Brett Ratner. With Jackie Chan, Chris Tucker, Tom Wilkinson. 97 minutes. Rated PG-13.
Formula "fluff" with "all the right moves", this actioner finds time for "comic relief" as a crime-fighting pair of "exact opposites" teams up to rescue a kidnapped kid; "high-kicking" Chan breaks out with some "inventive chop-socky sequences" and "exhilarating" stunts while playing it straight alongside outspoken "wild man" Tucker, so even if the "plot's not much", the "buddy pairing" offers enough crowd-pleasing "chemistry" to translate into "loads of fun."

Rushmore
23 | 25 | 22 | 22

1998. Directed by Wes Anderson. With Jason Schwartzman, Olivia Williams, Bill Murray. 93 minutes. Rated R.
A monument of "quality quirkiness", this "unabashedly unusual" comedy stars Schwartzman as an "arrogant and clever" but "dysfunctional" scholarship student at an elite prep school whose "coming of age" takes many a "droll" twist when he befriends a rich alumnus and falls for a teacher; the "smart", "character-driven" script is "expertly acted", leading to high marks for a "winning gem" with "real heart" "beneath the smarminess" – and how about that "killer soundtrack"?

Russians Are Coming, The Russians Are Coming, The
21 | 21 | 22 | 20

1966. Directed by Norman Jewison. With Alan Arkin, John Phillip Law, Jonathan Winters. 120 minutes. Not Rated.
Da, comrades, this "classic '60s comedy" is a "Cold War satire" that offers a "sweet take" on a paranoid period as a Red Navy sub goes aground off the Massachusetts coast and Soviet swabbie Arkin is sent into a Nantucket-like island community for a rescue boat, setting off rumors of an invasion; *Strangelove* it ain't, but the "very funny" situations are still "worth the time."

Ruthless People
20 | 19 | 19 | 17

1986. Directed by David Zucker, Jerry Zucker, Jim Abrahams. With Danny DeVito, Bette Midler. 93 minutes. Rated R.
Echt '80s in its send-up of "pure greed", this pretty "crass" but "sidesplitting" black comedy gets going when a couple of "inept kidnappers" snatch Midler (carrying on at her "bitchy best") and

demand ransom from DeVito, a "standout" as the "crude", double-dealing "spandex king" husband scheming to rid himself of a despised spouse; "lots of plot twists" ensue in a "silly", "hilarious" caper that anyone with a cynical side shouldn't overlook.

Ryan's Daughter ▽ | 22 | 23 | 23 | 24 |
1970. Directed by David Lean. With Robert Mitchum, Trevor Howard, Sarah Miles, John Mills. 176 minutes. Rated PG.
"Love and infidelity" are played out against a "magnificent Irish seacoast setting" in this "epic tearjerker" via David Lean, a "weak-in-the-knees romance" that's "gorgeously filmed" and set to memorably "haunting music"; its "bracing scenery" and truly "powerful" story – depicting "love as steadfastness rather than a cheap emotion" – lead many to call it "underrated."

Sabrina ◑ | 25 | 25 | 25 | 23 |
1954. Directed by Billy Wilder. With Humphrey Bogart, Audrey Hepburn, William Holden. 113 minutes. Not Rated.
Like an order of "first-class everything", this "delicious" "rags-to-riches" romance sparkles with "wit and couture" as an "ethereal" Hepburn plays a "beguiling", love-struck chauffeur's daughter in a "little black dress"; the "modern Cinderella" scenario finds Bogie in a "comedic role" as an all-business heir determined to beat out his "younger playboy brother" for Audrey's affections; as for Harrison Ford's 1995 remake, loyalists "consider it blasphemy."

Sahara | 17 | 16 | 16 | 20 |
2005. Directed by Breck Eisner. With Matthew McConaughey, Penélope Cruz, Steve Zahn. 124 minutes. Rated PG-13.
An "amusing" if "minor-league Indiana Jones rip-off", this "carefree" adventure yarn based on Clive Cussler's best-seller grafts the search for a "Civil War battleship in Africa" onto an "enviro-sensitive" story of a catastrophic plague threatening the worlds' oceans; though Matthew, Penélope and the "exotic locales" make for "beautiful scenery", the end result is "pretty to look at, but not much else."

Same Time, Next Year | 22 | 24 | 25 | 21 |
1978. Directed by Robert Mulligan. With Ellen Burstyn, Alan Alda, Ivan Bonar. 119 minutes. Rated PG.
Expect to go from "laughter to tears and back again" in this "decade-spanning romance", featuring "convincing" turns from Alda and Burstyn as a couple of "married lovers who meet once a year"; adapted from the Broadway stage, the "annual adultery" device tracks the two as they "change with the times", making for "sweet", "warm" entertainment – even if it does "promote affairs."

Sand Pebbles, The | 24 | 26 | 25 | 24 |
1966. Directed by Robert Wise. With Steve McQueen, Richard Crenna, Richard Attenborough, Candice Bergen. 179 minutes. Rated PG-13.
An "epic of China" told from the point of view of Yank sailors knee-deep in the revolutionary turmoil of 1926, this "powerful, pertinent" war drama features "authentic hero" McQueen "smoldering in top form" as a "tough-guy" Navy mechanic "with a heart of gold", manning an American patrol boat; if the tale "meanders like the Yellow River", it's still a "must-see" for History Channel addicts.

Santa Clause, The ❷
19 | 17 | 19 | 19

1994. Directed by John Pasquin. With Tim Allen, Judge Reinhold, Wendy Crewson. 97 minutes. Rated PG.

"Corny in a good way", this holiday comedy packages the "fantastic" with the "real world" when exec Allen takes over the reins from an abruptly retired Kris Kringle, mysteriously begins "fattening" and meets with complications in the custody of his young son; though it sleds along on a "sappy story", consensus calls it rather "original" as far as Yuletide yarns go.

Saturday Night Fever ❷
22 | 19 | 20 | 22

1977. Directed by John Badham. With John Travolta, Karen Lynn Gorney. 118 minutes. Rated R.

A paean to "polyester", this romance defines the "days of disco" with an "electric" Travolta as the blow-dried mook who lives to "look good" and "shake his groove thing" but has to boogie to "improve his life" when love comes to town; iconic "dance scenes" accentuate an "affecting" story with "dark" undercurrents that "perfectly evokes" "real life in Brooklyn" circa '77, even if some survivors of those "cheesy times" "feel embarrassed" about it now.

Satyricon 🄵
20 | 17 | 17 | 24

1969. Directed by Federico Fellini. With Martin Potter, Hiram Keller, Capucine, Alain Cuny. 129 minutes. Rated R.

"Nothing's sacred" in this "out-there" "hymn to decadence", a "provocative", "surreal" trip through Nero's Rome that's based on incomplete remnants of a satire by Petronius, which might explain its "oddly fragmented" structure ("can someone please tell me what it's about?"); definitely "not for everyone" (especially kids), this is "disturbing", ultra-"kinky" stuff – either "Fellini at his indulgent worst" or "awe-inspiring in its sheer extravagance."

Save the Last Dance
17 | 17 | 17 | 17

2001. Directed by Thomas Carter. With Julia Stiles, Sean Patrick Thomas, Kerry Washington. 112 minutes. Rated PG-13.

This "modern star-crossed-lovers" saga stars Stiles as a suburban teen transferred to an inner-city school where she falls into an interracial "across-the-tracks romance"; though the "textbook" set-ups "could have been more inventive", the picture imparts a "good message", abetted by a "great soundtrack", some "fancy footwork" and a climactic "hip-hop 'n' classical ballet."

SAVING PRIVATE RYAN ✉
26 | 26 | 24 | 28

1998. Directed by Steven Spielberg. With Tom Hanks, Tom Sizemore, Edward Burns. 170 minutes. Rated R.

"As intense as it gets", Steven Spielberg's "celluloid monument" to WWII evokes the fear of war with "in-your-face" footage like the "devastating" opening, a "masterful" montage of "graphic" death and mayhem on a D-day beachhead; thereafter Hanks leads a "superbly" cast unit through no-man's-land on a "compelling" quest for a missing grunt, and despite sniping that "the story bogs down", it's a "wrenching" oh-"so-real" reminder that "war is hell."

Saw ❷
18 | 17 | 22 | 19

2004. Directed by James Wan. With Leigh Whannell, Cary Elwes, Danny Glover. 100 minutes. Rated R.

"Graphic" and "gruesome", this "edge-of-your-seat thriller" is definitely "not for the squeamish" ("don't eat beforehand") in its story of two men chained in a lavatory with a hacksaw – for sawing off their own legs – their only means of escape; while hardcore aficionados dis the "lousy acting" and a "*Seven* rip-off" plot, many more praise its "real scares" and that "absolutely stunning ending" – "you won't see it coming."

Scarface
22 23 22 22

1983. Directed by Brian De Palma. With Al Pacino, Steven Bauer, Michelle Pfeiffer. 170 minutes. Rated R.
"Raw and fun all at once", this "benchmark" crime thriller about a Miami-based "Latin drug ring" is ultra-"intense" and "extravagantly bloody" ("close your eyes when they bring out that chainsaw!"); addicts attest that it's worth seeing for Pacino's "over-the-top" turn as the "kind of bad guy you could really like", but the unmoved sneer it's "ultimately unredeeming" – and too "profane" to boot ("how many times can you say the F-word?").

Scarlet Empress, The ◑
▽ 24 23 22 27

1934. Directed by Josef von Sternberg. With Marlene Dietrich, John Lodge, Sam Jaffe, Louise Dresser. 104 minutes. Not Rated.
"Spectacularly bizarre", this over-the-top take on the life of Catherine the Great is a "masterpiece of fantasy pretending to be biography" that's worth watching for its "dazzling" production values, period; La Dietrich enacts the title role in a "series of poses" lovingly lit by director von Sternberg, and even if it's "not *The Blue Angel*", this "delirious mess" is certainly "like nothing else you've ever seen."

Scenes from a Marriage 🅵
▽ 24 27 22 22

1973. Directed by Ingmar Bergman. With Liv Ullmann, Erland Josephson, Bibi Andersson. 168 minutes. Rated PG.
Originally a six-hour TV miniseries pared down to feature length, this still "powerful" portrayal of a "marriage breaking down" via Ingmar Bergman is a "real, poignant" tale told with such "rich execution" that it might "scare off all but the bravest from the altar"; though "hard to take for its intensity", this "talkathon" is worth seeing for its simply "astonishing performances."

Scent of a Woman ✉
21 25 21 21

1992. Directed by Martin Brest. With Al Pacino, Chris O'Donnell, Philip Seymour Hoffman. 157 minutes. Rated R.
Pacino's "bravura" Best Actor bit has him cast as a retired military man compensating for his visual impairment with an "abrasive personality" and "foghorn" pipes as he drags his "meek" preppy babysitter along for a wild weekend in the Naked City; where cynics see "hokum" that "tends to drag", fans of the "too-fabulous" Al find it worthwhile "for the tango scene" alone.

SCHINDLER'S LIST ✉◑
29 29 28 29

1993. Directed by Steven Spielberg. With Liam Neeson, Ben Kingsley, Ralph Fiennes. 197 minutes. Rated R.
Embarking on a "tour-de-force" "journey through a dark period", Spielberg's "direct", "painful" wartime drama "crystallizes" the "real-life horror" of the Holocaust in "stunning quasi-documentary" black-and-white, with Neeson as the man of "moral conscience" dealing with the Nazis in "shattering" circumstances; "beyond moving" and "tough to watch" in spite of its "understatement" and "touches of grace", it's a top Oscar honoree that's all-but-unanimously cited as "unforgettable required viewing."

School of Rock
20 | 20 | 20 | 19

2003. Directed by Richard Linklater. With Jack Black, Joan Cusack. 108 minutes. Rated PG-13.

"Jack Black's manic zeal" takes center stage in this comedy about a "selfish wannabe" pop star who learns "selflessness" and turns a "bunch of buttoned-up prep schoolers" into "rock monsters"; it's "cute" and "sappy" in a "predictable", "family-friendly" way, but the "infectious energy" embodies the "irreverent spirit of classic rock" well enough to appeal to "young and old alike."

Scream Ⅱ
20 | 16 | 21 | 19

1996. Directed by Wes Craven. With David Arquette, Neve Campbell, Courteney Cox. 111 minutes. Rated R.

In an "aptly titled" entry, *Nightmare on Elm Street*'s Wes Craven "revives" the horror genre by aiming "clever potshots" at a host of hackneyed "slasher-film" clichés, lending a "humorously self-aware twist" to a "fast-paced" story of a "slice-and-dice" psycho at large among suburban teens; sure, the picture "makes fun of itself", but it's still "scary stuff" that sets a suitably "bloody and gross" precedent for a "slew of imitators."

Seabiscuit
25 | 25 | 25 | 26

2003. Directed by Gary Ross. With Tobey Maguire, Jeff Bridges, Chris Cooper. 141 minutes. Rated PG-13.

Set against the "backdrop of the Great Depression", this "winning" adaptation of Laura Hillenbrand's best-selling pony tale trots out an "old-fashioned" story about a "little horse that could"; "moving" turns from Maguire, Bridges and Cooper (as jockey, owner and trainer) and "beautifully photographed", "suspenseful" racing sequences evoke cheers, even if a few find this gelding's gait a tad "slow", saying "it misses greatness by a nose."

SEARCHERS, THE
27 | 25 | 27 | 27

1956. Directed by John Ford. With John Wayne, Jeffrey Hunter, Vera Miles. 120 minutes. Not Rated.

"Not just a shoot-'em-up", this "thinking person's" Western boasts "peak" work from Wayne, who delivers a "gripping" portrayal of a "brooding" Civil War vet obsessed with tracking down his niece, abducted by Comanches; with its "spectacular" backdrops and "controversial" handling of "kinship and racism", it's much praised as "Ford's masterpiece", "perhaps the finest in the genre."

Secondhand Lions
22 | 25 | 22 | 22

2003. Directed by Tim McCanlies. With Michael Caine, Robert Duvall, Haley Joel Osment. 109 minutes. Rated PG.

A young boy spends the summer in the "middle of nowhere" with his "eccentric uncles" in this "family-friendly", "feel-good" flicker that teaches "moral lessons about integrity and honor", yet is still "fun to watch"; as two "grumpy old men" weaving "tall tales from truth", Caine and Duvall exhibit "perfect timing", despite a somewhat "corny", "predictable" premise.

Secretary
21 | 24 | 20 | 19

2002. Directed by Steven Shainberg. With James Spader, Maggie Gyllenhaal. 104 minutes. Rated R.

A "repressed" attorney "takes out his do-as-I-say delights on his all-too-willing secretary" in this "brilliant black comedy" (or is it a "kinky love story"?) that "makes you realize there's someone for everyone"; "hilarious characters", "interesting plot twists" and "superb acting" add up to an "ass-spanking good time."

Secret of NIMH, The ⑪   24 | – | 25 | 24
1982. Directed by Don Bluth. Animated. 82 minutes. Rated G.
From the all-pro pens of "former Disney artists" comes this "freaky", oft-"forgotten" "alternative to sugar-coated" animation, a "beautifully drawn gem" of a barnyard yarn about a mama mouse desperately seeking a new nest for her brood; the "captivating" depiction of farm life comes with "character development" and an "interesting" story designed to appeal to the "adult" in everyone.

Secrets and Lies   24 | 27 | 24 | 22
1996. Directed by Mike Leigh. With Brenda Blethyn, Marianne Jean-Baptiste. 136 minutes. Rated R.
Bad boy Leigh turns "accessible" in this "smart", "solid British drama" of "long-lost" family ties concerning a young black Londoner who "searches out her biological mother" only to find out that mum may be a working-class white woman; led by Blethyn's "pure, honest performance", the principals do a "terrific job" of making this tale "involving" and "heartbreaking."

Sense and Sensibility ✉   26 | 27 | 26 | 26
1995. Directed by Ang Lee. With Emma Thompson, Alan Rickman, Kate Winslet, Hugh Grant. 136 minutes. Rated PG.
"Jane Austen would have liked" this "bittersweet" story of two husband-hunting sisters that "captures the true flavor" of her novel "with wit and honesty" largely due to a "strong", Oscar-winning script from the "so-fine" Emma Thompson; sensitive types tout the "beautiful" scenery, director Lee's "brilliant" job and an ensemble cast that "rises to the occasion" – "this is what moviemaking should be."

Serenity   23 | 22 | 23 | 24
2005. Directed by Joss Whedon. With Nathan Fillion, Gina Torres, Alan Tudyk. 119 minutes. Rated PG-13.
A big-screen adaptation of the "short-lived" "cult" TV series *Firefly*, this "enjoyable" sci-fi/Western spins an "innovative" outer-space adventure enlivened by "solid" FX and a "memorable" cast of "relative unknowns" armed with a payload of "witty lines"; advice to the "uninitiated": viewing the original show "isn't mandatory", but it might make the "convoluted" story less "confusing."

Sergeant York ✉◐∅   ▽ 24 | 24 | 23 | 21
1941. Directed by Howard Hawks. With Gary Cooper, Walter Brennan, Joan Leslie. 134 minutes. Not Rated.
A "true story that needs no amplification", this "satisfying" biopic stars an Oscar-winning Cooper as the pacifist who became WWI's most decorated soldier after single-handedly dismantling an enemy regiment; a "complex" piece of pro-war propaganda, it's also a "great depiction" of a man of "quiet inner strength."

Serpico   23 | 26 | 24 | 21
1973. Directed by Sidney Lumet. With Al Pacino, John Randolph, Tony Roberts. 129 minutes. Rated R.
Honesty "doesn't pay" in this "gritty" true story starring a "superb" Pacino as a whistle-blowing NYPD do-gooder who becomes a "man alone" when his exposure of "cop corruption" threatens to

bring down the whole city; if all the "raw emotion" can grow "frustrating" and the milieu seems "a bit dated", it remains arresting as a "compelling commentary on the times."

Servant, The ◑
25 | 27 | 25 | 23
1963. Directed by Joseph Losey. With Dirk Bogarde, James Fox, Sarah Miles, Wendy Craig. 112 minutes. Not Rated.
The "British class structure" gets the Harold Pinter treatment in this "dark", "nasty piece of work" detailing the "power struggle" between a "menacing butler" and his "decadent", weak-willed master; in the title role, the "peerless" Bogarde is so "appropriately creepy" that some consider "giving up their household staff."

Seven
23 | 23 | 24 | 23
1995. Directed by David Fincher. With Brad Pitt, Morgan Freeman, Kevin Spacey. 123 minutes. Rated R.
All the "elegant nastiness" of a "guided tour through hell" surfaces in this "macabre psychological thriller" about two big-city detectives on the trail of an "ingenious" serial killer who dreams up "genuinely disturbing" torments "based on the seven deadly sins"; an "unrelenting" dose of "creepy modern noir" at its "darkest", it's wickedly "riveting" and "impressive" but "hard-to-take" and "gruesome" – with "no happy ending."

Seven Beauties 🅵
▽ 25 | 26 | 24 | 23
1976. Directed by Lina Wertmüller. With Giancarlo Giannini, Fernando Rey, Shirley Stoler. 115 minutes. Rated R.
Wertmüller's "extraordinary" exploration of "survival in WWII" stars Giannini as a Chaplin-esque romeo trying to stay alive in a German concentration camp; a "brilliant" "amalgam of comedy and drama", it's a "powerful introduction to foreign filmmaking."

Seven Brides for Seven Brothers
24 | 20 | 21 | 25
1954. Directed by Stanley Donen. With Howard Keel, Jane Powell, Russ Tamblyn. 103 minutes. Rated G.
Ok, it's "low on feasibility", but this "down-home" musical of "seven eligible backwoodsmen looking for love" with a septet of hillbilly "Sabine women" strikes "pure gold" with its "great Johnny Mercer" tunes and "extraordinary" choreography; fans dig its "exuberant" production numbers so "athletic" they "make dance macho", particularly that "barn-raising scene."

Seven Days in May ◑
26 | 24 | 28 | 22
1964. Directed by John Frankenheimer. With Burt Lancaster, Kirk Douglas, Fredric March. 118 minutes. Not Rated.
"It could happen here", or so says this "riveting 'what-if' drama", a "scary" Cold War story about disgruntled Pentagon brass who lay plans for a "military takeover"; soldiering along with "well-plotted" plausibility and "Douglas and Lancaster turning up the star heat", it's a "powerful nail-biter" that "political junkies" consider – gulp – "as timely today as ever."

SEVEN SAMURAI, THE ◑🅵
29 | 27 | 28 | 27
1956. Directed by Akira Kurosawa. With Toshiro Mifune, Takashi Shimura. 203 minutes. Not Rated.
Credited with "defining its own genre", Kurosawa's "awesome", "pivotal" Japanese adventure introduces the "original magnificent seven" as old-time samurai "warrior-heroes" who rise to the defense of a village menaced by a "vicious band of marauders";

the "epic running time melts away" before the "exciting" display of "honor", "courage" and "classic swordplay", and though there are "countless" reworkings, connoisseurs claim this "way-cool prototype" is "far superior."

1776 `22` `22` `24` `23`
1972. Directed by Peter H. Hunt. With William Daniels, Howard da Silva, Blythe Danner. 142 minutes. Rated G.
Put away the books and take an "entertaining shortcut" to U.S. history via this "faithful" rendering of the Broadway musical, a "patriotic pageant" wherein periwigged radicals assemble in Philly and wrangle over the Declaration of Independence, backed up by "wonderful music and lyrics"; it's a "smart", "informative" way to "put a face" on "those lovable founding fathers", and they turn out to be "such great singers" – "who knew?"

Seventh Seal, The ◑🅵 `27` `27` `26` `26`
1957. Directed by Ingmar Bergman. With Max von Sydow, Gunnar Björnstrand, Nils Poppe. 96 minutes. Not Rated.
An utterly foreign flick and staple of "college days", Bergman's "challenging" drama is a "dark allegory" with von Sydow as a "knight returning from the Crusades to plague-swept Europe" only to hunker down for a high-stakes "chess game with Death"; as a "cerebral" meditation on the "meaning of existence", it seals the deal with "some of the greatest visuals ever" and a "symbolic story" that "makes everything else look like a game of checkers."

7th Voyage of Sinbad, The `20` `12` `20` `22`
1958. Directed by Nathan Juran. With Kerwin Mathews, Kathryn Grant, Torin Thatcher. 88 minutes. Rated G.
"Amazing for its time", this "delightful" adventure "throwback" "makes myth real without computers" using '50s-era FX to summon up a host of "lovingly created monsters"; ok, the "Saturday-matinee" storyline is "standard cheese", but it's a "fondly remembered fantasy" for fans who happily "take it for what it is."

Seven Year Itch, The `23` `23` `20` `20`
1955. Directed by Billy Wilder. With Marilyn Monroe, Tom Ewell, Evelyn Keyes. 105 minutes. Not Rated.
Marilyn's billowing-dress "subway-grate scene" is the iconic moment in this "enjoyable" comedy, which finds "ordinary guy" Ewell "on his own" when the wife and kiddies split for summer vacation simultaneous with the arrival of his new neighbor, a most "memorable" Monroe in full "innocent-sexpot" mode, who brings on a major "midlife crisis"; sure, the repartee seems "dated and stagy", but it can still tickle the "funny" bone.

Sex, Lies and Videotape `19` `20` `20` `18`
1989. Directed by Steven Soderbergh. With James Spader, Andie MacDowell, Peter Gallagher. 98 minutes. Rated R.
Wounded libidos fight the "battles of the sexes" in this "fresh take" on the "deterioration of relationships", a "simple", "well-crafted" drama about a college chum visiting an unhappily married couple and getting some pretty spicy tell-all on videotape; it's an "intelligent", insightful look at the "permissive age" heated up by erotic "suspense" more than "actual" on-screen whoopee, though those who spurn "loser" characters find it "hard to care about."

Shadow of a Doubt ◐　　26 | 26 | 26 | 25
1943. Directed by Alfred Hitchcock. With Teresa Wright, Joseph Cotten, Macdonald Carey. 108 minutes. Not Rated.
Hitchcock's "first truly American film" (and his "personal favorite"), this "dark" thriller is set in a "sunny", "Norman Rockwell"–esque town that's home to a "young girl and her mysterious yet appealing uncle" who's suspected of murder; the "is-he-or-isn't-he" plot works thanks to the "spot-on" Cotten, whose performance is "chilling" enough for you to consider "background checks on your own family."

Shadow of the Vampire　　20 | 25 | 20 | 23
2000. Directed by E. Elias Merhige. With John Malkovich, Willem Dafoe, Cary Elwes. 92 minutes. Rated R.
Maybe it's "not scary", but this "behind-the-scenes" drama does apply a few shadowy "touches of horror" as it chronicles the "legendary production" of the fiendish '20s masterwork *Nosferatu*; Dafoe does a "great job" vamping as an undead actor with an "evil" hankering for hemoglobin, but foes call it a "disappointing" "art-house mess" that's "not sharp" enough to draw blood.

SHAKESPEARE IN LOVE ✉　　24 | 25 | 24 | 26
1998. Directed by John Madden. With Gwyneth Paltrow, Geoffrey Rush, Joseph Fiennes, Judi Dench. 122 minutes. Rated R.
"Whether it be true or not", this "lush, literate" romance is a "good-humored confection" that "lights up the screen" with "adorable" performances from Fiennes (an "ink-stained" Elizabethan scribe) whose "writer's block" is cleared by the "exquisitely attired" Paltrow (his not-so-secret admirer); a "rich" depiction of the age "laced with dialogue" from the plays, it's a "captivating", "rip-roaring" ride that's "accessible at any level."

Shampoo　　16 | 16 | 15 | 16
1975. Directed by Hal Ashby. With Warren Beatty, Julie Christie, Goldie Hawn, Lee Grant, Carrie Fisher. 109 minutes. Rated R.
Starring a "state-of-the-art Warren Beatty at his prettiest", this bedroom farce unfolds over election day, 1968, and follows the "hysterical" ups and downs of a randy hairdresser bouncing around Beverly Hills; both Christie and Hawn are a "blast", the premise is "very funny" and the "bittersweet" ending is a "touching" surprise.

Shane　　26 | 25 | 25 | 25
1953. Directed by George Stevens. With Alan Ladd, Jean Arthur, Van Heflin. 118 minutes. Not Rated.
There's "always a nuance to savor" in this "towering", "classic" Western, telling the "mythical American" tale of a "world-weary gunslinger forced out of retirement" when he sides with a homesteader family menaced by "ruthless cattle ranchers"; the "poignant" setup pays off with a "great finale" as Ladd walks tall in a showdown with "no-good" varmint Jack Palance, leading many oater voters to name it "best" in the West.

Shark Tale　　19 | – | 18 | 23
2004. Directed by Bibo Bergeron, Vicky Jenson, Rob Letterman. Animated. 90 minutes. Rated PG.
A "whale-size list of celeb voices" (Robert De Niro, Renée Zellweger, Angelina Jolie) adds buoyancy to this aquatic-themed cartoon that desperately "wants to be *Finding Nemo*" but just "isn't

in the same league"; still, it "tries hard" with a positive, "be-your-self" message for the kiddies and "cute sight gags" for their parents (e.g. the "characters' resemblance to the actors who voice them").

Shattered Glass | 21 | 23 | 24 | 19 |
2003. Directed by Billy Ray. With Hayden Christensen, Peter Sarsgaard, Chloë Sevigny. 95 minutes. Rated PG-13.
A "smart surprise" reminiscent of "*All the President's Men*", this story of a "gifted journalist who self-destructs" after "making up articles for the *New Republic*" is an "engrossing" look at "how the media manipulates what the public sees"; though it "drags a tad", Christensen delivers a "surprisingly mature performance."

Shaun of the Dead | 22 | 19 | 22 | 20 |
2004. Directed by Edgar Wright. With Simon Pegg, Kate Ashfield, Nick Frost. 99 minutes. Not Rated.
Leave it to "those crazy Brits" to concoct this "groovy" "send-up of zombie movies" combining equal doses of "campy fun" and "all-out horror bloodbath" to give you "giggles with your chills"; geeks advise watching some "George Romero flicks" first to "get all the references", but if that's not doable, "a few pints of ale" should be sufficient to prime your "brainnnnssss."

SHAWSHANK REDEMPTION, THE | 28 | 28 | 28 | 27 |
1994. Directed by Frank Darabont. With Tim Robbins, Morgan Freeman, Bob Gunton. 142 minutes. Rated R.
Finding the "stirring" in the stir and big hearts in the big house, this "first-rate" "gripper" of a prison drama goes behind the walls of a "dismal" state pen to follow fellow lifers Robbins and Freeman on a "long, dark journey" that pits "friendship", "ingenu-ity and inner strength" against a "brutal, corrupt system"; besides the "marvelous acting", there's a last-reel "surprise" to add a "feel-good factor" and even some "hope."

Sheltering Sky, The | 16 | 19 | 15 | 21 |
1990. Directed by Bernardo Bertolucci. With Debra Winger, John Malkovich, Campbell Scott. 138 minutes. Rated R.
"Morocco never looked so beautiful" as in this "gorgeously filmed" adaptation of Paul Bowles' existential novel about a couple's aim-less roaming around North Africa in the hope of rekindling their romance; many report it's "rambling" and "pretentious", with too much "sand" and not enough plot, so "to avoid disappointment, see the movie first and then read the book."

She Wore a Yellow Ribbon | 24 | 22 | 23 | 25 |
1949. Directed by John Ford. With John Wayne, Joanne Dru, John Agar, Ben Johnson. 103 minutes. Not Rated.
Ford's second bugle blast in his "cavalry trilogy" finds the direc-tor "at his best" in a tribute to the "honor and tradition" of horse soldiers posted to the frontier; the Duke is typically "bigger than life" as a stiff-brimmed but sympathetic old man about to hang up his hat after a career in Injun territory, all portrayed against boundlessly "beautiful" big-sky scenery – "what else does a Western need?"

Shine ✉ | 22 | 25 | 21 | 21 |
1996. Directed by Scott Hicks. With Geoffrey Rush, Armin Mueller-Stahl, Lynn Redgrave. 105 minutes. Rated PG-13.
"Mad musician makes good" in this "enlightening", "uplifting true story" about a gifted Australian pianist who succeeds in the

shadow of an inflexible father but succumbs to a "harrowing" bout with schizophrenia – only to return to the bench for a midlife comeback; Rush's "compelling" turn keeps things uptempo, and if some dub it an "overrated curiosity", more offer bravos for a portrait that "shines" from first movement to last.

Shining, The
25 | 26 | 25 | 25

1980. Directed by Stanley Kubrick. With Jack Nicholson, Shelley Duvall, Scatman Crothers. 146 minutes. Rated R.

The "supernatural and psychotic" collide in this "revolutionary horror film", a "downright scary" story from the Stephen King novel about a "snowbound caretaker of an old hotel" running amok; though voters agree that the "elevator scene", "Diane Arbus twin girls" and "gloriously unhinged Nicholson" all shine, Duvall gets mixed marks: "intensely annoying" vs. "profoundly brilliant"; best line, no contest: "heeere's Johnny!"

Ship of Fools ◑
23 | 25 | 24 | 23

1965. Directed by Stanley Kramer. With Vivien Leigh, Simone Signoret, José Ferrer, Lee Marvin, Oskar Werner, Elizabeth Ashley, George Segal, Michael Dunn. 149 minutes. Not Rated.

A "touching but loaded adaptation" of the Katherine Anne Porter novel, this "clever" drama follows a clutch of characters "aboard an ocean liner" traveling from Mexico to Germany "on the eve of WWII"; while sinkers shrug it off as "hammy", "soap operatic" stuff (think *Grand Hotel* at sea), far more feel the "all-star" international cast is worth watching, notably the "memorable" Signoret, "standout" Werner and "heartbreaking" Leigh, who's "too convincing as a faded beauty."

Shipping News, The
18 | 21 | 17 | 21

2001. Directed by Lasse Hallström. With Kevin Spacey, Julianne Moore, Judi Dench. 111 minutes. Rated R.

Based on the best-selling book, this drama tells the "strange story" of a "hopeless mope" doing drudge work at a small-town gazette who gets a "second chance" when his wife dies and he ships out to the Newfoundland coast; though it's praised as "ultimately optimistic", foes torpedo the "overblown", "contrived" production as a "lackluster" Miramax bid for the Oscar race.

Shirley Valentine
24 | 24 | 23 | 20

1989. Directed by Lewis Gilbert. With Pauline Collins, Tom Conti, Alison Steadman. 108 minutes. Rated R.

A real "charmer" with a "Liverpudlian accent", this "spirited" comedy sends a "terrific message" with its "sweet midlife fantasy" of a "bored English housewife" who flees to the Aegean "looking for love" and nets Greek sailor Conti; adapted from the "superb" stage show, it "loses nothing in the translation" as a "wise" celebration of "independence and self-respect."

SHOAH ▣
28 | – | 28 | 26

1985. Directed by Claude Lanzmann. Documentary. 563 minutes. Not Rated.

"Not a film to watch casually", this documentary addresses the "horror of the Holocaust" through "first-hand accounts" as a "necessary antidote" to "one of the worst episodes in human history"; Lanzmann uses witnesses from both sides of the "barbed-wire fence" to record their "intense", "shattering" memories of an entire society's "complicity", and "emotions pour out" over "eight hours of painful viewing" that are "impossibly sad and difficult" – but "worth all of it."

Shoot the Piano Player ❶⨍ | 25 | 24 | 23 | 22 |
1962. Directed by François Truffaut. With Charles Aznavour, Marie Dubois, Nicole Berger. 84 minutes. Not Rated.
Beside the "great title", Truffaut's "stylized" sophomore effort is a "slightly weird" combination of Gallic satire and American gangster picture that features a "not-so-romantic view of Paris"; its "unusual" story of a former concert pianist mixed up with hooligans may be "for movie lovers only", but cineasts advise "see it with small expectations and you'll be rewarded."

Shot in the Dark, A ⑪ | 23 | 22 | 20 | 20 |
1964. Directed by Blake Edwards. With Peter Sellers, Elke Sommer, George Sanders. 102 minutes. Rated PG.
Sort of a cub *Pink Panther,* this "laugh-aloud funny" comedy features a "brilliant" Sellers as the clueless Inspector Clouseau, bumbling his way through a "delicious red-herring salad" of a plot that finds him assigned to solve a murder pinned on a Parisian chambermaid; if the "charmingly quirky" setup has its "slow" moments, the "master" makes it watchable "for his accent alone."

Show Boat | 23 | 20 | 24 | 25 |
1951. Directed by George Sidney. With Kathryn Grayson, Ava Gardner, Howard Keel. 107 minutes. Not Rated.
The "schmaltzy" but "fabulous" Broadway hit gets the Technicolor treatment in this "sterling MGM musical" about a showgirl's entanglement with a riverboat gambler; the big wheel paddles along to "unforgettable" songs, "solid production numbers" and hoofers who "dance up a storm", and if purists prefer 1936's "glory-days" version, most can't help lovin' dat "beautiful, melodic" spectacle.

Showgirls | 5 | 4 | 4 | 10 |
1995. Directed by Paul Verhoeven. With Elizabeth Berkley, Kyle MacLachlan, Gina Gershon. 131 minutes. Rated NC-17.
Alright already, "nobody expected Shakespeare", but this "sorry" saga of a stripper hell-bent on becoming a Vegas showgirl is one truly "tacky", "pointless" enterprise, with "absolutely no redeeming value" and an NC-17 rating to boot; for "camp" followers, however, it's "unintentionally funny" (sort of a "nudie" version of *"All About Eve"*) and "so awful it's wonderful"; biggest howler: the "swimming pool sex scene."

SHREK ⑪ | 26 | – | 25 | 28 |
2001. Directed by Andrew Adamson, Vicky Jenson. Animated. 90 minutes. Rated PG.
They "added a category" on Oscar night to honor this "playfully creative original" that uses "exceptional" CGI animation and "great voicing" to rework a "hoary storyline" about an ogre saving a princess into "highly entertaining" fare; it challenges the "Disney fairy-tale formula" with adult-level "parody" and "inside jokes" underscored with a "positive message" for all.

Shrek 2 | 26 | – | 24 | 28 |
2004. Directed by Andrew Adamson, Kelly Asbury, Conrad Vernon. Animated. 92 minutes. Rated PG.
"Another ogre-achiever", this "worthy sequel" once again features "incredible animation so lifelike you forget it's animation",

"star voice actors" (Mike Myers, Eddie Murphy, Cameron Diaz) and a "laugh-out-loud" love story that sends up classic fairy-tale films; the "sly" satire and "clever" dialogue are "as much fun for adults as for the kids", and new addition Antonio Banderas — "purrfect as Puss 'n' Boots" — nearly "steals the movie."

Sid & Nancy
18 | 20 | 18 | 16

1986. Directed by Alex Cox. With Gary Oldman, Chloe Webb, David Hayman. 112 minutes. Rated R.
An "absolutely demented but totally compelling love story", this "gripping" slice of "rock history" details the rise and fall of the "Sex Pistols' wildest member", featuring a "convincing Oldman" as Sid Vicious and the "scarily real" Webb as his "crazy girlfriend"; though the story of their downward, drug-laden spiral is not for the faint-hearted, groupies dig it 'cause it's "dark, ugly and vibrant all at once."

Sideways
23 | 26 | 22 | 22

2004. Directed by Alexander Payne. With Paul Giamatti, Thomas Haden Church, Virginia Madsen, Sandra Oh. 123 minutes. Rated R.
Oenophiles toast this "intoxicatingly hilarious" road tripper pitting Giamatti's "shlub" against Church's "crack-up" for a Bacchian weekend of "middle-aged angst"–inspired "debauchery" in "scenic California wine country"; the "literate", Oscar-winning script uncorks some "wonderfully painful" scenes that are "so real" it's "like watching a train wreck", though a few whine it's just a "mundane soaper" with as much depth as a "glass of merlot."

Signs
18 | 20 | 18 | 20

2002. Directed by M. Night Shyamalan. With Mel Gibson, Joaquin Phoenix, Rory Culkin. 106 minutes. Rated PG-13.
Farmer Mel Gibson finds weird "crop circles" in his cornfields in this "paranormal" thriller from M. Night Shyamalan that delivers a "good number of jump-out-of-your-seat moments"; some say it's a really "religious movie disguised as science fiction" ("I've coughed up scarier things"), yet there's a "creepy realness" about it that keeps the mood "tense."

SILENCE OF THE LAMBS, THE ✉ ❶
27 | 28 | 27 | 26

1991. Directed by Jonathan Demme. With Jodie Foster, Anthony Hopkins, Scott Glenn. 118 minutes. Rated R.
Every subsequent "psych-profiling" flick owes something to this "masterful", "profoundly creepy" thriller that combines "heart-thumping suspense" with "premier" performances as Foster, an FBI greenhorn on a serial-killer hunt, is drawn into "intense mind games" with the "soft-spoken" madman Hopkins; its "well-deserved Oscars" speak for its "twisted", "truly terrifying" achievement, though some say it "gives fava beans a bad name."

Silkwood
22 | 26 | 25 | 21

1983. Directed by Mike Nichols. With Meryl Streep, Kurt Russell, Cher, Craig T. Nelson. 131 minutes. Rated R.
This "somewhat forgotten" drama generates a "great deal of tension" telling the fact-based story of a whistle-blowing nuclear plant worker who comes to a "mysterious end" when she tries to go public with hazardous goings-on at the facility; lit up by "terrific acting" from "marvelous" Meryl and "eye-opener" Cher, it's a "moving" picture of blue-collar good guys vs. white-collar baddies.

Silverado
| 24 | 24 | 23 | 24 |

1985. Directed by Lawrence Kasdan. With Kevin Kline, Scott Glenn, Kevin Costner. 127 minutes. Rated PG-13.

Boys, the "fun Western" rides again in this "well-made" "modern horse opera", a "true homage" that "throws in all the clichés" and delivers some "slick sequences" and "great one-liners" of its own; a "tremendous" cast "manages to upstage the glorious scenery", though it's best appreciated on the "biggest screen you can find."

Silver Streak
| 19 | 19 | 18 | 19 |

1976. Directed by Arthur Hiller. With Gene Wilder, Richard Pryor, Jill Clayburgh. 114 minutes. Rated PG.

"One of the best comedy teams on film" gets its "first pairing" in this "slick takeoff" on Hitchcock-style "train capers", featuring Wilder in the "amusing" role of an innocent railroaded in an art-world murder only to find himself on the run along with the "beyond-funny" Pryor; devotees call it "enjoyable" and "underappreciated."

Simple Plan, A
| 19 | 22 | 22 | 19 |

1998. Directed by Sam Raimi. With Bill Paxton, Bridget Fonda, Billy Bob Thornton. 121 minutes. Rated R.

B-movie maestro Raimi's "entry into respectable filmdom" is a "well-paced thriller" with a "convincing" scenario about a rustic threesome in the backwoods who stumble upon a wrecked plane and a bag of cash; "plot-twisting" and "suspense" ensue as lives "unravel" in a "tragic" parable of the "evils of ill-gotten gain" that makes it the "*Treasure of the Sierra Madre*" for the "*Fargo*" crowd.

Sin City
| 22 | 21 | 20 | 26 |

2005. Directed by Frank Miller, Robert Rodriguez, Quentin Tarantino. With Bruce Willis, Mickey Rourke, Jessica Alba, Clive Owen, Elijah Wood. 124 minutes. Not Rated.

"Not for the faint of heart", this "sin-tillating" noir take on a pulp comic book series is "gritty" and "ultra-violent", with a "meandering storyline" played out in a "wonderful" mix of black-and-white live action and colorful "comic animation"; a "'roided-up Rourke" makes his "comeback", Wood does "Frodo-turned-psycho" and a "scantily clad" Alba does tricks with a "lasso."

SINGIN' IN THE RAIN
| 28 | 26 | 25 | 28 |

1952. Directed by Stanley Donen, Gene Kelly. With Gene Kelly, Donald O'Connor, Debbie Reynolds. 103 minutes. Rated G.

"Giddy", "wet and wonderful", this "timeless" musical brightens the worst day with an "exuberant" "something-for-everyone" blend of "quintessential" song and dance, "satire" and a "sappy, funny love story"; the "flawless" Kelly plays a silent movie star in a "sweet send-up" of Hollywood's early talkie days and effortlessly executes the puddle-hopping "title number", leaving fans "awed."

Single White Female
| 16 | 18 | 17 | 15 |

1992. Directed by Barbet Schroeder. With Bridget Fonda, Jennifer Jason Leigh, Steven Weber. 107 minutes. Rated R.

"Watch your back!": this "roommate-from-hell thriller" "keeps you on edge" with its "sick vulgarity" and mounting "suspense"; though the trading-identities storyline might be "derivative", the picture's still "full of surprises" and "done well" enough to "make you think it could actually happen"; P.S. brace yourself for a particularly "nasty ending."

Sister Act ⓤ

18 | 18 | 17 | 17

1992. Directed by Emile Ardolino. With Whoopi Goldberg, Maggie Smith, Kathy Najimy. 100 minutes. Rated PG.
Whoopi gets a witness protection program in this "engaging" "fish-out-of-water comedy" about a lounge diva who sings for the cops after her beau commits homicide, only to find herself stashed in "nun other than" a convent; the verdict: a "guilty pleasure" that rises above the "run of the mill" with "cool" musical interludes.

Sisterhood of the Traveling Pants, The

19 | 19 | 20 | 19

2005. Directed by Ken Kwapis. With Amber Tamblyn, Alexis Bledel, America Ferrera, Blake Lively. 119 minutes. Rated PG.
The "angst"-ridden "summer adventures" of four "very different" teen girls are sewn together by a "pair of magical pants" in this "charming" coming-of-ager featuring an "adorable" cast of young actresses; sure, it's a "tear-jerking" "chick flick if there ever was one", but its one-size-fits-all spirit means "even males" may be reaching for a "hankie."

Sisters

▽ 22 | 21 | 23 | 20

1973. Directed by Brian De Palma. With Margot Kidder, Jennifer Salt, Charles Durning. 92 minutes. Rated R.
"De Palma does Hitchcock" ("again") in this "tense", "really scary" thriller about a pair of "warped" Siamese twins, recently separated; filmed on Staten Island for what looks like a "$2.50" budget, it's most "memorable" for Bernard Herrmann's "excellent score" and some "great acting" from a "pre–Lois Lane" Kidder.

Six Degrees of Separation

21 | 24 | 23 | 20

1993. Directed by Fred Schepisi. With Will Smith, Stockard Channing, Donald Sutherland. 112 minutes. Rated R.
"Great performances" ensure this "intriguing" "stage-to-screen" drama "adjusts quite nicely" to celluloid as a "sublime" Channing offers an encore of her theatrical role opposite a "young" Smith in the "challenging" part of a "charming hustler" posing as Sidney Poitier's son; it draws applause as a "clever" critique of "moneyed values" that's "surprisingly strong."

Sixteen Candles

22 | 18 | 21 | 19

1984. Directed by John Hughes. With Molly Ringwald, Justin Henry, Anthony Michael Hall. 93 minutes. Rated PG.
"Ringwald will steal your heart" in this "sweet coming-of-age classic", a "day-in-the-life" comedy that conveys the "teen angst" of high school, "first love and puberty" as seen through the eyes of a 16-year-old "birthday girl whom everyone forgot"; though its "damn funny" "Brat Pack" cast "characterizes the '80s to a tee", modernists who love this "brilliant" send-up "can still relate to it."

SIXTH SENSE, THE

26 | 25 | 27 | 25

1999. Directed by M. Night Shyamalan. With Bruce Willis, Haley Joel Osment, Toni Collette. 107 minutes. Rated PG-13.
A "tricky" one, this mega-hit thriller "surprises even the most astute" with its "perfectly crafted story" of a troubled boy with an "unwelcome gift" who finds a friend in Willis, leading to "really spooky" plot developments; it's hailed as an "unpredictable" sensation that rewards with "white-knuckle jolts" and a "stunning" "O. Henry"–esque ending.

Slap Shot ⑪

`22` `18` `19` `17`

1977. Directed by George Roy Hill. With Paul Newman, Michael Ontkean, Strother Martin. 122 minutes. Rated R.

Right up there with the "funniest sports flicks", this puckish comedy finds "Newman on skates" as the "foul-mouthed coach" of a "dark horse" minor-league hockey team with a "strange way" of turning every face-off into a riot on ice; it "epitomizes the goonery" of the high-sticking '70s, resulting in "crazy", "profane" and "fairly violent" fare that hard-core fans "cannot live without."

Sleeper

`23` `19` `23` `20`

1973. Directed by Woody Allen. With Woody Allen, Diane Keaton, John Beck. 89 minutes. Rated PG.

Orwell's wake-up call has nothing on this "inspired sci-fi spoof", a "hilarious" comedy of a nebbishy NYer who's cryogenically preserved then "defrosted in the future"; "laced with fast-paced verbal" cracks, it's "vintage" Allen at his "goofiest" and "most slapsticky" in a romp that generates "nonstop laughs" – the "orgasmatron alone is worth the price of admission."

Sleeping Beauty

`25` `–` `23` `25`

1959. Directed by Clyde Geronimi. Animated. 75 minutes. Rated G.

No snooze among the "old Disney greats", this "lushly animated" "princess movie" has a trio of good fairies protecting the titular knockout from an evil spell by zapping her into a sound nap, interrupted only after her true love battles it out with filmdom's most fearsome dragon lady; the very wicked witch may be "too scary for the little ones", but most say this "classic" only "gets better with age."

Sleeping with the Enemy

`17` `18` `18` `17`

1991. Directed by Joseph Ruben. With Julia Roberts, Patrick Bergin, Kevin Anderson. 99 minutes. Rated R.

"Harrowing scenes of spousal abuse" supply the "scary edge" in this "Julia Roberts vehicle" about a "murderous husband and the wife determined to get away from him"; though it strikes a few as "overwrought and cartoonish", this thriller makes others "think long and hard" about a problem that could be "more common than we think."

Sleepless in Seattle

`21` `22` `22` `21`

1993. Directed by Nora Ephron. With Tom Hanks, Meg Ryan, Rosie O'Donnell. 105 minutes. Rated PG.

Although pretty "predictable", this Ephron romance "works", renewing faith in the "soul-mate concept" as the "perfectly cast", "totally lovable" Hanks and Ryan make "a great match" in the story of a woman who pursues a lonely-hearts stranger cross country; sure, this "toothache-sweet trifle" is "a bit far-fetched" ("at least Harry *met* Sally"), but it's also a "funny", "male-tolerable chick flick" that's likely to spring eternal for "hopeless romantics."

Sleepy Hollow

`17` `18` `17` `23`

1999. Directed by Tim Burton. With Johnny Depp, Christina Ricci, Miranda Richardson. 105 minutes. Rated R.

All your "decapitation entertainment needs will be fulfilled" in this "engrossing" rendition of Washington Irving's "headless horseman fable", a "funny but gory" ride from Tim Burton that's a "wonderful update of the Hammer horror films"; Depp is "daringly unconventional", and the "eye-popping" cinematography is "visually splendid" – so it's alright to nod off during that "big Hollywood action finale."

Sleuth
25 | 28 | 26 | 23

1972. Directed by Joseph L. Mankiewicz. With Laurence Olivier, Michael Caine. 138 minutes. Rated PG.
It's no mystery why this suspense thriller based on the Broadway smash adapts "wonderfully to film": "masters-at-work" Olivier and Caine offer "witty", "subtle" work as a cuckolded writer and his rival engaged in a calculated confrontation in an English country manor; the "creative" story builds "numerous plot twists" that cross and double-cross, and "two of the greatest" muster up some of the liveliest back-and-forth volleys ever seen "outside of Wimbledon."

Sling Blade ✉
25 | 27 | 25 | 22

1996. Directed by Billy Bob Thornton. With Billy Bob Thornton, Dwight Yoakam, J.T. Walsh. 135 minutes. Rated R.
"Too convincing" in the role that lands him "on the map", "creepy Billy Bob" is "brilliantly believable" in this "tragedy from the real world" playing a slow-witted country boy who's sprung from the state booby hatch and taken in by a single mom; a "unique, touching" drama of man trouble, it "earns every accolade" with "excellent acting" and an "unforgettable punch" at the climax.

Smiles of a Summer Night ◑🅕
26 | 26 | 25 | 26

1957. Directed by Ingmar Bergman. With Ulla Jacobsson, Eva Dahlbeck, Gunnar Björnstrand. 108 minutes. Not Rated.
For "Bergman without the angst", check out his "rare venture" into romantic comedy, this "sumptuous" tale of love, desire and "what it means to be human" set in fin de siècle Sweden; probably the director's "lightest, most approachable" film, it was "most influential" to a generation of artists, and best known today as the inspiration for Sondheim's *A Little Night Music*.

Smokey and the Bandit ⓔ
16 | 13 | 15 | 15

1977. Directed by Hal Needham. With Burt Reynolds, Sally Field, Jackie Gleason. 96 minutes. Rated PG.
This "good ol' boys car chase" comedy is a rootin' tootin' good "road movie" about a cross-country "race against time"; sure, it's "corny", "cheaply made" stuff based on what appears to be an improvised script, but in the end, it's plain that "everyone's having fun", particularly the "dynamite duo" of Reynolds and Field.

Snake Pit, The ◑
25 | 28 | 25 | 24

1948. Directed by Anatole Litvak. With Olivia de Havilland, Mark Stevens, Leo Genn, Celeste Holm. 108 minutes. Not Rated.
"Daring for its time", this "hair-raising" depiction of conditions inside a mental institution was made during the postwar "heyday of psychoanalytic films" and is "still frightening" today; in addition to de Havilland's "sensitive", Oscar-nominated performance, many say it's most "memorable" for that "bird's-eye view" of the asylum's psycho ward.

Snatch
21 | 23 | 22 | 22

2000. Directed by Guy Ritchie. With Benicio Del Toro, Dennis Farina, Brad Pitt. 104 minutes. Rated R.
Fittingly "splashy" fare from Mr. Madonna, director Ritchie's sophomore effort is a "relentless crime comedy" with a substan-

tial cast of "wild" London gangsters who follow "interacting storylines" in a "quick-witted" "mix-'em-up heist" caper centered around a stolen diamond; the results are "bloody hilarious", and though you might need "subtitles" to decipher Pitt's "crazy-man accent", at least it's "never boring."

SNOW WHITE & THE SEVEN DWARFS 27 | – | 26 | 27

1937. Directed by David Hand. Animated. 83 minutes. Rated G.
The "one that started it all", this "true classic" is the "*Citizen Kane* of animation", the "first full-length feature" from the Disney drawing boards and "still the finest" of them all; this tale of a fair maiden hiding in the forest with a band of "cute little guys" to escape a "terrifying wicked queen" is a "masterpiece" of "charm, simplicity and beauty" that continues to "entertain generations" and leave 'em humming "hi ho, hi ho!"

SOME LIKE IT HOT ◑ 28 | 27 | 26 | 26

1959. Directed by Billy Wilder. With Marilyn Monroe, Tony Curtis, Jack Lemmon, Joe E. Brown. 120 minutes. Rated PG.
"Cross-dressing was never so hilarious" as in this "legendary" "laff riot" about "two patsies on the run from the mob" who don dresses and join an all-girl band as part of their escape plan; thanks to Wilder's "sure touch" and the "sidesplitting" script's "countless priceless scenes" ("Lemmon with the maracas", "Curtis' riff on Cary Grant", Monroe "running wild"), this is one hot contender for the "greatest comedy ever made" – with the "best closing line" in moviedom: "nobody's perfect."

Something's Gotta Give 23 | 26 | 22 | 23

2003. Directed by Nancy Meyers. With Jack Nicholson, Diane Keaton, Keanu Reeves. 128 minutes. Rated PG-13.
"People over 50 having sex" is the novel premise of this "middle-aged" romantic comedy positing that "growing old can be fun"; cynics nix the "lousy title" and "predictable", "sitcom-lite" plot, but the "*Architectural Digest*–worthy" settings and mighty "excellent chemistry" between Jack and Diane make it go down easy for "mature audiences"; just ignore the "lame", "too-bad-she-wound-up-with-the-wrong-guy" ending.

Something Wild 20 | 20 | 20 | 19

1986. Directed by Jonathan Demme. With Jeff Daniels, Melanie Griffith, Ray Liotta. 113 minutes. Rated R.
"You're never quite sure what's going on" when a "funky gal" meets a "conservative guy" in this "wild road movie", a "fast-paced", "fasten-your-seatbelt" ride that "starts funny", "ends tragically" and "constantly surprises at every turn"; the "pre–plastic surgery" Griffith "sizzles" as the "new wave femme fatale", Daniels "shines" as the good-natured chump and Liotta is just plain "scary as hell"; ultimately, the "title says it all" about this one.

Song of Bernadette, The ✉◑ 22 | 24 | 22 | 21

1943. Directed by Henry King. With Jennifer Jones, Charles Bickford, Gladys Cooper, Anne Revere. 156 minutes. Not Rated.
This "uplifting", "inspirational" tale of a French peasant girl who claims to have seen a vision of the Virgin Mary features a "sympathetic", Oscar-winning performance by Jones that will make you "believe her, even if no one else in the film does"; overall, the picture's a relic of "less cynical" times and may be too "syrupy" for modern audiences, but "it can still touch your heart, if you let it."

Song of the South ∅

23 | – | 22 | 26

1946. Directed by Wilfred Jackson, Harve Foster. Animated. With Ruth Warrick, James Baskett. 94 minutes. Rated G.

Yup, it's "corny and dated", but "Disney's version of the Uncle Remus stories" is also "one of the earliest" to offer an "animation–live action mix" as a young boy encounters Brers Rabbit, Fox and Bear; its "controversial" stereotyping of plantation life means it's currently "missing in action" on DVD, but music lovers say it will always be "tough to top 'Zip-A-Dee-Doo-Dah.'"

Sophie's Choice ✉

26 | 28 | 26 | 24

1982. Directed by Alan J. Pakula. With Meryl Streep, Kevin Kline, Peter MacNicol. 150 minutes. Rated R.

A "luminous" Streep with a "faint Polish accent" "shows her stuff" in this "haunting", highly "emotional" drama, which draws its "powerful story" from William Styron's novel about an Auschwitz survivor; though "wrenching" at points, it's a "compelling tour de force" that many see as Oscar-winner Meryl's "finest" hour.

SORROW AND THE PITY, THE ❶**F**

29 | – | 28 | 25

1972. Directed by Marcel Ophüls. Documentary. 251 minutes. Rated PG.

The "truth about the Nazi occupation of France" is revealed in this "devastating" but "essential" documentary that shows how "even civilized countries can fall victim to fascism"; *bien sûr*, it's "a bit long" (clocking in at just over four hours) and its "chilling depiction of neighbor against neighbor" is "not easy to take", but it's "required viewing for historical revisionists everywhere" thanks to its "relentlessly tenacious" director.

Sorry, Wrong Number ❶

25 | 25 | 25 | 23

1948. Directed by Anatole Litvak. With Barbara Stanwyck, Burt Lancaster. 89 minutes. Not Rated.

This "real thriller" adapted from a famed radio play stars Stanwyck as an "invalid heiress" who overhears a murder plot over crossed telephone wires; it's "pretty much a one-woman show" that relies on flashbacks to keep in motion, and if some say the "static" story is "stretched too thin", more report "enough twists" to keep your "spine tingling."

SOUND OF MUSIC, THE ✉

28 | 25 | 27 | 28

1965. Directed by Robert Wise. With Julie Andrews, Christopher Plummer, Eleanor Parker. 174 minutes. Rated G.

Everyone has an Alp-size "soft spot" for this "schmaltzy" Rodgers and Hammerstein musical, wherein a "charming" governess marries into a "do-re-mi" singing family and "stands on principle" after the Huns invade; the only Best Picture winner to feature "nuns, Nazis" and "kids in lederhosen", it's "shamelessly saccharine" but loved for its "uplifting" story, "fantastic" songs and "lush" scenery.

South Pacific

24 | 22 | 24 | 25

1958. Directed by Joshua Logan. With Mitzi Gaynor, Rossano Brazzi, John Kerr. 151 minutes. Not Rated.

"Incomparable music" washes up in a "tropical paradise" in this Rodgers and Hammerstein songfest, which finds American sea dogs and dames living and loving and singing along to "beautiful orchestrations" on a WWII Pacific atoll; though a huge hit in its day owing to those "eternal" tunes, some say it "doesn't hold up" anymore, pointing to the "filtered camera gels" that drown meaningful moments in "gaudy Technicolor" tints.

South Park
20 | – | 19 | 16

1999. Directed by Trey Parker. Animated. 81 minutes. Rated R.
Don't "blame Canada" for this "tasteless" full-length treatment of the "rude, crude" TV series, a "very un-PC" "equal-opportunity offender" with a "raunchy" mix of "lowbrow" laffs and "catchy" musical interludes; "rated R for a reason", it's "unbelievably funny" but "not for the kiddies" or "faint-of-heart" adults.

Spaceballs
18 | 15 | 17 | 17

1987. Directed by Mel Brooks. With Mel Brooks, John Candy, Rick Moranis. 96 minutes. Rated PG.
"Brooks strikes again" in this "goofy takeoff on *Star Wars*" that skewers sci-fi as a couple of space cowboys rocket to the rescue of a princess, setting up "cornball" gags that are the "hysterical" stuff of Mel's genre parodies; though hard-core fans find it "gets funnier every time", those unamused by the "tired", "obvious" humor contend it's "hard to believe" this is the work of a "genius".

Space Jam
16 | – | 14 | 19

1996. Directed by Joe Pytka. Animated. With Michael Jordan, Wayne Knight, Charles Barkley. 87 minutes. Rated PG.
The "Looney Tunes get their own movie" in this "fun fantasy" in which Bugs and crew play b-ball with über-hoopster Jordan and other stars to free themselves from alien kidnappers; despite "so-so" acting and storytelling, the "surprisingly good" matching of animation and live action makes this one "fun for the whole family."

Spanglish
19 | 20 | 18 | 18

2004. Directed by James L. Brooks. With Adam Sandler, Téa Leoni, Paz Vega, Cloris Leachman. 131 minutes. Rated PG-13.
Cultures clash in this "more-serious"-than-you'd-expect film from James L. Brooks about a privileged, "dysfunctional" family turned upside down when a "beautiful" Latina becomes their housekeeper; though there's applause for Sandler's "serious acting chops", critics say Téa's "too over the top" as the "control-freak wife" and "aren't sure about the ending", nor the "after-school-special" script.

Spartacus
26 | 24 | 25 | 26

1960. Directed by Stanley Kubrick. With Kirk Douglas, Laurence Olivier, Jean Simmons. 184 minutes. Rated PG-13.
"Elevated" by its "sweeping vision" and "superb all-star cast", Kubrick's "impressive" epic headlines Douglas as the "virile" leader of a "slave revolt against Rome"; pairing a "psychologically complex" story with plenty of "gory but good" action, it's an "exciting" box-office big-timer that's "matched by few" in the "classic" spectacle sweeps.

Speed ⓫
18 | 14 | 19 | 20

1994. Directed by Jan de Bont. With Keanu Reeves, Dennis Hopper, Sandra Bullock. 116 minutes. Rated R.
"*Die Hard* on a bus" is the "inanely simple" premise behind this "fast-moving" "high-concept actioner", with "sweetheart" Bullock and "studly SWAT boy" Reeves making a "cute and feisty" twosome as they find themselves "trapped" on a "tense", "nonstop" "thrill ride" aboard a "runaway bus" wired to "go boom";

though it's dismissed as "lightweight bubblegum" with "wooden" line readings from "Mr. Whoa", at least there's "no letup."

Spellbound ◑
24 | 25 | 23 | 24

1945. Directed by Alfred Hitchcock. With Gregory Peck, Ingrid Bergman, Leo G. Carroll. 111 minutes. Not Rated.

One of the first mainstream movies to tackle psychiatry, this "outstanding" Hitchcock thriller deals with unlocking a "repressed memory", and the "perfect Bergman" and "gorgeous Peck" are a "good match" as doctor and patient; but despite touches like the "ahead-of-its-time dream sequences" designed by Salvador Dali, some analysts dismiss it as "dated Freudian nonsense."

SPELLBOUND
28 | – | 27 | 26

2003. Directed by Jeffrey Blitz. Documentary. 97 minutes. Rated G.

A "fascinating commentary on American education", this "charming" documentary profiles eight grammar-school contestants bound for the National Spelling Bee in Washington, DC; most surveyors are "a-m-a-z-e-d" that such subject matter can be so much "fun to watch", but the word is this "letter perfect" picture is alternately "poignant", "uplifting" and "completely riveting."

Spider-Man ⑪
21 | 19 | 20 | 25

2002. Directed by Sam Raimi. With Tobey Maguire, Willem Dafoe, Kirsten Dunst, James Franco. 121 minutes. Rated PG-13.

Comic-book mavens marvel at how well this "adaptation captures the spirit of the original" – a literally "loopy tale" of "spider bites boy" (Maguire), who sprouts superpowers and "spins around town on threads", battling "campy, cackling nemesis" Dafoe and kissing "hot" honey Dunst upside down; heroes hail the "CGI effects seamlessly woven" into the "action-packed visuals" but hiss the "wooden acting and predictable plot"; overall, it's caught most folks "in its web."

Spider-Man 2
22 | 20 | 21 | 26

2004. Directed by Sam Raimi. With Tobey Maguire, Kirsten Dunst, James Franco, Alfred Molina. 127 minutes. Rated PG-13.

"Spidey tries to hang up his tights" and "live his own life" only to be bugged by "super villain" Doc Ock in this comic-book movie follow-up that's "as good as the original"; expect the usual "jaw-dropping" FX plus a "deeper" exploration of the webslinger's struggles with "guilt, sacrifice" and "love", and get ready for "further sequels" 'cause this franchise has legs.

Spirit: Stallion of the Cimarron
21 | – | 21 | 23

2002. Directed by Kelly Asbury, Lorna Cook. Animated. 83 minutes. Rated G.

A "gorgeous" combination of hand-drawn and computer animation "elevates" this "charming tearjerker" about a "spirited wild stallion and man's hapless efforts to tame him"; it's "great for kids and adults who grew up watching old Westerns", with "endearing characters" and a "sad" but "beautiful storyline."

Spirited Away 🇫
27 | – | 25 | 28

2002. Directed by Hayao Miyazaki. Animated. 125 minutes. Rated PG.

"Master storyteller" Miyazaki's "inventive", "visually stunning" Japanese version of "*The Wizard of Oz*" meets "*Alice in Wonderland*" "transcends the animation genre", bringing viewers to an "enchanted" "spirit world" filled with "bizarre characters", "unexpected sights" and "fantastic artwork"; it's "a tad long" and "has some pretty scary moments in it", so it may be best for "those 10 and up" – "unless you want to spend money on therapy" for the kids later.

Splash ⓘ 19 | 18 | 19 | 20

1984. Directed by Ron Howard. With Tom Hanks, Daryl Hannah, John Candy. 111 minutes. Rated PG.
More "sweet" than salty yet "not too mushy", this "fish-out-of-water love story" is an "engaging" comedy shored up by Hannah's starmaking splash as a "sexy mermaid" whom Hanks courts and transports to NYC; the fantasy is buoyed by a cast of "charming" characters "you can't help but like", including some "sterling support" from a "scene-stealing" Candy – so dive in and "enjoy."

Splendor in the Grass ✉ 25 | 25 | 24 | 22

1961. Directed by Elia Kazan. With Natalie Wood, Warren Beatty, Zohra Lampert. 124 minutes. Not Rated.
There's "heartbreak" in the heartland as "yearning" breeds "teen angst" in this "bittersweet" romance set in pre-Depression Kansas; the very "young" and very "gorgeous" Wood and Beatty supply some "real acting" as a "modern Romeo and Juliet" driven to "wrenching" extremes in this drama of "stolen dreams" and "lost love" that makes some sob sisters "cry just thinking about it."

Spy Kids ⓘ 19 | 17 | 19 | 21

2001. Directed by Robert Rodriguez. With Antonio Banderas, Carla Gugino, Alexa Vega, Daryl Sabara. 88 minutes. Rated PG.
Look for "good clean spy fun" in this "appealing" family adventure that's "empowering for kids" in its story of a bungling parental pair of agents "called back into duty", leaving it up to their "cute" tykes to "save the world"; there are plenty of "cool gadgets", so grown-ups might not want to "check their brain" after all.

Spy Kids 2: Island of Lost Dreams ⓘ 16 | 15 | 16 | 20

2002. Directed by Robert Rodriguez. With Antonio Banderas, Carla Gugino, Alexa Vega, Daryl Sabara. 100 minutes. Rated PG.
An eye-popping parade of "dazzling effects" and "great gizmos" heralds the return of pint-size secret agent sibs Carmen and Juni as they "once again try to save the world" in this "longer, louder" sci-fi sequel; if the consensus is it's "not nearly as good as the first", some still spy a "decent way to keep the kids quiet."

Spy Who Came in from the Cold, The ◑ 25 | 26 | 25 | 22

1965. Directed by Martin Ritt. With Richard Burton, Claire Bloom, Oskar Werner. 112 minutes. Not Rated.
"Spying isn't pretty" in this "very cold look at the Cold War" adapted from John Le Carré's "first major success"; Burton's "at his peak" as a "brooding" British secret agent who defects to East Germany, and his "brilliant" work is backed up by "taut direction" and a "stark", "realistic" screenplay – "James Bond, this is not."

Spy Who Loved Me, The 21 | 17 | 20 | 22

1977. Directed by Lewis Gilbert. With Roger Moore, Barbara Bach, Richard Kiel. 125 minutes. Rated PG.
When it comes to "popcorn" action fare, "nobody does it better" than Mr. Bond, and this is "one of Moore's better outings" as 007 pursues a nuclear blackmailer and fights off the "awesome", metal-

mouthed nemesis Jaws; if by now the scripts are "superfluous", it's still the leading franchise for "fast cars, fast women" in "clingy clothes" ("oh, James!") and "lots of things that blow up."

Squid and the Whale, The

21 | 25 | 20 | 20

2005. Directed by Noah Baumbach. With Jeff Daniels, Laura Linney, Jessie Eisenberg, Owen Kline. 81 minutes. Rated R.

"Ultra-real" performances (led by Daniels' "brilliant" turn as a "pompous", has-been writer) propel this "sharply observed" study of a "dysfunctional" family "riven by divorce"; though "often very funny" in its take on "self-involved parenting" and its "effects on the kids", it's painted with "uncomfortably realistic" strokes — some outright "bizarre" — that "ring so true."

Stagecoach ◑

27 | 24 | 26 | 25

1939. Directed by John Ford. With John Wayne, Claire Trevor, John Carradine. 96 minutes. Not Rated.

"Wayne's grand entrance" alone immortalizes this "archetypal" Ford Western about a group of stock frontier types "traversing hostile Indian territory" by rickety stage; featuring the young Duke in his "breakthrough role" as a fugitive convict, it rolls along on "great dialogue" and "well-acted" ensemble work interrupted by "viscerally exciting" action scenes, making it the "classic source" of countless tumbleweed "clichés."

STALAG 17 ✉◑

27 | 26 | 27 | 24

1953. Directed by Billy Wilder. With William Holden, Don Taylor, Otto Preminger. 120 minutes. Not Rated.

Wilder's "wonderful" adaptation of the stage drama supplies the "intrigue" of a "psychological thriller" with some comic relief in this story starring the "properly Oscarized" Holden as a "cynical prisoner" in a WWII POW camp who's "suspected of being a German spy"; thanks to "tremendous acting" and "tense" plotting that "keeps you guessing until the end", this study of military "camaraderie" and "mob judgment" is "not to be missed."

Stand and Deliver

20 | 22 | 22 | 17

1988. Directed by Ramon Menendez. With Edward James Olmos, Lou Diamond Phillips. 102 minutes. Rated PG.

Giving credit to the "common man", this "inspirational" drama presents Olmos as the real-life Jaime Escalante, a "math teacher who makes a difference" in a tough East LA school by tutoring a class of bad-attitude kids; tough graders say this "good fun flick" also scores as an "underrated" self-esteem booster.

Stand by Me

24 | 23 | 25 | 23

1986. Directed by Rob Reiner. With Wil Wheaton, River Phoenix, Corey Feldman. 89 minutes. Rated R.

This "wholesome" "coming-of-ager" focuses on preadolescent "best buddies" in '50s Oregon who set out "in search of a missing boy", bonding in the face of various perils and learning about the "real stuff" along the way; a platform for "young talent", it carries a "strong message" about the "struggle to grow up."

Stargate

18 | 17 | 20 | 22

1994. Directed by Roland Emmerich. With Kurt Russell, James Spader, Jaye Davidson. 121 minutes. Rated PG-13.

"Egypt" meets "outer space" in this "interesting" sci-fi flicker about a "portal" discovered in the desert that's an intergalactic wormhole to a "distant world" enslaved by the "powerful" Egyptian god Ra; the ensuing "face-off" is long on "thoughtless action" and "terrific" pyrotechnics but "never delivers" on the "great premise."

Star Is Born, A   25 | 26 | 26 | 26
1954. Directed by George Cukor. With Judy Garland, James Mason, Jack Carson. 181 minutes. Rated PG.
"Forget the other versions": this "heartbreaking" musical drama revisits the Tinseltown parable of fickle celebrity fortunes with the "best Judy ever", showcasing her "true range" as the nobody whose rise to fame is paralleled by her big-name hubby's descent; whether laughing, singing or "turning on the waterworks", the "mesmerizing" Garland gives the "performance of her life", leaving loyalists to lament the Oscar "that got away."

Starman   19 | 20 | 21 | 17
1984. Directed by John Carpenter. With Jeff Bridges, Karen Allen, Richard Jaeckel. 115 minutes. Rated PG-13.
A spacecraft falls to Earth and an "alien and earthling fall for each other" in this "overlooked date movie"; a "first-rate" Bridges plays an "E.T. in human form" who inhabits the bod of Allen's recently deceased husband, leading to "sentimental" getting-to-know-you sessions and a "romantic" road trip that draws to a "sweet" if "predictable" conclusion.

Starship Troopers   15 | 9 | 15 | 21
1997. Directed by Paul Verhoeven. With Casper Van Dien, Dina Meyer, Denise Richards. 129 minutes. Rated R.
"Robert A. Heinlein's classic yarn" about an invasion of "big bad bugs" gets a "campy" rendering in this "full-throttle sci-fi" flick loaded with "amazing" effects; while cynics nix the "cheesy acting", "trite" plot and "pointless violence", "nonstop action" fans say that this "critique of militarism" isn't "meant to be taken seriously."

Starsky & Hutch   14 | 15 | 12 | 16
2004. Directed by Todd Phillips. With Ben Stiller, Owen Wilson, Snoop Dogg. 101 minutes. Rated PG-13.
Proving yet again that it can't "leave the original alone", Hollywood unretires Bay City's "metrosexual" five-o's (and their "fun-to-look-at" Ford Torino) and sends them after a white-collar criminal in this "schlocky" spoof of the '70s TV series; P.S. forget Stiller and Wilson – Snoop Dogg as Huggy Bear is the "best casting" choice.

Star Trek II: The Wrath of Khan Ⅱ   23 | 19 | 24 | 24
1982. Directed by Nicholas Meyer. With William Shatner, Leonard Nimoy, DeForest Kelley, Ricardo Montalban. 113 minutes. Rated PG.
"Best villain + best story" = "best *Trek*": so say supporters of this "ripping" sci-fi sequel that hits warp speed when "scenery-chewing" outer-space outlaw Khan hijacks a starship and goes gunning for Admiral Kirk, back for yet one more mission with his familiar Starfleet crew; it offers all the "overblown acting" and "heart of the original", and the windup with Spock on the spot has enough "emotional punch" to "make a Trekkie out of anyone."

Star Trek IV: The Voyage Home Ⅱ   21 | 17 | 21 | 23
1986. Directed by Leonard Nimoy. With William Shatner, Leonard Nimoy, DeForest Kelley. 119 minutes. Rated PG.
The final frontiersmen send us a "message from the future" in this "easygoing", "most accessible" of the sci-fi spin-offs, with Kirk

and company "letting their hair down" to indulge in "tongue-in-cheek" interplay as they travel backward through the centuries to join a modern-day "scientific babe" in a mission to "save the whales"; it's a little "lightweight" despite the "timely ecological" theme, but as with the other "even-numbered" entries in the series, the voyaging is "not at all bad."

STAR WARS ⓤ
28 | 22 | 28 | 29

(aka Star Wars Episode IV: A New Hope)
1977. Directed by George Lucas. With Mark Hamill, Harrison Ford, Carrie Fisher. 121 minutes. Rated PG.
Lucas' "Force is strong" in this "visionary" blockbuster, the "quantum leap" that "redefined sci-fi" and established a "dynasty" by locating the "universal" in a "galaxy far, far away", where "original" "critters" and "futuristic samurais" side with a put-upon princess against an evil Empire; building to a "black hats/white hats" showdown, it's an "entertaining" mix of "modern myth" and "thrill-and-a-half" FX; subsequent space operas "can't touch" it.

Star Wars Episode I: The Phantom Menace ⓤ
18 | 16 | 18 | 26

1999. Directed by George Lucas. With Liam Neeson, Ewan McGregor, Natalie Portman. 133 minutes. Rated PG.
"After all the hype", here's the "good-looking" sci-fi prequel, which finds an earlier Jedi generation aiding a "planet under blockade" while setting some backstories straight as Obi-Wan and Skywalker *père* are groomed for knighthood; though denounced as a "giant misstep" that makes do with "so-so" storytelling while "pandering to the kiddies" with CGI "overkill" and "irritating" cast members ("why Jar Jar?"), "it's still *Star Wars*", and many "escapists" welcome it as a "worthy addition."

Star Wars Episode II: Attack of the Clones ⓤ
17 | 13 | 16 | 24

2002. Directed by George Lucas. With Hayden Christensen, Ewan McGregor, Natalie Portman. 143 minutes. Rated PG.
Unmoved by thunderous legions jeering the "magic is missing", franchise faithfuls stand by this "impressive" second act of the prequel trilogy, lauding its "mesmerizing visuals", "foreboding" moods and "many-questions-answered" plotlines; of course, even diehards don't deny Anakin and Padmé's courtship is a "cardboard"-acted, "dire attempt at romance", yet it's all "worthwhile" for the "showstopping" scene when Yoda fights.

Star Wars Episode III: Revenge of the Sith
23 | 16 | 23 | 28

2005. Directed by George Lucas. With Hayden Christensen, Ewan McGregor, Ian McDiarmid, Natalie Portman. 140 minutes. Rated PG-13.
"Even though you know" how it wraps up, seeing the "missing pieces of the puzzle" fall into place brings "closure" to a generation of fans who've waited "20-plus years" to learn how Jedi "badass" Anakin Skywalker falls from grace and "becomes Darth Vader" in this "very dark", "epic conclusion" to the beloved space saga; piling on more "dazzling" FX and "campy acting" than ever, it's the "stronger story" this time 'round ("it took Lucas three tries") that explains why it's widely considered "the best of the prequels."

STAR WARS EPISODE V: THE EMPIRE STRIKES BACK ⑪

26 | 21 | 26 | 28

1980. Directed by Irvin Kershner. With Mark Hamill, Harrison Ford, Carrie Fisher, Billy Dee Williams. 124 minutes. Rated PG.
The "darkest of the *Star Wars* series", this "worthy" first sequel features more "depth" in its characterizations and the "best story-line so far", "revealing many important secrets" as the "cosmic struggle continues"; "blissfully free of wooden dialogue", it might be the "most adult" of the "original trilogy", while that open-ended "cliff-hanger" of a finale makes for a suitably "spectacular" windup.

Star Wars Episode VI: Return of the Jedi

24 | 20 | 23 | 28

1983. Directed by Richard Marquand. With Mark Hamill, Harrison Ford, Carrie Fisher, Billy Dee Williams. 134 minutes. Rated PG.
Either a "worthy sequel" or "leftovers", this "wrap-up" episode of the *Star Wars* original trilogy finds the now-classic cast "comfortable in their roles", mugging their way through a "patented good-wins-over-evil storyline" with ample space for "cool special effects" and an "amazing final battle"; loyalists say the force is with it, but skeptics see a "weak entry" overrun with "cute, furry Ewoks", foreshadowing "toy tie-ins" and the "beginnings of Jar Jar."

Station Agent, The

25 | 27 | 23 | 23

2003. Directed by Thomas McCarthy. With Peter Dinklage, Patricia Clarkson, Bobby Cannavale. 88 minutes. Rated R.
"Putting the *Q* in quirky and the *S* in subtle", this "quiet little film" also puts the *I* in indie with its "arty" but "restrained" portrayal of the unlikely friendship between three "eccentrics" in rural New Jersey; while "not much happens" in this "meandering character study", a "great ensemble performance" (especially little person Dinklage's "charisma"-laden turn as a train enthusiast) makes for a "funny", "poignant" flick that "never falls off the track."

Steel Magnolias

24 | 25 | 24 | 23

1989. Directed by Herbert Ross. With Sally Field, Dolly Parton, Shirley MacLaine, Daryl Hannah. 117 minutes. Rated PG.
Break out the "Kleenex" for this "estrogen"-soaked drama, a "major tearjerker" smothered in "Southern-fried flavor", dashed with "laughs" and "memorable one-liners" and played "to the hilt and then some" by a "talented" bunch of "adorable" all-star "belles"; the story of "best girlfriends" in a Looziana beauty parlor bonding through "thick and thin", it's "captivating", "well-made" and "weepy" enough to qualify as the "ultimate chick flick."

St. Elmo's Fire

17 | 17 | 17 | 17

1985. Directed by Joel Schumacher. With Rob Lowe, Demi Moore, Andrew McCarthy, Judd Nelson. 110 minutes. Rated R.
This "nostalgic" '80s "cult classic" starring the "Brat Pack at its finest" addresses "issues faced in life just after college"; sure, there are some "weak spots" and a few moments that are now "unintentionally hilarious", but overall, it remains a "favorite" "coming-of-age flick", like "*The Big Chill* for Generation X."

STING, THE ✉⑪

27 | 26 | 27 | 26

1973. Directed by George Roy Hill. With Paul Newman, Robert Redford, Robert Shaw. 129 minutes. Rated PG.
"Deftly" charming its way to Best Picture honors, this "classy" comedy "caper" "succeeds in spades" as a "likable", "fast-

paced" vehicle for Newman and Redford, radiating "great rapport" as a pair of grifters playing a gangster for a sucker in Depression-era Chicago; a "funny, intriguing" "period piece" set to "elegant" Joplin rags, it raises the "suspense" stakes with "masterful" plotting and a final "zinger" that saves the sharpest sting for last.

Stir Crazy ▽ 18 | 19 | 16 | 16
1980. Directed by Sidney Poitier. With Gene Wilder, Richard Pryor, JoBeth Williams. 111 minutes. Rated R.
The second "outing from the estimable team of Pryor and Wilder" (after the successful *Silver Streak*), this buddy comedy concerns two wrongly imprisoned jokers out to clear their names; though some consider it somewhat downhill from the comedians' first matchup, it was popular enough to spawn a TV sitcom.

Stop Making Sense 25 | – | 14 | 24
1984. Directed by Jonathan Demme. Documentary. With Talking Heads. 88 minutes. Not Rated.
"Turn up the sound", because Demme's "alterna-rockumentary" presents a "superior" show from new wave faves the Talking Heads in their "heyday", burning down the house with "energetic music"; the flick proves the "exception to the rule that concerts don't translate" to the big screen and finds bandleader "David Byrne in top form", "swaying" in his trademark "enormous suit."

Story of Adele H., The 🄵 24 | 26 | 24 | 24
1975. Directed by François Truffaut. With Isabelle Adjani, Bruce Robinson. 96 minutes. Rated PG.
"Unrequited love" turns into "single-minded obsession" and then to flat-out "stalking" in this "intense" psychological drama from François Truffaut, the story of a 19th-century woman (based on "Victor Hugo's actual daughter") infatuated with one "cruelly oblivious man"; in the Oscar-nominated performance that made her an international star, Adjani is "near perfect", alternately "radiant, commanding and heartbreaking."

Straight Story, The 24 | 27 | 22 | 21
1999. Directed by David Lynch. With Richard Farnsworth, Sissy Spacek, Jane Galloway. 111 minutes. Rated G.
The "only G-rated" effort from malaise-meister Lynch goes straight for the heart in this "odd" but "compelling" drama of a septuagenarian "who rides his John Deere" power mower cross country to mend fences with his infirm brother; this "interesting" "character study" is polished into an "absolute gem" by "brilliant performances" and a "lovely" meditation on the "ending of the life cycle", but be warned that "travel by tractor" can be a "slow" ride.

Strangers on a Train ◑ 26 | 24 | 27 | 24
1951. Directed by Alfred Hitchcock. With Farley Granger, Robert Walker, Ruth Roman. 101 minutes. Rated PG.
Be careful "what you wish for" is the underlying theme of this "fascinating", "forward-thinking" Hitchcock thriller wherein a flippant "promise to exchange murders" spirals out of control into a "dark tale of unwanted bedfellows"; "spine-tingler" aficionados single out Walker's "chilling" turn as a "wacko" mama's boy, and among many "tense moments", the "carousel finale still amazes."

STREETCAR NAMED DESIRE, A ✉◑   27 28 26 25

1951. Directed by Elia Kazan. With Vivien Leigh, Marlon Brando, Kim Hunter, Karl Malden. 125 minutes. Rated PG.
Destined to "hold great forever", this "brilliant interpretation" of Tennessee Williams' "overwrought classic" showcases the "amazing" Brando "exploding onto the scene" ("hey, *Stella!*") in the "legendary" role of a "rugged" slob who engages in "shattering" "psychological warfare" with his delicate sister-in-law (the "wonderful", "so-sad" Leigh); fans say it's worth watching if only for a look at the "virile" Marlon when he was "still acting."

Strictly Ballroom   23 21 23 22

1992. Directed by Baz Luhrmann. With Paul Mercurio, Tara Morice, Bill Hunter. 94 minutes. Rated PG.
This "quirky" dose of "flash and flamenco" is a surprise charmer of a romantic comedy pairing a "hot" Aussie hoofer with an "ugly duckling", who proceed to shake up a dance championship with the question "to tango or not to tango?"; a "delightful send-up" of the "viciousness of the competitive ballroom circuit", it amuses with "well-executed" moves, even if onlookers "kinda know" how the strictly by-the-numbers story will turn out.

Stripes   21 18 18 18

1981. Directed by Ivan Reitman. With Bill Murray, Harold Ramis, Warren Oates. 101 minutes. Rated R.
"Red-blooded guys" are quick to salute this "service comedy" starring "cynical" Murray as a goldbricking civilian who joins the Army and endures basic training with the idea that it's "all about laughs"; with a "strong comic cast" and gags ranging from the truly "hilarious" to the sublimely "ridiculous", it ranks as "one of the funniest" in its class, though deserters say it "bogs down" midway and caution it's "no *Caddyshack*" – and "that's a fact, Jack."

Stuart Little ⑪   19 18 19 21

1999. Directed by Rob Minkoff. With Geena Davis, Hugh Laurie, Jonathan Lipnicki. 84 minutes. Rated PG.
Adapted from E.B. White's "sweet" children's classic, this "cute production" craftily combines "amazing animation" and live action to tell the tale of an "adorable" "talking mouse" who's adopted by humans only to be claimed by a couple of rodents posing as his "birth parents"; most can't help loving its "warm" "poignancy", though a few whiskers twitch at the "piffle"-ridden plot.

Stuart Little 2   19 18 18 22

2002. Directed by Rob Minkoff. With Geena Davis, Hugh Laurie, Jonathan Lipnicki. 78 minutes. Rated PG.
From the continuing chronicles of mice and men comes this "winner" of a sequel to E.B. White's classic tale, marking a respectable reprise for the "wonderfully animated" titular rodent as he teams up with a feathered friend and "tackles a new adventure"; though it's probably better suited for "grandkids" than grown-ups, keep a hawk's eye peeled for the "adult humor tucked in the dialogue."

Suddenly, Last Summer ◑   24 26 23 22

1959. Directed by Joseph L. Mankiewicz. With Elizabeth Taylor, Katharine Hepburn, Montgomery Clift. 114 minutes. Not Rated.
Alright, this "sensational" Tennessee Williams "stunner" about a wealthy woman scheming to have her niece lobotomized in order

to "silence her" is "a bit much" – and a little too "murky", "talky" and "icky" for the squeamish; but fans flip for its "baroque excess", Liz's "tight white bathing suit", the cast's "fine chewing of the scenery" and, most of all, that truly "shocking ending."

Sugarland Express, The | 18 | 20 | 18 | 18 |
1974. Directed by Steven Spielberg. With Goldie Hawn, William Atherton, Ben Johnson, Michael Sacks. 110 minutes. Rated PG.
"Spielberg's first movie" ("before he went CGI mad") is this "little-seen" true story that "concentrates on characters instead of effects" and even has a "downer ending"; it stars a "young" Goldie, who "runs away with the picture" as a "not-so-nice" gal who springs her hubby from prison in order to "reclaim their baby from foster care."

Sullivan's Travels ◗   ▽ 27 | 25 | 25 | 25 |
1941. Directed by Preston Sturges. With Joel McCrea, Veronica Lake, William Demarest. 90 minutes. Not Rated.
A Depression-era movie director suffering from a "mid-career crisis" "develops a conscience" and decides to shoot a truly "serious film" in this "profound comedy" from Preston Sturges; the result is a delightfully "inspirational" flick that not only has "something important to say about America", but also is one of the "best pictures ever made about Hollywood – even though it hardly takes place there."

Summer of '42 | 21 | 19 | 23 | 19 |
1971. Directed by Robert Mulligan. With Jennifer O'Neill, Gary Grimes, Jerry Houser. 103 minutes. Rated R.
Sentimental yearning and raging hormones drive this "coming-of-age" romance, which finds a trio of "pubescent boys" spending the first summer after Pearl Harbor goofing off until one of them hooks up with a young soldier's widow, who's "grasping at life"; the combination of "humor" and "heartbreak" is also a "moving" remembrance of a "time of war", while the Oscar-winning score alone is "worth the price of admission."

Sum of All Fears, The | 16 | 15 | 18 | 19 |
2002. Directed by Phil Alden Robinson. With Ben Affleck, Morgan Freeman, James Cromwell. 124 minutes. Rated PG-13.
"Neo-Nazis" seize a nuclear warhead and restart the Cold War in this "average" suspense thriller that boasts "good production values" but is certainly "not the best of the series" based on the Tom Clancy best-sellers; Affleck's "laughable" as Jack Ryan ("Harrison Ford he ain't"), and the "goodbye-Baltimore" finale "so implausible" that many advise "read the book, it's much better."

Sunday Bloody Sunday | 24 | 26 | 24 | 22 |
1971. Directed by John Schlesinger. With Peter Finch, Glenda Jackson, Murray Head. 110 minutes. Rated R.
"Very adult for its time", this "complex" film about "a man, a woman and their shared male lover" is "still very adult", starting with its "unflinching look at homosexuality"; Oscar nominees Jackson and Finch are "unforgettable" as "lost souls in the modern world" on the opposite sides of this "love triangle", while a "literate" script and "flawless" direction make this "groundbreaking" work "as relevant today as it was then."

SUNSET BOULEVARD ✉◖   28 | 28 | 27 | 27
1950. Directed by Billy Wilder. With William Holden, Gloria Swanson, Erich Von Stroheim. 110 minutes. Not Rated.
"Some of the greatest dialogue ever" (most famously, "I'm ready for my close-up, Mr. DeMille") graces this hybrid of "Gothic" and "film noir", a "scabrous take on Hollywood" from the standpoint of a "struggling screenwriter" trying to "resurrect the career of a silent movie star" who's "not exactly in touch with reality"; given Wilder's "acerbic" direction, an "'in'-joke"–laced script and "pitch-perfect" performances from a "larger-than-life Swanson" and "hunky Holden", "who needs a musical version?"

Sunshine Boys, The   21 | 23 | 19 | 18
1975. Directed by Herbert Ross. With Walter Matthau, George Burns, Richard Benjamin. 111 minutes. Rated PG.
The radiant screen rendition of Neil Simon's Broadway comedy presents Matthau and Burns (who reappears after decades off-screen and snags an Oscar) as a couple of crusty "vaudeville greats who must work together" on a TV reunion show, even though they're given to much bickering; the "funny story" makes for surefire yuks, but razzers report the act as a whole is "not so bright."

Sunshine State   18 | 22 | 18 | 18
2002. Directed by John Sayles. With Edie Falco, Jane Alexander, Ralph Waite, Angela Bassett. 141 minutes. Rated PG-13.
A "great ensemble cast" (notably the "terrific" Falco) is the bright ray of sunshine in this "thought provoking" "social drama" set in a moribund Florida community; devotees delight in the "ambitious script" that spins "lots of subplots" and leaves behind "untied loose ends", but detractors yawn "boring" and insist it's "not the best" effort from indie auteur Sayles.

Superman ⑪   22 | 19 | 22 | 23
1978. Directed by Richard Donner. With Christopher Reeve, Margot Kidder, Gene Hackman. 143 minutes. Rated PG.
"You'll really believe a man can fly" after a look at this "ahead-of-its-time" superhero fantasy, the "delightful", "campy" saga of a survivor from a doomed planet who grows up to be a "man of steel"; even if the "comic-book sensibility" is "a little silly" and the line readings "stiff", a super "heart shines through" as Reeve turns in the "definitive", "true-blue portrayal" of "all things good" – when he's not "sizing up telephone booths", that is.

Super Size Me   24 | – | 24 | 21
2004. Directed by Morgan Spurlock. Documentary. 96 minutes. Rated G.
Near-"suicide by gluttony" is both "disturbing" and "funny" in this "crowd-pleasing documentary" wherein director/star Spurlock submits himself to an all-McDonald's diet for a month; although "not the most researched study of fast food" and perhaps "lacking in nutritional substance", this "stomach-churning" "wake-up call" still might send you running for a "piece of fruit."

Suspect   ▽ 19 | 19 | 20 | 18
1987. Directed by Peter Yates. With Cher, Dennis Quaid, Liam Neeson. 121 minutes. Rated R.
Cher's an ambitious public defender in this "courtroom thriller" about a high-level conspiracy involving a slick lobbyist, a dead

Supreme Court justice and a deaf-and-dumb homeless man; though "predictable" and only "relatively involving" to the suspicious, others say it "keeps you wondering" until the "surprise ending."

Suspicion ✉️◗ 25 | 26 | 25 | 25

1941. Directed by Alfred Hitchcock. With Joan Fontaine, Cary Grant, Cedric Hardwicke, Nigel Bruce. 99 minutes. Not Rated.
A "poor little rich girl" hooks up with a "potential murderer" in this "top Hitchcock" thriller starring an appropriately "menacing" Grant and a "wimpy" (but Oscar-winning) Fontaine; if some find the picture "a bit tentative" for the master of suspense (who was famously forced to "change the ending"), all agree on its most unforgettable prop, the "scariest looking glass of milk in cinema history."

S.W.A.T. 15 | 15 | 15 | 18

2003. Directed by Clark Johnson. With Samuel L. Jackson, Colin Farrell, Michelle Rodriguez, LL Cool J. 117 minutes. Rated PG-13.
Hollywood's predictable pairing of "guns and testosterone" is the trigger for this "peek into the life of a SWAT agent", a "generic" guy flick bulging with "badass" cops and "through-the-roof" action; factor in the plot's "telegraphed twists" and most prefer their "fond memories of the original TV series" over this "tired revival."

Sweet Charity 20 | 21 | 19 | 23

1969. Directed by Bob Fosse. With Shirley MacLaine, John McMartin, Chita Rivera. 149 minutes. Rated G.
"Fosse's directorial debut" adapts a boffo Broadway show into an "exciting" musical featuring "MacLaine at her best" as a honey of a dance-hall damsel; look for "over-the-top production numbers" (especially Chita's raucous 'Big Spender') with "memorable staging" and "great tunes", and if the "quirky" story "drifts" when the music stops, charitable types cheer the players for "trying with all their might."

Sweet Hereafter, The 24 | 25 | 23 | 23

1997. Directed by Atom Egoyan. With Ian Holm, Sarah Polley, Bruce Greenwood. 112 minutes. Rated R.
"Haunting" in a "somber" way, this adaptation of Russell Banks' novel is a "beautifully shot", "terribly moving" drama about the "aftermath of a small-town tragedy" and the "dysfunction" it lays bare; the "terrific cast" sees the burg's "delicate balance" upset when some kids die in a bus crash, and the camera lends a "hypnotic" feel to material that's "smart" but "shrouded in sadness."

Sweet Home Alabama 17 | 18 | 16 | 18

2002. Directed by Andy Tennant. With Reese Witherspoon, Josh Lucas, Patrick Dempsey. 108 minutes. Rated PG-13.
A "country girl turned NYC fashionista" choosing between two suitors "returns to her roots" to make a decision in this "light-hearted", "pass-me-the-popcorn" romantic comedy that's "good for a girls' night out"; while "America's Sweetheart" Reese just "couldn't be cuter", the "no-surprises", "by-the-book" script and "stereotypical", "culture-clash humor" aren't as sweet.

SWEET SMELL OF SUCCESS, THE ◗ 27 | 28 | 26 | 26

1957. Directed by Alexander Mackendrick. With Burt Lancaster, Tony Curtis, Martin Milner. 96 minutes. Not Rated.
A "cookie full of arsenic" soaked in "hydrochloric acid", this extra-"tasty" morsel of "moody noir" unearths the "seamy side" of

showbiz with its "cynical" "character study" of the "slimy" sorts working the "publicity end": a "superb" Lancaster as a "brutal", Winchell-esque columnist and the "unctuous Curtis" as his publicist toady; brace yourself for "crackling dialogue" and some "beyond beautiful" NYC "nighttime shots" in this "timeless" but never "more timely" picture.

Swept Away 🅵   24 | 24 | 24 | 24

1975. Directed by Lina Wertmüller. With Mariangela Melato, Giancarlo Giannini. 116 minutes. Rated R.

Stranding strangers on a "sunbaked isle" long "before the arrival of *Survivor*", Wertmüller's "unforgettable" Italian comedy "steams up the screen" as a snobbish socialite and a coarsely "expressive" boatman develop a "passionate" "love/hate relationship" alone on a Mediterranean cay; the satire "speaks volumes" as a "comment on class" and the "battle of the sexes", though there's a strong undercurrent of "violence" running beneath the beautiful "scenery."

Swimming Pool   20 | 23 | 20 | 20

2003. Directed by François Ozon. With Charlotte Rampling, Ludivine Sagnier, Charles Dance. 103 minutes. Rated R.

A burnt-out "older British woman" and a "slutty French girl" share a house in the south of France in this "plenty sexy" psychological thriller that delineates some "wonderfully uncomfortable" "generational differences"; while the "cryptic" climax leaves cynics perplexed – "could someone please explain the ending?" – boobs say it's "worth renting for the nudity" alone.

Swingers   23 | 22 | 23 | 20

1996. Directed by Doug Liman. With Jon Favreau, Vince Vaughn, Heather Graham. 96 minutes. Rated R.

"Hooking up in the '90s" gets a "hilarious" but "realistic" spin in this "hip, kinetic" buddy comedy–cum–"cultural phenomenon" about two single guys "finding their mojo" on the "Los Angeles dating scene"; it's "immensely funny", universally "accurate in defining a generation" and "'so money' that it spawned its very own vernacular."

Swiss Family Robinson   ▽ 23 | 18 | 25 | 22

1960. Directed by Ken Annakin. With John Mills, Dorothy McGuire, James MacArthur. 126 minutes. Rated G.

"Action, romance, adventure and comedy" coexist amiably in this "absolute classic" from Walt Disney, a story of castaways shipwrecked on a tropical isle that "bears little resemblance to the novel"; an exercise in "good, clean fun", it's everything a "family movie should be", and that "terrific" treehouse set "still fascinates" smaller fry.

Sylvia   16 | 20 | 16 | 19

2003. Directed by Christine Jeffs. With Gwyneth Paltrow, Daniel Craig, Jared Harris, Blythe Danner. 110 minutes. Rated R.

"Troubled writer" Sylvia Plath is the subject of this "relentlessly morose" biopic that gets somewhat of a lift from Paltrow's "strong yet fragile" title turn; although it's an "even-handed treatment of an uneven marriage", many find the story too "depressing and pointless", wondering if "her life is interesting enough" to "deserve its own movie."

Syriana
21 | 24 | 20 | 22

2005. Directed by Stephen Gaghan. With Jeffrey Wright, George Clooney, Matt Damon. 126 minutes. Rated R.

Holding up a "mirror to current events", this "tough-minded" drama about "the Middle East", "Big Oil" and the "dirty tricks" that bind them together weaves a "complex" (if at times "confusing") tapestry of "intersecting plotlines" loaded with "twists"; Clooney's "fabulous" performance as a "disillusioned CIA agent" is one reason why this political "wake-up call" rewards "multiple viewings."

Take the Money and Run
21 | 18 | 21 | 17

1969. Directed by Woody Allen. With Woody Allen, Janet Margolin, Marcel Hillaire. 85 minutes. Rated R.

Woody's "first full-fledged feature" wings it with "pure slapstick" and "typical" self-deprecating shtick, depicting the escapades of a "hopeless nerd bank robber" into a phony documentary that's "basically a series of blackouts and sketches"; though a bit "threadbare" in between the "patches of brilliance", it packs in enough "anarchy and whimsy" to foretell things to come.

Talented Mr. Ripley, The
18 | 21 | 19 | 21

1999. Directed by Anthony Minghella. With Matt Damon, Jude Law, Gwyneth Paltrow. 139 minutes. Rated R.

A "lush thriller of mistaken identity" set in '50s Europe, this "unsettling", "underrated" study of a murderous "schmuck-turned-socialite" stars Damon as the "slippery" title character (in a performance that's either "unnervingly good" or totally "botched"); while the "disturbing storyline" played out against "spectacular scenery" enthralls many, critics see little talent in its "lack of warmth" and way-"too-long" running time.

Talk to Her ✉ 🄵
26 | 26 | 26 | 25

2002. Directed by Pedro Almodóvar. With Javier Cámara, Darío Grandinetti, Leonor Watling, Rosario Flores, Geraldine Chaplin. 112 minutes. Rated R.

"Don't think about it too much and it will captivate you" advise fans of this "brilliant piece of art" by the "risk-taking" Almodóvar, a "haunting", "highly original" "drama, comedy and mystery all in one" about "two women who have fallen into comas and the men who love them"; a "wonderful cast" tackles a "provocative" "multilayered storyline" that "allows fantasy to play with reality" – "finally, a film for mature audiences!"

Tarzan
22 | – | 21 | 24

1999. Directed by Chris Buck, Kevin Lima. Animated. 88 minutes. Rated G.

Some of "Disney's best work" "re-creates the magic" of a "classic" in this tale of man and monkey swinging through life via "phenomenally innovative" animation; a "fast-paced adventure" that takes time out for "character" but "keeps things relatively lighthearted", it adds some "thoughtful modern" angles and a "great score", including an Oscar-winning song from Phil Collins.

Tarzan and His Mate ◑ ⑪
21 | 16 | 19 | 20

1934. Directed by Cedric Gibbons. With Johnny Weissmuller, Maureen O'Sullivan. 104 minutes. Not Rated.

See "what movies were like before the censors" in this rather racy sequel to *Tarzan the Ape Man* flaunting barely there costumes, "nude underwater" frolicking and title characters living together sans holy matrimony; despite some "racist" undertones and acting that "leaves a lot to be desired", some consider it the "best" of the Weissmuller Tarzans.

Tarzan the Ape Man ◐ ⑪

| 21 | 16 | 21 | 18 |

1932. Directed by W.S. Van Dyke. With Johnny Weissmuller, Maureen O'Sullivan. 99 minutes. Not Rated.
An "old-fashioned" fave among the "first real adventure films", this "memorable" intersection of Hollywood and vine finds a Brit lady Jane abducted by the ape-bred hero only to civilize him; Olympic swimmer Weissmuller brings "definitive" bravura to the title character, and thus this "campy" but "trendsetting original" "holds up better" than all the sequels you can shake a banana at.

TAXI DRIVER

| 27 | 29 | 25 | 25 |

1976. Directed by Martin Scorsese. With Robert De Niro, Jodie Foster, Harvey Keitel, Cybill Shepherd. 113 minutes. Rated R.
Confirming "non-NYers' greatest fears" about the "brutal underbelly" of "modern urban life", Scorsese's vividly "cerebral" thriller rolls through "sleazy" streets and "neon" nights charged by De Niro's "monumental performance" as a "creepy", insomniac hack – "you talking to me?" – whose live-wire issues build to "harrowing" magnum force in the "steam-filled" city; overall, its depiction of "urban decay, rage and alienation" is "top-class" but "lurid" and very "intense."

10

| 17 | 16 | 16 | 17 |

1979. Directed by Blake Edwards. With Dudley Moore, Julie Andrews, Bo Derek, Robert Webber. 122 minutes. Rated R.
This "midlife crisis movie for men" might be "silly", but will always be a "time capsule of the American dream, circa 1979" thanks to one iconic image: "Derek in cornrows" bouncing on the beach in "slow motion" to the accompaniment of "Ravel's 'Bolero'"; sure, it has about as much depth as the "*Sports Illustrated* swimsuit issue", but it's "still funny" and proves that "short guys can be sexy."

Ten Commandments, The

| 24 | 21 | 25 | 27 |

1956. Directed by Cecil B. DeMille. With Charlton Heston, Yul Brynner, Anne Baxter, Edward G. Robinson. 220 minutes. Rated G.
"Let it be written" that DeMille's "over-the-top" biblical blockbuster is the "epic of all epics", a "Cliffs Notes" account of Exodus built on "Heston's finest" role as the "one and only Moses", performer of "monumental" miracles on land and Red Sea; though "fantastic sets" and Brynner's "badass" Egyptian king distract from the "kitschy" script and "overblown" production, it's "entertaining" enough to keep a "cast of thousands" in "constant circulation."

Terminal, The

| 18 | 22 | 18 | 20 |

2004. Directed by Steven Spielberg. With Tom Hanks, Catherine Zeta-Jones, Stanley Tucci. 128 minutes. Rated PG-13.
"Every traveler's nightmare" comes true in this story of an "Eastern European stranded for months at JFK" that divides viewers, with fans praising the "truly original" idea, "spare-no-expense" production and Tom's "gold-standard" performance ("he's good in anything"); but those who say it "just doesn't fly" find it "terminally dull", given the "strained", "*Castaway*-in-an-airport" story, "unsatisfying", "Capra-esque ending" and "zero chemistry" between the "not sexy" Hanks and "wasted" Zeta-Jones.

Terminator, The ⑪ | 24 | 18 | 24 | 24 |

1984. Directed by James Cameron. With Arnold Schwarzenegger, Michael Biehn, Linda Hamilton. 108 minutes. Rated R.

Buckle up for Cameron's "unstoppable breakthrough", this sci-fi/action "genre-maker" about an "evil cyborg sent from the future" to wreak havoc on the past via Ah-nuld's "seriously scary presence" alone; it "doesn't disappoint" in dispensing "awesome" "violent" mayhem all over '80s LA, and its most famous line – "I'll be back" – was a harbinger of the sequels to come.

Terminator 2: Judgment Day ⑪ | 23 | 17 | 22 | 26 |

1991. Directed by James Cameron. With Arnold Schwarzenegger, Linda Hamilton, Edward Furlong. 137 minutes. Rated R.

The Terminator's "baaack" as a "kinder, gentler" cyborg in this "outsize thrill ride" that deftly embellishes the initial premise of murderous, "time-traveling" robots; fans say it's a "rare sequel that fulfills the promise of the original", citing the "whiz-bang", "ahead-of-their-time" FX, Hamilton's "buff", "kick-butt" heroine and the one-and-only Arnold, whose "mechanical" performance makes him the "perfect choice to play an android."

Terminator 3: Rise of the Machines | 16 | 13 | 15 | 22 |

2003. Directed by Jonathan Mostow. With Arnold Schwarzenegger, Nick Stahl, Claire Danes. 109 minutes. Rated R.

"Staying true" to its origins, this third entry in the long-unfolding sci-fi series features the usual "bang-up" pyrotechnics and "breezy" plotting, along with a "twist": a fembot Terminatrix villainess; still, foes fret the "franchise has run out of steam", citing "retread special effects", "phoned-in" work from Arnold and that "downer" of an ending; in short, "they should have stopped at 2."

Terms of Endearment ✉⑪ | 25 | 26 | 24 | 22 |

1983. Directed by James L. Brooks. With Shirley MacLaine, Debra Winger, Jack Nicholson. 132 minutes. Rated PG.

A "four-hanky tearjerker" "worth its weight in Kleenex", this "engrossing" "weepie with a spine" starts off comically enough depicting a "tangled mother-daughter relationship" but takes a "serious" turn in the second act when "life-and-death" issues arise; quite the Oscar magnet, it took home Best Picture honors as well as statuettes for the "amazing" MacLaine and Nicholson.

Tess | 21 | 22 | 21 | 22 |

1980. Directed by Roman Polanski. With Nastassja Kinski, Peter Firth, Leigh Lawson. 172 minutes. Rated PG.

"Spectacularly beautiful", this "faithful rendition" of Thomas Hardy's "melancholy" classic *Tess of the D'Urbervilles* stars a "simply luminous" Kinski as a peasant girl trying to improve her station in life; some say it's "schmaltzy" and "overly long", but most praise Polanski's "really fine adaptation" and promise you'll "never look at strawberries the same way" after seeing it.

Texas Chainsaw Massacre, The ⑪ | 17 | 13 | 17 | 15 |

1974. Directed by Tobe Hooper. With Marilyn Burns, Allen Danziger, Paul A. Partain. 83 minutes. Rated R.

Something "like a car wreck", this "alternately repulsive and fascinating" "slashfest" is the "nightmarish" story of innocent folk "falling prey to a cannibalistic family" and is "creepy beyond belief" despite "surprisingly little overt gore"; aficionados call it the

"*Casablanca* of horror films" notwithstanding the "low-budget" looks and "bad acting" – but "truly amazing screaming."

Thank You for Smoking   23 | 23 | 23 | 21
2006. Directed by Jason Reitman. With Aaron Eckhart, Maria Bello, Rob Lowe, Robert Duvall, William H. Macy, Katie Holmes. 92 minutes. Rated R.
Eckhart's "killer" portrayal of a "smug" but "lovable" cigarette industry spin doctor has you "rooting for the bad guy" in this "hysterically sarcastic" send-up of "Big Tobacco" and the "art of lobbying"; packed with "intelligent commentary" and featuring a star-studded cast, it "throws some moral curveballs" that leave "plenty to talk about after the credits roll."

That's Entertainment! ❶   25 | – | – | 25
1974. Directed by Jack Haley Jr. Documentary. With Gene Kelly, Fred Astaire. 127 minutes. Rated G.
This "remarkable survey of MGM musicals" lays out a "delicious", "crème-de-la-crème" buffet of glorious "old clips" set up with "narration by some mighty big stars"; showcasing the likes of Kelly and Astaire at their "thrilling" peak, this compilation is "desert-island" viewing and an "entertaining introduction" for young folks to the bygone days of "real talent."

Thelma & Louise ✉   23 | 25 | 23 | 21
1991. Directed by Ridley Scott. With Susan Sarandon, Geena Davis, Brad Pitt, Harvey Keitel. 129 minutes. Rated R.
A "high-powered" "girl-power" flick focusing on a "feminist crime spree", this "groundbreaking" display of "female macho" "rocks" as two everyday gals "finally get back" at the men who've wronged them by becoming "devil-may-care outlaws"; the "superb storyline" and "stellar performances" keep things "involving" right up to the "heartbreaking", "*Butch Cassidy*"–esque "bad ending."

There's Something About Mary   21 | 19 | 20 | 19
1998. Directed by Bobby Farrelly, Peter Farrelly. With Cameron Diaz, Matt Dillon, Ben Stiller. 119 minutes. Rated R.
Proceed "at your own risk" as the "ultra-crude" Farrelly brothers "push the limits" of "gross-out comedy" in this "tacky laugh riot" about a "loser with a heart of gold" and the "good-sport" girl he loves that's an "oh-my-gosh" compendium of "high-school humor" and "vulgar" "sight gags" (the "dog", the "zipper", the "hair gel"); but foes moan this is a movie "made by morons for morons."

They Shoot Horses, Don't They?   21 | 24 | 22 | 21
1969. Directed by Sydney Pollack. With Jane Fonda, Michael Sarrazin, Susannah York. 120 minutes. Rated PG.
"Jane Fonda at her world-weariest" provides the glue in this "classic" Depression drama about "desperate" marathon dancers frantically trying to make a buck; though the story's "small" and the sentiments grim, its ensemble cast is "unforgettable" – particularly the "superlative" Gig Young, who copped an Oscar for the role of the slimy emcee.

Thief of Bagdad, The ◑   ▽ 25 | 24 | 23 | 24
1924. Directed by Raoul Walsh. With Douglas Fairbanks, Snitz Edwards, Julanne Johnston. 155 minutes. Not Rated.
This Arabian Nights fantasy is a "definitive swashbuckler", featuring an "athletic" Fairbanks "at his best" as a charming rogue

seeking a princess' hand; one of the most expensive silent movies ever made, it's a "lavish" spectacle with sets by William Cameron Menzies that are "still amazing by today's standards"; in short, it's simply "great."

Thing, The ◐　　　　　　　23 | 19 | 25 | 19
(aka The Thing from Another World)
1951. Directed by Christian Nyby. With Kenneth Tobey, Margaret Sheridan. 87 minutes. Not Rated.
This "serious" '50s sci-fi suspenser "still holds up" as a "smart" "flying-saucer" shocker about a group of scientists driven to "creepy" extremes in a "claustrophobic, paranoid" encounter with a murderous alien found frozen in the Arctic ice; despite "skimpy" special effects, the "tight script" builds enough "tension" to frighten the "daylights" out of fans, who spurn the "gory remake" – there's nothing like "the real *Thing*."

Thing, The　　　　　　　　23 | 19 | 23 | 23
1982. Directed by John Carpenter. With Kurt Russell, Wilford Brimley, David Clennon. 109 minutes. Rated R.
"Chills" abound in Carpenter's "excellent remake of the '51 classic", wherein the Antarctic's most "frigid science outpost" is beset by a "horrible alien" capable of disguising itself in human form; an "imaginative" contribution to the "sci-fi/horror pantheon", it supplies enough "true suspense" to keep the audience "guessing" as the "paranoia" mounts.

Thin Man, The ◐Ⅱ　　　　26 | 25 | 23 | 23
1934. Directed by W.S. Van Dyke. With William Powell, Myrna Loy, Maureen O'Sullivan. 93 minutes. Not Rated.
"Break out the martini glasses": "mystery meets screwball comedy" in this "snazzy" flicker featuring "cool detective" Nick Charles and his "classy wife", Nora, "drinking like fish" and "fluidly" spouting "snappy dialogue" ("double entendre, anyone?") as they investigate a murder; the "suave, sexy fun" is so "cosmopolitan" and "wonderfully evocative of the '30s" that it seems unsporting to point out that the "whodunit" plot is a bit thin.

Thin Red Line, The　　　　19 | 21 | 17 | 22
1998. Directed by Terrence Malick. With Sean Penn, George Clooney, John Cusack. 170 minutes. Rated R.
Malick's "experimental war epic" is made for those who "enjoy thinking about big questions", with Penn exuding "gravity" as a sarge facing the front lines at Guadalcanal with a "star-studded" company of "common soldiers"; "stunning visuals" "attempt to poeticize" the "horror and beauty" of battle and warfare's "emotional effects", though detractors grunt it's "incoherent."

THIRD MAN, THE ◐　　　　28 | 28 | 27 | 28
1949. Directed by Carol Reed. With Joseph Cotten, Alida Valli, Orson Welles, Trevor Howard. 104 minutes. Not Rated.
"Oh, that zither!"; this "masterful" piece of "postwar" noir simmers with shadowy "intrigue" as an "alienated" Cotten encounters "romance" and "betrayal" while searching "bombed-out" Vienna for a "mysterious" black marketeer (played by Welles, who makes the most of a "small" role with an "arresting" entrance); graced with "expressionist" lensing, Graham Greene's "clever, dark script" and a "memorable" final fade, it's hailed as "all-around perfect."

Thirteen
21 26 22 19

2003. Directed by Catherine Hardwicke. With Holly Hunter, Evan Rachel Wood, Nikki Reed. 100 minutes. Rated R.

"You won't want to let your kids out of the house" after a gander at this "disturbing" tale about a pair of "troubled" 13-year-olds who are "harder to control than Mike Tyson"; while critics hiss the "after-school-special" script and "weak ending", far more applaud this "wake-up call" for telling it like it is "without sugar coating."

39 Steps, The ◑
27 25 27 24

1935. Directed by Alfred Hitchcock. With Robert Donat, Madeleine Carroll. 86 minutes. Not Rated.

"You can't go wrong" with this "classic" "British period" Hitchcock nail-biter, a "virtuoso" "thriller diller" wherein an "innocent man wrongly accused" of murder tries to clear his name amid "chase scenes, foreign spy intrigue and romance" (with a woman he winds up "handcuffed" to); sure, the "dated" special effects are on the low-tech side, but this "tense mystery" delivers enough suspense to "keep you on the edge of your seat."

This Is Spinal Tap
26 24 25 22

1984. Directed by Rob Reiner. With Christopher Guest, Michael McKean, Rob Reiner. 82 minutes. Rated R.

"VH1's *Behind the Music*" pales before this "hysterical" "rock mockumentary", an "unbelievably authentic-feeling send-up" of the music industry and superstar "pretensions" that follows an "aging heavy-metal band" taking its act on the road; the "stellar cast" plays an "unforgettable" group of clueless musicians, simulating a "sidesplitting insider's view" that's alarmingly "like the real thing" – except "every single second is funny."

Thomas Crown Affair, The
23 23 24 22

1968. Directed by Norman Jewison. With Steve McQueen, Faye Dunaway, Paul Burke. 102 minutes. Rated R.

This "slick", "grown-up romance" offers a "cat-and-mouse" plot as millionaire McQueen engineers a bank heist for kicks until he encounters Dunaway, a "knockout" insurance sleuth in mad pursuit; their "smoldering", "high-tension" affair is a "stylish" standoff down to the final "checkmate" in that famed chess match, and as for the remake, "do not accept imitations."

Thoroughly Modern Millie
18 19 16 21

1967. Directed by George Roy Hill. With Julie Andrews, Mary Tyler Moore, Carol Channing. 138 minutes. Rated G.

"Roaring '20s" razzle-dazzle makes this musical comedy an "absolute hoot", with "Andrews at her peak" as a big-city rookie trying to land a man; it's played as a "slapstick farce set to song and dance" that alternates new tunes with "flapper-era" standards, and if "silly fluff", all that "jazzy fun" is "entertaining nonetheless."

Three Coins in the Fountain
▽ 20 20 20 21

1954. Directed by Jean Negulesco. With Clifton Webb, Dorothy McGuire, Jean Peters, Louis Jourdan. 102 minutes. Not Rated.

"Rome at its best" is the real "star" of this "good old-fashioned love story" about three husband-hunters making coin-tossing wishes in the Trevi Fountain; it's every 1950s "female's dream" and still "so much emotional fun" that it's easy to ignore the correspondingly overripe 1950s "sentimentality."

Three Faces of Eve, The ✉◐   24 | 27 | 24 | 20

1957. Directed by Nunnally Johnson. With Joanne Woodward, David Wayne, Lee J. Cobb. 91 minutes. Not Rated.

"Incredible" Oscar-winner Woodward delivers a "tour-de-force" turn in this "multiple-personality genre film", an "interesting drama" about a "woman tormented" by triple identities; switching from subdued homemaker to brazen party girl, Woodward does a "stellar" job of "bringing all three characters to life."

Three Kings   20 | 21 | 21 | 22

1999. Directed by David O. Russell. With George Clooney, Mark Wahlberg, Ice Cube. 114 minutes. Rated R.

Opening at the close of Desert Storm, this "bold and different" war flick offers a combo of "crackerjack action" and "surprisingly good" acting as "irreverent army guy" Clooney launches a "chase for stolen Kuwaiti gold" that morphs into a "morality tale" midway through; the "insightful" scenario and "creative" visuals make it royally "enjoyable on many levels", though a few are "not impressed" by the "chaotic storyline" and "preachy dialogue."

Three Men and a Baby ⑪   16 | 15 | 17 | 16

1987. Directed by Leonard Nimoy. With Tom Selleck, Steve Guttenberg, Ted Danson. 102 minutes. Rated PG.

Like the title implies, "three men care for a baby girl" in this "big-hearted" comedy with a "charming ensemble" cast; the un-amused suggest you "bring insulin" or hold out for the "much better" French film on which it's based: *Three Men and a Cradle.*

Three Musketeers, The ⑪   22 | 22 | 22 | 23

1974. Directed by Richard Lester. With Oliver Reed, Richard Chamberlain, Michael York. 105 minutes. Rated PG.

A "rollicking rendition" of the Dumas classic, this "rousing" "old-fashioned" adventure "stays faithful" to the original tale but spices up the swordplay with "slapstick" and "bawdy" humor as a brave band of swashbucklers defends the queen's honor against that crooked cardinal; the "lavish" 17th-century sets and all-for-one "charm" of the "great cast" ensure its place as the "quintessential" version by which all others "shall be judged."

Thunderball   22 | 21 | 21 | 23

1965. Directed by Terence Young. With Sean Connery, Claudine Auger, Adolfo Celi. 130 minutes. Rated PG.

Bringing the "basic Bond formula" to the Bahamas, this swimming entry in the superspy series has Connery breaking out his arsenal of "gadgets" and dry wisecracks against the "very real threat" of stolen nukes held for ransom; the "nonstop action" and "incredible underwater fight sequences" made it a thunderous success in its day, and if now "underappreciated", connoisseurs nevertheless rank it "near the top" of the 007 oeuvre.

Tie Me Up! Tie Me Down! 🄵   20 | 21 | 20 | 20

1990. Directed by Pedro Almodóvar. With Victoria Abril, Antonio Banderas, Loles Leon. 111 minutes. Rated NC-17.

"Madcap" director Almodóvar strikes again in this naughty knotty comedy about a kidnapped, trussed-up B-movie star that's a cross between *The Collector* and a soft-core bondage flick; its "sexy", "vivid characters" and "nice" Ennio Morricone soundtrack further spice up a storyline that's already "hysterically funny."

Time After Time
23 | 23 | 25 | 21

1979. Directed by Nicholas Meyer. With Malcolm McDowell, Mary Steenburgen, David Warner. 112 minutes. Rated PG.

A "clever" bit of "brainy entertainment", this "charming" sci-fi thriller recounts "H.G. Wells chasing Jack the Ripper to modern-day San Francisco" via a "functioning time machine"; a "witty" romp expertly blending "romantic" interludes between McDowell and Steenburgen with "suspenseful" sequencing, it's "well worth seeing" for Warner's "helluva performance" alone.

Time Bandits
21 | 19 | 23 | 22

1981. Directed by Terry Gilliam. With John Cleese, Sean Connery, Shelley Duvall. 116 minutes. Rated PG.

Gilliam's "warped-mind" "genius" shines in this "bittersweet" time-travel fantasy about the "classic struggle between good and evil", with a sprawling cast that includes a "band of midgets", a "fantastic villain" and a parade of "delightful" cameos; though the visual effects may be showing their age, there are still enough "juicy moments" to justify its "cult-classic" status.

Time Machine, The
22 | 17 | 26 | 23

1960. Directed by George Pal. With Rod Taylor, Alan Young, Yvette Mimieux. 103 minutes. Rated G.

"Faithful to both the letter and spirit of H.G. Wells' novel", this "granddaddy of time-travel movies" concerning a 19th-century scientist flabbergasted by the future is "nicely paced" and "fondly remembered" for its "thought-provoking storyline" and "good special effects for the era" (which won an Oscar); though the "remake isn't bad", the "much-better" original is the real "gem."

Time to Kill, A
18 | 18 | 22 | 19

1996. Directed by Joel Schumacher. With Matthew McConaughey, Sandra Bullock, Samuel L. Jackson. 149 minutes. Rated R.

"Very adult" and "suspenseful to the end", this "hard-hitting" Mississippi courtroom drama about racist violence and retribution is a "solid adaptation of the John Grisham novel"; despite the very "Hollywood ending", it's "captivating" thanks to "intelligent" turns from Bullock and McConaughey ("his best role").

Tin Drum, The ✉ 🄵
▽ 23 | 24 | 24 | 23

1979. Directed by Volker Schlöndorff. With David Bennent, Mario Adorf, Angela Winkler. 142 minutes. Rated R.

A "fine social commentary" about apathy and "life in Nazi Germany", this "disturbing" allegorical drama about a young boy who refuses to grow old "preserves the spirit of Günter Grass' novel" while charting the rise and fall of the Third Reich; the "well-deserved winner of the Best Foreign Film Oscar", it's a "surreal" work that remains "vivid and haunting" a generation later.

Titanic ✉
19 | 16 | 18 | 26

1997. Directed by James Cameron. With Leonardo DiCaprio, Kate Winslet, Billy Zane. 194 minutes. Rated PG-13.

Ok, it's "not highbrow stuff", but this "over-the-top spectacular" detailing a "doomed love story" aboard a "doomed ocean liner" thrills with "dazzling" special effects, including a "fantastic" "re-creation of the original ship" and icebergs so real "you can almost touch them"; some torpedo the "shallow" "cardboard characters", "soap opera"–esque script and "weak acting" as "all wet", and whether it's "deserving of its Oscars" – all 11 of them – is still hotly debated.

To Be or Not to Be ◑
▽ 25 | 25 | 25 | 23

1942. Directed by Ernst Lubitsch. With Carole Lombard, Jack Benny, Robert Stack. 99 minutes. Not Rated.
"Life in Nazi-occupied Europe" becomes "exhilarating comedy" in this "funny but poignant" war story, an "oft-overlooked gem" via the ever "clever" Ernst Lubitsch; playing married actors, Benny and Lombard supply "barrels of laughs" – particularly when Jack "does to Shakespeare what the Germans are doing to Poland."

To Catch a Thief
25 | 25 | 24 | 25

1955. Directed by Alfred Hitchcock. With Grace Kelly, Cary Grant, Jesse Royce Landis. 106 minutes. Not Rated.
"Slick, sophisticated and oh-so-cool", this romantic thriller may be "Hitchcock lite", but Grant and Kelly provide plenty of "dazzle" in an amusing trifle about a cat burglar prowling the south of France; maybe the "plot is secondary" to the "enjoyable scenery" and "fab clothes", but there's snappy patter aplenty, notably Grace's classic picnic query "would you prefer a leg or a breast?"

To Die For
18 | 21 | 19 | 18

1995. Directed by Gus Van Sant. With Nicole Kidman, Matt Dillon, Joaquin Phoenix. 106 minutes. Rated R.
A "true tabloid story" becomes "cuttingly observed satire" in this drama about "America's obsession with fame", a "wicked black comedy" due to "Buck Henry's brilliant script" and Van Sant's "incisive" direction; in her "most original role", Kidman "positively shines" as an "ambitious" TV weathergirl "trying to get ahead in her job and out of her marriage" – many say her performance alone is the "reason to see it."

To Have and Have Not ◑
26 | 27 | 24 | 24

1944. Directed by Howard Hawks. With Humphrey Bogart, Lauren Bacall, Walter Brennan. 100 minutes. Not Rated.
Bacall (in her screen debut) teams with future real-life hubby Bogart to "define star chemistry" in this dramatization of the Hemingway novel about WWII resistance runners; Martinique supplies a sultry backdrop for the two stars to "smolder", especially when Lauren "steams up the screen" with her legendary question "you know how to whistle, don't you?"

TO KILL A MOCKINGBIRD ✉◑
29 | 29 | 29 | 26

1962. Directed by Robert Mulligan. With Gregory Peck, Mary Badham, Robert Duvall. 129 minutes. Not Rated.
"After all these years", this Southern courtroom drama about racism and prejudice "told from the point of view of a young girl" "still packs the same emotional punch"; kudos go to Oscar-winning screenwriter Horton Foote "for not having strayed" from Harper Lee's "original text", and to an "im-peck-able" Peck at his "peak" as the "dad we wish we had"; in short, "Hollywood got this one right."

Tombstone
21 | 22 | 21 | 21

1993. Directed by George P. Cosmatos. With Kurt Russell, Val Kilmer, Sam Elliott. 130 minutes. Rated R.
More than an ok rendition of the "O.K. Corral story", this "slick retelling" brings legends Wyatt Earp and Doc Holliday up to date

with plenty of good old "modern-day violence"; starring a pistol-packing Russell and "fun-to-watch" Kilmer, it's a "worthy" enough stab at pure "entertainment" – "even if you don't like Westerns."

Tom Jones ✉   25 | 24 | 24 | 25

1963. Directed by Tony Richardson. With Albert Finney, Susannah York, Hugh Griffith. 121 minutes. Not Rated.
"Richly crafted and craftily acted" – with four Oscars to prove it – this hilariously "bawdy" "period piece par excellence" might be set in 18th-century England but moodwise is more like a "snap-shot of the Swinging '60s"; devotees are ever smitten with its "clever script", "lively direction" and Finney's "lusty" title turn, while gourmands eat up that "sexy food-seduction scene."

Tommy   16 | 14 | 16 | 20

1975. Directed by Ken Russell. With Roger Daltrey, Ann-Margret, Oliver Reed, Elton John. 111 minutes. Rated PG.
The Who's "seminal rock opera" goes Hollywood in this "over-the-top feast for the senses" that divides voters: ravers revel in the "great score", "Tina Turner as the Acid Queen" and that "scene with Ann-Margret and the baked beans", but bashers bawl it's a "disservice to both musicals and rock 'n' roll."

Tomorrow Never Dies   20 | 20 | 17 | 21

1997. Directed by Roger Spottiswoode. With Pierce Brosnan, Jonathan Pryce, Michelle Yeoh. 119 minutes. Rated PG-13.
" . . . and neither does James" joke 007 junkies of the juggernaut's 18th entry, wherein "Brosnan fills Connery's" custom-made shoes and "brings back" the secret agent's "cruel streak"; the "thoughtful plot" (something about a mad "media magnate" bent on starting WWIII) is buoyed by "high-tech special effects", though Bond-girl watchers say the picture belongs to the "fabulous" Yeoh.

Tootsie   25 | 27 | 24 | 23

1982. Directed by Sydney Pollack. With Dustin Hoffman, Jessica Lange, Bill Murray, Teri Garr. 119 minutes. Rated PG.
"Cross-dressing doesn't get much better" than this "brilliantly funny" comedy about a long-"struggling actor" who finally achieves success – "as an actress"; though Hoffman might be "one ugly" broad, his "sublime", "think-out-of-the-box" perfor-mance mixing "humor with humanity" is beautiful, while a "slick" but "unpredictable script" and an "outstanding" supporting cast make this one a "keeper, not a renter."

TOP GUN   22 | 18 | 20 | 24

1986. Directed by Tony Scott. With Tom Cruise, Kelly McGillis, Val Kilmer. 110 minutes. Rated PG.
"Sexy fighter pilots" populate this "absolutely irresistible" "'80s action icon", a roiling mix of "noise", "romance" and "aerial ma-neuvers"; Cruise "looks great in uniform" and that "volleyball scene" sure is "hot", but foes dis the "hokey" plot and "intermit-tent acting" and can't fathom why it's so "inexplicably popular."

TOP HAT ◑   27 | 23 | 21 | 26

1935. Directed by Mark Sandrich. With Fred Astaire, Ginger Rogers, Edward Everett Horton. 101 minutes. Not Rated.
"Heaven, I'm in heaven" sigh fans of this "classic '30s musical" spotlighting the big-city charms of a "debonair Astaire" opposite a "feather"-gowned Rogers; sure, there's an "all-hit Irving Berlin

score", "amazing production numbers" and a "witty French farce of a script", but in the end, it's "Fred and Ginger dancing cheek-to-cheek" that catapults it to "sublime"-ville.

Topkapi
24 | 22 | 25 | 21

1964. Directed by Jules Dassin. With Melina Mercouri, Peter Ustinov. 119 minutes. Not Rated.
Director "Dassin's '60s caper holds up well", managing to "avoid clichés the same way" its jewel-thief cast "avoid traps" as they engineer a heist in Istanbul; owing to a "clever script" and some "beautifully drawn characters" (like the "sophisticated" Mercouri and "priceless", "Oscar-winning" Ustinov), this "taut" thriller/comedy is reminiscent of an erstwhile "*Mission: Impossible.*"

Topper ◑ �**II**
20 | 21 | 21 | 19

1937. Directed by Norman Z. McLeod. With Roland Young, Constance Bennett, Cary Grant. 97 minutes. Not Rated.
Grant and Bennett "never miss a beat" in this "smart" romantic comedy about a pair of martini-swilling, madcap ghosts who must do a good deed to go to heaven; expect lots of laughs when the "delightful" phantoms select uptight banker Cosmo Topper as the beneficiary of their largesse in this "lighthearted" bit of "whimsy."

Topsy-Turvy
23 | 25 | 23 | 26

1999. Directed by Mike Leigh. With Jim Broadbent, Allan Corduner, Timothy Spall. 160 minutes. Rated R.
This "finely observed story about the stormy partnership of Gilbert and Sullivan" provides a "window into the Victorian age" as well as a "fascinating" glimpse into the "creative process" via a subplot about the first staging of *The Mikado*; "superb" acting (with an especially "grand Broadbent") and a "gorgeous production" make it a "joy to watch" for most, though a few yawn "boring."

Tora! Tora! Tora!
23 | 19 | 25 | 24

1970. Directed by Richard Fleischer, Kinji Fukasaku, Toshio Masuda. With Martin Balsam, Jason Robards, Joseph Cotten. 144 minutes. Rated G.
Surveyors split on this "intricate" war chronicle of the "Japanese attack on Pearl Harbor": defenders say this "ultimate docu-drama" is "well done historically", citing its "bilingual plotlines" and over-the-top "stunning" special effects, but curmudgeons counter it's a "comic-book" look at the tragedy.

To Sir, With Love �**II**
22 | 23 | 24 | 20

1967. Directed by James Clavell. With Sidney Poitier, Judy Geeson, Christian Roberts. 105 minutes. Not Rated.
The "always-excellent" Poitier stars in this "nice little piece of '60s" nostalgia as a "London high school teacher" passing on life lessons to "inner-city punks"; "sweet" and "timeless", it deals with "still-relevant" issues – "race, family conflicts, respect for authority" – in a "genuinely moving" fashion, and Lulu's smashing rendition of the title song "makes the movie."

Total Recall
18 | 14 | 21 | 22

1990. Directed by Paul Verhoeven. With Arnold Schwarzenegger, Rachel Ticotin, Sharon Stone. 113 minutes. Rated R.
"One of Ah-nuld's better" efforts may be this "exciting sci-fi adventure" flick, one of those "is-it-all-a-dream" stories about a secret agent implanted with someone else's memory chip; filmed

"just before the age of digital effects" dawned, this "visual tour de force" inspires diverse reactions – "original" vs. "mediocre" – though pacifists are peeved by all that "gratuitous violence."

Touch of Evil ◑
26 | 24 | 25 | 26

1958. Directed by Orson Welles. With Charlton Heston, Janet Leigh, Orson Welles. 95 minutes. Rated PG-13.
"Proof that Welles was more than a one-hit wonder", this "rococo" "pinnacle of film noir" stars the director as a "bloated" Texas border town cop feuding with his south-of-the-border counterpart (Heston in "Mexican blackface"); among its many memorable touches are the "sweeping" opening sequence and the "effortless scene-stealing" by Marlene Dietrich, who has the picture's best line: "lay off the candy bars"; P.S. the "restored version" is "much better" than the original release.

Towering Inferno, The
18 | 17 | 18 | 22

1974. Directed by John Guillermin, Irwin Allen. With Steve McQueen, Paul Newman, William Holden. 165 minutes. Rated PG.
"Make sure you know where all the exits are" before settling into this "big, bad '70s disaster" flick starring a skyscraper, a fire and a "rogues' gallery of great actors"; although the "passable" "special effects were top-drawer for its time", cynical sorts snort it's more of a "made-for-TV movie" by modern standards.

TOY STORY ⓫
27 | – | 25 | 28

1995. Directed by John Lasseter. Animated. 81 minutes. Rated G.
Ushering in a "new era of animation" with "breakthrough" computer-generated effects, this Pixar-produced "instant classic" is a bona fide "technical wonder"; its "humorous" storyline, "lovable characters" and the "great concept" of walking, talking toys add up to a picture that's not only "equally entertaining for adults and kids" but also "deserving of the franchise it started."

Trading Places
23 | 22 | 23 | 20

1983. Directed by John Landis. With Dan Aykroyd, Eddie Murphy, Jamie Lee Curtis. 118 minutes. Rated R.
This "hysterical" treatment of the "classic" "rags-to-riches" "switcheroo" has "pauper" Murphy turned into "prince" Aykroyd and vice-versa; "quickly paced and never boring", it's memorable for "early vintage" Eddie moments, some "funny" business from Dan and the spectacle of Jamie Lee's "exposed breasts."

Traffic ✉
23 | 24 | 23 | 25

2000. Directed by Steven Soderbergh. With Michael Douglas, Benicio Del Toro, Catherine Zeta-Jones. 147 minutes. Rated R.
Maybe "more realistic than you want", this "eye-opening portrait of the drug wars" is "poignant, intelligent" and "troubling", using "multiple storylines" to create a "stunning" hybrid of "thriller" and "cautionary tale"; the "amazing use of color", "documentary-like handheld" camerawork and Del Toro's deft, Oscar-winning turn all get the green light, though the highest praise is reserved for its "absolutely brilliant" director.

Training Day ✉
20 | 27 | 19 | 22

2001. Directed by Antoine Fuqua. With Denzel Washington, Ethan Hawke, Scott Glenn, Tom Berenger. 120 minutes. Rated R.
"Denzel shows his scary side" as a "profoundly bad" LA cop with "charisma" in his Oscar-winning role as a detective who has

"one day to teach the ropes" to a "rookie" (played by a "holding-his-own" Hawke); the "twisting" plot "grabs you from the very beginning" and takes you on one "wild ride."

Trainspotting
22 | 22 | 20 | 22

1996. Directed by Danny Boyle. With Ewan McGregor, Ewen Bremner, Robert Carlyle. 94 minutes. Rated R.

"Giddy and witty" but also "harrowing and intense", this "graphic" British drama depicting the "daily life of drug addicts" has a "kinetic rawness" about it that "gets right under your skin"; while "not for everyone", its "quirky" cinematography and "outstanding" '80s pop score make for "reality-check" viewing, but bring an "interpreter" – the "Scottish accents are thick."

TransAmerica
24 | 28 | 23 | 22

2005. Directed by Duncan Tucker. With Felicity Huffman, Kevin Zegers, Fionnula Flanagan. 103 minutes. Rated R.

Huffman's "fearless" portrayal of an "uptight" male-to-female transsexual who "learns she has a son" provides this "original" gender-bender dramedy with lots of "hilarious", "seat-squirming" moments mixed with "compelling", "raw emotion"; it "drags" in places, but its pro-"acceptance" message "pulls no punches."

TREASURE OF THE SIERRA MADRE, THE ⊠◑
27 | 27 | 26 | 24

1948. Directed by John Huston. With Humphrey Bogart, Walter Huston, Tim Holt. 126 minutes. Not Rated.

"Human nature poisoned by greed" is the theme of this "old-fashioned" "treasure hunt", a "wonderful adventure" that won Oscars for the father-and-son Hustons; Bogart exudes "masculine energy" showing "what gold will do to a man" in an "unforgettably powerful" performance that devolves into "paranoia" – and as for the "stunning" black-and-white photography, purists say "we don't need no stinkin' color."

Triplets of Belleville, The 🅵
24 | – | 23 | 26

2003. Directed by Sylvain Chomet. Animated. 80 minutes. Rated PG-13.

"Trippy and funny in a way that American animation isn't", this "art house" French cartoon sure "ain't Disney" with its "surreal" plot, "stylized" illustration and "nearly dialogue-free" soundtrack; having something to do with a kidnapped bicyclist rescued by his "grandmère", an "amazing" dog and the "wacky" Triplets of Belleville, it's both "innovative" and "offbeat", and probably more "for adults" than small fry.

Triumph of the Will ◑🅵
27 | – | 17 | 27

1935. Directed by Leni Riefenstahl. Documentary. 114 minutes. Not Rated.

"Perhaps the most powerful (and immoral) documentary" ever made, this "Leni Riefenstahl masterpiece" was commissioned to honor Germany's 1934 National Socialist Party Congress and the metaphorical "enthronement of Hitler"; the "superb" camera-work leads reluctant admirers to admit this "artful" propaganda piece is indeed a "triumph of filmmaking", if not subject matter.

Tron
18 | 14 | 18 | 22

1982. Directed by Steven Lisberger. With Jeff Bridges, Bruce Boxleitner, David Warner. 96 minutes. Rated PG.

Wired types tout this "underappreciated forerunner to today's special-effects" extravaganzas by dubbing it the "first real geek movie", owing to a storyline that posits what could happen "if you got sucked into your Nintendo"; ok, it could be a tad "dated" now, but it was the "coolest thing since sliced bread when it came out."

Troy   19 | 19 | 20 | 25
2004. Directed by Wolfgang Petersen. With Brad Pitt, Orlando Bloom, Eric Bana. 163 minutes. Rated R.
Homer's *Iliad* gets the "Hollywood treatment" in this "genuine epic" featuring lots of "oiled", "well-tanned" dudes in "miniskirts" engaged in battles that bear distinct "similarities to WWF wrestling"; wags say Brad's performance is the "only thing more wooden than the Trojan horse", but there's applause for the "action-packed" script and "excellent production values."

True Grit ✉ ⓪   22 | 23 | 21 | 22
1969. Directed by Henry Hathaway. With John Wayne, Glen Campbell, Kim Darby. 128 minutes. Rated G.
"Another Western for your library", this "classic" oater is made "especially for Wayne fans" because the Duke took home his first (and only) Oscar here; otherwise, it's standard stuff about a vengeful lawman, though early-in-their-career performances by Dennis Hopper and Robert Duvall keep things lively.

True Lies   19 | 16 | 20 | 22
1994. Directed by James Cameron. With Arnold Schwarzenegger, Jamie Lee Curtis. 144 minutes. Rated R.
"Arnold is Bond, James Bond" in this "tongue-in-cheek" spy flicker that's a "wonderful combo" of "comedy, action and intrigue"; as his "frumpy wife" turned "drop-dead gorgeous" siren, Jamie Lee is "smoking", while Tom Arnold's a "gas" as the "not-so-super secret-agent sidekick"; throw in "lots of explosions and weapons" and you've got a true "blockbuster" "blastfest."

True Romance   24 | 23 | 24 | 22
1993. Directed by Tony Scott. With Christian Slater, Patricia Arquette, Dennis Hopper, Christopher Walken. 120 minutes. Rated R.
Brace yourself for some "big-time gore" in this "ultraviolent" "true cult classic" about newlyweds on the run, scripted by a "pre-*Pulp Fiction* Quentin Tarantino" and featuring an "all-star" ensemble (including bits by Brad Pitt, Samuel L. Jackson and James Gandolfini "when they were little known"); sticklers note it "steals heartily from *Badlands*", but ultimately, it's "kinetic", "edgy" and just plain "cool."

Truman Show, The   21 | 22 | 23 | 22
1998. Directed by Peter Weir. With Jim Carrey, Laura Linney, Ed Harris. 103 minutes. Rated PG.
This "original", "thought-provoking" fantasy/comedy offers a "departure" for Carrey, who's "unusually restrained" (i.e. "doesn't act like a moron") in the role of an unwitting star of a 24/7 reality TV show set in a "phony world"; though some lookers find "little content" among all the "hype", intellectuals enthuse that this "Big Brother"–ish allegory leaves you "questioning what reality is."

Truth or Dare   15 | – | 14 | 17
1991. Directed by Alek Keshishian. Documentary. With Madonna. 118 minutes. Rated R.
"Ardent Madonna fanatics" say this "behind-the-scenes" documentary of her 1990 tour, a "warts-and-all" portrayal of the super-

star "not striking a pose", is "better than it has any right to be"; but knockers claim this "self-absorbed" "vanity project" is just "mugging for the camera", save for the cameo by Warren Beatty, who "looks appropriately embarrassed as her latest boy toy"; most amusing scene: "talking to Daddy on the phone."

Tucker: The Man and His Dream 20 | 21 | 23 | 21

1988. Directed by Francis Ford Coppola. With Jeff Bridges, Joan Allen, Martin Landau. 110 minutes. Rated PG.
For a "revealing look beneath the hood of the American auto industry", this "colorful", "stylish" film features a "terrific" Bridges in the sort of "true-ish story" of a "visionary '40s car maker and his sad defeat" at the hands of competitors and politicians; Coppola-ficionados say this "underrated" film "deserves more notice."

12 ANGRY MEN ◐ 28 | 28 | 27 | 23

1957. Directed by Sidney Lumet. With Henry Fonda, Martin Balsam, Lee J. Cobb, E.G. Marshall. 96 minutes. Not Rated.
"Human nature at its best and worst" is on display in this "brilliant courtroom drama" depicting the "hidden agendas" of jurors deciding the fate of a murder defendant; thanks to its "taut" script and an "unforgettable Fonda", this "study of American democracy" is alternately "suspenseful and compelling."

Twelve Monkeys 22 | 23 | 24 | 23

1995. Directed by Terry Gilliam. With Bruce Willis, Madeleine Stowe, Brad Pitt. 129 minutes. Rated R.
Gilliam's "master-of-the-bizarre" status is reinforced by this "complex", "super-ingenious" time-travel tale about the "release of a deadly virus" followed by a "post-apocalyptic" attempt to "save the world"; the sets are "dazzling", Brad 'n' Bruce prove they can "actually act" and if the "*Terminator*-meets-*Brazil*" sci-fi storyline is "confusing", it's "wonderfully" so.

Twelve O'Clock High ◑ 26 | 25 | 26 | 23

1949. Directed by Henry King. With Gregory Peck, Hugh Marlowe, Dean Jagger. 132 minutes. Not Rated.
"Peck is marvelous" as a WWII Brigadier General "placing terrible pressure on young American pilots" in this "accurate" depiction of the "burdens of command" and the "human side of war"; a "perfect screenplay" "rooted in historical reality" "manipulates the tension" right up to the compelling climax.

28 Days Later 18 | 17 | 19 | 18

2002. Directed by Danny Boyle. With Cillian Murphy, Naomie Harris. 113 minutes. Rated R.
"Modern-day horror" gets some "low-budget twists" in this "seriously scary" British import that "reinvents the zombie flick for the new millennium" in its story of a "viral disaster" that threatens civilization; while surveyors split on its digital video cinematography ("cool and grainy" versus "looks like it was shot with a bad camcorder"), most agree that the finale "wimps out" – although the DVD includes a number of "alternate endings."

25th Hour 21 | 25 | 20 | 21

2002. Directed by Spike Lee. With Edward Norton, Philip Seymour Hoffman, Barry Pepper. 135 minutes. Rated R.
A drug dealer "with one day left before prison turns to his friends for comfort" in this "captivating film that's even more poignant

given its tribute to post-9/11 NYC"; it's "not your typical Spike Lee, but still one of his best" thanks to "superb ensemble acting"; still, some say "it seemed like it was 25 hours long."

21 Grams
22 **27** **21** **21**

2003. Directed by Alejandro González Iñárritu. With Sean Penn, Naomi Watts, Benicio Del Toro. 124 minutes. Rated R.
"Not an easy watch", this "disturbing take on love and loss" details the lives of three people who meet as the result of a deadly accident; its "nonlinear storyline" told via "flashbacks and flashforwards" (à la *Memento* and *Pulp Fiction*") might be "intriguing" to some and "confusing" to others, but the "stellar" ensemble supplies enough "brain candy" to make for "compelling" viewing; in sum, be ready for an "emotionally draining downer" that's "moving, intelligent" and guaranteed to "keep you guessing."

20,000 Leagues Under the Sea
22 **18** **25** **23**

1954. Directed by Richard Fleischer. With Kirk Douglas, James Mason, Peter Lorre. 127 minutes. Rated G.
"Disney's live-action adaptation of the Jules Verne classic" is a "fabulous" undersea adventure starring a "singing", "tight shorts"—wearing Douglas as the heroic 19th-century seafarer who battles both Captain Nemo and a "scary giant squid" who "should have received an Oscar"; even though the special effects look "cheesy" today, overall it's a "real old-fashioned hoot."

Twister
15 **14** **14** **22**

1996. Directed by Jan de Bont. With Helen Hunt, Bill Paxton, Cary Elwes, Jami Gertz. 114 minutes. Rated PG-13.
"Mother nature" runs amok in this "far-fetched disaster movie" about Midwestern meteorologists tracking tornados; though the "fancy computer effects" make the "awesome" twisters "look so real", the "sleepwalking" actors and "easily forgettable" story with "no concern for logic" lead some to snore "major bore."

Two for the Road
24 **27** **24** **24**

1967. Directed by Stanley Donen. With Albert Finney, Audrey Hepburn. 111 minutes. Not Rated.
"Love isn't always easy" in this "bittersweet travelogue of the ups and downs of a married couple" that "jumps back and forth in time" as they "find, lose and rekindle" their relationship; Audrey's at her "most charming" and "marvelous" together with Finney amid all that "unmatched European scenery"; meanwhile, the "mesmerizing, melodious" Mancini music further "sustains the mood."

2001: A SPACE ODYSSEY 🔟
26 **19** **24** **27**

1968. Directed by Stanley Kubrick. With Keir Dullea, Gary Lockwood, William Sylvester. 139 minutes. Rated G.
The "*Citizen Kane* of science-fiction films", this "era-defining" Kubrick interpretation of an Arthur C. Clarke story "changed movies forever" with its "haunting view" of a future world of "machine domination"; sure, some modernists find it "slow" and "ponderous", but even those who have "no clue what it all means" say this "coldly magnificent" epic is "undeniably influential" – and add "you'll never hear Strauss' 'Blue Danube Waltz' the same way again"; P.S. "don't bother trying to figure out the ending."

2010
16 | 16 | 17 | 20

1984. Directed by Peter Hyams. With Roy Scheider, John Lithgow, Helen Mirren, Bob Balaban. 114 minutes. Rated PG.

"High-quality special effects" make this sequel to *2001* "relatively worthwhile", not to mention "less confusing", since a "more linear plot" "helps to explain the original storyline"; but foes insist it's "not in the same league at all", merely a "workmanlike" effort with "no transcendence", though admitting it "had an awful lot to live up to."

Two Weeks Notice
16 | 18 | 16 | 17

2002. Directed by Marc Lawrence. With Sandra Bullock, Hugh Grant. 101 minutes. Rated PG-13.

A "playboy" real estate tycoon and a "do-gooder" lawyer meet cute in this "soggy" romantic comedy, a "predictable" "bit of fluff" with an "obvious ending" and "only 10 minutes' worth of laughs"; further faults include a "flimsy script" and "no sense of true chemistry" between the otherwise "likable" leads – "no one in the real world behaves like this."

Two Women ✉◑🄵
▽ 25 | 28 | 25 | 22

1961. Directed by Vittorio De Sica. With Sophia Loren, Eleanora Brown, Raf Vallone. 99 minutes. Not Rated.

The "horror of war" from a "woman's viewpoint" is delineated in this "heartbreaking" Italian drama where a "protective mother and her daughter" bond after being "brutally raped" by a gang of soldiers; best remembered for Sophia's "riveting" performance, it's a "very emotional" film that's "seldom seen these days."

U-571
17 | 17 | 19 | 21

2000. Directed by Jonathan Mostow. With Matthew McConaughey, Bill Paxton, Harvey Keitel. 116 minutes. Rated PG-13.

This "tense" World War II "submarine flick" brings out plenty of "claustrophobia" in its story of a tightly quartered American crew duking it out with a German U-boat under high seas; while it's "no *Das Boot*" (given "so-so acting" and a "could-have-been-better" storyline "full of obvious holes"), it's still a "rousing", bona fide guy movie.

Umbrellas of Cherbourg, The 🄵
24 | 22 | 21 | 26

1964. Directed by Jacques Demy. With Catherine Deneuve, Nino Castelnuovo. 87 minutes. Not Rated.

Ultra-"bright Technicolor" and "captivating" music from Michel Legrand provide the uplift in this "sad story" of love in vain, an idiosyncratic French bonbon that's "entirely sung" (a "risky" proposition that ultimately "works"); starring a "fetching young Deneuve", it has the "courage" to turn a potentially "cheesy" premise into "inspiring" filmmaking.

Unbearable Lightness of Being, The
21 | 24 | 21 | 21

1988. Directed by Philip Kaufman. With Daniel Day-Lewis, Juliette Binoche, Lena Olin. 171 minutes. Rated R.

"Romance amid revolution" is the theme of this erudite picture about the "erotic" misadventures of a young Czech surgeon swept up in the '68 Russian invasion of Prague; while the light-headed like the "hottie" cast's "compelling" work, cynics sneer this "yawner" "leaves a lot to be desired" and suggest the title be cut to just plain "*Unbearable*."

Unbreakable   16 | 19 | 17 | 19
2000. Directed by M. Night Shyamalan. With Bruce Willis,
Samuel L. Jackson, Robin Wright Penn. 107 minutes.
Rated PG-13.
Ok, it's "hard to live up to *The Sixth Sense*", but this solid follow-
up from the Shyamalan/Willis team "keeps you wondering all the
time" with its "intriguing" story of a "man struggling with immor-
tality"; though surveyors split on the end result (a "noble failure"
vs. "terribly underrated"), holdouts insist it "warrants more than
one viewing" to be fully appreciated.

Uncle Buck   17 | 18 | 17 | 17
1989. Directed by John Hughes. With John Candy, Amy Madigan,
Jean Louisa Kelly. 100 minutes. Rated PG.
"Among John Candy's best", most "lovable" roles is his heavy-
duty turn as a "derelict turned babysitter" in this lightweight comedy; while the "movie itself is just ok", the "funny dialogue" and
heroic oafishness of the lead prevail – and an appearance by a
pre–*Home Alone* Macaulay Culkin adds to its family appeal.

Under Siege ⓤ   15 | 11 | 14 | 16
1992. Directed by Andrew Davis. With Steven Seagal, Tommy Lee
Jones, Gary Busey. 102 minutes. Rated R.
Think "*Die Hard* on a battleship" to get the gist of this "graphically
violent" Seagal vehicle where he "kicks some serious ass" to
keep his "reputation afloat"; maybe the plot about lunatic villains
thieving nukes is "moronic", but at least the "kill-first-ask-
questions-later" sensibility is "entertainingly dumb."

Under the Tuscan Sun   19 | 20 | 18 | 22
2003. Directed by Audrey Wells. With Diane Lane, Sandra Oh,
Raoul Bova. 113 minutes. Rated PG-13.
A newly divorced woman buys a house in "picturesque Tuscany"
to start her life anew and "find herself" in this "coming-into-
bloom" picture, a "feel-good" chick flick worth seeing for Lane's
"warm, genuine performance" alone; alright, "it isn't *Enchanted
April*" by a long shot, and there's "not much storyline", but it's still
"sweet and fun."

Unfaithful   21 | 24 | 20 | 20
2002. Directed by Adrian Lyne. With Diane Lane, Richard Gere,
Olivier Martinez. 124 minutes. Rated R.
Diane Lane is "spectacular" and "so convincing" as a modern
housewife "torn between guilt and thrills as she embarks on
an affair" with a "hot" stranger, and Richard Gere delivers the
"most mature, nuanced performance of his career" as the
"cuckold" in this "unexpectedly intense film" that's "disturbing in its credibility"; "now if only they'd found a better plot" and a
less "lame" ending.

Unforgiven ✉   26 | 26 | 24 | 25
1992. Directed by Clint Eastwood. With Clint Eastwood, Gene Hackman,
Morgan Freeman. 131 minutes. Rated R.
"Clint directs, Clint scores, Clint wins" a Best Picture statuette
with this "grim" "anti-Western" that manages to "revise every
convention and cliché of the genre" with a "superb script" and
cast of "unforgivable", "unforgettable" characters; indeed, it's so
"powerful" and "dark", you'll find "no white hats here."

Unmarried Woman, An
20 | 25 | 21 | 19

1978. Directed by Paul Mazursky. With Jill Clayburgh, Alan Bates, Michael Murphy. 130 minutes. Rated R.

This "very-much-of-its-time" portrait of a "New Yorkey" divorcée "in transition" offers a "thoughtful", "emotional" examination of a '70s "woman's lib"–style romance; the picture broke "new ground" when originally released, thanks to the "excellent" Clayburgh as the recently "single" gal, though postfeminists posit it may "seem dated now."

Unsinkable Molly Brown, The
21 | 20 | 20 | 21

1964. Directed by Charles Walters. With Debbie Reynolds, Harve Presnell, Ed Begley. 128 minutes. Not Rated.

"Think of it as the last big" MGM musical and "you'll be in for a good evening's entertainment" with this "rollicking" bio of a turn-of-the-century "bawdy broad who wants it all and gets it"; warblers adore the "rip-roarin'" Reynolds in the title role, who drowns all doubts about how "she got the name 'unsinkable.'"

Untouchables, The
22 | 22 | 22 | 22

1987. Directed by Brian De Palma. With Kevin Costner, Sean Connery, Robert De Niro. 119 minutes. Rated R.

"Sassy" '30s crime drama recounting the epic "good-vs.-evil" struggle between Eliot Ness and Al Capone, as interpreted by Costner and De Niro (wearing "amazing Armani suits" that nearly upstage them); while this "period piece" has "exciting action" and "style to spare", the most "compelling" work comes from the Oscar-winning Connery as a streetwise copper.

Upside of Anger, The
22 | 26 | 21 | 22

2005. Directed by Mike Binder. With Joan Allen, Kevin Costner, Erika Christensen, Evan Rachel Wood. 118 minutes. Rated R.

"Rage and depression" are about to overwhelm an abandoned housewife when a "washed-up baseball player" steps up to the plate to "suffer by her side" in this "acute observation" of "real people"; it pairs the "amazing" Allen with a "hang-loose" Costner, but apart from the "great screen chemistry", there's a downside: that "difficult-to-swallow" "surprise" ending.

Uptown Girls
14 | 16 | 15 | 15

2003. Directed by Boaz Yakin. With Brittany Murphy, Dakota Fanning. 92 minutes. Rated PG-13.

"Don't set your expectations too high" before watching this "feel-good" story of a "spoiled rich girl" who goes broke and becomes a nanny for a "poor little trust fund" kid; as "mindless" chick flicks go, it's appropriately "shallow" and "cutesy-pie", though it does attempt to teach a lesson about the "power of friendship" that makes sentimental types "cry like a baby."

Urban Cowboy
18 | 17 | 16 | 17

1980. Directed by James Bridges. With John Travolta, Debra Winger, Scott Glenn. 132 minutes. Rated PG.

Travolta "in tight jeans" plays opposite Winger at her most "adorable" in this "highly watchable" honky-tonk romance of "beer-swigging", "mechanical bull–riding" men and the women who love them; although Debra nearly "steals the show", she's almost bested by an appealing Houston setting.

USUAL SUSPECTS, THE ✉   27 | 28 | 28 | 25
1995. Directed by Bryan Singer. With Gabriel Byrne, Kevin Spacey, Benicio Del Toro, Stephen Baldwin. 106 minutes. Rated R.
"Don't blink" or you'll risk missing one of the many "imaginative" twists in this "tricky-as-hell" "instant classic" that may be one of the finest "whodunit" "thrill rides" ever made; fans "watch it at least twice" to absorb the "brilliant" story, admire the "flawless" Spacey and figure out what the heck "Benicio's saying"; as for that "unpredictable finale", you'll "never see it coming."

Van Helsing   15 | 15 | 14 | 21
2004. Directed by Stephen Sommers. With Hugh Jackman, Kate Beckinsale. 132 minutes. Rated PG-13.
"Superficially entertaining", this horror flick–cum–"thrill machine" about a bounty hunter hounding Dracula, Frankenstein and various werewolves should be "pure escapist fun" what with its "nonstop", "over-the-top" special effects, yet many call it a "big mess"; though Jackman "broods elegantly" in the title role, he's up against a "muddled storyline", Beckinsale's "awful accent" and an "overblown" production that seems more about "merchandising" than moviemaking.

Vanity Fair   17 | 19 | 18 | 23
2004. Directed by Mira Nair. With Reese Witherspoon, James Purefoy, Ramola Garai, Eileen Atkins. 141 minutes. Rated PG-13.
A "visually beautiful" interpretation of Thackeray's "bitingly satirical" novel, this "opulent" romance tells the story of a "conniving" social climber trying to "elevate herself into society" in 19th-century Britain; but many say this "less than faithful adaptation" suffers most from a "miscast Reece", who's "more cutesy than cunning" and "never ages" in a story that unwinds over 30 years.

Vera Drake   24 | 28 | 25 | 23
2004. Directed by Mike Leigh. With Imelda Staunton. 125 minutes. Rated R.
Wherever you stand on Roe vs. Wade, it's "hard not to be moved" by this "devastating portrait" of a "well-meaning abortionist who runs afoul of the law" in '50s London; "delicate" direction by Leigh keeps the "polarizing" material in check, while "flawless" performances by a "magnificent" ensemble (particularly Staunton's "unforgettable" title turn) ensure there's "never a false moment."

Verdict, The   23 | 25 | 23 | 20
1982. Directed by Sidney Lumet. With Paul Newman, Charlotte Rampling, Jack Warden. 129 minutes. Rated R.
A "David-vs.-Goliath" legal struggle is the underpinning of this "underrated" courtroom drama about a "burned-out lawyer trying one last case to keep from going under"; Newman's "intense", "tour-de-force" turn is one of his "greatest" roles (leaving many "stunned" that the Oscar eluded him), while the "mesmerizing" Rampling "excels" as the love interest.

Veronica Guerin   21 | 25 | 22 | 20
2003. Directed by Joel Schumacher. With Cate Blanchett, Gerard McSorley. 98 minutes. Rated R.
"Versatile" Blanchett "shines" as a "determined" Dublin journo "fighting the good fight" against drug lords in this "gripping"

thriller based on a true but "tragic" story; if the thick brogues are "hard to follow" and the overall message skews toward "heavy-handedness", most feel it's Guerin-teed to "make you wonder" about some tough issues.

VERTIGO
27 | 26 | 27 | 26

1958. Directed by Alfred Hitchcock. With James Stewart, Kim Novak, Tom Helmore. 128 minutes. Rated PG.

"Don't look down": this "dizzyingly complex" thriller offers lots of "twists and turns" as it details the "haunting" tale of an "obsessive" man who "tries to mold a woman into a vision of his lost love"; many call it "Hitchcock's crowning achievement" thanks to a Bernard Herrmann score that's "like perfume" as well as "spellbinding" work from a "bewitching Novak" and "Stewart at his darkest"; as for that "fever dream" of a plot, "it's not supposed to make sense."

Very Long Engagement, A F
22 | 24 | 22 | 25

2004. Directed by Jean-Pierre Jeunet. With Audrey Tautou, Gaspard Ulliel. 134 minutes. Rated R.

Amélie's "dynamic duo" (director Jeunet and "radiant" actress Tautou) reunite for this "beautifully done" French war saga whose "graphic" depictions of WWI trenches are tempered by a "tearful" story of "lost love"; with "so many characters", the "complex storyline" can be "hard to follow" and "takes time" to develop, leaving some to retitle it *A Very Long Movie.*"

V for Vendetta
22 | 22 | 22 | 24

2006. Directed by James McTeigue. With Natalie Portman, Hugo Weaving, Stephen Rea. 132 minutes. Rated R.

"Reminiscent of *1984*" with its "dark" depiction of a "totalitarian" society, this "provocative" futuristic thriller relating the exploits of a "Guy Fawkes–like" rebel is "V for very good" thanks to "spine-tingling" visuals, "swiftly paced" action and "well-acted" characterizations by Portman and Weaving; flirting with the "controversial subject of terrorism", it strikes many as a "not-so-subtle" allusion to "current events."

Victor/Victoria
23 | 24 | 23 | 23

1982. Directed by Blake Edwards. With Julie Andrews, James Garner, Robert Preston. 132 minutes. Rated PG.

"What a hoot!" holler fans who "never tire of watching" Blake Edwards' "hilarious" musical farce about Parisian nightlife denizens in the '30s; "Andrews lights up the screen" as the titular double-crossed cross-dresser, while Leslie Ann Warren's fabulous floozie is deliciously "over-the-top"; in sum, this "fast-paced", "madcap" tale of "jazz-age gender bending" is "just plain fun."

View to a Kill, A ⑪
14 | 13 | 14 | 18

1985. Directed by John Glen. With Roger Moore, Christopher Walken, Tanya Roberts, Grace Jones. 131 minutes. Rated PG.

"Old" Moore caps his 12-year run as 007 – and "not in the best way" – with this "forgettable" installment pitting the secret agent against a psycho industrialist, whose scheme "to corner the world market in microchips" was a silly premise "even in 1985"; granted, it may have "some of the best stunts and title music" of the series and a "scary" Bond girl in Grace Jones, but the final view on this one is "clunker."

Village of the Damned ◐ ⓤ

1960. Directed by Wolf Rilla. With George Sanders, Barbara Shelley, Michael Gwynn. 78 minutes. Not Rated.

An "unfortunate town" becomes host to an army of "alien children" with funny eyeballs in this "spooky" British sci-fi flick that "succeeds without a lot of fancy effects"; ever "cool" over 45 years later, it still "creeps out" viewers ("whoever thought kids could be so scary?") who advise "don't bother with the '95 version."

Wages of Fear ◐ 🄵

27 | 26 | 27 | 24

1953. Directed by Henri-Georges Clouzot. With Yves Montand, Charles Vanel. 148 minutes. Not Rated.

"Fasten your seatbelts for a bumpy" ride via this "nerve-racking" "nail-biter" about "down-and-outers" racing a "nitroglycerine-loaded truck" across the mountains of South America; Clouzot's knack for "oh-my-God" suspense and "social commentary" makes it one of the "best art-house action" flicks around.

Wag the Dog

19 | 22 | 22 | 19

1997. Directed by Barry Levinson. With Dustin Hoffman, Robert De Niro, Anne Heche. 97 minutes. Rated R.

Pundits praise this "biting black comedy" that "makes light (and dark) of media-oriented politics" via a "surreal" story about a "nonexistent war created by the government to divert attention" from a presidential scandal; though some wonder if it's a "documentary", others tout this "underrated" political satire for Hoffman and De Niro's "standout" turns.

Waiting for Guffman

25 | 26 | 24 | 23

1996. Directed by Christopher Guest. With Christopher Guest, Eugene Levy, Fred Willard, Catherine O'Hara. 84 minutes. Rated R.

"Anyone who loves the theater and loves to laugh" shouldn't miss this "hilarious" mockumentary about "community theater in the boonies" courtesy of "comic genius" Guest and his "usual incredibly talented ensemble"; it's a "laugh riot from the first frame to the last", with "classic" scenes you'll "quote lines from" – "I'm still searching for *My Dinner with Andre* action figures."

Wait Until Dark

25 | 26 | 27 | 23

1967. Directed by Terence Young. With Audrey Hepburn, Alan Arkin, Richard Crenna. 107 minutes. Not Rated.

This "unforgettable" thriller posits a "simple, nerve-shattering premise": a blind woman, all alone in her apartment, in a "game of cat-and-mouse" with a "brutal psychopath"; gird yourself for an "eerie Henry Mancini soundtrack" and a "twists-and-turns"–laden scenario with "one particularly electrifying moment" that's guaranteed to "have you out of your seat."

WALK THE LINE ✉

25 | 28 | 23 | 25

2005. Directed by James Mangold. With Joaquin Phoenix, Reese Witherspoon. 136 minutes. Rated PG-13.

The "Man in Black" walks again courtesy of this "evocative", "behind-the-music" biopic that pays "touching tribute" to country "legend" Johnny Cash and his "true love", June Carter, the "good woman" who "saved him" from a life of "drugs and temptation"; both Phoenix and Witherspoon are "phenomenal" (yep, "they do their own singing"), and the "foot-stomping" tunes "ain't bad", either; P.S. don't mind the unmistakable "similarity to *Ray*."

Wallace & Gromit in the Curse of the Were-Rabbit

24 | – | 22 | 27

2005. Directed by Steve Box, Nick Park. Animated. 85 minutes. Rated G.
Appearing in their first feature-length flick, "goofy" gadgeteer Wallace and his silently "expressive" pooch Gromit come to the neighborhood's rescue when a "mutated rabbit terrorizes its gardens" in this "jolly good", "for-all-ages" claymation comedy brimming with "Brit wit" and "inventive" visual spectacle; fans beg series creator Nick Park "please sir, may we have some more?"

Wall Street ✉

22 | 23 | 22 | 21

1987. Directed by Oliver Stone. With Michael Douglas, Charlie Sheen, Martin Sheen. 125 minutes. Rated R.
"Greed is good" in this "quintessential insider's view" of the "go-go '80s" as personified by "ruthless financier" Gordon Gecko, an "ever-so-cool" piece of "Wall Street slime", "brilliantly executed" by the Oscar-winning Douglas; the "world of high finance" in all its "moneymaking" excess is captured here "like in no other film."

War of the Roses, The

17 | 20 | 17 | 18

1989. Directed by Danny DeVito. With Michael Douglas, Kathleen Turner, Danny DeVito. 116 minutes. Rated R.
"You need a slightly off-color sense of humor" (namely, "black") to enjoy this "daring" comedy about the "disintegration of a marriage" and subsequent "over-the-top divorce shenanigans"; still, the "materialism, ego and folly" are played out with such a "mean-spirited", "venomous edge" that some find it "completely depressing and charmless."

War of the Worlds, The

23 | 16 | 24 | 23

1953. Directed by Byron Haskin. With Gene Barry, Ann Robinson, Les Tremayne. 85 minutes. Rated G.
Although the "Orson Welles radio broadcast" is "more famous", this "faithful" filming of the H.G. Wells "sci-fi classic" still clearly telegraphs its "frightening premise" of Martians run amok on Planet Earth; ok, it may be a bit "overstated" and "unintentionally funny today", but boob-tubers tune in "every time it's on television."

Wayne's World ⑪

17 | 14 | 15 | 15

1992. Directed by Penelope Spheeris. With Mike Myers, Dana Carvey, Rob Lowe. 95 minutes. Rated PG-13.
"One of the few *Saturday Night Live* skits to soar in a longer format", this parody of local access cable TV shows is an "inventive", "mindless" romp that was one of the biggest box office comedies of the '90s; it's also the breakout for the pre–*Austin Powers* Myers, who gives an "awesome" rendition of "stupidity at its finest."

Way We Were, The

24 | 25 | 25 | 23

1973. Directed by Sydney Pollack. With Barbra Streisand, Robert Redford, Bradford Dillman. 118 minutes. Rated PG.
"Still a tearjerker after all these years", this "improbable romance" pits a "brainy" Jewish girl opposite a "golden Wasp boy" and "tugs every heartstring available" in its "realistic" depiction of their "ill-fated" affair; Streisand and Redford "at their peak" are "beyond delicious" together, though the most indelible "memories" involve the "famous final scene" at the "Plaza Hotel" with that "sad", Oscar-winning song playing in the background.

Wedding Banquet, The 🎦 | 22 | 21 | 25 | 21 |

1993. Directed by Ang Lee. With Winston Chao, May Chin, Mitchell Lichtenstein. 106 minutes. Rated R.

"Family dynamics" get a "touching" twist in this "gently told" Taiwanese tale about a "marriage of convenience" between a "gay man" hoping to make his parents happy and his green card–seeking bride; this "funny charade" comes to a climax at the titular feast, where "unconditional love" comes "out of the closet" in a "warmhearted" if "bittersweet finale."

Wedding Crashers | 21 | 21 | 20 | 21 |

2005. Directed by David Dobkin. With Owen Wilson, Vince Vaughn, Christopher Walken. 119 minutes. Rated R.

Fast becoming the "Lemmon and Matthau" of the "overgrown frat boy" set, Wilson and Vaughn play a pair of "opportunistic womanizers" who "prey on weddings" to "get their groove on" in this "deliciously vulgar" comedy; despite some "mushy" messing around with a "semi-serious love story", overall it delivers enough "flashes of hilarity" to make for "easy viewing."

Wedding Singer, The | 17 | 16 | 16 | 16 |

1998. Directed by Frank Coraci. With Adam Sandler, Drew Barrymore. 96 minutes. Rated PG-13.

Take a "blast to the past" via this romantic comedy set in the "suburban '80s" whose real stars are its rocking retro soundtrack and obligatory "tasteless fashion" parade; beyond that, it's a "cute if insipid" "chick flick" about a down-and-out wedding singer, "dejected love" and its "sweet" redemption.

Welcome to the Dollhouse | 22 | 21 | 21 | 19 |

1995. Directed by Todd Solondz. With Heather Matarazzo, Matthew Faber, Eric Mabius. 88 minutes. Rated R.

A "dead-on look at the horrors" of junior high, this "scathing" study of a "dorky adolescent" "hits close to home" thanks to an "eerily real" performance by Matarazzo as the "picked-on" protagonist; both "cruelly funny" and "disturbingly accurate", it makes some oldsters "worry about young people today."

WEST SIDE STORY ✉ | 27 | 24 | 27 | 27 |

1961. Directed by Robert Wise, Jerome Robbins. With Natalie Wood, Richard Beymer, Rita Moreno, George Chakiris. 151 minutes. Not Rated.

Starting with that "opening bird's-eye view of NYC", this "remarkable musical" that transposes *Romeo and Juliet* to "urban" turf is "sheer perfection" thanks to "fiery acting", "superb" streetwise choreography and the "dynamic" Leonard Bernstein/Stephen Sondheim score; sure, Beymer might be "miscast" and it's "too bad they didn't let Natalie sing", but otherwise this Oscar magnet – 10 statuettes including Best Picture – is "forever fabulous."

Westworld 🎞 | 19 | 16 | 21 | 20 |

1973. Directed by Michael Crichton. With Yul Brynner, Richard Benjamin, James Brolin. 88 minutes. Rated PG.

You can "see where *Jurassic Park* came from" in this sci-fi thriller whose "irresistible premise" involves a futuristic resort where vacationers live out their Wild West fantasies with robot stand-ins; though sharp-shooters say Brynner is "perfect" as an "android gunslinger" gone haywire, cynics ponder the idea of a "wooden actor playing an automaton."

We Were Soldiers
21 | 22 | 21 | 23

2002. Directed by Randall Wallace. With Mel Gibson, Madeleine Stowe, Greg Kinnear, Sam Elliott. 138 minutes. Rated R.
The "first ground battle of the Vietnam War" is "authentically replicated", "graphic violence" and all, in this "powerful" profile of the "humanity and courage" of America's soldiers in the thick of "intense action"; with a special salute going to Gibson's portrayal of a "religious man" turned "battlefield leader", some grunt this is "one of the most overlooked" combat pics around.

Whale Rider
25 | 26 | 24 | 24

2003. Directed by Niki Caro. With Keisha Castle-Hughes, Rawiri Paratene, Vicki Haughton. 101 minutes. Rated PG-13.
Featuring "no stars, no explosions and no CGI effects", this nonetheless "powerful" film tells the "captivating" story of a Maori girl's struggle to help her tribe balance "tradition and the 21st century"; a "refreshing", family-friendly slice of "edutainment" complete with "beautiful" New Zealand vistas and "phenomenal" work by "up-and-comer" Castle-Hughes, this "achingly sad" story will "leave your soul touched."

What About Bob?
18 | 19 | 18 | 17

1991. Directed by Frank Oz. With Bill Murray, Richard Dreyfuss, Julie Hagerty. 99 minutes. Rated PG.
Proving that "life is indeed baby steps", this "dark" comedy about a "shrink driven nuts" by a "psycho patient" pairs the "screwball" Murray with the "hilarious" Dreyfuss; though the picture might be "as irritating as it is funny", your "sides will hurt" from laughter all the same.

What Dreams May Come
16 | 17 | 15 | 24

1998. Directed by Vincent Ward. With Robin Williams, Cuba Gooding Jr., Annabella Sciorra. 113 minutes. Rated PG-13.
"Extremely pleasing to the eye", this "beautiful fantasy of the afterlife" "based on the touching Richard Matheson novel" finds Williams desperately trying to rescue his wife's soul from the underworld; but realists report a "sappy", "schmaltzy script" and sum this one up as "visually exquisite, but little else."

Whatever Happened to Baby Jane? ◐
22 | 25 | 23 | 21

1962. Directed by Robert Aldrich. With Bette Davis, Joan Crawford, Victor Buono. 134 minutes. Not Rated.
"Campy and creepy", this "classic" exercise in Grand Guignol is the last hurrah of Hollywood's "two queen bees" in a "frightening" story of the "hate-hate relationship" between a pair of movie-star sisters; expect an "audacious" Crawford facing off against an "over-the-top" Davis, whose "grotesque" appearance is "too scary to think about" for too long; most memorable scene: Joan's "rat à-la-carte" din-din.

What Lies Beneath
16 | 18 | 16 | 18

2000. Directed by Robert Zemeckis. With Harrison Ford, Michelle Pfeiffer, Diana Scarwid. 126 minutes. Rated PG-13.
This "chilling" "Hitchcockian" thriller about a "sinister ghost" at loose in the house is a "slick" endeavor, with enough "scary moments" to "make you jump" out of your seat; but foes find the "cable-TV-caliber script" "silly" and "predictable", and wonder what "A-list actors" are doing in this "overwrought", "C-list movie."

What's Eating Gilbert Grape
22 | 25 | 22 | 21

1993. Directed by Lasse Hallström. With Johnny Depp, Juliette Lewis, Leonardo DiCaprio, Mary Steenburgen. 118 minutes. Rated PG-13.
An "original" study of an ultra-"dysfunctional" family, this "weirdly winning" dramedy features a "quietly intense" Depp opposite a "brilliant" DiCaprio "before he became a teen idol"; its "loving look at two fringe groups – the obese and the mentally challenged" – turns this "quirky" tale into "surprisingly good" moviemaking.

What's Love Got to Do with It
22 | 26 | 22 | 21

1993. Directed by Brian Gibson. With Angela Bassett, Laurence Fishburne. 118 minutes. Rated R.
That Tina Turner "never did anything nice and easy" is plain to see in this "perfect" biopic depicting how a "gifted" gal "got the strength to move on" from an abusive marriage to super-duper stardom; in a picture that's "all about the acting", Bassett is "outstanding", but be warned that it can be "painful to watch."

What's Up, Doc?
21 | 20 | 21 | 20

1972. Directed by Peter Bogdanovich. With Barbra Streisand, Ryan O'Neal, Madeline Kahn. 94 minutes. Rated G.
"Streisand's like butter" in this "zany" "modern screwball comedy" "reminiscent of *Bringing Up Baby*" wherein some "terrific Ryan-Babs chemistry" is brought to bear on a nutty storyline involving "igneous rocks", identical plaid suitcases and a "fantastic comic car chase through San Francisco"; P.S. "Kahn's a scream" in her film debut.

What Women Want
15 | 17 | 17 | 16

2000. Directed by Nancy Meyers. With Mel Gibson, Helen Hunt, Marisa Tomei. 126 minutes. Rated PG-13.
A misogynist is redeemed after becoming superhumanly "sensitized" to women's inner monologues in this "enjoyably light" chick flick; while it might "miss the mark" due to "predictable" plotting, it's an "original concept" that's "worth it just to see" "Mad Max Mel struggle with pantyhose."

WHEN HARRY MET SALLY . . .
26 | 25 | 25 | 24

1989. Directed by Rob Reiner. With Billy Crystal, Meg Ryan, Carrie Fisher, Bruno Kirby. 96 minutes. Rated R.
"Can a man and a woman be just friends?"; this romantic comedy – the "king of all date movies" – attempts to answer that question as it details a "terrific take on relationships" that "rings true for many"; written by Nora Ephron as an "ode to Manhattan", it stars an "adorable", "pre-pixie cut" Ryan opposite a "perfect" Crystal, both "forever remembered" for the "infamous orgasm scene" in Katz's Deli that inspired one of the best lines in moviedom: "I'll have what she's having."

Where's Poppa?
23 | 25 | 23 | 21

1970. Directed by Carl Reiner. With George Segal, Ruth Gordon, Trish Van Devere, Ron Leibman. 82 minutes. Rated R.
This "twisted" black comedy from Carl Reiner examines the "sick relationship" between a "senile" mom living with her "dutiful (up-to-a-point)" son; "painfully funny", it's acquired "cult" status over the years for set pieces like the "ape suit scene" and the "tush-biting" sequence; P.S. the jaw-dropping original ending, an extra on the DVD, is truly "insane."

While You Were Sleeping
18 | 19 | 20 | 18

1995. Directed by Jon Turteltaub. With Sandra Bullock, Bill Pullman, Peter Gallagher. 103 minutes. Rated PG.

"Token-booth worker" Bullock "falls in love with two brothers" in this "tender" romantic comedy, an "engaging", "Cinderella"-like "fairy tale" trading on "mistaken identity"; sure, it's "feel-good fluff", but the "unique storyline", "sweet" performances and "great chemistry" between the leads add up to an "all-around cute movie."

White Christmas
25 | 21 | 22 | 24

1954. Directed by Michael Curtiz. With Bing Crosby, Danny Kaye, Rosemary Clooney. 120 minutes. Not Rated.

"It wouldn't be Christmas" without a peek at this "sentimental" favorite, a virtual holiday "requirement" with "all the trimmings": "wonderful dance numbers", "essential" Irving Berlin tunes and "Der Bingle" crooning "kringle jingles"; in short, this "classic" is so "charming", it's almost "un-American not to love it"; P.S. sticklers note that Bing originally "made the title song famous in *Holiday Inn*."

White Heat ◑
25 | 28 | 24 | 23

1949. Directed by Raoul Walsh. With James Cagney, Virginia Mayo, Edmond O'Brien. 114 minutes. Not Rated.

One part "descent into madness", one part "valentine to mom", this schizophrenic, noirish thriller represents the "classic gangster film refined to the nth degree"; as a "homicidal nut job" "mama's boy", Cagney turns in one of his "greatest performances", though the flick's most remembered for the "best last line in movie history": 'made it, ma! top of the world!'

White Oleander
18 | 23 | 19 | 19

2002. Directed by Peter Kosminsky. With Michelle Pfeiffer, Renée Zellweger, Alison Lohman, Robin Wright Penn. 109 minutes. Rated PG-13.

A "manipulating" mom in prison and a "conflicted teen" shunted from foster home to foster home are the protagonists of this "solid coming-of-age drama" based on the "offbeat", Oprah-endorsed best-seller; maybe it "falls short of being really great" (many say the "book was better"), but at least this "interesting tale of growth and change" is "perfectly cast."

Who Framed Roger Rabbit
24 | – | 23 | 27

1988. Directed by Robert Zemeckis. Animated. With Bob Hoskins, Christopher Lloyd. 103 minutes. Rated PG.

This "one-of-a-kind treat" featuring a "glorious mix of live action and animation" boasts an all-star cartoon cast, with appearances by every 'toon from Mickey to Woody (though the "seductive" Jessica Rabbit runs away with the picture); set in the Hollywood of yore, the "classic" noir plot has Hoskins investigating a murder case, with "wonderfully entertaining" results.

Who's Afraid of Virginia Woolf? ✉◑
25 | 27 | 25 | 23

1966. Directed by Mike Nichols. With Elizabeth Taylor, Richard Burton, George Segal, Sandy Dennis. 134 minutes. Not Rated.

Maybe "Liz made up to look frumpy is a laugh", but otherwise this "scalding adaptation" of Edward Albee's "masterpiece" about an "unraveling marriage" is pretty serious stuff, "brilliantly acted" and "brutally honest"; it's "funny and mean and sad" all at once – "never has a play been converted into a movie" with such "power."

WILD BUNCH, THE | 27 | 26 | 25 | 27 |
1969. Directed by Sam Peckinpah. With William Holden, Ernest Borgnine, Robert Ryan. 134 minutes. Rated R.
Not for the faint of heart, this "blood-and-guts" Peckinpah "epic" is a "Western to end all Westerns" that "transcends the genre" with an "in-your-face style" that turns "violence into poetry"; starring Holden as the leader of a band of "honorable outlaws", it depicts a "changing world" at the "end of an era" in "unsentimental" terms and manages to be both "noble and perverse at the same time."

Wild One, The ◐ | 22 | 24 | 19 | 20 |
1953. Directed by László Benedek. With Marlon Brando, Mary Murphy, Lee Marvin. 79 minutes. Not Rated.
"Brando on a motorcycle" in "tight black leather" sums up the appeal of this '50s cautionary tale about a gang of bikers that terrorizes a small town; sure, it's "dated" and "mild by today's standards", yet Marlon's "bad-boy attitude" alone keeps it "compelling"; most "unforgettable" exchange: "what are you rebelling against? – whaddya got?"

Wild Strawberries ◐🅕 | 26 | 26 | 24 | 25 |
1959. Directed by Ingmar Bergman. With Victor Sjöström, Bibi Andersson, Ingrid Thulin. 91 minutes. Not Rated.
"Essential Bergman" that's not just for art movie mavens, this "elegiac" "road film about life, death and redemption" "continues to hold up well"; a "bittersweet" story of an "elderly doctor who learns how to love at the last minute of his life", it's ultimately "hopeful", even if it displays the director's signature "depressive" streak.

Willow | 20 | 18 | 20 | 22 |
1988. Directed by Ron Howard. With Val Kilmer, Joanne Whalley, Warwick Davis. 130 minutes. Rated PG.
"If you like *Princess Bride*", you'll like this "wonderfully escapist" fantasy featuring "appealing" characters in a sword-and-sorcery story that "seems familiar" to those who dub it a "*Lord of the Rings*" clone; "Kilmer's gorgeous" and there's plenty of "excitement", but some say that it's a "formulaic disappointment."

WILLY WONKA AND THE CHOCOLATE FACTORY | 26 | 22 | 26 | 26 |
1971. Directed by Mel Stuart. With Gene Wilder, Jack Albertson, Peter Ostrum. 100 minutes. Rated G.
Chocoholics cheer this "delicious family classic" adeptly adapted from the "brilliant Roald Dahl book" about an "underdog" kid who gets a "once-in-a-lifetime" chance to tour a "curious candy factory"; it's such a "blast to watch" (thanks to "psychedelic" sets, "imaginative" vignettes and "great songs") that it's almost become a "rite of passage" for the stroller set.

Wind and the Lion, The | 24 | 25 | 24 | 24 |
1975. Directed by John Milius. With Sean Connery, Candice Bergen, Brian Keith. 119 minutes. Rated PG.
This "old-fashioned, character-driven adventure" about an Arab chieftain's abduction of an American widow is loosely "based on a real incident during Teddy Roosevelt's presidency"; despite the

"wonderful desert romance" that blooms between the "charismatic" Connery and "watchable" Bergen, there's "still enough action for the guys" in this "obscure history lesson."

Winged Migration   26 | – | 21 | 28
2003. Directed by Jacques Perrin, Jacques Cluzaud, Michel Debats. Documentary. 98 minutes. Rated G.
"Soar with the birds" in this "breathtaking" documentary whose "amazing camerawork" puts you shoulder-to-wing with "flocks flying" around the globe; a "masterpiece" that will "awaken your appreciation" of nature's "avian heroes", it "should be required viewing" for budding environmentalists and cinematographers alike; P.S. one welcome feature: there's "no bad acting."

Wings of Desire ❶❷🄵   24 | 24 | 22 | 25
1988. Directed by Wim Wenders. With Bruno Ganz, Solveig Dommartin. 127 minutes. Rated PG-13.
A "charming meditation" about the "angels who watch over us", "longing to be human", this "haunting" German film "celebrates the human condition"; "dreamy cinematography" and an "amazing" cast elevate it to "pure poetry" – but don't "judge it by its self-conscious remake", Hollywood's "unfortunate" *City of Angels*.

Witches of Eastwick, The   17 | 20 | 18 | 18
1987. Directed by George Miller. With Jack Nicholson, Cher, Susan Sarandon, Michelle Pfeiffer. 118 minutes. Rated R.
Three small-town gals take on the devil himself in this "funny but disturbing" comedy, a variation on the "beauty-and-the-beast" theme based on the John Updike novel; no surprise, a "wicked Jack" walks away with the picture, triumphing over the occasionally "weird storyline" and "bizarre" denouement.

Witness ✉   23 | 24 | 23 | 22
1985. Directed by Peter Weir. With Harrison Ford, Kelly McGillis, Lukas Haas. 112 minutes. Rated R.
"One of Weir's finest", this "quiet" film offers a "sensitive portrayal" of a "small Amish community" that "collides with the violent outside world" in the aftermath of a murder; the actors have "perfect pitch" (particularly the "workmanlike" Ford, who "sizzles" against the "luminous McGillis"), and even if the story's somewhat "improbable", its overall "excellence sneaks up on you."

WITNESS FOR THE PROSECUTION ◑   27 | 28 | 28 | 25
1957. Directed by Billy Wilder. With Tyrone Power, Marlene Dietrich, Charles Laughton. 116 minutes. Not Rated.
Perhaps the "best murder mystery ever", this "Agatha Christie puzzler" is one of "Wilder's wiliest", featuring "two legends" – an "incredible" Laughton and an "outstanding" Dietrich – along with a courtroom-full of "compelling characterizations"; the dialogue "crackles" and the "plot twists and double twists" right up to the "still shocking ending."

WIZARD OF OZ, THE   28 | 26 | 28 | 29
1939. Directed by Victor Fleming. With Judy Garland, Ray Bolger, Jack Haley, Bert Lahr. 101 minutes. Rated G.
A "star is born" – the "iconic" "Judy, Judy, Judy" – in this "timeless", "transporting" musical about a Kansas girl "off to see the Wizard" that's been "adored for decades" thanks to its "tremendous" cast, "glorious", "rainbow"-hued score and "inspired"

moments involving a pair of "ruby slippers", a pack of "scary flying monkeys" and that "magical", "hello-Technicolor" transition; in Toto, this "landmark in family entertainment" is the ultimate proof that "there's no place like home."

Wolf Man, The ◑⓫   20 | 19 | 22 | 19
1941. Directed by George Waggner. With Lon Chaney Jr., Claude Rains, Ralph Bellamy. 70 minutes. Not Rated.
This "classic Universal monster" flicker set the "standard for fright" in its day with a hair-raising mix of ominous gypsies, howling werewolves and foreboding full moons; a "superb" Chaney stars as the fuzzy-faced lead, though a few howl about his "hammy" acting chops and "special effects that look damn silly" now.

WOMAN OF THE YEAR ✉◑   27 | 28 | 26 | 26
1942. Directed by George Stevens. With Katharine Hepburn, Spencer Tracy, Fay Bainter. 114 minutes. Not Rated.
The "war between the sexes was never more fun" than in this first matchup of legendary duo Hepburn and Tracy in what some call the "best" of their eight films together; its Oscar-winning script pits the "right-on" Kate as an "ahead-of-her-time" foreign correspondent against Spence's laid-back sportswriter, but the hands-down winner in this battle of wills is clearly the audience.

Woman Under the Influence, A   24 | 27 | 22 | 21
1974. Directed by John Cassavetes. With Peter Falk, Gena Rowlands. 155 minutes. Rated R.
"Raw, naturalistic performances" lie at the core of this "stunning", "hyper-real" drama about a "housewife's sad decline" into mental illness; a "heartbreaking" Rowlands plays the title role "like a Stradivarius", and even though some "overlong, meandering" scenes can be "difficult to watch", ultimately it's a "tender", "uncompromising" look at the "beautiful mess that is marriage."

Women, The ◑   ▽ 27 | 26 | 26 | 25
1939. Directed by George Cukor. With Norma Shearer, Joan Crawford, Rosalind Russell, Paulette Goddard. 133 minutes. Not Rated.
"Meow!": a "wonderful wallow" in "fabulous bitchiness", this "marvelous" MGM adaptation of Clare Boothe Luce's "clever" stage play about high-society divorcées boasts an all-star, all-gal cast rattling off "extraordinary fast-paced" dialogue; though the constant "cattiness" can be a turnoff, it's still "required viewing" for "chick flick" and camp followers.

Women in Love ✉   23 | 26 | 24 | 23
1969. Directed by Ken Russell. With Alan Bates, Oliver Reed, Glenda Jackson, Jennie Linden. 131 minutes. Rated R.
Ken Russell's "visually amazing", "erotically charged" take on the D.H. Lawrence novel "deals frankly" with two couples' struggle to conform to the sexual conventions of 1920s England; it's a "sensual", "memorable" picture that's most renowned for Jackson's Oscar-winning turn and its notorious "nude male wrestling scene."

Women on the Verge of a Nervous Breakdown 🇫   24 | 24 | 23 | 22
1988. Directed by Pedro Almodóvar. With Carmen Maura, Antonio Banderas. 90 minutes. Rated R.
Forget the "depressing" title: this "campy", "door-slamming farce" "put director Almodóvar on the map" and is one of the

"funniest foreign films" ever made; a "wacky" story of "neurotic characters with different agendas", it also introduced "eye-candy Banderas to the Western world."

Wonder Boys

`21` `24` `21` `20`

2000. Directed by Curtis Hanson. With Michael Douglas, Tobey Maguire, Frances McDormand. 111 minutes. Rated R.
Douglas shines in this "intelligent" if "overlooked" dramedy as a "humpy-shlumpy" college professor stultified by writer's block compounded by a "midlife crisis"; a "funny, smart and caring" piece of moviemaking, it supplies "many different interwoven storylines" – though calculators say its "parts prove greater than the sum of the whole."

Woodsman, The

`21` `27` `21` `20`

2004. Directed by Nicole Kassell. With Kevin Bacon, Kyra Sedgwick. 87 minutes. Rated R.
Venturing far afield from his *Footloose* beginnings, Bacon earns "high marks" for his "daring" turn as a "recovering pedophile" desperately "seeking a second chance" in this "honorably realistic" indie character study; fans warn if you're not in the mood to "feel sorry for" a "fragile" child molester, this one's gonna be "hard to watch."

Woodstock

`24` `–` `21` `23`

1970. Directed by Michael Wadleigh. Documentary. With Jimi Hendrix, The Who. 184 minutes. Rated R.
"Drop out, turn on and tune in" to this "seminal pop-culture event", a "groundbreaking" rockumentary about the fabled "peace-and-love" concert that's a "near-perfect snapshot" of the era, "minus the bad acid"; though ticked-off "tie-dyed flower children" sniff the "split-screen stuff gets old" and find "too much mud and not enough Hendrix", peaceniks maintain that this "marathon" movie provides "evidence that the summer of love was no pipe dream."

Working Girl

`20` `20` `21` `19`

1988. Directed by Mike Nichols. With Melanie Griffith, Harrison Ford, Sigourney Weaver. 109 minutes. Rated R.
"Workplace revenge" was never funnier than in this "Cinderella-by-way-of-Wall-Street" "chick flick" that "empowers every woman who's had to put up with a difficult boss"; Griffith's at her "dumb girl/smart girl best", Weaver's "delightfully loathsome" and Ford's "adorable" "not playing an action hero for a change"; favorite line: "I've got a head for business and a bod for sin."

World According to Garp, The

`21` `23` `22` `19`

1982. Directed by George Roy Hill. With Robin Williams, Mary Beth Hurt, Glenn Close. 131 minutes. Rated R.
An "unforgettable", "modern-day fairy tale" full of "bizarre characters", this adaptation of John Irving's best-seller relates the "weird life" of T.S. Garp, beginning with his conception "when his mother sleeps with a man on his death bed"; though "unusual" is putting it mildly, this "unforgettable" tale is ultimately "affecting."

World Is Not Enough, The

`19` `19` `18` `21`

1999. Directed by Michael Apted. With Pierce Brosnan, Denise Richards. 128 minutes. Rated PG-13.
Though admittedly "pure escapism", 007's 19th trip to the big screen divides voters: fans vow that Pierce is "as good as Sean",

but foes growl that "gadgets have replaced characterization and plot" and snicker at the "ludicrous" Richards playing a "short-shorts–wearing nuclear physicist."

WUTHERING HEIGHTS ◑ | 27 | 27 | 27 | 24 |
1939. Directed by William Wyler. With Laurence Olivier, Merle Oberon, David Niven. 103 minutes. Not Rated.
This "Gothic romance" is a "charter" member of the "pantheon" of silver screen weepies and the "ultimate" adaptation of the Brontë tale; Olivier's "soulful brooding" as a spurned, lower-caste lover is so "brilliantly intense" that it's inspired generations of maidens to "waste away from heartbreak on the moors" ever after.

X-Files, The | 17 | 17 | 16 | 19 |
1998. Directed by Rob Bowman. With David Duchovny, Gillian Anderson, Martin Landau. 120 minutes. Rated PG-13.
Both "fans and novices appreciate" this blockbuster adaptation of the TV series that's "just like the show" but with some "twists" and an "occasional dirty word" thrown in; it doesn't "answer any questions" and may be "muddled, disappointing" stuff to connoisseurs, but it does "serve as a bridge between seasons" with some "catchy" moments.

X-Men ⓫ | 19 | 18 | 18 | 23 |
2000. Directed by Bryan Singer. With Patrick Stewart, Hugh Jackman, Ian McKellen, Halle Berry, James Marsden. 104 minutes. Rated PG-13.
Even those "who've never read the comic book" chime in with their "ringing endorsement" of this "true-to-the-source" adaptation of the Marvel sci-fi series; most memorable for Jackman's "starmaking turn", it's such an obvious "setup for a franchise" that many "popcorn" eaters are hungrily "awaiting the sequels."

X-Men: The Last Stand | 20 | 19 | 19 | 25 |
2006. Directed by Brett Ratner. With Hugh Jackman, Halle Berry, Ian McKellen, Famke Janssen. 104 minutes. Rated PG-13.
The "choice to be normal or true to themselves" confronts movieland's mutant superheroes as they battle "discrimination" and each other in this "big bang" finale to the franchise – or is it?; piling on more "spectacular" effects than ever (i.e. the "Golden Gate Bridge ripped from its base"), this "boisterous" juggernaut doesn't let up until the "last scene *after* the credits."

X2: X-Men United ⓫ | 24 | 21 | 22 | 27 |
2003. Directed by Bryan Singer. With Patrick Stewart, Hugh Jackman, Ian McKellen, Brian Cox. 133 minutes. Rated PG-13.
"Finally, a sequel to sink your claws into": this "X-cellent" follow-up "tops the mediocre original" "in just about every way" – a "better storyline", "intriguing new characters", a "deservedly bigger role" for the "buff", "brooding" Jackman and "mega-cool special effects" . . . "what a bigger budget will do for a movie"; "can't wait for the next one – and there *will* be a next one."

XXX ⓫ | 15 | 12 | 14 | 20 |
2002. Directed by Rob Cohen. With Vin Diesel, Asia Argento, Samuel L. Jackson. 124 minutes. Rated PG-13.
"Check your brain at the door" and get snowed under by an avalanche of "terrific stunts" and "blowed-up stuff" in this "steroidal" refashioning of "James Bond" for the "slacker generation"; as for the acting, Vin's rendition of a "smartass" agent bent on

"saving the world" is "kinda stupid", though some Diesel disciples still stand by their man – provided he "zips his flap."

Yankee Doodle Dandy ✉ ◑   25 | 25 | 23 | 25

1942. Directed by Michael Curtiz. With James Cagney, Joan Leslie, Walter Huston. 126 minutes. Not Rated.

"Flag-waving", "red-white-and-blue" musical bio of the "all-American" showman George M. Cohan, starring Cagney in full "hoofer" bloom; the story's "whitewashed", but after a few bars of its "patriotic tunes" you'll understand why the "4th of July wouldn't be the same without it."

Year of Living Dangerously, The   24 | 25 | 25 | 24

1983. Directed by Peter Weir. With Mel Gibson, Sigourney Weaver, Linda Hunt. 117 minutes. Rated PG.

An outbreak of "civil war" during the "Sukarno regime" in '60s Indonesia comes alive in this "captivating" "political" drama following a journalist who's covering the conflict; though the "compelling" Gibson and Weaver cast "steamy sparks", Hunt took home an Oscar for her "tour-de-force", "gender-bending role" in this "tense" thriller.

Yellow Submarine   22 | – | 18 | 23

1968. Directed by George Dunning. Animated. 90 minutes. Rated G.

"Contagiously fun", this "lighthearted" "hallucination" of a cartoon supplies "eye-popping" "psychedelic" imagery aplenty in recounting a story about the Fab Four's battle to save Pepperland from the Blue Meanies; though the "actual Beatles don't provide" the speaking parts, their performance on the "foot-tapping" soundtrack is "more than enough" – and the music "won't drive parents crazy."

Yentl ∅   18 | 19 | 19 | 20

1983. Directed by Barbra Streisand. With Barbra Streisand, Mandy Patinkin, Amy Irving. 132 minutes. Rated PG.

"La Streisand" does it all – "acts, sings and directs" – in this "underrated", "impeccably made" musical about a turn-of-the-century Jewish girl masquerading as a "boy in order to study the Talmud"; though foes call it Babs at her "self-indulgent worst", fans counter her "incredible talent" and "amazing attention to detail" make this "emotionally stirring" picture "deserving of more credit."

Yojimbo ◑ⅡⒻ   ▽ 27 | 27 | 25 | 25

1961. Directed by Akira Kurosawa. With Toshiro Mifune, Tatsuya Nakadai. 110 minutes. Not Rated.

"Kurosawa's classic samurai film" stars Mifune as the "ultimate antihero" who "plays both sides" of a village feud between a silk merchant and a sake merchant, and then watches as the depraved "warring factions" destroy each other; the "inspiration" for myriad remakes (*A Fistful of Dollars, Last Man Standing,* etc.), this "far superior" original clearly "shows how great this director really is."

You Can Count on Me   23 | 26 | 22 | 20

2000. Directed by Kenneth Lonergan. With Laura Linney, Mark Ruffalo, Rory Culkin, Matthew Broderick, John Tenney. 109 minutes. Rated R.

Freshman director Lonergan "doesn't take a false step" in this "compelling", "character-driven" indie film about the "family bonds" between a "messed-up brother and sister" and the divergent paths their lives have taken; you can count on lots of "terrific acting" (with a "breakout performance from Linney") and a "lifelike lack of final resolution" that makes this a "sleeper with a heart."

YOUNG FRANKENSTEIN ◑   27 | 26 | 25 | 25
1974. Directed by Mel Brooks. With Gene Wilder, Peter Boyle, Marty Feldman, Madeline Kahn, Cloris Leachman. 108 minutes. Rated PG.
"Frankenstein Sr. would be proud" of this "insanely hysterical" "spoof of the Mary Shelley" horror classic that's Mel Brooks' "high-water mark"; Wilder is "pure genius" in the title role backed up by an "endlessly amusing" cast of characters spouting some of the "most quoted" dialogue in movie history; best line: a toss-up between "walk this way", "what knockers" and "hump? what hump?"; best song: Kahn's rendition of 'Ah! Sweet Mystery of Life', no contest.

Young Guns ⓫   15 | 12 | 15 | 17
1988. Directed by Christopher Cain. With Emilio Estevez, Kiefer Sutherland, Lou Diamond Phillips, Charlie Sheen. 107 minutes. Rated R.
This "good Wild West romp 'n' stomp flick" featuring the "Brat Pack" in all their glory chronicles the beginnings of Billy the Kid's felonious career with his band of misfits, the Regulators; though "hardly the best movie ever", it works when you're in the mood for "interesting escapist fun."

You Only Live Twice   22 | 21 | 20 | 22
1967. Directed by Lewis Gilbert. With Sean Connery, Mie Hama, Donald Pleasence. 117 minutes. Rated PG.
"Despite the absurdity of a six-foot-plus Scotsman as a spy in Japan", diehards declare this espionage flicker one of the "better Connery Bonds", given its amusing "'60s Tokyo" settings and that "great Nancy Sinatra" theme song; ok, it might be "cheesy", but camp followers claim that's what makes it "all the more fun now."

You've Got Mail   18 | 20 | 18 | 18
1998. Directed by Nora Ephron. With Tom Hanks, Meg Ryan, Parker Posey, Greg Kinnear, Jean Stapleton. 119 minutes. Rated PG.
Manhattan's "Upper West Side looks like Paris" in this "feel-good" romantic comedy, a "remake of *The Shop Around the Corner*" updated to "today's techie, e-mail-ish world"; though a tad too "cutesy pie" and "predictable" for cynics, "chick flick" fans find it "enchanting" thanks to that "great chemistry between Hanks and Ryan."

Y Tu Mamá También 🆔   24 | 24 | 23 | 21
2002. Directed by Alfonso Cuarón. With Maribel Verdu, Gael García Bernal, Diego Luna, Diana Bracho. 105 minutes. Rated R.
Two "upper-middle-class Mexican boys" "learn the facts of life" and then some from a "sexy older woman" during a road trip "that takes some unexpected turns" in this *muy caliente* "coming-of-age" character study; some say "everything takes a back seat (no pun intended)" to the "very explicit sex scenes" – whew! – but more cerebral types see it more as a "passionate film about life, youth and love" that's "far greater than the sum of its parts."

Z ✉🆔   26 | 25 | 26 | 24
1969. Directed by Costa-Gavras. With Yves Montand, Irene Papas, Jean-Louis Trintignant, Jacques Perrin. 127 minutes. Rated PG.
Unfortunately all "too true", this fact-based account of the assassination of a left-leaning scientist in a right-wing country is a

crackerjack "political thriller" that's "deeply affecting" and "not easy to watch"; Montand is "nothing less than superb" in the title role, while director Costa-Gavras makes this "documentary-like" "exposé" of corruption "captivating from the first scene."

Zelig ◑ | 20 | 20 | 21 | 21 |
1983. Directed by Woody Allen. With Woody Allen, Mia Farrow. 79 minutes. Rated PG.
What could be "Forrest Gump's ancestor" is the much "more charming (and neurotic) Zelig", a human chameleon who somehow manages to play a prominent role in 20th-century world events with "dryly comedic" results; it's an unusual, "technically complex" outing for the usually straightforward Allen that "warps history" by "digitally" inserting our hero into vintage "newsreel footage", but cynics say this "curiosity piece" has only "one clever idea" and "should have been funnier."

Zorba the Greek ◑ | 25 | 27 | 25 | 23 |
1964. Directed by Michael Cacoyannis. With Anthony Quinn, Alan Bates, Irene Papas, Lila Kedrova, Georges Foundas. 142 minutes. Not Rated.
There's ex-zorba-tant praise for this "still-fresh" drama about an Englishman visiting Crete on an existential quest, only to fall under the spell of a "person full of passion", the "flamboyant" Zorba; Quinn's "breakout" performance, plus some "memorable" theme music and dancing, keep this "feel-good" "affirmation of life" so "exciting and entertaining" that repeaters faithfully "see it every year."

Zulu Ⅱ | 24 | 24 | 25 | 24 |
1964. Directed by Cy Endfield. With Stanley Baker, Jack Hawkins, Michael Caine. 138 minutes. Not Rated.
The "true story of valor in the face of incredible odds", this "epic treatment of a 19th-century British military disaster" is played out against the "broad canvas of Africa" and features an "unknown Caine" in his "first big film"; "visually and viscerally stunning", it's "historically accurate without sacrificing dramatic appeal", and the "tension's unrelenting."

Indexes

DECADES
GENRES/SPECIAL FEATURES

DECADES

1910s/1920s
Birth of a Nation
Cabinet of Dr. Caligari
Cocoanuts, The
General, The
Gold Rush
Greed
Intolerance
Metropolis
Napoléon
Nosferatu
Potemkin
Thief of Bagdad

1930s
Adventures of Robin Hood
Alexander Nevsky
All Quiet on the Western Front
Angels with Dirty Faces
Animal Crackers
Awful Truth
Beau Geste
Blue Angel
Bride of Frankenstein
Bringing Up Baby
Captain Blood
Captains Courageous
City Lights
Dark Victory
David Copperfield
Day at the Races
Destry Rides Again
Dinner at Eight
Dracula (1931)
Duck Soup
42nd Street
Frankenstein
Freaks
Front Page
Fury
Gay Divorcee
Gone with the Wind
Goodbye, Mr. Chips
Grand Hotel
Grand Illusion
Gunga Din
Horse Feathers
Hound of the Baskervilles
Hunchback/Notre Dame (1939)
Invisible Man

It Happened One Night
King Kong (1933)
Lady Vanishes
Little Caesar
Lost Horizon
M
Modern Times
Monkey Business
Mr. Deeds Goes to Town
Mr. Smith Goes to Washington
Mummy, The (1932)
Mutiny on the Bounty (1935)
My Man Godfrey
Night at the Opera
Ninotchka
Nothing Sacred
Public Enemy
Rules of the Game
Scarlet Empress
Snow White
Stagecoach
Tarzan and His Mate
Tarzan the Ape Man
Thin Man
39 Steps
Top Hat
Topper
Triumph of the Will
Wizard of Oz
Women, The
Wuthering Heights

1940s
Adam's Rib
All the King's Men
Arsenic and Old Lace
Bambi
Beauty/Beast (1947)
Best Years of Our Lives
Bicycle Thief
Big Sleep
Bishop's Wife
Brief Encounter
Buck Privates
Casablanca
Children of Paradise
Citizen Kane
Double Indemnity
Duel in the Sun
Dumbo

Easter Parade
Fantasia
Fort Apache
For Whom the Bell Tolls
Fountainhead, The
Gaslight
Gentleman's Agreement
Ghost and Mrs. Muir
Gilda
Going My Way
Grapes of Wrath
Great Dictator
Great Expectations
Gun Crazy
Hamlet (1948)
Heaven Can Wait (1943)
High Sierra
His Girl Friday
Holiday Inn
How Green Was My Valley
It's a Wonderful Life
I Was a Male War Bride
Jane Eyre
Jungle Book (1942)
Key Largo
Killers, The
Kind Hearts and Coronets
Lady Eve
Lady from Shanghai
Laura
Letter, The
Lifeboat
Little Foxes
Lost Weekend
Magnificent Ambersons
Maltese Falcon
Man Who Came to Dinner
Mark of Zorro
Meet Me in St. Louis
Mildred Pierce
Miracle on 34th Street
Monsieur Verdoux
Mr. Blandings
Mrs. Miniver
Murder, My Sweet
National Velvet
Notorious
Now, Voyager
On the Town
Open City
Out of the Past
Ox-Bow Incident
Palm Beach Story

Philadelphia Story
Pinocchio
Postman Always Rings... (1946)
Pride and Prejudice (1940)
Pride of the Yankees
Rebecca
Red River
Red Shoes
Rope
Sergeant York
Shadow of a Doubt
She Wore a Yellow Ribbon
Snake Pit
Song of Bernadette
Song of the South
Sorry, Wrong Number
Spellbound (1945)
Sullivan's Travels
Suspicion
Third Man
To Be or Not to Be
To Have and Have Not
Treasure of the Sierra Madre
Twelve O'Clock High
White Heat
Wolf Man
Woman of the Year
Yankee Doodle Dandy

1950s

Affair to Remember
African Queen
Alice in Wonderland
All About Eve
American in Paris
Anastasia (1956)
Anatomy of a Murder
Around the World in 80 Days
Asphalt Jungle
Auntie Mame
Bad and the Beautiful
Bad Day at Black Rock
Bad Seed
Band Wagon
Bell, Book and Candle
Ben-Hur
Big Heat
Blackboard Jungle
Black Orpheus
Born Yesterday
Bridge on the River Kwai
Brigadoon
Bus Stop

Caine Mutiny
Carmen Jones
Carousel
Cat on a Hot Tin Roof
Cheaper By the Dozen (1950)
Christmas Carol
Cinderella
Damn Yankees
Day the Earth Stood Still
Desk Set
Diabolique
Dial M for Murder
Diary of Anne Frank
D.O.A.
East of Eden
Father of the Bride (1950)
5,000 Fingers of Dr. T.
Fly, The (1958)
Forbidden Planet
400 Blows
Friendly Persuasion
From Here to Eternity
Funny Face
Gentlemen Prefer Blondes
Giant
Gigi
Godzilla
Gunfight at O.K. Corral
Guys and Dolls
Harvey
High Noon
High Society
House of Wax
How to Marry a Millionaire
Imitation of Life
Invasion/Body Snatchers (1956)
I Want to Live!
Jailhouse Rock
Journey to Center of Earth
King and I
King Solomon's Mines
Kiss Me Deadly
Kiss Me Kate
Lady and the Tramp
Ladykillers, The (1956)
La Strada
Lavender Hill Mob
Lili
Limelight
Love in the Afternoon
Love Is a Many-Splendored
Man Who Knew Too Much
Marty

Mister Roberts
Mon Oncle
Moulin Rouge
Mouse That Roared
Mr. Hulot's Holiday
Niagara
Night of the Hunter
Nights of Cabiria
North by Northwest
No Time for Sergeants
Oklahoma!
Old Yeller
Oliver Twist
On the Beach
On the Waterfront
Operation Petticoat
Paths of Glory
Peter Pan (1953)
Peyton Place
Pickup on South Street
Picnic
Pillow Talk
Place in the Sun
Quiet Man
Rashomon
Rear Window
Rebel Without a Cause
Rio Bravo
Robe, The
Roman Holiday
Room at the Top
Sabrina
Searchers, The
Seven Brides/Seven Brothers
Seven Samurai
Seventh Seal
7th Voyage of Sinbad
Seven Year Itch
Shane
Show Boat
Singin' in the Rain
Sleeping Beauty
Smiles of a Summer Night
Some Like It Hot
South Pacific
Stalag 17
Star Is Born
Strangers on a Train
Streetcar Named Desire
Suddenly, Last Summer
Sunset Boulevard
Sweet Smell of Success
Ten Commandments

Thing, The (1951)
Three Coins in the Fountain
Three Faces of Eve
To Catch a Thief
Touch of Evil
12 Angry Men
20,000 Leagues Under the Sea
Vertigo
Wages of Fear
War of the Worlds
White Christmas
Wild One, The
Wild Strawberries
Witness for the Prosecution

1960s

Absent-Minded Professor
Alamo, The
Alfie
Apartment, The
Barbarella
Battle of Algiers
Becket
Bedazzled
Belle de Jour
Bells Are Ringing
Billy Liar
Birdman of Alcatraz
Birds, The
Blowup
Bob & Carol & Ted & Alice
Bonnie and Clyde
Born Free
Breakfast at Tiffany's
Breathless
Bride Wore Black
Bullitt
Butch Cassidy/Sundance Kid
Bye Bye Birdie
Cactus Flower
Camelot
Cape Fear (1962)
Cat Ballou
Charade
Charly
Cleopatra
Collector, The
Contempt
Cool Hand Luke
Counterfeit Traitor
Damned, The
Darling
Days of Wine and Roses

Dirty Dozen
Divorce Italian Style
Doctor Zhivago
Don't Look Back
Dr. No
Dr. Strangelove
Easy Rider
8½
El Cid
Elmer Gantry
Elvira Madigan
Exodus
Experiment in Terror
Faces
Fahrenheit 451
Fail-Safe
Fantastic Voyage
Finian's Rainbow
Fistful of Dollars
Flight of the Phoenix
For a Few Dollars More
Fortune Cookie
From Russia With Love
Funny Girl
Funny Thing Happened...
Goldfinger
Goodbye, Columbus
Good, the Bad and the Ugly
Graduate, The
Great Escape
Great Race
Guess Who's Coming...
Guns of Navarone
Gypsy
Hard Day's Night
Hatari!
Hello, Dolly!
Help!
Hiroshima, Mon Amour
How the West Was Won
Hud
Hustler, The
In Cold Blood
Inherit the Wind
In the Heat of the Night
Irma La Douce
It's a Mad Mad Mad World
Judgment at Nuremberg
Jules and Jim
Juliet of the Spirits
Jungle Book (1967)
King of Hearts
Knife in the Water

La Dolce Vita
L'Avventura
Lawrence of Arabia
Leopard, The
Lilies of the Field
Lion in Winter
Lolita
Longest Day
Lord of the Flies
Love Bug
Magnificent Seven
Man and a Woman
Manchurian Candidate (1962)
Man for All Seasons
Man Who Shot Liberty Valance
Mary Poppins
Midnight Cowboy
Miracle Worker
Misfits, The
Music Man
Mutiny on the Bounty (1962)
My Fair Lady
Never on Sunday
Night of the Living Dead
Nutty Professor (1963)
Ocean's Eleven (1960)
Odd Couple
Oliver!
Once Upon a Time/West
101 Dalmatians (1961)
One, Two, Three
On Her Majesty's Secret
    Service
Paint Your Wagon
Parent Trap
Pawnbroker, The
Persona
Pink Panther
Pit and the Pendulum
Planet of the Apes
Prime of Miss Jean Brodie
Producers, The
Psycho
Raisin in the Sun
Repulsion
Requiem for a Heavyweight
Romeo and Juliet
Rosemary's Baby
Russians Are Coming...
Sand Pebbles
Satyricon
Servant, The
Seven Days in May

Ship of Fools
Shoot the Piano Player
Shot in the Dark
Sound of Music
Spartacus
Splendor in the Grass
Spy Who Came in from Cold
Sweet Charity
Swiss Family Robinson
Take the Money and Run
They Shoot Horses, Don't They?
Thomas Crown Affair
Thoroughly Modern Millie
Thunderball
Time Machine
To Kill a Mockingbird
Tom Jones
Topkapi
To Sir, With Love
True Grit
Two for the Road
2001: A Space Odyssey
Two Women
Umbrellas of Cherbourg
Unsinkable Molly Brown
Village of the Damned
Wait Until Dark
West Side Story
Whatever Happened to...
Who's Afraid of V. Woolf?
Wild Bunch
Women in Love
Yellow Submarine
Yojimbo
You Only Live Twice
Z
Zorba the Greek
Zulu

1970s

Aguirre: The Wrath of God
Airport
Alice Doesn't Live Here
Alien
All That Jazz
All the President's Men
Amarcord
American Graffiti
Andromeda Strain
Animal House
Annie Hall
Apocalypse Now
Apprenticeship/Duddy Kravitz

Badlands
Bad News Bears
Bananas
Bang the Drum Slowly
Barry Lyndon
Being There
Benji
Black Stallion
Blazing Saddles
Breaking Away
Cabaret
Candidate, The
Carnal Knowledge
Carrie
China Syndrome
Chinatown
Cinderella Liberty
Claire's Knee
Clockwork Orange
Close Encounters
Coming Home
Conformist, The
Conversation, The
Cousin, Cousine
Cries and Whispers
Day for Night
Days of Heaven
Death in Venice
Death on the Nile
Death Wish
Deep, The
Deer Hunter
Deliverance
Diamonds Are Forever
Dirty Harry
Discreet Charm
Dog Day Afternoon
Don't Look Now
Enter the Dragon
Eraserhead
Exorcist, The
Fiddler on the Roof
Five Easy Pieces
Foul Play
Freaky Friday (1976)
French Connection
Funny Lady
Garden of the Finzi-Continis
Getaway, The
Gimme Shelter
Godfather, The
Godfather Part II
Goodbye Girl

Grease
Great Gatsby
Great Santini
Hair
Halloween
Harold and Maude
Heartbreak Kid
Heaven Can Wait (1978)
High Anxiety
High Plains Drifter
In-Laws, The
Invasion/Body Snatchers (1978)
Jaws
Jeremiah Johnson
Jerk, The
Jesus Christ Superstar
Julia
Klute
Kramer vs. Kramer
La Cage aux Folles
Lady Sings the Blues
Last Picture Show
Last Tango in Paris
Last Waltz
Lenny
Life of Brian
Little Big Man
Live and Let Die
Longest Yard (1974)
Looking for Mr. Goodbar
Lord of the Rings
Love Story
Manhattan
Man Who Fell to Earth
Man Who Would Be King
Man with the Golden Gun
Marathon Man
Marriage of Maria Braun
MASH
McCabe & Mrs. Miller
Mean Streets
Meatballs
Midnight Express
Monty Python/Holy Grail
Moonraker
Muppet Movie
Murder by Death
Murder on the Orient Express
My Brilliant Career
My Night at Maud's
Nashville
Network
New York, New York

1900
Norma Rae
North Dallas Forty
Nosferatu the Vampyre
Oh, God!
Omen, The
One Flew Over Cuckoo's Nest
Outlaw Josey Wales
Out-of-Towners
Paper Chase
Paper Moon
Papillon
Patton
Pete's Dragon
Pink Flamingos
Play It Again, Sam
Play Misty for Me
Poseidon Adventure
Pretty Baby
Prisoner of Second Avenue
Pumping Iron
Rescuers, The
Robin and Marian
Rocky
Rocky Horror Picture Show
Rose, The
Ruling Class
Ryan's Daughter
Same Time, Next Year
Saturday Night Fever
Scenes from a Marriage
Serpico
Seven Beauties
1776
Shampoo
Silver Streak
Sisters
Slap Shot
Sleeper
Sleuth
Smokey and the Bandit
Sorrow and the Pity
Spy Who Loved Me
Star Wars
Sting, The
Story of Adele H.
Sugarland Express
Summer of '42
Sunday Bloody Sunday
Sunshine Boys
Superman
Swept Away
Taxi Driver

10
Texas Chainsaw Massacre
That's Entertainment!
Three Musketeers
Time After Time
Tin Drum
Tommy
Tora! Tora! Tora!
Towering Inferno
Unmarried Woman
Way We Were
Westworld
What's Up, Doc?
Where's Poppa?
Willy Wonka/Chocolate Factory
Wind and the Lion
Woman Under the Influence
Woodstock
Young Frankenstein

1980s

Absence of Malice
Abyss, The
Accidental Tourist
Accused, The
After Hours
Agnes of God
Airplane!
Akira
Aliens
All Dogs Go to Heaven
Altered States
Amadeus
American Tail
American Werewolf in London
Annie
Arthur
Atlantic City
Au Revoir Les Enfants
Babette's Feast
Baby Boom
Back to the Future
Barfly
Batman
Beetlejuice
Beverly Hills Cop
Big
Big Business
Big Chill
Bill & Ted's
Blade Runner
Blood Simple
Blues Brothers

Blue Velvet
Body Heat
Born on the Fourth of July
Brazil
Breaker Morant
Breakfast Club
Broadcast News
Broadway Danny Rose
Brother from Another Planet
Bull Durham
Caddyshack
Cat People
Chariots of Fire
Children of a Lesser God
Christmas Story
Cinema Paradiso
Coal Miner's Daughter
Cocoon
Color of Money
Color Purple
Coming to America
Conan the Barbarian
Crimes and Misdemeanors
Crocodile Dundee
Dangerous Liaisons
Dark Crystal
Das Boot
Dead Poets Society
Dead Ringers
Desperately Seeking Susan
Die Hard
Diner
Dirty Dancing
Diva
Do the Right Thing
Down and Out in Beverly Hills
Down by Law
Dressed to Kill
Driving Miss Daisy
Drugstore Cowboy
Dune
Eating Raoul
Educating Rita
Elephant Man
Empire of the Sun
Escape from New York
E.T. The Extra-Terrestrial
Evil Dead
Fabulous Baker Boys
Fame
Fanny and Alexander
Fast Times at Ridgemont High
Fatal Attraction

Ferris Bueller's Day Off
Field of Dreams
First Blood: Rambo
Fish Called Wanda
Fitzcarraldo
Flashdance
Fletch
Fly, The (1986)
Footloose
48 HRS.
For Your Eyes Only
Fox and the Hound
Frances
French Lieutenant's Woman
Friday the 13th
Full Metal Jacket
Gallipoli
Gandhi
Ghostbusters
Gloria
Glory
Gods Must Be Crazy
Good Morning, Vietnam
Goonies, The
Gorillas in the Mist
Gremlins
Greystoke
Hairspray
Hannah and Her Sisters
Heartburn
Heathers
Heavy Metal
Henry V
Honey, I Shrunk the Kids
Hoosiers
House of Games
Hunger, The
Indiana Jones/Last Crusade
Indiana Jones/Temple of Doom
Innerspace
Jagged Edge
Jean de Florette
Karate Kid
Killing Fields
King of Comedy
Kiss of the Spider Woman
Last Emperor
Last Metro
Last Temptation of Christ
Legend
Lethal Weapon
License to Kill
Little Mermaid

Little Shop of Horrors
Living Daylights
Local Hero
Lost in America
Mad Max
Married to the Mob
Mask
Melvin and Howard
Missing
Mission, The
Mississippi Burning
Mommie Dearest
Moonstruck
Mr. Mom
My Beautiful Laundrette
My Bodyguard
My Dinner with Andre
My Favorite Year
My Left Foot
My Life As a Dog
Mystic Pizza
Naked Gun
National Lampoon's Vacation
Natural, The
Never Say Never Again
Nightmare on Elm Street
9½ Weeks
9 to 5
No Way Out
Octopussy
Officer and a Gentleman
Once Upon a Time/America
On Golden Pond
Ordinary People
Out of Africa
Outrageous Fortune
Outsiders, The
Parenthood
Paris, Texas
Pee-wee's Big Adventure
Peggy Sue Got Married
Places in the Heart
Platoon
Poltergeist
Postman Always Rings... (1981)
Pretty in Pink
Princess Bride
Private Benjamin
Prizzi's Honor
Purple Rose of Cairo
Radio Days
Raging Bull
Raiders of the Lost Ark

Rain Man
Raising Arizona
Ran
Reds
Repo Man
Right Stuff
Risky Business
Road Warrior
RoboCop
Roger & Me
Romancing the Stone
Room with a View
Roxanne
Runaway Train
Ruthless People
Scarface
Secret of NIMH
Sex, Lies and Videotape
Shining, The
Shirley Valentine
Shoah
Sid & Nancy
Silkwood
Silverado
Sixteen Candles
Something Wild
Sophie's Choice
Spaceballs
Splash
Stand and Deliver
Stand by Me
Starman
Star Trek II
Star Trek IV
Star Wars V/Empire Strikes
Star Wars VI/Return of Jedi
Steel Magnolias
St. Elmo's Fire
Stir Crazy
Stop Making Sense
Stripes
Suspect
Terminator, The
Terms of Endearment
Tess
Thing, The (1982)
This Is Spinal Tap
Three Men and a Baby
Time Bandits
Tootsie
Top Gun
Trading Places
Tron

Tucker
2010
Unbearable Lightness of Being
Uncle Buck
Untouchables, The
Urban Cowboy
Verdict, The
Victor/Victoria
View to a Kill
Wall Street
War of the Roses
When Harry Met Sally...
Who Framed Roger Rabbit
Willow
Wings of Desire
Witches of Eastwick
Witness
Women on the Verge
Working Girl
World According to Garp
Year of Living Dangerously
Yentl
Young Guns
Zelig

1990s

Ace Ventura
Addams Family
Adventures of Priscilla
Affliction
Age of Innocence
Air Force One
Aladdin
All About My Mother
American Beauty
American History X
American Pie
American President
Amistad
Analyze This
Anastasia (1997)
Anna and the King
Antonia's Line
Antz
Apollo 13
Armageddon
As Good As It Gets
Austin Powers
Awakenings
Babe
Backdraft
Barton Fink
Basic Instinct

Basquiat
Batman Returns
Beauty/Beast (1991)
Beethoven
Being John Malkovich
Big Lebowski
Big Night
Birdcage, The
Boogie Nights
Boys Don't Cry
Boys on the Side
Boyz N the Hood
Braveheart
Breaking the Waves
Bridges of Madison County
Buena Vista Social Club
Bug's Life
Bugsy
Bullets Over Broadway
Cape Fear (1991)
Casino
Casper
Celluloid Closet
Chasing Amy
Cider House Rules
City Slickers
Clear and Present Danger
Clerks
Client, The
Clueless
Con Air
Contact
Cool Runnings
Crimson Tide
Crying Game
Dances with Wolves
Dave
Dead Again
Dead Man Walking
Deconstructing Harry
Deep Impact
Dick Tracy
Donnie Brasco
Double Jeopardy
Dracula (1992)
Dr. Dolittle
Dumb and Dumber
Eat Drink Man Woman
Edward Scissorhands
Ed Wood
Election
Elizabeth
Emma

Enchanted April
End of the Affair
Enemy of the State
English Patient
Evita
Eyes Wide Shut
Face/Off
Fantasia 2000
Farewell My Concubine
Fargo
Father of the Bride (1991)
Fear and Loathing in Las Vegas
Few Good Men
Fifth Element
Fight Club
Firm, The
First Wives Club
Fisher King
Fly Away Home
Forrest Gump
Four Weddings and a Funeral
Free Willy
Fried Green Tomatoes
Fugitive, The
Full Monty
George of the Jungle
Ghost
Girl, Interrupted
Glengarry Glen Ross
Godfather Part III
Gods and Monsters
GoldenEye
Goodfellas
Good Will Hunting
Grand Canyon
Green Mile
Grifters, The
Groundhog Day
Grumpy Old Men
Hamlet (1996)
Hand That Rocks the Cradle
Happiness
Heat
Heavenly Creatures
Henry & June
Hercules
Hilary and Jackie
Hoffa
Home Alone
Hook
Hoop Dreams
Horse Whisperer
Howards End

Hunchback/Notre Dame (1996)
Hunt for Red October
Hurricane, The
Il Postino
In & Out
Independence Day
Indochine
Insider, The
Interview with the Vampire
In the Company of Men
In the Line of Fire
In the Name of the Father
Iron Giant
James and the Giant Peach
Jerry Maguire
JFK
Jumanji
Jurassic Park
L.A. Confidential
La Femme Nikita
Last of the Mohicans
L.A. Story
Last Seduction
League of Their Own
Leaving Las Vegas
Legends of the Fall
Liar Liar
Life Is Beautiful
Like Water for Chocolate
Lion King
Little Princess
Little Women
Lock, Stock and Two...
Lone Star
Longtime Companion
Love! Valour! Compassion!
Madness of King George
Magnolia
Malcolm X
Man on the Moon
Mask, The
Mask of Zorro
Matrix, The
Maverick
Mediterraneo
Men in Black
Metropolitan
Mighty Aphrodite
Miller's Crossing
Misery
Mission: Impossible
Mr. Holland's Opus
Mrs. Brown

Mrs. Doubtfire
Mulan
Mummy, The (1999)
My Best Friend's Wedding
My Cousin Vinny
My Girl
My Own Private Idaho
Nightmare Before Christmas
Notting Hill
Nutty Professor (1996)
101 Dalmatians (1996)
Outbreak
Out of Sight
Patch Adams
Patriot Games
Pelican Brief
People vs. Larry Flynt
Phenomenon
Philadelphia
Piano, The
Player, The
Pleasantville
Pocahontas
Postcards from the Edge
Presumed Innocent
Pretty Woman
Primal Fear
Primary Colors
Prince of Egypt
Prince of Tides
Pulp Fiction
Quiz Show
Ransom
Reality Bites
Red Violin
Remains of the Day
Reservoir Dogs
Reversal of Fortune
River Runs Through It
Robin Hood: Prince of Thieves
Rock, The
Romeo + Juliet
Run Lola Run
Rush Hour
Rushmore
Santa Clause
Saving Private Ryan
Scent of a Woman
Schindler's List
Scream
Secrets and Lies
Sense and Sensibility
Seven

Shakespeare in Love
Shawshank Redemption
Sheltering Sky
Shine
Showgirls
Silence of the Lambs
Simple Plan
Single White Female
Sister Act
Six Degrees of Separation
Sixth Sense
Sleeping with the Enemy
Sleepless in Seattle
Sleepy Hollow
Sling Blade
South Park
Space Jam
Speed
Stargate
Starship Troopers
Star Wars I/Phantom Menace
Straight Story
Strictly Ballroom
Stuart Little
Sweet Hereafter
Swingers
Talented Mr. Ripley
Tarzan
Terminator 2: Judgment Day
Thelma & Louise
There's Something About Mary
Thin Red Line
Three Kings
Tie Me Up! Tie Me Down!
Time to Kill
Titanic
To Die For
Tombstone
Tomorrow Never Dies
Topsy-Turvy
Total Recall
Toy Story
Trainspotting
True Lies
True Romance
Truman Show
Truth or Dare
Twelve Monkeys
Twister
Under Siege
Unforgiven
Usual Suspects
Wag the Dog

Waiting for Guffman
Wayne's World
Wedding Banquet
Wedding Singer
Welcome to the Dollhouse
What About Bob?
What Dreams May Come
What's Eating Gilbert Grape
What's Love Got to Do with It
While You Were Sleeping
World Is Not Enough
X-Files, The
You've Got Mail

2000s

About a Boy
About Schmidt
Adaptation
A.I.: Artificial Intelligence
Almost Famous
Along Came a Spider
Amélie
American Splendor
Analyze That
Anger Management
Anniversary Party
Antwone Fisher
Atlantis
Auto Focus
Aviator, The
Bad Education
Bad Santa
Barbershop
Batman Begins
Beautiful Mind
Before Night Falls
Before Sunset
Being Julia
Bend It Like Beckham
Best in Show
Beyond the Sea
Big Fish
Billy Elliot
Black Hawk Down
Bourne Identity
Bourne Supremacy
Bowling for Columbine
Bridget Jones's Diary
Bringing Down the House
Brokeback Mountain
Brother Bear
Bruce Almighty
Calendar Girls

Capote
Cast Away
Catch Me If You Can
Changing Lanes
Charlie's Angels
Cheaper By the Dozen (2003)
Chicago
Chicken Little
Chicken Run
Chocolat
Chronicles of Narnia
Cinderella Man
City of God
Closer
Coach Carter
Coffee and Cigarettes
Cold Mountain
Collateral
Confessions/Dangerous Mind
Constant Gardener
Contender, The
Cooler, The
Corpse Bride
Count of Monte Cristo
Crash
Crouching Tiger
Dancer in the Dark
Daredevil
Da Vinci Code
Day After Tomorrow
De-Lovely
Die Another Day
Dinosaur
Dirty Pretty Things
Divine Secrets/Ya-Ya
   Sisterhood
Dogville
Donnie Darko
Door in the Floor
Down with Love
8 Mile
Elephant
Elf
Emperor's New Groove
Enron/Smartest Guys in Room
Erin Brockovich
Eternal Sunshine
Fahrenheit 9/11
Family Man
Far From Heaven
Fever Pitch
50 First Dates
Finding Nemo

Finding Neverland
Fog of War
40 Year Old Virgin
Freaky Friday (2003)
Frequency
Frida
Friday Night Lights
Gangs of New York
Garden State
Ghost World
Girl with a Pearl Earring
Gladiator
Good Girl
Good Night, and Good Luck
Gosford Park
Gothika
Hannibal
Harry Potter/Chamber of
   Secrets
Harry Potter/Goblet of Fire
Harry Potter/Prisoner of
   Azkaban
Harry Potter/Sorcerer's Stone
Hero
Hidalgo
History of Violence
Hitch
Holes
Hollywood Ending
Hotel Rwanda
Hours, The
House of Flying Daggers
House of Sand and Fog
How the Grinch Stole Christmas
How to Lose a Guy in 10 Days
Hustle & Flow
I Am Sam
Ice Age
Ice Age: The Meltdown
Identity
Igby Goes Down
Importance of Being Earnest
In America
Incredibles, The
Inside Man
Insomnia
Interpreter, The
In the Bedroom
Intolerable Cruelty
Iris
I, Robot
Italian Job
Jackass: The Movie

Junebug
Just Like Heaven
Kid Stays in the Picture
Kill Bill Vol. 1
Kill Bill Vol. 2
King Kong (2005)
Kinsey
Kissing Jessica Stein
Kung Fu Hustle
Ladder 49
Ladykillers, The (2004)
Last Samurai
Laurel Canyon
Legally Blonde
Lemony Snicket's/Unfortunate
Life Aquatic/Steve Zissou
Life of David Gale
Lilo & Stitch
Longest Yard (2005)
Lord of the Rings/Fellowship
Lord of the Rings/Return
Lord of the Rings/Two Towers
Lost in Translation
Love Actually
Madagascar
Magdalene Sisters
Maid in Manhattan
Manchurian Candidate (2004)
Man from Elysian Fields
Man on Fire
Man Who Wasn't There
March of the Penguins
Maria Full of Grace
Master and Commander
Match Point
Matchstick Men
Matrix Reloaded
Matrix Revolutions
Mean Girls
Meet the Fockers
Meet the Parents
Melinda and Melinda
Memento
Memoirs of a Geisha
Men in Black II
Mighty Wind
Million Dollar Baby
Minority Report
Miracle
Miss Congeniality
Missing, The
Mona Lisa Smile
Monsoon Wedding

Monster
Monster's Ball
Monsters, Inc.
Motorcycle Diaries
Moulin Rouge!
Mrs. Henderson Presents
Mulholland Dr.
Munich
Murderball
My Big Fat Greek Wedding
Mystic River
Napoleon Dynamite
National Treasure
Nicholas Nickleby
North Country
Notebook, The
Nurse Betty
O Brother, Where Art Thou?
Ocean's Eleven (2001)
Old School
Once Upon a Time in Mexico
One Hour Photo
Others, The
Over the Hedge
Panic Room
Passion of the Christ
Patriot, The
Pearl Harbor
Perfect Storm
Peter Pan (2003)
Phantom of the Opera
Phone Booth
Pianist, The
Pieces of April
Pirates of the Caribbean
Polar Express
Pollock
Pride & Prejudice (2005)
Princess Diaries
Punch-Drunk Love
Quiet American
Rabbit-Proof Fence
Radio
Ray
Real Women Have Curves
Recruit, The
Red Dragon
Remember the Titans
Rent
Requiem for a Dream
Ring, The

Road to Perdition
Robots
Roger Dodger
Rookie, The
Royal Tenenbaums
Runaway Jury
Sahara
Save the Last Dance
Saw
School of Rock
Seabiscuit
Secondhand Lions
Secretary
Serenity
Shadow of the Vampire
Shark Tale
Shattered Glass
Shaun of the Dead
Shipping News
Shrek
Shrek 2
Sideways
Signs
Sin City
Sisterhood/Traveling Pants
Snatch
Something's Gotta Give
Spanglish
Spellbound (2003)
Spider-Man
Spider-Man 2
Spirit: Stallion of the Cimarron
Spirited Away
Spy Kids
Spy Kids 2
Squid and the Whale
Starsky & Hutch
Star Wars II/Attack of Clones
Star Wars III/Revenge of Sith
Station Agent
Stuart Little 2
Sum of All Fears
Sunshine State
Super Size Me
S.W.A.T.
Sweet Home Alabama
Swimming Pool
Sylvia
Syriana
Talk to Her
Terminal, The

Terminator 3: Rise of Machines
Thank You for Smoking
Thirteen
Traffic
Training Day
TransAmerica
Triplets of Belleville
Troy
28 Days Later
25th Hour
21 Grams
Two Weeks Notice
U-571
Unbreakable
Under the Tuscan Sun
Unfaithful
Upside of Anger
Uptown Girls
Van Helsing
Vanity Fair
Vera Drake

Veronica Guerin
Very Long Engagement
V for Vendetta
Walk the Line
Wallace & Gromit/Were-Rabbit
Wedding Crashers
We Were Soldiers
Whale Rider
What Lies Beneath
What Women Want
White Oleander
Winged Migration
Wonder Boys
Woodsman, The
X-Men
X-Men: The Last Stand
X2: X-Men United
XXX
You Can Count on Me
Y Tu Mamá También

GENRES/SPECIAL FEATURES

Action/Adventure

Adventures of Robin Hood
Aguirre: The Wrath of God
Around the World in 80 Days
Backdraft
Batman
Batman Begins
Batman Returns
Benji
Beverly Hills Cop
Black Stallion
Bourne Identity
Bourne Supremacy
Captain Blood
Captains Courageous
Cast Away
Catch Me If You Can
Charlie's Angels
Chronicles of Narnia
Con Air
Conan the Barbarian
Contact
Count of Monte Cristo
Crimson Tide
Crocodile Dundee
Crouching Tiger
Daredevil
Day After Tomorrow
Deep, The
Deep Impact
Deliverance
Die Hard
Easy Rider
Enter the Dragon
Evil Dead
Face/Off
Fantastic Voyage
Fifth Element
First Blood: Rambo
Fitzcarraldo
Flight of the Phoenix
Fly Away Home
Getaway, The
Gladiator
Gods Must Be Crazy
Goonies, The
Great Escape
Great Race
Greystoke
Hatari!

Hero
Hidalgo
House of Flying Daggers
Independence Day
Indiana Jones/Last Crusade
Indiana Jones/Temple of Doom
I, Robot
Journey to Center of Earth
Jumanji
Jurassic Park
Kill Bill Vol. 1
Kill Bill Vol. 2
King Kong (1933)
King Kong (2005)
King Solomon's Mines
Kung Fu Hustle
Ladder 49
Last Samurai
Lawrence of Arabia
Legend
Lethal Weapon
Longest Yard (1974)
Lord of the Rings/Fellowship
Lord of the Rings/Return
Lord of the Rings/Two Towers
Mad Max
Magnificent Seven
Man Who Would Be King
Mark of Zorro
Mask of Zorro
Master and Commander
Matrix, The
Matrix Reloaded
Matrix Revolutions
Men in Black
Men in Black II
Minority Report
Mission, The
Mummy, The (1999)
Mutiny on the Bounty (1935)
Mutiny on the Bounty (1962)
National Treasure
Once Upon a Time in Mexico
Papillon
Pearl Harbor
Peter Pan (2003)
Pirates of the Caribbean
Planet of the Apes
Poseidon Adventure
Raiders of the Lost Ark

Rio Bravo
Road Warrior
Robin and Marian
Robin Hood: Prince of Thieves
RoboCop
Rocky
Romancing the Stone
Romeo + Juliet
Rush Hour
Sahara
Seven Samurai
7th Voyage of Sinbad
Smokey and the Bandit
Spartacus
Spider-Man
Spider-Man 2
Spy Kids
Spy Kids 2
Stargate
Starship Troopers
Starsky & Hutch
Star Trek II
Star Trek IV
Star Wars
Star Wars I/Phantom Menace
Star Wars II/Attack of Clones
Star Wars III/Revenge of Sith
Star Wars V/Empire Strikes
Star Wars VI/Return of Jedi
Sum of All Fears
Superman
S.W.A.T.
Swiss Family Robinson
Tarzan and His Mate
Tarzan the Ape Man
Terminator, The
Terminator 2: Judgment Day
Terminator 3: Rise of Machines
Thief of Bagdad
Three Kings
Three Musketeers
Time Machine
Top Gun
Topkapi
Total Recall
Treasure of the Sierra Madre
Tron
Troy
True Lies
Twister
Under Siege
Van Helsing
V for Vendetta

Wages of Fear
War of the Worlds
Wind and the Lion
X-Men
X-Men: The Last Stand
X2: X-Men United
XXX
Yojimbo
Young Guns
Zulu

Additions
(Movies added since the last edition of the book)

Aguirre: The Wrath of God
Analyze That
Anger Management
Anniversary Party
Auto Focus
Bad and the Beautiful
Barbarella
Barbershop
Batman Begins
Beyond the Sea
Big Business
Billy Liar
Bride Wore Black
Brigadoon
Bringing Down the House
Brokeback Mountain
Brother from Another Planet
Bruce Almighty
Capote
Carmen Jones
Changing Lanes
Charlie's Angels
Cheaper By the Dozen (2003)
Chicken Little
Chronicles of Narnia
Cinderella Man
Claire's Knee
Closer
Coffee and Cigarettes
Confessions/Dangerous Mind
Constant Gardener
Contempt
Corpse Bride
Counterfeit Traitor
Count of Monte Cristo
Damned, The
Daredevil
Darling
Da Vinci Code

Day After Tomorrow
Death in Venice
De-Lovely
Desk Set
Destry Rides Again
Dick Tracy
Divine Secrets/Ya-Ya
   Sisterhood
Divorce Italian Style
Dogville
Donnie Darko
Don't Look Now
Door in the Floor
Down by Law
Down with Love
Duel in the Sun
Dune
Elephant
Experiment in Terror
Eyes Wide Shut
Faces
Fever Pitch
50 First Dates
Fitzcarraldo
For a Few Dollars More
40 Year Old Virgin
Freaks
Freaky Friday (2003)
Fury
Getaway, The
Gloria
Good Girl
Good Night, and Good Luck
Gothika
Great Expectations
Great Gatsby
Gun Crazy
Harry Potter/Goblet of Fire
Heartbreak Kid
Heartburn
Heaven Can Wait (1943)
Hiroshima, Mon Amour
History of Violence
Hollywood Ending
How Green Was My Valley
How to Lose a Guy in 10 Days
Hud
Hustle & Flow
Ice Age: The Meltdown
Identity
Inside Man
Insomnia
Intolerable Cruelty

I, Robot
I Want to Live!
I Was a Male War Bride
Jackass: The Movie
Jailhouse Rock
Junebug
Just Like Heaven
King Kong (2005)
King of Hearts
Kiss Me Deadly
Knife in the Water
Ladder 49
Ladykillers, The (1956)
Ladykillers, The (2004)
Last Metro
Laurel Canyon
Lemony Snicket's/Unfortunate
Lenny
Leopard, The
License to Kill
Life Aquatic/Steve Zissou
Limelight
Little Caesar
Living Daylights
Longest Yard (2005)
Longtime Companion
Love! Valour! Compassion!
Maid in Manhattan
Manchurian Candidate (2004)
Man from Elysian Fields
March of the Penguins
Marriage of Maria Braun
Match Point
Matchstick Men
Mean Girls
Meet the Fockers
Melinda and Melinda
Melvin and Howard
Memoirs of a Geisha
Men in Black II
Misfits, The
Missing
Missing, The
Mona Lisa Smile
Monsieur Verdoux
Mr. Deeds Goes to Town
Mrs. Henderson Presents
Mrs. Miniver
Munich
Murderball
Murder, My Sweet
My Brilliant Career
My Night at Maud's

330

Napoleon Dynamite
National Treasure
Niagara
Nicholas Nickleby
North Country
North Dallas Forty
Nosferatu the Vampyre
Old School
Oliver Twist
Once Upon a Time in Mexico
Once Upon a Time/West
One Hour Photo
On the Beach
Out of the Past
Over the Hedge
Palm Beach Story
Panic Room
Paris, Texas
Pearl Harbor
Peyton Place
Phone Booth
Pickup on South Street
Pretty Baby
Pride & Prejudice (2005)
Prime of Miss Jean Brodie
Prisoner of Second Avenue
Pumping Iron
Punch-Drunk Love
Raisin in the Sun
Recruit, The
Red Dragon
Rent
Requiem for a Heavyweight
Ring, The
Roger Dodger
Room at the Top
Ruling Class
Sahara
Satyricon
Saw
Scarlet Empress
Serenity
Servant, The
Shadow of a Doubt
Shark Tale
Sheltering Sky
Ship of Fools
Shoot the Piano Player
Showgirls
Sisterhood/Traveling Pants
Sisters
Smiles of a Summer Night
Snake Pit

Something Wild
Song of Bernadette
Sorrow and the Pity
Sorry, Wrong Number
Spanglish
Spellbound (2003)
Spy Kids 2
Spy Who Came in from Cold
Squid and the Whale
Starsky & Hutch
Story of Adele H.
Stuart Little 2
Suddenly, Last Summer
Sugarland Express
Sum of All Fears
Sunday Bloody Sunday
Sunshine State
Suspicion
S.W.A.T.
Sweet Home Alabama
Sylvia
Syriana
Tarzan and His Mate
Terminal, The
Terminator 2: Judgment Day
Terminator 3: Rise of Machines
Tess
Thank You for Smoking
TransAmerica
True Romance
Two Weeks Notice
Uptown Girls
Van Helsing
Vanity Fair
Veronica Guerin
V for Vendetta
View to a Kill
Walk the Line
Wallace & Gromit/Were-Rabbit
Wedding Crashers
We Were Soldiers
Where's Poppa?
White Oleander
Wild One, The
Woman Under the Influence
Women in Love
X-Men: The Last Stand
XXX

Adults Only
American History X
Auto Focus
Bad Education

Bad Seed
Basic Instinct
Belle de Jour
Blue Velvet
Body Heat
Boogie Nights
Damned, The
Dead Ringers
Grifters, The
Happiness
Henry & June
Hunger, The
Kill Bill Vol. 1
Kill Bill Vol. 2
Last Tango in Paris
Last Temptation of Christ
Lolita
Looking for Mr. Goodbar
Midnight Cowboy
Monster
Passion of the Christ
Pink Flamingos
Pretty Baby
Requiem for a Dream
Reservoir Dogs
Satyricon
Secretary
Showgirls
Woodsman, The

Americana

Alamo, The
All the King's Men
American Graffiti
Amistad
Badlands
Best Years of Our Lives
Blue Velvet
Bull Durham
Cheaper By the Dozen (1950)
Christmas Story
Dances with Wolves
Days of Heaven
East of Eden
Far From Heaven
Forrest Gump
Friday Night Lights
Friendly Persuasion
Giant
Grapes of Wrath
Guys and Dolls
It's a Wonderful Life
Last Picture Show

League of Their Own
Meet Me in St. Louis
Mr. Deeds Goes to Town
Mr. Smith Goes to Washington
Music Man
Nashville
Natural, The
O Brother, Where Art Thou?
Oklahoma!
Old Yeller
Picnic
Places in the Heart
Pleasantville
Radio Days
River Runs Through It
Seabiscuit
1776
Shadow of a Doubt
Stand by Me
Straight Story
Summer of '42
To Kill a Mockingbird
Tucker
Yankee Doodle Dandy

Animated

(* Not for children)
Akira*
Aladdin
Alice in Wonderland
All Dogs Go to Heaven
American Tail
Anastasia (1997)
Antz
Atlantis
Bambi
Beauty/Beast (1991)
Brother Bear
Bug's Life
Chicken Little
Chicken Run
Cinderella
Corpse Bride
Dinosaur
Dumbo
Emperor's New Groove
Fantasia
Fantasia 2000
Finding Nemo
Fox and the Hound
Heavy Metal*
Hercules
Hunchback/Notre Dame (1996)

Ice Age
Ice Age: The Meltdown
Incredibles, The
Iron Giant
James and the Giant Peach
Jungle Book (1967)
Lady and the Tramp
Lilo & Stitch
Lion King
Little Mermaid
Lord of the Rings
Madagascar
Monsters, Inc.
Mulan
Nightmare Before Christmas
101 Dalmatians (1961)
Over the Hedge
Peter Pan (1953)
Pete's Dragon
Pinocchio
Pocahontas
Polar Express
Prince of Egypt
Rescuers, The
Robots
Secret of NIMH
Shark Tale
Shrek
Shrek 2
Sleeping Beauty
Snow White
Song of the South
South Park*
Space Jam
Spirit: Stallion of the Cimarron
Spirited Away
Tarzan
Toy Story
Triplets of Belleville*
Wallace & Gromit/Were-Rabbit
Who Framed Roger Rabbit
Yellow Submarine

Biographies

Alexander Nevsky
Amadeus
American Splendor
Anastasia (1956)
Antwone Fisher
Auto Focus
Aviator, The
Basquiat
Becket

Before Night Falls
Beyond the Sea
Birdman of Alcatraz
Bonnie and Clyde
Born Free
Bugsy
Capote
Cinderella Man
Cleopatra
Coal Miner's Daughter
Confessions/Dangerous Mind
De-Lovely
Diary of Anne Frank
Ed Wood
Elephant Man
Elizabeth
Evita
Finding Neverland
Frances
Frida
Funny Girl
Funny Lady
Gandhi
Gods and Monsters
Gorillas in the Mist
Gypsy
Henry & June
Hoffa
Hurricane, The
Iris
Julia
Kid Stays in the Picture
Kinsey
Lady Sings the Blues
Last Emperor
Lawrence of Arabia
Lenny
Madness of King George
Malcolm X
Man for All Seasons
Man on the Moon
Miracle Worker
Mommie Dearest
Mrs. Brown
Napoléon
Patton
People vs. Larry Flynt
Pocahontas
Pollock
Pride of the Yankees
Raging Bull
Ray
Reds

Genres/Special Features

Reversal of Fortune
Scarlet Empress
Sergeant York
Sid & Nancy
Song of Bernadette
Sylvia
Tucker
Unsinkable Molly Brown
Walk the Line
What's Love Got to Do with It
Yankee Doodle Dandy
Young Guns

Black Comedies

After Hours
Arsenic and Old Lace
Bad Santa
Beetlejuice
Being John Malkovich
Being There
Brazil
Clerks
Discreet Charm
Divorce Italian Style
Dr. Strangelove
Eating Raoul
Ed Wood
Election
Fear and Loathing in Las Vegas
Fortune Cookie
Gremlins
Groundhog Day
Happiness
Harold and Maude
Heathers
Kind Hearts and Coronets
King of Comedy
Ladykillers, The (1956)
Ladykillers, The (2004)
Life of Brian
Lolita
MASH
Monsieur Verdoux
Monty Python/Holy Grail
Nurse Betty
Pink Flamingos
Prizzi's Honor
Producers, The
Royal Tenenbaums
Ruling Class
Russians Are Coming...
Ruthless People
Secretary

Something Wild
Time Bandits
To Die For
Wag the Dog
War of the Roses
Welcome to the Dollhouse
What About Bob?
Where's Poppa?

Blockbusters

(Annual highest grossing
movies with year of release)
Aladdin (1992)
Armageddon (1998)
Back to the Future (1985)
Bambi (1942)
Batman (1989)
Ben-Hur (1959)
Best Years of Our Lives (1946)
Birth of a Nation (1915)
Blazing Saddles (1974)
Bridge on the River Kwai (1957)
Butch Cassidy/Sundance Kid
    (1969)
Cleopatra (1963)
Duel in the Sun (1946)
E.T. The Extra-Terrestrial (1982)
Exorcist, The (1973)
Forrest Gump (1994)
French Connection (1971)
Funny Girl (1968)
Ghostbusters (1984)
Godfather, The (1972)
Going My Way (1944)
Gone with the Wind (1939)
Graduate, The (1967)
Grease (1978)
Harry Potter/Sorcerer's Stone
    (2001)
Home Alone (1990)
Honey, I Shrunk the Kids (1989)
How the Grinch Stole Christmas
    (2000)
Independence Day (1996)
Jaws (1975)
Jurassic Park (1993)
King Kong (1933)
King Solomon's Mines (1950)
Kramer vs. Kramer (1979)
Lawrence of Arabia (1962)
Lord of the Rings/Return (2003)
Love Story (1970)
Mary Poppins (1964)

Mister Roberts (1955)
Mrs. Miniver (1942)
Night at the Opera (1935)
Peyton Place (1957)
Raiders of the Lost Ark (1981)
Rain Man (1988)
Red River (1948)
Robe, The (1953)
Robin Hood: Prince of Thieves
   (1991)
Rocky (1976)
Saving Private Ryan (1998)
Sergeant York (1941)
Shrek 2 (2004)
Snow White (1937)
Sound of Music (1965)
South Pacific (1958)
Spartacus (1960)
Spider-Man (2002)
Star Wars (1977)
Star Wars I/Phantom Menace
   (1999)
Star Wars III/Revenge of Sith
   (2005)
Star Wars V/Empire Strikes
   (1980)
Star Wars VI/Return of Jedi
   (1983)
Ten Commandments (1956)
Terminator 2: Judgment Day
   (1991)
Thin Man (1934)
Three Men and a Baby (1987)
Titanic (1997)
Top Gun (1986)
Toy Story (1995)
Twister (1996)
Under Siege (1992)
West Side Story (1961)
White Christmas (1954)

Buddy Films
About a Boy
Analyze That
Analyze This
Auto Focus
Blues Brothers
Breaking Away
Brokeback Mountain
Butch Cassidy/Sundance Kid
City Slickers
Down by Law
Easy Rider

48 HRS.
Ghost World
Gloria
Gunga Din
Lethal Weapon
Man Who Would Be King
Mean Streets
Men in Black
Men in Black II
Midnight Cowboy
Motorcycle Diaries
North Dallas Forty
Odd Couple
Outrageous Fortune
Roger Dodger
Rush Hour
Sahara
Starsky & Hutch
Stir Crazy
Swingers
Thelma & Louise
Wedding Crashers

Camp Classics
Adventures of Priscilla
Auntie Mame
Barbarella
Birdcage, The
Bride of Frankenstein
Conan the Barbarian
Duel in the Sun
Eating Raoul
Evil Dead
Fly, The (1958)
Gentlemen Prefer Blondes
Godzilla
Grease
Hairspray
How to Marry a Millionaire
Imitation of Life
I Want to Live!
La Cage aux Folles
Little Shop of Horrors
Mildred Pierce
Mommie Dearest
9½ Weeks
Pee-wee's Big Adventure
Peyton Place
Pillow Talk
Pink Flamingos
Poseidon Adventure
Rocky Horror Picture Show

Showgirls
Texas Chainsaw Massacre
Whatever Happened to...
Women, The
Women on the Verge

Capers
Asphalt Jungle
Bourne Supremacy
Catch Me If You Can
Fish Called Wanda
Getaway, The
Inside Man
Italian Job
Ladykillers, The (1956)
Ladykillers, The (2004)
Lavender Hill Mob
Lock, Stock and Two...
Matchstick Men
National Treasure
Ocean's Eleven (1960)
Ocean's Eleven (2001)
Out of Sight
Pink Panther
Reservoir Dogs
Ruthless People
Silver Streak
Snatch
Sting, The
Thomas Crown Affair
Topkapi

Chick Flicks
(See also Romance)
Affair to Remember
Amélie
Baby Boom
Boys on the Side
Breakfast at Tiffany's
Bridges of Madison County
Bridget Jones's Diary
Calendar Girls
Clueless
Desperately Seeking Susan
Dirty Dancing
Divine Secrets/Ya-Ya
  Sisterhood
Down with Love
Enchanted April
English Patient
Father of the Bride (1991)
First Wives Club

Four Weddings and a Funeral
Fried Green Tomatoes
Funny Face
Ghost
How to Lose a Guy in 10 Days
Kissing Jessica Stein
Legally Blonde
Little Women
Love Actually
Love Is a Many-Splendored
Love Story
Maid in Manhattan
Mean Girls
Miss Congeniality
Mona Lisa Smile
My Best Friend's Wedding
Mystic Pizza
Notebook, The
Notting Hill
Now, Voyager
Officer and a Gentleman
Out of Africa
Outrageous Fortune
Peyton Place
Pretty Woman
Pride and Prejudice (1940)
Private Benjamin
Real Women Have Curves
Roman Holiday
Sense and Sensibility
Shakespeare in Love
Sisterhood/Traveling Pants
Sleepless in Seattle
Something's Gotta Give
Splendor in the Grass
Steel Magnolias
Sweet Home Alabama
Terms of Endearment
Thelma & Louise
Two Weeks Notice
Under the Tuscan Sun
Unmarried Woman
Uptown Girls
Way We Were
Wedding Singer
What Women Want
When Harry Met Sally...
White Oleander
Women, The
Working Girl
You've Got Mail

Children/Family

(See also Animated)

Annie
Babe
Bad News Bears
Beethoven
Big
Black Stallion
Born Free
Casper
Cheaper By the Dozen (2003)
Christmas Carol
Christmas Story
Cool Runnings
Dark Crystal
David Copperfield
Dr. Dolittle
Elf
E.T. The Extra-Terrestrial
Father of the Bride (1950)
Father of the Bride (1991)
Fly Away Home
Freaky Friday (1976)
Freaky Friday (2003)
Free Willy
George of the Jungle
Goonies, The
Great Race
Harry Potter/Chamber of
   Secrets
Harry Potter/Goblet of Fire
Harry Potter/Prisoner of
   Azkaban
Harry Potter/Sorcerer's Stone
Hidalgo
Holes
Honey, I Shrunk the Kids
Hook
How the Grinch Stole Christmas
It's a Wonderful Life
Journey to Center of Earth
Jungle Book (1942)
Lemony Snicket's/Unfortunate
Lili
Little Princess
Love Bug
Mary Poppins
Mrs. Doubtfire
National Velvet
Old Yeller
Oliver!
101 Dalmatians (1996)

Parent Trap
Pee-wee's Big Adventure
Peter Pan (2003)
Princess Bride
Princess Diaries
Remember the Titans
Rookie, The
Santa Clause
Sound of Music
Spy Kids
Spy Kids 2
Stuart Little
Stuart Little 2
Swiss Family Robinson
Three Men and a Baby
Tron
20,000 Leagues Under the Sea
Whale Rider
Willow
Willy Wonka/Chocolate Factory
Wizard of Oz

City Settings

LA Stories

Adaptation
Bad and the Beautiful
Barfly
Barton Fink
Beverly Hills Cop
Big Sleep
Boyz N the Hood
Chinatown
Clueless
Crash
D.O.A.
Down and Out in Beverly Hills
Ed Wood
Gods and Monsters
Grand Canyon
L.A. Confidential
L.A. Story
Mulholland Dr.
Player, The
Postcards from the Edge
Pretty Woman
Princess Diaries
Reservoir Dogs
Shampoo
Singin' in the Rain
Starsky & Hutch
Sunset Boulevard
Swingers

Genres/Special Features

Las Vegas Stories
Bugsy
Casino
Cooler, The
Diamonds Are Forever
Fear and Loathing in Las Vegas
Leaving Las Vegas
Ocean's Eleven (1960)
Ocean's Eleven (2001)
Showgirls

London Stories
About a Boy
Alfie
American Werewolf in London
Austin Powers
Bedazzled
Blowup
Bridget Jones's Diary
Elephant Man
End of the Affair
Fish Called Wanda
Gaslight
Lock, Stock and Two...
Love Actually
Man Who Knew Too Much
Mary Poppins
Match Point
My Fair Lady
Notting Hill
Oliver!
101 Dalmatians (1996)
Patriot Games
Secrets and Lies
Snatch
28 Days Later

New York Stories
Affair to Remember
After Hours
Age of Innocence
All About Eve
All That Jazz
Angels with Dirty Faces
Annie Hall
Apartment, The
Arthur
Basquiat
Bells Are Ringing
Big
Breakfast at Tiffany's
Broadway Danny Rose
Bullets Over Broadway
Changing Lanes

Crimes and Misdemeanors
Crocodile Dundee
Day After Tomorrow
Death Wish
Desperately Seeking Susan
Dog Day Afternoon
Donnie Brasco
Do the Right Thing
Dressed to Kill
Elf
Escape from New York
Fame
Fisher King
42nd Street
French Connection
Gangs of New York
Ghostbusters
Gloria
Godfather, The
Godfather Part II
Guys and Dolls
Hair
Hannah and Her Sisters
Hitch
Hustler, The
Igby Goes Down
Inside Man
Interpreter, The
King Kong (1933)
King of Comedy
Kissing Jessica Stein
Klute
Madagascar
Maid in Manhattan
Manhattan
Marathon Man
Marty
Mean Streets
Melinda and Melinda
Metropolitan
Midnight Cowboy
Mighty Aphrodite
Miracle on 34th Street
Moonstruck
My Favorite Year
Network
New York, New York
Odd Couple
Once Upon a Time/America
On the Town
On the Waterfront
Out-of-Towners
Pawnbroker, The

Pieces of April
Pollock
Prizzi's Honor
Quiz Show
Radio Days
Ransom
Rear Window
Rent
Rosemary's Baby
Saturday Night Fever
Serpico
Six Degrees of Separation
Spider-Man
Sunshine Boys
Sweet Smell of Success
Taxi Driver
Tootsie
25th Hour
Unfaithful
Unmarried Woman
Wall Street
West Side Story
When Harry Met Sally...
Working Girl
You've Got Mail

Paris Stories
Amélie
American in Paris
Before Sunset
Belle de Jour
Bourne Identity
Breathless
Charade
Children of Paradise
Da Vinci Code
Diva
400 Blows
Funny Face
Gigi
Henry & June
Hunchback/Notre Dame (1939)
Irma La Douce
Last Tango in Paris
Love in the Afternoon
Moulin Rouge
Moulin Rouge!
Shoot the Piano Player
Victor/Victoria

Rome Stories
Ben-Hur
Bicycle Thief
Cleopatra

Funny Thing Happened...
Gladiator
La Dolce Vita
Open City
Roman Holiday
Satyricon
Spartacus
Talented Mr. Ripley
Three Coins in the Fountain

San Francisco Stories
Basic Instinct
Birdman of Alcatraz
Birds, The
Bullitt
Conversation, The
Dead Man Walking
Dirty Harry
Experiment in Terror
48 HRS.
Foul Play
Invasion/Body Snatchers (1978)
Jagged Edge
Love Bug
Rock, The
Time After Time
Towering Inferno
Vertigo
What's Up, Doc?

Comedies
(See also Black Comedies,
Dramedies, Screwball
Comedies)
Absent-Minded Professor
Ace Ventura
Adam's Rib
Addams Family
Adventures of Priscilla
Airplane!
Amarcord
American Pie
American Werewolf in London
Analyze That
Analyze This
Anger Management
Animal House
Annie Hall
Apprenticeship/Duddy Kravitz
Arthur
Auntie Mame
Austin Powers
Baby Boom

Bad News Bears
Bananas
Barbershop
Bedazzled
Beethoven
Bell, Book and Candle
Best in Show
Beverly Hills Cop
Big
Big Business
Big Lebowski
Bill & Ted's
Birdcage, The
Bishop's Wife
Blazing Saddles
Breakfast Club
Bridget Jones's Diary
Bringing Down the House
Broadway Danny Rose
Brother from Another Planet
Bruce Almighty
Bullets Over Broadway
Cactus Flower
Caddyshack
Cat Ballou
Charlie's Angels
Chasing Amy
Cheaper By the Dozen (1950)
Cheaper By the Dozen (2003)
City Slickers
Clueless
Coming to America
Cool Runnings
Crocodile Dundee
Dave
Deconstructing Harry
Desk Set
Desperately Seeking Susan
Down and Out in Beverly Hills
Down with Love
Dr. Dolittle
Dumb and Dumber
Eat Drink Man Woman
Elf
Emma
Family Man
Fast Times at Ridgemont High
Father of the Bride (1950)
Father of the Bride (1991)
Ferris Bueller's Day Off
Fever Pitch
50 First Dates
First Wives Club

Fish Called Wanda
Fletch
40 Year Old Virgin
Foul Play
Four Weddings and a Funeral
Freaky Friday (1976)
Freaky Friday (2003)
Full Monty
General, The
George of the Jungle
Ghostbusters
Gods Must Be Crazy
Gold Rush
Goodbye, Columbus
Goodbye Girl
Graduate, The
Great Dictator
Great Race
Gremlins
Grumpy Old Men
Hairspray
Harvey
Hatari!
Heartbreak Kid
Heaven Can Wait (1943)
High Anxiety
Hitch
Hollywood Ending
Home Alone
Honey, I Shrunk the Kids
How to Lose a Guy in 10 Days
How to Marry a Millionaire
Importance of Being Earnest
In & Out
Innerspace
It's a Mad Mad Mad World
I Was a Male War Bride
Jackass: The Movie
Jerk, The
Jungle Book (1967)
Just Like Heaven
Kissing Jessica Stein
Kung Fu Hustle
La Cage aux Folles
L.A. Story
Lavender Hill Mob
Legally Blonde
Liar Liar
Little Big Man
Local Hero
Lost in America
Love Actually
Love Bug

Maid in Manhattan	Postcards from the Edge
Manhattan	Pretty in Pink
Man Who Came to Dinner	Pretty Woman
Married to the Mob	Princess Diaries
Mask, The	Private Benjamin
Matchstick Men	Purple Rose of Cairo
Maverick	Radio Days
Mean Girls	Repo Man
Meatballs	Risky Business
Mediterraneo	Roxanne
Meet the Fockers	Rush Hour
Meet the Parents	Santa Clause
Mighty Aphrodite	School of Rock
Mighty Wind	Seven Year Itch
Miss Congeniality	Shampoo
Mister Roberts	Shaun of the Dead
Modern Times	Shirley Valentine
Monkey Business	Shot in the Dark
Mon Oncle	Silver Streak
Mouse That Roared	Sister Act
Mr. Blandings	Sixteen Candles
Mr. Deeds Goes to Town	Slap Shot
Mr. Hulot's Holiday	Sleeper
Mr. Mom	Sleepless in Seattle
Mrs. Doubtfire	Smiles of a Summer Night
Muppet Movie	Smokey and the Bandit
Murder by Death	Some Like It Hot
My Best Friend's Wedding	Something's Gotta Give
My Big Fat Greek Wedding	South Park
My Cousin Vinny	Spaceballs
My Favorite Year	Starsky & Hutch
Naked Gun	Stir Crazy
Napoleon Dynamite	Strictly Ballroom
National Lampoon's Vacation	Stripes
9 to 5	Sunshine Boys
No Time for Sergeants	Swingers
Notting Hill	Take the Money and Run
Nutty Professor (1963)	10
Nutty Professor (1996)	Thank You for Smoking
O Brother, Where Art Thou?	There's Something About Mary
Odd Couple	This Is Spinal Tap
Oh, God!	Three Men and a Baby
Old School	Tie Me Up! Tie Me Down!
One, Two, Three	Tom Jones
Operation Petticoat	Tootsie
Out-of-Towners	Topkapi
Outrageous Fortune	Topper
Parent Trap	Trading Places
Pee-wee's Big Adventure	Two for the Road
Peggy Sue Got Married	Two Weeks Notice
Pillow Talk	Uncle Buck
Pink Panther	Unmarried Woman
Play It Again, Sam	Waiting for Guffman

Wayne's World
Wedding Banquet
Wedding Crashers
Wedding Singer
What Women Want
When Harry Met Sally...
While You Were Sleeping
Witches of Eastwick
Woman of the Year
Working Girl
Young Frankenstein
You've Got Mail
Zelig

Comic Book Adaptations
Addams Family
Akira
American Splendor
Annie
Barbarella
Batman
Batman Begins
Batman Returns
Casper
Daredevil
Dick Tracy
Ghost World
Heavy Metal
History of Violence
Men in Black
Men in Black II
Road to Perdition
Sin City
Spider-Man
Spider-Man 2
Superman
V for Vendetta
X-Men
X-Men: The Last Stand
X2: X-Men United

Coming of Age
Almost Famous
Bambi
Billy Elliot
Breaking Away
Coming Home
David Copperfield
Empire of the Sun
Fast Times at Ridgemont High
400 Blows
Graduate, The
Igby Goes Down

Karate Kid
Last Picture Show
Metropolitan
My Bodyguard
My Brilliant Career
My Life As a Dog
Mystic Pizza
National Velvet
Outsiders, The
Pretty Baby
Prime of Miss Jean Brodie
Real Women Have Curves
Risky Business
Rushmore
Sisterhood/Traveling Pants
Sixteen Candles
Stand by Me
St. Elmo's Fire
Summer of '42
What's Eating Gilbert Grape
White Oleander
Y Tu Mamá También

Crime
(See also Film Noir)
Anatomy of a Murder
Angels with Dirty Faces
Arsenic and Old Lace
Badlands
Batman Begins
Big Lebowski
Bonnie and Clyde
Boyz N the Hood
Bugsy
Capote
Casino
Chicago
City of God
Clockwork Orange
Death on the Nile
Diabolique
Dial M for Murder
Dick Tracy
Dirty Harry
Dirty Pretty Things
Dog Day Afternoon
Donnie Brasco
Elephant
Experiment in Terror
Fletch
48 HRS.
French Connection
Gangs of New York

Getaway, The
Gloria
Godfather, The
Godfather Part II
Godfather Part III
Goodfellas
Heat
Heavenly Creatures
History of Violence
Hoffa
Hustle & Flow
In Cold Blood
Inside Man
In the Heat of the Night
I, Robot
Italian Job
I Want to Live!
Ladykillers, The (1956)
Ladykillers, The (2004)
Lavender Hill Mob
Lethal Weapon
Little Caesar
Lock, Stock and Two...
M
Married to the Mob
Matchstick Men
Mean Streets
Miller's Crossing
Monsieur Verdoux
Monster
Mystic River
Nurse Betty
Ocean's Eleven (1960)
Ocean's Eleven (2001)
Once Upon a Time/America
On the Waterfront
Out of Sight
Panic Room
Prizzi's Honor
Public Enemy
Pulp Fiction
Rear Window
Red Dragon
Reservoir Dogs
Road to Perdition
Scarface
Serpico
Shoot the Piano Player
Snatch
Sting, The
Sugarland Express
To Catch a Thief
Traffic

Training Day
True Romance
25th Hour
Untouchables, The
Usual Suspects

Cross-Dressing
Adventures of Priscilla
All About My Mother
Bad Education
Birdcage, The
Boys Don't Cry
Celluloid Closet
Crying Game
Damned, The
Ed Wood
Farewell My Concubine
Hairspray
I Was a Male War Bride
Kind Hearts and Coronets
La Cage aux Folles
Life of Brian
Love! Valour! Compassion!
Monty Python/Holy Grail
Mouse That Roared
Mrs. Doubtfire
Pink Flamingos
Psycho
Rocky Horror Picture Show
Some Like It Hot
Tootsie
TransAmerica
Victor/Victoria
World According to Garp
Yentl

Cult Films
Adventures of Priscilla
After Hours
Akira
All About Eve
American Splendor
Barbarella
Barfly
Being John Malkovich
Big Lebowski
Bill & Ted's
Blade Runner
Blue Velvet
Brazil
Breakfast at Tiffany's
Breakfast Club
Brother from Another Planet

Casablanca
Children of Paradise
Clerks
Clockwork Orange
Crying Game
Dirty Dancing
Donnie Darko
Down by Law
Dr. Strangelove
Dune
Eating Raoul
8½
Enter the Dragon
Eraserhead
Eternal Sunshine
Evil Dead
Fantasia
Fear and Loathing in Las Vegas
Ferris Bueller's Day Off
Fight Club
5,000 Fingers of Dr. T.
Fletch
Forbidden Planet
Freaks
Friday the 13th
Gods Must Be Crazy
Grease
Gun Crazy
Harold and Maude
Heathers
Heavy Metal
It's a Wonderful Life
Kill Bill Vol. 1
Kill Bill Vol. 2
King of Hearts
Life of Brian
Little Shop of Horrors
Mad Max
Manchurian Candidate (1962)
Melvin and Howard
Monty Python/Holy Grail
Mulholland Dr.
My Dinner with Andre
Napoleon Dynamite
Night of the Living Dead
Pee-wee's Big Adventure
Pink Flamingos
Princess Bride
Raising Arizona
Red Shoes
Repo Man
Repulsion
Road Warrior

Rocky Horror Picture Show
Royal Tenenbaums
Ruling Class
Rushmore
Serenity
7th Voyage of Sinbad
Shawshank Redemption
Showgirls
Sin City
Sound of Music
Star Wars
St. Elmo's Fire
Texas Chainsaw Massacre
Time Bandits
True Romance
28 Days Later
Village of the Damned
Waiting for Guffman
Welcome to the Dollhouse
Where's Poppa?
Willy Wonka/Chocolate Factory
Wizard of Oz

Date Movies

Amélie
Annie Hall
Before Sunset
Big Chill
Bull Durham
Casablanca
Chocolat
Dirty Dancing
Eternal Sunshine
Fabulous Baker Boys
Fever Pitch
Four Weddings and a Funeral
Ghost
How to Lose a Guy in 10 Days
Jerry Maguire
Just Like Heaven
Love Actually
Love Story
Man and a Woman
Mediterraneo
Moonstruck
My Big Fat Greek Wedding
Notting Hill
Officer and a Gentleman
Pretty Woman
Prince of Tides
Romancing the Stone
Roman Holiday
Romeo and Juliet

Saturday Night Fever
Shakespeare in Love
Sideways
Sleepless in Seattle
Something's Gotta Give
Starman
Strictly Ballroom
Summer of '42
Titanic
Way We Were
Wedding Singer
What Women Want
When Harry Met Sally...
You've Got Mail

Disaster Flicks

(See also End of the World)
Airplane!
Airport
Backdraft
China Syndrome
Perfect Storm
Poseidon Adventure
Titanic
Towering Inferno
Twister

Documentaries

Bowling for Columbine
Buena Vista Social Club
Celluloid Closet
Don't Look Back
Enron/Smartest Guys in Room
Fahrenheit 9/11
Fog of War
Gimme Shelter
Hoop Dreams
Kid Stays in the Picture
Last Waltz
March of the Penguins
Murderball
Pumping Iron
Roger & Me
Shoah
Sorrow and the Pity
Spellbound (2003)
Stop Making Sense
Super Size Me
That's Entertainment!
Triumph of the Will
Truth or Dare
Winged Migration
Woodstock

Dramas

(See also Crime, Dramedies,
Film Noir)
Absence of Malice
Accidental Tourist
Affliction
Age of Innocence
Agnes of God
Alfie
Alice Doesn't Live Here
All That Jazz
All the King's Men
All the President's Men
American History X
Amistad
Antonia's Line
Atlantic City
Au Revoir Les Enfants
Aviator, The
Awakenings
Babette's Feast
Bad and the Beautiful
Bad Education
Bang the Drum Slowly
Barfly
Barry Lyndon
Beautiful Mind
Belle de Jour
Best Years of Our Lives
Bicycle Thief
Billy Elliot
Blackboard Jungle
Black Orpheus
Blowup
Blue Angel
Blue Velvet
Boogie Nights
Breaker Morant
Breaking Away
Breaking the Waves
Breathless
Caine Mutiny
Candidate, The
Carnal Knowledge
Cat on a Hot Tin Roof
Changing Lanes
Chariots of Fire
Charly
Children of a Lesser God
Cider House Rules
Cinderella Liberty
Cinema Paradiso

Citizen Kane
Closer
Coach Carter
Cold Mountain
Color of Money
Color Purple
Coming Home
Conformist, The
Contempt
Contender, The
Conversation, The
Crash
Cries and Whispers
Crying Game
Damned, The
Dancer in the Dark
Dangerous Liaisons
Darling
David Copperfield
Day for Night
Days of Wine and Roses
Dead Man Walking
Dead Poets Society
Death in Venice
Deer Hunter
Dogville
Door in the Floor
Driving Miss Daisy
Drugstore Cowboy
East of Eden
Educating Rita
8½
8 Mile
Elmer Gantry
Enchanted April
End of the Affair
English Patient
Erin Brockovich
Eyes Wide Shut
Faces
Fail-Safe
Fame
Fanny and Alexander
Far From Heaven
Few Good Men
Field of Dreams
Finding Neverland
Flashdance
Flight of the Phoenix
Footloose
Fountainhead, The
400 Blows
Free Willy

French Lieutenant's Woman
Friday Night Lights
Friendly Persuasion
From Here to Eternity
Fury
Garden of the Finzi-Continis
Gentleman's Agreement
Girl, Interrupted
Girl with a Pearl Earring
Glengarry Glen Ross
Goodbye, Mr. Chips
Good Night, and Good Luck
Grand Canyon
Grand Hotel
Grand Illusion
Grapes of Wrath
Great Expectations
Great Santini
Greed
Green Mile
Greystoke
Hamlet (1948)
Hamlet (1996)
Henry V
High Noon
Hilary and Jackie
Hiroshima, Mon Amour
Hoosiers
Horse Whisperer
Hotel Rwanda
Hours, The
House of Games
House of Sand and Fog
Howards End
How Green Was My Valley
Hunchback/Notre Dame (1939)
Hustler, The
I Am Sam
Il Postino
Imitation of Life
In America
Inherit the Wind
Insider, The
In the Bedroom
In the Company of Men
In the Name of the Father
Jailhouse Rock
Jane Eyre
Jean de Florette
JFK
Judgment at Nuremberg
Kinsey
Kiss of the Spider Woman

Knife in the Water
Kramer vs. Kramer
La Dolce Vita
Last Metro
Last Picture Show
La Strada
Last Tango in Paris
Last Temptation of Christ
Laurel Canyon
L'Avventura
Leaving Las Vegas
Leopard, The
Lilies of the Field
Lion in Winter
Little Foxes
Little Women
Lone Star
Longtime Companion
Looking for Mr. Goodbar
Lord of the Flies
Lost Weekend
Love Is a Many-Splendored
Love Story
Magdalene Sisters
Magnificent Ambersons
Magnolia
Man from Elysian Fields
Maria Full of Grace
Marriage of Maria Braun
Marty
Mask
McCabe & Mrs. Miller
Midnight Cowboy
Million Dollar Baby
Miracle
Miracle on 34th Street
Misfits, The
Missing
Mission, The
Mississippi Burning
Monster's Ball
Motorcycle Diaries
Moulin Rouge
Mr. Holland's Opus
Mrs. Miniver
Mulholland Dr.
My Beautiful Laundrette
My Bodyguard
My Brilliant Career
My Dinner with Andre
My Left Foot
My Life As a Dog
My Night at Maud's

My Own Private Idaho
National Velvet
Natural, The
Never on Sunday
New York, New York
Nicholas Nickleby
Nights of Cabiria
9½ Weeks
Norma Rae
North Country
Notebook, The
Now, Voyager
Oliver Twist
On Golden Pond
Open City
Ordinary People
Out of Africa
Outsiders, The
Ox-Bow Incident
Paris, Texas
Passion of the Christ
Paths of Glory
Pawnbroker, The
Persona
Peyton Place
Phantom of the Opera
Phenomenon
Philadelphia
Pianist, The
Piano, The
Place in the Sun
Places in the Heart
Pretty Baby
Primal Fear
Prime of Miss Jean Brodie
Prince of Tides
Quiet American
Quiet Man
Quiz Show
Rabbit-Proof Fence
Radio
Rain Man
Raisin in the Sun
Rashomon
Ray
Rebel Without a Cause
Red Shoes
Red Violin
Remains of the Day
Remember the Titans
Requiem for a Dream
Requiem for a Heavyweight
Reversal of Fortune

Right Stuff
River Runs Through It
Robe, The
Rocky
Roger Dodger
Romeo and Juliet
Rookie, The
Room at the Top
Room with a View
Rose, The
Runaway Jury
Sand Pebbles
Satyricon
Save the Last Dance
Scenes from a Marriage
Schindler's List
Seabiscuit
Secrets and Lies
Servant, The
Seven Days in May
Seventh Seal
Sex, Lies and Videotape
Shadow of the Vampire
Shattered Glass
Shawshank Redemption
Sheltering Sky
Shine
Ship of Fools
Shipping News
Showgirls
Silkwood
Six Degrees of Separation
Sling Blade
Snake Pit
Sophie's Choice
Splendor in the Grass
Stand and Deliver
Stand by Me
Star Is Born
Story of Adele H.
Straight Story
Streetcar Named Desire
Suddenly, Last Summer
Sunday Bloody Sunday
Sunshine State
Suspect
Sweet Hereafter
Swimming Pool
Talented Mr. Ripley
Talk to Her
Taxi Driver
Thelma & Louise
They Shoot Horses, Don't They?

Thirteen
Three Faces of Eve
Time to Kill
Tin Drum
To Have and Have Not
To Kill a Mockingbird
Tommy
Topsy-Turvy
To Sir, With Love
12 Angry Men
21 Grams
2010
Two Women
Unbearable Lightness of Being
Unfaithful
Urban Cowboy
Vera Drake
Verdict, The
Very Long Engagement
Wall Street
Whale Rider
Whatever Happened to...
White Oleander
Who's Afraid of V. Woolf?
Wild One, The
Wild Strawberries
Witness
Witness for the Prosecution
Woman Under the Influence
Women in Love
Woodsman, The
Wuthering Heights
Year of Living Dangerously
Yentl
Yojimbo
You Can Count on Me
Zorba the Greek

Dramedies

(Part comedy, part drama)
About a Boy
About Schmidt
Adaptation
African Queen
All About Eve
All About My Mother
Almost Famous
American Beauty
American Graffiti
American Splendor
Anniversary Party
Apartment, The
As Good As It Gets

Barton Fink
Being Julia
Bend It Like Beckham
Big Chill
Big Fish
Big Night
Billy Liar
Bob & Carol & Ted & Alice
Boys on the Side
Breakfast at Tiffany's
Broadcast News
Bull Durham
Bus Stop
Calendar Girls
Charade
City Lights
Coffee and Cigarettes
Confessions/Dangerous Mind
Cooler, The
Cool Hand Luke
Cousin, Cousine
Crimes and Misdemeanors
Diner
Dinner at Eight
Divine Secrets/Ya-Ya
    Sisterhood
Do the Right Thing
Down by Law
Fargo
Fight Club
Fisher King
Five Easy Pieces
Forrest Gump
Fried Green Tomatoes
Front Page
Garden State
Ghost World
Going My Way
Good Girl
Good Morning, Vietnam
Good Will Hunting
Gosford Park
Guess Who's Coming...
Hannah and Her Sisters
Heartburn
Heaven Can Wait (1978)
Igby Goes Down
Irma La Douce
It's a Wonderful Life
Jerry Maguire
Juliet of the Spirits
Junebug
King of Comedy

King of Hearts
Lady Vanishes
League of Their Own
Life Aquatic/Steve Zissou
Life Is Beautiful
Limelight
Longest Yard (1974)
Longest Yard (2005)
Lost in Translation
Love in the Afternoon
Love! Valour! Compassion!
Madness of King George
Man Who Wasn't There
Melinda and Melinda
Melvin and Howard
Metropolitan
Mona Lisa Smile
Monsoon Wedding
Moonstruck
Mrs. Henderson Presents
Mr. Smith Goes to Washington
My Girl
Mystic Pizza
Nashville
Network
Ninotchka
North Dallas Forty
One Flew Over Cuckoo's Nest
Paper Chase
Paper Moon
Parenthood
Pieces of April
Player, The
Pleasantville
Pride and Prejudice (1940)
Primary Colors
Prisoner of Second Avenue
Punch-Drunk Love
Reality Bites
Real Women Have Curves
Royal Tenenbaums
Rules of the Game
Rushmore
Sabrina
Same Time, Next Year
Scent of a Woman
Secondhand Lions
Sense and Sensibility
Seven Beauties
Shakespeare in Love
Sideways
Sisterhood/Traveling Pants
Snatch

Spanglish
Squid and the Whale
Stalag 17
Station Agent
Steel Magnolias
St. Elmo's Fire
Sting, The
Sullivan's Travels
Sweet Home Alabama
Swept Away
Terminal, The
Terms of Endearment
Three Musketeers
To Be or Not to Be
Trainspotting
TransAmerica
Triplets of Belleville
Truman Show
Under the Tuscan Sun
Upside of Anger
Uptown Girls
Vanity Fair
What's Eating Gilbert Grape
Women, The
Wonder Boys
World According to Garp
Y Tu Mamá También

DVD Not Available
African Queen
Apprenticeship/Duddy Kravitz
Becket
Bedazzled
Cinderella Liberty
Conformist, The
Cousin, Cousine
El Cid
Enchanted April
Fountainhead, The
Greed
Jane Eyre
Kiss of the Spider Woman
Lili
Looking for Mr. Goodbar
Magnificent Ambersons
Mediterraneo
Mutiny on the Bounty (1962)
Napoléon
1900
No Time for Sergeants
Sergeant York
Song of the South
Yentl

End of the World
(See also Disaster Flicks)
A.I.: Artificial Intelligence
Andromeda Strain
Armageddon
Day After Tomorrow
Deep Impact
Dr. Strangelove
Escape from New York
Independence Day
Mad Max
Matrix, The
Matrix Reloaded
Matrix Revolutions
On the Beach
Planet of the Apes
Road Warrior
Terminator, The
Terminator 2: Judgment Day
Terminator 3: Rise of Machines
28 Days Later
War of the Worlds

Epics
Alexander Nevsky
Around the World in 80 Days
Ben-Hur
Birth of a Nation
Braveheart
Bridge on the River Kwai
Cleopatra
Dances with Wolves
Doctor Zhivago
Duel in the Sun
El Cid
Empire of the Sun
Evita
Exodus
Gandhi
Giant
Gladiator
Gone with the Wind
Gunga Din
Hamlet (1996)
How the West Was Won
Intolerance
It's a Mad Mad Mad World
King Solomon's Mines
Last Emperor
Last Samurai
Lawrence of Arabia
Legends of the Fall
Leopard, The

Longest Day
Master and Commander
Mutiny on the Bounty (1935)
Mutiny on the Bounty (1962)
Napoléon
1900
Once Upon a Time/America
Once Upon a Time/West
Patriot, The
Pearl Harbor
Ran
Reds
Robe, The
Ryan's Daughter
Sand Pebbles
Seven Samurai
Spartacus
Ten Commandments
Titanic
Tora! Tora! Tora!
Troy
2001: A Space Odyssey
Zulu

Fantasy

Addams Family
Back to the Future
Batman
Batman Returns
Beauty/Beast (1947)
Beetlejuice
Being John Malkovich
Big Fish
Bill & Ted's
Brazil
Brigadoon
Bruce Almighty
Casper
Cat People
Christmas Carol
Chronicles of Narnia
Conan the Barbarian
Corpse Bride
Crouching Tiger
Daredevil
Dark Crystal
Donnie Darko
Edward Scissorhands
Eraserhead
Eternal Sunshine
Fantastic Voyage
Field of Dreams
Finian's Rainbow

Fisher King
5,000 Fingers of Dr. T.
Freaky Friday (1976)
Freaky Friday (2003)
Ghost
Ghost and Mrs. Muir
Gremlins
Harry Potter/Chamber of
    Secrets
Harry Potter/Goblet of Fire
Harry Potter/Prisoner of
    Azkaban
Harry Potter/Sorcerer's Stone
Harvey
Heaven Can Wait (1978)
Heavy Metal
Holes
Hook
How the Grinch Stole Christmas
Hunger, The
Indiana Jones/Last Crusade
Indiana Jones/Temple of Doom
Juliet of the Spirits
Jumanji
King Kong (1933)
King Kong (2005)
Legend
Lemony Snicket's/Unfortunate
Little Princess
Lord of the Rings
Lord of the Rings/Fellowship
Lord of the Rings/Return
Lord of the Rings/Two Towers
Lost Horizon
Mad Max
Man Who Fell to Earth
Mary Poppins
Mask, The
Miracle on 34th Street
Nightmare Before Christmas
Peggy Sue Got Married
Pete's Dragon
Phenomenon
Pirates of the Caribbean
Pleasantville
Polar Express
Princess Bride
Purple Rose of Cairo
Raiders of the Lost Ark
Repo Man
7th Voyage of Sinbad
Space Jam
Spider-Man

Spider-Man 2
Spirited Away
Splash
Stuart Little
Stuart Little 2
Superman
Time Bandits
Topper
Truman Show
Unbreakable
What Dreams May Come
Willow
Willy Wonka/Chocolate Factory
Wings of Desire
Witches of Eastwick
Wizard of Oz

Film Noir

Asphalt Jungle
Big Heat
Big Sleep
Blade Runner
Blood Simple
Body Heat
Cape Fear (1962)
Cape Fear (1991)
Chinatown
Dead Again
D.O.A.
Double Indemnity
Fargo
Gilda
Grifters, The
Gun Crazy
High Sierra
Key Largo
Killers, The
Kiss Me Deadly
L.A. Confidential
Lady from Shanghai
Last Seduction
Laura
Letter, The
Maltese Falcon
Man Who Wasn't There
Memento
Mildred Pierce
Murder, My Sweet
Niagara
Night of the Hunter
Out of the Past
Pickup on South Street
Postman Always Rings... (1946)

Postman Always Rings... (1981)
Seven
Sin City
Sorry, Wrong Number
Strangers on a Train
Sunset Boulevard
Sweet Smell of Success
Third Man
Touch of Evil
White Heat
Who Framed Roger Rabbit

Food-Themed

Babette's Feast
Big Night
Chocolat
Diner
Dinner at Eight
Discreet Charm
Eat Drink Man Woman
Fried Green Tomatoes
Like Water for Chocolate
My Big Fat Greek Wedding
Mystic Pizza
9½ Weeks
Spanglish
Super Size Me
Tom Jones
Wedding Banquet

Foreign Films

Australian

Adventures of Priscilla
Babe
Breaker Morant
Crocodile Dundee
Gallipoli
Mad Max
My Brilliant Career
Piano, The
Rabbit-Proof Fence
Road Warrior
Shine
Strictly Ballroom
Year of Living Dangerously

Brazilian

City of God
Motorcycle Diaries

British

About a Boy
Alfie
Barry Lyndon
Becket

Bedazzled
Bend It Like Beckham
Billy Elliot
Billy Liar
Blowup
Born Free
Brazil
Bridge on the River Kwai
Bridget Jones's Diary
Brief Encounter
Calendar Girls
Chariots of Fire
Christmas Carol
Clockwork Orange
Constant Gardener
Crying Game
Darling
Death on the Nile
Diamonds Are Forever
Die Another Day
Dirty Pretty Things
Don't Look Now
Dr. No
Educating Rita
Elizabeth
Enchanted April
English Patient
Fahrenheit 451
For Your Eyes Only
Four Weddings and a Funeral
French Lieutenant's Woman
From Russia With Love
Full Monty
Gandhi
Girl with a Pearl Earring
GoldenEye
Goodbye, Mr. Chips
Great Expectations
Greystoke
Hamlet (1948)
Hamlet (1996)
Hard Day's Night
Help!
Henry V
Hilary and Jackie
In America
In the Name of the Father
Killing Fields
Kind Hearts and Coronets
Ladykillers, The (1956)
Lady Vanishes
Lavender Hill Mob
Lawrence of Arabia

Legend
Life of Brian
Lion in Winter
Live and Let Die
Local Hero
Lock, Stock and Two...
Lord of the Flies
Love Actually
Madness of King George
Magdalene Sisters
Man for All Seasons
Man with the Golden Gun
Mission, The
Monty Python/Holy Grail
Moonraker
Mouse That Roared
Mrs. Brown
Mrs. Henderson Presents
Murder on the Orient Express
My Beautiful Laundrette
My Left Foot
Notting Hill
Octopussy
Oliver!
Oliver Twist
On Her Majesty's Secret
   Service
Pride & Prejudice (2005)
Prime of Miss Jean Brodie
Red Shoes
Remains of the Day
Repulsion
Robin and Marian
Rocky Horror Picture Show
Romeo and Juliet
Room at the Top
Room with a View
Ruling Class
Ryan's Daughter
Secrets and Lies
Sense and Sensibility
Servant, The
Shaun of the Dead
Sheltering Sky
Snatch
Spy Who Came in from Cold
Spy Who Loved Me
Sunday Bloody Sunday
Third Man
39 Steps
Time Bandits
Tom Jones
Tommy

Tomorrow Never Dies
Topsy-Turvy
To Sir, With Love
Trainspotting
28 Days Later
Vanity Fair
Vera Drake
Village of the Damned
Wallace & Gromit/Were-Rabbit
Women in Love
World Is Not Enough
Yellow Submarine
You Only Live Twice
Zulu

Canadian
Apprenticeship/Duddy Kravitz
Heavy Metal
Meatballs
Red Violin
Sweet Hereafter

Chinese
Crouching Tiger
Farewell My Concubine
Hero
House of Flying Daggers
Kung Fu Hustle

Danish
Babette's Feast
Breaking the Waves
Dancer in the Dark
Dogville

Dutch
Antonia's Line

French
Amélie
Au Revoir Les Enfants
Barbarella
Beauty/Beast (1947)
Belle de Jour
Black Orpheus
Breathless
Bride Wore Black
Children of Paradise
Claire's Knee
Contempt
Cousin, Cousine
Day for Night
Diabolique
Discreet Charm
Diva
400 Blows
Grand Illusion

Hiroshima, Mon Amour
Indochine
Jean de Florette
Jules and Jim
King of Hearts
La Cage aux Folles
La Femme Nikita
Last Metro
Man and a Woman
March of the Penguins
Mon Oncle
Mr. Hulot's Holiday
My Night at Maud's
Napoléon
Pianist, The
Rules of the Game
Shoah
Shoot the Piano Player
Sorrow and the Pity
Story of Adele H.
Swimming Pool
Tess
Triplets of Belleville
Umbrellas of Cherbourg
Very Long Engagement
Wages of Fear
Winged Migration
Z

German
Aguirre: The Wrath of God
Blue Angel
Cabinet of Dr. Caligari
Das Boot
Fitzcarraldo
M
Marriage of Maria Braun
Metropolis
Nosferatu
Nosferatu the Vampyre
Paris, Texas
Run Lola Run
Tin Drum
Triumph of the Will
Wings of Desire

Greek
Never on Sunday
Zorba the Greek

Indian
Monsoon Wedding

Italian
Amarcord
Battle of Algiers

Bicycle Thief
Cinema Paradiso
Conformist, The
Damned, The
Death in Venice
Divorce Italian Style
8½
Fistful of Dollars
For a Few Dollars More
Garden of the Finzi-Continis
Good, the Bad and the Ugly
Il Postino
Juliet of the Spirits
La Dolce Vita
La Strada
Last Tango in Paris
L'Avventura
Leopard, The
Life Is Beautiful
Mediterraneo
Nights of Cabiria
1900
Once Upon a Time/West
Open City
Satyricon
Seven Beauties
Swept Away
Two Women

Japanese
Akira
Godzilla
Ran
Rashomon
Seven Samurai
Spirited Away
Yojimbo

Mexican
Like Water for Chocolate
Y Tu Mamá También

New Zealand
Whale Rider

Russian
Alexander Nevsky
Potemkin

Spanish
All About My Mother
Bad Education
Talk to Her
Tie Me Up! Tie Me Down!
Women on the Verge

Swedish
Cries and Whispers
Elvira Madigan
Fanny and Alexander
My Life As a Dog
Persona
Scenes from a Marriage
Seventh Seal
Smiles of a Summer Night
Wild Strawberries

Taiwanese
Eat Drink Man Woman
Wedding Banquet

Guy Movies
(See also Sports, War)
Airplane!
Animal House
Beverly Hills Cop
Big Fish
Big Lebowski
Blazing Saddles
Blues Brothers
Breaker Morant
Caddyshack
Con Air
Conan the Barbarian
Cool Hand Luke
Diner
Dirty Harry
Dumb and Dumber
Escape from New York
Face/Off
Few Good Men
Fight Club
First Blood: Rambo
Fistful of Dollars
48 HRS.
French Connection
Gladiator
Glengarry Glen Ross
Goodfellas
Heat
High Plains Drifter
Hunt for Red October
Jackass: The Movie
Lock, Stock and Two...
Mad Max
Meatballs
Naked Gun
Ocean's Eleven (2001)
Old School

Outlaw Josey Wales
Papillon
Reservoir Dogs
Road Warrior
Rush Hour
Scarface
Serpico
Snatch
South Park
Stir Crazy
Stripes
Swingers
10
Terminator, The
Terminator 2: Judgment Day
Terminator 3: Rise of Machines
Top Gun
Total Recall
Under Siege
Wild Bunch
Wild One, The
X-Men
X-Men: The Last Stand
X2: X-Men United
Young Guns

High School
American Graffiti
American Pie
Bill & Ted's
Blackboard Jungle
Breakfast Club
Carrie
Clueless
Coach Carter
Dead Poets Society
Donnie Darko
Election
Elephant
Fame
Fast Times at Ridgemont High
Ferris Bueller's Day Off
Friday Night Lights
Goodbye, Mr. Chips
Grease
Heathers
In & Out
Mean Girls
Mr. Holland's Opus
My Bodyguard
Napoleon Dynamite
Pretty in Pink
Prime of Miss Jean Brodie

Remember the Titans
Rushmore
Save the Last Dance
Sixteen Candles
Stand and Deliver
Thirteen
To Sir, With Love

Holiday
Christmas
Bad Santa
Bishop's Wife
Christmas Carol
Christmas Story
Elf
Holiday Inn
How the Grinch Stole Christmas
It's a Wonderful Life
Miracle on 34th Street
Nightmare Before Christmas
Polar Express
Santa Clause
White Christmas
Easter
Easter Parade
Last Temptation of Christ
Passion of the Christ
Robe, The
Independence Day
Born on the Fourth of July
Patriot, The
1776
Yankee Doodle Dandy

Horror
American Werewolf in London
Bride of Frankenstein
Cabinet of Dr. Caligari
Carrie
Cat People
Dracula (1931)
Dracula (1992)
Evil Dead
Exorcist, The
Fly, The (1958)
Fly, The (1986)
Frankenstein
Freaks
Friday the 13th
Godzilla
Gothika
Halloween
House of Wax

Hunger, The
Identity
Interview with the Vampire
Invasion/Body Snatchers (1956)
Invasion/Body Snatchers (1978)
Invisible Man
Mummy, The (1932)
Mummy, The (1999)
Nightmare on Elm Street
Night of the Living Dead
Nosferatu
Nosferatu the Vampyre
Omen, The
Pit and the Pendulum
Poltergeist
Ring, The
Rosemary's Baby
Saw
Scream
Shadow of the Vampire
Shaun of the Dead
Shining, The
Sisters
Sleepy Hollow
Texas Chainsaw Massacre
Thing, The (1951)
Thing, The (1982)
28 Days Later
Van Helsing
Village of the Damned
Wolf Man
Young Frankenstein

Independents

(See also Documentaries)
American Splendor
Anniversary Party
Barfly
Basquiat
Before Night Falls
Being John Malkovich
Being Julia
Benji
Blood Simple
Brokeback Mountain
Brother from Another Planet
Capote
Clerks
Coffee and Cigarettes
Cooler, The
Crash
Deconstructing Harry
Donnie Darko

Door in the Floor
Down by Law
Eating Raoul
Eraserhead
Evil Dead
Faces
Far From Heaven
Frida
Garden State
Girl with a Pearl Earring
Gods and Monsters
Gods Must Be Crazy
Good Night, and Good Luck
Happiness
Henry V
Hustle & Flow
In the Company of Men
Junebug
Kissing Jessica Stein
Laurel Canyon
Longtime Companion
Lost in Translation
Love! Valour! Compassion!
Man from Elysian Fields
Metropolitan
Monster
Monster's Ball
Monty Python/Holy Grail
My Beautiful Laundrette
My Big Fat Greek Wedding
My Dinner with Andre
Night of the Living Dead
One Hour Photo
Passion of the Christ
Pieces of April
Pink Flamingos
Pollock
Real Women Have Curves
Requiem for a Dream
Reservoir Dogs
Roger Dodger
Room with a View
Saw
Secretary
Sex, Lies and Videotape
Shattered Glass
Sideways
Squid and the Whale
Station Agent
Sunshine State
Swingers
Texas Chainsaw Massacre
This Is Spinal Tap

TransAmerica
21 Grams
Upside of Anger
Welcome to the Dollhouse
Whale Rider
Woman Under the Influence
Woodsman, The
You Can Count on Me

James Bond

Diamonds Are Forever
Die Another Day
Dr. No
For Your Eyes Only
From Russia With Love
GoldenEye
Goldfinger
License to Kill
Live and Let Die
Living Daylights
Man with the Golden Gun
Moonraker
Never Say Never Again
Octopussy
On Her Majesty's Secret
   Service
Spy Who Loved Me
Thunderball
Tomorrow Never Dies
View to a Kill
World Is Not Enough
You Only Live Twice

Literary Adaptations

About a Boy
About Schmidt
Accidental Tourist
Adaptation
Adventures of Robin Hood
Affliction
Age of Innocence
A.I.: Artificial Intelligence
Airport
Aladdin
Alice in Wonderland
All Quiet on the Western Front
All the King's Men
All the President's Men
Along Came a Spider
Altered States
Andromeda Strain
Anna and the King
Apprenticeship/Duddy Kravitz

Around the World in 80 Days
Babette's Feast
Barry Lyndon
Beau Geste
Beautiful Mind
Beauty/Beast (1947)
Bedazzled
Being There
Ben-Hur
Big Fish
Big Sleep
Black Stallion
Blade Runner
Bourne Identity
Bourne Supremacy
Breakfast at Tiffany's
Bride Wore Black
Bridge on the River Kwai
Bridges of Madison County
Bridget Jones's Diary
Caine Mutiny
Captain Blood
Captains Courageous
Carrie
Catch Me If You Can
Christmas Carol
Christmas Story
Cider House Rules
City of God
Clear and Present Danger
Client, The
Clockwork Orange
Clueless
Cold Mountain
Collector, The
Color of Money
Color Purple
Conan the Barbarian
Contact
David Copperfield
Da Vinci Code
Death in Venice
Death on the Nile
Death Wish
Deep, The
Deliverance
Diamonds Are Forever
Dirty Dozen
Divine Secrets/Ya-Ya
   Sisterhood
Doctor Zhivago
Don't Look Now
Door in the Floor

Dracula (1931)
Dracula (1992)
Dr. Dolittle
Dr. No
Dune
East of Eden
Elmer Gantry
Emma
Empire of the Sun
End of the Affair
English Patient
Exodus
Exorcist, The
Fahrenheit 451
Fast Times at Ridgemont High
Fear and Loathing in Las Vegas
Firm, The
First Blood: Rambo
First Wives Club
Fletch
Forbidden Planet
Forrest Gump
For Whom the Bell Tolls
Fountainhead, The
Frances
Frankenstein
French Lieutenant's Woman
Fried Green Tomatoes
Friendly Persuasion
From Here to Eternity
From Russia With Love
Gentleman's Agreement
Giant
Gigi
Girl, Interrupted
Godfather, The
Goldfinger
Gone with the Wind
Goodbye, Columbus
Goodbye, Mr. Chips
Graduate, The
Grand Hotel
Grapes of Wrath
Great Expectations
Great Gatsby
Great Santini
Greed
Green Mile
Greystoke
Grifters, The
Gunga Din
Guns of Navarone
Hamlet (1948)

Hamlet (1996)
Hannibal
Harry Potter/Chamber of
    Secrets
Harry Potter/Goblet of Fire
Harry Potter/Prisoner of
    Azkaban
Harry Potter/Sorcerer's Stone
Heartburn
Henry & June
Henry V
High Sierra
Holes
Hook
Horse Whisperer
Hound of the Baskervilles
Hours, The
House of Sand and Fog
Howards End
How the Grinch Stole Christmas
Hud
Hunchback/Notre Dame (1939)
Hunchback/Notre Dame (1996)
Hunt for Red October
Imitation of Life
Importance of Being Earnest
In Cold Blood
Interview with the Vampire
Invisible Man
Iris
I, Robot
James and the Giant Peach
Jane Eyre
Jaws
Jean de Florette
Journey to Center of Earth
Julia
Jungle Book (1942)
Jungle Book (1967)
Jurassic Park
Killers, The
King Solomon's Mines
Kiss Me Deadly
Kiss of the Spider Woman
Lady Vanishes
Last of the Mohicans
Last Picture Show
Laura
Lemony Snicket's/Unfortunate
Like Water for Chocolate
Lili
Little Big Man
Little Princess

Little Women
Live and Let Die
Lolita
Looking for Mr. Goodbar
Lord of the Flies
Lord of the Rings
Lord of the Rings/Fellowship
Lord of the Rings/Return
Lord of the Rings/Two Towers
Lost Horizon
Lost Weekend
Love in the Afternoon
Love Story
Maltese Falcon
Manchurian Candidate (1962)
Man Who Fell to Earth
Man Who Would Be King
Man with the Golden Gun
Marathon Man
Mary Poppins
Master and Commander
Memoirs of a Geisha
Mildred Pierce
Misery
Mommie Dearest
Moonraker
Motorcycle Diaries
Murder, My Sweet
Murder on the Orient Express
Mutiny on the Bounty (1935)
Mutiny on the Bounty (1962)
Mystic River
National Velvet
Never Say Never Again
Nicholas Nickleby
Night of the Hunter
Nosferatu
Notebook, The
Octopussy
Oh, God!
Oliver!
Oliver Twist
One Flew Over Cuckoo's Nest
On Her Majesty's Secret
    Service
Ordinary People
Out of Africa
Out of Sight
Outsiders, The
Ox-Bow Incident
Paper Chase
Papillon
Passion of the Christ

Patch Adams
Patriot Games
Pelican Brief
Perfect Storm
Peyton Place
Pianist, The
Pit and the Pendulum
Place in the Sun
Planet of the Apes
Polar Express
Postcards from the Edge
Postman Always Rings... (1946)
Postman Always Rings... (1981)
Presumed Innocent
Pride and Prejudice (1940)
Pride & Prejudice (2005)
Primary Colors
Prime of Miss Jean Brodie
Prince of Tides
Princess Diaries
Prizzi's Honor
Quiet American
Rabbit-Proof Fence
Rebecca
Remains of the Day
Rescuers, The
Reversal of Fortune
Right Stuff
Robe, The
Romancing the Stone
Room with a View
Rosemary's Baby
Roxanne
Runaway Jury
Sense and Sensibility
Serpico
Seven Days in May
Shawshank Redemption
Sheltering Sky
Shining, The
Ship of Fools
Shipping News
Sideways
Silence of the Lambs
Single White Female
Sisterhood/Traveling Pants
Sleeping with the Enemy
Sleepy Hollow
Sophie's Choice
Spy Who Came in from Cold
Spy Who Loved Me
Starship Troopers
Strangers on a Train

Sum of All Fears
Sweet Hereafter
Swiss Family Robinson
Talented Mr. Ripley
Tarzan
Tarzan and His Mate
Tarzan the Ape Man
Terms of Endearment
Tess
They Shoot Horses, Don't They?
Thin Man
Thin Red Line
Three Coins in the Fountain
Three Musketeers
Thunderball
Time Machine
Time to Kill
Tin Drum
To Have and Have Not
To Kill a Mockingbird
Tom Jones
Topper
Treasure of the Sierra Madre
Troy
25th Hour
20,000 Leagues Under the Sea
2010
Two Women
Unbearable Lightness of Being
Under the Tuscan Sun
Vanity Fair
Village of the Damned
War of the Roses
War of the Worlds
Whale Rider
What Dreams May Come
Willy Wonka/Chocolate Factory
Witches of Eastwick
Wizard of Oz
Women in Love
World According to Garp
Wuthering Heights
You Only Live Twice

Martial Arts

Crouching Tiger
Enter the Dragon
Hero
House of Flying Daggers
Karate Kid
Kill Bill Vol. 1
Kill Bill Vol. 2
Kung Fu Hustle

Last Samurai
Magnificent Seven
Matrix, The
Matrix Reloaded
Matrix Revolutions
Ran
Rush Hour
Seven Samurai
Yojimbo

Movies About Movies

Adaptation
Anniversary Party
Aviator, The
Bad and the Beautiful
Bad Education
Barton Fink
Boogie Nights
Cinema Paradiso
Contempt
Day for Night
Ed Wood
8½
Frances
Kid Stays in the Picture
Mommie Dearest
Mulholland Dr.
Notting Hill
Player, The
Postcards from the Edge
Purple Rose of Cairo
Shadow of the Vampire
Singin' in the Rain
Star Is Born
Sullivan's Travels
Sunset Boulevard

Musicals

All That Jazz
American in Paris
Annie
Band Wagon
Bells Are Ringing
Beyond the Sea
Blues Brothers
Brigadoon
Buck Privates
Bye Bye Birdie
Cabaret
Camelot
Carmen Jones
Carousel
Chicago

Damn Yankees
Dancer in the Dark
De-Lovely
Easter Parade
Evita
Fame
Fiddler on the Roof
Finian's Rainbow
5,000 Fingers of Dr. T.
42nd Street
Funny Face
Funny Girl
Funny Lady
Funny Thing Happened...
Gay Divorcee
Gentlemen Prefer Blondes
Gigi
Grease
Guys and Dolls
Gypsy
Hair
Hard Day's Night
Hello, Dolly!
Help!
High Society
Holiday Inn
Jailhouse Rock
Jesus Christ Superstar
King and I
Kiss Me Kate
Little Shop of Horrors
Mary Poppins
Meet Me in St. Louis
Moulin Rouge!
Music Man
My Fair Lady
New York, New York
Oklahoma!
Oliver!
On the Town
Paint Your Wagon
Phantom of the Opera
Rent
Rocky Horror Picture Show
Seven Brides/Seven Brothers
1776
Show Boat
Singin' in the Rain
Sound of Music
South Pacific
Sweet Charity
That's Entertainment!
Thoroughly Modern Millie

Tommy
Top Hat
Umbrellas of Cherbourg
Unsinkable Molly Brown
Victor/Victoria
West Side Story
White Christmas
Wizard of Oz
Yankee Doodle Dandy
Yentl

Occupations
Doctors
Awakenings
Charly
Dark Victory
Dead Ringers
Dr. Dolittle
Elephant Man
Girl, Interrupted
Greed
Marathon Man
MASH
Nurse Betty
One Flew Over Cuckoo's Nest
Outbreak
Patch Adams
Spellbound (1945)
Three Faces of Eve

Journalists
Absence of Malice
All the President's Men
Almost Famous
Broadcast News
Capote
Chicago
China Syndrome
Citizen Kane
Fear and Loathing in Las Vegas
Fletch
Front Page
Gentleman's Agreement
Good Morning, Vietnam
Good Night, and Good Luck
Groundhog Day
Heartburn
His Girl Friday
Insider, The
It Happened One Night
Killing Fields
La Dolce Vita
Life of David Gale
Love Is a Many-Splendored

Mighty Aphrodite
Nashville
Network
Nothing Sacred
Pelican Brief
Philadelphia Story
Quiet American
Reds
Roger & Me
Roman Holiday
Shattered Glass
Shipping News
Superman
Sweet Smell of Success
Talk to Her
To Die For
Veronica Guerin
Woman of the Year
Year of Living Dangerously

Lawyers
Absence of Malice
Accused, The
Anatomy of a Murder
Body Heat
Breaker Morant
Caine Mutiny
Changing Lanes
Chicago
Client, The
Enemy of the State
Erin Brockovich
Few Good Men
Firm, The
Fortune Cookie
I Am Sam
Inherit the Wind
Intolerable Cruelty
Jagged Edge
Judgment at Nuremberg
Kramer vs. Kramer
Legally Blonde
Liar Liar
Man for All Seasons
My Cousin Vinny
Paper Chase
Pelican Brief
Philadelphia
Presumed Innocent
Primal Fear
Reversal of Fortune
Runaway Jury
Secretary

Suspect
Time to Kill
To Kill a Mockingbird
12 Angry Men
Two Weeks Notice
Verdict, The
Witness for the Prosecution

Politicians
Air Force One
All the King's Men
All the President's Men
American President
Being There
Candidate, The
Contender, The
Dave
Evita
Fahrenheit 9/11
Gandhi
Good Night, and Good Luck
Great Dictator
JFK
Malcolm X
Manchurian Candidate (1962)
Mississippi Burning
Mrs. Brown
Mr. Smith Goes to Washington
Nashville
Pelican Brief
Primary Colors
Reds
Seven Days in May
1776
Taxi Driver
Wag the Dog
Z

Prostitutes
Belle de Jour
Cinderella Liberty
Dressed to Kill
Eating Raoul
8½
Elmer Gantry
Farewell My Concubine
Irma La Douce
Klute
Leaving Las Vegas
Man from Elysian Fields
McCabe & Mrs. Miller
Midnight Cowboy
Mighty Aphrodite
Monster

My Own Private Idaho
Never on Sunday
Nights of Cabiria
Pretty Baby
Pretty Woman
Risky Business
Sweet Charity
Taxi Driver
Trading Places

Spies
(See also James Bond)
Austin Powers
Bourne Identity
Bourne Supremacy
Clear and Present Danger
Confessions/Dangerous Mind
Conversation, The
Counterfeit Traitor
Donnie Brasco
General, The
Hunt for Red October
In-Laws, The
La Femme Nikita
Man Who Knew Too Much
Mission: Impossible
Notorious
No Way Out
Outrageous Fortune
Patriot Games
Recruit, The
Spy Kids
Spy Kids 2
Spy Who Came in from Cold
Sum of All Fears
Syriana
39 Steps
True Lies
XXX

Teachers
Anna and the King
Au Revoir Les Enfants
Beautiful Mind
Billy Elliot
Blackboard Jungle
Blue Angel
Charly
Children of a Lesser God
Coach Carter
Dead Poets Society
Diabolique
Educating Rita
Election

Fame
Goodbye, Mr. Chips
Harry Potter/Chamber of
    Secrets
Harry Potter/Goblet of Fire
Harry Potter/Prisoner of
    Azkaban
Harry Potter/Sorcerer's Stone
In & Out
Inherit the Wind
King and I
Looking for Mr. Goodbar
Miracle Worker
Mona Lisa Smile
Mr. Holland's Opus
My Fair Lady
Nutty Professor (1963)
Nutty Professor (1996)
Oliver!
Paper Chase
Piano, The
Prime of Miss Jean Brodie
Red Shoes
Rushmore
School of Rock
Stand and Deliver
To Sir, With Love
Wonder Boys

Office Politics
Apartment, The
Baby Boom
Broadcast News
Desk Set
Front Page
Glengarry Glen Ross
His Girl Friday
In the Company of Men
Network
9 to 5
Secretary
Wall Street
Working Girl

Oscar Winners
Best Picture
All About Eve (1950)
All Quiet on the Western Front
    (1930)
All the King's Men (1949)
Amadeus (1984)
American Beauty (1999)

American in Paris (1951)
Annie Hall (1977)
Apartment, The (1960)
Around the World in 80 Days (1956)
Beautiful Mind (2001)
Ben-Hur (1959)
Best Years of Our Lives (1946)
Braveheart (1995)
Bridge on the River Kwai (1957)
Casablanca (1943)
Chariots of Fire (1981)
Chicago (2002)
Crash (2005)
Dances with Wolves (1990)
Deer Hunter (1978)
Driving Miss Daisy (1989)
English Patient (1996)
Forrest Gump (1994)
French Connection (1971)
From Here to Eternity (1953)
Gandhi (1982)
Gentleman's Agreement (1947)
Gigi (1958)
Gladiator (2000)
Godfather, The (1972)
Godfather Part II (1974)
Going My Way (1944)
Gone with the Wind (1939)
Grand Hotel (1932)
Hamlet (1948) (1948)
How Green Was My Valley (1941)
In the Heat of the Night (1967)
It Happened One Night (1934)
Kramer vs. Kramer (1979)
Last Emperor (1987)
Lawrence of Arabia (1962)
Lord of the Rings/Return (2003)
Lost Weekend (1945)
Man for All Seasons (1966)
Marty (1955)
Midnight Cowboy (1969)
Million Dollar Baby (2004)
Mrs. Miniver (1942)
Mutiny on the Bounty (1935) (1935)
My Fair Lady (1964)
Oliver! (1968)
One Flew Over Cuckoo's Nest (1975)
On the Waterfront (1954)
Ordinary People (1980)

Out of Africa (1985)
Patton (1970)
Platoon (1986)
Rain Man (1988)
Rebecca (1940)
Rocky (1976)
Schindler's List (1993)
Shakespeare in Love (1998)
Silence of the Lambs (1991)
Sound of Music (1965)
Sting, The (1973)
Terms of Endearment (1983)
Titanic (1997)
Tom Jones (1963)
Unforgiven (1992)
West Side Story (1961)

Best Actor
F. Murray Abraham
  Amadeus
Roberto Benigni
  Life Is Beautiful
Humphrey Bogart
  African Queen
Ernest Borgnine
  Marty
Marlon Brando
  Godfather, The
  On the Waterfront
Adrien Brody
  Pianist, The
Yul Brynner
  King and I
Nicolas Cage
  Leaving Las Vegas
James Cagney
  Yankee Doodle Dandy
Gary Cooper
  High Noon
  Sergeant York
Broderick Crawford
  All the King's Men
Bing Crosby
  Going My Way
Russell Crowe
  Gladiator
Daniel Day-Lewis
  My Left Foot
Robert De Niro
  Raging Bull
Robert Donat
  Goodbye, Mr. Chips

Michael Douglas
  Wall Street
Richard Dreyfuss
  Goodbye Girl
Peter Finch
  Network
Henry Fonda
  On Golden Pond
Jamie Foxx
  Ray
Clark Gable
  It Happened One Night
Alec Guinness
  Bridge on the River Kwai
Gene Hackman
  French Connection
Tom Hanks
  Forrest Gump
  Philadelphia
Rex Harrison
  My Fair Lady
Charlton Heston
  Ben-Hur
Dustin Hoffman
  Kramer vs. Kramer
  Rain Man
Philip Seymour Hoffman
  Capote
William Holden
  Stalag 17
Anthony Hopkins
  Silence of the Lambs
William Hurt
  Kiss of the Spider Woman
Jeremy Irons
  Reversal of Fortune
Ben Kingsley
  Gandhi
Burt Lancaster
  Elmer Gantry
Fredric March
  Best Years of Our Lives
Lee Marvin
  Cat Ballou
Ray Milland
  Lost Weekend
Paul Newman
  Color of Money
Jack Nicholson
  As Good As It Gets
  One Flew Over Cuckoo's Nest

Laurence Olivier
  Hamlet (1948)
Al Pacino
  Scent of a Woman
Gregory Peck
  To Kill a Mockingbird
Sean Penn
  Mystic River
Sidney Poitier
  Lilies of the Field
Cliff Robertson
  Charly
Geoffrey Rush
  Shine
Paul Scofield
  Man for All Seasons
George C. Scott
  Patton
Kevin Spacey
  American Beauty
Rod Steiger
  In the Heat of the Night
James Stewart
  Philadelphia Story
Spencer Tracy
  Captains Courageous
Jon Voight
  Coming Home
Denzel Washington
  Training Day
John Wayne
  True Grit

Best Actress
Julie Andrews
  Mary Poppins
Anne Bancroft
  Miracle Worker
Kathy Bates
  Misery
Ingrid Bergman
  Anastasia (1956)
  Gaslight
Halle Berry
  Monster's Ball
Ellen Burstyn
  Alice Doesn't Live Here
Cher
  Moonstruck
Claudette Colbert
  It Happened One Night

Joan Crawford
  Mildred Pierce
Faye Dunaway
  Network
Sally Field
  Norma Rae
  Places in the Heart
Louise Fletcher
  One Flew Over Cuckoo's Nest
Jane Fonda
  Coming Home
  Klute
Jodie Foster
  Accused, The
  Silence of the Lambs
Glenda Jackson
  Women in Love
Greer Garson
  Mrs. Miniver
Audrey Hepburn
  Roman Holiday
Katharine Hepburn
  Guess Who's Coming...
  Lion in Winter
  On Golden Pond
Judy Holliday
  Born Yesterday
Holly Hunter
  Piano, The
Helen Hunt
  As Good As It Gets
Jennifer Jones
  Song of Bernadette
Joan Fontaine
  Suspicion
Julie Christie
  Darling
Diane Keaton
  Annie Hall
Nicole Kidman
  Hours, The
Vivien Leigh
  Gone with the Wind
  Streetcar Named Desire
Sophia Loren
  Two Women
Shirley MacLaine
  Terms of Endearment
Maggie Smith
  Prime of Miss Jean Brodie

Marlee Matlin
  Children of a Lesser God
Frances McDormand
  Fargo
Liza Minnelli
  Cabaret
Gwyneth Paltrow
  Shakespeare in Love
Patricia Neal
  Hud
Julia Roberts
  Erin Brockovich
Susan Sarandon
  Dead Man Walking
Simone Signoret
  Room at the Top
Sissy Spacek
  Coal Miner's Daughter
Meryl Streep
  Sophie's Choice
Barbra Streisand
  Funny Girl
Susan Hayward
  I Want to Live!
Hilary Swank
  Boys Don't Cry
  Million Dollar Baby
Jessica Tandy
  Driving Miss Daisy
Elizabeth Taylor
  Who's Afraid of V. Woolf?
Charlize Theron
  Monster
Emma Thompson
  Howards End
Reese Witherspoon
  Walk the Line
Joanne Woodward
  Three Faces of Eve

Best Director
All About Eve
All Quiet on the Western Front
Amadeus
American Beauty
Annie Hall
Apartment, The
Awful Truth
Beautiful Mind
Ben-Hur
Best Years of Our Lives
Born on the Fourth of July

Braveheart
Bridge on the River Kwai
Brokeback Mountain
Cabaret
Casablanca
Dances with Wolves
Deer Hunter
English Patient
Forrest Gump
French Connection
From Here to Eternity
Gandhi
Gentleman's Agreement
Giant
Gigi
Godfather Part II
Going My Way
Gone with the Wind
Graduate, The
Grapes of Wrath
How Green Was My Valley
It Happened One Night
Kramer vs. Kramer
Last Emperor
Lawrence of Arabia
Lord of the Rings/Return
Lost Weekend
Man for All Seasons
Marty
Midnight Cowboy
Million Dollar Baby
Mr. Deeds Goes to Town
Mrs. Miniver
My Fair Lady
Oliver!
One Flew Over Cuckoo's Nest
On the Waterfront
Ordinary People
Out of Africa
Patton
Pianist, The
Place in the Sun
Platoon
Quiet Man
Rain Man
Reds
Rocky
Saving Private Ryan
Schindler's List
Silence of the Lambs
Sound of Music
Sting, The
Terms of Endearment

Titanic
Tom Jones
Traffic
Treasure of the Sierra Madre
Unforgiven
West Side Story

Best Screenplay
All About Eve
Almost Famous
Amadeus
American Beauty
American in Paris
Annie Hall
Apartment, The
Around the World in 80 Days
Bad and the Beautiful
Beautiful Mind
Becket
Best Years of Our Lives
Breaking Away
Bridge on the River Kwai
Brokeback Mountain
Butch Cassidy/Sundance Kid
Candidate, The
Casablanca
Chariots of Fire
Chinatown
Cider House Rules
Citizen Kane
Coming Home
Crash
Crying Game
Dances with Wolves
Dangerous Liaisons
Darling
Dead Poets Society
Divorce Italian Style
Doctor Zhivago
Dog Day Afternoon
Driving Miss Daisy
Elmer Gantry
Exorcist, The
Fargo
Forrest Gump
French Connection
From Here to Eternity
Gandhi
Ghost
Gigi
Godfather, The
Godfather Part II
Gods and Monsters

Going My Way
Gone with the Wind
Good Will Hunting
Gosford Park
Guess Who's Coming...
Hannah and Her Sisters
Howards End
How the West Was Won
In the Heat of the Night
It Happened One Night
Judgment at Nuremberg
Julia
Kramer vs. Kramer
L.A. Confidential
Last Emperor
Lavender Hill Mob
Lion in Winter
Lord of the Rings/Return
Lost in Translation
Lost Weekend
Man and a Woman
Man for All Seasons
Marty
MASH
Melvin and Howard
Midnight Cowboy
Midnight Express
Miracle on 34th Street
Missing
Moonstruck
Mr. Mom
Mrs. Miniver
Network
One Flew Over Cuckoo's Nest
On Golden Pond
On the Waterfront
Ordinary People
Out of Africa
Patton
Philadelphia Story
Piano, The
Pillow Talk
Place in the Sun
Places in the Heart
Producers, The
Pulp Fiction
Rain Man
Roman Holiday
Room at the Top
Room with a View
Schindler's List
Sense and Sensibility
Shakespeare in Love

Silence of the Lambs
Sling Blade
Splendor in the Grass
Sting, The
Sunset Boulevard
Talk to Her
Terms of Endearment
Thelma & Louise
To Kill a Mockingbird
Tom Jones
Traffic
Treasure of the Sierra Madre
Usual Suspects
Witness
Woman of the Year

Best Foreign Language Film
All About My Mother
Amarcord
Antonia's Line
Babette's Feast
Bicycle Thief
Black Orpheus
Cinema Paradiso
Crouching Tiger
Day for Night
Discreet Charm
8½
Fanny and Alexander
Garden of the Finzi-Continis
Indochine
La Strada
Life Is Beautiful
Man and a Woman
Mediterraneo
Mon Oncle
Nights of Cabiria
Tin Drum
Z

Religion
Agnes of God
Ben-Hur
Bruce Almighty
Da Vinci Code
Elmer Gantry
Exorcist, The
Going My Way
Hunchback/Notre Dame (1939)
Intolerance
Jesus Christ Superstar
Last Temptation of Christ
Life of Brian
Magdalene Sisters

Oh, God!
Passion of the Christ
Prince of Egypt
Robe, The
Song of Bernadette
Ten Commandments
Yentl

Road Movies

Adventures of Priscilla
Boys on the Side
Easy Rider
Lost in America
Motorcycle Diaries
National Lampoon's Vacation
Paris, Texas
Smokey and the Bandit
Something Wild
Straight Story
Sugarland Express
Thelma & Louise
Y Tu Mamá También

Rock 'n' Roll

Almost Famous
Bill & Ted's
Blues Brothers
Bye Bye Birdie
Don't Look Back
Fame
Footloose
Gimme Shelter
Grease
Hair
Hard Day's Night
Help!
Jailhouse Rock
Jesus Christ Superstar
Last Waltz
Rocky Horror Picture Show
Rose, The
Saturday Night Fever
School of Rock
Sid & Nancy
Stop Making Sense
This Is Spinal Tap
Tommy
Truth or Dare
Wayne's World
What's Love Got to Do with It
Woodstock
Yellow Submarine

Romance

(See also Chick Flicks)
Accidental Tourist
Adventures of Robin Hood
African Queen
Almost Famous
American in Paris
American President
Anna and the King
Annie Hall
Apartment, The
Arthur
As Good As It Gets
Awful Truth
Barry Lyndon
Before Sunset
Bell, Book and Candle
Bishop's Wife
Breaking the Waves
Brief Encounter
Bringing Up Baby
Broadcast News
Broadway Danny Rose
Brokeback Mountain
Bull Durham
Bus Stop
Cactus Flower
Camelot
Carousel
Casablanca
Charade
Chasing Amy
Children of a Lesser God
Children of Paradise
Chocolat
Cinderella Liberty
Claire's Knee
Cold Mountain
Cooler, The
Cousin, Cousine
Dangerous Liaisons
Dark Victory
Days of Heaven
Desk Set
Doctor Zhivago
Dracula (1992)
Easter Parade
Elvira Madigan
Emma
End of the Affair
Eternal Sunshine
Fabulous Baker Boys

Family Man
Farewell My Concubine
Far From Heaven
Fever Pitch
50 First Dates
Flashdance
40 Year Old Virgin
For Whom the Bell Tolls
Fountainhead, The
French Lieutenant's Woman
From Here to Eternity
Garden State
Gay Divorcee
Ghost and Mrs. Muir
Gigi
Gone with the Wind
Goodbye, Columbus
Goodbye Girl
Graduate, The
Great Gatsby
Hannah and Her Sisters
Harold and Maude
Heartbreak Kid
Heartburn
Hello, Dolly!
Henry & June
His Girl Friday
Hitch
Holiday Inn
Horse Whisperer
House of Flying Daggers
How Green Was My Valley
How to Marry a Millionaire
Importance of Being Earnest
Indochine
It Happened One Night
I Was a Male War Bride
Jane Eyre
Jerry Maguire
Jules and Jim
Just Like Heaven
Kiss Me Kate
Lady and the Tramp
Lady Eve
L.A. Story
Last Tango in Paris
Laura
Like Water for Chocolate
Lili
Lost Horizon
Love in the Afternoon
Man and a Woman
Manhattan

Marty
Match Point
Memoirs of a Geisha
Misfits, The
Monster's Ball
Moonstruck
Moulin Rouge
Moulin Rouge!
Mrs. Brown
My Big Fat Greek Wedding
My Brilliant Career
My Fair Lady
My Girl
9½ Weeks
Ninotchka
Nothing Sacred
Notorious
Out of Sight
Pearl Harbor
Philadelphia Story
Piano, The
Picnic
Pillow Talk
Place in the Sun
Play It Again, Sam
Pretty in Pink
Pride & Prejudice (2005)
Prince of Tides
Punch-Drunk Love
Quiet Man
Reality Bites
Rebecca
Reds
Red Shoes
Remains of the Day
Rent
Robin and Marian
Romancing the Stone
Romeo and Juliet
Romeo + Juliet
Room with a View
Roxanne
Ryan's Daughter
Sabrina
Same Time, Next Year
Saturday Night Fever
Save the Last Dance
Shine
Sid & Nancy
Smiles of a Summer Night
South Pacific
Spanglish
Spellbound (1945)

Splash
Starman
St. Elmo's Fire
Story of Adele H.
Strictly Ballroom
Summer of '42
Talk to Her
10
Tess
Thomas Crown Affair
Three Coins in the Fountain
Titanic
To Catch a Thief
To Have and Have Not
Tootsie
Top Hat
Topper
Two for the Road
Umbrellas of Cherbourg
Unbearable Lightness of Being
Upside of Anger
Urban Cowboy
Vanity Fair
Vertigo
Walk the Line
West Side Story
What Dreams May Come
While You Were Sleeping
White Christmas
Witness
Women in Love
Wuthering Heights

Sci-Fi

Abyss, The
A.I.: Artificial Intelligence
Akira
Alien
Aliens
Altered States
Andromeda Strain
Back to the Future
Barbarella
Blade Runner
Brother from Another Planet
Close Encounters
Cocoon
Contact
Day After Tomorrow
Day the Earth Stood Still
Deep Impact
Donnie Darko
Dune

Escape from New York
E.T. The Extra-Terrestrial
Fahrenheit 451
Fifth Element
Fly, The (1958)
Fly, The (1986)
Forbidden Planet
Frequency
Ghostbusters
Godzilla
Heavy Metal
Independence Day
Innerspace
Invasion/Body Snatchers (1956)
Invasion/Body Snatchers (1978)
I, Robot
Journey to Center of Earth
Jurassic Park
Man Who Fell to Earth
Matrix, The
Matrix Reloaded
Matrix Revolutions
Men in Black
Men in Black II
Metropolis
Minority Report
Nutty Professor (1996)
On the Beach
Planet of the Apes
Repo Man
RoboCop
Serenity
Signs
Sleeper
Spaceballs
Stargate
Starman
Starship Troopers
Star Trek II
Star Trek IV
Star Wars
Star Wars I/Phantom Menace
Star Wars II/Attack of Clones
Star Wars III/Revenge of Sith
Star Wars V/Empire Strikes
Star Wars VI/Return of Jedi
Terminator, The
Terminator 2: Judgment Day
Terminator 3: Rise of Machines
Thing, The (1951)
Thing, The (1982)
Time After Time
Time Machine

Total Recall
Tron
Twelve Monkeys
28 Days Later
20,000 Leagues Under the Sea
2001: A Space Odyssey
2010
V for Vendetta
Village of the Damned
War of the Worlds
Westworld
X-Files, The
X-Men
X-Men: The Last Stand
X2: X-Men United

Screwball Comedies

Animal Crackers
Awful Truth
Born Yesterday
Bringing Up Baby
Cocoanuts, The
Day at the Races
Duck Soup
His Girl Friday
Horse Feathers
In-Laws, The
Intolerable Cruelty
It Happened One Night
Lady Eve
My Man Godfrey
Night at the Opera
Nothing Sacred
Palm Beach Story
Philadelphia Story
Raising Arizona
Thin Man
What's Up, Doc?
Women on the Verge

Silent

Birth of a Nation
Cabinet of Dr. Caligari
City Lights
General, The
Gold Rush
Greed
Intolerance
Metropolis
Modern Times
Napoléon
Nosferatu
Potemkin
Thief of Bagdad

Soundtracks

(See also Musical; * Best
Score Oscar winner)
Adventures of Robin Hood*
Aladdin*
Alexander Nevsky
Alfie
All That Jazz*
Almost Famous
Amadeus
Amarcord
American Beauty
American Graffiti
American in Paris*
Anatomy of a Murder
Around the World in 80 Days*
Barry Lyndon*
Basquiat
Beauty/Beast (1991)*
Bells Are Ringing
Ben-Hur*
Beyond the Sea
Big Chill
Blackboard Jungle
Black Orpheus
Blue Velvet
Born Free*
Braveheart
Breakfast at Tiffany's*
Bridge on the River Kwai*
Brief Encounter
Brokeback Mountain*
Buena Vista Social Club
Butch Cassidy/Sundance Kid*
Cabaret*
Camelot*
Cat Ballou
Cat People
Charade
Chariots of Fire*
Chinatown
Cinema Paradiso
Clockwork Orange
Cold Mountain
Crouching Tiger*
Damn Yankees
Dances with Wolves*
Days of Heaven
Days of Wine and Roses*
Death in Venice
De-Lovely
Desperately Seeking Susan

Diner
Dinosaur
Dirty Dancing
Diva
Doctor Zhivago*
Donnie Darko
Don't Look Back
Down by Law
Dracula (1931)
Dumbo*
Easter Parade*
Easy Rider
8½
8 Mile
El Cid
Elvira Madigan
Emma*
Empire of the Sun
English Patient*
E.T. The Extra-Terrestrial*
Exodus*
Fame*
Fantasia
Fantasia 2000
Far From Heaven
Fear and Loathing in Las Vegas
Fiddler on the Roof*
Fight Club
First Blood: Rambo
Flashdance
Footloose
Forbidden Planet
Forrest Gump
Frida*
Full Monty*
Funny Thing Happened...*
Garden State
Gigi*
Gimme Shelter
Gladiator
Godfather, The
Godfather Part II*
Goldfinger
Gone with the Wind
Good, the Bad and the Ugly
Graduate, The
Great Escape
Great Gatsby
Hard Day's Night
Harold and Maude
Harry Potter/Sorcerer's Stone
Hatari!
Heavy Metal

Hello, Dolly!*
High Noon*
Hunger, The
Hustle & Flow
I Am Sam
Il Postino*
In Cold Blood
Irma La Douce*
I Want to Live!
Jailhouse Rock
Jaws*
Journey to Center of Earth
Jungle Book (1967)
King and I*
Lady Sings the Blues
Last Emperor*
Last of the Mohicans
La Strada
Last Tango in Paris
Last Waltz
Lawrence of Arabia*
Life Is Beautiful*
Lili*
Limelight*
Lion in Winter*
Lion King*
Little Mermaid*
Local Hero
Lock, Stock and Two...
Lord of the Rings/Fellowship*
Lord of the Rings/Return*
Lord of the Rings/Two Towers
Love Is a Many-Splendored*
Love Story*
Magnificent Seven
Magnolia
Man and a Woman
Man Who Knew Too Much
Mark of Zorro
Mary Poppins*
Mean Streets
Mediterraneo
Midnight Cowboy
Midnight Express*
Mighty Wind
Mission, The
Music Man*
My Fair Lady*
Nashville
Natural, The
Nightmare Before Christmas
Night of the Hunter
1900

North by Northwest
Now, Voyager*
O Brother, Where Art Thou?
Oklahoma!*
Oliver!*
Omen, The*
Once Upon a Time/West
On the Town*
Out of Africa*
Phantom of the Opera
Piano, The
Pink Panther
Place in the Sun*
Pleasantville
Pocahontas
Pretty in Pink
Princess Bride
Psycho
Pulp Fiction
Raiders of the Lost Ark
Ray
Red Shoes*
Red Violin*
Repo Man
Repulsion
Rescuers, The
Right Stuff*
Rocky
Romeo and Juliet
Room with a View
Rose, The
Run Lola Run
Rushmore
Saturday Night Fever
Schindler's List*
School of Rock
Seven Brides/Seven Brothers*
7th Voyage of Sinbad
Shakespeare in Love*
Shine
Shrek
Sisters
Sleepless in Seattle
Snow White
Song of Bernadette
Sound of Music*
South Park
Spartacus
Spellbound (1945)*
Stagecoach*
Stand by Me

Star Trek II
Star Wars*
Star Wars V/Empire Strikes
Star Wars VI/Return of Jedi
St. Elmo's Fire
Sting, The*
Stop Making Sense
Strictly Ballroom
Summer of '42*
Sunset Boulevard*
Superman
Sweet Smell of Success
Talk to Her
Tarzan
Taxi Driver
Third Man
This Is Spinal Tap
Thoroughly Modern Millie*
Thunderball
Tie Me Up! Tie Me Down!
Titanic
To Kill a Mockingbird
Tom Jones*
Tommy
Top Gun
To Sir, With Love
Touch of Evil
Trainspotting
Truth or Dare
Two for the Road
2001: A Space Odyssey
Urban Cowboy
Vertigo
Victor/Victoria*
Wait Until Dark
Walk the Line
Way We Were*
Wedding Singer
West Side Story*
What's Love Got to Do with It
When Harry Met Sally...
Wild Bunch
Willy Wonka/Chocolate Factory
Wind and the Lion
Wizard of Oz*
Woodstock
Yankee Doodle Dandy*
Yellow Submarine
Young Frankenstein
Zorba the Greek
Zulu

Sports

Baseball
Bad News Bears
Bang the Drum Slowly
Bull Durham
Damn Yankees
Fever Pitch
League of Their Own
Natural, The
Pride of the Yankees
Rookie, The

Basketball
Hoop Dreams
Hoosiers
Space Jam

Boxing
Cinderella Man
Hurricane, The
Million Dollar Baby
Raging Bull
Requiem for a Heavyweight
Rocky

Football
Ace Ventura
Fortune Cookie
Jerry Maguire
Longest Yard (1974)
Longest Yard (2005)
North Dallas Forty
Radio
Remember the Titans

Hockey
Miracle
Slap Shot

Other
Bend It Like Beckham
Chariots of Fire
Color of Money
Cool Runnings
Hustler, The
Murderball
Pumping Iron
Seabiscuit

Stage Adaptations

Amadeus
Animal Crackers
Annie
Arsenic and Old Lace
Auntie Mame
Awful Truth
Bad Seed

Becket
Bell, Book and Candle
Bells Are Ringing
Birdcage, The
Born Yesterday
Brief Encounter
Brigadoon
Bus Stop
Bye Bye Birdie
Cabaret
Cactus Flower
Camelot
Carmen Jones
Carousel
Cat on a Hot Tin Roof
Chicago
Children of a Lesser God
Cocoanuts, The
Damn Yankees
Desk Set
Dial M for Murder
Diary of Anne Frank
Dinner at Eight
Driving Miss Daisy
Educating Rita
Elephant Man
Evita
Fiddler on the Roof
Finian's Rainbow
Front Page
Funny Girl
Funny Thing Happened...
Gaslight
Gay Divorcee
Glengarry Glen Ross
Grease
Guys and Dolls
Gypsy
Hair
Hamlet (1948)
Hamlet (1996)
Harvey
Heaven Can Wait (1943)
Hello, Dolly!
Henry V
High Society
His Girl Friday
Inherit the Wind
Irma La Douce
Jesus Christ Superstar
Key Largo
King and I
Kiss Me Kate

La Cage aux Folles
Letter, The
Lion in Winter
Little Foxes
Little Shop of Horrors
Love! Valour! Compassion!
Madness of King George
Man for All Seasons
Man Who Came to Dinner
Miracle Worker
Mister Roberts
Music Man
My Fair Lady
Odd Couple
Oklahoma!
Oliver!
One, Two, Three
On Golden Pond
On the Town
Paint Your Wagon
Peter Pan (1953)
Peter Pan (2003)
Phantom of the Opera
Philadelphia Story
Picnic
Play It Again, Sam
Prisoner of Second Avenue
Raisin in the Sun
Real Women Have Curves
Rent
Rocky Horror Picture Show
Romeo and Juliet
Rope
Roxanne
Ruling Class
Same Time, Next Year
1776
Seven Year Itch
Shirley Valentine
Show Boat
Six Degrees of Separation
Sleuth
Sound of Music
South Pacific
Stalag 17
Steel Magnolias
Streetcar Named Desire
Suddenly, Last Summer
Sunshine Boys
Sweet Charity
Unsinkable Molly Brown
Wait Until Dark
West Side Story

Who's Afraid of V. Woolf?
Witness for the Prosecution
Women, The

Swashbucklers
Adventures of Robin Hood
Captain Blood
Count of Monte Cristo
Mark of Zorro
Mask of Zorro
Master and Commander
Mutiny on the Bounty (1935)
Mutiny on the Bounty (1962)
Pirates of the Caribbean
Robin and Marian
Robin Hood: Prince of Thieves
7th Voyage of Sinbad
Thief of Bagdad
Three Musketeers

Thrillers
(See also James Bond)
Accused, The
Air Force One
Airport
Alien
Aliens
Along Came a Spider
Apollo 13
Armageddon
Bad Day at Black Rock
Bad Seed
Basic Instinct
Birds, The
Blood Simple
Body Heat
Bourne Identity
Bourne Supremacy
Bride Wore Black
Bullitt
Cape Fear (1962)
Cape Fear (1991)
China Syndrome
Clear and Present Danger
Client, The
Collateral
Collector, The
Constant Gardener
Counterfeit Traitor
Da Vinci Code
Dead Again
Dead Ringers
Death Wish

Deep, The
Diabolique
Dial M for Murder
Dirty Pretty Things
Diva
Dog Day Afternoon
Don't Look Now
Double Jeopardy
Dressed to Kill
Enemy of the State
Experiment in Terror
Fail-Safe
Fatal Attraction
Firm, The
Forbidden Planet
Foul Play
Frequency
Fugitive, The
Gaslight
Gothika
Hand That Rocks the Cradle
Hannibal
History of Violence
Hound of the Baskervilles
Hunt for Red October
Identity
Inside Man
Insider, The
Insomnia
Interpreter, The
In the Line of Fire
Invasion/Body Snatchers (1956)
Invasion/Body Snatchers (1978)
Jagged Edge
Jaws
Kiss Me Deadly
Klute
Lady Vanishes
La Femme Nikita
Last Seduction
Lifeboat
Life of David Gale
Manchurian Candidate (1962)
Manchurian Candidate (2004)
Man on Fire
Man Who Knew Too Much
Marathon Man
Match Point
Memento
Midnight Express
Misery

Mission: Impossible
Munich
Murder on the Orient Express
Nightmare on Elm Street
Night of the Hunter
North by Northwest
Notorious
No Way Out
Omen, The
One Hour Photo
Others, The
Outbreak
Panic Room
Patriot Games
Pelican Brief
Perfect Storm
Phone Booth
Play Misty for Me
Poltergeist
Poseidon Adventure
Presumed Innocent
Primal Fear
Psycho
Pulp Fiction
Ransom
Rear Window
Recruit, The
Red Dragon
Repulsion
Rock, The
Rope
Rosemary's Baby
Runaway Jury
Runaway Train
Run Lola Run
Saw
Seven
Seven Days in May
Shadow of a Doubt
Signs
Silence of the Lambs
Simple Plan
Sin City
Single White Female
Sixth Sense
Sleeping with the Enemy
Sleepy Hollow
Sleuth
Speed
Spellbound (1945)
Spy Who Came in from Cold

Strangers on a Train
Sum of All Fears
Suspect
Suspicion
Swimming Pool
Syriana
Talented Mr. Ripley
Taxi Driver
Texas Chainsaw Massacre
Third Man
39 Steps
Time After Time
To Catch a Thief
Towering Inferno
Training Day
Twelve Monkeys
Twister
Unbreakable
Veronica Guerin
Vertigo
Wages of Fear
Wait Until Dark
Westworld
Whatever Happened to....
What Lies Beneath
X-Files, The
Z

War
Alamo, The
Alexander Nevsky
All Quiet on the Western Front
Apocalypse Now
Battle of Algiers
Beau Geste
Black Hawk Down
Born on the Fourth of July
Braveheart
Bridge on the River Kwai
Caine Mutiny
Casablanca
Cold Mountain
Coming Home
Das Boot
Deer Hunter
Diary of Anne Frank
Dirty Dozen
El Cid
Empire of the Sun
Exodus
For Whom the Bell Tolls
Full Metal Jacket

Gallipoli
Glory
Gone with the Wind
Good Morning, Vietnam
Good, the Bad and the Ugly
Grand Illusion
Great Escape
Gunga Din
Guns of Navarone
Henry V
Hotel Rwanda
Killing Fields
Last of the Mohicans
Longest Day
MASH
Mister Roberts
Mrs. Miniver
Open City
Paths of Glory
Patriot, The
Patton
Pearl Harbor
Pianist, The
Platoon
Potemkin
Ran
Sand Pebbles
Saving Private Ryan
Schindler's List
Sergeant York
South Pacific
Stalag 17
Thin Red Line
Three Kings
Tin Drum
Tora! Tora! Tora!
Troy
Twelve O'Clock High
Two Women
U-571
Very Long Engagement
We Were Soldiers
Year of Living Dangerously

Weddings
Bride Wore Black
Father of the Bride (1950)
Father of the Bride (1991)
Four Weddings and a Funeral
Godfather, The
In-Laws, The
Monsoon Wedding
My Best Friend's Wedding

My Big Fat Greek Wedding
Philadelphia Story
Sixteen Candles
Wedding Banquet
Wedding Crashers
Wedding Singer

Westerns
Alamo, The
Blazing Saddles
Butch Cassidy/Sundance Kid
Cat Ballou
City Slickers
Dances with Wolves
Destry Rides Again
Duel in the Sun
Fistful of Dollars
For a Few Dollars More
Fort Apache
Good, the Bad and the Ugly
Gunfight at O.K. Corral
High Noon
High Plains Drifter
How the West Was Won
Hud
Jeremiah Johnson

Legends of the Fall
Little Big Man
Magnificent Seven
Man Who Shot Liberty Valance
Maverick
McCabe & Mrs. Miller
Misfits, The
Missing, The
Oklahoma!
Once Upon a Time/West
Outlaw Josey Wales
Ox-Bow Incident
Paint Your Wagon
Red River
Rio Bravo
Searchers, The
Shane
She Wore a Yellow Ribbon
Silverado
Spirit: Stallion of the Cimarron
Stagecoach
Tombstone
True Grit
Unforgiven
Wild Bunch
Young Guns

On the go.
In the know.

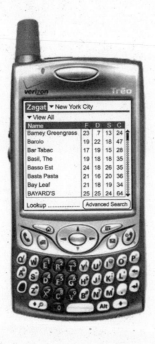

ZAGAT TO GO^{SM}

or Palm OS®, Windows Mobile®,
lackBerry® and mobile phones

Unlimited access to Restaurant and Nightlife guides in over 65 world cities.

Search by ratings, cuisines, locations and a host of other handy indexes.

Up-to-the-minute news and software updates.

Available at mobile.zagat.com